ALL · IN · ONE

SHRM-CP®/SHRM-SCP® Certification

EXAM GUIDE

Second Edition

Beverly N. Dance, MBA, SHRM-SCP,
SPHR, PHRca, CCP, CEBS
Dory Willer, SHRM-SCP, SPHR
William H. Truesdell, SHRM-SCP, SPHR
William D. Kelly, SHRM-SCP, SPHR-CA

New York   Chicago   San Francisco
Athens   London   Madrid   Mexico City
Milan   New Delhi   Singapore   Sydney   Toronto

McGraw Hill books are available at special quantity discounts to use as premiums and sales promotions, or for use in corporate training programs. To contact a representative, please visit the Contact Us pages at www.mhprofessional.com.

SHRM-CP®/SHRM-SCP® Certification All-In-One Exam Guide, Second Edition

1 2 3 4 5 6 7 8 9   LCR   28 27 26 25 24 23

Library of Congress Control Number: 2023931657

ISBN   978-1-265-02151-1
MHID   1-265-02151-1

Sponsoring Editor	Technical Editor	Production Supervisor
Lisa McClain	Leslie Jarvis	Thomas Somers
Editorial Supervisor	**Copy Editor**	**Composition**
Patty Mon	Bart Reed	KnowledgeWorks Global Ltd.
Project Editor	**Proofreaders**	**Illustration**
Rachel Fogelberg	KaTrina Jackson, Richard Camp	KnowledgeWorks Global Ltd.
Acquisitions Coordinator	**Indexer**	**Art Director, Cover**
Caitlin Cromley-Linn	Kevin Broccoli	Jeff Weeks

We dedicate this book to all HR professionals who constantly strive to do better.

I dedicate this book to the memories of the six remarkable women my family collectively call the Lincoln Ladies. They were strong, determined, and intelligent women. Two of these women in particular, my mother Marian Lincoln Dance and maternal grandmother Leona Parminter Lincoln, held and passed on the admirable value and habit that one should learn something new every single day. My sincerest thanks for the influence of these very special women.

—*Beverly*

I dedicate this book to two career-impactful bosses of mine: Peter Raisbeck, CEO, and Jim Benson, COO. They understood the value of what the HR function could be as a business partner for an organization. They mentored me with the foundational knowledge and experience of tying HR operations and strategies into the organization's overall vision, grasping business acumen, and earning a seat at the executive round table.

—*Dory*

This book is dedicated to the HR professionals who choose to do an increasingly difficult job as our world becomes more complex every day. You are carrying the banner for your employees and employers. Best wishes for a wonderful career.

—*Bill T.*

ABOUT THE AUTHORS

Beverly N. Dance, MBA, SHRM-SCP, SPHR, PHRca, CCP, CEBS, is a human resource (HR) professional with significant HR management and independent consulting experience. She is the founder and principal of Dance Associates, providing HR consulting support for a variety of clients, including nonprofits, commercial businesses, and higher education institutions, plus coaching for executives and individuals.

Beverly joined the Society for Human Resources Management (SHRM) faculty in 2007. In addition to leading SHRM's certification preparation classes, Beverly both developed and delivered SHRM compensation classes. Beverly continues to facilitate via HR.com and has taught more than 120 certification classes. She has presented at the HR West conference three times and at a SHRM annual conference.

Beverly earned a master's degree in business administration (MBA) from the Haas School of Business at the University of California, Berkeley, with a concentration in organizational design and industrial relations. She did this after graduating magna cum laude with a BA from the University of California, San Diego, in communication and sociology and as the student of the year. In addition to her SHRM and HRCI certifications, Beverly has earned the Certified Compensation Professional (CCP) and Certified Employee Benefit Specialist (CEBS) certifications. If you would like to contact Beverly, you may reach her at dance@mba.berkeley.edu.

Dory Willer, SHRM-SCP, PCC, is a certified executive coach with more than 30 years of experience as a senior HR executive, keynote speaker, and strategic planning facilitator. She has broad and diverse experience working for blue chip and Fortune 100 companies, leaving her last corporate position as a vice president of HR to open Beacon Quest Coaching. Dory coaches clients in leadership enhancement, performance improvement, and career renewal. Additionally, she facilitates strategic planning sessions that stretch paradigms, align activities with behaviors, and hold groups accountable to produce end results. She was among the first graduating class from Stanford's Executive HR certification program (Graduate School of Business, 1994). Dory achieved the designation of SPHR more than 25 years ago, has a BS degree in behavioral science from the University of San Francisco, and earned several advanced certifications in professional coaching. If you would like to contact Dory for speaking engagements or individual and team coaching, you may reach her at Dory@BeaconQuest.com.

William H. Truesdell, SHRM-SCP, is retired from HR consulting following a 32-year practice. He had previously retired from corporate management following 20 years with the legacy AT&T company. He is an expert on the subjects of personnel practices, employee handbooks, equal opportunity, affirmative action, and performance management programs. He is a past president of the Northern California Employment Round Table and former HR course instructor at the University of California, Berkeley, extension program. He holds the SPHR certification and a BS in business administration from California State University, Fresno. He authored many books for The Management Advantage, Inc., and coauthored several books for McGraw Hill.

William D. Kelly, SHRM-SCP, SPHR, has sadly passed away. He was the owner of Kelly HR, an HR consulting services firm specializing in providing generalist HR consulting services and support for small business enterprises. Bill's experience included more than 40 years of professional-level HR responsibilities that included 22 years within industry at Bechtel and later at Brown and Caldwell as an environmental engineer. His credentials included experience in employee relations, state and federal legal compliance, staffing and recruitment, equal employment opportunity and affirmative action, compensation, benefits, training and development, health and safety, and government contract management. Bill also had 20 years' HR consulting experience that included providing HR services, support, and advice to a wide range of Northern California clients. He also had 17 years' experience as an instructor for the University of California, Berkeley, extension program teaching Management of Human Resources; Recruiting, Selection, and Placement; California Employment Law; and professional HR certification preparation courses. Bill had more than 18 years' experience teaching the Professional PHR/SPHR Certification Preparation Course as well as 7 years' experience teaching the California HR Certification Preparation Course for the Society for Human Resource Management (SHRM) and the Northern California HR Association (NCHRA). He played a key role in the development of California's HR certification credential; also, he was the project manager for the team of California HR professionals who developed SHRM's first California Learning System in support of the California certification. Bill's professional leadership also included roles on the board of directors and national vice president for the Society for Human Resource Management; the board of directors and president for the HR Certification Institute (HRCI); state director, California State Council of SHRM; the board of directors and president for the Northern California HR Association (NCHRA); and commissioner and chair, Marin County Personnel Commission. Bill received his BS in political science from Spring Hill College in Mobile, Alabama, and undertook post-graduate studies in organizational management at the College of William and Mary in Williamsburg, Virginia, and the University of Virginia in Richmond, Virginia. Prior to HR, Bill had a military career, achieving the rank of major in the United States Army, with tours of duty in the United States, Germany, Thailand, and Vietnam. You are missed Bill.

About The Technical Editor

Leslie Jarvis left her role in early 2022 as the corporate human resources director for a Kentucky-based business conglomerate to pursue her true passion of leadership development and coaching. In her most recent HR role, Leslie's department provided HR services to a group of companies employing more than 2100 employees, specializing in the areas of banking, insurance, long-term care facilities, broadcasting, and IT services.

Leslie holds a BS degree and an MBA and has spent her 25-year HR career working in both the public and private sectors, the last 15 years spent at the executive level.

In addition, Leslie is an adjunct instructor with Bluegrass Community and Technical College in Lexington, Kentucky, teaching the SHRM Learning Course and serves as the past-president for the Bluegrass SHRM Chapter and as the Eastern District Director for the Kentucky State SHRM Council. She also serves on various boards in the Lexington, Kentucky area.

CONTENTS AT A GLANCE

CONTENTS

ACKNOWLEDGMENTS

I'd like to thank Heather Phelps and Pandora Patterson for their never-ending support as I prepared the second edition of this book. My thanks to Dory and the Bills for the huge task of writing the first edition. Special thanks to the late Bill Kelly, who suggested I be brought on to write the scenario questions for that first edition.

My thanks to the many talented people at McGraw Hill for helping this become a written reality. First, to Tim Green, who suggested I author the second edition. To Lisa McClain, who accepted that suggestion and guided the project. Finally, in order of my interactions in the many-step process of getting a book into print, thanks to Caitlin Cromley-Linn, Rachel Fogelberg, Bart Reed, KaTrina Jackson, and Richard Camp.

Human resources is most likely part of our DNA makeup; we've lived it and breathed it for many decades. We are proud to share the knowledge and tactics we believe will help you pass your SHRM-CP or SHRM-SCP. This book is our way to continue mentoring developing HR professionals. We've tried to design our book not only to help the SHRM certification exam taker but also to create a resource that will have a prominent place on the HR bookshelf as a "go-to" reference book. We hope we've succeeded with that intention.

In Memory of Bill Kelly

From Dory Willer:

"Mr. HR" was how many of us referred to Bill Kelly in the SFO HR community. When I first met Bill, I was newly promoted to an HR management position for a large organization, some 35 years ago. I was mesmerized by a presentation that Bill had made for our HR professional association chapter. I recall he invited audience members to "call on him," and I certainly did. Many times when I was seeking out best practices and what options there might be, Bill was always happy to share what he knew. Fast-forward to 2013 when I needed an HR expert to be a technical editor for an HR certification book I was co-authoring for McGraw Hill, and "Mr. HR" Bill Kelly was at the top on my list. I miss Bill, yet I continue to hear his wisdom in my mind when I think, "What would Mr. HR say?"

From Bill Truesdell:

I first met Bill Kelly in the early 1990s when we were both instructing classes for the Council on Education in Management, the largest HR training organization in the United States at the time. Later we both served as consulting partners with Merit Resource Group, supporting client HR needs of various sorts.

Bill was always humble and a gentleman. He had a depth of knowledge about human resource management and labor management requirements that was matched by very few others. He never stopped working. Bill worked with a partner to create online HR training programs to help new people in the profession.

He was a congenial colleague, willing to share whatever he knew with others of us in the consulting profession. He was a great author and communicator. I will miss our conversations. He is, no doubt, helping organize the human resource management function in Heaven.

INTRODUCTION

Allow us to be the first to congratulate you on deciding to sit to earn your SHRM Certified Professional (SHRM-CP) or SHRM Senior Certified Professional (SHRM-SCP) certification! Professional certification is a mark of distinction that sets you apart in the profession and speaks volumes about your commitment to your vocation. It is our belief that HR professional certifications are important to you as an HR professional because they endorse your knowledge and expertise to employers, clients, and the world at large.

Through this book, we can help you ready yourself for the type of material you will be expected to master. You bring your own professional experience to the process. Combining the two, you will be better equipped to answer situational-based and knowledge-based questions that you may find on the exam.

We want you to be successful. Having a professional certification is more critical every day in the world of work. It may be a requirement of your next job assignment or the promotional opportunity you are pining for in your organization. We wish you the best professional regards and success in passing your exam and earning the prestigious designation of SHRM-CP or SHRM-SCP.

SHRM Certifications

This book is now in its second edition to be current with the changes SHRM made in 2022. This book was first written in 2015, which was the first year of the new SHRM exams. We hope you find this book of immense help in your preparations to pass your exam.

How to Use This Book

We believe this book covers the entire SHRM Body of Applied Skills and Knowledge (BASK) identified in the three specific domains in which topics are organized and the nine behavioral competencies identified by SHRM for application. The manner in which we present the information is based on a learning principle we call *foundational knowledge*. This means we've purposefully organized this book to ensure that the reader first grasps the foundational knowledge items required of the profession. That is why we have placed U.S. laws as one of the first chapter topics, followed by the BASK knowledge domain chapters of "People," "Organization," and "Workplace," and then the behavioral competency information.

Additionally, within the writing, we have presented the essential "guts" of the information that we feel is minimally necessary for the exams and have pointed you to additional resources to discover more information on topics such as theories. It is our belief that as readers progress through the material and progressively move through with a sure-footed understanding of the "what," they will then be able to progress to the "how" of applying the topics. We know that in spite of being over 600 pages, the information presented in this book for passing the exam is concise. Studying for the exam is no cakewalk. The presentation of material was specifically designed to help the self-directed learner cover information they may already be well familiar with, and yet offer new information in a succinct manner for ease of learning.

Chapter 1

In Chapter 1, we explain everything you need to know about the different types of HR certifications and the benefits of professional certification (such as boosting your credibility as an HR professional and providing a platform to show you're ready to take on the next-level challenge for your career.)

Chapter 2

In Chapter 2, we explain everything you need to know about the SHRM exams, the development process of the exams, eligibility for each exam, and criteria to decide which certification is right for you. Know that the SHRM-CP exam is correlated with HR administration, and the SHRM-SCP is associated more with strategy. SHRM offers the Academic Eligibility Program, which allows students in a bachelor's or master's degree program in good standing at an academically aligned school to apply for and take the SHRM-CP exam. This boosts HR students' value prior to graduating and provides opportunities to be as marketable as possible. Additionally, you'll find information about the process of registering, the actual exam experience, and the style of exam questions.

Chapter 3

Chapter 3 provides a list of all the current U.S. laws and regulations you need to know. We placed this information as one of the early chapters, rather than as an appendix, to emphasize the importance of reviewing the laws and regulations prior to diving into the knowledge areas. This should make it easier for you to grasp the reasoning behind the material that is presented in Chapters 4–6. While the exams will only ask about federal laws, remember that laws and regulations change, and it's important that you stay current on all applicable laws that impact your organization.

Chapters 4–6

Chapters 4–6 go into the detailed topics of HR technical knowledge (that is, HR expertise), grouped into the domains of People, Organization, and Workforce. These domains are defined as the principles, practices, and function of effective HR management and are associated with the expertise required for the HR profession. The explanations are designed to be concise and yet effectively communicate the information you'll need for the exam. Their application is facilitated by the behavioral competencies identified in Chapter 7. SHRM suggests that to be a successful HR practitioner, one must be in command of both the technical HR knowledge (*what* you know) and the behavioral components of an effective HR practice (*how* you apply what you know).

The People domain covers HR strategic planning, talent acquisition, employee engagement and retention, learning and development, and total rewards.

The Organization domain covers the structure of the HR function, organizational effectiveness and development, workforce management, employee and labor relations, and technology management.

The Workplace domain covers HR in the global context, risk management, corporate and social responsibility, and the application of U.S. employment laws and regulations from Chapter 3.

Chapter 7

Chapter 7 consists of the nine behavioral competencies that have been defined by SHRM as needed for success in any HR role, regardless of organization size or sector. These behavioral competencies provide the foundation for talent management throughout the HR lifecycle. They are grouped into three clusters: Leadership, Interpersonal, and Business. Each competency cluster is further divided into subcompetencies that specifically describe its components and is composed of proficiency key behavior indicators—the statements that illustrate effective use in the HR role. Pay close attention to the SHRM BASK related to the behavioral competencies we have outlined in this chapter. The situational judgment test questions (SJTs) rely heavily on those descriptions.

Notes   Specially called-out *Notes* are part of each chapter, too. These are interesting tidbits of information that are relevant to the topic and point out helpful information.

Practice Questions and Answers   At the end of Chapters 3 through 7, you will find a set of questions and answers to help you test your knowledge and comprehension. Practice, practice, and then practice some more, as it will pay off on exam day.

Appendixes

We have created appendixes to supplement the information you need to know.

Appendix A   Appendix A lists acronyms used in the HR profession. The HR profession is notorious for using jargon in HR language, and these acronyms have flowed into the everyday business language of employers, employees, and the public at large. Will there be exam questions related to acronyms? We think questions and answers may have acronyms in them but do not expect a question as simple as "What does ABC stand for?"

Appendix B   In Appendix B we have listed associated legal cases you should know and review. They are organized under each chapter's functional area and include a brief synopsis of what the case addressed. A URL is provided to review the case in more detail, and we recommend you delve into more information about the cases if you have the time.

Appendix C   Appendix C lists additional resources that are not only helpful for your exam study but are also helpful as you navigate through the lifecycle of your HR career. You should treat this resource list as a "living document," adding new listings as new theories and best practices are developed over the course of your HR career.

Appendix D   Appendix D provides details about the accompanying online practice exams. There are 134 questions each for the SHRM-CP and SHRM-SCP, with answers that relate to each possible response, both correct and incorrect. These practice opportunities should help prepare you for sitting for the same number of questions on your SHRM exam. Refer to Appendix D for more details, and follow the instructions to access the online practice exams.

Glossary

The glossary is composed of HR terms you may encounter. Not only will using this glossary help you review and learn the key terms contained in this material, it will help you move through your HR career lifecycle in human resource management. We recommend you study the glossary, not just review or reference it, because several exam questions may pertain to glossary terms. The glossary also points out when more than one term refers to the exact same thing.

Index

In the back of the book is an index that will guide you to the appropriate pages where a term is mentioned or discussed.

The Examinations

The SHRM-CP and SHRM-SCP exams are neither simple multiple-choice nor memory-recall exams. Your exam will be in two parts, each up to an hour and 50 minutes long. During that time you will answer 134 questions. There will be complex situational judgement questions, short situational questions, formula-based questions, knowledge-based questions, and interpretive questions. Knowing how to get the most out of each question is crucial.

The questions will come in clusters; you'll see a group of knowledge questions and then a group of scenario-based situational judgment questions. For scenario questions, a second page will display, like a book. The scenario stays on the left side of the screen for reference, and the questions with their answer choices will appear on the right side of the screen, one at a time.

Situational Questions

Situational questions will test your ability to identify the relevant content and are associated with the behavioral competencies. These questions will be lengthy and make up 40 percent of the exam weighting. Pay particular attention to reading and accurately identifying the question so that you can eliminate irrelevant and insignificant information. Using the highlighting feature, which is intuitive and will be explained prior to exam, is a great way to mark what you read as the most relevant information for a correct answer.

Formula-Based Questions

Formula-based questions are more thought-provoking. You must know both the formula and how to perform the calculation to reach a correct answer. No, you may not bring your calculator with you into the test center. Yes, a calculator will be on your monitor screen for use if you need it. A whiteboard with a marker or numbered blank sheets of paper with a pencil will be provided so you may write, but you cannot write down anything to take with you after the exam.

Knowledge-Based Questions

The knowledge-based questions will require you to know your facts. These questions test your knowledge of HR theories and laws. Sometimes you are asked to identify an example chart or graph, so pay attention to the figures included in the chapters.

Interpretational Questions

Interpretational questions will seek to test your ability to deduce a situation or condition and select the best, most appropriate answer. All answers may actually be correct, yet selecting the *best* answer could apply. Sometimes these questions, as well as the situational questions, seek to determine if you know the right sequence of actions to take, so pay attention to hints like the words *first, next,* and *last.*

Preparing for the Exam

Preparing for any type of certification exam is not about memorizing information. Certification exams require that an HR professional be able to demonstrate that they can apply their experience and knowledge in a host of different situations. You have already invested in an education for your career. Investing in serious study time and preparation will pay off when you pass your exam.

For those with more limited or minimal experience, we suggest you begin studying at least 6 months prior to your exam date. For those with significantly more experience as an HR professional, a 3-month minimum should be your yardstick. If you want to "shoot from the hip" and not study the material outlined in this book, your odds of passing will be low—even if you have been in an exempt HR position for eons. We aren't saying that it can't be done, but we know that your chances are much better if you use the information in this book and its accompanying practice exams to prepare. Guessing strategies are hardly foolproof and not a good substitute for solid study habits in preparation for an exam.

Preparing Ahead of Time

Here are our tips on actions to take between now and your exam. We will follow this section with tips directly related to studying.

- Control your self-talk. "I CAN PASS! I WILL PASS! I SUCCESSFULLY MAKE TIME TO STUDY!" ought to be part of your vocabulary. If you need reinforcement, put up sticky notes on the side of your monitor or on your bathroom mirror.
- Focus on understanding the *concepts*. Remember, the exam is experience based.
- Solicit support from your boss, co-workers, family, and friends to ensure preparation for your exam remains a priority until your test date.
- Set study goals and get study time on your calendar, *plus* fit it in whenever you can. If the person coming to you for a 10 o'clock meeting is late, open the book and review the glossary until they arrive.

- Schedule your exam at a time consistent with your personal biorhythms and at a time that works with the other demands in your life. Saturday morning timeslots fill up first, so if that is your preferred time, sign up early.

- Some folks feel better doing a practice drive to their test center, timing how long it takes and checking out the parking situation. Make sure your parking spot is one where you can be for enough hours with a little cushion. You do not want to risk the distraction of worrying about a potential parking ticket.

- If you have a disability that needs an accommodation, speak up early in the process to report this and ask for what accommodation you need.

- Know that nothing that has occurred in the last 18 months will be covered on your exam in a question that is scored. It can take a year or two to process the questions and include them as scored questions on an exam. Therefore, don't worry about current events or a new law that just passed.

- The night before the exam, pamper yourself so that you go into the exam refreshed. Get the appropriate amount of rest. Do not cram late into the night. Studies prove that a REM state of sleeping is extremely helpful for brain functions.

Studying

Here are our tips directly related to studying:

- Before studying, go for a brief walk to take in some air and clear your mind in preparation for being focused. Put all your other thoughts, projects, and responsibilities on a back burner and allow your mind to be a clean slate exclusively for attentive SHRM studying.

- Make sure your "do not disturb" sign is on your door if you are at home or in the office and that others clearly know nothing is to disturb you during your study time. One passing student worked in a downtown building next to a bar. She wanted to study at lunchtime, but knew she'd get interrupted if she stayed in her office. She made a deal with the bartender, and at lunchtime Monday through Friday she took the back booth and studied with her standing diet soda order. No one would image her in a bar during the day, so she achieved her private, uninterrupted study time.

- Do some studying 5 to 6 days a week versus waiting and cramming at the end. Even 10 minutes here and there reinforces what you've learned. Most exam takers find an hour a day is enough time to devote to their regular study schedule when they commit enough weeks to preparation.

- Clear your study area. It should be void of anything else that might capture your attention and distract you from studying, especially your phone. Keep the focus on the studying at hand, and to add a little incentive, create a bit of visual incentive for yourself—the desired end result, which would be a letter stating you have successfully passed your exam. Spoof a letter from SHRM, print it, put it in a nice picture frame, and place it in front of you every time you begin your study time. What the mind can conceive, you can achieve!

- Make regular time to study and select a time of day that is optimal for you. Are you best in the wee hours of the early morning with a cup of coffee prior to work, or perhaps it's the noon hour? Maybe your rhythm is one of a person who kicks in just after dinner. Find that sweet hour and make the appointment on your calendar listing it as VIP-SHRM. You are the very important person, and this appointment will cause you to think twice before allowing another activity to slip into your time slot.

- Give additional focus to areas that have the heaviest weighting on your exam and areas where you know you lack expertise.

- As you study the material, you may want to make flash cards to help you shore up areas of knowledge that will help you pass the exam. You can make flash cards using the website http://www.kitzkikz.com/flashcards/, or you can use old-fashion index cards or, better yet, business card stock. This is particularly useful if you are a kinetic learner and learn best by touching things. Punch a hole in the corner of your cards and keep them on a ring, so if you drop them, there is only one item to pick up, not multiple cards flying all over.

- As you work through this exam guide and discover a term that is new to you, pause long enough to flip to the glossary and look it up. Knowing how a word or phrase is used can be helpful in discovering its application or meaning. Consider adding those terms to your flash cards.

- We strongly recommend you consider using the complement publication to this exam guide, *SHRM-CP®/SHRM-SCP® Certification Practice Exams,* by Beverly N. Dance, William D. Kelly, and Joanne Simon-Walters, to further help you with an assessment of your HR knowledge strengths and weaknesses. Time yourself as you take the mock exams.

- Physically train by sitting and answering test questions at your computer for 4 hours with no food or beverage, ideally at the same time of day your exam is scheduled. (Four hours to account for the pretest before and survey at the end, in addition to the two parts of the exam.) See what it feels like. Learn if you will need the 15-minute break after an hour and 50 minutes or if you would prefer to launch immediately into the second half of your exam. We highly recommend taking the full 15 minutes to stretch your body and refresh yourself. Know what pace you need to go to complete the exam without rushing.

- Now that you've focused on learning and studying *what* concepts and content the exam is going to test you on *how* you can apply that knowledge. Practice asking yourself, "How could they ask me to apply this knowledge?" "How can I eliminate wrong answers to increase my odds of choosing the most correct answer?"

- Know your federal legislation by the full name, the acronym, and its nickname if it has one (such as the Wagner Act).

Action for Your Exam Day

- Set an additional alarm or arrange for a phone call to ensure you are awake when you need to be if you have a morning exam slot. Have your entrance information organized and your photo ID ready to go. If you use reading glasses, have them ready too.

- Plan to get to your test center 30 minutes early for check-in. Allow plenty of time for bad traffic so you do not add any anxiety. If you're taking public transportation, have one backup connection that could still get you to your test center on time.

- Strategize your caffeine and fluid consumption. You want to be hydrated for maximum brain capacity. Water is good for the body but even better for the brain. It brings oxygen that helps your brain functions improve. No food or drink of any kind is allowed inside the testing room.

- Use the bathroom immediately prior to entering the testing room. Yes, if needed you can take a break during the exam, yet every minute you use on a break is a minute you are not using to answer questions since the clock keeps running throughout any break requested during either part of the exam. Also realize that a mid-test break will consume additional time due to flagging the proctor and getting your monitor locked, plus getting reseated and your monitor unlocked at the proctor's convenience.

- Eat an appropriate breakfast or lunch, depending on your exam time.

- Wear comfortable clothing. Leave your watch, jewelry, and scarves at home, or be prepared to take them off and secured in your assigned locker. (Wedding rings are tolerated.) If you are dressed in layers, assess the room temperature and decide which layers you will keep on during your test. Most test centers will not allow you to shed a layer during the exam—crazy, we know.

- Pack and bring with you any snacks and fluids you may want to use during your time at the test center.

- Use your assigned locker for your snacks, phone, purse, watch, and so on. Do *not* bring study notes into the test center with you. If a proctor sees those notes while you are accessing your water bottle, you will be disqualified and automatically failed.

- Relax and mentally prepare for security, similar to what you would go through at an airport. Be prepared to show them you haven't stuffed notes into your socks or written answers on your arms and that your pockets are empty.

- Take one of the center's tissues to have at hand. If you have it handy, you probably won't need it. You won't lose precious time flagging the proctor to get one later. Realize you may need to hand it back at the end to prove you didn't write on it to sneak out notes.

Taking the Exam

Here is our advice to apply once you are escorted into the exam center's testing room.

- Feel free to do a core dump of notes onto your white board as soon as you are seated. Jot down any concepts, definitions, or formulas you want.

- Take the pre-test where the highlighting, marking, and strikethrough features are explained. Don't rush since you don't get to apply that time to your exam. Use that period to get used to your surroundings by checking the height of your chair, the correct brightness of the computer screen, your mouse, and try out the calculator on the screen. Decide if you are most comfortable with or without the headphones or earplugs. If the onscreen calculator is not working, flag the proctor and insist on another station.

- After reading a question, extract the key elements. Think of what answer you'd give if the exam were all fill-in-the-blank format prior to reading the answers. When your answer is one of the four options, that is a good sign.

- Even when the first answer looks right, discipline yourself to read all four of the answer choices before making your selection. It may be that you need to select the *best* answer because all answers are correct.

- Respond to your learning style. If you are an oral learner, move your lips while reading. If you are kinetic learner, move your mouse cursor across the screen as you read.

- If a word or concept has momentarily left you, leave the test question unanswered, mark it, and come back to it. That phrase may come to you through a subsequent question.

- Use the strikethrough feature to eliminate distracters and narrow your choices. Using the strikethrough feature is particularly useful for those questions you mark to return to later, as you won't have to read all four options again. Mark as many questions to return to as you want.

- For scenario questions, read the first question that you will need to answer from the passage prior to reading the passage. That way, you may read the material in a more targeted and efficient way.

- Watch and slow down to catch key words and phrases that could change your answer if you missed reading them, such as the following:
  - Most/least
  - Always/never
  - All/except
  - Will/will not
  - Employer or employee

- Look for the one answer that differs from the other three.

- If two options are essentially identical, they must both be wrong since there is always one best answer. Don't use the length of an answer as a clue.

- Trust your gut, your first impression. A first impression of the correct answer is many times the best choice. This should not be confused with "guessing." This refers to topics you know that you know.

- If you encounter two "right" answers, with one matching the Body of Knowledge and one matching your company policies, choose the Body of Knowledge answer. This is particularly important if you know your organization does not follow best practices.

- There will be no patterns, so don't even look for them. The psychometric exam process used for the SHRM exam prevents questions from falling into patterns. Federal laws are the only laws on the exams. Check your knowledge of state, international, and local laws outside the door of the exam center. If you must guess at an answer, pick the answer that is the *most employer* friendly and the *least employee* friendly to get away from a state bias.

- Avoid over-analyzing. The most common weakness of HR test takers is over-analyzing the options. Do not read into a question variables that are not there. If you are looking at two "right" answers, ask yourself, "Which of these two do I get to most directly?" Pick the one with the shortest number of logic steps to get there. Be thorough, but be reasonable in your analysis and answer selection.

- Start each question by eliminating the obvious "not best" answers and then focus on what remains.

- Resist the urge to change your answers. Only change an answer if you are *absolutely, positively 100% sure* your initial choice was wrong based on new information. Trust your first impression. Resist the urge to second-guess yourself and change answers.

- Manage your time. Do not rush. A timer will be on the screen in the top-right corner, counting down how much time you have left. You will have a little over a minute and a half for each question, but allot more time for your scenario questions.

- Answer every question. Use the computer report to check that you have answered all your questions prior to submitting your exam for grading. Your exam does not penalize for wrong answers.

- Remember to breathe. Periodically take a deep breath in and out. Also engage in shoulder and neck exercises to keep tension at bay.

- Stay calm, confident, and relaxed.

After the Exam

After you submit your exam for grading, you will need to complete a survey to get to the screen to learn your preliminary results. Once you know them and leave the test center, here are our tips for after the exam.

- Plan a fun activity after your exam to decompress and *celebrate!*

- Regardless of the exam scoring, know that *you are already a winner!* Think about how much you have learned on this journey.

- Establish your online recertification account with SHRM right away and record your continuing education and other recertification credits as you earn them to keep yourself certified after all this hard work. Bookmark this page so it is easy find again. Sixty units in 3 years is quite doable.

Remember, This Book Is a Resource

Finally, this book has been designed not only to assist SHRM exam takers but also to be a reliable reference book on the shelf in any HR professional's office. There is a lot to remember in the discipline of human resources. It is our desire that you find this book to be a quick resource that guides you in times when something pops up that you haven't encountered before or for which you may need a refresher. At a minimum, we hope it provides you with direction to gather more information for your particular HR circumstances.

Finally, dear reader, thank you for selecting this book. We sincerely hope your SHRM exam goes well and wish you the absolute best on your exam day and throughout your career in HR!

PART I

The Human Resource Profession

CHAPTER 1

Human Resource Certification

The skills and abilities a professional in human resources (HR) uses to produce desired results require a variety of proficiencies. Proficiency in any profession will involve a continuous career-long commitment to learning, and that is a foundational truth within the HR profession. HR has been, and continues to be, an evolving component of an organization because its basic focus is on people, otherwise referred to as the human capital of an organization. The constant changes and outside influences on an organization's workforce increase the demands on HR professionals. HR professionals today walk a tight line and must master the art of staying two steps ahead while having one foot firmly planted in the present. Today's HR department needs to be perceived as a strategic player within an organization, tasked with developing business approaches while solving problems and being more than a cost center.

Professional Human Resource Management Certification

Earning your certification as an HR professional demonstrates to your colleagues, your organization, and the world that you are committed to a higher standard and dedicated to the HR profession. When you pass your HR certification exam, it signals your proficiency of core competencies and key functional areas in HR management, raising the confidence of an employer and your peers in your knowledge and abilities. Because the HR profession is constantly changing and evolving, it is important for HR professionals to constantly update their HR competencies and knowledge. Achieving certification and recertification is a good way to do so.

A professional certification should not be confused with a certificate program. HR professional certifications are based on a highly defined body of applied skills and knowledge, along with recertification requirements. Certificate programs do not require recertification. Competency-based certifications address a critical need in our global marketplace because employers expect more today from their internal experts, and the HR profession must be ready to meet those expectations.

Benefits of Certification

Earning an HR certification give you a significant level of recognition as an expert in the HR profession. This certification is a distinction that sets you apart in the profession, indicating you have an elevated level of knowledge and skills. It adds value to your career and to your organization. Your HR certification could mean the difference between you or your competition being hired. In fact, 96 percent of employers say that an HR-certified candidate applying for a job would have an advantage over a noncertified candidate. Also, HR professionals who hold certifications tend to make more money than their peers who do not.[1] According to PayScale Human Capital, this pattern is true for all industries and metropolitan areas in the United States. HR certification is becoming an important means for employers to recognize HR expertise and for HR professionals to increase their value and worth.

Earning an HR credential can help you in the following ways:

- Boost your confidence
- Create recognition for you as an HR expert
- Give you expert knowledge in the HR profession
- Protect your organization from risk via regulatory compliance
- Stand out from other HR candidates in job searches and promotions
- Broaden your perspective in the HR field
- Keep up with HR innovations, developments, and legislative/law changes
- Demonstrate your commitment to the HR profession

For human resources professionals who want to advance, evidence shows the higher the career level the greater likelihood of having an HR certificate.[2] More than half of Chief Human Resources Officers (CHRO) or Vice Presidents of HR are certified. If an individual wants to be considered for a senior-level HR position, then certification is a growing expectation.

HR Certification Organizations

HR professionals can receive their certifications from two certifying organizations: the HR Certification Institute (HRCI) and the Society for Human Resource Management (SHRM). Determining whether to pursue the SHRM Certified Professional (SHRM-CP) or SHRM Senior Certified Professional (SHRM-SCP) or the HRCI certifications is a major decision. Both organizations' certifications test knowledge that the profession requires as their baseline. While they both test knowledge, the SHRM certifications focus 50 percent of their test content on applying that knowledge and the importance of behavioral competencies, even as they include a more expansive global perspective. The SHRM exams cost slightly less than the HRCI exams. The SHRM exams have also significantly relaxed their eligibility requirements, which are discussed in more detail in Chapter 2. Both sets of exams have their merits, which is why your authors hold both certifications.

The HR Certification Institute

The HR Certification Institute (www.hrci.org) was established in 1976 as an internationally recognized certifying organization for the human resource profession. Its mission is to develop and deliver the highest-quality certification programs that validate proficiency in the field of human resource management and contribute to the continued improvement of individual and organizational performance. More than 500,000 HR professionals in more than 100 countries have earned a certification from HRCI. Both HRCI and SHRM are accredited certifying organizations.

HRCI exists to enhance the professionalism of the HR profession with its various certification processes. The institute is a nonprofit (501)(c)(3) organization[3] (an IRS designation) separate from the Society of Human Resource Management, which is a (510)(c)(6) organization.[4] HRCI was accredited by the National Commission for Certifying Agencies (NCCA) in 2008. SHRM's exams have been accredited by the Buros Center for Testing.

HRCI's Body of Knowledge (BoK) is a complete set of knowledge and responsibilities required to successfully understand and perform generalist HR-related duties associated with each of its eight certifications: Associate Professional in Human Resources (aPHR), Associate Professional in Human Resources, International (aPHRi), Professional in Human Resources (PHR), Professional in Human Resources, California (PHRca), Professional in Human Resources, International (PHRi), Senior Professional in Human Resources (SPHR), Senior Professional in Human Resources, International (SPHRi), and Global Professional in Human Resources (GPHR). The BoK is periodically updated, typically every 5 to 7 years, to ensure it is consistent with and reflects current practices in the HR field. Our book *PHR/SPHR Professional in Human Resources Certification All-in-One Exam Guide, Second Editon*[5] provides in-depth preparation for the PHR and SPHR exams. Of the eight exams, the PHR and SPHR are the most popular.

The Society for Human Resource Management

For more than 65 years, the Society for Human Resource Management (www.shrm.org) has served the human resource profession and HR professionals worldwide. Founded in 1948, SHRM is the world's largest HR membership organization devoted to human resource management. Representing more than 300,000 members in 165 countries, SHRM is the leading provider of resources to serve the needs of HR professionals and advance the professional practice of human resource management. SHRM has more than 575 affiliated chapters in more than 125 countries.

HR professionals look to SHRM for resources to help them do their jobs, progress their careers, and partner with government and public and private industries. SHRM focuses on advancing the whole HR profession, ensuring that as business needs involving human capital evolve, HR evolves to meet those needs. That was the driving force behind the development of a Body of Competency and Knowledge (BoCK) supporting next-generation certifications in the HR field: the SHRM Certified Professional and the SHRM Senior Certified Professional certifications. That BoCK was updated in 2022 to the Body of Applied Skills and Knowledge (BASK).

SHRM has a commitment to developing the HR profession globally. SHRM provides resources, global best practices, and a network of members around the globe. In addition to delivering certification preparation courses and other educational products and services to members and nonmembers around the world, SHRM partners with volunteers in select countries to lead member forums and encourage local networking among members. SHRM is an active member of the North American Human Resource Management Association (NAHRMA) and the World Federation of People Management Associations (WFPMA) and currently serves as the secretariat for both organizations.

Chapter Review

The number of HR professionals needed in the coming years to manage the human capital in organizations will continue to expand. The U.S. Bureau of Labor Statistics anticipates that the number of HR manager positions will grow 9 percent this decade.[6] In addition, employer selection criteria will increasingly use certification as an employment screening factor. Whether you choose to obtain a certification from SHRM or HRCI, or both, is not going to be as relevant as when you will achieve your certification. The value of certification is being recognized in all levels of the organization and throughout the HR profession. SHRM's Body of Applied Skills and Knowledge and certification exams raise the stakes for professionals by requiring exam takers to demonstrate an ability to apply the knowledge they know, not simply identify what they know. We're confident that adding the SHRM certification to your résumé will draw special attention to your achievement due to the time and discipline involved in attaining this professional goal.

References

1. PayScale Human Capital research report, "The Market Value of PHR and SPHR Certifications," https://www.payscale.com/research-and-insights/market-value-of-phr-sphr-infographic/.

2. "HR Certifications: How They Impact Pay and Career Trajectory, 2018 U.S. Edition," www.payscale.com/research-and-insights/hr-certifications-pay/

3. To be tax-exempt under section 501(c)(3) of the Internal Revenue Code, an organization must be organized and operated exclusively for exempt purposes set forth in section 501(c)(3), and none of its earnings may inure to any private shareholder or individual. In addition, it may not be an action organization (i.e., it may not attempt to influence legislation as a substantial part of its activities), and it may not participate in any campaign activity for or against political candidates. Organizations described in section 501(c)(3) are commonly referred to as charitable organizations. Organizations described in section 501(c)(3), other than testing for public safety organizations, are eligible to receive tax-deductible contributions in accordance with Code section 170. IRS Code (https://www.irs.gov/charities-non-profits/charitable-organizations/exemption-requirements-section-501-c-3-organizations).

4. IRC 501(c)(6) provides for exemption of business leagues, chambers of commerce, real estate boards, boards of trade, and professional football leagues (whether or not administering a pension fund for football players), which are not organized for profit, and no part of the net earnings of which inures to the benefit of any private shareholder or individual. IRS Code (https://www.irs.gov/pub/irs-tege/eotopick03.pdf).

5. Willer, Dory, Christina Nishiyama, and William H. Truesdell, *PHR/SPHR Professional in Human Resources Certification All-in-One Exam Guide, Second Edition* (McGraw-Hill Education, 2019).

6. Bureau of Labor Statistics, U.S. Department of Labor, *Occupational Outlook Handbook, 2022 Edition,* Human Resources Managers, www.bls.gov/ooh/management/human-resources-managers.htm.

SHRM's Certification Program

Today, we live and work in a global economy in which geographic borders are virtually nonexistent, with innovation, agility, and strategy as critical success factors. The HR profession operates at the core of this global economy, ensuring the alignment of organizational strategy with a high-performing workforce. The Society for Human Resource Management (SHRM) certification program[1] offers two exams—the SHRM Certified Professional (SHRM-CP) and the SHRM Senior Certified Professional (SHRM-SCP)—for senior practitioners with strategic experience.

In 2011, SHRM decided to invest in the advancement of the HR profession by developing a new competency framework to serve as a foundational resource for all HR professionals. The SHRM Competency Model originally identified eight key behavioral competencies: Leadership & Navigation, Business Acumen, Ethical Practice, Relationship Management, Consultation, Critical Evaluation, Global & Cultural Effectiveness, and Communication. In 2022, SHRM added a ninth behavioral competency—Diversity, Equity & Inclusion (DE&I)—elevating it from its former functional area status. SHRM also changed the names of two of its remaining functional areas: Critical Evaluation is now Analytical Aptitude, and HR in the Global Context is now Global Mindset. SHRM also identified one technical competency: HR Expertise (HR Knowledge). SHRM's studies indicate that these competencies comprise the foundation of a successful HR career.

The SHRM Competency Model[2] is fundamental to SHRM's two certifications: the SHRM-CP for early-to-mid-career practitioners and the SHRM-SCP for senior-level practitioners. These certifications address two basic goals:

- For HR professionals, these certifications recognize the importance of both competencies and knowledge as essential elements for successful job performance.
- For employers, they affirm the need to look for competencies and knowledge as key indicators of successful HR job performance.

As a function of its studies, SHRM identified a bank of knowledge topics that are essential and a list of behaviors that are critical to HR professionals' success. SHRM originally called these the Body of Competency and Knowledge (BoCK). SHRM's 2022 updates now call these the Body of Applied Skills and Knowledge (BASK).

SHRM's certifications are designed to demonstrate to the global business community that the holder has strong HR capabilities for effective job performance.

As part of its research, SHRM conducted more than 100 focus groups involving more than 1000 HR practitioners to identify the critical competencies necessary for success as an HR professional. Focus group participants included HR professionals from 33 countries, representing a diversity of both personal and organizational attributes.

SHRM then confirmed the relevance and universality of the SHRM Competency Model through a content validation survey, which drew responses from more than 32,000 HR professionals worldwide. Finally, a series of large-scale multiorganizational criterion validation studies were conducted involving a highly diverse sample of more than 1500 HR professionals and their supervisors, the purpose of which was to establish that proficiency in these competencies is intricately linked to successful job performance. Figure 2-1 illustrates SHRM's current Body of Applied Skills and Knowledge[3] building blocks of proficiency for the HR professional.

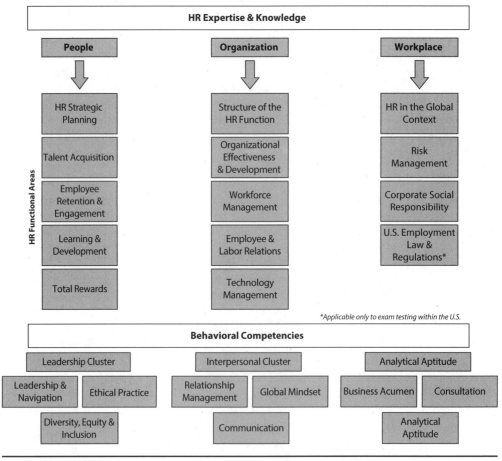

Figure 2-1 2022 SHRM Body of Applied Skill and Knowledge

The SHRM-CP and SHRM-SCP exams were accredited by the Buros Center for Testing in late 2016, a pronouncement that the HR certifications meet the highest standards in testing.

HR Expertise/Knowledge

A competency model is a set of competencies defining the requirements for effective performance in a specific job, profession, or organization. As mentioned before, there are now nine behavioral competencies and one technical competency, HR Expertise/Knowledge, in the SHRM Competency Model.

SHRM conducted a knowledge specification exercise to identify the key areas of HR functional knowledge and expertise. SHRM consulted academic and employer surveys regarding the basic functional knowledge needed for participation in the HR field.

SHRM's BoCK Advisory Panel

Since 2014, HR and business leaders from various industries, including retail, research, consulting, health care, and manufacturing, have served on SHRM's BoCK Advisory Panel, which was established to validate this framework. The panel reviewed the proposed HR technical knowledge framework for accuracy and comprehensiveness, defined key responsibility statements and knowledge topic areas associated with each knowledge domain and functional area, and developed importance rankings and weights for each knowledge domain. Upon completion, SHRM adopted this framework as the basis for the knowledge component of the SHRM BoCK, which was updated to the BASK in 2022.

Next, SHRM approached the development of behavioral competencies, as outlined in Table 2-1. Competencies can be either technical or behavioral. Technical competencies reflect the knowledge required to perform a specific role. Behavioral competencies describe the knowledge, skills, abilities, and other characteristics (KSAOs) that facilitate the application of technical knowledge to job-related behavior. In other words, technical competencies reflect the knowledge HR professionals apply to their jobs, and behavioral competencies reflect how they apply this knowledge. SHRM's motto is "Knowledge + Behavior = Success."

Another SHRM 2022 update was the expansion of sub-competencies (see Table 2-2).

The SHRM BASK documents the HR behavioral competencies and knowledge domains tested on the SHRM-CP and SHRM-SCP certification exams. The SHRM BASK is also the basic resource for item writers developing questions and individuals developing exam preparation materials. SHRM operates exam development and study material development as separate, independent functions and has established a strict firewall between these activities to protect the integrity and credibility of the certification exams.

Cluster	Competency	Definition
Leadership	Leadership & Navigation	The KSAOs needed to create a compelling vision and mission for HR that align with the strategic direction and culture of the organization, accomplish HR and organizational goals, lead and promote organizational change, navigate the organization, and manage the implementation and execution of HR initiatives.
	Ethical Practice	The KSAOs needed to maintain high levels of personal and professional integrity and to act as an ethical agent who promotes core values, integrity, and accountability throughout the organization.
	Diversity, Equity & Inclusion	The KSAOs needed to create a work environment in which all individuals are treated fairly and respectfully, have equal access to opportunities and resources, feel a sense of belonging, and use their unique backgrounds and characteristics to contribute fully to the organization's success.
Interpersonal	Relationship Management	The KSAOs needed to create and maintain a network of professional contacts within and outside of the organization, to build and maintain relationships, to work as an effective member of a team, and to manage conflict while supporting the organization.
	Communication	The KSAOs needed to effectively craft and deliver concise and informative communications, to listen to and address the concerns of others, and to transfer and translate information from one level or unit of the organization to another.
	Global Mindset	The KSAOs needed to value and consider the perspectives and backgrounds of all parties, to interact with others in a global context, and to promote a culturally diverse and inclusive workplace.
Business	Business Acumen	The KSAOs needed to understand the organization's operations, functions, and external environment as well as to apply business tools and analyses that inform HR initiatives and operations consistent with the overall strategic direction of the organization.
	Consultation	The KSAOs needed to work with organizational stakeholders in evaluating business challenges and identifying opportunities for the design, implementation, and evaluation of change initiatives as well as to build ongoing support for HR solutions that meet the changing needs of customers and the business.
	Analytical Aptitude	The KSAOs needed to collect and analyze qualitative and quantitative data as well as to interpret and promote findings that evaluate HR initiatives and inform business decisions and recommendations.

Table 2-1   SHRM Behavioral Competency Definitions[4]

Competency	Sub-competency	Definition
Leadership & Navigation	Navigating the Organization	Works within the parameters of the organization's hierarchy, processes, systems, and policies
	Vision	Defines and supports a coherent vision and long-term goals for HR that support the strategic direction of the organization
	Managing HR Initiatives	Implements and supports HR projects that align with HR and organizational objectives
	Influence	Inspires colleagues to understand and pursue the strategic vision and goals of HR and the organization
Ethical Practice	Personal Integrity	Demonstrates high levels of integrity in personal relationships and behaviors
	Professional Integrity	Demonstrates high levels of integrity in professional relationships and behaviors
	Ethical Agent	Cultivates the organization's ethical environment and ensures that policies and practices reflect ethical values
Diversity, Equity & Inclusion	Creating a Diverse and Inclusive Culture	Cultivates a work environment in which every person in an organization feels welcomed, respected, supported, and a sense of belonging
	Ensuring Equity Effectiveness	Ensures fair treatment in access, opportunity, and advancement for all individuals in the workplace
	Connecting DE&I to Organizational Performance	Demonstrates the importance of DE&I efforts in achieving organizational goals and key objectives
Relationship Management	Networking	Effectively builds a network of professional contacts both within and outside of the organization
	Relationship Building	Effectively builds and maintains relationships both within and outside of the organization
	Teamwork	Participates as an effective team member as well as builds, promotes, and leads effective teams
	Negotiation	Reaches mutually acceptable agreements with negotiating parties within and outside of the organization
	Conflict Management	Manages and resolves conflicts by identifying areas of common interest among the parties in conflict
Communication	Delivering Messages	Develops and delivers, to a variety of audiences, communications that are clear, persuasive, and appropriate to the topic and situations
	Exchanging Organizational Information	Effectively translates and communicates messages among organizational levels or units
	Listening	Understands information provided by others and seeks feedback

Table 2-2   SHRM Behavioral Sub-competency Definitions[5] *(continued)*

Competency	Sub-competency	Definition
Global Mindset	Operating in a Culturally Diverse Workplace	Demonstrates openness and respect when working with people from different cultural traditions
	Operating in a Global Environment	Effectively manages globally influenced workplace requirements to achieve organizational goals
	Advocating for a Culturally Diverse and Inclusive Workplace	Designs, implements, and promotes organizational policies and practices that encourage cultural diversity and inclusion in the workplace
Business Acumen	Business and Competitive Awareness	Understands the organization's operations, functions, products, and services as well as the competitive, economic, social, and political environments in which the organization operates
	Business Analysis	Applies business metrics, principles, and technologies to inform and address business needs
	Strategic Alignment	Aligns HR strategy, communications, initiatives, and operations with the organization's strategic direction
Consultation	Evaluating Business Challenges	Works with business partners and leaders to identify business challenges and opportunities for HR solutions
	Designing HR Solutions	Works with business partners and leaders to design HR solutions and initiatives that meet business needs
	Advising on HR Solutions	Works with business partners and leaders as they implement and support HR solutions and initiatives
	Change Management	Leads and supports maintenance of or changes in strategy, organization, and/or operations
	Service Excellence	Provides high-quality service to all stakeholders and contributes to a strong customer service culture
Analytical Aptitude	Data Advocate	Understands and promotes the importance and utility of data
	Data Gathering	Understands how to determine data utility as well as identifies and gathers data to inform organizational decisions
	Data Analysis	Analyzes data to evaluate HR initiatives and business challenges
	Evidence-Based Decision-Making	Uses the results of data analysis to inform the best course of action

Table 2-2   SHRM Behavioral Sub-competency Definitions[5]

SHRM Certification Commission

The SHRM Certification Commission[6] functions as a technical advisory committee established by SHRM to serve as a governance body for SHRM's certifying activities. The commission is composed of volunteers who have extensive HR and business expertise from industries and organizations throughout the world. The commission's mission is to ensure the highest quality and impartiality of SHRM's certification program. Its responsibilities include reviewing certificant eligibility, approving exam specifications and scoring, ensuring impartiality in certification activities, and ensuring due consideration of appeals and complaints.

Commission members are not financially compensated for their involvement but are reimbursed for their fair and reasonable expenses that are directly related to the commission's business activities.

The SHRM Body of Applied Skills and Knowledge

Increasingly, business leaders understand that effective people management is a strategic imperative. Employers expect that HR professionals will demonstrate, in addition to a basic knowledge of HR concepts and requirements, the behavioral competencies required to effectively apply their knowledge in the modern workplace. Because the HR profession is constantly changing and evolving, it is important for certified professionals to continually update their HR knowledge and competencies. Achieving the SHRM-CP or SHRM-SCP certification is a major step in this process.

The 2022 SHRM Body of Applied Skills and Knowledge[7] (SHRM BASK) is the basis for the SHRM certifications. The SHRM BASK draws heavily from the SHRM Competency Study, as it describes the behavioral competencies and functional areas of knowledge needed for effective job performance. The SHRM BASK explains not only what HR professionals need to know but also how they must apply this expertise to perform effectively in the workplace.

SHRM-CP and SHRM-SCP Exam Eligibility

Formerly, exam applicants were required to meet specific educational levels and work experience when submitting their applications.[8] As of 2022, eligibility has been significantly broadened. SHRM membership is not required, and you do not need to be currently employed to sit for either exam. Note the absence of required educational levels.

For the SHRM-CP:

- The SHRM-CP certification is for individuals who perform general HR/HR-related duties, or for those pursuing a career in Human Resource Management.

- Candidates for the SHRM-CP certification are not required to hold an HR title and do not need a degree or previous HR experience to apply; however, a basic working knowledge of HR practices and principles is recommended.

- The SHRM-CP exam is designed to assess the competency level of those who engage in HR work at the operational level. Work at this level includes duties such as implementing HR policies, supporting day-to-day HR functions, and serving as an HR point of contact for staff and stakeholders.

- Refer to the SHRM BASK for detailed information on proficiency standards (that is, Proficiency Indicators Only For All HR Professionals).

For the SHRM-SCP:

- The SHRM-SCP certification is for individuals who have a work history of at least 3 years performing strategic-level HR/HR-related duties; or for SHRM-CP certification holders who have had it for at least 3 years and are working in, or are in the process of transitioning to, a strategic level role.

- Candidates for the SHRM-SCP certification are not required to hold an HR title and do not need a degree to apply.

- The SHRM-SCP exam is designed to assess the competency level of those who engage in HR work at the strategic level. Work at this level includes duties such as developing HR policies and/or procedures, overseeing the execution of integrated HR operations, directing an entire HR enterprise, and leading the alignment of HR strategies to organizational goals.

- Applicants must be able to demonstrate that they devoted at least 1000 hours per calendar year (January–December) to strategic-level HR/HR-related work. More than 1000 hours in a calendar year does not equate to more than 1 year of experience.

- Part-time work qualifies as long as the 1000-hour-per-calendar-year standard is met.

- Experience may be either salaried or hourly.

- Individuals who are HR consultants may demonstrate qualifying experience through the HR/HR-related duties they perform for their clients. Contracted hours must meet the 1000-hour standard.

- Refer to the SHRM BASK for detailed information on proficiency standards (that is, Proficiency Indicators For All HR Professionals and For Advanced HR Professionals).

Which Certification Is Right for You?

Which certification to choose is an important decision that involves several factors. It is important to consider a number of variables when choosing your exam for the best odds of success. While education requirements have been eliminated, it is a factor for your personal consideration. While the SHRM-SCP now requires only 3 years of strategic HR experience, you well might want more experience before taking on that challenge. Factor in your HR experience and the variety of your HR responsibilities. The following are general guidelines to consider:

- SHRM-SCP certification is designed for HR professionals at a senior level who operate primarily in a strategic role developing policies and strategies, overseeing the execution of HR operations, analyzing performance metrics, planning, and contributing to the alignment of HR strategies to organizational goals.

- SHRM-CP certification is designed for HR practitioners who are engaged primarily in an operational HR role implementing policies, serving as the HR point of contact for staff and stakeholders, and performing day-to-day HR functions. If this is your focus, the SHRM-CP is likely your better option, even if you meet the eligibility criteria for the SHRM-SCP.

To ensure that you take the exam that best reflects your experience, compare your core responsibilities as reflected in your experience with the key proficiencies highlighted in the SHRM BASK. This should help you, as a test taker, make the choice most appropriate for achieving success. If you are still uncertain, shrmcertification.org provides an eligibility assessment tool you can use called "Which certification is right for you?"

 NOTE During the winter testing window each year (December 1 to February 15), SHRM offers both exams in Spanish. Applicants must specifically request the Spanish version when they apply for the exam.

Application Deadlines and Exam Windows

Currently, SHRM offers two 2.5-month-long exam windows—one in the winter beginning December 1, and one in the spring beginning May 1.[9] Candidates register for their exam between the application's accepted starting date and the regular application deadline. As of this writing, the application fees are US$375 for SHRM members and US$475 for non-SHRM members for either the SHRM-CP or SHRM-SCP exam. Discounts are available for early-bird, military, student, and corporate team registrations. Candidates who apply after the regular application deadline but before the late application deadline will incur a late application fee. Applications submitted after the late application deadline will not be accepted.

Go to www.shrm.org/certification/apply for detailed information.

Exam Delivery, Duration, and Format

Prometric is SHRM's test delivery vendor and provides computerized exam administration at more than 8000 secure testing centers in more than 180 countries.[10] The format and the time allowed for both exams is as follows:

- Both exams now consist of 134 multiple-choice questions. Eighty are stand-alone, knowledge-based questions and approximately 54 are situational judgement items to test your behavioral competencies.

- The exams are now divided in two parts: Section 1 and Section 2. For each section, you have up to 1 hour and 50 minutes. Once you submit Section 1, you may not access it again. You have the option to immediately begin Section 2 or take a break of up to 15 minutes.

- The computer test begins with a 2-minute Confidentiality Reminder. Then there is an Introduction/Tutorial that takes up to 10 minutes, but if you finish early, you are not allowed to apply that time elsewhere. The time for these do not take away from your 110 minutes for each exam section.

- The experience concludes with 8 minutes at the end of the exam for a survey.

Exam Content Outline

The SHRM-CP and SHRM-SCP exams are based on the SHRM BASK and its two major aspects of modern HR practice: competencies and knowledge. Accordingly, the exams contain two types of questions:[11]

- **Knowledge items**   These questions cover the three knowledge domains (People, Organization, and Workplace) associated with the SHRM BASK's HR technical competency. There are two categories of stand-alone knowledge-based items on the exams. Items in the first category are referred to as HR-specific *knowledge items (KIs)*, covering key concept topics associated with the 14 HR functional areas. KIs assess the candidate's understanding of factual information. Examinees are asked questions on particular subject areas. Items in the second category, referred to as *foundational knowledge items (FKIs)*, cover key concept topics considered foundational to the nine behavioral competencies. Correct answers receive full credit. Incorrect answers receive no credit.

- **Situational judgment items**   These questions cover the KSAOs (knowledge, skills, abilities, and other characteristics) associated with the SHRM BASK's behavioral competencies. *Situational judgment items (SJIs)* assess candidate KSAO capabilities and decision-making skills, which are not easily measured using traditional knowledge-based questions. Examinees are presented with realistic work-related scenarios and asked to choose the best of four strategies to resolve or address the issues described in each scenario.

Answers to these questions determine the final score for the exams. In addition, both exams contain "field test" items, the answers for which will not be scored. Field test items are unscored because they are being presented for the first time for the purpose of statistically determining their validity and reliability. Field test items are randomly distributed throughout the exam. Candidates' answers to field test questions will not count toward any part of their final exam scores, but there is no indicator as to whether a question will be counted or is a field question.

Table 2-3 shows the score weighting for each subject area.

HR Knowledge Domains	Item Type
People (18%)	
Organization (18%)	HR-specific knowledge (50%)
Workplace (14%)	
Behavioral Competency Clusters	**Item Type**
Leadership (17%)	
Business (16.5%)	Situational judgment (40%) Foundational knowledge (10%)
Interpersonal (16.5%)	

Table 2-3   Exam Score Content Weighting

Exam Identification and Conduct Guidelines

The SHRM certification exams are administered in highly secure testing centers.[12] All exam candidates are required to provide proof of identity with an unexpired government-issued photo identification with signature, such as a driver's license, a passport, or a military ID. The name on the ID must be an exact match to the name on the candidate's authorization to test (ATT) letter; otherwise, they will be turned away.

If the ID used does not have a photo or signature, a second form of identification must be provided that contains the missing information. The name on the second ID must be the same as the name on the first ID. The following are acceptable forms of secondary identification:

- Valid employer identification card
- Valid credit card with signature
- Valid bank card with photo

If you do not have the appropriate form of ID, contact SHRM at least 5 business days before your scheduled exam appointment date to determine your options.

Trained proctors, called *test center administrators (TCAs)*, supervise the Prometric testing centers. Irregularities observed or suspected by the proctors or identified by subsequent statistical analysis of your answers on the exam may result in your removal from participation in the test or invalidation of your score. Irregularities include, but are not limited to, creating a disturbance, giving or receiving unauthorized information or aid to or from other examinees, and attempting to remove materials from the testing room. SHRM has the right to investigate each incident of misconduct or irregularity.

Testing center rules of conduct include the following:

- You must present an unexpired government-issued ID with a photo and signature to be admitted to the exam.
- Arrive at the testing center at least 30 minutes before your scheduled exam appointment time to check in. Late arrivals are not admitted, so plan your transportation accordingly.
- Note-taking and the use of audible beepers, mobile phones, or memory-capable devices are prohibited in the testing room.
- You will be asked to empty and turn out your pockets.
- Candidates who must leave the testing room for an added break will not be given extra time on the exams. Once the exam clock begins, it keeps running until the end of Section 1, then again for Section 2.
- Candidates cannot leave the testing center during a break.
- Accessing your mobile phone or study materials after your arrival at the testing center or during breaks is prohibited. Therefore, do not bring any study materials with you to the testing center.

- Smoking is prohibited at the testing center and during breaks.

- Religious headwear can be worn into the testing room; however, it may be subject to inspection by a TCA before entry into the testing room is permitted.

- All exams are monitored and may be recorded in both audio and video format.

- Prometric will provide lockers for exam candidates to store their personal items such as purses, cell phones, jackets, food, drinks, and medical supplies.

My Experience Taking the SHRM-SCP Examination

While the exam timing and number of questions has changed since Bill Kelly wrote about his exam experience in 2015, we think you'll still enjoy hearing from an actual exam taker.

To be honest, I was "drafted" into taking the new SHRM-SCP examination as one of the SHRM Study Group instructors. The intention was to use my exam experience as an opportunity to share my insights with people preparing to take the SHRM-CP or SHRM-SCP exam for the first time. It was many years ago that I first took my SHRM SPHR exam (then called the "ASPA SPHR exam"), well before there was a Prometric to administer the exam nationwide using the wonderful capabilities of technology.

Following my first exam experience, I promised myself I would never do that again; I would always ensure I had sufficient credits to be able to recertify when the time came for recertification. Now, not only was I being asked to take the exam again, but, even scarier, this was SHRM's new certification program with a heightened presence of international subject matter and focus on behavioral competencies. I had been active in the HR profession for many years, but what if now I failed to pass the new SHRM-SCP exam? Well, it was too late to back out. Certainly, as a program instructor, my only choice was to accept this "opportunity" to take the exam.

First, I had to register with SHRM and then with Prometric. I chose a date late in the registration window more out of a lack of excitement (to put it mildly) than anything else. Finally, I registered to take the exam on June 24, scheduled from 1 P.M. to 5 P.M. (to be honest, the four-hour exam window was a bit intimidating by itself). My test location was Alameda, California. Okay, now I am committed, I thought, there was no backing out, unless maybe there was an earthquake. Actually, I didn't have much hope that would happen in a timely way. Oh well, time to prepare.

Although I carefully laid out a vigorous study plan (I wasn't going to be embarrassed if I could help it), as I suspected, a thousand unexpected things distracted me. I don't know if that was just my way of avoiding the issue or whether those things were real. Who knows? In any case, I found that the test date was just a week away and I still was only halfway through SHRM's Learning System. By the way, the Learning System is an excellent resource. It is an easy read and covers the subject matter well. But, not surprisingly, I found myself in panic mode a week before my test date. I decided to block big chunks of whatever time there was left to at least read all of the Learning System.

Well, June 24 arrived. Yes, I did read all of the Learning System material, but not as well as I should have. There was no backing out now, though. Normally, driving from Walnut Creek, where I live, to Alameda takes no more than an hour in the middle of a workday. I allowed two hours just to be safe. Actually, I drove the distance in less than 45 minutes. The good news was that I had time to kill; the bad news was that I had time to kill, but I was too nervous to do any last-minute studying. Even experienced HR professionals who have been around the block a few decades can be nervous when being tested on our knowledge and capabilities.

Prometric turned out to be well organized. The staff members were professional but thorough. Test takers really will do well to think of the airport security screening process to mentally prepare for the test center experience. No watches are allowed, not even the lowest-tech models. A metal-detecting wand was used all over, and there was a requirement to lift each pant leg to see whether anything was stashed in socks. We were allowed to take two tissues but instructed to keep them on the surface of the desk. A security camera is focused on every test taker.

The exam provides 3 hours and 40 minutes for answering 180 questions. Test takers are warned, so they don't feel cheated, especially if they had been timing themselves during their practice runs prior to the real thing. There is a pretest that takes up to 11 minutes, but if you finish early, you are not allowed to use the extra minutes elsewhere. By the way, the pretest is there to help you become familiar with the hardware and software. The remaining time is for survey questions, such as picking the three most important reasons you are testing for your SHRM certification.

A nice feature with the 90 scenario questions is an intuitive highlighter function. It is explained during the pretest. When test takers get to a scenario question, they should hit the "Next" button so they are able to read the first question they will need to answer from the scenario paragraphs. They should feel free to highlight anything that strikes them as being important. The scenario is on the left, and the questions are on the right side of the screen.

For the SHRM-SCP exam, the questions were grouped by styles—that is, knowledge followed by behavioral scenario and then knowledge again followed by scenario. As I recall, it went 30 knowledge questions, followed by 45 scenario questions, followed by 30 more knowledge questions, followed by 45 scenario questions, and finishing with 30 knowledge questions. There were 10 to 15 scenarios in total with several (two to five) multiple-choice questions attached to each of them.

SHRM-SCP test takers would be well served to know their balanced score cards, SWOT analysis, Perlmutter's HQ orientations, details of the WARN Act, and compa-ratios, but I didn't need to do any math.

There is a huge emphasis/bias in the material on large global institutions and big data. This bias may make many HR practitioners with mostly small-to-medium-size domestic organization experience feel overwhelmed, lost, or frustrated when preparing for this exam. (How do I make sense of this when our HRIS system is an Excel spreadsheet, or what if I don't have a corporate social responsibility manager like the text describes as an answer?)

(continued)

> Well, it turns out that after all was said and done, I passed!
>
> My closing thoughts are that this exam is really not for everyone. Even the experienced HR practitioner whose work experience is mainly with small-to-medium-size organizations may find the exam experience overwhelming. On the other hand, HR practitioners with large global organization experience will find the experience stimulating. Those who pass the exam certainly can say that they "earned" their certification.
>
> William D. Kelly, author

More on the Test Center

Wear layers to the test center since you don't know if where you are seated will feel warm or cool to you. Know you will not be allowed to take off a sweater or a jacket during the exam. Leave scarves and all jewelry other than wedding and engagement rings at home since there is a known history of making people take these items off.

Bring with you any snack and beverage you might want to consume during your exam day. No food or beverage may be taken into the testing room. Some test centers have an open shelf for easy access to these items just outside of the testing room. Others have you keep your snacks in your assigned locker.

Before you enter the testing room, make sure you have used the restroom. While of course you can leave the testing room to use the facilities, once the clock starts, it does not stop for any bathroom break. Also, the break will take more time than you think since you need to flag down a proctor who then goes through a specific protocol to secure your workstation during this interruption as well as makes sure you have no access to study materials. Plan so that this interruption is unnecessary.

As soon as you are escorted to your assigned workstation, do your own ergonomics check to make sure your chair is at the most comfortable height and that the screen does not have an uncomfortable glare.

There will be a calculator onscreen, and you should make sure it is working prior to beginning Section 1, even though it probably won't be needed. Your own calculator is not allowed. You will have the ability to write, but not the option to write anything down and take it out of the testing room with you. Most test centers provide a whiteboard with marker and eraser, but some provide a pencil with numbered sheets of paper that are returned at the end of the exam. It is completely legitimate if you want to write down any notes for yourself before the timed exam begins.

How Exams Are Scored

The SHRM certification exams are designed to distinguish candidates who have the appropriate levels of competency and knowledge from those who do not.

Your performance on the certification exam is measured against a predetermined standard. The SHRM-CP standard is the level of competency and knowledge that can be expected of individuals with basic competence in HR management. The SHRM-SCP standard is the level of competency and knowledge that can be expected of individuals with senior-level competence in HR management.

Your performance is not measured against the performance of other individuals taking the test. Therefore, if everyone who takes the test meets the knowledge and competency standards, everyone will pass.

Everyone who passes now gets a score of 200. It is 200 whether you scored just one question above failing or were perfect; you will never know. The range of scores is 120 to 200. Candidates will receive a Candidate Score and Feedback Report. In addition to your official score, the report will also have a diagnostic graph with performance information on the three HR knowledge domains of People, Organization, and Workplace, plus the behavioral competency clusters of Interpersonal, Business, and Leadership.[13]

SHRM has multiple versions of each exam for each exam window. While it's completely counterintuitive, you want the most difficult exam because it is scored the most generously.

Candidates will receive a provisional onscreen pass/did-not-pass decision at the testing center upon completion of the exam. An electronic version of the provisional report will be e-mailed to the address provided when the exam was scheduled. Approximately 3 to 4 weeks after sitting for the exam, candidates will receive an e-mail directing them to retrieve their official results from the SHRM online portal. Those who pass their exam will be able to download a PDF file of their certificate.

Official test results will be sent by postal mail to the primary address in the candidate's online account. To protect confidentiality, results are not provided by e-mail, phone, or fax.

Candidates who pass the exam receive an official score report plus a certificate and a lapel pin. The report confirms that they passed the exam, successfully completing the certification process. The newly certified also receive a laminated certification card the size of a credit card, which they may carry with them in their wallet.

Candidates who do not pass the exam receive an official score report with their actual score below 200, plus a diagnostic report outlining their performance. This information is provided to help candidates focus their preparations prior to retaking the exam.

Chapter Review

Human resource management has evolved over the years into a complex, multidimensional endeavor with expansive global as well as domestic implications. The need to establish competency in today's world requires HR professionals to apply both knowledge and behavioral competencies to carry out their responsibilities. The SHRM-Certified Professional (CP) and SHRM-Senior Certified Professional (SCP) certifications are designed to test and validate the HR professional's capabilities at all levels to meet today's requirements on a global scale.

References

1. 2022 SHRM Body of Applied Skills and Knowledge (BASK), Introduction, page 3.

2. 2022 SHRM Body of Applied Skills and Knowledge (BASK), Development of the SHRM BoCK, pages 6–9.

3. 2022 SHRM Body of Applied Skills and Knowledge (BASK), Competency, Sub-competency, and Domain Definitions, pages 5–85.

4. 2022 SHRM Body of Applied Skills and Knowledge (BASK), Competency Model, pages 3–4.

5. 2022 SHRM Body of Applied Skills and Knowledge (BASK), Sub-domain Definitions, pages 12–85.

6. https://www.shrm.org/certification/about/certification-commission/pages/default.aspx

7. SHRM Certification Handbook, The SHRM Skills and Knowledge (BASK), page 3.

8. SHRM Certification Handbook, Exam Eligibility Criteria, pages 7–8.

9. SHRM Certification Handbook, Application Deadlines and Exam Windows, page 10.

10. SHRM Certification Handbook, Preparing for the Exam, page 17.

11. SHRM Certification Handbook, Exam Composition, page 19.

12. SHRM Certification Handbook, Taking the Exam, page 21.

13. SHRM Certification Handbook, Test Results, page 23.

U.S. Laws and Regulations

In this chapter, we introduce the federal laws and legislation that the HR professional needs to know and understand. It is our belief that thoroughly reading these laws and regulations will help you understand the material written in Part II of this book. Knowing these laws can sometimes make the difference for the exam-taker on selecting the right answer on the SHRM Certified Professional (SHRM-CP) exam or the SHRM Senior Certified Professional (SHRM-SCP) exam. After studying this chapter and completing the practice questions, you should understand the relevance of these laws in the employment relationship. HR professionals in both small and large companies play a key role in dealing with day-to-day employment issues relating to the recruiting, hiring, managing, and training of employees. Ensuring that an employer's policies and actions follow the law and keeping employers out of legal jeopardy are essential functions valued by employers.

What You Need to Know
Concerning Employee Management

We have structured this chapter so that it not only covers the necessary knowledge needed for the Society for Human Resource Management (SHRM) exams but also includes additional laws. This way, the chapter can also be used as a reference tool for your day-to-day needs while working in human resources. The laws are summarized and listed in groupings according to the number of employees an organization employs, from 1 to 100+. Included is a reference uniform resource locator (URL) that points to the law's full description. For your ease of use, the laws appear in alphabetical order within each grouping. Legal regulation constantly evolves, so when using this guide as a reference book, be sure to check with your attorney about specific state laws that govern your work locations. The laws and regulations mentioned above are being presented by the number of employees on your payroll.

- If you have from 1 to 14 employees, there are 54 federal laws and regulations by which you must abide.
- If you have from 15 to 19 employees, there are an additional ten federal laws for your attention.
- If you have from 20 to 49 employees, add another four laws to the list.

- If you have from 50 to 99 employees, add another six laws to the list.

- If you have 100 or more employees, there are a total of 75 federal laws you must know and follow to stay in compliance.

- If you are in a federal agency, you must comply with six laws specifically focused on your employee management issues.

In other chapters, we will direct you back to this chapter's specific laws for reference. We suggest that you thoroughly explore this chapter's information before moving into subsequent chapters. Gauge your understanding of the laws by using the practice questions at the end of this chapter.

Please also note that while we share the year the legislation became law, it is for your understanding only. Neither the SHRM-CP nor the SHRM-SCP have any test questions about the years in which legislation became law.

For all the laws that follow, in addition to the resources provided for more information, you may of course always go to an Internet search engine and search for the law by name. We recommend gravitating toward government-sponsored websites for the most accurate information.

1. When You Have One or More Employees

Employers sometimes forget that the moment they hire their first employee, they become subject to a host of legal requirements. Here are 54 laws that will impact an employer with one or more employees on the payroll.

1.1. The Clayton Act (1914)

This legislation modified the Sherman Anti-Trust Act by prohibiting mergers and acquisitions that would lessen competition. It also prohibited a single person from being a director of two or more competing corporations. The act also restricts the use of injunctions against labor and legalized peaceful strikes, picketing, and boycotts.

For more information, see 15 U.S.C. Sec. 12 (www.law.cornell.edu/uscode/text/15/12).

1.2. The Consumer Credit Protection Act (1968)

Congress expressed limits to the amount of wages that can be garnished or withheld in any one week by an employer to satisfy creditors, usually a maximum of 25 percent. This law also prohibits employee dismissal because of garnishment for any one indebtedness.

For more information, see https://www.law.justia.com

1.3. The Copeland "Anti-Kickback" Act (1934)

This act precludes a federal contractor or subcontractor from inducing an employee to give up any part of his or her wages to the employer for the benefit of having a job. For more information, see https://www.dol.gov/agencies/whd/government-contracts/copeland-anti-kickback.

1.4. The Copyright Act (1976)

The Copyright Act offers protection of "original works" for authors so others may not print, duplicate, distribute, or sell their work. In 1998, the Copyright Term Extension Act further extended copyright protection to the duration of the author's life plus 70 years for general copyrights and to 95 years for works made for hire and works copyrighted before 1978. If anyone in the organization writes technical instructions, policies and procedures, manuals, or even e-mail responses to customer inquiries, it would be a prudent idea to speak with your attorney and arrange copyright agreements to clarify whether the employer or the employee who authored those documents will be designated the copyright owner. Written agreements can be helpful in avoiding any misunderstandings. For more information, see www.copyright.gov/title17/92appa.pdf.

1.5. The Davis-Bacon Act (1931)

This law requires contractors and subcontractors on certain federally funded or assisted construction projects over $2000 in the United States to pay wages and fringe benefits at least equal to those prevailing in the local area where the work is performed. This law applies only to laborers and mechanics. It also allows trainees and apprentices to be paid less than the predetermined rates under certain circumstances. For more information, see https://www.dol.gov/agencies/whd/government-contracts/construction.

1.6. The Dodd-Frank Wall Street Reform and Consumer Protection Act (2010)

This law offers a very wide range of mandates affecting all federal financial regulatory agencies and most parts of the nation's financial services industry. It includes a non-binding vote for shareholders on executive compensation, golden parachutes, and return of executive compensation based on inaccurate financial statements. Also included are requirements to report chief executive officer (CEO) pay compared to the average employee compensation and provision of financial rewards for whistleblowers. The U.S. Securities and Exchange Commission (SEC) reports the adoption of 67 mandatory rulemaking provisions stemming from the Dodd-Frank Act. For more information, see www.sec.gov/about/laws/wallstreetreform-cpa.pdf.

1.7. The Economic Growth and Tax Relief Reconciliation Act (EGTRRA) (2001)

Here we find modifications to the Internal Revenue Code for adjusting pension vesting schedules, increasing retirement plan limits, permitting pre-tax catch-up contributions by participants over the age of 50 in certain plans (which are not tested for discrimination when made available to the entire workforce), and changing distribution and rollover rules. For more information, see www.irs.gov/pub/irs-tege/epchd104.pdf.

1.8. The Electronic Communications Privacy Act (ECPA) (1986)

This is a unique law composed of two pieces of legislation: the Wiretap Act and the Stored Communications Act. Combined, they provide rules for access, use, disclosure, interpretation, and privacy protections of electronic communications, and they provide the possibility of both civil and criminal penalties for violations. They prohibit interception of e-mails in transmission and access to e-mails in storage. The implications for HR have to do with recording employee conversations. Warnings such as "This call may be monitored or recorded for quality purposes" are intended to provide the notice required by this legislation. Having cameras in the workplace to record employee or visitor activities is also covered, and notices must be given to anyone subject to observation or recording. Recording without such a notice can be a violation of this act. If employers make observations of employee activities and/or record telephone and other conversations between employees and others and proper notice is given to employees, then employees will have no expectation of privacy during the time they are in the workplace. For more information, see www.justice.gov/jmd/ls/legislative_histories/pl99-508/pl99-508.html.

1.9. The Employee Polygraph Protection Act (1988)

Before 1988, it was common for employers to use a "lie detector" as a tool in investigations of inappropriate employee behavior. That changed when this act prohibited the use of lie detector tests for job applicants and employees of companies engaged in interstate commerce. Exceptions are made for certain limited conditions:

- The test is part of an ongoing investigation of losses suffered by the employer.
- The tested employee had access to the property in question.
- The employer had reasonable suspicion of the employee's involvement.
- The employer provides a statement of the basis for the preceding conditions.

There is also an exception to allow testing of job applicants when the job is either with a certain type of security firm or with a manufacturer or distributor of controlled substances and the employee would have direct access to said controlled substances. There is a federal poster requirement. Be aware that if an employee voluntarily agrees to the polygraph test, they may change their mind at any time without any repercussions. Note that many state laws also prohibit the use of lie detector tests.

For more information, see https://www.dol.gov/agencies/whd/polygraph.

1.10. The Employee Retirement Income Security Act (ERISA) (1974)

This law doesn't require employers to establish pension plans, but instead governs how those plans are managed once they are established. It establishes uniform minimum standards to ensure that employee benefit plans are established and maintained in a fair and financially sound manner. It also protects employees covered by a pension plan from losses in benefits due to job changes, plant closings, bankruptcies, or mismanagement, and it protects plan beneficiaries. It covers most employers engaged in interstate commerce. Public-sector employees and churches are not subject to ERISA. Employers that offer retirement plans must also conform with the Internal Revenue Service (IRS) code to receive tax advantages.

ERISA also established the PBCG, Pension Benefit Guaranty Corporation. The PBGC acts as insurance for pension plans, and all corporations offering employee pension plans are required to make payments into it.

Another ERISA provision establishes minimum vesting schedules. A company may choose either cliff vesting or graduated vesting. The former is zero vesting until the employee's third work anniversary, when they change to 100 percent vested. Graduated, step, or stair (all interchangeable terms) vesting must begin with at least 20 percent vested after 2 years, followed by 20 percent more each year, thus going from 20 percent, to 40 percent, to 60 percent, to 80 percent, to 100 percent at six years. For more information, see https://www.dol.gov/agencies/ebsa/about-ebsa/about-us/history-of-ebsa-and-erisa.

1.11. The Equal Pay Act (EPA) (Amendment to the FLSA) (1963)

Equal pay requirements apply to all employers. The act is an amendment to the FLSA and is enforced by the Equal Employment Opportunity Commission (EEOC). It prohibits employers from discriminating on the basis of sex by paying wages to employees at a rate less than the rate paid to employees of the opposite sex for equal work on jobs requiring substantially equal skill, effort, and responsibility, and performed under similar working conditions. It does not address the concept of comparable worth. For more information, see www.eeoc.gov/laws/statutes/epa.cfm.

1.12. The FAA Modernization and Reform Act (2012)

Congress took action in 2012 to amend the Railway Labor Act to change union certification election processes in the railroad and airline industries and impose greater oversight of the regulatory activities of the National Mediation Board (NMB). This law requires the Government Accountability Office (GAO) initially to evaluate the NMB's certification procedures and then audit the NMB's operations every 2 years. For more information, see https://www.law.justia.com

1.13. The Fair and Accurate Credit Transactions Act (FACT) (Amendment to the FCRA) (2003)

The financial privacy of employees and job applicants was enhanced in 2003 with these amendments to the Fair Credit Reporting Act, providing for certain requirements in third-party investigations of employee misconduct charges. Employers are released from obligations to disclose requirements and obtain employee consent if the investigation involves suspected misconduct, a violation of the law or regulations, or a violation of preexisting written employer policies. A written plan to prevent identity theft is required. For more information, see https://www.ftc.gov/legal-library/browse/statutes/fair-accurate-credit-transactions-act-2003.

1.14. The Fair Credit Reporting Act (FCRA) (1970)

This was the first major legislation to regulate the collection, dissemination, and use of consumer information, including consumer credit information. It requires employers to notify any individual in writing if a credit report may be used in making an employment decision. Employers must also get a written authorization from the subject individual before asking a credit bureau for a credit report. The Fair Credit Reporting Act also protects the privacy of background investigation information and provides methods for ensuring that information is accurate. Employers who take adverse action against a job applicant or current employee based on information contained in the prospective or current employee's consumer report will have additional disclosures to make to that individual. For more information, see https://www.ftc.gov/legal-library/browse/statutes/fair-credit-reporting-act.

1.15. The Fair Labor Standards Act (FLSA) (1938) and Provisions Effective January 1, 2020

The FLSA is one of a handful of federal laws that establishes the foundation for employee treatment. It is a major influence in how people are paid, young people are employed, and records are to be kept on employment issues such as hours of work. The law introduced a maximum 44-hour, 7-day workweek, established a national minimum wage, guaranteed "time-and-a-half" for overtime in certain jobs, and prohibited most employment of minors in "oppressive child labor," a term that is defined in the statute. It applies to employees engaged in interstate commerce or employed by an enterprise engaged in commerce or in the production of goods for commerce, unless the employer can claim an exemption from coverage. It is interesting to note that FLSA, rather than the Civil Rights Act of 1964, is the first federal law to require employers to maintain records on employee race and sex identification.

Provisions and Protections

Employers covered under the "enterprise" provisions of this law include the following:

- Public agencies
- Private employers whose annual gross sales exceed $500,000
- Those operating a hospital or a school for mentally or physically disabled children, or gifted children
- Preschools, elementary and secondary schools, and institutions of higher education (profit or nonprofit)

Individuals can still be covered even if they don't fit into one of the enterprises listed. If the employees' work regularly involves them in commerce between states, they would be covered. These include employees who work in communications or transportation; regularly use the mail, telephone, or telegraph (as originally written) for interstate communication or keep records of interstate transactions; handle the shipping or receiving of goods moving in interstate commerce; regularly cross state lines in the course of employment; or work for independent employers who contract to do clerical, custodial, maintenance, or other work for firms engaged in interstate commerce or in the production of goods for interstate commerce. The FLSA establishes a federal minimum wage that has been raised from time to time since the law was originally passed. The FLSA prohibits the shipment of goods in interstate commerce that were produced in violation of the minimum wage, overtime pay, child labor, or special minimum wage provisions of the law.

Exempt Employees

FLSA sets a three-part criteria how employees may be classified as exempt from the FLSA rules:

- The employee must be paid on a salary basis.
- The employee must be engaged in "exempt" duties. The different exempt categories are defined within the statute and are executive, administrative, professional, computer, outside sales, and highly compensated.
- The employee must earn a minimum amount. This amount was raised January 1, 2020 by the Department of Labor to at least $684 per week, which is equal to an annual salary of $35,568.

Recordkeeping

FLSA proscribes methods for determining whether a job is exempt or nonexempt from the overtime pay requirements of the act. If a job is exempt from those requirements, incumbents can work overtime as the job requires without receiving additional pay. Exempt versus nonexempt status attaches to the job, not the incumbent. Therefore, someone with an advanced degree who is working in a clerical job may be nonexempt because of the job requirements, not their personal qualifications. Employers are permitted to be more generous than the FLSA and have a policy that calls for paying exempt employees when they work overtime. That is a voluntary option in excess of federal requirements. State laws may have additional requirements. People who work in nonexempt jobs must be paid overtime according to the rate computation methods provided for in the act. Usually, this is a requirement for overtime after 40 hours of regular time worked during a single workweek. The act also describes how a workweek is to be determined.

Each employer covered by the FLSA must keep records for each covered, nonexempt worker. Those records must include the following:

- Employee's full name and Social Security number.
- Address, including ZIP code.
- Birth date, if younger than 19.

- Sex.
- Occupation.
- Time and day of week when employee's workweek begins.
- Hours worked each day and total hours worked each workweek. (This includes a record of the time work began at the start of the day, when the employee left for a meal break, the time the employee returned to work from the meal break, and the time work ended for the day.)
- Basis on which the employee's wages are paid (hourly, weekly, piecework).
- Regular hourly pay rate.
- Total daily or weekly straight-time earnings.
- Total overtime earnings for the workweek.
- All additions or deductions from the employee's wages.
- Total wages paid each pay period.
- Date of payment and the pay period covered by the payment.

There is no limit in the FLSA to the number of hours employees age 16 and older may work in any workweek. There is a provision for employers to retain all payroll records, collective bargaining agreements, sales, and purchase records for at least 3 years. Any timecard, piecework record, wage rate tables, and work and time schedules should be retained for at least 2 years. A workplace poster is required to notify employees of the federal minimum wage, even if the state minimum wage is higher.

The federal child labor provisions of the FLSA, also known as the child labor laws, were enacted to ensure that when young people work, the work is safe and does not jeopardize their health, well-being, or educational opportunities. These provisions also provide limited exemptions. Workers under 14 years of age are restricted to jobs such as newspaper delivery to local customers; babysitting on a casual basis; acting in movies, TV, radio, or theater; and working as a home worker, gathering evergreens and making evergreen wreathes. Under no circumstances, even if the business is family owned, may a person this young work in any of the 17 most hazardous jobs. See Figure 3-1 for a list of the 17 most hazardous jobs.

For workers 14 and 15 years of age, all work must be performed outside school hours, and these youth may not work

- More than 3 hours on a school day, including Friday.
- More than 18 hours per week when school is in session.
- More than 8 hours per day when school is not in session.
- More than 40 hours per week when school is not in session.
- Before 7 A.M. or after 7 P.M. on any day, except from June 1 through Labor Day, when nighttime work hours are extended to 9 P.M.

- Manufacturing or storing of explosives
- Driving a motor vehicle or working as an outside helper on motor vehicles
- Coal mining
- Forest fire fighting and forest fire prevention, timber tract, forestry service, and occupations in logging and sawmilling
- Using power-driven woodworking machines
- Exposure to radioactive substances and ionizing radiation
- Using power-driven hoisting apparatuses
- Using power-driven metal-forming, punching, and shearing machines
- Mining, other than coal

- Using power-driven meat-processing machines, slaughtering, meat and poultry packing, processing, or rendering
- Using power-driven bakery machines
- Using balers, compactors, and power-driven paper-product machines
- Manufacturing brick, tile, and related products
- Using power-driven circular saws, band saws, guillotine shears, chain saws, reciprocating saws, woodchippers, and abrasive cutting discs
- Working in wrecking, demolition, and ship-breaking operations
- Roofing and work performed on or about a roof
- Trenching or excavating

Source: U.S. Department of Labor, eLaws Advisors, "Fair Labor Standards Act Advisor"

Figure 3-1 The 17 most dangerous jobs that may not be performed by workers under 18 years of age

Until employees reach the age of 18, it is necessary for them to obtain a work permit from their school district. For workers 16 and 17 years of age, there are no restrictions on the number of hours that can be worked per week. There continues to be a ban on working any job among the 17 most hazardous industries. All of these conditions must be met, or the employer will be subject to penalties from the U.S. Department of Labor.

Overtime Computation

Overtime is required at a rate of 1.5 times the normal pay rate for all hours worked over 40 in a single workweek for nonexempt employees. An employer may designate that their workweek begins at a given day and hour and continues until that same day and hour 7 days later. Once selected, that same workweek definition must be maintained consistently until there is a legitimate business reason for making a change. That change must be clearly communicated in advance to all employees who will be affected by the change. No pay may be forfeited because the employer changes its workweek definition. Compensating time off in lieu of overtime pay is permitted only for the public sector under the FLSA if it is given at the same rates required for overtime pay.

Enforcement

Provisions of the FLSA are enforced by the U.S. Department of Labor's Wage and Hour Division. With offices around the country, this agency can interact with employees on complaints and follow up with employers by making an on-site visit if necessary. If violations are found during an investigation, the agency has the authority to make recommendations for changes that would bring the employer into compliance.

An employer that retaliates against any employee for filing a complaint under the FLSA or in any other way availing himself or herself of the legal rights it offers is subject to additional penalties. Willful violations may bring criminal prosecution and fines up to $10,000. Employers convicted a second time for willfully violating the FLSA can find themselves in prison.

The Wage and Hour Division may, if it finds products produced during violations of the act, prevent an employer from shipping any of those goods. It may also "freeze" shipments of any product manufactured while overtime payment requirements were violated. A 2-year limit applies to recovery of back pay unless there was a willful violation, which triggers a 3-year liability. For more information, see www.dol.gov/whd/regs/statutes/FairLaborStandAct.pdf.

1.16. The Foreign Corrupt Practices Act (FCPA) (1997)

The FCPA prohibits American companies from making bribery payments to foreign officials for the purpose of obtaining or keeping business. Training for employees who are involved with international negotiations should include a warning to avoid anything even looking like a bribery payment to a foreign company or its employees. For more information, see www.justice.gov/criminal/fraud/fcpa/.

1.17. The Health Information Technology for Economic and Clinical Health Act (HITECH) (2009)

The HITECH Act requires that anyone with custody of personal health records send notification to affected individuals if their personal health records have been disclosed, or the employer believes they have been disclosed, to any unauthorized person. Enacted as part of the American Recovery and Reinvestment Act (ARRA), this law made changes to the Health Insurance Portability and Accountability Act (HIPAA), including the establishment of a federal standard for security breach notifications that requires covered entities, in the event of a breach of any personal health information (PHI), to notify each individual whose PHI has been disclosed without authorization. For more information, see www.hhs.gov/ocr/privacy/hipaa/administrative/enforcementrule/hitechenforcementifr.html.

1.18. The Health Insurance Portability and Accountability Act (HIPAA) (1996)

This law ensures that individuals who leave or lose their jobs can obtain health coverage even if they or someone in their family has a serious illness or injury or is pregnant. It also provides privacy requirements related to medical records for individuals as young as 12 years old. It limits exclusions for preexisting conditions and guarantees renewability of health coverage to employers and employees, allowing people to change jobs without the worry of loss of coverage. It also restricts the ability of employers to impose actively-at-work requirements as preconditions for health plan eligibility, as well as a number of other benefits. For more information, see https://www.law.justia.com.

1.19. The Immigration and Nationality Act (INA) (1952)

The INA is the first law that pulled together all the issues associated with immigration and is considered the foundation on which all following immigration laws have been built. It addresses employment eligibility and employment verification. It defines the conditions for the temporary and permanent employment of aliens in the United States.

The INA defines an *alien* as any person lacking citizenship or status as a national of the United States. The INA differentiates aliens as follows:

- Resident or nonresident

- Immigrant or nonimmigrant

- Documented and undocumented

The perceived need to curtail illegal immigration led to the enactment of the Immigration Reform and Control Act (IRCA). For more information, see https://www.dol.gov/agencies/whd/immigration.

1.20. The Immigration Reform and Control Act (IRCA) (1986)

This is the first law to require new employees to prove both their identity and their right to work in this country. Regulations implementing this law created the Form I-9,[1] which must be completed by each new employee and the employer. Form I-9 has been updated many times since 1986. Be sure you are using the most current version of the form and note the documents presented by your new employee to confirm both identification and right to work in the United States. These documents must be current and not expired. Also, there are document retention requirements. The law prohibits discrimination against job applicants based on national origin or citizenship. It establishes penalties for employers who hire undocumented immigrants. For more information, see https://www.congress.gov/bill/99th-congress/senate-bill/1200.

1.21. The IRS Intermediate Sanctions (2002)

Here we find guidelines for determining reasonable compensation for executives of nonprofit organizations. It was enacted by the IRS and applied to nonprofit organizations. Quoting from the sanctions, "The purpose of IRC (Internal Revenue Code) 4958 is to impose sanctions on the influential persons in charities and social welfare organizations who receive excessive economic benefits from the organization, rather than to punish the exempt organization itself." These rules allow the IRS to impose penalties when it determines that top officials have received excessive compensation from their organizations. Intermediate sanctions may be imposed either in addition to or instead of revocation of the exempt status of the organization. For more information, see www.irs.gov/pub/irs-tege/eotopice03.pdf.

1.22. The Labor-Management Relations Act (LMRA) (1947)

Also called the Taft-Hartley Act, this is the first national legislation that placed controls on unions. It prohibits unfair labor practices by unions and outlaws closed shops, where union membership is required to get and keep a job. Employers may not form closed-shop agreements with unions. It requires both parties to bargain in good faith and covers nonmanagement employees in private industry who are not covered by the Railway Labor Act.

For more information, see https://www.justice.gov/jm/jm-9-132000-labor-management-relations-act-29-usc-186.

1.23. The Labor-Management Reporting and Disclosure Act (LMRDA) (1959)

Also called the Landrum-Griffin Act, this law outlines procedures for redressing internal union problems, protects the rights of union members from corrupt or discriminatory labor unions, and applies to all labor organizations. Specific requirements include the following:

- Unions must conduct secret elections, the results of which can be reviewed by the U.S. Department of Labor.
- A bill of rights guarantees union members certain rights, including free speech.
- Convicted felons and members of the Communist Party cannot hold office in unions.
- Annual financial reporting from unions to the Department of Labor is required.
- All union officials have a fiduciary responsibility in managing union assets and conducting the business of the union.
- Union power to place subordinate organizations in trusteeship is limited.
- Minimum standards for union disciplinary action against its members are provided.

For more information, see https://www.dol.gov/agencies/olms/laws.

1.24. The Mine Safety and Health Act (MSHA) (1977)

Following a series of deadly mining disasters, the American people demanded that Congress take action to prevent similar events in the future. This law converted the existing Mine Enforcement Safety Administration (MESA) to the Mine Safety and Health Administration (MSHA). For the first time, it brought all coal, metal, and nonmetal mining operations under the same Department of Labor jurisdiction. Regulations and safety procedures for the coal mining industry were not altered, just carried into the new agency for oversight. For more information, see https://www.msha.gov/.

Provisions and Protections

This law requires the secretaries of labor and health, education, and welfare to create regulations governing the country's mines. All mines are covered if they are involved in commerce, which any active mining operation would be. Regulations that implement this law specify that employees must be provided with certain personal protective equipment (PPE) while working in a mine. These devices relate to respiration and fire prevention, among other protections. Protecting against "black lung disease" is a key concern, even today, in the coal mining industry.

Recordkeeping Requirements

Employers engaged in mining operations must inspect their worksites and document the results, reflecting hazards and actions taken to reduce or eliminate the hazards. Employees are to be given access to information related to accident prevention, fatal accident statistics for the year, and instructions on specific hazards they will face while working in the mine. Employers are required to detail the content of written emergency response plans, emergency mapping, and rescue procedures. Individual employee exposure records must be maintained. Each mine operator is required to conduct surveys of mine exposures and hazards, have a plan to deal with those problems, and keep a record of the results. This information must be made available to MSHA inspectors if they request it.

MSHA Standards

The agency enforces mine safety standards that involve ventilation, chemical exposure, noise, forklifts, and other mining equipment, mine shoring, and more. Safety data sheets (SDSs) must be available to employees in mining as they are in other industries overseen by the OSHA agency.

MSHA Enforcement

MSHA has a team of federal inspectors that conduct on-site audits of mining operations. MSHA has the authority to cite mine operators for violations of its regulations, and citations can carry a $1000-per-day penalty in some circumstances.[2]

1.25. The National Industrial Recovery Act (1933)

This was an attempt to help the country get out from the Great Depression. It proposed the creation of "Codes of Fair Competition" for each of several different industries. Essentially, every business would have to identify with and belong to a trade association. The association would then be required to create a Code of Fair Competition for the industry. Antitrust laws would be suspended in favor of the code. Of course, the code would have to be approved by the president of the United States, and the administration would issue federal licenses to every business in the country. If a business refused to participate in the code, its license could be suspended, and that would be the signal for that business to end all operations. There were financial penalties as well. This law didn't fare very well. It was declared unconstitutional by the U.S. Supreme Court in 1935 and was replaced by the National Labor Relations Act later that same year.

For more information, see https://www.archives.gov/milestone-documents/national-industrial-recovery-act.

1.26. The National Labor Relations Act (NLRA) (1935)

This is the "granddaddy" of all labor relations laws in the United States. It initially provided that employees have a right to form unions and negotiate wage and hour issues with employers on behalf of the union membership. Specifically, the NLRA grants to employees the right to organize, join unions, and engage in collective bargaining and other "concerted activities." It also protects against unfair labor practices by employers.

Following on the heels of the National Industrial Recovery Act's failures, this law stepped into the void and addressed both union and employer obligations in labor relations issues. It established the National Labor Relations Board (NLRB), which would help define fair labor practices in the following decades. The NLRB has the power to accept and investigate complaints of unfair labor practices by either management or labor unions. It plays a judicial role within an administrative setting. This law is sometimes called the Wagner Act. The following are its key provisions:

- The right of workers to organize into unions for collective bargaining
- The requirement of employers to bargain in good faith when employees have voted in favor of a union to represent them
- Requirement that unions represent all members equally
- Covers nonmanagement employees in private industry who are not already covered by the Railway Labor Act
- Established the National Labor Relations Board to oversee elections of unions seeking recognition to represent employees, plus hear and rule on charges of unfair labor practices.

For more information, see https://www.nlrb.gov/guidance/key-reference-materials/national-labor-relations-act.

1.27. The Needlestick Safety and Prevention Act (2000)

This law modifies the Occupational Safety and Health Act (OSHA) by introducing a new group of requirements in the medical community. Sharps, as they are called, are needles, puncture devices, knives, scalpels, and other tools that can harm either the person using them or someone else. The law and its regulations provide rules related to handling these devices, disposing of them, and encouraging invention of new devices that will reduce or eliminate the risk associated with injury due to sharps. Injuries by sharps are to be recorded on the OSHA 300 log with "privacy case" listed instead of the employee's name. Blood-borne pathogens and transmission of human blood–borne illnesses such as AIDS/HIV and hepatitis are key targets of this law. Reducing the amount of injury and subsequent illness due to puncture, stab, or cut wounds is a primary objective. There are communication requirements, including employment poster content requirements.

For more information, see https://www.congress.gov/bill/106th-congress/house-bill/5178.

1.28. The Norris-LaGuardia Act (1932)

Remember that when this law was enacted, it was still 3 years before the NLRA was enacted. When unions tried to use strikes and boycotts, employers would trot into court and ask for an injunction to prevent such activity. More often than not, employers were successful, and judges provided the injunctions. Congress had been pressured by organized labor to restore their primary tools that could force employers to bargain on issues unions saw as important. The following are key provisions of this law:

- It prohibited "yellow-dog" contracts. Those contracts were agreements in which employees promised employers that they would not join unions. This new law declared such contracts to be unenforceable in any federal court.

- It prohibited federal courts from issuing injunctions of any kind against peaceful strikes, boycotts, or picketing when used by a union in connection with a labor dispute.

- It defined labor dispute to include any disagreement about working conditions.

For more information, see http://legislation.lawi.us/norris-laguardia-act/.

1.29. The Occupational Safety and Health Act (OSHA) (1970)

Signed into law by President Richard M. Nixon on December 29, 1970, the Occupational Safety and Health Act created an administrative agency within the U.S. Department of Labor called the Occupational Safety and Health Administration (OSHA). It also created the National Institute of Occupational Safety and Health (NIOSH), which resides inside the Centers for Disease Control and Prevention (CDC).

Provisions and Protections

Regulations implementing this legislation have grown over time. They are complex and detailed. It is important that HR professionals understand the basics and how to obtain additional detailed information that applies to their particular employer circumstances. There are many standards that specify what employers must do to comply with their legal obligations. Overall, however, the law holds employers accountable for providing a safe and healthy working environment. The "General Duty Clause" in OSHA's regulations says employers shall furnish each employee with a place of employment free from recognized hazards that are likely to cause death or serious injury. It also holds employees responsible for abiding by all safety rules and regulations in the workplace. Some provisions require notices to be posted in the workplace covering some of the OSHA requirements. Posters are available for download from the OSHA website without charge. The law applies to all employers, regardless of the employee population size.

Recordkeeping Requirements

OSHA regulations require that records be kept for many purposes. It is necessary to conduct and document inspections of the workplace that look for safety and health hazards. It is necessary to document and make available to employees records about hazardous materials and how they must be properly handled. Employers with ten or more people on the payroll must summarize all injury and illness instances and post that summary in a conspicuous place within the workplace. That report must remain posted from February 1 to April 30 each year. Certain employers are exempt from some OSHA recordkeeping requirements. They generally are classified by industry Standard Industrial Classification (SIC) code. A list is available on OSHA's website at www.osha .gov. Any time there is a serious or fatal accident, a full incident report must be prepared by the employer and maintained in the safety file. These records must be maintained for a minimum of 5 years from the date of the incident. Known as a log of occupational injury or illness, it must include a record of each incident resulting in medical treatment (other than first aid), loss of consciousness, restriction of work or motion, or transfer or termination of employment. If you are in the medical industry, construction industry, or manufacturing industry, or you use nuclear materials of any kind, there are additional requirements you must meet. Key to compliance with OSHA rules is communication with employees. Employers often provide training to meet this hazard communication requirement. In summary, then, OSHA recordkeeping involves the following:

- Periodic safety inspections of the workplace
- Injury or illness incident reports
- Annual summary of incidents during the previous calendar year
- Injury and illness prevention program (if required by rules governing your industry)
- Employee training on safety procedures and expectations
- Records of training participation
- Safety data sheets for each chemical used in the workplace (made available to all employees in a well-marked file or binder that can be accessed at any time during work hours)

Occupational Safety and Health Act Enforcement

OSHA inspections may include the following:

- **On-site visits that are conducted without advance notice**   Inspectors can just walk into a place of employment and request that you permit an inspection. You don't have to agree unless the inspector has a search warrant. In the absence of the warrant, you can delay the inspection until your attorney is present. Note that OSHA inspectors have printers in their cars and know which judges are most likely to grant a warrant. This means turning away an inspector until a search warrant is in hand may only buy you 15 to 30 minutes, and now the inspector views you as less cooperative.

- **On-site inspections or phone/fax investigations**   Depending on the urgency of the hazard and the agreement of the person filing the complaint, inspectors may telephone or fax inquiries to employers. The employer has 5 working days to respond with a detailed description of inspection findings, corrective action taken, and additional action planned.

- **Highly trained compliance officers**   The OSHA Training Institute provides training for OSHA's compliance officers, state compliance officers, state consultants, other federal agency personnel, and the private sector.

Inspection priorities are in the following order, starting with most important:

- **Imminent danger**   Situations where death or serious injury are highly likely. Compliance officers will ask employers to correct the conditions immediately or remove employees from danger.

- **Fatalities and catastrophes**   Incidents that involve a death or the hospitalization of three or more employees. Employers must report these incidents to OSHA within 8 hours, so it doesn't hurt to put OSHA's telephone number in your contacts: 800-321-OSHA.

- **Worker complaints**   Allegations of violations of OSHA standards, workplace hazards, unsafe or unhealthful working conditions. Employees may request anonymity when they file complaints with OSHA. OSHA forbids discrimination against employees who request inspections.

- **Referrals**   Other federal, state, and local agencies as well as individuals, organizations, and the media can make referrals to OSHA, so the agency may consider making an inspection.

- **Follow-ups**   Checks for abatement of violations cited during previous inspections are also conducted by OSHA personnel in certain circumstances.

- **Planned or programmed investigations**   OSHA can conduct inspections aimed at specific high-hazard industries or individual workplaces that have experienced high rates of injuries and illnesses. These are sometimes called *targeted investigations*.

Two Types of Standards

The law provides for two types of safety and health standards. The agency has therefore developed its regulations and standards in those two categories.

Normal Standards   If OSHA determines that a specific standard is needed, any of several advisory committees may be called upon to develop specific recommendations. There are two standing committees, and ad hoc committees may be appointed to examine special areas of concern to OSHA. All advisory committees, standing or ad hoc, must have members representing management, labor, and state agencies, as well as one or more designees of the secretary of Health and Human Services (HHS). The occupational safety and health professions and the general public also may be represented.[3]

Emergency Temporary Standards   "Under certain limited conditions, OSHA is authorized to set emergency temporary standards that take effect immediately. First, OSHA must determine that workers are in grave danger due to exposure to toxic substances or agents determined to be toxic or physically harmful or to new hazards and that an emergency standard is needed to protect them. Then, OSHA publishes the emergency temporary standard in the Federal Register, where it also serves as a proposed permanent standard. It is then subject to the usual procedure for adopting a permanent standard except that a final ruling must be made within six months. The validity of an emergency temporary standard may be challenged in an appropriate U.S. Court of Appeals."[4] For more information, see https://www.osha.gov/.

1.30. The Omnibus Budget Reconciliation Act (OBRA) (1993)

Signed into law by President Bill Clinton on August 10, 1993, this legislation reduces compensation limits in qualified retirement programs and triggers increased activity in nonqualified retirement programs. It also calls for the termination of some plans. For more information, see https://www.congress.gov/bill/103rd-congress/house-bill/2264.

1.31. The Pension Protection Act (PPA) (2006)

Focused solely on pensions, this law requires employers that have underfunded pension plans to pay a higher premium to the Pension Benefit Guarantee Corporation (PBGC). It also requires employers that terminate pension plans to provide additional funding to those plans. This legislation impacted nearly all aspects of retirement planning, including changes to rules about individual retirement accounts (IRAs). For more information, see https://www.dol.gov/agencies/ebsa/laws-and-regulations/laws/pension-protection-act.

1.32. The Personal Responsibility and Work Opportunity Reconciliation Act (1996)

This law requires all states to establish and maintain a new hire reporting system designed to enhance enforcement of child support payments. It requires welfare recipients to begin working after 2 years of receiving benefits. States may exempt parents with children younger than 1 from the work requirements. Parents with children younger than 1 may use this exemption only once; they cannot use it again for subsequent children. These parents also are still subject to the 5-year time limit for cash assistance. HR professionals will need to establish and maintain reporting systems to meet these tracking requirements. For more information, see www.acf.hhs.gov/programs/css/resource/the-personal-responsibility-and-work-opportunity-reconcilliation-act.

1.33. The Portal-to-Portal Act (1947)

By amending the Fair Labor Standards Act (FLSA), this law defines "hours worked" and establishes rules about payment of wages to employees who travel before and/or after their scheduled work shift. The act provides that minimum wages and overtime are not required for "traveling to and from the actual place of performance of the principal activity or activities which such employee is to perform" or for "activities which are preliminary to or postliminary to said principal activity or activities," unless there is a custom or contract to the contrary. For more information, see https://uscode.house.gov/view.xhtml?path=/prelim@title29/chapter9&edition=prelim.

1.34. The Railway Labor Act (1926)

Originally, this law was created to allow railway employees to organize into labor unions. Over the years, it has been expanded in coverage to include airline employees. Covered employers are encouraged to use the Board of Mediation, which has since morphed into the National Mediation Board, a permanent independent agency. For more information, see https://uscode.house.gov/view.xhtml?path=%2Fprelim%40title45%2Fchapter8&edition=prelim.

1.35. The Rehabilitation Act (1973)

This replaced the Vocational Rehabilitation Act and created support for states to create vocational rehabilitation programs. The term originally used in this legislation was *handicapped*. The law was later modified to replace that term with *disabled*.

Table 3-1 notes the most important sections of the Rehabilitation Act.

For more information, see https://www.dol.gov/agencies/ofccp/section-503.

1.36. The Retirement Equity Act (REA) (1984)

Signed into law by President Ronald Reagan on August 23, 1984, the REA provides certain legal protections for spousal beneficiaries of qualified retirement programs. It prohibits changes to retirement plan elections, spousal beneficiary designations, and in-service withdrawals without the consent of a spouse. Changing withdrawal options does not require spousal consent. It permits plan administrators to presume spousal survivors' annuity and reduce primary pension amounts accordingly. Specific written waivers are required to avoid spousal annuity. For more information, see www.law.cornell.edu/uscode/text/29/1055.

1.37. The Revenue Act (1978)

This law added two important sections to the Internal Revenue Tax Code relevant to employee benefits: Section 125, Cafeteria Benefit Plans, and Section 401(k), originally a pre-tax savings program for private-sector employees known as individual retirement accounts (IRAs), subsequently expanded to a second plan opportunity known as "Roth IRA" that permitted funding with after-tax savings. For more information, see https://www.congress.gov/bill/95th-congress/house-bill/13511.

Section	Requirement
Section 501	Requires nondiscrimination and affirmative action in hiring disabled workers by federal agencies within the executive branch
Section 503	Requires nondiscrimination and affirmative action by federal contractors and subcontractors with contracts valued at $10,000 or more
Section 504	Requires employers subject to the law to provide reasonable accommodation for disabled individuals who can perform the major job duties with or without accommodation

Table 3-1 Key Employment Provisions of the Rehabilitation Act of 1973

1.38. The Sarbanes-Oxley Act (SOX) (2002)

In response to corrupt practices in the financial industry and the economic disasters they created, particularly the behavior of the Enron executives, Congress passed the Sarbanes-Oxley Act to address the need for oversight and disclosure of information by publicly traded companies.

Provisions and Protections

This law brought additional strict oversight to corporate governance and financial reporting for publicly held companies. It holds corporate officers accountable for proper recordkeeping and reporting of financial information, including internal control systems to ensure those systems are working properly. There are also requirements for reporting any unexpected changes in financial condition, including potential new liabilities such as lawsuits. Those lawsuits can involve things such as employee complaints of illegal employment discrimination.

It requires administrators of defined contribution plans to provide notice of covered blackout periods and provides whistleblower protection for employees.

This law protects anyone who reports wrongdoing to a supervisor, appointed company officials who handle these matters, a federal regulatory or law enforcement agency, or a member or committee of Congress. This protection even extends to claims that prove to be false if the employee reasonably believed the reported conduct was a violation of Security Exchange Commission (SEC) rules or a federal law involving fraud against shareholders.

On March 4, 2014, the U.S. Supreme Court issued its opinion in the case of *Lawson v. FMR LLC.* (No. 12–3).[5] The 6–3 decision held that all contractors and subcontractors of publicly held companies are subject to the Sarbanes-Oxley Act, even if they are not publicly held. The takeaway from this ruling is that nearly everyone is now subject to the whistleblower provisions of the Sarbanes-Oxley Act. As Justice Sotomayor suggested in her dissenting opinion:

> For example, public companies often hire "independent contractors," of whom there are more than 10 million, and contract workers, of whom there are more than 11 million. And they employ outside lawyers, accountants, and auditors as well. While not every person who works for a public company in these nonemployee capacities may be positioned to threaten or harass employees of the public company, many are.
>
> Under [the majority opinion] a babysitter can bring a ... retaliation suit against his employer if his employer is a checkout clerk for the local PetSmart (a public company) but not if she is a checkout clerk for the local Petco (a private company). Likewise, the day laborer who works for a construction business can avail himself of [this ruling] if her company has been hired to remodel the local Dick's Sporting Goods store (a public company), but not if it is remodeling a nearby Sports Authority (a private company).

Recordkeeping Requirements

Internal control systems are required to ensure that public disclosure of financial information is done as required. The registered accounting firm responsible for reviewing the company's financial reports must attest to the proper implementation of internal control systems and procedures for financial reporting.

SOX Enforcement

Enforcement of the law is done by private-firm audits overseen by the Public Company Accounting Oversight Board (PCAOB). The PCAOB is a nonprofit corporation created by the act to oversee accounting professionals who provide independent audit reports for publicly traded companies. It audits the auditors.

Companies and corporate officers in violation of the act can find themselves subject to fines and/or up to 20 years imprisonment for altering, destroying, mutilating, concealing, or falsifying records, documents, or tangible objects with the intent to obstruct, impede, or influence a legal investigation. For more information, see https://sarbanes-oxley-act.com/.

1.39. The Securities and Exchange Act (1934)

When companies "go public" by issuing common stock for trade, it is done on the "primary market." This law provides for governance in the "secondary market," which is all trading after the initial public offering. It also created the Securities and Exchange Commission (SEC), which has oversight authority for the trading of stocks in this country. It extends the "disclosure" doctrine of investor protection to securities listed and registered for public trading on any of the U.S. exchanges. For more information, see www.law.cornell.edu/wex/securities_exchange_act_of_1934.

1.40. The Service Contract Act (SCA) (1965)

Applying to federal contractors (and subcontractors) offering goods and services to the government, this law calls for payment of prevailing wages and benefit requirements to all employees providing service under the agreement. All contractors and subcontractors, other than construction services, with contract value in excess of $2,500 are covered. Safety and health standards also apply to such contracts.

The Wage and Hour Division in the U.S. Department of Labor (DOL) enforces the compensation requirements of this law. The SCA safety and health requirements are enforced by the Occupational Safety and Health Administration, also an agency within the DOL. For more information, see https://https://www.law.justia.com.

1.41. The Sherman Anti-Trust Act (1890)

If you travel back in time to the latter part of the nineteenth century, you will find that big business dominated the landscape. There was Standard Oil, Morgan Bank, U.S. Steel, and a handful of railroads. They were huge by comparison with other similar enterprises at the time, and people were concerned that they were monopolizing the marketplace plus holding prices high just because they could. John Sherman, a Republican senator from Ohio, was chairperson of the Senate Finance Committee. Sherman suggested that the country needed protections against monopolies and cartels. Thus, this law was created and subsequently used by federal prosecutors to break up the Standard Oil Company into smaller units. Over the years, case law has developed that concludes that attempting to restrict competition or fix prices can be seen as a violation of this law. Restraint of trade is also prohibited. For more information, see 15 U.S.C. Secs. 1–7 (www.law.cornell.edu/uscode/text/15/1).

1.42. The Small Business Job Protection Act (SBJPA) (1996)

This law increased federal minimum wage levels and provided some tax incentives to small business owners to protect jobs and increase take-home pay. It also amended the Portal-to-Portal Act for employees who use employer-owned vehicles. It created the SIMPLE 401(k) retirement plan to make pension plans easier for small businesses. Other tax incentives created by this law include the following:

- Employee education incentive—allowed small business owners to exclude up to $5250 from an employee's taxable income for educational assistance provided by the employer
- Increased the maximum amount of capital expense allowed for a small business to $7000 per year
- Replaced the Targeted Jobs Tax Credit with the Work Opportunity Tax Credit
- Provided a tax credit to individuals who adopted a child (up to $5000 per child) and a tax credit of up to $6000 for adoption of a child with special needs

For more information, see www.ssa.gov/legislation/legis_bulletin_082096.html.

1.43. The Social Security Act (1935)

The Social Security program began in 1935 in the heart of the Great Depression. It was initially designed to help senior citizens when that group was suffering a poverty rate of 50 percent. It was also intended to encourage retirement at age 65 so younger workers could take those jobs and reduce the extraordinarily high unemployment at the time. It currently includes social welfare and social insurance programs that can help support disabled workers who are no longer able to earn their wages.

The Social Security program is supported through payroll taxes with contributions from both the employee and the employer. Those payroll tax rates are set by the Federal Insurance Contributions Act (FICA) and have been adjusted many times over the years. There are multiple programs currently under the control of the Social Security Act and its amendments. These include the following:

- Federal old-age benefits (retirement)
- Survivors' benefits (spouse benefits, dependent children, and widow/widower benefits)
- Disability insurance for workers no longer able to work

- Temporary Assistance for Needy Families
- Medicare Health Insurance for Aged and Disabled
- Medicaid Grants to States for Medical Assistance Programs
- Supplemental Security Income (SSI)
- State Children's Health Insurance Program (SCHIP)
- Patient Protection and Affordable Care Act

There is currently a separate payroll deduction for Medicare health insurance, which is also funded by both the employee and employer. The Patient Protection and Affordable Care Act (Obamacare) has been implemented. Congress continues to try to find ways to modify it so the cost of medical health insurance can be reduced to individuals. As with other laws and regulations, events can change rapidly. You must keep up with the news of how health care insurance programs are evolving.

A personal Social Security number is used as a tax identification number for federal income tax, including bank records, and to prove work authorization in this country. Social Security numbers can be used in completing Form I-9, which must be completed for every new employee on the payroll. Also required for the I-9 is proof of identity. For more information, see www.ssa.gov/history/35act.html.

1.44. The Tax Reform Act (1986)

This law made extensive changes to the Internal Revenue Service tax code, including a reduction in tax brackets and all tax rates for individuals. Payroll withholdings were affected, many passive losses and tax shelters were eliminated, and changes were made to the alternative minimum tax computation. This is the law that required all dependent children to have Social Security numbers. That provision reduced the number of fraudulent dependent children claimed on income tax returns by 7 million in its first year. For HR professionals, answers to employee questions about the number of exemptions to claim on their Form W-4 are influenced by this requirement for dependent Social Security numbers. For more information, see http://archive.org/stream/summaryofhr3838t1486unit/summaryofhr3838t1486unit_djvu.txt.

1.45. The Taxpayer Relief Act (1997)

Congress wanted to give taxpayers a couple of ways to lower their tax payments during retirement, so the Taxpayer Relief Act was passed to create new savings programs called Roth IRAs and Education IRAs. Many individuals were able to achieve a better tax position through these tools. For more information, see www.gpo.gov/fdsys/pkg/BILLS-105hr2014enr/pdf/BILLS-105hr2014enr.pdf.

1.46. The Trademark Act (1946)

This is the legislation that created federal protections for trademarks and service marks. A trademark offers protection for a symbol, logo, phrase, word, design, or name for goods or products, and service marks offer similar protection for services. Officially it was called the Lanham (Trademark) Act, and it set forth the requirements for registering a trademark or service mark to obtain those legal protections. HR professionals may well have a role to play in training employees in how to properly handle organizational trademarks and the policies that govern those uses. For more information, see www.uspto.gov/trademarks/law/tmlaw.pdf.

1.47. The Unemployment Compensation Amendments Act (UCA) (1992)

This law established 20 percent as the amount to be withheld from payment of employee savings accounts when leaving an employer and not placing the funds directly (rolling over) into another tax-approved IRA or 401(k). For more information, see www.socialsecurity.gov/policy/docs/ssb/v56n1/v56n1p87.pdf.

1.48. The Uniformed Services Employment and Reemployment Rights Act (USERRA) (1994)

USERRA provides instructions for handling employees who are in the reserves and receive orders to report for active duty. The law protects the employment, reemployment, and retention rights of anyone who voluntarily or involuntarily serves or has served in the uniformed services. It requires that employers continue paying for the employee's benefits to the extent they paid for those benefits before the call to duty. It also requires that employers continue giving credit for length of service as though the military service was equivalent to company service and to hold the job for a service member for 5 years. There are specific detailed parameters for how long an employee may wait to engage the employer in return-to-work conversations after being released from active military duty.

This law and its provisions cover all eight U.S. military services and other uniformed services:

- Army
- Navy
- Air Force
- Marines
- Public Health Service Commissioned Corps
- National Oceanic and Atmospheric Administration Commissioned Corps
- Coast Guard
- National Guard groups that have been called into active duty

For more information, see www.dol.gov/sites/dolgov/files/VETS/legacy/files/USERRA_Annual_FY2020.pdf.

1.49. The Vietnam Era Veterans Readjustment Assistance Act (VEVRAA) (1974) [As Amended by the Jobs for Veterans Act (JVA) (2008)]

Current covered veterans include the following:

- Disabled veterans.
- Veterans who served on active duty in the U.S. military during a war or campaign or an expedition for which a campaign badge was awarded.
- Veterans who, while serving on active duty in the Armed Forces, participated in a U.S. military operation for which an Armed Forces service medal was awarded pursuant to Executive Order 12985.
- Recently separated veterans (veterans within 36 months from discharge or release from active duty). Note that due to this provision, the Vietnam Era Veterans Readjustment Assistance Act applies today. Do not get fooled into thinking it is merely historical due to "Vietnam Era" being in the name of the act.

These requirements apply to all federal contractors with a contract valued at $25,000 or more, regardless of the number of total employees.

This veteran support legislation requires all employers subject to the law to post their job openings with their local state employment service. The following are the three exceptions to that requirement:

- Jobs that will last 3 days or less
- Jobs that will be filled by an internal candidate
- Jobs that are senior executive positions

Affirmative action outreach and recruiting of veterans are required for federal contractors meeting the contract value threshold. For more information, see www.dol.gov/agencies/ofccp/vevraa.

1.50. The Wagner-Peyser Act (1933), As Amended by the Workforce Investment Act (WIA) (1998) and the Workforce Innovation and Opportunity Act (WIOA) of 2014

The Wagner-Peyser Act created a nationwide system of employment offices known as Employment Service Offices. They were run by the U.S. Department of Labor's Employment and Training Administration (ETA). These offices provided job seekers with assistance in their job search, assistance in searching jobs for unemployment insurance recipients, and recruitment services for employers.

The Workforce Investment Act created the "One Stop" centers within Employment Service Offices. The federal government contracts with states to run the Employment Service Offices and One Stop centers. Funds are allocated to states based on a complicated formula. For more information, see www.doleta.gov/programs/w-pact_amended98.cfm.

1.51. The Walsh-Healey Act (Public Contracts Act) (1936)

President Franklin Roosevelt signed this into law during the Great Depression. It was designed to ensure the government paid a fair wage to manufacturers and suppliers of goods for federal government contracts in excess of $15,000 each, as amended. The provisions of the law included the following:

- Overtime pay requirements for work done over 8 hours in a day or 40 hours in a week.

- A minimum wage equal to the prevailing wage.

- Prohibition on employing anyone under 16 years of age or a current convict.

- The Defense Authorization Act (1968) later excluded federal contractors from overtime payments in excess of 8 hours in a day.

For more information, see https://www.dol.gov/agencies/whd/government-contracts/pca.

1.52. The Work Opportunity Tax Credit (WOTC) (1996)

This law provides federal income tax credits to employers who hire from certain targeted groups of job seekers who face employment barriers. The amount of tax credit is adjusted from time to time and currently stands at $9600 per employee.

Targeted groups include the following:

- Qualified recipients of Temporary Assistance to Needy Families (TANF).

- Qualified veterans receiving food stamps (referred to as Supplemental Nutrition Assistance Program [SNAP] today) or qualified veterans with a service-connected disability who

  - Have a hiring date that is not more than 1 year after having been discharged or released from active duty, or

  - Have aggregate periods of unemployment during the 1-year period ending on the hiring date that equals or exceeds 6 months.

- WOTC also includes family members of a veteran who received food stamps (SNAP) for at least a 3-month period during the 15-month period ending on the hiring date, or a disabled veteran entitled to compensation for a service-related disability hired within a year of discharge or unemployed for a period totaling at least 6 months of the year ending on the hiring date.

- Ex-felons hired no later than 1 year after conviction or release from prison.

- Designated Community Residents—individuals who are between the ages of 18 and 40 on the hiring date and who reside in an Empowerment Zone, Renewal Community, or Rural Renewal County.

- Vocational rehabilitation referrals, including Ticket Holders with an individual work plan developed and implemented by an Employment Network.

- Qualified summer youth ages 16 through 17 who reside in an Empowerment Zone, Enterprise Community, or Renewal Community.
- Qualified SNAP recipients between the ages of 18 and 40 on the hiring date.
- Qualified recipients of Supplemental Security Income (SSI).
- Long-term family assistance recipients.

These categories change from time to time as well.

In addition to these specific federal laws, there are laws dealing with payroll that HR professionals need to understand. While it is true that accounting people normally handle the payroll function in an employer's organization, occasionally HR professionals get involved and must work with accounting people to explain deductions and provide input about open enrollment for health care benefit programs, among other things. Those things can include garnishments, wage liens, savings programs, and benefit premium contributions as well as income tax, FICA, and Medicare withholdings. For more information, see www.gao.gov/new.items/d01329.pdf.

1.53. Labor-Management Reporting and Disclosure Act (LMRDA)(1959)

This law provides for the reporting and disclosure of certain financial transactions and administrative practices of labor organizations and employers to prevent abuses in the administration of trusteeships by labor organizations and to provide standards with respect to the election of officers of labor organizations. It created a bill of rights for members of labor organizations (29 U.S.C. 401-402; 411-415; 431-441; 461-466; 481-484; 501-505).

For more information, see www.dol.gov/olms/regs/statutes/lmrda-act.htm.

1.54. Whistleblowing

It is important to highlight the issue of whistleblowing. Whistleblowing is speaking up to an authority figure or an external agency about perceived wrongdoing or unethical activities. Protections against retaliation for whistleblowing are embedded in various laws we cover in this chapter; laws with those provisions and protections include the Civil Rights Acts, OSHA, MSHA, the Sarbanes-Oxley Act, ADA, the Whistleblower Protection Ace of 1989, the Whistleblower Protection Enhancement Act (WPEA) of 2012, and more.

Whistleblower laws usually apply to public-sector employees and employees of organizations contracting with the federal government or state governments. They are designed to protect individuals who publicly disclose information about corrupt practices or illegal activities within their employer's organization. Often, such events occur when someone is mishandling money, contracts, or other assets. Construction projects not being built to specifications can result in whistleblowing by governmental employees. Employees of financial services companies (banks, credit unions, stock brokerages, and investment firms) have been in the headlines during recent years. They uncovered and disclosed misbehavior among people in their companies and were protected under whistleblower provisions of various laws. Whistleblowers are protected from disciplinary action, termination, or other penalty. For more information, see https://www.dol.gov/general/topics/whistleblower.

2. When You Have 15 or More Employees

Once employers have added 15 or more employees to their payroll, it becomes necessary to comply with an additional ten major federal laws.

2.1. Americans with Disabilities Act (ADA) (1990)

Prior to this legislation, the only employees who were protected against employment discrimination were the ones working for the federal, state, or local government and federal government contractors. They were safeguarded by the Rehabilitation Act. In fact, it was the Rehabilitation Act that was used as a model for developing the ADA. Five years after the Rehabilitation Act, the Developmental Disabilities Act of 1978 spoke specifically to people with developmental disabilities. It provided for federally funded state programs to assist people in that category of the population. The ADA had been first proposed in 1988, and it was backed by thousands of individuals around the country who had been fighting for rights for their family members, friends, and co-workers. They thought it was only appropriate for those people to have equal access to community services, jobs, training, and promotions. It was signed into law by President George H. W. Bush on July 26, 1990. It became fully effective for all employers with 15 or more workers on July 26, 1992.

Provisions and Protections

Title I, Employment, applies to employers with 15 or more workers on the payroll. Those employers may not discriminate against a physically or mentally disabled individual in recruitment, hiring, promotions, training, pay, social activities, and other privileges of employment. Qualified individuals with a disability are to be treated as other job applicants and employees are treated. If a reasonable job accommodation is required for a qualified individual to perform the assigned job, employers are required to provide that accommodation or recommend an alternative that would be equally effective. The interactive process between employers and employees should result in an accommodation or explanation about why making the accommodation would provide an undue hardship on the employer. Title I is enforced by the Equal Employment Opportunity Commission (EEOC). Part of the interactive discussion about accommodation requests involves the employer investigating other accommodations that may be equally effective yet lower in cost or other resource requirements. Employers are not obligated to accept the employee's request without alteration.

U.S. Supreme Court Interpretation of the ADA

Several U.S. Supreme Court cases interpreted the ADA very narrowly. They limited the number of people who could qualify as disabled under the Court's interpretation of Congress's initial intent. Reacting to those cases, Congress enacted the ADA Amendments Act in September 2008. It became effective on January 1, 2009.

ADA Amendments Act (ADAAA) (2008)

Following the U.S. Supreme Court decisions in *Sutton v. United Airlines*[6] and in *Toyota Motor Manufacturing, Kentucky, Inc., v. William*,[7] Congress felt that the Court had been too restrictive in its interpretation of who qualifies as disabled. It was the intent of Congress to be broader in that definition. Consequently, Congress passed the ADA Amendments Act to capture a wider range of people in the disabled classification. A disability is now defined as "an impairment that substantially limits one or more major life activities, having a record of such an impairment, or being regarded as having such an impairment." Although the words remain the same as the original definition, the Amendments Act went further. It said that, when determining whether someone is disabled, there may be no consideration of *mitigating circumstances*. In the past, we used to say people who had a disability under control were not disabled. An employee with a prosthetic limb did everything a whole-bodied person could do. An employee with migraines that disappeared with medication wasn't considered disabled. Under the old law, epilepsy and diabetes were not considered disabilities if they were controlled with medication. Now, because the law prohibits a consideration of either medication or prosthesis, they are considered disabilities. You can see that a great many more people are captured within the definition of disabled as a result of these changes. The only specifically excluded condition is the one involving eyeglasses and contact lenses. Congress specifically said having a corrected vision problem if eyeglasses or contact lenses are worn may not constitute a disability under the law.

An individual can be officially disabled but quite able to do his or her job without an accommodation of any sort. Having more people defined as disabled doesn't necessarily mean there will be more people asking for job accommodations. For more information, see www.eeoc.gov/laws/statutes/adaaa.cfm.

"Substantially Limits"

Employers are required to consider as disabled anyone with a condition that "substantially limits" but does not "significantly restrict" a major life activity. Even though the limitation might be reduced or eliminated with medication or other alleviation, the treatment may not be considered when determining the limitations. Therefore, people who use shoe inserts to correct a back problem or who take prescription sleeping pills may now be classified as disabled. The same might be said of people who are allergic to peanuts or bee stings. Yet, there may be no need for any of them to request a job accommodation.

"Major Life Activities"

Caring for oneself, seeing, hearing, touching, eating, sleeping, walking, standing, sitting, reaching, lifting, bending, speaking, breathing, learning, reading, concentrating, thinking, communicating, interacting with others, and working are all considered "major life activities." Also included are major bodily functions such as normal cell growth, reproduction, immune system, blood circulation, and the like. Some conditions are specifically designated as disabilities by the EEOC. They include diabetes, cancer, HIV/AIDS (human immunodeficiency virus and acquired immunodeficiency syndrome), MS (multiple sclerosis), CP (cerebral palsy), and CF (cystic fibrosis) because they interfere with one or more of our major life activities.

"Essential Job Function"

An essential job function is defined as "a portion of a job assignment that cannot be removed from the job without significantly changing the nature of the job." An essential function is highly specialized, and the incumbent has been hired because he or she has special qualifications, skills, or abilities to perform that function, among others.

"Job Accommodation"

Someone with a disability doesn't necessarily need a job accommodation. Remember that we select people and place them in jobs if they are qualified to performance the essential functions, with or without a reasonable job accommodation. Someone with diabetes may have the disease under control with medication and proper diet. No accommodation would be required. However, if it were essential that the employee had food intake at certain times of the day, there could be a legitimate request for accommodating that need. The employer might be asked to consistently permit the employee to have meal breaks at specific times each day.

Job accommodations are situationally dependent. First, there must be a disability and an ability to do the essential functions of the job. Next, there must be a request for accommodation from the employee. If there is no request for accommodation, no action is required by the employer. It is perfectly acceptable for an employer to request supporting documentation from medical experts identifying the disability. There might even be recommendations for specific accommodations, including those requested by the employee.

Once an accommodation is requested, the employer is obliged to enter into an interactive discussion with the employee. For example, an employee might ask for something specific, perhaps a new piece of equipment (a special ergonomic chair) that will eliminate the impact of their disability on their job performance. The employer must consider that specific request. Employers are obligated to search for alternatives that could satisfy the accommodation request only when the specific request cannot be reasonably accommodated. This is the point where the Job Accommodation Network (JAN)[8] can become a resource. It can often provide help for even questionable and unusual situations (https://askjan.org/).

The employer must consider if making that accommodation would be an "undue hardship" considering all it would involve. You should note that most job accommodations carry a very low cost. Often they cost nothing. The larger an employer's payroll headcount, the more difficult it is to fully justify using "undue hardship" as a reason for not agreeing to provide an accommodation. Large corporations or governments have vast resources, and the cost of one job accommodation, even if it does cost a large dollar amount, won't likely cause an undue hardship on that employer.

Recordkeeping Requirements

There is nothing in the Americans with Disabilities Act of 1990, or its amendments, that requires employers to create job descriptions. However, smart employers are doing that to identify physical and mental requirements of each job. Job descriptions also make it easy to identify essential job functions that any qualified individual would have to perform, with or without a job accommodation. It is easier to administer job accommodation request procedures and to defend against false claims of discrimination when an employer has job descriptions that clearly list all of the job's essential requirements. It also makes screening job applicants easier because it shows them in writing what the job will entail. Then, recruiters may ask, "Is there anything in this list of essential job functions that you can't do with or without a job accommodation?" That question ought to be asked consistently of all applicants, not just some.

If a job requires an incumbent to drive a delivery truck, driving would be an essential function of that job. A disability that prevented the incumbent from driving the delivery truck would likely block that employee from working—unless an accommodation could be found that would permit the incumbent to drive despite the disability.

People are sometimes confused about temporary suspension of duty being a permanent job accommodation. If that temporary suspension means the incumbent no longer is responsible for performing an essential job function, the job could not be performed as the employer designed it. It is not necessary for an employer to redesign job content to make a job accommodation. It is possible for such voluntary efforts to be made on behalf of an employee the organization wants to retain. Those situations are not job accommodations, however. They are job reassignments.

EEOC procedures prohibit employers from inviting job applicants to identify their disability status prior to receiving a job offer. Federal regulations related to affirmative action requirements for disabled workers[9] require contractors to invite job applicants to identify their status as disabled and then provide the same invitation to identify themselves as disabled once they have been hired. Federal contractors are also required to conduct a general survey of the entire employee population every 5 years (at a minimum) with an invitation to self-identify as disabled. At any time, employees are permitted to identify themselves as disabled to their employer.

Annual review of job description content is required under the EEOC guidelines. It is important to maintain accurate listings of essential job functions and physical and mental job requirements. Annual review will help ensure that you always have current information in your job descriptions.

ADA Enforcement

The EEOC enforces Title I of the ADA. That agency will accept complaints of illegal discrimination based on mental or physical disability. Once an employee has established that they are disabled and claims that they have been prohibited any employment benefit because of the disability (hiring, promotion, access to training, or inappropriate termination), there is a *prima facie* case (meaning it is true on its surface). Then the EEOC notifies the employer of the complaint and asks for the employer's response. This process can work back and forth from employer response to employee response for multiple cycles. Ultimately, the agency will determine that the case has cause (was a valid claim of discrimination), the case has no cause (the claim could not be substantiated), or the case was closed for administrative purposes (either the employee asked for the case to be closed or the time for an investigation expired). Each of those three outcomes is followed by a "right to sue" letter, allowing the employee to get an attorney and file a lawsuit in federal court seeking remedies under the law.[10]

Once a complaint (called a *charge of illegal discrimination*) is filed with the EEOC, employers are instructed to cease talking about that issue directly with their employee. All conversation about the complaint must be directed through the EEOC. Unfortunately, that complicates the communication process, and it provides a strong incentive for employers to resolve complaints internally before they reach the formal external complaint stage. Working directly with an employee about accommodation, or any other personnel issue, is preferable to working through an agency such as the EEOC. For more information, see www.ada.gov.

2.2. Civil Rights Act (Title VII) (1964)

Although this was not the first federal civil rights act in the country,[11] it came to us through a great deal of controversy. It was signed into law by President Lyndon Johnson on July 2, 1964. Following the assassination of President John F. Kennedy the previous November, President Johnson took it upon himself to carry the civil rights banner and urge Congress to pass the law.

For more information, see www.eeoc.gov/laws/statutes/titlevii.cfm.

Employment Protections

Title VII of the act speaks to employment discrimination and cites five protected classes of people. Before the final days when Congress was discussing the issues, there were only four protected classes listed: race, color, religion, and national origin. There was a great deal of opposition in the Senate from Southern states. They decided that they would strategically add another protected category to the list. They thought that if "sex" were added to the list, the bill would surely fail because no one would vote for having women protected in the workplace. Well, it passed…with all five protected categories in place. From that time forward, when making employment decisions, it has been illegal to consider any employee's membership in any of the protected classifications.

Penalties for Violations

Penalties can be assessed by a federal court. Protocol requires a complaint be filed with the Equal Employment Opportunity Commission (EEOC), the administrative agency tasked with the duty to investigate claims of illegal employment discrimination. Regardless of the outcome of that administrative review, a "right to sue" letter is given to the complaining employee so the case can move forward to federal court if that is what the employee wants to do next.

Penalties that can be assessed if an employer is found to have illegally discriminated include the following:

- **Actual damages**   Costs for medical bills, travel to medical appointments, equipment loss reimbursement, lost wages (back pay), lost promotional increase, and lost future earnings (front pay). The limitation is usually 2 years into the past and unlimited number of years into the future.

- **Compensatory damages**   Dollars to reimburse the victim for "pain and suffering" caused by this illegal discrimination.

- **Punitive damages**   Dollars assessed by the court to "punish" the employer for treatment of the employee that was egregious in its nature. This is usually thought of as "making an example" of one case to send a message to other employers that doing such things to an employee or job applicant will be severely punished.

2.3. The Civil Rights Act (1991)

This act modified the 1964 Civil Rights Act in several ways:

- It provided for employees to receive a jury trial if they wanted. Up to this point, judges always heard cases and decided them from the bench.
- It established requirements for any employer defense.
- It placed a limitation on punitive damage awards by using a sliding scale, depending on the number of the employees in the organization (payroll headcount):
  - For employers with 15 to 100 employees, damages are capped at $50,000.
  - For employers with 101 to 200 employees, damages are capped at $100,000.
  - For employers with 201 to 500 employees, damages are capped at $200,000.
  - For employers with more than 500 employees, damages are capped at $300,000.

For more information, see https://www.eeoc.gov/statutes/civil-rights-act-1991.

2.4. Drug-Free Workplace Act (1988)

This legislation requires some employers to maintain a drug-free workplace. Subject employers must ensure employee compliance.

Provisions and Protections

This law applies to federal contractors and all organizations receiving grants from the federal government. If you are covered, you are required to ensure that all the employees working on the contract or grant are in compliance with its drug-free requirements. Covered employers are required to have a drug-free policy that applies to its employees. To determine that an employer is in compliance with the requirements, drug testing is often performed on employees and applicants who have received a job offer. Random drug testing is also used in some organizations to ensure employees subject to the law or policy are continuing to comply with the requirements. As written, however, this legislation does not require drug testing. Those federal requirements do not go away even if laws in your state permit the use of recreational or medical marijuana. The employer is still permitted to have a policy prohibiting the use of drugs by applicants and employees. Any federal contractor under the jurisdiction of the Office of Federal Contract Compliance Programs (OFCCP) in the Department of Labor must comply with this legislation.

Employee notification about the policy must include information about the consequences of failing a drug test or other noncompliance with the drug-free policy. Whenever an employee has been convicted of a criminal drug violation in the workplace, the employer must notify the contracting or granting agency within 10 days.

Recordkeeping Requirements

Covered employers are required to publish a written policy statement that clearly covers all employees or just those employees who are associated with the federal contract or grant. Each covered employee must be given a copy of the policy statement, and it is a good idea, although it is not required, to have employees sign for receipt of that policy statement. The statement must contain a list of prohibited substances. At a minimum it must cite controlled substances.[12]

Some employers choose to include in the policy prohibition of alcohol and prescription drug misuse, although that is not a requirement. Subject employers must also establish a drug-free awareness training program to make employees aware of a) the dangers of drug abuse in the workplace; b) the policy of maintaining a drug-free workplace; c) any available drug counseling, rehabilitation, and employee assistance programs; and d) the penalties that may be imposed on employees for drug abuse violations. Records should be maintained showing each employee who received the training and the date it occurred.

Drug-Free Workplace Act Enforcement

Federal contractors under the jurisdiction of the OFCCP will find that the agency requires proof of compliance when it conducts a general compliance evaluation of affirmative action plans. Any employee who fails a drug test must be referred to a treatment program or given appropriate disciplinary action. Care should be given to treating similar cases in the same way. It is fairly easy to be challenged under Title VII for unequal treatment based on one of the Title VII protected groups.

Each federal agency responsible for contracting or providing grants is also responsible for enforcing the Drug-Free Workplace Act requirements. These responsibilities are spelled out in the Federal Acquisition Regulation (FAR). Failing to maintain a drug-free workplace can result in the following:[13]

- Suspension of payments for contract or grant activities
- Suspension or cancellation of grant or contract
- Up to 5 years' prohibition from any further contracts or grants

For more information, see https://www.congress.gov/bill/100th-congress/house-bill/4719.

2.5. The Equal Employment Opportunity Act (EEOA) (1972)

The EEOA amended the Civil Rights Act of 1964 by redefining some terms. It also required a new employment poster for all subject work locations explaining that "EEO is the law."

For more information, see https://www.guidelinesandprinciples.org/wiki/index.php/Equal_Employment_Opportunity_Act_of_1972.

2.6. The Genetic Information Nondiscrimination Act (GINA) (2008)

In general terms, GINA prohibits employers from using genetic information to make employment decisions. This legislation was brought about by insurance companies using genetic information to determine who would likely have expensive diseases in the future. That information allowed decisions to exclude those individuals from hiring or enrollment in medical insurance programs. With the implementation of this law, those considerations are no longer legal. The protection from GINA extends back to great-grandparents and also extends to adopted children.

For more information, see www.eeoc.gov/laws/statutes/gina.cfm.

2.7. Guidelines on Discrimination Because of Sex (1980)

The Equal Employment Opportunity Commission (EEOC) published these guidelines to help employers understand what constituted unwanted behavior and harassment. They were issued long before the U.S. Supreme Court considered the leading cases on sexual harassment. This is about the only thing at the time that employers were able to turn to for help in managing the problem of sexual harassment in the workplace.

2.8. The Lilly Ledbetter Fair Pay Act (2009)

This was the first piece of legislation signed by President Barack Obama after he was inaugurated the 44th president of the United States. It was passed in reaction to the U.S. Supreme Court decision in *Ledbetter v. Goodyear Tire & Rubber Co., Inc.*, 550 U.S. 618 (2007).

This law amends the Civil Rights Act of 1964 and states that the clock will begin running anew with each new paycheck for time to file a charge of an illegal act of discrimination experienced by an employee. In Lilly Ledbetter's situation, her pay was significantly less than that of men doing the same supervisor job. The old law didn't permit her to succeed in her complaint of discrimination because she failed to file 20 years earlier on the first occasion of her receiving a paycheck for less than her male counterparts. It didn't matter that she did not know about the pay difference until late in her career. Under the new law, the 180-day statute of limitations (or 300 days in deferral states) for filing an equal-pay lawsuit regarding pay discrimination resets with each new paycheck affected by that discriminatory action. For more information, see www.eeoc.gov/laws/statutes/epa_ledbetter.cfm.

2.9. The Pregnancy Discrimination Act (PDA) (1978)

This law modified (amended) the Civil Rights Act of 1964. It defined pregnancy as protected within the definition of "sex" for the purpose of coverage under the Civil Rights Act. It also specifically said that no employer shall illegally discriminate against an employee due to pregnancy. It defines pregnancy as a temporary disability and requires accommodation on the job if it is necessary. It guarantees the employee the right to return to work to the same or similar job with the same pay following her pregnancy disability. For more information, see https://www.eeoc.gov/statutes/pregnancy-discrimination-act-1978.

2.10. Uniform Guidelines on Employee Selection Procedures (1976)

Employers and HR professionals alike often overlook this set of regulations. For covered employers with 15 or more people on the payroll, this set of requirements is essential in preventing claims of discrimination.

There are two types of illegal employment discrimination: disparate adverse treatment and adverse or disparate impact. The former is purposely treating a protected class differently. The latter almost always results from seemingly neutral policies having a statistically adverse impact on a specific protected group of people. To avoid illegal discrimination, the guidelines require that all steps in a hiring decision be validated for application to the job being filled. Validity of a selection device can be determined through a validity study or by applying a job analysis to demonstrate the specific relationship between the selection device and the job requirements. Selection devices include things like a written test, an oral test, an interview, a requirement to write something for consideration, and a physical ability test.

Employers can get into trouble when they use selection tools that have not been validated for their specific applications. For example, buying a clerical test battery of written tests and using it to make selection decisions for administrative assistants as well as general office clerks may not be supportable. Only a validity analysis will tell for sure. What specific validation studies have been done for the test battery by the publisher? Any publisher should be able to provide you with a copy of the validation study showing how the test is supposed to be used and the specific skills, knowledge, or abilities that are analyzed when using it. If you can't prove that the test measures things required by your job content, don't use the test. According to the Uniform Guidelines, "While publishers of selection procedures have a professional obligation to provide evidence of validity which meets generally accepted professional standards, users are cautioned that they are responsible for compliance with these guidelines."[14] That means the employer, not the test publisher, is liable for the results. For more information, see www.eeoc.gov/policy/docs/factemployment_procedures.html.

3. When You Have 20 or More Employees

The next threshold for employers occurs when they reach a headcount of 20 employees. At that point, another four major federal laws begin their influence on the organization.

3.1. The Age Discrimination in Employment Act (ADEA) (1967)

When this law was first passed, it specified the protected age range of 40 to 70. Anyone younger than 40 or older than 70 was not covered for age discrimination in the workplace. Amendments were made a few years later that removed the upper limit. Today, the law bans employment discrimination based on age if the employee is 40 years old or older. Remedies under this law are the same as under the Civil Rights Act. They include reinstatement, back pay, front pay, and payment for benefits in arrears.

Some exceptions to the "unlimited" upper age exist. One example is the rule that airline pilots may not fly commercial airplanes after the age of 65.[15] Also, upper age limits apply for first responders. For more information, see https://www.eeoc.gov/statutes/age-discrimination-employment-act-1967.

3.2. The American Recovery and Reinvestment Act (ARRA) (2009)

The thrust of this legislation was to create government infrastructure projects such as highways, buildings, dams, and such. It was an attempt to find ways to re-employ many of the workers who had become unemployed since the Great Recession began in 2007. There was a provision that provided partial payment of COBRA (The Consolidated Omnibus Budget Reconciliation Act) premiums for people who still had not found permanent job placement. It applied to individuals who experienced involuntary terminations prior to May 31, 2010.

ARRA also modified HIPAA privacy rules. It applies HIPAA's security and privacy requirements to business associates. Business associates are defined under ARRA as individuals or organizations that transmit protected medical data, store that data, process that data, or in any other way have contact with that private medical information. All parties are responsible for proper handling and compliance with the HIPAA rules. For more information, see https://www.fcc.gov/general/american-recovery-and-reinvestment-act-2009.

3.3. The Consolidated Omnibus Budget Reconciliation Act (COBRA) (1986)

This law requires employers with group health insurance programs to offer terminating employees the opportunity to continue their health plan coverage after they are no longer on the payroll or no longer qualify for benefits coverage due to a change in employment status (that is, reduction in hours). COBRA can be for dependents, too, if there has been a qualifying event, such as divorce or death of the employee. The cost must be at group rates, and the employer can add a small 2 percent administrative service charge. It turns out that many employers turn these programs over to vendors who administer the COBRA benefits for former employees. They send out billing statements and provide collection services. The total cost of COBRA premiums and administrative fees is paid by employees participating in COBRA. The duration of coverage is dependent on some variables, so it may be different from one person to another. For more information, see www.dol.gov/dol/topic/health-plans/cobra.htm.

3.4. The Older Workers Benefit Protection Act (OWBPA) (1990)

In the 1980s, it was common for employers, particularly large ones, to implement staff reduction programs as a means of reducing expenses. Often those programs were targeted at more senior workers because, generally speaking, their compensation was greater than that of new employees. Reducing one senior worker could save more money than the reduction of a more recently hired worker. Congress took action to prevent such treatment based on age when it passed this law.

The key purposes of the OWBPA are to prohibit an employer from the following:

- Using an employee's age as the basis for discrimination in benefits
- Targeting older workers during staff reductions or downsizing
- Requiring older workers to waive their rights without the opportunity for review with their legal advisor

For more information, see https://www.congress.gov/bill/101st-congress/senate-bill/1511.

4. When You Have 50 to 99 Employees

Once the employee headcount reaches 50 to 99 employees, the following additional legal obligations become effective for employers. Some of them only apply if the employer is subject to affirmative action requirements as a federal contractor.

4.1. Executive Order 11246—Affirmative Action (1965)

This is the presidential order that created what we now know as employment-based affirmative action. In 1965, President Johnson had already approved the Civil Rights Act, and he was in the process of examining how it was being implemented around the country by employers. He concluded that the law was pretty much being ignored. He needed something to stimulate implementation of the employment provisions in the Civil Rights Act, Title VII. His staff suggested they require affirmative action programs from federal contractors. A new program was born. President Johnson said that if a company wanted to receive revenue by contracting with the federal government, it would have to implement equal employment opportunity and establish outreach programs for minorities and women. At the time, minorities and women were for the most part being excluded from candidate selection pools for desirable jobs. If they couldn't get into the selection pools, there was no way for them to be selected.

Therefore, affirmative action programs were created. Outreach and recruiting was the name of the game in these programs. Analysis of the incumbent workforce, the available pool of qualified job candidates, and the training of managers involved in the employment selection process all contributed to a slow movement toward fuller equality for minorities and women.

The Office of Federal Contract Compliance Programs (OFCCP) is the law enforcement agency that currently has responsibility for enforcing the executive order, along with other laws. Federal contractors must meet several conditions in return for the contracting privilege. One is the requirement to abide by a set of rules known as the Federal Acquisition Regulation (FAR). In addition, there is affirmative action for the disabled and veterans. Any business that doesn't want to abide by these requirements can make the business decision to abandon federal revenues and contracts. If you want the contracts, you also must agree to the affirmative action requirements.[16] For more information, see https://www.dol.gov/agencies/ofccp/about/executive-order-11246-history.

4.2. The Family and Medical Leave Act (FMLA) (1993) and Amendments from the National Defense Authorization Act of 2010

In general, the Family and Medical Leave Act set in place new benefits for some employees in the country. Qualifying employees could for the first time take a leave of absence with a guaranteed return to work to the same or equivalent job, at the same pay, under the same conditions as prior to the leave of absence. If their employer has 50 or more people on the payroll working within 75 miles of one another, then they are required to permit FMLA leave of absence for their workers. FMLA provides for leaves lasting up to 12 weeks in a 12-month period, and it is unpaid unless the employer has a policy to pay for the leave time. The 12-month period begins on the first day of leave. A new leave availability will occur 12 months from the date the first leave began. During the leave, it is an obligation of the employer to continue paying any benefit plan premiums that the employer would have paid if the employee had remained on the job. If there is a portion of the premium for health insurance that is normally paid by the employee, that obligation for co-payment continues during the employee's leave time. The 12-weeks leave may be taken in increments of 1 day or less.

To qualify, employees must have more than 1 year of service. The leave is authorized to cover childbirth, adoption, or a foster care placement; to care for a seriously ill child, spouse, or parent; or to attend to the employee's own serious illness.

The National Defense Authorization Act of 2010 created two additional FMLA leaves. These leaves are the first time an employee may apply for and qualify for FMLA when no one is sick, and they are not adding a child to the family. The first is for an employee preparing for a family member to deploy to active duty. The second includes provisions for "Military Caregiver Leave," lasting up to 26 weeks of unpaid leave of absence for employees with family members needing care due to a military duty–related injury or illness. The 26-week limit renews every 12 months. The law provides for "National Guard and Military Reserve Family Leave." Employees who are family members of the National Guard or military reservists who are called to active duty may take FMLA leave to assist with preparing financial and legal arrangements and other family issues associated with rapid deployment or post-deployment activities. An employer may agree to any non-listed condition as a qualifier for FMLA leave as well. This is the only circumstance when FMLA expands from 12 weeks to 26. Also, this "Military Caregiver Leave" may also be taken to care for "next of kin," which is broader than the usual FMLA for parents, spouse, self, and children. Spouses who work for the same employer can use no more than 26 weeks combined for this leave. To be clear, this is not 26 additional weeks added to the original 12, for a total of 38 weeks away. If an employee had used 3 weeks of FMLA when requesting this type of leave, they would qualify for up to 23 weeks of leave (26 minus 3).

FMLA provides for "Light Duty Assignments." It clarifies that "light duty" work does not count against an employee's FMLA leave entitlement. It also provides that an employee's right to job restoration is held in abeyance during the light duty period. An employee voluntarily doing light duty work is not on FMLA leave.

Also, there is an employment poster requirement. The notice must be posted at each work location where employees can see it without trouble. A "Medical Certification Process" is part of the new provisions. DOL regulations have specified who may contact the employee's medical advisor for information, written or otherwise, and specifically prohibits the employee's supervisor from contacting the employee's medical advisor.

Specific prohibitions are made against illegal discrimination for an employee taking advantage of the benefits offered under this law. These provisions are enforced by the EEOC. For more information, see https://www.dol.gov/agencies/whd/laws-and-regulations/laws/fmla and for the military-related leaves see https://www.dol.gov/agencies/whd/fmla/military-families.

4.3. The Mental Health Parity Act (MHPA) (1996)

This legislation requires health insurance issuers and group health plans to adopt the same annual and lifetime dollar limits for mental health benefits as for other medical benefits. For more information, see https://www.congress.gov/bill/104th-congress/house-bill/4058/text.

4.4. The Mental Health Parity and Addiction Equity Act (MHPAEA) (2008)

This is an amendment of the Mental Health Parity Act of 1996. It requires that plans that offer both medical/surgical benefits and mental health and/or substance abuse treatment benefits provide parity between both types of benefits. All financial requirements (for example, deductibles, copayments, coinsurance, out-of-pocket expenses, and annual limits) and treatment requirements (for example, frequency of treatment, number of visits, and days of coverage) must be the same for treatment of both mental and physical medical problems. For more information, see https://www.hhs.gov/guidance/document/mental-health-parity-and-addiction-equity-act.

4.5. The National Defense Authorization Act (2008)

This is the origin of benefit provisions under FMLA for leaves of absence due to military reasons. Qualifying events include notice of deployment, return from deployment, and treatment for an injury sustained while on deployment. The provision is for up to 26 weeks, which can be taken in increments of a day or less if, for example, treatment is required for a service-related injury. For more information, see https://www.congress.gov/bill/110th-congress/house-bill/4986.

4.6. The Patient Protection and Affordable Care Act (PPACA) (2010)

Signed into law by President Barack Obama on March 23, 2010, this law is commonly referred to as the Affordable Care Act (ACA), or Obamacare. It has created health insurance trading centers in each state where employees and those who are unemployed can shop for health insurance coverage. These trading centers are the American Health

Benefit Exchanges and Small Business Health Options Program (SHOP). Individuals and business owners of organizations with fewer than 100 workers can purchase insurance through these exchanges.

It applies to all employers with 50 or more full-time workers on the payroll. Employers with fewer than 50 full-time workers are exempt from coverage under the law. Effective January 1, 2014, covered employers must either provide minimum health insurance coverage to their full-time employees or face a fine of $2000 per employee, excluding the first 30 from the assessment. Employers with fewer than 25 employees will receive a tax credit if they provide health insurance to their workers. In 2014, that credit amounted to 50 percent of the employer's contribution to the employee's health care program, if the employer pays at least that amount for insurance costs. A full credit is available for employers with fewer than ten workers earning an average annual wage of less than $25,000. The credit will last for 2 years. One of its most popular provisions is allowing parents to keep adult children on their health plans until the adult children reach age 26. For more information, see https://www.healthcare.gov/glossary/patient-protection-and-affordable-care-act/.

5. When You Have 100 or More Employees

The final major threshold for employers is reached when the payroll reaches 100 employees. At that time, employers become subject to the WARN Act and are required to submit annual reports to the EEOC summarizing their race and sex demographics. (See Chapter 5 for more information about the Standard Form 100 reports.)

5.1. The Worker Adjustment and Retraining Notification Act (WARN) (1988)

This was the first attempt by Congress to involve local communities early in the private sector's downsizing process. It also prevented employers from just shutting the door and walking away without any worker benefits. It applies to all employers with 100 or more full-time workers at a single facility. The law specifies a qualifying employer to be one that has 100 or more employees who in the aggregate work at least 4000 hours per week (exclusive of hours of overtime).

Definitions

The term *plant closing* refers to the permanent or temporary shutdown of a single site of employment, or one or more facilities or operating units within a single site of employment, if the shutdown results in an employment loss at the single site of employment during any 30-day period for 50 or more employees, excluding any part-time employees.

The term *mass layoff* refers to a reduction in force that is not the result of a plant closing and results in an employment loss at the single site of employment during any 30-day period when (1) at least 500 employees are to be laid off from a workforce of 500 or more; or (2) at least 33 percent of the workforce (excluding any part-time employees) is going to be removed from the payroll in a layoff where there is a total of 50 to 499 workers before the layoff.

Required Actions

The law requires 60 days' advance notice to employees of plant closing or mass layoffs. Any employment loss of 50 or more people, excluding part-time workers, is considered a trigger event to activate the requirements. Notification of public officials in the surrounding community in addition to notification of employees is a requirement. The local community leaders must be informed and invited to participate in the process of finding new jobs for laid-off workers. There is a provision that says an employer can pay 60 days' separation allowance if it gives no notice to workers who will be terminated.

Exemptions to Notice Requirement

Notice is not required, regardless of the size of layoff, if the layoff, downsizing, or terminations result from the completion of a contract or project that employees understood would constitute their term of employment. It is not uncommon for workers to be hired in a "term" classification that designates them as employees for the life of a project. If they understand that from the beginning of their employment, their termination will not trigger the WARN Act.

WARN is not triggered in the following cases:

- In the event of strikes or lockouts that are not intended to evade the requirements of this law.
- In the event the layoff will be for less than 6 months.
- If state and local governments are downsizing. They are exempt from the notice requirement.
- In the event that fewer than 50 people will be laid off or terminated from a single site.
- If 50 to 499 workers lose their jobs and that number is less than 33 percent of the active workforce at the single site.

For more information, see https://www.dol.gov/general/topic/training/warn-reg-preamble.

6. For Federal Government Employees

The federal government is subject to some of the same laws as the private-sector employers, yet there are additional obligations that government employers have. Some of those obligations stem from the United States Constitution. Others come from the following laws.

6.1. The Civil Service Reform Act (1978)

This legislation eliminated the U.S. Civil Service Commission and created three new agencies to take its place:

- **The Office of Personnel Management (OPM)**   This is the executive branch's human resources department. It handles all HR issues for agencies reporting to the president.

- **The Merit Systems Protection Board (MSPB)**   This part of the law prohibits consideration of marital status, political activity, or political affiliation in dealing with federal civilian employees. It also created the Office of Special Counsel, which accepts employee complaints and investigates and resolves them.

- **The Federal Labor Relations Authority (FLRA)**   This is the agency that enforces federal civilian employee rights to form unions and bargain with their agencies. It establishes standards of behavior for union officers, and these standards are enforced by the Office of Labor-Management Standards in the U.S. Department of Labor.

For more information, see https://www.congress.gov/bill/95th-congress/senate-bill/2640.

6.2. The Congressional Accountability Act (1995)

Until this law was implemented, the legislative branch of the government was exempt from nearly all employment-related requirements that applied to other federal agencies and private employers. This law requires Congress and its affiliated agencies to abide by 11 specific laws that are already applied to other employers, in and out of government:

- Americans with Disabilities Act of 1990
- Age Discrimination in Employment Act of 1967
- Employee Polygraph Protection Act of 1988
- Federal Service Labor-Management Relations Statute of 1978
- Rehabilitation Act of 1973
- Civil Rights Act of 1964 (Title VII)
- Fair Labor Standards Act of 1938
- Family and Medical Leave Act of 1993
- Occupational Safety and Health Act of 1970
- Veterans Employment Opportunities Act of 1998
- Worker Adjustment and Retraining Notification Act of 1989

For more information, see https://www. https://law.justia.com

6.3. The False Claims Act (1863)

During the Civil War, people were selling defective food and arms to the Union military. This law, sometimes referred to as the Lincoln Law, prohibits such dishonest transactions. It prohibits making and using false records to get those claims paid. It also prohibits selling the government goods that are known to be defective. For HR professionals today, it is wise to train all employees about the need to avoid creating records that are inaccurate or, even worse, fictitious. Doing things that are illegal, just because the boss says you should, is still illegal. Employees need to understand that concept.

For more information, see www.justice.gov/civil/docs_forms/C-FRAUDS_FCA_Primer.pdf.

6.4. The Homeland Security Act (2002)

Congress and President George W. Bush created this Cabinet-level organization (Department of Homeland Security) to consolidate security efforts related to protecting the U.S. after the 9/11 attack. Immigration and Customs Enforcement (ICE) is a part of this department. The E-Verify system resides here. Used by federal contractors as part of their affirmative action obligations and other private employers on a voluntary basis, the system is intended to assist in rapid verification of Social Security numbers (SSNs) and confirm that the individuals attached to the SSNs have a valid right to work in this country. For more information, see https://www.dhs.gov/homeland-security-act-2002.

6.5. The Privacy Act (1974)

This law provides that governmental agencies must make known to the public their data collection and storage activities and must provide copies of pertinent records to the individual citizen when requested—with some specific exemptions. Those exemptions include law enforcement, congressional investigations, Census use, "archival purposes," and other administrative purposes. In all, there are 12 statutory exemptions from disclosure requirements. If employees are concerned about employers using their Social Security numbers in records sent to the government, this act ensures privacy. Although such privileged information is required by the government, the government is prohibited from releasing it to third parties without proper authorization or court order. For more information, see www.justice.gov/opcl/privstat.htm.

6.6. The USA PATRIOT Act (2001)

The USA PATRIOT Act (Uniting and Strengthening America by Providing Appropriate Tools Required to Intercept and Obstruct Terrorism Act) was passed immediately following the terrorist attacks in New York City and at the Pentagon in Virginia on September 11, 2001. It gives the government authority to intercept wire, oral, and electronic communications relating to terrorism, computer fraud, and abuse offenses. It also provides the authorization for collecting agencies to share the information they collect in the interest of law enforcement. This law can have an impact on private-sector employers in the communications industry. It can also have an impact on any employer when the government asks for support to identify and track "lone wolves" suspected of terrorism without being affiliated with known terrorist organizations. HR professionals may find themselves involved in handling the collection and release of personal, confidential information about one or more employees. When legal documents such as subpoenas and court orders are involved, it is always a prudent step to have the organization's attorney review them before taking any other action. For more information, see www.justice.gov/archive/ll/highlights.htm.

Employment Visas for Foreign Nationals

Under some circumstances, it is possible for people from other countries to come work in the United States. There are several classifications of workers that can be used, depending on the type of work to be done and the level of their responsibilities.

E Nonimmigrant Visas

There are two types of E Nonimmigrant Visas: E-1 Treaty Traders and E-2 Treaty Investors. For more information on E Nonimmigrant Visas, see www.uscis.gov/portal/site/uscis.

E-1 Treaty Traders

The individual must be a citizen of the treaty country; there must be substantial trade; the trade must be principally with the treaty country; the individual must have executive, supervisory, or essential skills; and the individual must intend to depart the United States when the trading is completed.

E-2 Treaty Investors

The individual must be a citizen of the treaty country and be invested personally in the enterprise. The business must be a bona fide enterprise and not marginal, and the investment must be substantial. E-2 employees must have executive, supervisory, or essential skills, and E-2 investors must direct and develop the enterprise. The E-2 investor must depart the United States when the investment is concluded.

H Visas

These are visas available to employers and employees for specialized talent or educational requirements.

H1-B Special Occupations and Fashion Models

These visas require a bachelor's or higher degree or its equivalent. The job must be so complex that it can be performed only by a person with the degree. The employer normally requires a degree or its equivalent for this job. Fashion models also fall into this category.

H1-C Registered Nurse Working in a Health Professional Shortage Area

This requires a full and unrestricted nursing license in the country where your nursing education was obtained. Or, you must have received your nursing education and license in the United States. It also requires that you have appropriate authorization from the U.S. state's Board of Nursing to practice within the United States. H1-C requires that you have passed the examination given by the Commission on Graduates for Foreign Nursing Schools (CGFNS) or have a full and unrestricted license to practice as a registered nurse in the state where you will work.

H-2A Temporary Agricultural Workers

The employer must be able to demonstrate that there are not sufficient U.S. workers who are able, willing, qualified, and available to do the temporary seasonal work. The employer must also show that the employment of H-2A workers will not adversely affect the wages and working conditions of similarly employed U.S. workers.

H-2B Temporary Non-Agricultural Workers

The employer must show that there are not enough U.S. workers who are able, willing, qualified, and available to do the temporary work and that the employment of H-2B workers will not adversely affect the wages and working conditions of similarly employed U.S. workers. The employer must also show that the need for the prospective worker's services is temporary, regardless of whether the underlying job can be described as temporary.

H-3 Nonimmigrant Trainee

To qualify, employees must be trainees receiving training in any field of endeavor, other than graduate medical education, which is not available in their home country. Or they must be a Special Education Exchange Visitor who will participate in a special education training program focused on the education of children with physical, mental, or emotional disabilities.

L-1 Intra-Company Transferee

This allows a qualifying organization to move an employee from another qualifying country into the United States for a temporary assignment either that is managerial in nature or that requires specialized knowledge.

L1-A Managers and Executives

These are intracompany transferees coming to the United States to work in a managerial or executive capacity. The maximum stay in the United States allowed under this visa is 7 years.

Specialized Knowledge

This is someone with specialized knowledge of the employer's product, service, research, equipment, techniques, management, or other interests and its application in international markets, or an advanced level of knowledge or expertise in the organization's processes and procedures. An L1-B visa holder may stay in the United States for only 5 years.

O-1 Alien of Extraordinary Ability in Arts, Science, Education, Business, Athletics

These people have a level of expertise indicating that they are among the small percentage who have risen to the very top of their field of endeavor. Alternatively, they represent extraordinary achievement in motion picture and television productions, or they have extraordinary ability and distinction in the arts.

P Visa Categories

There are seven variations of athletics-based or art-based visas:

- P1-A Individual Athletes or Athletic Teams
- P1-B Entertainment Groups

- P1-S Essential Support needed for P1-A or P1-B
- P2 Artist or Entertainer Under a Reciprocal Exchange Program
- P2-S Essential Support for P2
- P3 Artist or Entertainer Under a Culturally Unique Program
- P3-S Essential Support for P3

EB Employment-Based Visas

There are five levels of employment-based visas. They are prioritized so that once the first-level immigrant applicants are processed, the next level of priority will be considered. That will continue until the maximum allotment of visas is reached. In recent years, about 140,000 employment-based visas were permitted each year.

EB-1 Alien of Extraordinary Ability

The employer must demonstrate that the alien has extraordinary ability in the sciences, arts, education, business, or athletics, which has been demonstrated by sustained national or international acclaim and whose achievements have been recognized in the field through extensive documentation. It must also be shown that the work to be done in the United States will continue in the individual's area of extraordinary ability. It must also be shown how the alien's entry into this country will benefit the United States; 28.6 percent of the total employment-based visas are allocated to this category.

EB-2 Alien of Extraordinary Ability

This is a classification that applies to any job that requires advanced degrees and persons of exceptional ability; 28.6 percent of the employment-based visas are allocated to this category.

EB-3 Skilled Workers

This category requires professionals and even unskilled workers who are sponsored by employers in the United States; 28.6 percent of the employment-based visas are allocated to this category.

EB-4 Certain Special Immigrants

Included here are some broadcasters, ministers of religion, employees, or former employees of the U.S. government, Iraqi or Afghan interpreters and translators, and other similar workers; 7.1 percent of the employment-based visas are allocated to this category.

EB-5 Immigrant Investors

These are people who will create new commercial enterprises in the United States that will provide job creation; 7.1 percent of the employment-based visas are allocated to this category.

Chapter Review

While this chapter is not meant to be a comprehensive statement of each law, studying and learning these laws will help you understand the basics as you perform your human resource management responsibilities. As you read the other chapters in this book, it's important to remember that one or more of these laws will be the underlying basis for SHRM's Body of Applied Skills and Knowledge subject matter. Additionally, while using this chapter as a reference guide in your day-to-day application as an HR professional, please consult the statutes and regulations themselves via the URLs we have provided. A thorough understanding of the various laws and regulations that impact the employment relationship will enhance your ability to protect your organization in matters involving employment and employee relations.

Questions

The following are all questions about U.S. laws and regulations concerning employee management.

1. John, a new employee, has just arrived at the orientation program where everyone completes their payroll forms and signs up for health care benefits. He brings his W-4 form to you and says he isn't subject to payroll withholding because he pays his taxes directly each quarter. What is your response?

    A. "That's okay. We won't process a W-4 form for you. We will give you a Form 1099."

    B. "I'll check with the accounting department to find out whether you can do that."

    C. "Unfortunately, all employees are subject to payroll tax withholding."

    D. "If you can show me a W-10 form you have submitted to the IRS, we can block your paycheck withholding."

2. The Wagner-Peyser Act protects workers who are:

    A. Unemployed

    B. Injured on the job

    C. Unable to work because of pregnancy

    D. Have two or more jobs

3. Mary, age 42, has had a bad encounter with her supervisor, Henry. Henry has, yet again, changed her work schedule from days to evenings. It seems that Henry won't let Mary work the same shift more than two shifts in a row, making Mary's childcare arrangements almost impossible. Mary notices that no other employees are subject to these perpetual shift changes. What might be happening?

    A. As Mary's supervisor, Henry has every right to staff company shifts as needed.

    B. The law says shifts must be maintained and not changed for at least 6 months.

    C. The company is protected against Mary's dissatisfaction since she is not disabled.

    D. Henry may be violating Mary's ADEA rights and creating a hostile work environment, inviting constructive discharge.

4. Pete is sensitive about the security of his personal identity information since his credit card has been stolen twice in the past year. He is trying to clear up his credit rating because of the problems with the stolen cards. Now, he has approached the HR manager at his organization and requested that his Social Security number be removed from all of the company records. He thinks that a mistake could cause him more grief if the Social Security number were to be obtained by thieves. As the HR manager, what should you do?

A. The company can and should delete the Social Security number from its records to protect Pete.

B. There is a need for the company to keep the Social Security number for tax reporting.

C. There is a need for the company to keep the Social Security number for Census reporting.

D. The company has no need for the Social Security number but should keep it regardless.

5. Pat works at a company with 120 employees and is talking with her colleagues about illegal discrimination at work. Someone mentions that the company is going to be sending out a request for updated race and sex information. Pat says that isn't legal. The company isn't supposed to track any of that information. Which of the following is true?

A. Pat has not understood the EEOC reporting requirements that employers keep race and sex data on employees.

B. The EEOC has issued guidelines that agree with Pat's belief that it is illegal to maintain that information in company records.

C. Only federal contractors are required to maintain the race and sex identification for employees.

D. It is only the public-sector employees who are exempt from providing their race and sex identification to employers.

6. The Tractor and Belt Company (TBC) handles conveyor belt installations for small firms. Each of the customer projects begins on a day that is most convenient for the customer. Sometimes, that's Monday; sometimes it's Thursday or another day. The HR manager says that the company will adjust its workweek to begin when the customer's project starts. That way, each installation team has a separate workweek, and those workweeks can shift several times a month. What is your advice about this strategy?

A. The HR manager is taking advantage of the FLSA's provisions for flexible workweeks that support small business. No change is required.

B. Once the workweek has been designated to begin on a certain day of the week, the HR manager should not change it.

C. It depends on state laws and regulations whether the workweek begins on any specific day of the week.

D. The FLSA says a workweek should always begin on Sunday.

7. Sandy is 15 years old and a sophomore at Central High School. She gets a job at the local hamburger drive-in. Her boss says he needs her to work the following schedule during the Spring Break week: 4 hours at lunch time every day, 9 hours on Saturday, and 6 hours on Sunday. Is that schedule acceptable for Sandy given that she has a work permit from the school?

   A. Because it is a school vacation week, there are no restrictions on the hours that Sandy can work.

   B. Only state laws impact what hours Sandy can work because it happens during a vacation week.

   C. Federal law says Sandy cannot work more than 8 hours a day when it is a vacation week.

   D. Because Sandy won't be working more than 40 hours for the week, there is no problem.

8. Gary is a junior at Buenaventura High School. He is 17 years old. The school needs help in its warehouse during the summer, and Gary needs a job so he can save money for college. His boss is the Facilities Manager. Gary is assigned to work 9 hours every day during the week because one of the other employees is on disability leave. And, because the other employee was the forklift driver, Gary has been given training in how to drive that equipment around the warehouse and loading dock. He likes that duty because he has been driving a car for only a few months. The forklift is cool. Is there any difficulty with the Facilities Manager's requirements of Gary?

   A. Everything the Facilities Manager has required Gary to do is permissible under federal laws.

   B. No. Since Gary is a minor, he shouldn't be working 9 hours per day.

   C. Whatever the Facilities Manager wants Gary to do is okay because it's only a summer job.

   D. Even though Gary can work unlimited hours, he cannot be assigned to drive the forklift.

9. Hank puts in the following hours at work at the Department of Labor: Sunday, 0; Monday, 8; Tuesday, 8; Wednesday, 9; Thursday, 8; Friday, 8; Saturday, 7. His boss says he will give Hank compensating time off for every hour of overtime Hank works. How many compensating hours off should Hank receive for this work time?

   A. 1 day of compensating time off.

   B. 1.5 days of compensating time off.

   C. 7 hours of compensating time off.

   D. Compensating time off is not permitted under the FLSA.

10. The Tractor and Belt Company (TBC) doesn't have an HR Manager. HR is handled by the Payroll Clerk. When a new employee is assigned to the Production Department as an Assembler, the Payroll Clerk raises a question. Should the new person be paid the same as all the other employees, all women in the department, or is it okay to pay her more because she made more at her former job?

    A. There are no restrictions on the amount a new employee can be paid. It is market driven.

    B. The Fair and Decent Treatment Act requires all people doing the same work to be paid the same amount.

    C. There is no restriction on the amount paid because all the incumbents are women.

    D. Once a valid market survey has been done, it can be used to determine starting pay for new people.

11. Finding a life insurance company to provide benefits to its workforce has been difficult for Joan, the HR Manager. She decides to recommend that her company offer a self-insured plan. What controls might Joan have to consider in her planning?

    A. There are no federal restrictions on a company providing its own life insurance plan to employees.

    B. The Employee Retirement Income Security Act regulates welfare benefit plans, including life insurance.

    C. The Life Insurance Benefit Plans Act has control over what Joan can do with her idea.

    D. Only state laws will have an influence on Joan's development of a self-insured benefit plan.

12. Simone has just been hired and is asked to complete a Form I-9. She offers her driver's license as proof of her identity. What else is required for her to complete the document?

    A. She may offer any document authorized on the Form I-9 instructions as proof of her authorization to work in this country.

    B. She must have a Social Security number to submit on the form.

    C. Simone has an expired U.S. passport but is told that she can't use it for her Form I-9.

    D. If Simone offers to get a Social Security number in the next 30 days, she can submit her Form I-9.

13. Steve is the HR Director for a Crane Operations company. He just got a phone call from one of his Field Supervisors with tragic news. One of their units has collapsed and 3 of their employees are in the hospital with serious injuries. What should Steve do first with that information?

    A. Steve should immediately call the hospital to be sure all the insurance information is on file for their employees.

    B. He should notify the Occupational Safety and Health Administration about the accident and the injuries.

    C. He should notify the Crane Safety Institute of America to be sure they are able to add this accident to their database.

    D. Steve should call the employees' emergency contacts to share news about the tragedy.

14. Every year Donna must attend training on the use of the company vehicles she drives. She thinks this is a silly waste of time. Donna knows how to drive, and she knows the company vehicles. Why should she attend training every year?

    A. There is no federal requirement for Donna to take yearly training.

    B. OSHA requires training be done only once for vehicle operation.

    C. Only state safety provisions govern how frequently training must be done in Donna's situation.

    D. Safety programs must be developed that provide for refresher training on all equipment operating procedures.

15. Jerry just arrived at work and found a sink hole in the parking lot. He is early enough that other people have not yet begun arriving for work. Because the hole is about 10 feet across now, what should Jerry be doing about the problem?

    A. If Jerry is a management employee, he should take charge of the situation and begin the process of alerting others to the danger posed by the sink hole.

    B. If Jerry is a nonmanagement employee, he should give his boss a call and leave a voice mail message, if necessary, about the sink hole.

    C. If the sink hole poses an immediate danger of death or serious injury, Jerry should call 911 and report it. He should barricade the perimeter of the sink hole with tape or something else to prevent people from falling in.

    D. Jerry should first test the edges of the sink hole to see whether it could grow. Then he should barricade the perimeter of the sink hole so no one will fall in.

16. Theresa attended a seminar recently that pointed out the need to post a yearly summary of injury and illness cases. Her boss doesn't want to do that, saying he doesn't want to publicize the problems the organization has had. What should Theresa tell him?

    A. Posting requirements call for display of the report in a prominent location if there are ten or more people on the payroll.

    B. Posting requirements can be met by putting a report on the back of the closet door in the employee lounge.

C. Posting requirements can be met by making the report available in a binder in the HR manager's office.

D. Posting requirements is optional, but good employers are using the report as a "best practice" in safety programs.

17. An employer routinely works with hazardous chemicals, trucking them for delivery to various customer locations. After each load, the truck must be cleaned before being loaded with a different chemical. Cleaning must be done by someone inside the tanker using special absorbent materials. What else should be considered?

A. Personal protective equipment should be provided by the employer, including breathing apparatus and hazmat suits.

B. Standard coveralls and boot covers should be provided for employees to use if they want.

C. Workers should never be sent into a tanker truck for any reason.

D. Breathing equipment is absolutely a requirement if someone will be in the tanker truck for longer than 30 minutes.

18. Shelly has worked for the same dentist for more than 10 years. In all that time, there has been no mention of any special requirements for handling syringes. She arranges the doctor's equipment trays every day and cleans them up after they have been used. She just tosses the used equipment into the autoclave or into the trash if it won't be used again. If you were advising Shelly about the practices used in her dental office, what would you say?

A. Needles should be broken off before they are thrown into the trash can.

B. Sharps should be triple wrapped in a stiff paper to protect from sticking someone handling the trash.

C. Any possible harm can be prevented if used syringes are placed into an approved sharps container.

D. Putting used syringes into any solid container that is wrapped in red paper is sufficient to meet requirements.

19. The price of gold is climbing, and folks at the Golden Nugget Mine are planning to reopen their operation. They know that safety is an important consideration. But what about federal regulations for gold mines? Are there such things?

A. There are only OSHA regulations in general. All of those rules still apply.

B. There are MSHA regulations to be considered, but because they are not in the coal mining business, the Golden Nugget Mine won't have to worry about them.

C. MSHA rules apply to all mining operations in the United States. The Golden Nugget Mine will have to study those rules and get ready for inspections by the government.

D. MSHA can tell the mine what to do, but it has no authority to conduct inspections because the Golden Nugget is not a coal mine.

20. Leslie is thrilled to have landed a job at a firm that still offers a pension plan for retirement. She wants to fully understand the moment she will be vested in the plan. Which of the following is the only legal vesting option?

   A. Zero vesting changing to 100 percent vesting on her fourth anniversary with the company

   B. Step or graduated vesting, immediately beginning with 10 percent upon hire, then 10 percent more each anniversary until 100 percent is reached

   C. Step or graduated vesting, waiting 2 years and then vesting 25 percent, repeating every 2 years she vests 25 percent more, so fully vested in 8 years

   D. Zero vesting changing to 100 percent vesting on her third anniversary with the company

21. For the past 6 years, Sam's company has been a federal contractor working on equipment for the Department of Defense. The company has additional contract opportunities coming up, and Sam isn't sure if there will be an extra burden related to disabled workers because they are subject to both the Americans with Disabilities Act and the Rehabilitation Act. What should Sam do?

   A. Sam should rest easy. The ADA and the Rehabilitation Act are identical in their content and requirements.

   B. Sam's company has already met its recruiting obligations and so now Sam must only worry about meeting ADA requirements.

   C. Handling job accommodation requests is a requirement of the ADA but not the Rehabilitation Act. Things should be easier for Sam only needing to comply with the ADA.

   D. Whatever Sam thinks, the ADA and Rehabilitation Act requirements have applied to his company for 6 years already. Adding more contracts won't change Sam's current obligations which he must fulfill for both pieces of legislation.

22. Arthur has applied for a job with the AB Transit Company. He is told he must take and pass a urine drug test. If he fails the test and any subsequent random drug test after he is hired, he will be dismissed from the company. Arthur reacts loudly and says, "That's an invasion of my privacy! I won't do it." What happens now?

   A. Arthur can call his lawyer and have the drug test waived since he doesn't want to take it.

   B. Arthur can discontinue his participation in the AB Transit Company's employment process.

   C. Arthur can take the test now and still refuse to participate in random tests later.

   D. Arthur can have his friend take the test for him.

23. Cynthia works for a large multistate manufacturing company and approaches her boss one morning to tell him that her husband has just received orders from the Coast Guard to report for deployment to the Middle East. They have a week to get everything ready for his departure. She wants to know if she can have excused time off during the coming week. If you were her boss, what would you tell her?

   A. Cynthia can take the time off, but it will be unexcused because she didn't give more than a week's notice.

   B. Jennifer has already requested the week off for vacation and only one person can be off at any one time; otherwise, the unit won't be able to function optimally. Cynthia's request is denied with regrets.

   C. Since only one person may be off for vacation, Jennifer must be told her vacation time off is canceled so Cynthia may take that vacation slot to spend time with her husband prior to deployment.

   D. Cynthia can have the time off, but it will be logged as unpaid and charged as FMLA leave, since Jennifer already has taken the vacation slot.

24. Robert works for a congressional representative and suffers a disabling injury in an automobile accident. Robert cannot work more than 3 hours per day according to his doctor. Weeks later, when he returns to work, he asks for a job accommodation and is told that it can't be done. When Robert presses the point, his supervisor states which of the following as the reason?

   A. The ADA does not cover congressional staff people, so they don't even have to discuss his request.

   B. The request he has made would exempt him from so many of his job's key responsibilities that it is not a reasonable accommodation.

   C. The request he has made would set a precedent that other representatives' offices would have to follow, and they don't want that.

   D. Because congressional staff members must meet the public every day, they can't have people seeing disabled workers in the office. It doesn't look good.

25. Jimmy has heard that he will be getting health care coverage from his company because of the Affordable Care Act. His company employs only ten people, but Jimmy is excited that he will finally get health insurance. He hasn't been feeling particularly good lately. How will the Affordable Care Act impact Jimmy?

   A. Jimmy might have to wait until he can arrange for insurance through one of the exchanges.

   B. Jimmy should get an enrollment form from his boss because all employees will be covered by the new requirement that employers provide health care coverage to workers.

   C. Jimmy is out of luck. The new law only covers employers with 50 or more people, and there is no way Jimmy will be getting health insurance under the new law.

   D. Jimmy's boss just ran out of forms, but he will get some more from HR and then have Jimmy sign up for his coverage.

Answers

1. **C**. If the new worker is classified as an employee on the payroll, the IRS demands that income tax, Social Security tax, and Medicare tax be withheld. People are not allowed to opt out because they want to file their own tax payments each quarter.

2. **A**. The Wagner-Peyser Act of 1933 provides for federal unemployment insurance and sets guidelines for state unemployment insurance programs.

3. **D**. Mary may indeed be singled out for shift changes due to her age, violating her ADEA rights. Creating a hostile work environment to encourage any worker of any age to exit is a no-no.

4. **B**. Both the FLSA and the IRS regulations require employers to obtain and report Social Security numbers from all employees. A Social Security number is required for completion of the Form I-9 to prove authorization to work in this country. The company may not remove it from its records, regardless of how concerned Pete may be.

5. **A**. Race and sex data is specifically required to be reported annually to the EEOC for all companies with 100 employees or more. For employers with 15 or more people on the payroll who are engaged in interstate commerce, EEOC regulations also require maintenance of those data records.

6. **B**. The FLSA requires employers to designate a day as the beginning of the workweek. To change that designation, there should be a significant business reason. Moving the start of the workweek based on projects is not acceptable. FLSA requires consistency because of the need to pay overtime for hours in excess of 40 in a workweek. Constantly moving a workweek could deprive employees of earned overtime.

7. **C**. The FLSA prohibits people aged 14 and 15 from working more than 8 hours in a day, even when school is not in session.

8. **D**. Driving a "power-driven hoisting apparatus" is one of the 17 most dangerous jobs that may not be performed by workers younger than 18. At Gary's age, the FLSA has no restriction on the hours he may work in a week.

9. **B**. The FLSA requires all hours of work in excess of 40 in a week be paid overtime at the rate of 1.5 times the normal hourly pay rate. Compensating time off, in lieu of overtime pay, must be given at the rate of 1.5 hours for every overtime hour and may only be granted by government organizations. Compensating time off in lieu of paying overtime is not an option in the private sector. Therefore, a day of overtime (8 hours) should be compensated for with 12 hours of compensating time off in the public sector.

10. **C**. The Equal Pay Act requires men and women doing the same work to be paid the same rate. If there are no men in the job, only women, there is no Equal Pay Act issue. If all the incumbents are women, there is no employment discrimination based on sex because there is only one sex represented. Therefore, with those conditions, there is no barrier to paying the new employee more based on her previous job's compensation.

11. B. ERISA specifically regulates welfare benefit plans such as health insurance and life insurance. That is in addition to regulation of pension and retirement plans offered by employers. It makes no difference who underwrites the life insurance—the employer or a vendor. ERISA will still provide requirements.

12. A. Any documents listed on the I-9 form are acceptable. The employer may not designate certain documents as requirements. A Social Security number is one way to demonstrate authorization to work in this country. A valid U.S. passport is also a way to demonstrate both identity and work authorization. No expired documents may be accepted.

13. B. The company has only 8 hours after the accident to file its report of serious injury with OSHA. We don't know how long ago the accident happened, but it was long enough that employees are now in the hospital. Steve should gather all the information needed for the report and get it called in to the OSHA office first, then immediately notify the families.

14. D. OHSA requires Injury and Illness Prevention Programs. Part of the identification and remediation of workplace hazards is employee training. Even if employees have been trained on equipment operation, periodic refresher programs can help overcome bad habits that might have developed. Refresher programs conducted on a yearly basis represent a reasonable interval for Donna's situation.

15. C. It doesn't matter if Jerry is a manager or not. All employees should be trained to react to imminent dangers by taking immediate action to prevent anyone from serious injury. Walking up to the edge to see if it is going to collapse is just nuts.

16. A. If she must, Theresa should show her boss the requirement in OSHA regulations. A prominent display location excludes places such as the back of a closet door or inside a binder somewhere in the manager's office.

17. A. Working inside an enclosed space with dangerous fumes calls for hazmat equipment and adequate breathing equipment. OSHA regulations specify the personal protective equipment (PPE) necessary in this and other working conditions.

18. C. The Needlestick Safety and Prevention Act requires all sharps be disposed of in approved sharps containers. It also requires the posting of warnings and information about blood-borne pathogens.

19. C. The Mine Safety and Health Administration has jurisdiction over all mining operations, not just coal mines. It handles safety complaints and conducts inspections of both above ground and underground mining operations. All mine operators are required to conduct their internal safety inspections and maintain records of those inspections.

20. D. ERISA has two defined vesting schedules, and firms offering a pension must pick one. In this example, cliff vesting was chosen, going from zero to 100 percent on the third work anniversary. The company alternatively could have chosen a graduated vesting schedule, which begins at the second anniversary with 20 percent, followed by 20 percent more annually until 100 percent is reached. Yes, firms may be more generous in their vesting schedule, but never less than the ERISA regulations.

21. D. Sam's company will not incur any additional obligations for disabled workers if they seek additional government contracts. They have been obligated under both laws for 6 years.

22. B. Arthur must decide whether he wishes to continue seeking employment with the AB Transit Company. If so, he must participate in their drug testing program. If he wants to avoid testing, he must drop out of the job application process and seek employment elsewhere.

23. D. Under the FMLA, Cynthia is entitled to unpaid leave of absence as a spouse of a covered military service worker. It will be logged as unpaid time off, unless company policy allows Cynthia to use her accrued paid time off. It will also be logged in her record as FMLA leave.

24. B. Even the congressional offices are subject to the ADA's requirement to consider and discuss requests for job accommodations. Reasonable job accommodations must be made to make it easier for an employee to perform one of the job's essential functions. If he can't do that, even with an accommodation, he is not eligible for that job assignment. If there is no other job available, the employer can't return him to work until his status changes.

25. A. Employers are required to provide health insurance coverage, or pay a penalty in lieu of that insurance, only if they have 50 or more full-time workers. With only ten employees, Jimmy's employer is not obligated to provide health insurance coverage. Jimmy may purchase it for himself through one of the exchanges set up for that purpose.

References

1. "Instructions for Employment Eligibility Verification," U.S. Department of Homeland Security, U.S. Citizenship and Immigration Services, accessed June 20, 2016, www.uscis.gov/files/form/i-9.pdf

2. "Federal Mine Safety & Health Act of 1977, Public Law 91-173, as amended by Public Law 95-164," U.S. Department of Labor, Mine Safety and Health Administration, accessed June 20, 2016, www.msha.gov/regs/act/acttc.htm

3. "OSH Act, OSHA Standards, Inspections, Citations and Penalties," U.S. Department of Labor, Occupational Safety and Health Administration, accessed June 20, 2016, www.osha.gov (search for "Inspections, Citations, and Proposed Penalties")

4. Ibid.

5. *Lawson v. FMR LLC*, U.S. No. 12-3, accessed June 20, 2016, http://www.supremecourt.gov/opinions/13pdf/12-3_4f57.pdf

6. *Sutton v. United Air Lines, Inc.*, 527 U.S. 471 (1999)

7. *Toyota Motor Manufacturing, Kentucky, Inc. v. Williams*, 534 U.S. 184 (2002)

8. The Job Accommodation Network (JAN), 800-526-7234 or www.askjan.org (accessed on June 20, 2016). The Job Accommodation Network is a free resource for employers, provided by the U.S. Department of Labor's Office of Disability Employment Policy (ODEP). JAN has been providing services for over 25 years.

9. 41 C.F.R.60-741.42(c)

10. "Disability Discrimination," U.S. Equal Employment Opportunity Commission, accessed on June 20, 2016, https://www.eeoc.gov/laws/types/disability.cfm

11. The first was the Civil Rights Act of 1866, which protected the right to enter into contracts regardless of race.

12. A list of controlled substances can be found in Schedules I through V of Section 202 of the Controlled Substances Act (21 U.S.C. 812) and as further defined in Regulation 21 C.F.R. 1308.11-1308.15.

13. "eLaws – Drug-Free Workplace Advisor," U.S. Department of Labor, accessed June 20, 2016, http://webapps.dol.gov/elaws/asp/drugfree/screenr.htm

14. 41 C.F.R. 60-3.7

15. Fair Treatment of Experienced Pilots Act (December 13, 2007), Public Law 110-135

16. 41 C.F.R. 60

PART II

HR Knowledge and Behavior Competencies

CHAPTER 4

People

The People knowledge domain counts toward 18 percent for both exams. This domain covers the essential HR knowledge needed for relating to people. The following are the functional areas that fall within the People knowledge domain:

- Functional Area 1: HR Strategy
- Functional Area 2: Talent Acquisition
- Functional Area 3: Employee Engagement & Retention
- Functional Area 4: Learning & Development
- Functional Area 5: Total Rewards

HR professionals are expected to know how to perform the following Body of Applied Skills and Knowledge (BASK) statements for the People knowledge domain:

- **01** Creating and setting the strategic direction of the HR function
- **02** Acquiring and developing the talent necessary for pursuing organizational goals
- **03** Maintaining a satisfied and engaged workforce while minimizing unwanted employee turnover
- **04** Developing a total rewards program that maximizes the effectiveness of the organization's compensation and benefits.

Functional Area 1: HR Strategy

Here is SHRM's BASK definition: "HR Strategy involves the activities necessary for developing, implementing, managing and evaluating the strategic direction required to achieve organizational success and to create value for stakeholders."[1]

All career levels of HR are expected to support and contribute to the strategic direction and role of HR. HR professionals must be able to identify and understand the organization's strategic initiatives, plans, and direction for decision-making as well as contribute to the organization's overall strategy. All of that involves understanding the internal and external environments and utilizing the organization's mission and vision as a focus for determining where HR can support goals and sustain a competitive advantage.

Key Concepts

- Approaches to project management (for example, traditional, Lean Six Sigma, agile, critical chain, design thinking, Kaizen) and processes (for example, initiating, planning and designing, launching/executing, monitoring and controlling, closing)
- Project planning, monitoring, and reporting methods and tools (for example, critical path analysis, Gantt charts, variance analysis, outcome monitoring)
- Project leadership, governance, and structures (for example, team roles, team management, work breakdown structures)
- Systems thinking (for example, related parts, systems theory, and input-processes-output) and components of an organizational system (for example, interdependence, necessity of feedback, differentiation of units)
- Strategic planning analysis frameworks (for example, PESTLE analysis, SWOT analysis, industry analysis, location-specific analysis, planning, growth-share matrix, real time, and blue ocean)
- Strategic planning process (for example, formulation, goal setting, implementation, evaluation)

The following are SHRM-identified proficiency indicators:

For All HR Professionals	For Advanced HR Professionals (SCP Exam)
Uses the perspective of systems thinking to understand how the organization operates	Identifies the ways in which the HR function can support the organization's strategy and goals
Informs business decisions with knowledge of the strategy and goals of HR and the organization	Aligns strategic management and planning activities with organizational mission, vision, and values
Develops and implements an individual action plan for executing HR's strategy and goals	Engages business leaders in strategic analysis and planning
Uses benchmarks, industry metrics, and workforce trends to understand the organization's market position and competitive advantage	Evaluates HR's critical activities in terms of value added, impact, and utility, using cost-benefit analysis, revenue, profit-and-loss estimates, and other leading or lagging indicators
Informs HR leadership of new or overlooked opportunities to align HR's strategy with the organization's	Provides HR-focused expertise to business leaders when formulating the organization's strategy and goals
Provides HR leadership with timely and accurate information required for strategic decision-making	Develops and implements HR strategy, vision, and goals that align with and support the organization's strategy and goals
	Ensures that HR strategy creates and sustains the organization's competitive advantage

The Role of Strategy

The role of strategy is one that aligns all functions in an organization to "row together" toward defining the organization's goals and direction. The creation of strategic goals requires a vision of growth that is associated with the organization's mission and, of course, includes the result of value for stakeholders. The development of goals, initiatives, and objectives is a necessary part of strategy to make sure everyone is on the same page, leading in the direction of attaining the defined strategy.

What Is Strategy?

Strategy is the planning of long-range goals and actions to attain those goals. Initiatives, objectives, and tactics are outlined in detail for each specific function in the organization and coordinated over a defined period of time. Strategy will look within the walls of the organization at its strengths, weaknesses, and vulnerabilities, along with looking outward at competition, opportunities, and external issues and influences.

Some theorists believe that strategy emerges in response to environmental threats and opportunities and cannot be planned rationally—because no one person can foresee everything about the future. Theorist Henry Mintzberg[2] is associated with this strategy approach. Others believe that the gathering of data is its core source for setting and choosing direction—much like a control system that would have targets to aim toward. Michael Porter's perspective of the five forces on an industry in planning is aligned with this process.[3] Both concepts and processes have value. Strategy is necessary to set the direction and path for an organization, and strategic management is required in leadership of the organization to ensure that the functions in the organization are aligning their activities to help move the organization toward its goals and strategic plans.

Requirements for Strategy and Management   Several strategic-planning processes begin with the extension of the annual operating budget into a typical 5-year projection. This can be a valuable exercise, particularly for organizations that have operated on a yearly or even monthly planning cycle. Most organizations soon discover that 5-year operational and financial forecasts, in and of themselves, are ineffective as strategic-planning tools because they are predicated on the assumption of no significant change in environmental, economic, and competitive conditions.

There are certain concepts for the creation of strategy and the management of it.

- **Aligning effort**   It's important to ensure that all functions are aligned with the organization's mission and goals. This is where a 10,000-foot helicopter ride is of benefit to have a broader view, ensuring that policies and practices are aligned with the strategy and intention.

- **Controlling drift**   This is important to ensure that an organization is not coasting along, doing what it has always done, and missing the boat or, at worse, becoming blindsided because of disruption in its marketplace or industry.

- **Focusing on core competencies**   This means knowing what the organization is good at for its customer base and being sure to focus efforts using those competencies.

- **Systems thinking**   Keep in mind the inter-relations of both internal and external factors, such as stakeholders, industry forces, and the other influences on an organization. This includes looking at both opportunities and the corresponding risks or conflicts and knowing what degree of risk is acceptable to the organization.

- **Using structure as a strategic level**   Does the structure of the organization support the strategy, or does it hamper it because of current policies and expectations within the organization?

- **Using culture as a strategic level**   Does the culture align itself with the intended strategy? As an example, if the strategy is to have frontline employees make return decisions on the spot with a customer, is the organization's orientation program providing training and demonstrated shadowing for new frontline hires to develop the desired behaviors?

Benefits of Strategy   The benefits of strategy include helping everyone in the organization focus on the future with a written plan that contains goals to further the organization's existence. From the top to rank and file, strategy provides a map that gives direction and intention on where the organization plans to spend its resources. Strategy helps keep decision-making and activities aligned. Strategy also provides a spotlight to prioritize how to deploy resources.

Mistakes to Avoid   Organizations can fail to obtain the benefits of strategy through their process and/or the management of strategy. They can avoid failing by remembering not to take shortcuts with the process of strategy. Analysis such as SWOT (discussed later in this chapter) and an honest look inward, along with valid research externally, are absolutely necessary. Being too comfortable with the status quo and not challenging or assessing the potential risks are other mistakes to avoid. Lacking follow-through and alignment of the plan throughout the organization is one of the most common mistakes—creating "the plan" and putting it in a binder on the shelf to just dust it off at next year's planning retreat is a waste of time, effort, and execution. Insufficient involvement or commitment from management will sideline a good strategic plan in its tracks. Lastly, lack of communication throughout the organization on what the strategic plan is, and what it means to each employee and function in the organization, will thwart efforts and should be avoided.

Levels of Strategy   There are three levels of strategy:

- **Organizational level**   This level involves a general vision of the future—typically, what the organization plans to grow into—as an umbrella over the entire organization.

- **Business unit level**   This level focuses on how and where the organization will focus to create value for its shareholders. The focus is on the business units such as sectors, divisions, regions, and product units.

- **Operational level**   This level focuses on the activities and actions the functions within the organization will take to progress it toward its vision. Finance, manufacturing, R&D, marketing, HR, and so on are operational-level examples.

Role of HR in Strategy   With HR, the operational level is going to be the main focus to support the entire organization. HR's policies, programs, and processes need to correlate, collaborate, and align with the organization's business units. HR's resources need to be spent on the activities that add value and assist the business units in fulfilling their work toward the strategic plans. This may include workforce planning, talent development, and incentive compensation programs.

HR professionals need to develop strategy skills—which are discussed in the following sections—such as scanning the environment, formulating strategy, assessing risks, and setting SMARTER goals and objectives. This role that HR fulfills is the biggest growing role that organizations demand today, which is why the HR job title of "HR Business Partner" was created.

HR's role includes building bridges with both internal and external stakeholders, where they exist. HR needs to view issues from differing perspectives and seek resolutions to help bridge the differing functions in a collaborative effort. There may be a policy within the payroll function of finance that conflicts with a new compensation incentive plan being developed with the sales unit to help account management personnel achieve goals that fit the strategic plan. The HR professional will need to address the conflicting issues and seek a resolution that is best for the organization and its strategy.

Role of Value in Strategy

The basic premise with strategy and management is to lead activities that yield a great value. Understanding how an organization creates value with its mission is the first step. By *value,* we are not talking cultural values; we are referencing the value brought to stakeholders. What causes the organization to be successful for our stakeholders—that is the value. How well is the organization achieving the defined mission, and does that mission still make sense?

Value Chain   The value chain is another model by Michael Porter.[4] It describes the process by which a business receives materials and then adds value to the materials through processes that create their finished products or services, which are then sold to customers. Organizations will conduct their value-chain analysis by looking at the steps in their production process that are utilized to create their products or services and then identifying a way to increase the efficiency of the production chain. The end goal is to create maximum value for the least possible cost, which creates the organization's competitive advantage. Figure 4-1 illustrates Porter's concept of the value chain with five primary and four secondary activities. It demonstrates the interconnections of various functions in delivering value to the end customer or the organization.

Primary activities, which will vary according to the type of the organization's activities, contribute directly to the value that is created for the customer. An example is a food manufacturer that uses distributors and retailers for its product. The value of the primary activities depends on the secondary activities that provide services to the primary functions. HR administration as well as finance and IT are examples of secondary activities.

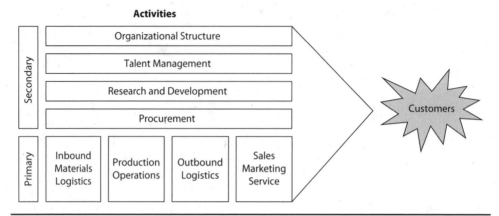

Figure 4-1 Porter value chain concept

NOTE Not all businesses will find this value chain concept realistic because their business does not control the entire chain of production and distribution.

A strategist, be it an HR professional or an internal or outside consult, needs to understand the flow in creating value. They need to know which activities in the organization are considered central to its mission, reflecting its *core* activities, and which ones are the most profitable activities or could be profitably outsourced.

Stakeholder Concept   R. Edward Freeman offered the stakeholder concept in the mid-1980s[5] as another perspective to the shareholder view of a corporation (which was to create wealth for the shareholders). Freeman's stakeholder concept recognizes the different types of value an organization creates. Yes, there may be monetary value as viewed by investors, but there is also value that a community may perceive via the employment taxes or corporate social responsibility contributions it makes. Figure 4-2 depicts Freeman's stakeholder concept. Understanding the various perceptions from the view of each stakeholder is especially challenging for a global organization. The customer's expectations will vary. Employees in various countries will have differing perspectives based on their cultural norms. This stakeholder concept encompasses all the relationships that impact the organization, plus all the people, groups, and entities that the organization impacts. It is a two-way relationship.

HR's Role in Defining and Creating Value   The biggest role HR has in defining and creating value for its organization is knowing the workforce. Knowing core competencies of talent, where to find the talent that is needed, and the legal environment in which the organization employs its workforce—these are critical value-producing activities for HR.

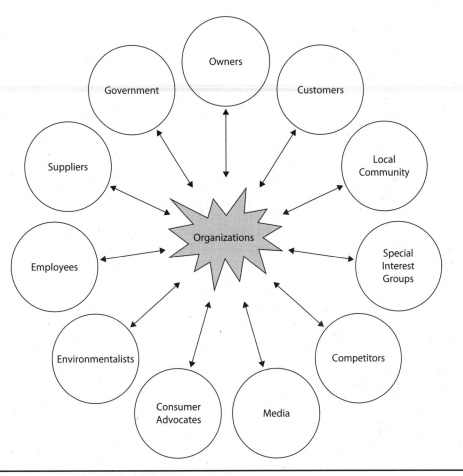

Figure 4-2 Freeman stakeholder concept

The Strategy Process

As we've explained, the strategic planning process is about designing the organization for the future. Whether that is a plan that is for 1 year, 5 years, or longer, it will always involve the following four basic stages and will be continually dynamic and changing as conditions change for an organization:

- **Formulation of the strategy**   Gathering the critical and necessary data to analyze and assess the current situation

- **Development of the strategy**   Creating your plan to gain a competitive advantage in the markets in which you compete

- **Implementation stage**   The enactment of specific objectives and initiatives that produce outcomes associated with the goals

- **Evaluation stage**   The final stage, where metrics and achievements are accessed and reported upon to stakeholders

Strategy Formulation

Strategy formulation is the process by which an organization chooses the most appropriate courses of action to achieve its defined goals.

Information Gathering and Analysis

A major part of strategy is the process of gathering data. It should be done prior to and during the creation of the strategic plan and continue through implementation and the monitoring process of the strategic plan. Data can be secondary or primary data and gathered through internal or external sources.

Improving Your Business and Organizational "Radar"   Information is the key to business success. When something is "on the radar," it is being tracked. That means someone believes the information is important to the organization's success. Therefore, the question becomes, "What should we be tracking or monitoring?" Get this right and you will be able to keep your eye on all the critical elements surrounding your organization, sort the critical from the mundane, and decide on future movements with greater accuracy.

Environmental Scanning

Seeing what is happening in the environment around you is important. Identifying the important information among the plethora of unimportant stuff becomes a challenge.

PESTLE Analysis   An environmental scanning technique that helps businesses assess particular factors that may have an impact on their operations is known by the acronym PESTLE. It can help look at external factors with six different focuses.
   PESTLE stands for:

   P—Political
   E—Economic
   S—Social
   T—Technological
   L—Legal
   E—Environmental

Develop ways you can gather information in each of these categories, and you will be well out in front of your competitors in your ability to make well-informed decisions. According to the Professional Academy, these are the elements to look for when gathering information:[6]

- **Political factors**   These are all about how and to what degree a government intervenes in the economy. This can include government policy, political stability or instability in overseas markets, foreign trade policy, tax policy, labor law, environmental law, trade restrictions, and so on.

   It is clear from the earlier list that political factors often have an impact on organizations and how they do business. Organizations need to be able to respond to the current and anticipated future legislation and adjust their marketing policy accordingly.

- **Economic factors** Economic factors have a significant impact on how organizations do business and how profitable they are. Factors include economic growth, unemployment rates, interest rates, exchange rates, inflation, disposable income of consumers and businesses, and so on.

  These factors can be further broken down into macroeconomic and microeconomic factors. Macroeconomic factors deal with the management of demand in any given economy. Governments use interest rate control, taxation policy, and government expenditure as their main mechanisms to influence these demand factors.

  Microeconomic factors are all about the way people spend their incomes. This has a large impact on business-to-consumer organizations in particular.

- **Social factors** Also known as sociocultural factors, these are the areas that involve the shared belief and attitudes of the population as well as demographic information. These factors include population growth, age distribution, health consciousness, career attitudes, and so on. These factors are of particular interest, as they have a direct effect on how marketers understand customers and what drives them.

- **Technological factors** We all know how fast the technological landscape changes and how this impacts the way we market our products. Technological factors affect marketing of our products and our HR services in three distinct ways:

  - **New ways of producing goods and services** Using remote access for employee updates directly to the human resource information system (HRIS) or enterprise resource planning (ERP) software, providing employees online access to their own employee records so they can request updates, such as when they move to a new address.

  - **New ways of distributing goods and services** Scanning barcodes to track where products are.

  - **New ways of communicating with target markets** Using e-mail, text messages, social media, and even a company emergency messaging system to notify employees of critical changes in the work environment.

- **Environmental factors** These factors have only really come to the forefront since the turn of the century. They have become important because of the increasing scarcity of raw materials, pollution reduction targets, doing business as an ethical and sustainable company, and carbon footprint targets set by governments. If HR were to reduce or eliminate paper records, that could have an impact on the environment (less paper used, fewer trees cut) and cost to the organization (a higher profit, however small a contribution). Increasingly, consumers are demanding that the products they buy are sourced ethically and, when possible, from a sustainable source. HR can contribute to that effort and be cited by corporate as an example of how the organization is reducing its impact on the environment.

- **Legal factors**   Legal factors include, but are not limited to, patent law and intellectual property protection, health and safety, equal opportunity, advertising standards, consumer rights and laws, product labeling, and product safety. It is clear that HR professionals need to know what is and what is not legal in order to avoid fines, embarrassment, or serious reputational damage.

SWOT Analysis

A SWOT analysis looks at both the internal and external environment and identifies pros and cons in each. It can be conducted for the entire organization or a subset of it. In the following example, we will use a subset of the HR department. SWOT stands for the following:

- **Strengths**   What are the strengths of your HR organization? What do you do really well? What do you want to continue doing into the future? It could be HRIS, sexual harassment prevention, or onboarding.

- **Weaknesses**   These are the areas you know need improvement. Maybe it is the amount and quality of employee training, recruiting for diversity, time to fill critical vacancies, or benefit program analysis.

- **Opportunities**   These are positives in the environment. A merger or acquisition offers opportunities to examine all HR systems in both organizations and determine which will serve the new employer group best in the future.

- **Threats**   These are negative challenges we face in the environment. For example, an outside vendor may propose to deliver benefit program management more cheaply than we currently do in-house. Our closest competitors may have just raised the compensation they pay dramatically. Initially, new government requirements can be perceived as threats. Effectively managed, they can sometimes be converted into opportunities.

Industry Analysis

Industry analysis is a tool that facilitates a company's understanding of its position relative to other companies that produce similar products or services. Understanding the forces at work in the overall industry is an important component of effective strategic planning. Industry analysis enables HR professionals to identify the threats and opportunities facing their businesses and to focus their resources on developing unique capabilities that could lead to a competitive advantage.[7] How are HR professionals throughout our industry conducting their business? What are they doing that can be applied within our organization?

Industry Lifecycle   There are four generally recognized phases to the lifecycle of a business or industry:

- **Introduction**   This is the beginning of the organization. It's the entrepreneurial phase where everything is new. Policies and systems are being created only as they are needed.

- **Growth**   After the new organization has gotten a foothold in its marketplace, it begins to grow. Growth is influenced by all the factors we have explored in the SWOT and PESTLE analyses.

- **Maturity**   This is the time when the organization is comfortable with its size, its influence, and its income. Policies and procedures become well-documented at this phase.

- **Decline**   The phase when systems have gotten surpassed by technological advances, and products and services have become passé. Without updates to its core reasons for being, the organization will ultimately cease to exist.

Porter's Five Forces   Each employer organization has pressures from both internal and external sources. Those pressures impact the competitiveness the organization will be able to apply to the world in which it operates. Porter first published his suggestion that these five forces are what influence competitiveness in a *Harvard Business Review* article in 1979.[8] These pressures consist of forces close to a company that affect its ability to serve its customers and make a profit.

The five forces are as follows:

- **Threat of new entrants**   When a company does so well that their success attracts new competitors who want to get in on that success, the competition can drive down profits.

- **Threat of substitutes**   In modern terms, these are the "knock-off" products that may even be legal if the original product patents have expired. Other people use different products or services to address the same need that the original product or service solved. Examples are digital watches versus analog watches and cell phones versus land lines.

- **Bargaining power of customers**   When customer orders are large, they can force the lowering of price. Consider the big-box stores and how their orders influence suppliers.

- **Bargaining power of suppliers**   If there are few options for sourcing component parts, raw materials, or other supplies, the supplier can have a strong influence on the cost of end products.

- **Industry rivalry**   Industry competitors greatly influence our ability to succeed in the marketplace. They can often drive our price to end users and force us to clearly differentiate how our products and services are superior to the other industry players.

Strategic Investment Decisions   In evaluating capital expenditure decisions, we should consider three techniques to see how investment decisions are evaluated: accounting rate of return, payback, and discounted cash flow techniques. In HR terms, investments should be evaluated based on the period of time it takes to reclaim the investment (using a new applicant-tracking software system), what the payback amount will be (savings in HR payroll expense from new software application), and what impact there will be on cash flow (reduction in HR budget that can put cash back into the organizational P&L statement).

Growth Share Matrix   Sometimes called the *Boston box* or *Boston matrix,* the growth share matrix was created by Bruce D. Henderson for the Boston Consulting Group in 1970 to help corporations analyze their product lines. The growth share matrix can be created with plotting on two axes. The x-axis is the relative market share, and the y-axis is market growth. Those two axes create four quadrants. When market share increases and market growth does too, the companies are "stars." When market growth is high, but market share is low, companies are questionable for investment. When market share is high, but growth is low, companies can be good cash cows. Finally, when both market growth and market share are low, companies can be described as "investment dogs." Figure 4-3 is an example of a growth share matrix.

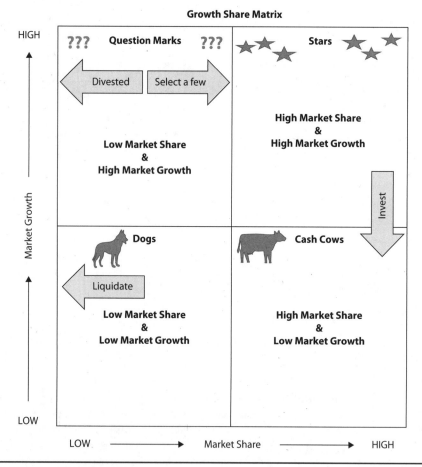

Figure 4-3   Growth share matrix

Figure 4-4
The GE-McKinsey
nine-box matrix
chart

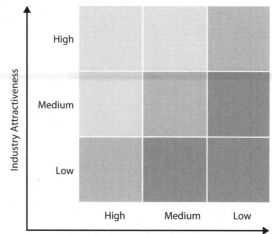

The GE-McKinsey Nine-Box Matrix   The *nine-box matrix,* shown in Figure 4-4, offers a systematic approach for the decentralized corporation to determine where best to invest its cash. Rather than rely on each business unit's projections of its future prospects, the company can judge a unit by two factors that will determine whether it's going to do well in the future: the attractiveness of the relevant industry and the unit's competitive strength within that industry.[9]

Defining Mission, Vision, and Values

According to SHRM, mission, vision, and values can be defined as follows:

- **Mission**   A concise explanation of the organization's reason for existence. It describes the organization's purpose and its overall intention. The mission statement supports the vision and serves to communicate purpose and direction to employees, customers, vendors, and other stakeholders.

- **Vision**   Looks forward and creates a mental image of the ideal state that the organization wants to achieve. Vision is inspirational and aspirational and should challenge employees.

- **Values**   The core principles that guide and direct the organization and its culture. In a values-led organization, the values create a moral compass for the organization and its employees.

Mission and Vision Statements   A mission statement answers these questions: What is our organization's purpose? Why does our organization exist? A vision statement answers these questions: What problem are we seeking to solve? Where are we headed? If we achieved all strategic goals, what would we look like 10 years from now?

PART II

Organizational Values Organizational values will answer these questions: What values do we embrace to guide the behavior and decision-making of our organization? What conduct should our employees uphold?

Articulating the HR Mission, Vision, and Values HR professionals are accountable for making sure senior executives create the HR mission, vision, and values statements. Beyond that, HR is responsible for communicating them to the general employee body in terms that can be well understood. When creating a presentation about the HR role and its place in the overall organization, consider these questions: What will be the impact on me [the executive or employee]? Why should I care about the role of HR in the organization? How will this make my job easier?

Setting Goals

Setting HR goals within the construct of articulated mission, vision, and values statements is the next step. What do we want to accomplish in the coming period of time? The time period could be a month or a year. What contributions can be made by HR to the overall organization's efforts? HR can make a financial impact, for example.

Using the SMARTER method will ensure that the goals created stand a chance of actually being achieved. Here's an example of an achievable goal:

> *Implement a new telecommunicating policy that complies with new ERGO standards for the IT department by end of second quarter.*

SMARTER goal setting stands for the following:

- **Specific** Know exactly what you want to accomplish. A goal must be well-defined, clear, and unambiguous.
- **Measurable** Have a yardstick to measure the specific intention.
- **Attainable** Make the goal achievable.
- **Realistic** Make the goal realistic to achieve in the time frame and relevant to align with the organization's strategic plan.
- **Timed** Specify whether this goal has an implementation date.

The preceding is the classic SMART model. SHRM has updated it to "SMARTER" by adding the following:

- **Evaluated** Measure how we did compared to what we set out to accomplish.
- **Revised** This is part of a commitment to continuous improvement. Consider what has happened, learn from it, and revise the goal going forward.

Composing goals with the SMARTER outline and using action verbs such as *identify, describe, create, implement,* and *define* will guide the objective of the goal's direction.

A word of caution when goal setting: be careful of the smorgasbord effect, which means getting so excited about creating SMARTER goals for the HR plan that too many goals are selected, which can cause a dilution of focus and resources.

Aligning HR Goals and Objectives   Once HR goals are set, it is necessary for a final step in the process, which is to check that HR goals are aligned with organizational goals and objectives. If HR isn't going to be supporting the overall goals of the employer organization, adjustments should be made. There is no room for "grandstanding" or building personal "kingdoms." HR must be a team player with the other executives in the leadership group. HR's contributions must be clear to the executive team.

Developing Strategy

A strategy is a statement of *how* we are going to get things done. It is less specific than an *action plan.* Once the mission, vision, and values have been established, the logical next step is to ask, "How will we accomplish these things?" It is a broad statement about what approach we will take to implement the mission at each point. Then, later, will come the action plan that answers the questions of who, when, and what.

Developing Strategies That Fit

This is according to Community Tool Box: "A good strategy will consider existing barriers and resources (people, money, power, materials, etc.). It will also stay with the overall vision, mission, and objectives of the initiative. Often, an initiative will use many different strategies—providing information, enhancing support, removing barriers, providing resources, etc.—to achieve its goals.

"Objectives [goals] outline the aims of an initiative—what success would look like in achieving the vision and mission. By contrast, strategies suggest paths to take (and how to move along) on the road to success. That is, strategies help you determine how you will realize your vision and objectives through the nitty-gritty world of action."[10]

It wouldn't make much sense to plan how to do something that isn't part of the mission, vision, or values of the organization. Follow the mission and stay within the boundaries of the vision and values. Strategy will allow you to determine how to implement your mission. If you discover a strategy that isn't speaking to the mission, get rid of it. It will be a distraction at best and a waste of resources at worst.

Business Strategy: How We Will Compete

Each enterprise must assess for itself the missions and strategies that it needs to accomplish its goals. Competing in an open market requires that assessment be updated periodically. After all, world conditions change with time. Employer organizations need to be flexible to accommodate those shifts.

In HR terms, should the HR functions be performed by in-house staff or by hiring a consultant from the outside? Perhaps contracting with a large vendor would be the more cost-effective approach. Payroll is the obvious example. Oftentimes, vendors can perform the payroll function more cheaply than internal staff. Other examples are HRIS management and benefit management (employee assistance programs). If you want to compete for rights to deliver any given HR function to your employees, it will be necessary for you to develop a business plan explaining how you will be able to do it better than the external vendors.

PART II

Types of Differentiation	Methods of Differentiation
Product differentiation	Features, performance, efficacy, conformance, durability, reliability, warranty
Service differentiation	Ordering ease, delivery, installation, customer training, customer consulting, other miscellaneous services
Channel differentiation	Coverage, expertise, performance
Relationship differentiation	Competence, courtesy, credibility, reliability, responsiveness, communication
Reputation/image differentiation	Perception, communication, advertising
Price differentiation	By customer, by quantity, by segment

Table 4-1 Six Ways to Differentiate Your Product or Service

Creating Competitive Advantage Delivering HR services using people on the payroll gives you flexibility because they can often spend a portion of their time working on projects that are not the primary focus of their other work. If you have HR professionals assigned to compensation analysis, they may have some time while waiting for compensation data input that could be used to review policies as part of a 2-year review cycle. That efficiency wouldn't be available to you if you hired an outsider to do the compensation analysis.

According to the Priority Metrics Group,[11] there are six ways to differentiate your organization within a competitive marketplace, regardless of where in the world you are located (see Table 4-1).

Porter's Competitive Strategies What forces drive competition in an industry? What moves will competitors make? How will one's industry evolve? How do strategic planners respond to competitive actions? How can a firm be best positioned to compete for the long run?

In 1985, Porter suggested that there are four primary competitive strategies that organizations can rely on when plotting their future business course.[12] Porter called the generic strategies cost leadership (no frills), differentiation (creating uniquely desirable products and services for which you may charge a premium price), and focus (offering a specialized service or product in a niche market). He then subdivided the focus strategy into two parts: cost focus and differentiation focus (see Table 4-2).[13]

Cost Leadership Within the cost leadership strategy, profits can be increased by reducing costs while maintaining prices at industry average. Market share can be increased by both reducing costs and lowering prices, taking sales away from competitors.

Table 4-2 Porter's Competitive Strategies	Scope	Broad	Cost Leadership	Differentiation
		Narrow	Cost Focus	Differentiation Focus
			Cost	Differentiation
			Source of Competitive Advantage	

The no-frills retailers have opted to cut costs to a minimum and pass their savings on to customers via lower prices. This helps them grab market share and ensures their stores are as full as possible, further driving down cost. Think of Walmart, Home Depot, and Lowes. This same thinking can be applied to the HR department if being the lowest-cost HR department in the industry is a mission of the group.

Differentiation   Differentiation involves making your products or services different from and more attractive than those of your competitors, allowing you to charge a premium price. How will you set yourself apart from your competition? Your competition in the HR world are the HR managers in other companies within your industry. Are they running a group that delivers HR services to their employees with a 1:150 HR professional-to-employee ratio? What if, at the same time, your HR professional-to-employee ratio was running 2:150? You are spending twice as much for HR professionals as your competitors. If you can differentiate your services based on cost, you should be able to do so based on quality. Being a full-service HR department means you "hold the hand of employees" as they ask for help with benefits enrollment, discrimination complaint processing, and training enrollment. Unless you can be better in either cost or quality, you will lose out to the competition. Important to this approach is that you can actually deliver the differentiated product or service, with high quality and in the time promised. The marketplace will long remember the broken promises made to customers, so beware of making promises you cannot keep.

Focus   When you focus on niche markets, it is possible to use focus as a strategy. Making something that no one else does that serves a specific requirement is one way. Examples are making dog collars using all natural materials and creating a seashell shop that imports seashells from all over the world so that customers can have a one-stop shopping experience. It costs customers less time and money to search the world for what they want when you have it all conveniently located in your offerings.

Companies that use focus strategies concentrate on a particular niche market and, by understanding the dynamics of that market and the unique needs of the customers within it, develop uniquely low-cost or well-specified products for the market. Because they serve customers in their market uniquely well, they tend to build strong brand loyalty among their customers. This makes their particular market segment less attractive to competitors.[14]

Impact of Business Strategies on HR Strategy   Business strategy is paramount. HR strategy must support that business strategy. So, begin with questions like these: What is the business mission? What strategies will be used to accomplish that mission? How can HR support those business strategies? HR is one component of the organization, as is finance, accounting, marketing, production, and research. If all of these components are not supporting the business strategy, there is little likelihood that business goals will be accomplished.

Your HR organization and its strategies can have an impact on the overall business strategies if you follow these ten steps to make it happen:[15]

1. *Understand your organization's business.* Spend time every day talking with sales, production, quality, and accounting. Make sure you know what is going on in that bigger world.

2. *Share responsibility for business goals and plans.* The overall business goals are your goals, too. When you make plans for your department, they should be directed to achieving overall business objectives as well as human resource goals. Developing a performance culture is a goal you'll likely own.

3. *Know the human resource business thoroughly.* Your customers rely on you for correct and insightful information and advice. What more is there to say? You are dependable, credible, trustworthy, and knowledgeable, and you have deep integrity.

4. *Run your department like a business.* Your goals must contribute to the accomplishment of the overall business objectives. Your action plans to achieve the goals need to translate into daily to-do lists for your staff. Every significant activity requires a feedback loop or audit so you know that it is being accomplished.

5. *Measure outcomes and goal achievement, not work processes.* Employee and executive surveys are often used to identify how these people see HR performance.

6. *Remember the people in human resources.* Is your office a magnet for people who need help, advice, or a sounding board? Are some of your visitors your senior managers? Even the CEO? If so, you remember that you are there to serve your organization's people so that they can meet your business goals.

7. *Express thoughtful opinions backed by data and study.* You have to understand the numbers. How else can you offer a substantial, intelligent opinion about business direction? Learn everything you can so that you have opinions and so your opinions are backed up with data. You need to understand the effect of decisions that your office makes on the work of the rest of the company. (For example, don't schedule meetings with plant personnel on the last day of their shipping month.)

8. *Harness the benefits of technology.* You'll provide better customer service and free your time for dreaming up new value-added strategies. You cannot overestimate the impact of an effective HRIS. Need reports about attendance? How about salary reports for your whole organization? Interested in turnover and retention figures?

9. *Recommend programs for people who continually improve the business.* When you propose new programs or problem-solve people issues, suggest solutions that support the accomplishment of business goals. You have reasons for suggesting a new variable pay system such as encouraging managers to accomplish business objectives. What's better—the thank-you card system that appears to help employee motivation and productivity or the attendance system that has reduced absenteeism by 4 percent?

10. *Learn and grow every day through every possible method.* Use your knowledge of how people develop to do what is necessary to continue your growth curve.

   - Seek out a more experienced mentor or sounding board. You need someone you can confide in and learn from.

   - Attend professional HR conferences, webinars, and events.

   - Attend executive leadership and management meetings in addition to your HR professional associations. You seek knowledge that goes beyond the bounds of your discipline and department.

- Attend at least 40 hours of training and education every year. Make sure your staff members attend too. Cover all aspects of the business and running a business.

- Seek out people who will ask you questions and challenge your beliefs so you can continue to grow. For example, a woman works with a CEO who asks her questions. She may not always like them, but the questions challenge her to think things through and to follow issues to their logical conclusion. He repeatedly asks, "How will you know if that is working? Happening? Bringing the results you want?" She needs to be able to respond.

Corporate Strategy: Where We Will Compete   Whatever the corporate strategy, we need to be able to support it from the HR department. Remember, strategy is how we will meet our goals and objectives. Once we identify how we will get there (what strategies we will use), we can begin developing the action plan that will assign individual responsibilities for each element of the strategy.

Determining which markets to address is a question business strategy must address. If the answer is that expansion into international locations is appropriate, then the HR strategy will need to address those requirements.

Growth Strategy Options   Growth can happen through market penetration (capturing a greater portion of the existing market with current products/services), market expansion (selling current products in a new market), diversification (selling new products to new markets), and acquisition (purchasing another company to gain broader product or service offerings or new market presence.).[16] Growth requires financial support. HR can contribute by controlling expenses. Here are some ways that growth strategy can be a viable option:

- **Market penetration**   Increasing market share through options such as lowering prices

- **Market expansion**   Developing new markets where current products and services can be sold

- **Product expansion**   Increasing the number of products or product features

- **Diversification strategies**   Selling new products to new markets

- **Acquisition strategies**   Purchasing another organization in an effort to expand product line or markets

Managing Growth Options   The key to a long, healthy corporate life is steady growth. According to a 1998 survey, of the companies that enjoyed greater than 10 percent sales growth per year, about 78 percent were still around six years after starting. Of the companies with flat or decreasing sales, only 27.5 percent survived for six years.[17]

Managing growth requires substantial market intelligence. Researching the needs of the target market, receptivity to product names or applications, and financial requirements of the expansion effort are all concerns that need to be addressed. HR can contribute to those research efforts through identification of employee benefit packages and their costs, specification of employee recruiting techniques and costs, and cultural challenges that will be faced because of the expansion.

Mergers and Acquisitions   Mergers and acquisitions (M&As) are transactions in which the ownership of companies, other business organizations, or their operating units are transferred or combined. As an aspect of strategic management, M&As can allow enterprises to grow, and change the nature of their business or competitive position. From a legal point of view, a merger is a legal consolidation of two entities into one entity, whereas an acquisition occurs when one entity takes ownership of another entity's stock, equity interests, or assets. M&As are means to new markets, new products or services, or new human capital. All could figure strategically into your future plans.

Sometimes it makes good business sense to purchase another organization or merge with another organization. When markets are different and a combined organization can offer both entities a broader sales base, there is synergy. When product lines can be added through M&As, there is synergy. Then HR interventions, such as the following, are needed to address cultural blending and employee support systems:

- **HR's role in the mergers and acquisitions strategy**   HR is almost always called upon to perform due diligence in the investigative phase prior to finalizing a merger or acquisition. What union agreements does the new company have? How will those provisions fit into our organization? What policies does the new company have, and how will they blend with our policies? (Examples are holiday and vacation computations, sick leave policies, and parental leave policies.)

- **Planning the HR integration strategy**   An estimated 70 percent to 90 percent of all M&As fail to achieve their anticipated strategic and financial objectives.[18] This rate of failure is often attributed to various HR-related factors, such as incompatible cultures, differing management styles, poor motivation, loss of key talent, lack of communication, diminished trust, and uncertainty of long-term goals.

Both mergers and acquisitions present significant challenges to HR professionals. The M&A process requires management of both organizations to consider all implications of a proposed merger or acquisition before agreeing to one—which necessarily involves consideration of the "people issues" created by a proposed merger or acquisition. HR professionals are often involved in the process by advising management on human resource matters, including using surveys and other metrics to gather relevant data, identifying potential conflicts or HR challenges between the two companies, integrating HR practices and company cultures after an M&A, and managing talent decisions such as layoffs, to name a few.[19]

Developing an integration strategy is like developing any other strategy. It requires asking who the stakeholders are (our company, their company, customers, stockholders, employees) and what benefits can be achieved by successfully completing the merger or acquisition (expanding markets, expanding product line, reducing expenses/costs, gaining customers/market share, and improving customer perception of our business).

Next, follow the same basic steps used in other strategy sessions:[20]

1. *Identify the vision.* What is the desired future? What is the inspiration? What are our aspirations now?

2. *Identify the mission.* What is the clear and compelling objective for the integration?

3. *Identify the goals.* What must be achieved? What needs should be met?

4. *Identify the strategies.* What is the plan that will lead us to achieving our mission and goals?

5. *Identify the initiatives.* What tactical and operational plans will be necessary to successfully implement the strategy?

Implementing Once established, the HR strategy for a merger or acquisition needs to be implemented. That requires further analysis of the tactics and operational plans that will be needed for achieving success. All of the basic support programs needed in running a business must be either blended or transitioned to one of the existing systems.

Here are a few of the keys needed to make a merger/acquisition successful based on the principles of the Accelerating Implementation Methodology (AIM):[21]

- **Define the changes in terms of human behavior** The speed of an integration is determined by how you manage the human elements of the change. Remember to define the changes in terms of what people need to be doing differently. What are we doing? Why are we doing it, and what are the consequences if we don't succeed?

- **Generate sponsorship** Sponsorship is the single most important factor in ensuring a fast and successful implementation. Every sponsor, from senior management down to the line managers, must express, model, and reinforce their commitment to the change. You will not get a cultural change with minor changes in sponsor behavior!

- **Manage resistance** Resistance is inevitable, even when people see the merger as positive. Resistance is a function of disruption, and a merger or acquisition can be very disruptive. Make sure you have a plan on how to manage resistance, including responding quickly to concerns, rumors, and questions.

- **Tighten up communications** Every communication sent must include a feedback loop. This way, when a communication goes out, feedback will come back in. Use a variety of communication channels, with an emphasis on the face-to-face method.

- **Manage reinforcements** The only way to implement actual culture change is to integrate the behavioral elements of the new culture into the daily business activities and then dramatically change the reinforcements—that is, the positive and negative consequences that managers apply on a daily basis with their direct reports.

Monitoring and Evaluating It is fine to know where we want to go and how we want to get there. However, it is equally important to know if we are actually walking the path we outlined for ourselves in the strategy we implemented. That is what monitoring and evaluating will tell us. Monitoring is the process of continually measuring the progress achievements of a project. It also assesses results that matter. Evaluation is the process of measuring the success of project achievements and the quality of those achievements. Establishing milestones for an M&A project will help you understand if you are on schedule, and quality measures will provide feedback about the success you have had so far with your implementation.

Measuring our incremental success can be great feedback to help us make adjustments so we can get back on track when necessary. HR can monitor recruiting and staffing functions, benefit design and implementation functions, employee relocation, policy development and implementation, and legal compliance requirements. Each of those functions should be evaluated for progress toward the goal. How many requisitions were filled within 10 days, 30 days, or longer? How quickly were policies developed when they were needed? What compliance requirements were met or not met (EEO discrimination complaint rate, compliance evaluation closures with "no violation" determination from the Department of Labor)? What is the retention rate of new hires? What is the turn-over rate at each compensation level within the organization? All these and more are valid measurements that can be used by HR to monitor the progress toward the goal of completing a merger or acquisition.

Divestiture Strategies   The opposite of merger is divestiture. Divestiture is the removal of assets or processes that are no longer needed and that can be converted into cash. As a strategy, "spinning off" pieces of an organization can leave the remainder of the company in a healthier state financially. Splitting up a company can be equally painful and complicated.

For example, in 1982, Judge Green ordered the bifurcation of the Bell System. It was necessary to create a new enterprise that had the legacy telephone company businesses and a new company that would be unregulated and allowed to compete openly in the business communication marketplace. On January 1, 1983, American Bell was born. It was staffed by 100,000 employees who had been transitioned from the 23 legacy operating companies in the Bell System—and the new company had no revenue. It survived the first year or so on loans from the former telephone operating companies. Also, it was necessary to pay those 100,000 people from the very beginning. The plan called for employee records to be transferred from the 23 operating companies to the new American Bell accounting center in Lakeland, Florida. Well, unfortunately, there were large differences among the record storage systems among the 23 companies. Therefore, data fields and formatting requirements were all different. Blending the imported records was not working on a practical level. It was necessary for HR to create a staff that would scrub the employee records to be sure they were both accurate and properly formatted for the new accounting system in Lakeland. Once that was done, things began to run smoothly. In the beginning, approximately 10 to 25 percent of the American Bell staff was not receiving paychecks. Branch sales managers were writing checks on the branch account to their employees as substitute paychecks. It took almost an entire year to unravel all of the payments that were made and to reconcile them with payroll.

Identifying how we will accomplish the divestiture seems like a reasonable step to take, and HR professionals can contribute to that planning process by identifying how they will add value to the end result.

Communicating Strategy Going through all the work of creating a strategy is a wasted effort if you don't then communicate through your organization so people know what the strategy is and can take actions to support it. "If you don't communicate your strategy in a way that your people understand and find compelling, how can you expect them to help you succeed with it? Research suggests only 5 percent of the people in an organization understand its strategy."[22] According to *Harvard Business Review*, there are eight ways to effectively communicate your strategy:[23]

- *Keep the message simple but deep in meaning.* Most organizations have a deeper meaning as to why they exist. This tends to influence strategy, decision-making, and behaviors at executive levels but often isn't well articulated for employees. What you call it doesn't matter—your purpose, your why, your core belief, your center. What does matter is that you establish the message's relevance with employees in a way that makes them care more about the company and about the job they do.

- *Build behavior based on market and customer insights.* For employees to fully understand how your strategy is different and better than the competition, they need to be in touch with market realities. The challenge is in how to effectively convey those realities so that your people can act on them. By building internal campaigns based on market and customer insights, you bring your strategy to life for your employees through this important lens. Package your content so that it can be shared broadly with all departments in your organization but in a hands-on way.

- *Use the discipline of a framework.* Inspire, educate, reinforce.

- *Think broader than the typical CEO-delivered message, and don't disappear.* Employees are more likely to believe what leaders say when they hear similar arguments from their peers, and conversations can be more persuasive and engaging than one-way presentations. Designate a team of employees to serve as ambassadors responsible for delivering important messages at all levels.

- *Put on your "real person" hat, and take off your "corporate person/executive" hat.* The fact is, few people are deeply inspired by the pieces of communication that their companies put out. Much of it ignores one of the most important truths of communication, especially communication in the early twenty-first century: be real. "Corporate speak" comes off as hollow and lacking in meaning. Authentic messages from you will help employees see the challenges and opportunities as you see them and understand and care about the direction in which you're trying to take the company.

- *Tell a story.* Facts and figures won't be remembered. Stories and experiences will. Use storytelling as much as possible to bring humanity to the company and to help employees understand the relevance of your strategy and real-life examples of progress and shortfalls in relation to it. Ask employees to share stories as well and use these as the foundation for dialogues that foster greater understanding of the behaviors that you want to encourage and enhance versus those that pose risks.

- *Use twenty-first century media and be unexpected.* Consider the roles of social media, networking, blogs, and games to get the word out in ways that your employees are used to engaging in. Where your message shows up also says a lot. Aim to catch people somewhere that they would least expect it. Is it in the elevator or stairwell? On their mobile phones?

- *Make the necessary investment.* Most executives recognize how important their employee audience is. They are the company's largest expense. They often communicate directly with your customers. They single-handedly control most perceptions that consumers have about the brand. Therefore, if this is a given, why are we so reluctant to adequately fund internal communication campaigns?

Implementing Strategy Production

 Implementation is the process that turns strategies and plans into actions to accomplish strategic objectives and goals. Implementing your strategic plan is as important as, or even more important than, your strategy.[24]

Implementation of Strategy

Implementation requires an action plan. It may be called an *implementation plan*. Regardless of its name, it is a document that assigns responsibility to individuals or specific groups, determines due dates, and sets periodic progress meetings to see whether you are still on track, what unexpected problems have arisen, and what other resources might be needed to fully complete the action plan.

Consider Elon Musk and his company SpaceX. Its mission has been to build and fly a rocket that would launch payloads and then return with a soft landing on a barge in the ocean. Of course, SpaceX wanted to reuse the rocket and reduce overall costs in the process. Therefore, the company developed a strategic plan (determining how it would reach its goals) and then assigned responsibilities to specific individuals and groups (to carry out the plan) and had routine meetings to confirm everyone was still on track with the plan. When the first two rockets landed too hard and blew up as a result, the company went back to the drawing board to determine the problem and try again. The third launch was successful. After that, the company began sending government and private payloads into space.

What Organizations Need for Effective Implementation   First there are objectives, which are the goals we want to accomplish. Then comes strategy, which is a statement of how we will reach each objective. Then comes the implementation plan (action plan) that answers the questions of how, who, and when. Think of it as a spreadsheet or a table that can be expanded as needed. Table 4-3 provides an example.

Allocating Resources

Resources come down to the budget, but there are many components that can be identified and managed along the way to that bottom-line budget impact. To determine how we will succeed, it is necessary to develop a business case to present to the executive team.

Strategic Action Plan				
Goal	**Strategy (How?)**	**Assigned To (Who?)**	**Complete Target (When?)**	**Actual Complete**
Obtain new medical insurance provider.	Perform background checks on at least five vendors.	HR benefit manager	5/12/2025	?
Upgrade HRIS.	Attend vendor training program.	HRIS manager	2/15/2025	2/10/2025
Offload employee relocation to a vendor.	Analyze at least three vendors for presentation to HR committee.	HR director	4/15/2015	?

Table 4-3   Strategic Action Plan

Making a Business Case   A major responsibility falling on the shoulders of HR professionals these days is the development and presentation of a business case for the organizational programs that will solve specific problems. For example, a business case is needed when recommending certain medical insurance programs, particularly if the employer has not provided such benefits in the past.

A business case is a written or oral presentation that identifies a problem, analyzes the various possible solutions, and makes a recommendation for implementing one of them. It will almost always have an analysis of financial impact, personnel impact, and customer impact. It is designed and presented using business terminology. For example, a recommendation for medical insurance would include the current cost plus a forecast of future costs, both in total dollars and in dollars per employee. It will have specific information about the way in which the recommendation will solve the problem that has been identified. (For example, the retention of employees is significantly improved if the employer offers medical insurance to workers. Higher retention means less turnover and lower recruiting and training costs.) All the benefits will have dollar values assigned to them in a business case presentation.

Making a business case means assembling business reasons for taking some action. The case will be ultimately presented to the decision-maker, be it an executive or the board of directors. There is a standardized expectation of what content a business case will include and in what order, which follows.

Business Case Content	
Executive summary	Short statement that summarizes the problem and recommendation with key reasons for choosing the recommended solution.
Definition of the problem	Identifying the issue that is being addressed in the business case. It could be changes in employee benefits, alterations in payroll, policy changes, or other HR-related issues. The definition should include a statement of how the organization is impacted by the problem.

Business Case Content	
Objectives	Statements of key results expected in solving the stated problem.
Possible solutions	List of key solutions possible for the stated problem.
Recommended solution	Identification of the solution that is being recommended and why. The list of reasons for making the choice should include statements of impact on the organization, its workforce, its customers/clients, and its other stakeholders. Those impacts should be quantified if possible.
Implementation plan	The steps needed to implement the solution and solve the problem. It could be a short list of steps or something quite complicated. An action plan should always include an action to be taken, who is responsible for that action, and the target date for completion of that action.
Support documents	All documents related to the selection decision. They might include financial analysis, statements of impact on profit and loss or the balance sheet, analysis of HR impacts (for example, turnover, diversity, and morale), organizational branding impacts, influences on competitive advantage, corporate responsibility changes, and staffing required for implementation.

Project Management Principles and Practices   Projects come and go in the life of HR professionals. There are projects for the implementation of new benefit programs, assessment of new recruiting sources, and all the projects associated with new paths of business on which the organization is embarking. Being able to juggle all those things at the same time while ensuring that each item gets the proper amount of attention and moves toward a conclusion is the mark of a good project manager.

A project consists of a series of activities and tasks that have been identified that need to be performed to accomplish an outcome. Dates are identified, people are assigned to the tasks, and resources, such as budget and people, are allocated. Overseeing a project is project management.

Project Management Tools   A standard tool used in project management is the Gantt chart, also known as an *activity log* or *milestone chart,* and it is widely available as a template on dedicated software programs. A Gantt chart normally identifies in chronological bar graph order what needs to occur first and simultaneously in a step fashion (see Figure 4-5). The benefit of a Gantt chart is the visual monitoring and communication of who is on first base and doing what task, what needs to occur before progression to second base, and then third base, and where the results must be before a run is counted at home plate.

Managing Change

Suffice it to say that managing change is the largest driving force behind employee relations. Change is a process that people and organizations undergo as a response; it is a transformation toward flexibility. HR is involved in managing the people issues resulting from change, either planned change or a reactive change, such as something occurring from an external source like an employment-related law regulating behavior in the workplace.

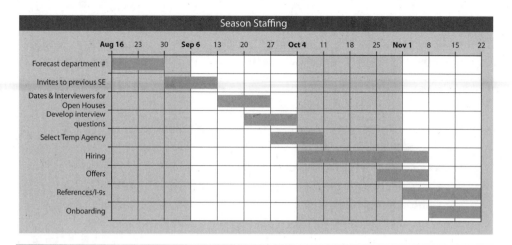

Figure 4-5   Sample Gantt chart

Helping both employees and management in an organized process through the roller-coaster ride of change, as identified by Elisabeth Kubler-Ross in her book *On Death and Dying*,[25] is an emotional intelligent (EQ) competency skill for HR professionals and leaders. First, shock and denial about the change is awakened within people. Next is the response of anger. Depression eventually sets in about the "loss" of status quo resulting from the change. Then movement toward bargaining and dialogue occurs related to the change. Finally, the roller-coaster ride ends with reaching a level of acceptance about the change. The key knowledge is in understanding the change and the management of the anticipated reactions.

Donald Kirkpatrick's *How to Manage Change Effectively*[26] discusses a model with the seven basic steps in the change management process for HR and organizations to prepare:

- Determining the need or desire for change
- Preparing the tentative plans for change
- Discussing alternative and probable reactions to the change
- Making a final decision about the change
- Establishing a project plan and associated timetable
- Communicating the change
- Implementing the change and evaluation

Response to Change   Employees are people, and people react to change differently. Fear of the unknown can bring on some strong emotional responses. Here are some of the possibilities of neutral or negative reactions:[27]

- **"Not me!"**   This is when somebody else is better suited for the new job assignment, or it's when there's denial that they are able to make the changes necessary.
- **"What will this do to my job security?"**   Will my job survive the changes?

- **Anger** Frustration can build to anger when employees believe they are losing control over their work.

- **Gossip** Uncertainty and frustration can result in employees gossiping about the change. Sometimes this turns to viciousness and vindictiveness, which are problematic.

- **"Who's in charge here?"** Uncertainty of reporting relationships can be frustrating also. One group during resizing used to say, "If the boss calls, get her name."

- **Panic** Emotional upset about the change can cause a severe lack of confidence that can even cause physical illness.

- **"I quit!"** This is the ultimate response to change by an employee. Unfortunately, the cost to the employee is greater than the cost to the organization.

Here are some examples of positive reactions:

- **"This is a challenge."** Open-minded about the new work arrangement, some employees are confident they can gain the necessary knowledge to do the work ahead.

- **Enthusiasm** Eager to accept new assignments, these workers can't wait to dig in.

- **"Maybe I could adjust to this change."** After a period of observation, they agree to give the change a chance.

- **Positive vision** These are people who see the bigger picture and have confidence in the organization's leadership.

Conditions That Make Change Possible Ken Blanchard and Scott Blanchard have listed six steps to ensuring successful change implementation for any organization:[28]

- **Beat communication breakdown** People don't want to be "sold" by executives on the advantages of the changes to come. They want to be able to understand what will be happening and why.

- **Get personal** Help employees answer these questions: What's in it for me to change? Will I win or lose? Will I look good? How will I find the time to implement this change? Will I have to learn new skills? Can I do it?

- **Plan your action** Leaders need to be able to drive forward with answers to these questions: What do I do first, second, third? How do I manage all the details? What happens if it doesn't work as planned? Where do I go for help? How long will this take? Is what we are experiencing typical? How will the organizational structure and systems change?

- **Sell the change** If leaders have done a good job on the previous steps, employees will often sell themselves on the change as a good thing.

- **Collaborate smartly** People begin turning outward to ask who else should be involved with questions such as these: How can we work with others to get them involved in what we are doing? How do we spread the word?

- **Refine for success**   Refinement questions are a good sign and show that the people in the organization are focused on continuous improvement. How can we improve on our original idea? How do we make the change even better?

Models for Managing Change   If the list of conditions that make change possible aren't enough, you can find more information about managing change in your industry from industry associations and even from your competitors who may already have gone through something similar to your challenge. Specific industry models can be extremely helpful because they are constructed with the language of your industry, not someone else's. HR associations such as SHRM can be helpful, with both written reports available and offerings of live expert help to counsel you through your planning and executing of change management.

HR's Role in Change Management   SHRM suggests that there are four roles HR professionals must play in change management. How that is done will vary according to the type of change being addressed.[29] Here are the four basic roles HR can play under the circumstances:

- **Leader**   With management, establish a vision and clear direction as well as shape the culture to minimize obstacles.
- **Educator**   Coach managers to implement and drive change on their teams, provide necessary training and tools to prepare employees for change, and build a communication road map to resonate with different audiences.
- **Advisor**   Create transparency as a liaison between executives and employees.
- **Demonstrator**   Design methods to reinforce the change, create a mindset of change by modeling, and encourage other executives to do the same.

When you put them together, the acronym is LEAD.

Evaluating Strategic Performance

Performance management is a systematic process that helps improve organizational effectiveness by providing feedback to employees on their performance results and improvement needs. When individual performance is linked to organizational strategic objectives, employees can see how they help impact accomplishments at the organizational level. It is employee accomplishments and contributions that drive the business results of an organization, so a regular feedback system discussing individual performance is at the core of a good performance management system. It ensures that employees are on course for the completion of tasks and goals that are aligned with the organization's goals and that the resources and support are provided for the employee to perform such functions.

Performance Evaluation and Reporting

Creating and communicating the organization's vision, mission, strategies, specific goals, and values form the foundation needed for the performance management system. Then, performance standards are agreed upon by both the line management and the employee on what the job requires and what will be measured. At this stage, it is essential that employees clearly understand the standards, including expected behavior standards set forth, for their jobs. Feedback is the next stage and can be both informal and formal. Formal feedback can entail a written performance appraisal.

Defining Performance Objectives

Employees need to know and understand what specific performance is expected of them in performing their jobs and the acceptable behavior. This communication begins with the very first discussion in a job interview and certainly with the job offer and new-hire orientation. The discussion continues on a consistent basis, both with the reinforcement of the organizational standards outlined in employee handbooks and other written material and with performance appraisal review sessions. The clearer the expectations set for employees, the greater the success in having expectations met.

Effective Performance Measurement Key to successfully using performance management are the following touchstones:

- Focus on results.
- Develop a culture of accountability.
- Align all organizational activities with overall organizational goals.
- Provide a common language for success.
- Make measurements simple to use.

Figure 4-6 will likely help you find these concepts easier to grasp.[30]

Using a Balanced Scorecard to Align Objectives with Strategy According to Howard Rohm, CEO of the Balanced Scorecard Institute, "The balanced scorecard is a robust organization-wide, strategic planning, management, and communications system. These are strategy-based systems that align the work people do with organization vision and strategy, communicate strategic intent throughout the organization and to external stakeholders, and provide a basis for better aligning strategic objectives with resources. In strategy-based scorecard systems, strategic and operational performance measures (outcomes, outputs, processes, and inputs) are only one of several important components, and the measures are used to better inform decision making at all levels in the organization. In strategy-based systems, accomplishments and results are the focus, based on good strategy executed well. A planning and management scorecard system uses

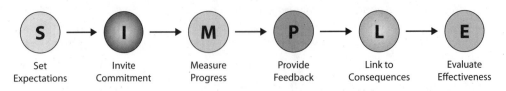

Figure 4-6   Effective performance management touchstones

strategic and operational performance information to measure and evaluate how well the organization is performing with financial and customer results, operational efficiency, and organization capacity building."[31]

Using Benchmarking to Set Performance Objectives   According to the Construction Industries Institute (CII), "Benchmarking is the systematic process of measuring one's performance against recognized leaders for the purpose of determining best practices that lead to superior performance when adapted and utilized.

"To be successful, benchmarking should be implemented as a structured, systematic process. It will not be successful if applied in an ad hoc fashion on a random basis. In most cases benchmarking is best-practice-oriented and is part of a continuous improvement program that incorporates a feedback process. Benchmarking requires an understanding of what is important to the organization (sometimes called critical success factors) and then measuring performance for these factors."[32]

Benchmarking can be internal or external. Strategic objectives usually establish comparisons with external sources. An example is found in compensation. Using salary surveys, employers can determine where they rate on compensation scales for any given job content. If the goal is to be in the second quartile, it is easy to determine whether that objective is being met by looking at the external pay for survey participants and the pay offered for the same job content.

SMART/SMARTER Goals/Objectives   SMART is an acronym you can use to guide your goal setting. Its criteria are commonly attributed to Peter Drucker's *Management by Objectives* concept, as discussed in the earlier "Setting Goals" section of this chapter. Remember, SHRM has subsequently added Evaluate and Revise to make the acronym SMARTER.

How Many and How Often   Examine your organizational goals and strategies for achieving those goals. You should have as many objectives as you need to identify the work you must do to properly contribute to achieving those organizational goals. Your goals should focus on HR issues, and there should be at least one goal for each of the major HR functions. Without them, you won't be able to tell how you are really doing in your HR efforts.

Common Organizational Metrics   Here are some common ways that organizations measure their own performance:

- **Marketing metrics**   Search engine optimization (SEO) keyword ranking, web traffic sources
- **Sales metrics**   Sales growth, average sale value, average profit margin
- **Financial metrics**   Debt-to-equity ratio, working capital
- **Social media metrics**   Social followers versus target
- **Customer feedback metrics**   End-of-transaction survey responses, quarterly survey responses
- **Employee metrics**   Cost per hire, retention rate, healthcare costs

Financial Statement and Metrics   Financial metrics reveal characteristics of financial data that might not be apparent from a simple review of the numbers:[33]

- **Cash flow metrics**   Businesspeople evaluate streams of cash flow events, such as investment outcomes or business case cash flow estimates.
- **Financial statement metrics**   Businesspeople use these metrics to evaluate a firm's financial position and financial performance, such as liquidity, payback period, and return on investment (ROI).

Nonfinancial Organizational Performance Metrics   These are any measurements that do not have a financial component, such as the following:

- Customer satisfaction trends
- Supplier delivery date accuracy
- Recruiting source candidate submission acceptance
- Workplace security and safety performance

Countless other possibilities exist. The challenge is to identify those things that can contribute strategically to your organizational goal achievement. Measure the things that matter. Measuring things that don't matter, or that you have no control over, will only dilute your focus and bring a sense of failure and lower morale.

Using Business Intelligence   Business intelligence (BI) refers to the tools, technologies, applications, and practices used to collect, integrate, analyze, and present an organization's raw data to create insightful and actionable business information. BI as a discipline and as a technology-driven process is made up of several related activities, including the following:

- Data mining
- Online analytical processing
- Querying
- Reporting

Today's trend toward using "big data" (huge databases with hundreds or even thousands of data elements) makes it essential that employers can reach into those databases and extract only those elements that will be useful in monitoring business activities and accomplishments.

Data Analysis Methods   Data can come in large or small files—and the large files can be really large files. The "cloud" is home to many examples of exceptionally large databases. Consider the U.S. Bureau of the Census as one such source. Its 2010 Occupational Database has information about individuals with accompanying information about race, gender, work industry, job category (EEO-1, EEO-3, EEO-4, EEO-5), job title, work location, home location (city, state, ZIP code), and more. If you only want to know about people working in a specific county in the HR professionals job category, you would need some method for extracting that information from the database before you could analyze it. Once you have the data in hand, the following are some ways in which you could analyze the smaller components of interest.

Variance Analysis   Variance analysis is the quantitative investigation of the difference between actual and planned behavior. This analysis is used to maintain control over a business. For example, if you budget for sales to be $10,000 and actual sales are $8000, variance analysis yields a difference of $2000. Variance analysis is especially effective when you review the amount of a variance on a trend line so that sudden changes in the variance level from month to month are more readily apparent.[34]

Regression Analysis   This is a technique for isolating which factors really have an impact on the issue you are studying. Does time in service have an impact on current compensation levels? To know, it is necessary to isolate time in service and take away consideration of other variables such as employee age, race, gender, years of experience in the industry, starting compensation amount, and any other variable that might interfere with the analysis of time in service. Regression analysis is generally accepted as the most accurate analysis tool available for assessing such things as employment discrimination like disparate impact.

Trend Analysis   Trend analysis is the process of comparing business data over time to identify any consistent results or trends. You can then develop a strategy to respond to these trends in line with your business goals.

Trend analysis helps you understand how your business has performed and predict where current business operations and practices will take you. Done well, it will give you ideas about how you might change things to move your business in the right direction.[35]

Let's say you are experiencing what you believe is unfavorable turnover among your production workforce. To begin the process of determining why that may be happening, it can be helpful to determine whether there actually is a turnover trend. Plotting the turnover rates for each month (or year) can allow you to see graphically what is actually happening. If there is an increasing slope in the results, you can begin the process of identifying causes for the trend. If you determine that the results are more or less consistent with an occasional spike in the turnover rate, you may decide that no action is required beyond what you are already doing to control turnover.

Graphic Presentation of Data Analysis   Let's assume we want to see the trend of our job requisitions during the past year. Table 4-4 shows the data.

Figures 4-7 and 4-8 show a couple of ways you might want to display the data in graph format. The months are represented by the numbers 1 through 12. The number of requisitions is shown on the left y-axis.

Communicating Data Analysis   Once you have determined that your data is as accurate as you can get it, you can then determine what the data says to you. What message is there from the data? Next, determine how you will present the data message to your audience. Different audiences sometimes require different presentations. If you are explaining the cost of benefit plans to the general employee body, you may use general cost charts. The same discussion with senior executives or the board of directors may be more detailed. While the subject is the same, the way you convey the message can be different.

Table 4-4
Requisition by
Month 1

Requisitions by Month	
25	January
15	February
12	March
21	April
18	May
14	June
10	July
8	August
16	September
13	October
24	November
19	December

Figure 4-7
Requisition by
Month 2

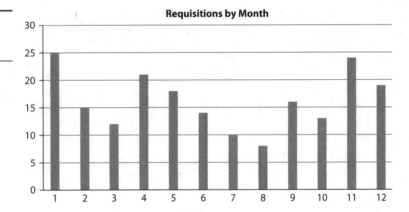

Figure 4-8
Requisition by
Month 3

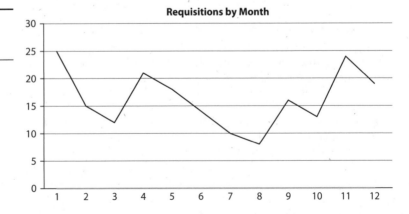

Providing Leadership and Strategy

SHRM-SCP
Leaders' critical focus should be on providing guidance and vision, controlling risks, and providing working environments where employees can contribute their best performance rather than just following directions. Leaders who manage employees should have the key skills of planning, staffing, organizing, controlling yet motivating people, and managing resources and budgets.

The HR professional as a leader will have a dual focus: being a leader for the HR function and being able to assist in identifying and developing the organization's leaders.

Leadership Characteristics

The key characteristics and skills for leadership have been written about for decades by many well-known and published authors. The skill set that began as hierarchical in design, where coercion and intimidation were main factors, has clearly changed in today's organizations. The models and opinions of successful leadership characteristics in the twenty-first century that you'll find associated with the SHRM exam are those of James Kouzes and Barry Posner,[36] Erica Fox,[37] Daniel Goleman,[38] and Marshall Goldsmith.[39]

In their studies and research, Kouzes and Posner found that the following practices made successful leaders:

- **Practice 1: Challenging the process** Successful leaders will recognize when there is a need for change.

- **Practice 2: Inspiring a shared vision** Successful leaders will have a vision and get their employees to be inspired by the same vision.

- **Practice 3: Enabling others to act** Successful leaders will empower their employees to do their best work, bringing out their full potential and encouraging collaboration in the workforce.

- **Practice 4: Modeling the way** Successful leaders will walk the talk and lead by example.

- **Practice 5: Encouraging the heart** Successful leaders will help their work groups celebrate the achievements and yet learn from their disappointments and matters of adversity.

Daniel Goleman's research report about emotional intelligence, focused on psychology and neuroscience, offers insight about our "two minds"—the rational and the emotional. Goleman delineates the five crucial skills of emotional intelligence for leaders and shows how they determine leaders' success in relationships, work, and physical well-being. The following are the five key emotional intelligence skills associated with successful leadership characteristics:

- **Self-awareness** A leader knows how they feel and how their emotions or actions can affect people around them.

- **Self-regulation** This key skill is about staying in control and regulating your actions and communications.

PART II

- **Motivation**   A self-motivated leader will work consistently toward goals and have high standards for the quality of their own work.

- **Empathy**   A leader who has empathy is essential for managing people and teams in today's work environment. They have the ability to put themselves in someone else's shoes. Through empathic skills, they can help develop the people they manage, challenge others who are acting unfairly, give constructive feedback, and also listen deeply for the meaning in conversations.

- **Social skills**   Leaders with emotional intelligence are great communicators. They're just as open to hearing the bad news as the good news. They are great at inspiring their people to a vision, and they are also good at managing change or resolving conflicts diplomatically.

In Erica Fox's research, she sees the successful leader as having a multifaceted personality, what she calls an "inner team." This inner team draws on the following strengths of characteristics to lead: intuition, reason, emotion, and willpower. As depicted in Figure 4-9, Fox labels these "inner team" members as follows: CEO as the inspirational dreamer, CFO as the analytical thinker, COO as the practical warrior, and the CPO as the emotional lover.

Marshall Goldsmith identifies 21 habits of behavior that derail the effectiveness of leaders and hold us back. These behaviors have to change and adapt to the level of leadership our careers grow into. The 21 bad habits are as follows:

1. **Winning too much**   The need to win at all costs and in all situations.

2. **Adding too much value**   A desire to add two cents to every discussion.

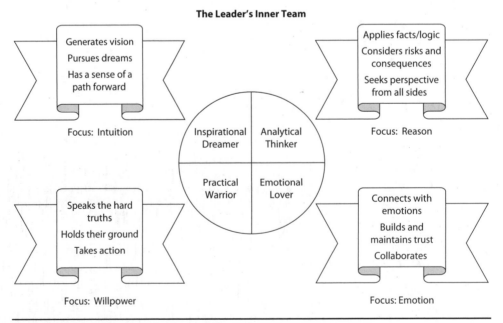

The Leader's Inner Team

Figure 4-9   Fox's inner team leader model

3. **Passing judgment**   The need to evaluate others and impose our standards/values on them.

4. **Making destructive comments**   Sarcasm and cutting remarks.

5. **Starting with "no," "but," or "however"**   The overuse of these negative qualifiers, which conveys "I'm right. You're wrong."

6. **Telling the world how smart we are**   The need to show people we're smarter than they think we are.

7. **Speaking when angry**   Using emotional volatility in communications.

8. **Negativity ("Let me explain why that won't work.")**   The need to share our negative thoughts.

9. **Withholding information**   The refusal to share information for an advantage over others.

10. **Failing to give proper recognition**   The inability to provide praise, rewards, and compliments.

11. **Claiming credit we do not deserve**   The overestimation of our contribution to some success.

12. **Making excuses**   The need to excuse annoying behavior as a permanent fixture so others will excuse us for it.

13. **Clinging to the past**   The need to deflect blame away from ourselves; this is a subset of blaming everyone else.

14. **Playing favorites**   Failing to see that we treat someone unfairly.

15. **Refusing to express regret**   The inability to take responsibility for our actions.

16. **Not listening**   The most passive-aggressive form of disrespect for others.

17. **Failing to express gratitude**   The most basic form of bad manners.

18. **Punishing the messenger**   The misguided need to attack the innocent who are providing information.

19. **Passing the buck**   Blaming everyone but ourselves.

20. **An excessive need to be "me"**   Exalting our faults as virtues simply because they embody who we are.

21. **Refusing to accept any responsibility for needing to change**   "That's just the way I am. Take it or leave it."

Theories About Leadership

In this section on leadership theories, we recognize that your formal education may have gone into great depth about each of the theories. What follows is a refresher on the basics of the leadership theories that will help you with your organizational design and HR initiatives. There are five basic schools of leadership theories: trait theory, behavioral school, contingency or situational school, leaders and followers, and dispersed leadership.

Trait Theory The theory of trait leadership was developed from early leadership research, which focused primarily on finding a group of attributes that differentiated leaders from nonleaders. Basically, it asserted that leaders were born and not made, and the focus was on personal characteristics and attributes that included mental and physical abilities. Although this perspective has been criticized immensely over the past century, scholars still continue to study the effects of personality traits on leader effectiveness. Past research has demonstrated that successful leaders differ from other people and possess certain core personality traits that significantly contribute to their success. It has been called the "great person leadership theory," with its assumption that leaders are different from the average person. The five traits identified are as follows:

- Intelligence
- Dominance
- Self-confidence
- High levels of energy and vitality
- Task or technical relevance knowledge

More current research has failed to identify one set of traits that *always* differentiates a leader.

Behavioral School The behavioral school theory focuses on a leader's ability to manage the performance and contribution of those they manage. Douglas McGregor and Blake-Mouton apply to the behavioral school theory. Behavioral school identifies two dimensions of leadership behavior—focused on the employee and focused on the job or tasks to do. Consideration is the employee-centered behavior; initiating structure is the job-oriented behavior.

McGregor's theory[40] offers two approaches to motivating employees: Theory X, which suggests an authoritative management style because it assumes that employees inherently do not like to work and must be controlled and closely monitored, and Theory Y, which suggests a participative style of management, under the belief that employees dislike controls and inherently want to do their best. It is obvious to see that a Theory Y type of supervisor will provide better leadership and produce greater satisfaction.

Another theory in the behavioral school is the situational leadership model developed originally in 1964 by Robert R. Blake and Jane Mouton[41] and later updated by them. It is a managerial grid model that identifies five different leadership styles based on the concern for people and the concern for production. Figure 4-10 illustrates the Blake-Mouton behavioral leadership theory and the resulting leadership styles.

 NOTE The ideal position is a 9 on production and 9 on people.

Figure 4-10
Blake-Mouton
behavioral
leadership theory

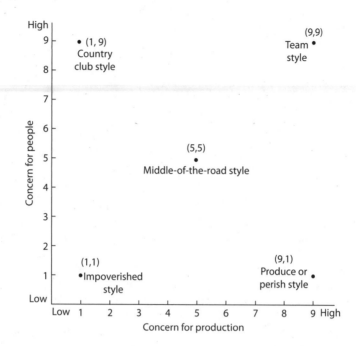

The types of leaders/managers are as follows:

- **Impoverished style (1, 1): evade and elude**   In this style, managers have low concern for both people and production. Managers use this style to preserve job and job seniority, protecting themselves by avoiding getting into trouble. The main concern for the manager is not to be held responsible for any mistakes, which results in less innovative decisions.

- **Country club style (1, 9): yield and comply**   This style has a high concern for people and a low concern for production. Managers using this style pay much attention to the security and comfort of the employees, in hopes that this will increase performance. The resulting atmosphere is usually friendly but not necessarily very productive.

- **Produce or perish style (9, 1): control and dominate**   With a high concern for production and a low concern for people, managers using this style are controlling and find employee needs unimportant; they provide their employees with money and expect performance in return. Managers using this style also pressure their employees through rules and punishments to achieve the company goals. This style is often used in cases of crisis management.

- **Middle-of-the-road style (5, 5): balance and compromise**   Managers using this style try to balance between company goals and workers' needs. By giving some concern to both people and production, managers who use this style hope to achieve suitable performance, but doing so gives away a bit of each concern so that the needs of neither production nor people are met.

- **Team style (9, 9): contribute and commit** In this style, high concern is paid both to people and to production. Managers choosing to use this style encourage teamwork and commitment among employees. This method relies heavily on making employees feel like they're constructive parts of the company.

- **The opportunistic style: exploit and manipulate** Individuals using this style, which was added to the grid theory before 1999, do not have a fixed location on the grid. They adopt whichever behavior offers the greatest personal benefit.

- **The paternalistic style: prescribe and guide** This style was added to the grid theory before 1999. Managers using this style praise and support but discourage challenges to their thinking.

Contingency or Situational School The well-known theories for contingency and situational leadership are the ones that accept differing leadership styles and adapt to the situations or people involved.

Widely referred to as the *Hersey-Blanchard situational leadership theory*, the fundamental underpinning of the theory is that there is no single "best" style of leadership. Effective leadership is task-relevant, and the most successful leaders are those who adapt their leadership style to the maturity of the individual or group they are attempting to lead or influence (for example, the capacity to set high but attainable goals, the willingness and ability to take responsibility for the task, and the relevant education and/or experience of the individual or group for the task). Effective leadership varies, not only with the person or group being influenced, but also for the task, job, or function that needs to be accomplished. The Hersey-Blanchard situational leadership theory rests on two fundamental concepts: leadership style and the individual or group's maturity level. Figure 4-11 depicts the situational leadership model.

The Hersey-Blanchard situational leadership theory[42] identifies four levels of maturity, M1 through M4:

High	Moderate		Low
M4	M3	M2	M1
Very capable and confident	Capable but unwilling	Unable but willing	Unable and insecure

- **M1** Employees still lack the specific skills required for the job at hand and are unable and unwilling to do the job or to take responsibility for the job or task.

- **M2** Employees are unable to take on responsibility for the task being done; however, they are willing to work at the task. They are novices but enthusiastic.

- **M3** Employees are experienced and able to do the task but lack the confidence or the willingness to take on responsibility.

- **M4** Employees are experienced at the task and comfortable with their own ability to do it well. They are able and willing to not only do the task but also to take responsibility for the task.

Figure 4-11
Situational
leadership model

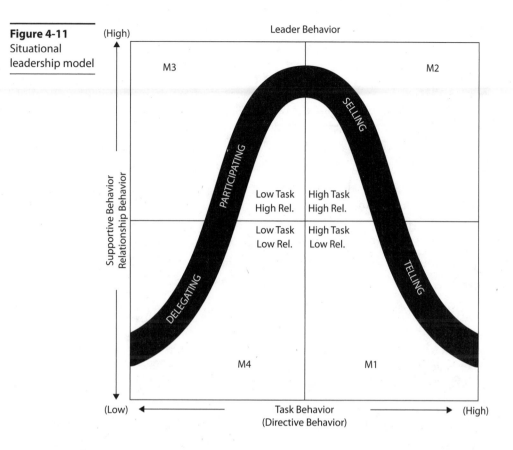

Leadership has four tasks based on an employee's maturity:

- **Delegating**   The leader is still involved in decisions; however, the process and responsibility have been passed to the individual or group. The leader stays involved to monitor progress.
- **Participating**   This is where shared decision-making with the work group about how a task is accomplished takes place; the leader is providing less task direction while maintaining high relationship behavior with the group.
- **Selling**   While the leader is still providing the direction, the leader is now using two-way communication and providing the socioemotional support that will allow the individual or group being influenced to buy into the process.
- **Telling**   Characterized by one-way communication in which the leader defines the roles of the individual or group and provides the what, how, why, when, and where to do the task.

Fred Fiedler developed the most popular situational contingency theory.[43] The Fiedler contingency theory holds that group effectiveness depends on an appropriate match between a leader's style (essentially a trait measure) and the demands of the situation.

Fiedler considers situational control the extent to which a leader can determine what their group is going to do to be the primary contingency factor in determining the effectiveness of leader behavior.

Fiedler's contingency model is a dynamic model where the personal characteristics and motivation of the leader are said to interact with the current situation that the group faces. Thus, the contingency model marks a shift away from the tendency to attribute leadership effectiveness to personality alone.

Fiedler asserts that there are three factors determining the favorableness of the environment for the leader:

- **Leader-member relations** The degrees of trust, confidence, and respect that employees have in their leader
- **Task structure** The extent to which the tasks the employees are engaged in are defined (clear or ambiguous, structured or unstructured)
- **Position power** The degree of power and influence the leader has over their subordinates

Changing one of the three factors is a more effective route rather than trying to change the leadership's trait.

Action-Centered Leadership Action-centered leadership is a model created by John Adair.[44] This model states that effective leaders accomplish goals and tasks through the efforts of the team they lead. To be effective, they must do three things in their leadership:

1. Structure the task and make sure everyone knows what is expected.
2. Develop each team member, review and evaluate their outcomes, coach/motivate them, and support them.
3. Coordinate the team's workflow, resolve disputes, ensure compliance with rules, and encourage collaboration.

Leaders and Followers Jon Katzenback and Douglas Smith's leadership theory of "leaders and followers" recognizes that the leader is not a hero per se but rather a team leader and servant to the team. With this leadership theory, leaders ask more questions rather than simply provide answers—a coaching tactic. They share opportunities to lead the team. Working with each other to solve problems is high with this style, along with building a solid foundation of the problems and issues before jumping into work on a resolution. Modern organizations generally rely heavily on team leaders and thus this style of leadership.

Dispersed Leadership Sometimes referred to as *emergent leadership*, with the dispersed leadership theory, leaders will emerge from a working group because of their expertise or experience to lead and influence the group working on a situation or task.

This typically is not a person who is given authority by way of title, such as manager or supervisor, within the hierarchy. Instead, the leader is someone the group has chosen to follow. This style of leadership has grown in the twenty-first century because of more self-managed teams in flat organizational structures.

Transformational and Transactional Leadership   Leadership can be either transformational or transactional in nature. A transformational leadership approach is one that stimulates and inspires people to work together toward achieving a common goal. Transformational leaders are charismatic (which instills pride, respect, and trust in the leader's sense of mission and vision); inspirational, with the communication skills necessary to gain engagement; stimulating, where the promotion of intelligence and challenge are at play; and attentive to individual needs, giving personal attention in manners of coaching or mentoring.

Transactional leadership has characteristics associated with contingent reward (effort is rewarded via accomplishment), management by exception (corrective action is taken when standards are not met or protocol is broken), and laissez-faire (responsibility is abdicated and decision-making is delayed or avoided).

Transactional leadership has been widely used and the norm historically for decades; transformational leadership has been proven to improve productivity and morale in the long run. A blend of both transactional and transformational leadership is typically warranted and the most effective.

Global Leadership Models   There are key issues to be aware of in global organizations that apply to global leadership models. Things become more complex because of cultural and language barriers as well as geographical and time zone differences. Managing the diverse global workplaces becomes complicated with laws, regulations, and practices differing from country to country. In 2004 and 2007, results from the Global Leadership and Organizational Behavior Effectiveness (GLOBE) research program found the data to support the shared cultural dimensions that were derived from Dr. Geert Hofstede and other cultural researchers.[46]

Cultural Issues   Two cultural constructs have a great influence on communication and training/development activities: power distance and high-context/low-context culture. Hofstede,[47] well-known for his pioneering research of cross-cultural groups in organizations, conducted a study of how workplace values were influenced by culture. He developed a model that identifies five primary dimensions to differentiate cultures:

- **Power distance**   The extent to which less-powerful members of organizations expect and accept that power is distributed unequally. In high-power distance organizations, the less powerful employee accepts autocratic structures.

- **Individualism**   The extent to which people are expected to stand up for themselves. With high individualism, an individual's rights are most important.

- **Uncertainty avoidance**   The extent to which members of a society cope with anxiety by minimizing uncertainty. High uncertainty avoidance cultures like structure and rules.

Global Leader Competencies				
Agility	Collaborating with peers	Managing virtual teams	Managing with a matrixed organization	Cross-cultural employee engagement
Managing innovation in multicultural setting	Applying ethical standards in multiple cultures	Proficiency in latest advances in virtual technology	Proficiency in social network technology	Multicountry supply chain management

Table 4-5 AMA's Global Leader Competencies

- **Masculinity (which also includes femininity)** The value placed on male or female values and traditional roles from a Western culture perspective. Feminine cultures place more value on relationships and harmony, whereas masculine cultures value competitiveness and assertiveness.

- **Long-term orientation** The degree to which the society embraces long-term devotion to traditional values. High long-term orientation has a respect for loyalty commitments, and work ethic is strong.

The American Management Association (AMA) developed a list of global leadership skills, listed in Table 4-5. This list was developed in 2012 via a survey conducted of more than 1000 global practitioners and emphasizes the essential need for having fluency in local cultures for global organizations.

Key Leadership Skills More than just business knowledge and expertise, leaders require a number of skills to manage a workforce. Leadership is an ability to influence others toward a strategy, results, and goals. It entails keeping the organization's vision and mission in sight and associated with its strategy, providing the direction on how that mission and vision will be accomplished as well as providing the tools and means to attain them, while motivating or encouraging people to work toward the vision.

Throughout this book, we discuss the multitude of key leadership skills. Those that are associated directly with strategy are focused on motivating a work group, making ethical decisions, having communications skills for aligning with stakeholders, and managing conflicts.

Ethical Behavior One of the key leadership competencies is being the role model for ethical decisions and actions. Being consistent and thoughtful with the challenging ethical decisions is at the core of this key leadership skill. To do so, a leader needs to recognize the ethical situations when they arise. They need to dig in to fully establish the facts about a given situation and their various options. Next, they need to evaluate the ethical dimensions of possible actions they can take. These might include religious or cultural beliefs/ norms. Then the leader would apply the relevant codes of ethics and behavior toward each option that has been presented in the situation. Consulting with others, either inside the organization (such as HR and other senior management levels) or outside (such as legal consultants), should be one of the options. The last parameter is owning the decision once it is made and perhaps learning from the mistakes/errors made from the issue/situation—all so that future decisions can be made better.

Communication   Communication is absolutely essential for effective leadership—sharing the vision, the strategy, the direction in which the organization is headed, at every level of function. It requires a thorough understanding of what is needed for the listeners to "hear the message" and uses various means to communicate matters appropriately.

Understanding a Listener's Needs and Expectations

The leader as a communicator needs to consider the message they want to send, who the "receiver" is intended to be, and in what manner they intend to provide it. A rule of thumb to use in all communications is recalling "MIM," which stands for Message, Intended receiver, Medium to be used. First, the communicator should "be in the shoes" of the intended receiver and consider all the varying perspectives that the receiver might have. Consider how the receiver might misunderstand the message and what their perception might be.

Planning Communication

What is the best manner for the communication to occur for the intended receiver (for example, verbal, meeting presentation, written)? If the receiver does not have easy access to the Internet or an intranet, that is going to hamper the timeliness of the communication. In planning the communication of strategy, the following questions are the first ones to consider: What information is needed to be communicated, in what order, on what dates, by whom, and specifically to whom? Next, what medium is to be used? Finally, what feedback mechanism is in place to ensure the intended communication was received and understood? This feedback will provide an awareness of what may need altering in the message to improve understanding and impact.

Managing Conflict

Conflict is natural, and it is bound to happen in all work settings. In most conflicts, neither party is right or wrong; instead, different opinions collide to create disagreement. Is conflict a bad thing? Not necessarily. Conflict can help lead to new discoveries of methods and improvements in matters such as policies and procedures. Interpersonal conflicts are bound to occur when groups of people are working together. There need to be rules of behavior associated with conflict, such as conflict of culture, personal differences, communication styles, and treatment of others. If there is constant conflict, that will surely erode collaboration and relationships in the workplace. Leaders, including HR professionals, should know how to approach conflict proactively and have the skills to resolve it effectively.

Conflict-Resolution Modes

When conflicts need to be resolved, the process of conflict resolution involves techniques to resolve issues and maintain effective working relationships. When a direct supervisor is unable to resolve the conflict, HR is normally brought in as an intervention and mediator. Clear and open communication is the cornerstone of successful conflict resolution; therefore, HR professionals must be skilled communicators. This includes creating an open communication environment that encourages the disconnected parties to talk. Listening and probing with nondefensive inquiries will help dissipate the conflict.

Whether it is co-workers jockeying for the desk next to the window or one employee wanting the room cooler while the other doesn't, immediate conflict resolution is essential. Steps for conflict resolution by a leader include the following:

- *Acknowledge that an opposing situation exists.* Acquaint yourself with what's happening and be open about the problem.

- *Let the individuals express their feelings.* Emotions fly and feelings of anger and/ or hurt usually accompany conflicts. Before any kind of probing can take place, acknowledge the emotions and feelings.

- *Define the problem.* What is the issue? What is the negative impact on the work or relationships? Are different personality styles part of the problem? Meet with the opposing parties separately at first and gain their perspectives about the situation.

- *Determine the underlying need.* There is no goal of deciding which person is right or wrong; the goal is to reach a solution that everyone can live with. Looking first for needs, rather than solutions, is a powerful tool for generating win-win options. To discover needs, you must try to find out why people want the solutions they initially propose. Once you understand the advantages their solutions have for them, you have discovered their needs.

- *Find common areas of agreement.* Agree on the problem; agree on some small change to give a feeling of compromise.

- *Find solutions to satisfy needs.*

- *Generate multiple alternatives.*

- *Determine which actions will be taken.*

- *Make sure involved parties buy into actions.* (Total silence may be a sign of passive resistance.) Be sure you get real agreement from everyone.

- *Determine follow-up to monitor actions and sustained agreements.* Schedule a follow-up check-in to determine how the solutions are working and how those involved feel about how the solutions are working.

What if the conflict goes unresolved? If the conflict is causing a disruption in the workplace and it remains unresolved, you may need to explore other avenues. An outside consultant such as a mediator may be able to offer other insights on solving the conflict problem. In some cases, the conflict becomes a performance issue and may become a topic for coaching sessions, performance appraisals, or disciplinary action.

Negotiation Methods   Some conflict may be to a level that it requires negotiation for a compromise. The methods used in negotiation methods are similar to some used in conflict resolution. Discussed more thoroughly in Chapter 5, negotiation involves knowing the needs and wants of both sides of the conflict. There are several different negotiating styles, yet the most common are the three that are known as *soft, hard,* and *principled.*

Soft negotiations have a focus that is based on the value of the relationship. Hard negotiations have a focus that is associated with win over lose at all costs to the relationship. Principled negotiations have a focus that is aimed at mutual gain for both sides.

Principled negotiations are what most organizations expect from their leadership—collaboration and relationship building.

Functional Area 2: Talent Acquisition

This is SHRM's BASK definition: "Talent Acquisition encompasses the activities involved in identifying, attracting, and building a workforce that meets the needs of the organization." [48]

Talent acquisition involves all the HR strategies and processes involved in attracting, recruiting, and selecting talent with the skills, knowledge, and abilities needed in the workforce to meet the organization's needs. HR professionals will analyze and understand the organization's workforce requirements and staffing needs to enable them to assist management with assessing current and future labor needs.

Key Concepts

- Methods for creating and maintaining a positive employer value proposition (EVP) and employment brand (for example, culture, opportunity for growth, purpose, varied work assignments)

- Job analysis and identification of job requirements (for example, job requirements and qualifications, task inventory analysis, critical incident technique, position analysis questionnaire)

- Methods for external and internal employee recruitment (for example, job ads, career fairs, social media, college/university relationships, talent pipelines, internal job postings, employee referrals)

- Methods for selection assessment (for example, ability, job knowledge, personality tests, assessment centers, individual or panel interviews)

- Employment categories (for example, full time, part time, contract, temporary workers, interns)

- Job offer contingencies (for example, background investigations, credit checks, physical or psychological evaluations)

- Job offer negotiations (for example, salary, relocation assistance, telecommuting, variable job share)

- Approaches to employee onboarding (for example, orientation, buddy system, personalization)

- Talent acquisition metrics (for example, cost per hire, time to fill, applicant-to-offer ratio, candidate yield from proactive sourcing)

- Talent acquisition technologies (for example, applicant tracking system [ATS], chatbots, artificial intelligence resume screening, social media to identify passive talent)

- Methods for supporting a positive candidate experience (for example, streamlined application process, limited rounds of interviews, fair consideration of applicant's time, frequent communication)

The following are the proficiency indicators that SHRM has identified as key concepts:

For All HR Professionals	For Advanced HR Professionals (SCP Exam)
Understands the talent needs of the organization or business unit	Analyzes staffing levels and projections to forecast workforce needs
Uses a wide variety of talent sources and recruiting methods to attract a qualified and diverse pool of applicants	Develops strategies for sourcing and acquiring a workforce that meets that organization's needs
Uses technology to support effective and efficient approaches to sourcing and recruiting employees	Establishes an EVP and employment brand that supports recruitment or high-quality job applicants
Promotes and uses the EVP and employment brand for sourcing and recruiting applicants	Designs and oversees effective strategies for sourcing, recruiting, and evaluating qualified job candidates
Uses the most appropriate hiring methods and assessments to evaluate a candidate's technical skills, organizational fit, and alignment with the organization's competency based upon job requirements	Designs and oversees employee onboarding processes
Conducts appropriate pre-employment screening	Designs and oversees valid and systematic programs for assessing the effectiveness of talent acquisition activities that meet the organization's needs
Implements effective onboarding and orientation programs for new employees	
Designs job descriptions to meet the organization's resource needs	
Complies with local and country-specific laws and regulations governing talent acquisition (such as avoiding illegal interview questions)	
Advises and coaches hiring managers on best practices related to job descriptions, interviews, onboarding, and candidate experience.	

Organizational Staffing Requirements

Getting the right people into the right jobs is the function known as *staffing*. This is the lifeblood of an organization, as people are required to make any organization run.

Staffing Challenges

At any time, one or more of these challenges can appear, to the dismay of HR professionals. Dealing with them effectively is the measure of a skilled HR manager.

Changing Demographics   When housing becomes too expensive for job applicants to live close to the job and commute distances are greater than people want to undertake, the workforce demographics can shift, sometimes rapidly. Look at any major metropolitan area these days, and it is easy to identify this problem. Employer responses may be too expensive for practical purposes. Raising the pay scale so new hires have enough money to either rent or buy a home could just be too expensive.

Lack of Skilled Labor   According to a Manpower Group survey, 75 percent of companies have reported talent shortages and difficulty hiring.[49]

Government and Regulatory Barriers to Hiring   The moment an employer hires its first worker, it becomes subject to more than 50 federal laws that require compliance—everything from safety to payroll and credit reporting. There are untold numbers of state laws that also demand attention, depending on the work locations being used.

Brain Drain   The departure of educated or professional people away from an employer to another employer usually is for better pay or living conditions. Particularly in industries such as high technology and engineering, there is a high cost for key personnel exodus.

Availability of Reliable Data   Workforce planning and strategic staffing initiatives become problematic when there is a lack of current, reliable data. A lack of reliability in either the forecast of job openings or the ability to develop high-quality talent pools from which to draw job candidates will quickly bring the recruiting process to a halt.

Economic Cycles   Economic cycles impact employer headcount levels. Employers are often faced with the challenge of identifying qualified recruits from a scarcity of resources when things get better through growth and demand. Likewise, when the economy turns down, layoffs are often the result.

Business Lifecycles   Recruiting and retention strategies will necessarily change as a business moves through four stages, or lifecycles, of existence. In the beginning (startup) and through its growth years, recruiting is typically hectic. Expansion means hiring. In its maturity and decline years, layoffs and downsizing/resizing are frequent impacts. Specific strategies are required for each of these four cycles.

PESTLE Factors   PESTLE (that is, political, economic, social, technological, legal, and environmental) factors must be considered when conducting an environmental scan or being engaged in other forecasting efforts. World events often drive, or at least influence, environmental scans conducted by using the PESTLE factors.

Employee Lifecycles   Staffing challenges are greatly influenced by employee lifecycles. Here are the relationships:

- **Recruitment and selection**   Finding the best fit between a job and an employee
- **Onboarding and orientation**   Gaining information and tools necessary to succeed on the job and getting acclimated to the organization's culture
- **Training and development**   Promoting engagement and retention by developing an employee's skills and commitment

- **Performance management**   Working with employees to help them achieve their goals and objectives and prime them to become stronger employees
- **Transition**   Achieving the best match of an employee's capabilities with an organization's needs through transfer, promotion, demotion, resignation, and retirement

Technology Shifts   In years past, recruiting was done with the aid of "position available" advertisements in the local newspaper. Today, social media is the primary source of job candidates. This is a paradigm shift. An example can be found when wristwatches were no longer made with springs but transitioned to models with electronic quartz movements. When robots entered the workplace, helping handle dangerous and repetitive tasks in the automobile industry, employees were tasked with feeding the robots materials and receiving from them the completed subassembly, which was another paradigm shift. When the Bell System used live operators to handle long-distance calls, emergency calls, and questions that are now handled by computer, another paradigm shift took place.

Cherry Picking: Pressure on Salary Levels   Offering more money beyond the approved pay range can effectively entice a desirable job candidate to accept a job offer but can also cause issues for other parts of an organization. If the hiring manager makes a job offer above the pay range maximum, something must happen to bring that individual back into the proper compensation range. Usually, this requires management to "freeze" the new hire's pay level until natural escalation pressures enable the company's pay structure to catch up. The short-term benefit of attracting a desirable job candidate this way is often overcome by general employee discontent and, as a result, discouragement. In addition, state and federal pay requirements, when applicable, must be followed in any case.

Creating a Job vs. Hiring for Work   When an engineering firm encounters an engineer with a certain specialty, experience, and educational credentials to back it up, the company may want to hire that person rather than let them go on to some other firm. In that case, it becomes necessary to create a job opening for the new engineer. As opposed to that scenario, often the practice is to have a job opening identified and then seek candidates for that job with the intent to hire the best qualified out of the batch. Filling a job need is quite different from creating a job for someone special we must hire to save the talent within our employee ranks.

Strategic Staffing

Staffing according to the business strategies requires understanding what those strategies are. Even if strategic plans are not formalized, successful employers need some form of organizational goals to effectively manage their business. HR professionals are uniquely positioned to help managers understand the importance of measurable strategic goals to be successful as HR business partners, providing appropriate job candidates to the operations units. When accounting is undertaking a conversion of its financial records processing system or when operations is installing a new computer-centric milling system, the HR professional supporting them will need to understand the importance of those changes to accomplish business goals. HR professionals cannot simply enjoy sitting in the HR world. They must be fluent in the language of their brothers and sisters in other parts of the business. Until they are, they will not be as helpful in staffing jobs in those other organizations as they otherwise could be.

Planning for Talent Acquisition on a Global Basis

Global staffing depends on recognizing and acquiring talent with precisely the job skills needed in a given work location, even when that work location happens to be halfway around the world.

Global Integration vs. Local Responsiveness Strategy

Strategically, it may be determined that recruiting, processing, and hiring people can be done from a remote location such as at a company's headquarters. Certainly, any talent acquisition program must be able to embrace global requirements. It will come as no surprise that maintaining a local responsiveness to acquisition requirements is also a key to success. It is important that people processing job candidates have the same level of empathy for local needs as local staff. Responsiveness to local management will go a long way toward building a strong working relationship. In the end, it is a customer service relationship that is important.

Orientation and Talent Staffing

Nancy Simonelli at Reliance Staffing and Recruiting says, "Employees who attend a structured orientation program are more likely to remain with the company after 3 years than those who do not. If you are going to spend money and time acquiring top talent and paying them to work, why not prepare them to succeed and stay?"[50] Therefore, a solid strategy for orientation training after a new hire accepts the job offer is to use a structured orientation program. Be sure to cover everything on your checklist, not just payroll and benefit information. Be sure to include things like, "How we do things around here."

Growth Strategies

Identifying growth in workforce needs will allow strategic preparation for recruiting and acquisition of talent that will be needed to permit the growth to be successful. It can take weeks or months to identify specific job candidate needs and then to create a recruiting program that will assimilate those candidates as active participants in the selection process. Starting before you have a specific requisition can be a good strategy for being ready when the time comes.

Maturity of the Global Location

How well can your global locations continue to serve your business needs? Is there a ready workforce with the talent necessary to satisfy your job requirements? In the face of an economic downturn, can you continue to maintain a branding program so that the job candidate market will react positively when openings occur again? Are there competitors in the same locations? Do they seek to attract the same type of talent to their workforce as you want to have in yours? The broader the supply and demand in your areas of talent need, the more likely you will be able to find what you want when you actually start looking.

External Factors

Influences from outside the employer's organization can include such things as local employment laws for wage and hour issues, minimum wage levels, mandated benefit requirements, cultural impacts on production schedules (for example, holidays), and local commute patterns. All of these and more must be considered as part of your strategic talent acquisition process.

Social Responsibility

Do subcontractors or suppliers participate in pay disparities or racial discrimination because of local cultural practices? It is incumbent upon the employer to determine whether it should even create a work location where those problems exist. And, if so, what will it take to address changes in those cultural standards?

Information Technology

What type of Internet connections are available in the work location chosen for your organization's needs? What types of computer support are available? Will you be using off-the-shelf software programs or something your in-house programmers have created or modified? Is there local support talent that can address these and other related types of infrastructure needs?

Visa Requirements

What type of visa requirements exist in your prospective work location? Can international candidates come and go without difficulty, or are there special work permit requirements they must meet? Are certain countries barred from sending workers to your location? How will you be able to work within those requirements? Talent acquisition can be made more difficult if there are these types of impediments.

Employment Branding

Branding is another word for reputation. What do people in your target workforce think about your company? How can you influence that?

Employment Branding Defined

According to Chris Mossevelde, "Employer branding is the process of promoting a company, or an organization, as the employer of choice to a desired target group, one which a company needs and wants to recruit and retain."[51]

Building a Brand

Mossevelde continues, "The company can only attract current and future employees if it has an identity that is true, credible, relevant, distinctive and aspirational. To achieve this, extensive research needs to be conducted." What does the public think of your organization? What does the group of people you consider a target recruiting source group think of your organization as an employer? Learning what exists will enable you to determine what action steps must be taken to mold your brand into the perceptions you want others to have.

Employee Value Proposition

An employee value proposition (EVP) is the unique set of benefits that an employee receives in return for the skills, capabilities, and experience they bring to a company.

Harnessing Social Media

In mid-2017, CareerBuilder.com posted the results of its latest study regarding the use of social media in the employment process. Here is what that study found: "70 percent of employers use social media to screen candidates before hiring, up significantly from 60 percent last year and 11 percent in 2006."[52] The lesson is clear. Employers must be using social media outlets to find the best talent available. Also, social media can influence the employer's brand in the eyes of those it will eventually want to recruit.

Best Practices for Employment Branding

To influence your brand, it is necessary to manage the expectations and perceptions of your job candidate target group. The first step is to identify key words that describe your company as a good place to work. If you say things like exciting, flexible, genuine, and challenging, you may advance to the next step. If you say things like old-fashioned, slow (to change), manipulative, and boring, you may have some work to do before moving to the next step. If you need to work on your employment brand, begin with a task force (group) of employees who can help identify key actions that will be needed to improve your organization's image. Consider focus groups for people in your prime employment recruiting populations to determine what they really think about your organization as an employer.

1. What changes might be necessary if you are to move forward? How can social media become a tool in that change process?

2. Develop and implement your action plan to bring about the changes your organization needs.

3. Evaluate the impact of changes you have created.

4. Repeat as necessary.

Job Analysis and Job Documentation

Establishing job content and determining how the job interacts with other jobs are important. Documenting the results can become what we know as a *job description*. That job description can become the foundation for analyzing its content and plotting its fit into compensation structures.

Job Analysis

Determining the level of responsibility embedded in the job and how it impacts the overall organization is what can be called *job analysis*. In addition to tasks and areas of responsibility assigned to the job, analysis should include the types of physical and mental conditions under which the job operates. That can vary widely from job to job. Consider the physical and mental requirements for an electrical high-tension line technician with those of the computer program coder. One faces the outside weather elements year around. The other sits inside using a computer keyboard to convert thought patterns into code the machine can use. Someone who doesn't like heights or working in rain and snow would probably not be a great candidate for the technician's job. Also, someone who has a high need for being outside, working on different job sites each day, would likely not do well in the computer programmer's job.

Job Documentation

Written descriptions of the key elements of a job, its working conditions, and its mental and physical demands will eventually constitute the documentation of the job and its content.

Job Descriptions   Job descriptions follow a general template for content. The same template can be used in constructing a CEO's job description as for an airline pilot. It is the content that falls within the template that varies.

Elements of Job Descriptions   Here is a typical job description template:

Administrative

- Date the job description was prepared
- Title of the job
- Reporting relationship: Which other title does this position report to?
- Department
- FLSA status: Exempt or nonexempt
- Objective: What does the job accomplish and how does it impact other jobs in the organization? In other words, what is the reason for having this job?
- Job code

Summary of job content with examples

- **Essential job functions**: Brief description of the specific tasks, duties, and responsibilities
- **Mental and educational requirements**: Formal education (degrees), certifications, licensing, journey-level craft training, extensive mathematical training (essential job requirements; the job cannot be done without these educational requirements)
- **Skill requirements**: Typing, welding, swimming, running harvesting equipment, docking spacecraft

- **Physical factors**: Hearing, seeing (watching/inspecting), touching, operating, standing, bending, squatting, reaching, lifting, carrying
- **Environmental factors**: Outside weather conditions, inside workplace conditions, confined spaces, heat, cold, wet, dry, odors, dust, hazardous materials
- **Hours**: Number of 8-hour shifts per week, overtime requirements, lunch/break requirements
- **Unplanned activities**: Duties or tasks that could come up, interactions, and support of other jobs
- **Approvals**: Reviews and approvals of management people authorized to design job content

Job Descriptions in the Global Environment   Global consistency can be helpful over time. While compensation rates may vary from country to country, the same job content may apply across borders. Having job content consistency may be helpful in the outreach and recruiting efforts your organization makes. Be sure, however, that the wording used accurately communicates the message. Expectations for honesty and forthrightness exist at many locations around the world. Yet, depending on the work location, how the message is expressed may be quite different. For example, in France, value is often placed on open disagreement as discussions move toward consensus. In Mexico, open disagreement is considered rude and disrespectful. In Indonesia, an open disagreement would be considered aggressive and negative because the reputation of the other person can be damaged. International differences do matter.

Job Specifications   A job specification states the minimum qualifications required for the individual performing a job. What education is required? What physical and mental abilities are necessary? What experience is essential? Those answers are posted in the job requisition so potential candidates will be able to assess the match they may have with the job requirements. Note job specifications are the minimum qualifications for the individual to be successful; not what the superstar might bring.

Writing and Updating Job Descriptions and Job Specifications   It is the duty of the supervisor and/or manager to develop and maintain accurate job descriptions and job specifications. Often this is done with the help of HR professionals. In larger organizations, there is a staff of HR people who are responsible for evaluating, rating, and assigning pay levels to job descriptions and compensation classifications as appropriate. They support line managers and supervisors in documenting their subordinate jobs. An annual review is mandated for all federal contractors who are required to maintain affirmative action plans for the disabled. Those requirements are focused on the need for accurate descriptions of physical and mental job requirements. Essential tasks, duties, and responsibilities are considered in order to determine whether a reasonable job accommodation can be made or circumstances call for it.

Accurate job specifications are important when a job opening occurs because the hiring manager often needs to move quickly. Pausing the process to be sure job specifications are accurate will be unnecessary if the specifications are already reviewed and updated.

Employment Categories   The term *employment categories* is used by many to mean often conflicting things. The two most often referenced are categories evolving from the Fair Labor Standards Act (FLSA) and those based on company policy. Therefore, SHRM generally considers the following FLSA classifications to be employment categories:

- **Nonexempt**   Workers on your payroll whose job content is not exempt from the requirements for minimum wage and overtime requirements.

- **Exempt**   Workers on your payroll who satisfy the 3 criteria of (1) being paid a minimum of $684 per week or $35,568 per year, (2) paid on a salary basis, and (3) engage in FLSA defined exempt job duties.

The following are the company policy classifications:

- *Regular full-time employees* are regularly scheduled to work the company's full-time schedule. Usually, they are eligible for company benefit programs, depending on eligibility conditions.

- *Regular part-time workers* are regularly scheduled to work less than the company's full-time schedule. They may be eligible for some company benefit programs.

- *Temporary full-time employees* are interim workers assigned to specific projects or scheduled to work for a specific limited duration. Benefits may or may not be offered.

- *Temporary part-time employees* are hired to temporarily supplement the workforce or to help with a specific project. They are regularly scheduled to work less than the company's full-time schedule for a limited duration. They are usually not eligible for company benefit programs.

- *On-call employees* are scheduled as needed for a nonspecified time period. Normally there is no eligibility for company benefit programs.

- *Interns* may be college or university students, high school students, or post-graduate adults who perform work for a specified period of time (that is, summer, academic semester, and so on).

Sourcing and Recruiting

Geoff Webb writes the following on LinkedIn:

"A Sourcer finds the passive candidates, the ones not applying through the corporate website or posting on the job boards. A Sourcer is a hunter. A Sourcer creates interest and drives talent to the organization. This means doing research: pouring over organizational charts, job descriptions, and social media profiles, while sourcing talent by accessing search engines and competitor web pages. This means engaging potential candidates: messaging through social media, sending emails, picking up the phone.

And because a hunt often involves a chase, this means repeating, tweaking, and refining these activities—until you have a slate of qualified prospects to hand off to…

"…the Recruiter. The Recruiter manages the relationships, guiding the candidates and the hiring manager through the screening, selection, and hiring process. This means phone calls, meetings, and interviews. This also means administration—a lot of it: posting jobs, reviewing applicant submissions through the corporate website, coordinating schedules, uploading documents, extending offers—going back and forth until all the details come together and the job opening has been filled."[53]

Sourcing and Recruiting in Diverse Markets

McKinsey & Company studied the relationship between diversity and financial returns in business terms. Among their findings were the following:[54]

- "In the United States, there is a linear relationship between racial and ethnic diversity and better financial performance: for every 10 percent increase in racial and ethnic diversity on the senior-executive team, earnings before interest and taxes (EBIT) rise 0.8 percent."

- "In the United Kingdom, greater gender diversity on the senior-executive team corresponded to the highest performance uplift in our data set: for every 10 percent increase in gender diversity, EBIT rose by 3.5 percent."

The conclusion is that sourcing and recruiting in diverse markets is a positive thing for the employer and its financial returns.

Recruiting Methods

Finding the right job candidate is a process that has changed little over time. What has changed is where we go to look for that stellar candidate. Two words say it all for external sourcing: social media.

Internal Recruiting   Looking for people who can fill openings often begins by looking internally. Notifying current employees about job openings can be done in any of several ways: sending an e-mail blast to all employees with the announcement, posting the opening announcement on the employee bulletin board, posting the opening announcement on the organization's website or employee channels, and asking all managers and supervisors to announce the opening to their employee groups. Some organizations believe it is good for morale to give current employees the opportunity to apply for new job openings, especially if it would mean a promotion to the candidate. Whatever the reason, selecting someone from the current employee ranks will cost less than searching for and screening a group of people from outside the organization.

External Recruiting   The following are proven external recruiting methods:

- **Job boards**   A partial list includes services such as Indeed, Glassdoor, Monster, CareerBuilder, ZipRecruiter, CareerBliss, Recruit.net, Jobs2Careers, and CareerJet.

- **Social media**   This includes LinkedIn, Facebook, Twitter, YouTube, Instagram, and more.

- **Website**   The employer's own Internet site is a perfect place to post job openings, where potential candidates may complete an application form.
- **Referrals**   Employee referrals are a wonderful source of job candidates, and they don't discount referrals from clients, customers, vendors, and the general public.

Other Recruiting Strategies   Employment agencies and temporary help agencies are more traditional, but they still have appeal today. Temporary help workers can "test-drive" the company to see whether it is a good match with their objectives, and the company can "test-drive" the employee to see whether they would be a good match for the employer's culture.

Robust Sourcing Strategy   Sourcing, as you know, is the art of seeking candidates before they apply for a job. *Hunting* may be a better term. If your sourcing strategy is robust, you have an active presence in the employment market looking for organizations, Internet sites, and social media accounts that represent the type of individual knowledge, skills, and abilities that you believe you will require now or in the future.

Recruiting Effectiveness

Establishing and maintaining a recruiting program is not cheap. It requires the investment of an internal staff of people dedicated to that activity or the time and effort of consulting support that can offer the same services. The trick is to be sure you are getting your money's worth in the bargain.

Measuring Recruitment Effectiveness   The classic measurement for this is Time to Fill, or Days to Fill.[55] This is the time between opening the requisition and a qualified candidate accepting a job offer.

HR Metrics   In addition to the recruiting measurement time to fill, we can measure the quality of new hires through various measures such as job performance ratings, the percentage of new hires promoted within a year, and the percentage of new hires retained after a year. Metrics related to turnover costs (unemployment insurance expense, workers' compensation expense, cost of training a replacement, and cost of recruiting and hiring a new employee) are also a useful yardstick.

Cautions Regarding Metrics   We need to be careful that the metrics we choose to use actually report on something that truly matters in our recruiting program. It is easy to get sidetracked into believing something is important when it really isn't. Who really cares about things like the number of typos in a job requisition or the number of people who don't know how to use social media? Be precise in what you measure because if it doesn't tell you something that can help you manage the process, it shouldn't be in your portfolio of metrics.

Peoplepower Reporting   Slicing and dicing the demographics of your workforce can have some value if you are interested in identifying representations of various groups for your diversity program. Here are some things that can be computed and reported.

Headcount   These are the number of people on the payroll, the number of people in candidate pools, the number of people who come from each recruiting source, and so on.

Groups and Subgroups   Numbers can be analyzed for group or unit representations such as department, division, unit, work location, or country. Within these there can be subgroups that might offer additional focus on your recruiting efforts. Focus on what will provide you with the most valuable feedback for the process. You must be able to "do" something with the information you compute. If you don't, there is no point in doing the analysis.

Demographics   Race, gender, disability, veteran status, and national origin are some of the affinity groups that can offer insight into the nature of your workforce composition and the effectiveness of such sourcing options such as employee referrals. You may have reporting requirements as part of your affirmative action program compliance. Be sure that there is value in collecting and analyzing the data and that someone will be doing something with it.

Cost of Hire/Cost per Hire   The American National Standards Institute (ANSI) has some standards for hiring metrics. Along with its partner, the Society for Human Resource Management (SHRM), ANSI has developed and published the following standards.

Cost of Hire   This measurement uses external costs and internal costs to determine overall cost per person hired during any given time period. This formula looks at the number of hires and the costs to obtain them. It enables us to derive expenses for each new hire stated as an average.

$$\text{Cost per Hire} = \frac{(\text{External Costs}) + (\text{Internal Costs})}{(\text{Total Number of Hires in a Time Period})}$$

External costs are those expenses such as external agency fees, advertising costs, job fair costs, travel costs, and other similar expenses for the time period being analyzed. Internal costs are expenses that can include fully loaded salary and benefits of the recruiting team and fixed costs such as physical infrastructure. Here is an example.

$$\text{Cost per Hire} = \frac{(\text{External Costs} = \$100,000) + (\text{Internal Costs} = \$100,000)}{(\text{Total Number of Hires in Time Period} = 50)}$$

Cost per Hire = $4,000

Cost per Hire Internal/Comparable   Determining the internal cost per hire uses the same formula but includes only internal costs in the formula numerator. It is possible to compute external cost per hire and compare the two results.

Days to Fill   From the time a requisition is posted until the employment offer has been accepted can be called the Days to Fill measurement.

Attrition   Several analyses could prove helpful when looking at attrition. Consider the following ones:

- Number of employees leaving before the first service anniversary
- Number of employees leaving before the fifth service anniversary
- Number of employees leaving total
- Number of employees leaving voluntarily (within a job or group)
- Number of employees leaving involuntarily (within a job or group)

Recruitment Cost and Yield Ratios   Ratios are the numerical representation of comparisons. They are normally stated as a percentage. The recruiting cost ratio (RCR) is one of those measurements. It looks at the cost per hire based on compensation rather than headcount.

$$\text{Recruiting Cost Ratio} = \frac{(\text{External Costs} = \$100,000) + (\text{Internal Costs} = \$100,000)}{(\text{Total First Year Compensation of Hires in Time Period})} \times 100$$

The RCR tells you how much you spent recruiting for every dollar of first-year compensation paid to the new hires.

$$\text{Recruiting Cost Ratio} = \frac{(\text{External Costs} = \$100,000) + (\text{Internal Costs} = \$100,000)}{(\text{Total First Year Compensation} = \$2,000,000)} \times 100$$

RCR = 10 percent

Obviously, the lower the percentage, the better (more efficient) the result.

Another measure of recruiting efficiency and effectiveness is the recruitment yield ratio. It can be calculated at each step of the recruiting and hiring process to determine how successful you are at each stage of the process.

- How many people were minimally qualified compared to total responses?
- How many people were sent to the hiring manager compared to minimally qualified?
- How many people were interviewed compared to those sent to the hiring manager?
- How many people were hired compared to those interviewed?

At each state, you can compare a ratio or percentage. The greater the percentage, the better.

$$\text{Recruitment Yield Ratio (RYR)} = \frac{\text{Number of Hires}}{\text{Number of Interviews}}$$

RYR = 3 / 15 = 20 percent

Achieving a higher ratio (percentage) means your yield is greater for whatever comparative group you are using. Here is another example:

> We have hired 25 new computer programmers. It took an average of four interviews for each new hire. Therefore, our recruitment yield ratio is 25 / 4 = 6.25. If we only required an average of three interviews per new hire, the RYR would be 25 / 3 = 8.33. The higher our RYR, the better. It allows us to recognize that many interviews in the hiring process add to the cost of hiring. Lowering the average number of interviews per hire will raise our ratio.

Workforce Analytics   Looking at the existing incumbent population, we can parse the numbers to tell us things like the representation of PhDs in a given job title or the number of people by gender in trade jobs (carpenter, plumber, electrician, landscaper, and so on). Recruiting cost ratio can be computed for job titles, job groups, departmental units, and more.

Leveraging Technology in Sourcing and Recruiting

Even if you are a small employer and don't have access to expensive computer programs, it is still possible to use Excel spreadsheets to provide yourself with periodic analysis results. Once you have established your spreadsheet to track things like the number of requisitions per month, the time between requisition and job offer, and the cost of hiring at each occupational level, you can create pivot tables that will provide automatic analysis charts once they are set up. Be sure you learn how to create and use pivot tables. They can make your life easier.

Internet Recruiting   Getting candidates from your own organization's website is a great way to recruit. Other sources can be the state employment service website, the website run by your industry, or the websites run by colleges and universities. All of those activities can be tracked and the data analyzed.

Social Media   Social media sites have become a primary recruiting aid in many organizations. It is estimated that at least 70 percent of jobs are being filled through networking and social media sources. If you are not using networking or social media in your recruiting efforts, realize your competitors are.

Selection

Once the recruiting effort has yielded proper candidates qualified for the open position, it is incumbent upon the hiring manager to determine who will get the job offer. That offer should go to the person who is best qualified for the job. That is the best business decision. The best qualified will provide your organization with the greatest return on your investment. Selecting someone other than the best qualified will cost your organization more in the final analysis.

Talent Selection Process

It is helpful sometimes to use a matrix constructed of the job qualifications specified in the job posting. An example is shown in Table 4-6.

Job	Candidate			
	1	2	3	4
Knowledge/Skills/Talents—"Can Do" Items				
Work Experience	+	OK	–	+
Education	OK	OK	OK	OK
Technical Skills	+	+	–	OK
Communication Skills	OK	–	–	OK
Specialized Training	+	+	OK	OK
Analytical Skills	+	OK	+	OK
Behaviors—"Will Do" Items				
Motivation	+	+	–	OK
Interests	+	+	OK	OK
Goals	+	OK	–	OK
Drive/Energy	+	+	–	–
Reliability	+	+	OK	OK
Initiative	+	+	–	OK
Working Conditions—"Compatibility" Issues				
Team Orientation	OK	OK	–	+
Independence	OK	–	+	–
Social Effectiveness	+	OK	–	OK
Interpersonal Style	+	OK	–	OK
Stress Tolerance	OK	OK	OK	OK
Travel	OK	OK	–	–
Overtime	OK	OK	+	OK
Relocation	OK	OK	OK	OK
Weekend Work	OK	OK	OK	OK

Legend:
+ is "better than required."
OK is "meets requirements."
– is "less than required."

Table 4-6   Candidate Selection Factors Chart

You can easily tell which candidate is the best match for your job requirements when you look at the chart. Candidate 1 is clearly better qualified than the others. Candidate 2 is running a strong second, and should you be unable to hire your first choice, you might feel quite comfortable with Candidate 2 as your alternate. The only possible downside to that individual is their communication skills and independence. Candidate 3 is clearly the poorest of the four candidates. Having fallen asleep during the interview, this candidate received a "minus" score for "Drive/Energy." Candidate 4 is good and solid but not quite as good as the first two. And then, there is the problem with Candidate 4's ability to travel, which is something the job will require.

Screening

Screening is the process of presorting job candidates to determine who meets minimum eligibility requirements of the job opening.

Screen The first pass in screening should be to determine whether the candidate meets the job qualifications as specified in the job requisition posting. Anyone who does not meet the job requirements should be removed from the group. No further processing of that candidate is needed. Sometimes a telephone interview is next in the screening process. Then comes an "in-person" interview, with the hiring manager and, possibly, with the HR manager too. There may be other interviews with people who would be in the same work group or other supervisors. The process should contain decision points that match your organization's requirements.

Lately, video interviews have become popular. That can be helpful to job candidates who are a far distance from the work location or if those doing the interview are working remotely.

Tracking Applicants Data on job applicants is really important. Keeping track of it is even sometimes required. If you are a federal contractor, you will be required to maintain specific applicant-tracking data points. It will be used to analyze disparity in the selection process, comparing females to males and minorities to nonminorities. Disparity analysis can suggest that there is more investigation required, and you will want to do more follow-up to learn more about the specifics of given selections. Ultimately, an enforcement agency, such as the Equal Employment Opportunity Commission (EEOC) or the Office of Federal Contract Compliance Programs (OFCCP), would be doing the same type of analysis if a complaint is filed with either or both agencies.

According to EEOC guidelines, it is all right to invite job applicants to self-identify their race/ethnicity and gender. You should use the standard EEOC categories for each:

- **Race/ethnicity** White, Black/African American, Hispanic, Asian, Native Hawaiian/Pacific Islander, Native American/American Indian, two or more races
- **Gender** Male, female

Inviting self-identification suggests the information being given is voluntary. If an applicant doesn't want to self-identify, they don't have to. Also, employers are not required to have the information for job applicants. Its only use is in disparity analysis. Race/ethnicity information will become mandatory for employer tracking once the applicant accepts a job offer and joins the payroll. The laws enforced by the EEOC require employers with 100 or more employees to collect and keep employee race and gender information.

Application Forms Application forms are not required by any federal law. In addition to being a handy device that can mitigate an employer's risk of discrimination claims, they are a useful way to collect information about job candidates that an employer would like to have. They can also be a test for honesty. It is estimated that as many as 60 percent of job applications have exaggerations or false information in them. Using application forms is a best practice, as you get to ask for the information you want. Include a statement approved by your legal counsel asking candidates to sign, affirming that what they have included on their application is truthful and accurate, with the potential for immediate dismissal if not.

Résumés and Curricula Vitae   Résumés and curricula vitae (CV) are documents prepared by individuals to describe their educational and employment history. Résumés are normally used with employers other than educational institutions. CVs are documents with far more detailed information, with a different format used in educational employment settings. Both résumés and CVs are intended to offer potential employers an overview of the individual's background with a positive "spin." They almost never contain compensation information, information about gaps in the employment timeline, or contact information for reference checking.

Potential Problem Warning Signs   There are some common behaviors in an interview that may indicate the candidate is not the fit for your position as they claim. These are common job interview red flags.[56]

1. Strange body language.
2. Rudeness, sloppiness, or tardiness.
3. Lack of passion for the role, product, or company.
4. Lack of ownership over past mistakes or experiences.
5. Asking no questions of the recruiter or hiring manager.
6. Being unprepared.
7. Complaining or gossiping.
8. Poor listening skills.
9. Offers no learning experiences.
10. Can't explain their previous work.

Additional red flags in the selection process may include:

- Grossly inappropriate email address.
- Reason for leaving a position consistently a variation of "bad boss."
- A work history that does not follow a logical pattern of job progression or conveniently have the exact requirements of your opening.
- Too many jobs where the supervisor who the applicant worked for is gone with no forwarding address or the entire firm has gone out of business.
- The experience is so long ago that any references would normally have moved on, retired, or died.
- Volunteer experience for an extended period of time when a means of support would have been required for the applicant. Also volunteer experience for a company that probably would not have such an arrangement.

- A job at a company that has since been merged with another company and a record of the position having existed cannot be found.

- Spelling mistakes that are inconsistent with what the candidate purports to know. For example, the psychology major who does not spell psychology correctly.

How should you react when you discover one of these flags waving at you from your applicant's résumé? Mark it for follow-up with the applicant, perhaps in an interview. If you know that a claim is untrue, you would be justified in putting that applicant's documentation in a "Suspect" file folder without further consideration.

Interviewing

Interviews are conducted so you can get more information from an applicant and impart information to them about your organization. Sometimes interviews are conducted by HR professionals and other times by hiring managers or groups of people from the hiring department. Interviews can be conducted face to face, on the telephone, or by a video hookup. Often, these days, more than one interview is conducted before a selection decision is made.

Type of Interviews   There are many types of interviews. They are named for the characteristics applied to the process of interviewing. The following are the primary types of interviews used today.

Structured Interview   An interviewer asks every applicant the same questions along with follow-up probes that may be different depending on the initial response. Structured interviews make it possible to gather similar information from all candidates and use it to comparatively measure relative job-based attributes. It affords great consistency and is the most reliable. Since you have developed a list of questions, minimal training of your hiring managers is required. This type of interview is sometimes called *patterned*.

Unstructured Interview   While not exactly "freewheeling," these interviews follow threads of information as they are revealed. That means no two interviews are alike, making comparisons of candidates more difficult. The interviewer must discern key information from the overall discussion. It requires less preparation time than the structured interview.

Behavioral Interview   In a behavioral interview, an interviewer focuses on how the applicant previously handled actual situations (real, not hypothetical). The interviewer probes specific situations, looking for past behaviors and how the applicant handled those experiences. The questions probe the knowledge, skills, abilities, and other personal characteristics identified as essential to success of the job. The interviewer looks for three things: a description of an actual situation or task, the action taken, and the result or outcome. The principle behind behavioral interviewing is that past performance is the best predictor of future performance.

Competency-Based Interview   In this type of interview, each question probes a specific skill or competency. Candidates are asked about their behavior in certain circumstances. Then, they are asked to explain how that happened in a real-life example.

Group Interview   Group interviews happen when multiple job candidates are interviewed at the same time. Group interviews are used in specific situations where several candidates are being considered for the same job in which the duties are limited and clearly defined, such as a merry-go-round operator. A *fishbowl* interview brings multiple candidates together to work with each other in an actual group activity or exercise. It is similar to an in-basket exercise, except it involves a group of candidates. A *team interview* typically involves a group of interviewers with a perspective of the actual interactions associated with the job. This might include supervisors, subordinates, peers, customers, and so on. It is like a 360-degree exercise. Finally, in a *panel interview*, questions are distributed among a group of interviewers—typically those most qualified in a particular area. At the end of the panel interview, the panel caucuses with the purpose of coming to a consensus regarding the result.

Stress Interview   In this type of interview, an interviewer creates an aggressive posture—in other words, deliberately creating some type of stress to see how the candidate reacts or thinks on their feet in uncomfortable situations. For example, using a room where the candidate has to face an open window with the sun in their eyes can put the candidate under stress. (That could also be problematic if the candidate has serious vision problems that rise to the level of a disability.) This type of interview is used more often in law enforcement, air traffic control, and similar high-stress occupations. The stress interview was more common in the 1970s and 1980s. Today, it is not recommended because of the likelihood that it will be interpreted as personal bias.

Guidelines for Interviews   The University of Nebraska at Kearney offers these tips for interviewers:[57]

- Directly observe certain aspects of an applicant's behavior, such as ability to communicate, alertness, self-confidence, understanding of necessary technical concepts, and so on.

- Obtain additional information regarding the applicant's education, work experience, relevant community activities, or job-related interests that can supplement or fill gaps on written application materials.

- Identify and assess the extent of the applicant's knowledge, skills, and other characteristics or competencies by inquiring about past performance and achievements.

- Preview the job and what the organization expects of employees, and what employees can expect in return, so that the applicants can determine whether they are interested in the position.

- Identify the need for any accommodation that might be required to enable the applicant with a disability to perform the functions of the position.

- Promote a good public image of the institution.

Interview Questions   Questions you can and can't ask in an employment interview are described in Table 4-7.[58]

Acceptable	Subject	Not Acceptable
• Street address of residence. • Length of time at current or former residence.	**Address of Residence**	• Inquiries into foreign addresses that would indicate national origin. • Do you own or rent your residence?
• If you are hired, can you show proof that you are 18 or older? • If you are younger than 18, can you provide a work permit from your school?	**Age**	• How old are you? • What is your birthday? • When did you graduate from elementary or high school? • Requirement for birth certificate or baptismal record *before* hiring. • Advertisement using words like *young, girl, boy, college student, retired person,* and so on.
• If you are hired, can you furnish proof of your right to work in this country?	**Ancestry, Birthplace, or National Origin**	• Where were you born? • Where were your parents born? • How did you learn your languages? • Do you have relatives in any other country?
• Have you ever been *convicted* of a crime that may be related to this job content or responsibilities? • "Ban-the-box" laws, both state and local, have restricted employer rights to inquire about conviction records. Be sure you speak with your attorney to know if this is still appropriate in your jurisdiction.	**Arrests or Convictions**	• Any question related to arrest record. • Some state and local laws and ordinances prohibit employers from inquiring about conviction records. Speak with your attorney about the prohibitions in your jurisdiction.
• Are you a U.S. citizen? (Use if citizenship is a job requirement because of security clearances and such.)	**Citizenship**	• Are you a native-born or naturalized citizen? • When did you become a citizen? • Show proof of citizenship or naturalization before hiring.
• Employers may tell applicants that any job offer is made contingent upon their passing a physical examination if such a requirement is made of everyone hired into that specific job. • Requiring applicants to pass a drug screen is usually permitted. • It is acceptable to ask if an applicant is able to perform the essential functions of the job, with or without a job accommodation.	**Disability or Medical Condition**	• Have you ever filed a workers' compensation claim? • Do you have any serious medical condition or disability? • Has anyone in your family ever had cancer, heart disease, or other serious illness? • Have you ever had a job accommodation?

Table 4-7 Questions You Can and Can't Ask in an Employment Interview *(continued)*

Acceptable	Subject	Not Acceptable
• Please list the college degrees you have earned and the institutions attended. • Please list any continuing education programs, certification, or vocational training you have received related to this job.	**Education**	• Any inquiry into the nationality or racial makeup of the institution. • When did you graduate from elementary or high school?
• There are usually no acceptable questions about financial status.	**Financial Status**	• Have you ever had your wages garnished? • What is your credit rating? • Have you ever filed for bankruptcy? • What is your net worth?
• Will you please demonstrate how you would perform job-specific tasks (duties)?	**Height and Weight**	• Almost no question about height and/or weight is acceptable.
• Almost no pre-employment inquiry is acceptable.	**Marital Status or Parental Status**	• Are you single, married, divorced, separated, and so on? • What are the names and ages of your spouse and children? • Where does your spouse work? • Are you planning to have more children?
• Please describe any military service experience you believe will help you on this specific job.	**Military Service**	• Have you served in the military of any country other than the United States? • What type of discharge did you receive?
• Have you ever used another name that would enable us to check on your employment or education records?	**Name**	• What is your maiden name? • Are you a Mr., Mrs., Miss, Ms., or other designation?
• Please indicate any job-related organizations, clubs, professional societies, or other associations to which you belong. You may omit those that indicate your race, religious creed, color, national origin, ancestry, sex, or age.	**Organization Memberships**	• List all organizations, clubs, societies, and lodges to which you belong. • Do not ask about *paid* work experience without also asking about *unpaid* or *volunteer* work experience.
• Statement that a photograph may be required *after* hiring.	**Physical Description or Photograph**	• Any request for a photograph or physical description prior to a job offer.

Table 4-7   Questions You Can and Can't Ask in an Employment Interview *(continued)*

Acceptable	Subject	Not Acceptable
• Identifying race following the job offer is often a requirement for governmental reporting. • Inviting applicant self-identification of race and sex is a requirement for affirmative action employers (government contractors). The data must be kept away from the hiring manager.	**Race or Color**	• Any inquiry about skin color, hair or eye color, and so on. • Any inquiry about race, color, or ethnicity.
• Who referred you to us? • Names of individuals who can provide either personal or professional references for the job applicant.	**References**	• Any request for references that might indicate applicant's race, religion, color, sex, national origin, age, or disability status.
• Name and contact information of person you want to have notified in the event of an emergency. • Name of applicant's relatives who work for the employer. • Names and addresses of guardians of a minor job applicant.	**Relatives or Emergency Contact Information**	• What is the name of the relative you want us to notify in the event of an emergency? • Who is your nearest living relative, and how can we contact them? • Do your relatives speak English?
• Other than absences from work for religious observances, will you be available for work at the following times?	**Religion**	• Who is your pastor (minister, rabbi, or other religious leader)? • What church do you attend? • What religious holidays do you observe?
• Inviting applicant self-identification of race and sex is a requirement for affirmative action employers (government contractors). The data must be kept away from the hiring manager.	**Sex**	• Any inquiry that would indicate preference for one sex over the other. • Advertisement indicating "Men Wanted" or "Women Wanted." • Any preference other than those based on a bona fide occupational qualification.
• Explanation of work schedule requirements and inquiry about willingness to meet that schedule.	**Work Schedule**	• How will you get to work? • Everyone works through the weekend. Are you willing to do that, too? • Are you willing to work on Christmas, Easter, and Good Friday? • Who will look after your kids while you're at work?

Table 4-7   Questions You Can and Can't Ask in an Employment Interview

Interview Biases   Hiring managers who interview may inadvertently create EEO problems or make ill-fated selection choices without the proper training and guidance from HR. Hiring is typically not a frequent responsibility of a line manager; it may have been several years since they had to hire an employee. A discussion of some common factors that may create problems in interviewing would be helpful from HR, including the following:[59]

- **Stereotyping**   This involves forming a generalized opinion about how candidates of a particular gender, religion, or race may think, act, feel, or respond. An example would be presuming a woman would prefer to work indoors rather than outdoors.

- **Inconsistency in questioning**   This involves asking different questions of different candidates. An example would be asking only the male candidates to describe a time when they used critical-thinking skills in their last job.

- **First-impression error**   This is when the interviewer makes a snap judgment and lets their first impression (be it positive or negative) cloud the entire interview. An example is where added credence is given to a candidate because the person graduated from an Ivy League college.

- **Negative emphasis**   This involves rejecting a candidate on the basis of a small amount of negative information. An example is when a male candidate is wearing a large earring plug, and in the interviewer's judgment this is inappropriate, yet the job the candidate is interviewing for is a phone customer service position, where there is no customer visual contact.

- **Halo/horn effect**   This is when the interviewer allows one strong point that they value to overshadow all other information about the candidate. Halo is in the candidate's favor, and horn is in the opposite direction.

- **Nonverbal bias**   An undue emphasis is placed on nonverbal cues that are unrelated to potential job performance. An example is a distracting mannerism such as biting one's nails.

- **Contrast effect**   This is when a strong candidate has interviewed after a weak candidate, making the person appear more qualified than they actually are—only because of the contrast.

- **Similar-to-me error**   The interviewer selects candidates based on personal characteristics that they share, rather than job-related criteria. An example would be that both the interviewer and the candidate attend the same local NFL team's home games.

- **Cultural noise**   This is when a candidate is masking their response, providing what is considered "politically correct" and not revealing anything or being factual.

Assessing and Evaluating

Assessing candidates and evaluating their assessment tests is helpful in screening to ensure those best qualified for the job position are forwarded on for the hiring manager's consideration.

Assessment Methods   The following are measurement approaches for behavior:

- **Personality tests**   These tests are self-reporting, projective techniques (ink blots) and behavioral assessment (role play).
- **Ability tests**   These tests tend to have high reliability but risk disparity results for race or gender.
- **Performance tests and work samples**   Candidates are asked to perform one or more of the tasks required by the job opening. If the job involves writing, the candidate is given a pencil, paper, and an allotted amount of time to write a sample for consideration. Performance tests can be set up in a workstation model so working conditions can be much the same as on the actual job.
- **Integrity tests**   These are designed to assess the applicant's tendency to be honest, trustworthy, and dependable.
- **Structured interview**   The aim of this approach is to ensure that each interview subject is presented with the same questions in the same order.

Discretionary Assessment Methods   Other methods are used to separate those who will receive a job offer from the other finalists; they might include consideration of the following:

- The person's match to the organization
- Personal motivation level
- Behaviors complementary to organizational personality, such as doing work in the community outside the individual's assigned job

Contingent Assessment Methods   Job offers can be made contingent upon the applicant succeeding in an assessment exercise. That may be a visit to the job site and interaction with current employees or successful participation in a formal assessment process structured for the job in question.

Cross-Cultural Assessment Tools   This can be a self-assessment tool used extensively in training, consulting, and program evaluation, as well as employment screening, that is designed to address a person's ability to adapt to different cultures. The assessment process should be designed to respond to several needs or practical concerns that are expressed by both culturally diverse and cross-culturally oriented populations.

Criteria for Selecting and Evaluating Selection Methods   There are four important criteria for selecting and evaluating selection methods:

- **Validity**   The extent to which the assessment can accurately predict job behavior (performance)
- **Adverse impact**   The extent to which protected group members (race, gender, age, national origin, disabled, veteran, and other minority groups) score lower on the assessment than those in majority groups

- **Cost**   The cost to develop and administer
- **Applicant reactions**   The extent to which applicants react positively rather than negatively to the assessment process

Establishing Reliability   Reliability is consistency of results and is important in the face of an observation or assessment being made by multiple people within the same circumstances. There are two main types of reliability:

- **Inter-rater or inter-observer reliability**   Assesses the degree to which different raters/observers give consistent estimates of the same phenomenon
- **Test-retest reliability**   Assesses the consistency of measurements from one time to another

Establishing Validity   Since 1978, the government has had specific expectations for employers to offer validation of their employment selection devices. An employment selection device can be a written or oral test, job interview, assessment center participation, or job skill demonstration requirement. Regulations were established by the Equal Employment Opportunity Commission (EEOC) and are known as the *Uniform Guidelines on Employee Selection Procedures*. Validity can be determined in several ways:

- **Construct validity**   The extent to which a test actually measures what it claims to measure
- **Content validity**   The extent to which a test measures all facets of a job
- **Test-retest or stability**   The extent to which a test produces stable and reliable results and the results remain consistent from test to retest

Establishing Equity   Establishing equity involves determining that the employment test treats people equally, regardless of their personal group membership. Groups include race, gender, age, pregnancy, mental and physical disability, national origin, veteran status, religion, sexual orientation, and additional state-protected groupings.

Establishing Cost-Effectiveness   Cost-effectiveness is the relationship between the cost to develop and administer a test and the benefit derived by it.

Background Investigations and Reference Checks   Job offers are often conditioned upon successful completion of background checks, reference checks, and sometimes even credit checks. In some instances, a job offer could be conditioned on passing a medical evaluation or drug screening.

Before conducting background checks or credit checks, review the current legal limitations on their use. The EEOC has issued guidelines on consideration of conviction records because the population of convicted felons is so heavily skewed with Blacks and Hispanics. Considering conviction records[60] has a disparate impact on those two racial/ethnic groups. Therefore, only if the conviction has a direct relationship to the job content will considering it in the hiring decision be permitted by the EEOC.[61]

International Background Checks Employers will typically use international background checks only if a candidate has lived abroad or if the company has facilities abroad.

Employment, Education, and Reference Checks Résumés and job applications usually contain information about educational background and employment history. While not always successful, verification calls should be made to the organizations on the résumé or job application to confirm the accuracy of the claims.

Select and Offer

Once all screening has been done, a decision must be made. When the best qualified candidate has been selected, a job offer should be made.

Decision Process There are several steps in the employment decision process:

1. **Summarize information** Use a summary sheet or matrix to pull together comparative key points about each finalist.
2. **ID and rank candidates** Using a tool such as the Candidate Selection Factors Chart, it is possible to summarize and rank each candidate against the others.
3. **Collect additional information** Additional information can include the candidate's willingness to accept the standard benefit package, verification of a professional license, and a pending certification. They all are loose ends that need to get tied up.
4. **Make an offer** Offers can be made verbally or in writing. Many employment attorneys counsel their clients to put a job offer in writing.

Contingent Job Offer A job offer can be made contingent upon any number of conditions:

- Legal right to work in the United States
- Verification of educational degrees
- Verification of professional licensing (medical doctor, lawyer, accountant)
- Confirmation of certification for the job duties (highway flagger, elevator repair technician, HR professional, certified professional accountant)
- Receipt of national security clearance

Employment Offer An employment offer should include start date, hourly wage for nonexempt employees or salary (in weekly or monthly amount[62]) for exempt employees, benefits, job title, work location, name of supervisor, restatement that the offer is made under an "employment at will" understanding, and any other pertinent information. In practical terms, phone calls are made to the applicant for confirmation that they are still available and interested in the job. Then, a written offer can be sent to confirm all of the details. A written offer should have a provision for the applicant to sign, accepting the offer and acknowledging the conditions specified. The offer is not considered completed until the signed acceptance is received and any contingency is met. Yes, DocuSign (or equivalent) makes this paperwork doable and legal electronically.

Employment Contract   You will recall that the alternative to employment at will is an employment contract. A contract can be either oral or written, express or implied. Oral contracts can be created even inadvertently if the employer isn't careful. When a hiring manager tells the newly hired employee something like, "This is a great company. You can spend your whole career here without worry of getting laid off," you run the risk of creating an implied oral contract.

Handing Nonselected Candidates

There may be a few or there may be many job candidates who did not receive a job offer. What do you do with them? Some employers just ignore them. Best HR practices, however, suggests that it is courteous to notify each individual who did not receive a job offer. You do not need to be specific about the reason each person was not selected, but a kind letter can go a long way to boosting your organization's reputation in the marketplace. People will remember for a long time how they felt about their application experience with you and your organization. You can make that a positive memory for them.

Special Considerations: Reasonable Accommodation

According to the U.S. Department of Labor's Office of Disability Employment Policy (ODEP),[63] "A reasonable accommodation is any change in the work environment or in the way things are usually done that enables an individual with a disability to participate in the application process, to perform the essential functions (or fundamental duties) of a job, or to enjoy equal benefits and privileges of employment that are available to individuals without disabilities."

Applicants and employees must make their request for a reasonable accommodation in writing, explaining how the accommodation will help them accomplish the duties of the job or the application process. Then the employer is obligated to review the request, enter into an interactive dialogue about the request, and explore any other accommodations that may be more appealing to the employer (for example, less expensive) while still permitting the applicant or employee to accomplish the tasks involved in the job or the application process. If the employer feels it cannot make the accommodation requested, it is permitted to decline the request and notify the applicant or employee of the decision.

Job Previewing

A job preview is a way for candidates to see how the job is actually performed. The preview itself can be presented in several different ways:

- **Video preview**   Incumbents can express their thoughts about what they like and dislike about the job.
- **Simulation**   Workstation mock-ups and task processing that can last 8 hours or longer can provide the candidate with a feel for how the job is actually accomplished.
- **Shadowing**   Candidates can spend time on the job with an incumbent to see what happens during the course of a normal workday.

Characteristics of Realistic Job Previews   Job previews must provide an honest picture of the job content. What physical and mental effort is required? What skills are used? What happens when something goes wrong? Honest representation of the job in all respects will give the candidate an opportunity to accept or not accept your invitation to go further in the process. Job previewing can be done after a contingent job offer is made, or it can be done earlier in the employment process. Simulation and shadowing can both be expensive if there are more than a few candidates. Video previews can be much more cost-effective, but they lack the "hands-on" view that a live presence on the job site can provide.

Benefits of a Job Preview   The candidate gets to experience the next best thing to actually performing the job. Seeing incumbents working on the tasks, having a chance to ask questions, and even doing parts of the job can be a great way to gain exposure to how it feels to do that work. It can give candidates the chance to determine whether they will like doing that work. If not, they can resign from further consideration. It also gives the employer a chance to observe each candidate in the working environment and judge their reactions to the work's demands.

Orientation and Onboarding

Orientation and onboarding are two activities that will set the tone for the balance of an employee's career with this employer. If we get off on the right foot with people, the chance for retention success goes up. If we skip this step, we miss the opportunity to define the new employee's image of us as an employer. Also, we miss the opportunity to establish the employee's expectations for the rest of their experience with this employer.

It is a common belief that the first 90 days of a worker's experience on a new job will determine how the relationship goes for the balance of their employment. One way to get off on the right foot is to provide a quality orientation followed by an onboarding program for every new employee.

A strong orientation program will include such things as the following:

- **Welcome by the CEO/senior executive**   This shows a new hire that senior management cares about employees. Senior executives who believe it isn't worth their time convey a strong message also.

- **Discussion about culture**   An opportunity to discuss "the way we do things around here." What does the employer value? What gets rewarded in the organization? What type of image does the employer want to project to the world? What are expectations of ethics? Assimilating and socializing the new hire into the culture and expectations of behavior that is expected of them while working in the organization are necessary and important steps for orientation and onboarding.

- **Enrollment in benefit programs**   This is an opportunity to complete payroll tax forms, benefit enrollment forms, and self-identification forms for race, sex, disability, and veteran status.

- **Tour of employee common areas**   This can include the cafeteria or break room, the location for labor law compliance posters, and restrooms.

- **Safety equipment and emergency exits**   This is often overlooked when it should be on the orientation agenda. If there are emergency breathing apparatus, eye wash stations, emergency shutdown switches, first-aid stations, or other important safety points of interest, this is the time to show each new worker where they are. Safety training in how to use emergency equipment will come later.

- **Introduction to co-workers and supervisors**   Guide the employees to their new work locations and introduce them to their new co-workers and supervisors, even if they may have met some of them during the interviewing process. Have someone designated to explain where to get office supplies, how to access computer terminals, and whom to ask when questions come up. These things are just common employment courtesies.

Onboarding

Onboarding new employees is the process of integrating them to the organization and its specific culture, as well as getting a new hire the tools and information needed to become a productive, contributing member of the organization. Onboarding should be a strategic process because how employers handle the first few days and months of a new employee's experience is crucial to ensuring a smooth transition into the organization and high retention. How long that onboarding is will vary depending on the job duties.

Getting Started with the Onboarding Process   The process of onboarding new employees can be one of the most critical factors in ensuring recently hired talent will be productive and happy workers. Not to be confused with orientation, onboarding is quite different. Orientation involves paperwork and routine tasks to place new hires in the organization's payroll and organization chart. Onboarding is a more comprehensive process that helps assimilate new hires faster and addresses the following:

- What impression do you want new hires to walk away with at the end of the first day? First month? First quarter? First year?

- What do new employees need to know about the culture and work environment? Do you use a vocabulary of acronyms that will be unfamiliar? If so, it would help to explicitly define them.

- What role will HR play in the process? What about direct managers? Co-workers?

- What kind of expectations, especially behavioral, do you want to set for new employees?

- Who will be the new employee's sponsor (generally someone out of the direct line of command)?

- How will you gather feedback on the program and measure its success?

- Who are you assigning as this new employee's "buddy" or mentor as a go-to resource different from the direct supervisor?

Once these questions have been addressed, HR professionals and upper management can devise a plan of action to help new employees quickly assimilate company policies and workflow while getting fully acquainted with the organization's culture.

Functional Area 3:
Employee Engagement & Retention

Here is SHRM's BASK definition: "Employee Engagement & Retention refers to activities aimed at retaining talent, solidifying and improving the relationship between employees and the organization, creating a thriving and energized workforce, and developing effective strategies to address appropriate performance expectations from employees at all levels."[64]

Key Concepts

The following are the SHRM identified key concepts for Employee Engagement & Retention:

- Approaches to developing and maintaining a positive organizational culture (for example, learning strategies, communication strategies, building values, personalized employee experience)

- Influence of culture on organizational outcomes (for example, organizational performance, organizational learning, innovation, risk-taking)

- Workplace flexibility programs (for example, telecommuting, alternative work schedules, job sharing)

- Methods for assessing employee engagement and satisfaction (for example, focus groups, stay interviews, surveys)

- Job attitude theories and basic principles (for example, engagement, satisfaction, commitment, involvement)

- Job-design principles and techniques (for example, job enrichment, job enlargement, job rotation, work simplification)

- Employee lifecycle phases (for example, recruitment, integration, development, departure)

- Employee retention concepts and best practices (for example, realistic job previews, suggestion mechanisms, identifying causes of turnover, prediction attrition analysis, personalized onboarding)

- Key components of, and best practices associated with, performance management systems (for example, dashboard, calibration, user training, goal recording)

- Principles of effective performance appraisal (for example, goal setting, frequent feedback)

- Retention and turnover metrics (for example, quality of hire, voluntary turnover rate, turnover at a specific location or level, vacancy rate)

- Types of organizational cultures (for example, authoritarian, mechanistic, participative, learning, high performance)

- Approaches to recognition (for example, performance or service awards, spot awards, point-based system, peer-to-peer recognition, personalized rewards)
- Approaches to supporting employee wellness (for example, mental health programs, financial wellness programs, stress management programs, work/life integration)

The following are the proficiency indicators that SHRM has identified:

For All HR Professionals	For Advanced HR Professionals (SCP Exam)
Designs, administers, analyzes, and interprets surveys of employee engagement, job satisfaction, and culture practices	Collaborates with business leaders to define an organizational strategy to create a positive employee experience and an engaged workforce
Administers and supports HR and organizational programs designed to improve the employee experience, including engagement and culture (for example, social events, telecommuting policies, recognition, job design, workplace flexibility)	Implements best practices for employee retention in HR programs, practices, and policies (for example, RJP, career development programs, employee socialization)
Identifies program opportunities to create more engaging or motivating jobs (for example, job enrichment/enlargement).	Designs, oversees, and communicates an action plan to address the findings of surveys on employee engagement, job satisfaction, and culture
Monitors changes in turnover and retention metrics and ensures that leadership is aware of such changes	Communicates the results of surveys of employee attitudes and culture
Coaches supervisors on creating positive working relationships with their employees	Designs and oversees HR and organizational programs designed to improve employee engagement and satisfaction (for example, social events, telecommuting policies, recognition, job design, workplace flexibility)
Trains stakeholders to use the organization's performance management systems	Holistically monitors the organization's metrics on employee attitudes, turnover and retention, and other information about employee engagement and retention
Helps stakeholders understand the elements of satisfactory employee performance and performance management	Designs and oversees best practices–based on employee performance management systems that meet the organization's talent management needs
Implements and monitors processes that measure the effectiveness of performance management systems	Designs and oversees processes to measure the effectiveness of performance management systems

Maintaining an engaged and satisfied workforce and a culture that employees perceive to be positive is an important function for HR. Employee turnover, along with poor performance, is costly and also disruptive. HR's practices can help mitigate these potential problems by monitoring and improving organizational performance and the retention of key talent.

Understanding Employee Engagement

Employee engagement is a broad outcome-driven concept that recognizes certain characteristics that contribute to behaviors that will positively influence employee job performance. HR authorities often define employee engagement in terms of "commitment"—that is, the identification with an organization and the commitment to active participation in its future. Engagement is the degree to which employees are psychologically invested in the organization and motivated to contribute to it success. It can also be described as the discretionary effort toward attaining organizational goals.[65]

There are three types of professional HR engagement:

- **Trait engagement**   The personality-based elements that make an individual inclined to be involved, to have a natural curiosity, and to have an interest in addressing and solving problems.

- **Stage engagement**   The influence of the workplace environment on an individual's inclination to become involved. Organizational interventions can directly influence this type of engagement.

- **Behavioral engagement**   The effect of individual effort that creates the satisfaction from a job well done. Behavioral engagement can occur in cases when both trait and stage engagement are present.

Employee Engagement Levels

While individual surveys differ to some degree, all indicate that the U.S. workforce is typically less engaged than employers expect or hope for. Most results show a relatively low level of employee engagement of about 30 to 40 percent. Other parts of the world show even less engagement.

Benefits of Employee Engagement

A 2013 Gallup study[66] on employee engagement involving 142 countries indicates only 13 percent of employees worldwide are engaged at work; further, 63 percent are not engaged, while 24 percent are actively disengaged. At a regional level, the United States and Canada have the highest proportion of workers who are engaged, 29 percent, followed by Australia and New Zealand. Significant observations indicate that actively disengaged employees outnumber engaged employees by nearly two to one. Gallup describes *engaged employees* as those employees who work with a passion and feel a profound connection to their company. They drive innovation and move their company forward. *Not engaged* employees are essentially "checked out." They're "sleepwalking" through their workday, putting in time but not energy or passion into their work. *Active disengaged* employees are just unhappy at work; they're busy acting out their unhappiness. Every day, these workers work to undermine what their engaged co-workers accomplish.

In 2012, Gallup conducted a meta-analysis of its research data across 192 organizations, 49 industries, and 34 countries. This study confirmed a well-established connection between employee engagement and a number of performance outcomes. The median differences between top-quartile and bottom-quartile units were as follows:

- 10 percent in customer ratings
- 22 percent in profitability
- 21 percent in productivity
- 25 percent in turnover (high-turnover organizations)
- 65 percent in turnover (low-turnover organizations)
- 48 percent in safety incidents
- 37 percent in absenteeism
- 41 percent in quality defects

Drivers and Role of Organizational Culture in Engagement

Organizational culture is a system of shared assumptions, values, and beliefs that govern how people behave in organizations. These shared values have a significant influence on people in the organization and dictate how they dress, act, and perform their jobs. An organization's ultimate goal is to align its culture and strategy.

Global Engagement Drivers

There are four drivers of engagement from an international perspective:

- The work itself as well as the development opportunities the work provides
- Stability and the confidence that is placed in an organization's leadership
- Rewards and recognition
- The upward and downward flow of communications

These drivers vary from country to country in a global context. Whereas the confidence that career interests can be met, a sense of personal satisfaction and confidence in the organization's success are primary in the United States; top drivers in Canada include a good work-life balance and being respectfully treated. Other countries value other drivers.

Some international drivers include the need for achievement and competence, but there is a difference between individualist cultures and collectivist cultures. Individualist cultures prefer personal feedback, whereas collectivist cultures prefer group feedback. A need for control is universal, but personal control is preferred in an individualist culture, whereas collective control is preferred in collectivist cultures.

Effective Management and Employee Engagement

Management's behavior is critical to employee engagement and to an employee's well-being. Managers who manage in ways that encourage employee engagement are essential to the engagement of their employees. Recent studies conclude that there is a link between employee engagement and leadership practices that encourage and support employee performance rather than dictate employee performance. The following are three leadership practices that encourage and support employee performance:

- **Transformational leadership**   This is a style of leadership where the leader is charged with identifying the needed change, creating a vision to guide the change through inspiration, and executing the change in tandem with committed members of the group.

- **Authentic leadership**   This is an approach to leadership that emphasizes building the leader's legitimacy through honest relationships with followers who value their input and that is built on an ethical foundation.

- **Supportive leadership**   This is one of the leadership styles found in path-goal theory (a theory based on specifying a leader's style or behavior that best fits the employee and work environment to achieve goals). A supportive leader attempts to reduce employee stress and frustration in the workplace.

Challenges to Employee Engagement

Many external factors present obstacles to effective employee engagement, including global competition, economic conditions, continuous innovation, and new technology. In addition, the blurred line between work and nonwork conditions exacerbates the difficulties faced by employers whose goal is to maximize conditions that support effective employee engagement.

Global competition coupled with less-than-ideal economic conditions places significant pressure on organizational managers to aggressively target production goals. Along with this, continuous innovation and new technology add another layer of pressure on work performance, even as they offer new capabilities to the workplace. Further, technology in the form of the Internet and mobile interconnectivity creates a new gray area as to where work time ends and nonwork time begins.

All of this places a new role on HR to create a business case for the need now, more than ever, for managers to invest in the issue of employee engagement.

HR's Employee Engagement Strategy

As part of its strategic management role, HR is tasked with developing effective strategies incorporating good employee engagement practices designed to best achieve the organization's business goals.

Assessing Employee Engagement

Employee engagement is the level of personal investment an employee has in their work. According to the *Harvard Business Review,* "Much has been studied about the impact of employee engagement on company performance, and there is general agreement that increased engagement drives results: Gallup, for example, suggests a 20% or better boost to productivity and profitability for companies with high engagement. Such companies, however, may be few and far between: Gallup also reports that only 30% of American workers, and 13% of global workers, are engaged in their jobs."[67]

Gathering Information About Employee Engagement

If you want to measure employee engagement, consider employee surveys or focus groups. Both can produce a great deal of information about how people feel about their jobs and their contributions to the organization.

Employee Surveys

Perhaps the most frequently used device for gathering information about employee engagement is the employee survey. It can be used to work on issues in the entire employer organization or in a subset like a department or division. When the accounting department is having problems and a new manager is appointed to manage the department, an employee survey of accounting personnel could be helpful to identify the issues employees want to see improved. Help your employees with the issues they believe are important, and they will react by being nicer to the customers they contact and other employees within the company.

Benefits of Conducting Employee Surveys   Why use an employee survey to measure employee engagement? Well, they are reasonable in cost, can be done fairly quickly, and can provide some great insights into the thinking of your employees. Surveys are versatile and can be done anonymously.

Survey Questions   Questions are constructed so there are no right or wrong answers (unlike the SHRM certification exam). Here are a few examples:

- On a scale of 1 to 10, where 10 is the best, please rate the quality of supervision in your work group.
- What word would you use to describe the company's strategy?
- On a scale of Strongly Agree to Strongly Disagree, how would you rate your views of this statement? The company executive team is open and accessible to all employees.
- Please rank in order the following five things, from 1 to 5, with 1 being first. Use each number only once.

Developing Surveys   To begin a survey project, you should identify the goals you want to meet by having a survey. If it is to determine levels of employee satisfaction with the new company headquarters building, that would be worthwhile. If it is to see what employees thought of the new office binder supplier, there may be less value to be gained. Once you have the goal in mind, identify the population that you want to invite to participate in the survey. Is it the entire employee body or only the group that is working at a given location? Then determine whether you want to build and implement the survey internally or hire an outside vendor to build and implement the survey for you. Construct the survey questions and test them with your HR staff (and even executives). Once all edits have been made, finalize the survey document and plan for its dissemination to your target audience. Gather and summarize the responses. Prepare a report on your results, and don't forget to share it with survey participants in addition to senior management.

Autonomy/empowerment	Are people able to act on their own authority and innovate on the job?
Career progression	Are there opportunities for people to grow and develop in the company?
Collaboration	Are they able to easily work with other teams or colleagues without barriers, and to what extent are people from diverse backgrounds or with diverse opinions able to collaborate?
Communication	Are they able to easily work with other teams or colleagues without barriers?
Company leadership	Do they believe in and trust their senior leaders?
Pay and benefits	Do people feel they're fairly compensated?
Quality of product or services	Do people believe in what they (and/or the organization) provide to their customers?
Recognition	Do people feel that they're recognized and appreciated?
Resources	Do they have the right tools (computers, systems, and so on) to do their jobs, and are there enough people on the team for them to achieve a work-life balance?
Strategy alignment	Do they buy into where the company is going, or do they even know?
Supportive management	Are managers supporting their teams to be successful? (This can also include good performance management.)
Training and development	Do people feel they have the training they need to do their jobs?

Table 4-8   Employee Engagement Survey

Guidelines for Employee Engagement Surveys   Table 4-8 describes the critical drivers to consider when building an employee engagement survey, according to Qualtrics.com.[68]

Online Survey   Turn on your computer and start cruising the World Wide Web, and you will be presented with a great many opportunities to participate in customer surveys. There are plenty of companies willing to help you prepare your online survey. Survey fraud is likely the greatest disadvantage of online surveys. You can't be positively sure about who is completing the survey. It could be someone who wants to distort your results, such as a competitor or unscrupulous employee. Yet, the costs are low for using online surveys. If you can be sure that only specific people are able to participate, you may find that this is a survey method you can use in your organization.

Managing Effective Employee Survey Projects   Aside from being careful in the construction of your survey, the most important part of the process is to get senior executive support both for the survey process and for taking the actions necessary once results have been tabulated. Employee trust can be lost as quickly as you can blink if you ask people for their opinions and then do nothing to fix problems unveiled in the process. By conducting the survey, you are raising employee expectations that you will take action based on the survey results. Therefore, you put yourself in the best position for success by getting a commitment in advance of the survey that you will be able to act based on the results.

Using Focus Groups and Interviews to Gather Engagement Information

When you're surveying employees, the last question should generally be, "May we contact you to discuss your responses?" Those people who say "yes" become candidates for follow-up interviews or participation in focus groups. Focus groups are designed to gain input from people who meet your defined criteria to help with the research you are doing. As an example, you might want to focus on employees with less than a year of service to help improve your orientation and onboarding programs. The focus group can discuss any subject and is highly structured, led by a facilitator who presents questions to get responses from group participants. Usually the sessions are recorded for later study. Participants need to be told that to avoid legal complications. Some consulting firms specialize in focus group facilitation. They assist with designing the questions, the photos or written slogans, advertising, or other company options, and they run the focus group sessions.

One-on-One Interviews   This is a technique for delving more deeply into the opinions expressed by individuals who responded to the employee survey. It can also be used to explore comments and opinions expressed during a focus group session. Someone who has a strong belief that the company benefit program should include paid parental leave could have some valuable input if discussed in a personal interview.

Analyzing Data on Employee Engagement

How do you feel when you are asked for your opinion and then ignored when you give it? That is what happens when employees sense the survey was just an exercise for show—in other words, a PR stunt. When the results are compiled and analyzed and action plans developed based on those results, employees will sense that their opinions actually matter.

Communicating Survey Results   One common failing of employee survey projects is that employees don't get any feedback about what the survey showed. Remember the communication cycle? We must complete the cycle by providing feedback to the employees about the survey results. How that is done can be quite creative—or it can be simple. Just be sure to do it. Also, let employees know before sending out a press release explaining the results to the world. That sends the message to employees that their input is just being used for a publicity stunt.

Determining Actions from Survey Results   How do you determine what should be done with the survey results? First, summarize the responses so there is a composite view of employee thoughts. Then, analyze those composites to determine what they are saying. Separate them into "urgent," "important," and "later" categories to reflect how quickly the employer should address the issues. Finally, build an action plan to determine what is to be done, who is assigned the tasks, and when those tasks should be completed. Follow up to check on progress and eventually resurvey the workforce to see how they feel after you have taken the action based on their first input.

Selecting Employee Engagement Initiatives   It is sometimes difficult to know where to start fixing employee engagement problems. Using employee survey results, you can analyze areas of need and then build some plans to address them. Rank ordering the problems is a way to set priorities. Involving employees in the action plan is a way to further their involvement and engagement. Start with the most important priority and work your way down the list, no matter how long it may take. Keep at it and tell employees what you are doing from time to time.

Business Case for Engagement

Employee engagement affects nine performance outcomes. Compared with bottom-quartile units, top-quartile units have the following:[69]

- 37 percent lower absenteeism
- 25 percent lower turnover (in high-turnover organizations)
- 65 percent lower turnover (in low-turnover organizations)
- 28 percent less shrinkage (that is, theft or breakage due to carelessness)
- 48 percent fewer safety incidents
- 41 percent fewer patient safety incidents
- 41 percent fewer quality incidents (defects)
- 10 percent higher customer metrics
- 21 percent higher productivity
- 22 percent higher profitability

It should be rather easy to convert these percentages to dollars in your organizational impact statement. Once that is done, a cost analysis to determine the budget requirements for spending to accomplish those results will help you prove the impact your employee engagement project will have on the financial bottom line.

Engaging Employees—From Hiring to Separation

Employee engagement is not only integral to your organization's workforce satisfaction, but also imperative to the bottom line. According to the 2015 *Journal of Corporate Finance,* organizations with employee engagement programs saw a 26 percent year-over-year increase in annual company revenue, compared to those that did not have formal programs. Making employees feel like their contribution makes an impact, facilitating opportunities for them to form relationships, and collecting feedback are ways to engage employees.

If you've been tasked with implementing employee engagement initiatives at your organization with a large number of employees, or a company with multiple locations, the task may seem daunting. Start with feedback. Collecting feedback is a great place to begin engaging your employees because you can use this feedback to inform the rest of your employee engagement strategy moving forward. For example, new hires are an important group to gather feedback from so you can refine your onboarding process, as are employees who are exiting the organization—they can give you insight into how you can better retain your current employees, if they will be candid with you. There are many different tools you can use to collect feedback. Using Glassdoor to collect feedback gives you a forum by which you can collect and respond to feedback.

Engaging Employees Throughout the Employee Lifecycle

There are critical key points in an employee lifecycle with the organization. Engagement begins with the first contact with the new employee and continues throughout their employment. HR plays an important role in increasing employee overall satisfaction and engagement from the get-go.

Engagement Practices During Hiring and Onboarding

HR professionals have a great amount of influence with employee engagement, beginning with the hiring and onboarding phase. The period that begins with the hiring is an important opportunity to start the engagement process. Gallup's report "State of the American Workplace: Employee Engagement Insights for U.S. Business Leaders" clearly points out that new hires are more engaged in their first 6 months on the job than they are at any other time during their employment. Five practices can be employed and used by HR during the hiring and onboarding processes:

- Make the job application process simple and informative.
- First impressions count—create an accurate first impression.
- Make the first day on the job organized and meaningful.
- Have a structured onboarding process to provide new hires with 90 days of onboarding and fitting in.
- Define and communicate a path to success for the new hires so they are aware of the career advancement paths.

Engagement Practices During an Employee's Career

In the same Gallup report cited earlier, after the first 6 months are done, the honeymoon is over. Gallup stated that engagement fell to 44 percent by the tenth year of employment. There is plenty of opportunity for HR to shift those percentages by developing programs and leadership training specifically focused on employee engagement throughout the lifecycle of an employee's career. We address some of the approaches in the functional areas of Learning and Development and Total Rewards in this chapter. They include the topics of job enrichment, compensation, noncompensatory rewards, and career management.

Developing Policies and Procedures to Promote Engagement   By helping to create policies, HR professionals are supporting how the organization defines roles and explains what actions and behaviors are acceptable and those that are not. Policies are meant to cover the majority of situations, yet there will always be an exception to a policy that will occur. Policies lead to the creation of procedures and processes for implementing those policies. HR needs to regularly assess its current policies and how they impact employee engagement. Work-life balance policies are an example of a type of policy that has great impact on employee engagement and that requires review on at least an annual basis.

Work-Life Balance   Because of technology growth and social pressures/changes within the family or community, work-life balance (WLB) is growing as an engagement issue for employees and organizations alike. Many organizations offer a number of WLB programs and policies that greatly enhance employee engagement. Telecommuting, childcare on-site, gym memberships or gyms on-site, concierge services, and PTO flexibility—the list is growing in innovation.

Developing Policies   When developing policies associated with work-life balance, the HR professional can rely on other organizations' best practices. These include having clear guidelines for management to apply and addressing a variety of situations (employee positions/roles) to which they apply. Policies are created to address a "real need"—be sure that the WLB policies do just that in the business unit of the organization. First, identify the "need" for the WLB policy. Next, determine what the policy's content will be in simple language. Avoid rigid rules that must be followed exactly in all circumstances. Move to the next phase of development, which is to obtain stakeholder support. Share the draft with those who will need to apply the policy and look to see where refinement may be needed. Now that the policy is ready to be implemented, go to your communication plan—the when, who, what, where, and how for the policy's launch. As mentioned earlier, keep an eye on the policy to determine when it needs refinement, refreshment, and/or revision.

How Policies Can Affect Employee Engagement   Policies can be one of the greatest sources of disenchantment for employee engagement. Notice what is brought up on the list of enhancements during labor relationship and contract negotiations. Pay attention to the exit interviews and preferably the "stay interviews" that provide feedback pointing to ineffective or behind-the-times policies. When it comes to employee engagement, HR can be the keeper of the keys when it comes to policies that affect employee satisfaction.

Using Motivation Theories to Increase Engagement   Motivation is essential for engaging employees in their work. Three underlying principles of human behavior are directly linked to motivation:

- All human behavior is caused. This means people have a reason for doing what they do.

- All behavior is focused on achieving an end result or goal. People do things to attain something tangible or intangible. Their behavior is not random, though it could be unconscious.

- Every person has a unique fingerprint and is unique in that no one has the exact experience, heredity, or environmental/relationship influences.

Understanding these principles of human behavior will assist you as an HR professional with motivational pursuits, not just in the learning process but in all matters related to the work and employment relationship, especially engagement.

Motivation is like a shower: it eventually wears off, and you need another in a couple of days. Inspiration, however, lights up like a fire and grows—it comes from deep within people. Transformational leaders cause people to be inspired, inspiring their employees to take action and providing them with self-esteem versus "shelf-esteem." As an HR professional and one who trains organizational leaders, try to seek the authentic inspirational skills to motivate and engage employees. The event will be lasting and sustained.

There are several other long-standing motivational theories, and we will briefly review them to refresh your memory about what you most likely learned in your secondary educational endeavors.

Maslow's Hierarchy of Needs Maslow's theory arranges the five basic human needs into a pyramid, necessitating that the first level (bottom of the pyramid) be met first before moving up the pyramid. Figure 4-12 shows Maslow's hierarchy of needs. Lower-level needs on the pyramid will always have some influence on behavior.[70]

You can fulfill these needs in the workplace through the following:

- **Physiological** Work environment and work shifts
- **Safety and security** Employment security such as an employment contract, pay and benefits, and working conditions
- **Belonging and love** Teams, good leadership, participation in groups, employee associations, customer base assignments
- **Esteem** Training, recognition, awards, special assignments
- **Self-actualization** Job growth opportunities, project team participation, becoming a mentor

 NOTE It's important to recognize that not all motivational models of Western culture, like Maslow's hierarchy of needs, are going to apply in many of the global and diverse organizations of today.

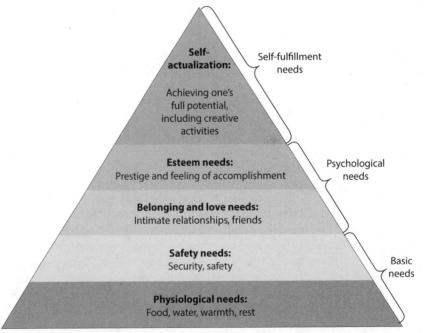

Figure 4-12 Maslow's hierarchy of needs

Herzberg's Motivation-Hygiene Theory   This theory asserts that employees have two different categories of needs and that they are essentially independent of each other, but they affect behavior in differing ways: hygiene factors, which are considered extrinsic, and motivational factors, which are considered intrinsic. The latter is associated with recognition, achievement, and personal growth–related events in the job, whereas the former is associated with factors around the positions (job security, pay, working conditions, supervision, co-worker relations) that can quickly lead to job dissatisfaction.

Theory X, Y, and Z   McGregor's theories X and Y offer two approaches to motivating employees. Theory X suggests an authoritative management style because it assumes that employees inherently do not like to work and must be controlled and closely monitored. Theory Y suggests a participative style of management, under the belief that employees dislike controls and inherently want to do their best. It is obvious to see that a theory Y type of supervisor will provide better leadership and produce greater satisfaction.

According to the search engine Bing, Theory Y is a participative style of management that "assumes that people will exercise self-direction and self-control in the achievement of organizational objectives to the degree that they are committed to those objectives." It is management's main task in such a system to maximize that commitment.

Theory Z management tends to promote stable employment, high productivity, and high employee morale and satisfaction. Theory Z is Dr. William Ouchi's[71] theory, called *Japanese management style,* popularized during Japan's economic boom of the 1980s. In the 1980s there was a huge demand for Japanese products and imports in America, mostly within the automotive industry. Why were U.S. consumers clambering for cars, televisions, stereos, and electronics from Japan? It was because of two reasons: high-quality products and low prices. The Japanese had discovered something that was giving them the competitive edge. The secret to their success was not what they were producing but how they were managing their people—Japanese employees were engaged, empowered, and highly productive. Ouchi studied Japan's approach to workplace teamwork and participative management. The result was his theory Z: a development beyond McGregor's theory X and theory Y that blended the best of Eastern and Western management practices. For Ouchi, theory Z focused on increasing employee loyalty to the company by providing a job for life, with a strong focus on the well-being of the employee, both on and off the job.

Theory Z makes certain assumptions about workers. One assumption is that they seek to build cooperative and intimate working relationships with their co-workers. In other words, employees have a strong desire for affiliation. Another assumption is that workers expect reciprocity and support from the organization. According to theory Z, employees want to maintain a work-life balance, and they value a working environment in which things like family, culture, and traditions are considered to be just as important as the work they do. Under theory Z leadership, not only do workers have a sense of affiliation with their fellow workers, but they also develop a sense of order, discipline, and a moral obligation to work hard. Finally, theory Z assumes that given the right leadership, workers can be trusted to do their jobs and look after their own and their co-workers' well-being.

Skinner's Behavioral Reinforcement Theory   One of the most influential American psychologists, B. F. Skinner, developed the theory of behavioral reinforcement, which deals with shaping behavior. Skinner found that behavior modification has four intervention strategies that are reactions used to eventually shape behavior: positive reinforcement, negative reinforcement, punishment, and extinction.

- Positive reinforcement involves providing an employee with a desired or appreciated reward to encourage the desired behavior.

- Negative reinforcement involves avoiding an undesirable consequence by giving the employee an appreciated reward when they exhibit a desired behavior.

- Punishment is just as it sounds—something negative occurs when an undesirable behavior occurs by the employee.

- Extinction involves no response. When the behavior is not reinforced through positive reinforcement, negative reinforcement, or punishment, the employee's behavior will diminish and become nonexistent.

Intrinsic Motivation   *Intrinsic motivation* is behavior that is driven by internal rewards. The *motivation* to engage in a behavior arises from within the employee because it is satisfying to them. Author Daniel Pink writes about the research that has been done globally on the topic of motivation. In his book *Drive: The Surprising Truth About What Motivates Us,* Pink states that rewards (pay-for-performance) work well for tasks where there is a simple set of rules and a clear destination, such as accounting and computer programming (the left-brain work).[72] For the tasks that exercise more of the right brain—which would be creative, research, and conceptual work—a pay-for-performance plan actually leads to poorer performance. Science has determined that intrinsic motivation is far more effective for the right-brain types because it is associated with doing tasks, work, and things that matter; because it is interesting; or because the employee likes it.

Using Rewards and Recognition to Increase Engagement   The purpose of having employee recognition and reward programs is to acknowledge the value of employees, their contributions, or some other identification. The intention is to show gratitude, appreciation, loyalty, and trust, as well as to continue engagement and motivation. An effective program highlights valued and desired behaviors. Of course, forms of recognition address the psychological needs of people.

Forms of Rewards and Recognition   There are financial rewards and nonfinancial rewards (explored in the Total Rewards functional area in this book). Rewards need to demonstrate appreciation and are more effective when they are customized to an individual employee, such as tickets to an interest or hobby they may have. HR can be highly effective with designing appropriate recognition rewards through innovation and creativity, looking to other organizations for their best practices, and simply getting to know the employees in their organization. Awards can run the gamut—from plaques, jewelry, and certificates to flex time off, conference attendance, tickets to events, and opportunities to fill in for an advanced position on a temporary/interim basis.

Recognition in Multinational Organizations   SHRM conducted research in 2006 that linked performance management and employee engagement in multinational enterprises operating across developed and developing economies. This research had the following key findings:[73]

- Having a broad range of performance appraisal outcomes was positively linked to engagement.

- Key elements of high levels of job/company resources were linked to employee engagement.

- Employee involvement in setting goals is linked positively to engagement.

Consistency and transparency in HR practices were highlighted as being critical to success.

Role of HR in Employee Recognition   In the 2016 SHRM/Globoforce Employee Recognition Survey,[74] HR professionals reported the following findings:

- Organizations that had strategic recognition programs reported less frustrated and more engaged employees.

- Programs tied to the organization's values were more effective than programs without ties.

- Empowering employees to give and receive formal recognition had good results.

- When more than 1 percent of payroll was spent on employee recognition, employee engagement was better.

Engagement Practices During Separation

Employee separations happen. It's a fact of the employment cycle. It may be for reasons that are positively focused, such as retirement, or for reasons that are unpleasant, such as terminations for cause or reductions in workforce (RIF). How these separations happen can have a positive or negative effect on employee engagement for those remaining in the workforce. HR can support fair, humane, and yet compliant processes with regard to separation. Exit interviews, as mentioned earlier, can be helpful for feedback on employee engagement. Also, well-done separations for cause can actually attract better employees capable of engagement and contribution, whereas the departing employee were not. In many organizations, especially in the tech industries, it is not uncommon for former employees to return to the organization with new skills, providing new value at higher-level positions. The level of engagement and treatment at the separation can influence the possibility of key valued employees returning to the organization.

Performance Management

Performance management is a systematic process that helps improve organizational effectiveness by providing feedback to employees on their performance results and improvement needs. Employee accomplishments and contributions drive the business results of an organization, so a regular feedback system discussing individual performance is at the core of a good performance management system. It ensures that employees are on course for the completion of tasks and goals that are aligned with the organization's goals and that the necessary resources and support are provided for the employee to perform such functions.

Employee performance management systems include the following:

- Delegating and planning work
- Setting expectations for performance results
- Continually monitoring performance
- Developing a capacity to perform to new levels for personal and professional growth
- Periodically rating performance in a summary fashion
- Providing recognition and rewarding good performance

Organizational Values and Goals

Creating and communicating the organization's vision, mission, strategies, specific goals, and values form the foundation needed for the performance management system. Then performance standards are agreed upon by both the line management and the employee on what the job requires and what will be measured. At this stage, it is essential that employees clearly understand the standards, including expected behavior standards set forth for their jobs. Feedback is the next stage and can be both informal and formal. Formal feedback would entail a written performance appraisal.

When it comes to performance management within a global organization, there are additional considerations. Different cultural values and societal norms will affect the definition of standards and performance criteria as it relates to a global workforce. Different languages will also have to be considered for the interpretation of performance definitions and standards. Recognizing that there are differing behaviors for different cultures can be a challenge for setting the behavioral standards and expectations of individuals.

Performance Standards

Employees need to know and understand what specific job performance is expected of them and what's considered acceptable behavior. This communication begins with the very first discussion in a job interview, and certainly with the job offer and new-hire onboarding orientation. The discussion continues on a consistent basis, both with the reinforcement of organizational standards outlined in employee handbooks and other written material and with performance appraisal review sessions. The clearer the expectations set for employees, the greater the success in having expectations met.

Employee Performance

Job performance means the extent to which an employee generates work output that meets expectations for quality and quantity.

Measurement and Feedback

Everything can be measured, even if it is inherently subjective. Once a measurement is taken, feedback should be provided to the employees so they can know how they are doing in their job efforts.

Appraisal Methods   Performance appraisals satisfy three purposes:

- Providing feedback and coaching
- Justifying the allocation of rewards and career opportunities
- Helping with employee career planning and development plans

For the organization, performance appraisals can foster commitment and align people to contribute to initiatives with their upcoming performance contributions. The most common performance appraisal method involves just two people: the employee and their direct supervisor. In some companies, others are asked to be involved in the appraisals, such as peers, another level of management, and sometimes colleagues in the organization whose job function interacts with the employee. These are known as *360-degree appraisals*.

Methods for rating the performance can be completely narrative, management by objectives (MBO), behaviorally anchored ratings (BARS), category rating scales (such as 1–5), and comparative ratings with others in like functions.

The least complex of the methods is the category rating where the reviewer simply checks a level of rating on a form. These three types of rating formulas are typically used in category ratings:

- **Graphic scale**   The most common type, where the appraiser checks a place on the scale for the categories of tasks and behaviors that are listed. A typical scale is 5 points, where 1 means not meeting expectations (or low) and 5 means exceeding expectations (or high). These types of performance appraisals normally have a comments section the appraiser completes that provides justification for the rating.

- **Checklist**   This is another common appraisal rating in which the appraiser is provided with a set list of statements/words to describe performance. The appraiser selects the one word or statement that best describes the performance—for example, "Employee consistently meets all deadlines" or "Employee consistently misses deadlines." Typically, with this method, the appraiser is required to check two of four statements.

- **Forced choice**   This is a variation of the checklist approach. One check is for the statement that is most like the employee's performance, and the other check is for the statement that is least like the employee's performance—a combination of positive and negative statements. This method can be difficult to convey to employees and understand from an employee's perspective. It also doesn't lend itself to a summary of performance.

With comparative methods, employee performance is compared directly with others in the same job. The appraiser will rank the employees in a group from highest to lowest in performance. This causes a forced distribution known as a *bell curve*. Ten percent will fall within the highest and lowest of the rating scale, another 20 percent will fall on either side, and then 40 percent will meet job standards and expectations. An obvious fault with

Figure 4-13
Bell curve
distribution

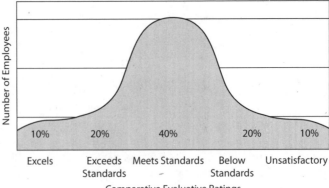

this type of system is suggesting that a percentage of employees will fall below expectations. Figure 4-13 displays a bell curve distribution.

Narrative evaluations are time-consuming for an appraiser to complete, yet they can be the most meaningful to the employee being evaluated. The following three methods are the most common for the narrative appraisal:

- **Essay format**   The appraiser writes an essay describing each category of performance.

- **Critical incident**   The appraiser logs the dates and details of both good and not-so-good performance incidents. This method requires the appraiser to keep good, detailed notes on a routine basis during the appraisal period and not rely solely on an employee's most recent performance.

- **Behaviorally anchored rating scale**   Referred to as BARS, this appraisal method describes desirable behavior and undesirable behavior. Examples are then compared with a scale of performance level for the rating. BARS works well in circumstances in which several employees perform the same function. A BARS appraisal system requires extensive time to develop and maintain to keep the performance dimensions up to date as the job functions change. However, the BARS method offers a more accurate gauge of performance measurement, provides clearer standards to employees, and has more consistency in rating.

- **Self-assessment**   Coupled with the direct supervisory management evaluation, many employees are asked to self-assess their performance. This approach assists with creating a truly two-way dialogue in the evaluation interview and offers an opportunity for the employee to provide their own perception of performance. Additionally, it engages employees in a proactive means of creating goals and objectives, along with triggering a discussion about career development. Figure 4-14 provides an example of a self-assessment, which features both a category rating and open-ended questions to elicit a narrative commentary.

Self-Assessment Performance Appraisal
For the appraisal period of January 1, 2024 – December 31, 2024

Employee Name: _____ EE # _____

Department: _____
Position Title: _____
Supervisor: _____
Facility: _____

Instructions:
Please complete your self-assessment evaluation and return it to your supervisor by (date)_____.
Your participation in the annual performance appraisal process helps to facilitate a comprehensive
evaluation of your performance and accomplishments against set standards, goals, and objectives.

1. Describe your accomplishments and contributions since last review period.
2. Describe the activities you have participated in that have produced favorable outcomes.
3. Since your last appraisal, what new skills have you acquired?
4. Describe skills that you have increased and provide an example of their effective application on the job.
5. List new training and/or development programs you have completed.
6. Describe areas you wish to improve to enhance your job performance and capabilities.
7. State three or more job objectives for this next year and how you plan to achieve them.

Please provide your self-assessment rating in the following categories using the rating scale below.

Rating Scale:

4 - Outstanding **3** - Very Competent or High Level **2** - Satisfactory **1** - Inexperienced or Improvement Needed

Category	Self-Rating
a. Technical Skills (job specific)	_____
b. Job Knowledge (up to date on industry, articles, and best practices)	_____
c. Quality of Work Product (comprehensive, accurate, timely)	_____
d. Productivity	_____
e. Professionalism (punctuality, attendance; conduct; responsiveness and follow-through)	_____
f. Collaboration & Teamwork	_____
g. Computer Skill Applications	_____
h. Time Management & Organizational Skills	_____
i. Interpersonal Skills	_____
j. Communication Skills – Verbal/Written	_____
k. Innovation or Creativity	_____

Date: _____   Employee Signature: _____

Figure 4-14 Self-assessment performance appraisal

Errors in Performance Appraisal As with any subjective system, performance appraisals are subjective because they are based on people's perceptions and opinions, so there can be shortcomings. Here are the most common errors made on the part of appraisers:

- **Halo** This occurs when the employee is doing well in one area and is therefore rated high in all areas.

- **Horn** This occurs when an employee is demonstrating a significant weakness and is therefore rated low in all other areas.

- **Bias** This happens when the evaluator's bias (consciously or unconsciously) influences and distorts their perspective.

- **Recency** A recency error occurs when more emphasis is placed on a recent occurrence and all earlier performances during the review period are discounted. It is particularly common to weigh more heavily the performance of the last 6 weeks and discount the prior 46 weeks for an annual review.

- **Primacy** The opposite of recency. The evaluator gives more weight and emphasis to earlier performance, discounting more recent performance.

- **Strictness** An evaluator is reluctant to give high ratings, and their standards are higher than other evaluators.

- **Leniency** The evaluator does not provide low scores and instead gives all employees high ratings on their appraisals.

- **Central** An evaluator rates all their employees in the same range and does not consider differences of actual performances among the group rated.

- **Contrast** The evaluator is providing an employee rating based solely on a comparison to that of another employee and not objective standards.

 NOTE These common errors can be avoided with narrative format methods.

Appraisal Meeting Once you have completed the written evaluation of your employee's performance, there are some key factors to consider in planning for the success of your feedback session with the employee. Here is an agenda outline for that meeting:

- Review the purpose of the feedback meeting and the importance of the appraisal process.

- Review results or accomplishments achieved against objectives and explain how these contributed to the work group's efforts.

- Identify reasons for success and causes of problems.

- Agree on action to be taken by you and by the employee, and discuss ideas for development.
- Summarize the discussion and express confidence in the employee's ability to succeed.

Documenting Employee Performance   Some performance evaluation systems have elaborate forms that must be filled in by the supervisor. Some require the employee to fill in forms because self-evaluation is part of their system of performance evaluation. Other documentation requirements are rather simple. A simple table with the information shown in Table 4-9 might suffice.

Business Results and Employee Growth

Business results and employee success are tightly linked. Employee growth can occur with chances to increase knowledge (learn something new), develop new skills (practice welding), or develop abilities that are new (enhance ability to take off and land an airplane). When a flight school's success depends on the ability of its instructors to help student pilots achieve their licenses, the level of business success cannot be separated from the level of instructor success.

Business Results   Business results can be measured in a host of possible ways. Some of the most common are profit and loss, ranking in the industry among competing companies, number of clients served during the year, and the return on investment for employee training.

Employee Growth and Rewards   In May of 2022, Workhuman and Gallop[75] partnered, looking at the impact of recognition on employee morale and engagement. Their results concluded only one in four employees strongly agree that they feel connected to their culture and only one in three strongly agree that they belong at their organization. Efforts to purposely engage employees can make a difference.

People want recognition for their work and accomplishments. They want real responsibility, and they want a chance to feel they are achieving good things on their job. All of those are possible if, first, the basic working conditions, policies, supervisor relationships, regular feedback, and compensation/benefits are acceptable.

Rewarding employees by simply and sincerely thanking them for their contributions can go a long way toward their feeling engaged in their work.

Responsibility	Objective	Result/Accomplishment	Action Plan
Produce monthly employee newsletter.	Complete publication by the 15th of each month.	All 12 issues this past year were published on time.	Continue with current performance.
Respond to media inquiries about company.	Respond to each inquiry within 1 day.	46 of 48 media inquiries were handled within 24 hours.	Ask for backup if it appears the target will be missed.

Table 4-9   Example of Simple Performance Documentation

Retention

The best business outcome is for a new hire to stick around for a while. Depending on the level of the job in your organization's structure, you can determine how long it will take to reach a "break-even" point for the organization to cover the cost of recruiting and hiring.

$$\text{Break-Even Point for New-Hire Retention} = \frac{\text{Monthly Value of New Hire on the Job}}{\text{Cost of Recruiting and Hiring}}$$

$$\text{Break-Even Point for New-Hire Retention} = \frac{\$5,000 \text{ per month}}{\$2,000^*}$$

Break-Even Point for New-Hire Retention = 2.5 months

*Cost of recruiting and hiring includes things such as search fees, HR recruiter expense (salary for time involved), and hiring manager expense (salary for interviews, paper reviews, discussions about candidates).

Business Case for Retention

While many employers say, "employees are our greatest asset," in fact, actual business practices have often been inconsistent with this concept. When there is a relatively high unemployment rate, in many cases employers have adopted a casual attitude toward talent acquisition. In some cases, they have gone so far as to think that a focus on retention is not so important; after all, employees should be happy they are employed. This is a false premise. Companies that don't continuously focus on attracting and retaining the absolute best talent are companies that will soon find themselves at the "back of the line" when it comes to being a competitive force in the marketplace.

Increasing employee engagement with the goal of keeping key talent on board is not just a matter of making employees feel good. It's about challenging them, asking them to reach their peak productivity, and providing them with meaningful work in which they can take pride. In other words, a poor retention rate means that the business is losing money it could otherwise save.

Satya Radjasa, a reward practice lead with the Hay Group, outlined just how costly it can be when essential employees fly the coop. He noted that there are expenses that come up when a valued staff member leaves. The first is the financial cost, which can be particularly high for people tasked with bringing in and keeping revenue streams, such as salespeople and account managers. The second layer of monetary impact, the cost of finding someone to fill the vacated role, can be even more dramatic. "Replacing an employee can cost from 30 to 200 percent of annual salary, depending on their level. So, if 15 percent of your 'critical' people are leaving, what would the cost be?"[76]

There is always a need for good talent regardless of whether there is a high unemployment rate or other adverse employment factors causing a large labor pool. Companies that don't recognize this fact will soon find themselves uncompetitive in the market.

Why Retention Matters   Retention has some level of correlation with morale. If people are constantly coming and going from the payroll, lack of consistency can be a deterrent to productivity. When such things make doing a job more difficult, frustration builds, and people soon become unhappy. Having an organization where people stay for long periods of time means consistency is higher in all respects. Then there is the cost of turnover, which can be controlled or eliminated if the revolving door can be slowed or stopped altogether.

Retention Practices and Strategies

HR professionals don't generally leave retention to chance. There is usually a written plan that describes how the organization will address retention issues.

Drivers of Retention   According to Robert Half, the following are some of the contributors to retention success:[77]

- Onboarding and orientation
- Mentorship programs
- Employee compensation
- Recognition and reward systems
- Work-life balance
- Training and development
- Communication and feedback
- Dealing with change
- Fostering teamwork
- Team celebration

Retention Initiatives   Retention is something that can be addressed like other HR issues. It needs focus and definition. It needs content in business case terms. Then, it needs to be addressed with goals and action planning.

Other Retention Practices   Providing these things can go a long way toward producing better retention results:

- Clear and consistent job expectations
- Supervision
- Training and development
- Promotional opportunities
- Recognition
- Respect
- Perceived equity

Evaluating Retention

Of course, the most obvious means of evaluating a retention program is to monitor the retention rate. That can be done for the organization as a whole or for components like departments, divisions, or service units. Another method for evaluating retention programs is to conduct exit interviews with people who are leaving the payroll. The reasons why they are leaving are really important for survey input. Stay interviews are another source for information. These types of interviews survey key employees and what is causing them to stay with the organization. Analysis of those pieces of intelligence can help identify weaknesses in the employer's organization that can be fixed to bring positive improvement in retention. In the end, it is employees who decide to stay or go. It is up to us as HR professionals to influence their decision to the fullest extent possible.

Retention Measurements   Employee retention is the positive side of employee turnover. You will recall that turnover costs can be computed and, over time, can give an indication of the impact your retention programs may be having. Therefore, employee turnover is a solid indicator for retention. Absenteeism is another such indicator. Employees who are absent a lot tend to have a lower sense of dedication to their work. Production levels are another indicator of retention program results. Look around, and you will find many more.

Evaluating Employee Engagement

So, you have conducted your employee survey, analyzed the results, and implemented your action plan to improve employee engagement. Ultimately, conducting another employee survey can give you more data about how far you have come in your employee engagement efforts.

Measuring Engagement

Employee engagement is measurable, just like other HR variables are measurable. Remember, if you can't measure it, you shouldn't be spending time on it. There is no specific metric called *employee engagement*. We use substitutes based on indicators that employee engagement is rising or falling. Those indicators can be measured. They revolve around what happens in the workplace when employees are happy with their work versus when they are not happy with their work. Absenteeism and turnover are two key variables in that regard. Earlier in this chapter we cited nine outcomes that can represent the effectiveness of an employee engagement program.

Engagement Metrics

To measure your results, you need to have a "stake in the ground" from which to stretch your tape. Before you begin the program, take a reading of things such as your absenteeism rate, turnover rate, product/supplies shrinkage, accident rates, customer metrics, quality scores, and productivity rates. Then, once your program is implemented and given time to work, take the same measurements again. That will tell you with empirical clarity how your program is doing.

Functional Area 4: Learning & Development

Here is SHRM's BASK definition: "Learning and Development activities enhance the knowledge, skills, abilities and other characteristics (KSAOs) and competencies of the workforce to meet the organization's current and future business needs."[78]

Key Concepts

- Needs analysis types (for example, person, organizational, training, cost-benefit) and techniques (for example, surveys, observations, interviews)

- Learning and development program design and implementation (for example, ADDIE model of analysis, design, development, implementation and evaluation, successive approximation model, action mapping, Bloom's taxonomy)

- Adult learning theories (for example, learning everywhere model, visual, auditory, and kinesthetic learning styles, 7-20-10 model)

- Learning and development approaches and techniques (for example, e-learning, just-in-time learning, micro-learning, blended learning, self-paced learning, self-directed learning, experiential learning, peer-to-peer training, webinars, gamification, infographics, podcasts, rotational programs)

- Developmental assessments (for example, 360-degree assessments, simulations, high-potential assessments, personality assessments, skills assessments, competency assessments)

- Goal-setting best practices (for example, individual development pans, specific, measurable, achievable, relevant and time-based [SMARTER] goals)

- Career development techniques (for example, career pathing, career mapping, mentorship, cross-training, on-the-job training, apprenticeship, job expansion, job enlargement)

- Knowledge-sharing techniques and facilitation (for example, knowledge maps, knowledge cafes)

- Leadership development and planning (for example, high-potential development programs, stretch assignments)

- Approaches to coaching and mentoring (for example, formal and informal mentorship programs, executive coaching, encouraging a growth mindset)

- Learning and development technologies (for example, learning management systems, artificial intelligence, virtual reality, chatbots)

The following are the proficiency indicators that SHRM has identified for Learning & Development:

For All HR Professionals	For Advanced HR Professionals (SCP Exam)
Uses best practices to evaluate data on gaps in employees' competencies and skills	Designs and oversees efforts to collect data on critical gaps in employees' competencies and skills
Uses best practices to develop and deliver learning and development activities that close gaps in employees' competencies and skills	Provides guidance to identify and develop critical competencies that meet the organization's talent needs
Uses all available resources (for example, vendors) to develop and deliver effective learning and development programs	Monitors the effectiveness of programs for emerging leaders and leadership development
Creates internal social networks (such as employee resource groups) to facilitate knowledge sharing among employees	Creates long-term organizational strategies to develop talent
Creates individual development plans (IDPs) in collaboration with supervisors and employees	Creates strategies to ensure the retention of organizational knowledge
Administers and supports programs to promote knowledge transfer	

The key function of learning and development plays a vital role for an organization. HR professionals lend their expertise and guidance to enhance the capabilities of employees, aligning their contributions with organizational goals. HR professionals will use their understanding of learning techniques and theories to assess, design, and implement training and learning activities as well as evaluate them to develop the workforce for the organization's needs today and in their future.

Learning and Development in Today's Organizations

While the fundamental underpinnings of the learning organization remain aligned to Peter Senge's five disciplines,[79] approaches to organizational learning are changing.

A shrinking supply of leaders is driving these changes, in part because of the aging of the "baby boomers," an increasing need to constantly develop and train workers to meet the demands of constantly evolving technology, a growing global marketplace, and issues of reducing turnover as employees seek environments better aligned with their personal values, such as the desire for more flexibility.

A 2014 survey by the Brandon Hall Group[80] states that more than 50 percent of the companies studied had examined their learning strategy less than twice in 5 years, rendering learning, for the most part, stagnant.

This wake-up call has propelled new interest in organizational learning techniques, the most powerful being the use of mobile learning solutions, including mobile learning apps and mobile performance web-based sites. Mobile learning approaches meet the need for global accessibility for employees and excite greater engagement. Current research reveals that only between 4 and 10 percent of companies have adopted these technologies despite the obvious advantages they would bring to attracting and retaining outstanding talent and addressing the increasing demands of the global marketplace.

Further, many companies have only nominally adopted social media tools as a way to enhance continuous learning for their employees. The most powerful of these tools—video and microblogs—are the least used! Less effective tools such as discussion forums are often thought sufficient.

Younger employees expect the latest technologies that allow for flexibility in communication; this group will ultimately be the new breed of leaders needed for sustained business success. Traditional approaches to learning alone cannot inspire employee engagement and retention.

Factors Affecting Learning and Development

Learning doesn't happen in a vacuum. Adult learning takes place in the midst of what is taking place in our personal lives, our work lives, and the stresses associated with both of those environments.

The Learning Organization and Organizational Learning Organizational learning is the process of improving actions through greater knowledge and understanding. Learning organizations are those that support the learning and development of organization members.

Talent Management Talent management is the forecasting of future people required by organizational needs and then developing plans for meeting those needs.

Knowledge Management Knowledge management involves actions that capture, develop, share, and effectively use organizational knowledge. According to the University of North Carolina at Chapel Hill, organizational knowledge includes on-the-job discussions, formal apprenticeships, discussion forums, corporate libraries, professional trainings, and mentoring programs.

Competency Models Competency models identify the specific competencies needed in each job within the organization. They emphasize basic competencies, or those that are important to everyone in the field, and areas of expertise, which are the specialized knowledge and actions required by specific roles. Sophisticated organizations develop databases that contain standardized competency lists for each job within the organization. When searching for candidates, the organization uses these competencies to advertise for candidates and screen applicants.

Impact of Globalization Globalization impacts training and development for the simple reason that there is an impact on the organization's competitiveness in the marketplace. When call center staffs are better trained in language skills related to their target audience, the company can achieve a better reputation for support efforts. When sales staff is better trained in cultural expectations for personal interactions, the revenue produced can increase. These are issues that must first be identified and then addressed in the training and development plans of the organization.

Cultural Issues   Learning environments must allow for people to practice and make mistakes. Some high-context cultures place extraordinary importance on expressions and body language during interactions. People in those cultures will be hesitant to practice their learning if they are afraid of making a mistake. Convincing them that mistakes are not only accepted but also expected can take some time. It is wise to explore all cultural issues that will impact a training and development program before implementation begins.

Global Talent Management   There are global implications in talent management because there are cultural differences among global work locations. Cultural differences influence learning and development efforts. They can impact the learning process (expectations for promptness) and the achievement of training objectives (management of confrontation issues). How talent is managed is impacted by the training and development programs available for people within an organization (for example, growing talent internally versus shopping for talent in the open job market).

Adult Learning

Adult learning principles have a single-track focus: trainability. Trainability is concerned with the readiness to learn and its associated motivation. Andragogy is the study of how adults learn, and it is based on five assumptions about learning in adults versus children. As people mature, they shift to the following:

- **Self-concept**   Their beliefs about themselves move toward becoming more self-directed and self-sufficient.
- **Experience**   They accumulate more experience that they tuck away and can access in learning situations.
- **Readiness to learn**   They adjust to a readiness state of learning because of developmental requirements for their stage of life and social roles (for example, parent, homeowner).
- **Orientation to learning**   They shift from subject-focused to problem-focused learning that has immediate applicability.
- **Motivation to learn**   Motivation for learning comes from an internal source rather than external.

As training programs are being designed and delivered, these needs of adult learning should be incorporated. Real-world examples and emphasis on how the training is going to be immediately applied are helpful.

Understanding the Adult Learner

All adults have a particular learning style that best suits their ability to learn. Understanding these learning styles will assist you in the creation of a learning environment within your organization, allowing you to accommodate each style with the delivery of training.

Additionally, as a presenter or trainer, knowing your own learning style will enhance your ability to adjust your preference of delivery methods so you won't fall into the comfort of just your style and can shift your delivery to meet the needs of all participants.

Also, knowing your own learning style will assist you in your career with problem-solving, conflict management, negotiations, teamwork, and career planning.

There are three primary learning styles: auditory, visual, and kinesthetic.

- *Auditory learners* process information best by hearing it, so they tend to benefit most from a lecture style. Present information by talking so they can listen. Auditory learners succeed when directions are read aloud, or information is presented and requested verbally because they interpret the underlying meanings of speech through listening to tone of voice, pitch, speed, and other nuances.

- *Visual learners* gather information best by seeing it, so rely upon viewing a presentation style: "Show me and I'll understand." These learners do best when seeing facial expressions and body language. It helps them understand content of what is being taught because they think in pictures, diagrams, charts, videos, computer training, and written directions. These students will value to-do lists, flip charts, and written notes. They need and want to take detailed notes to absorb the information.

- *Kinesthetic learners* are also called *tactile learners* because they absorb material best when touching it. They learn via a hands-on approach and prefer to explore the physical aspects of learning. Sitting for long periods of time is difficult for these learners because they need activity to learn. Kinesthetic learners are most successful when totally engaged with the learning activity such as in role playing, practicing, and with topics that can use the senses of feeling and imagining. These learners can benefit by having flashcards to hold. In a testing center, these learners would do well to move their mouse over the words as they read them.

Active Learning and Retention

The National Training Laboratories in Bethel, Maine have conducted studies on the subject of learning and retention.[81] Table 4-10 reflects the retention rates measured for each of several different types of learning methods.

Greater retention comes with greater participation in the learning process—a lesson that should not be lost to any professional trainer.

Table 4-10
Average Learning
Retention Rates

Average Learning Retention Rates*		
Teaching Method	**Method**	**Retention**
Passive teaching	Lecture	5 percent
	Reading	10 percent
	Audiovisual	20 percent
	Demonstration	30 percent
Participatory teaching	Group discussion	50 percent
	Practice	75 percent
	Teaching others	90 percent

*Adapted from National Training Laboratories, Bethel, Maine

Obstacles to Learning

According to K. P. Cross, there are three barriers to adult participation in learning:[82]

- **Situational**   Those that arise from one's situation or environment at a given point
- **Institutional**   Those practices and procedures that exclude or discourage adults from participating in organized learning activities
- **Dispositional**   Those related to the attitudes and self-perceptions about oneself as a learner

Learning Styles

Besides having different learning preference styles, adults also learn at different rates. This is referred to as *learning curves* (see Figure 4-15). A learning curve is a graphical representation of the increase of learning (vertical axis) with the experience (horizontal axis). The following are the factors that determine how quickly an adult will learn:

- The person's motivation for learning
- The person's prior knowledge or experience

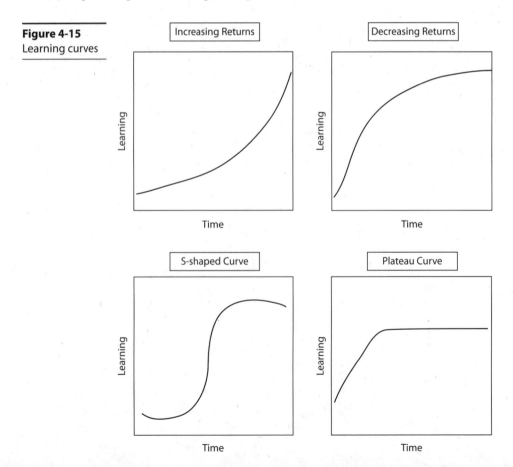

Figure 4-15
Learning curves

- The specific knowledge or task that is to be learned

- The person's aptitude and attitude about the knowledge or skill to learn

- **Increasing returns**   This is the pattern that comes into play when a person is learning something new. The start of the curve is slow while the basics are being learned. The learning increases and takes off as knowledge or skills are acquired. This curve assumes that the individual will continue to learn as time progresses. An example would be when an IT programmer needs to learn a new coding language. Learning will be slow at first until they grasp the new coding protocol, and after mastering the basics, the learning becomes easier and/or quicker as they learn more about the coding language.

- **Decreasing returns**   This pattern is when the amount of learning increases rapidly in the beginning and then the rate of learning slows down. The assumption with this learning curve is that once the learning is achieved, the learning then stops. This occurs with routine tasks learning and is the most common type of learning curve. An example is when a data entry clerk learns how to enter a sales order—the learning is complete.

- **S-shaped**   This learning curve is a blend of the increasing and decreasing returns curves. The assumption with this learning curve is that the person is learning something difficult, such as problem solving or critical thinking. Learning may be slow at the beginning until the person learning becomes familiar with the material, and at that point, learning takes off. The cycle continues with a slow to faster progression as new material is presented. An example of this is when a production lead is trained on new equipment, yet this equipment has not been utilized in the production of the product before. There might be trial and error for adjustments until the new production equipment is working as expected and is adjusted to the new product. Then, when another product is introduced, the equipment and process need adjusting again until everything works smoothly.

- **Plateau curve**   Just as the name suggests, learning on this curve is quick in the beginning and then flattens or plateaus. The assumption is that the plateau is not permanent and that with additional coaching, training, and support, the person learning can ramp up again. With this curve, it can be frustrating to the learner if they are not getting the support and additional training needed to master the task. An example of the plateau curve is a salesperson who has met quotas in the past, and when a new line of equipment is introduced into the product line, the salesperson is provided a minimal level of training/knowledge about it but not enough training to answer all the questions of the prospective customers. The anticipation of additional sales with the new product is not being achieved because the salesperson requires more training to pitch the new product and convince the customer to purchase it.

Training and Development

Large and many medium-sized employers have one group dedicated to employee training and development. When it doesn't make good economic sense to have a staff dedicated to that function, the programs required for employee training can be purchased "by the seat" from outside consulting organizations, law firms, or industry associations.

Training Design and Development (ADDIE Model)

Originally, this model was developed by Florida State University to explain instructional systems development (ISD) for military applications. It has since been adopted by many in the world of training development. ADDIE, as it is known, stands for Analyze, Design, Develop, Implement, and Evaluate. In practice, evaluation can happen at each of the four primary stages of activity. Also, modifications of revisions to the training program can result from each evaluation undertaken.

Analysis

In this phase, data is received and collected to identify where there may be a lack of productivity or gaps in desired performance. Individually, or within groups, this assessment will point the way to what specific knowledge, skills, and abilities are lacking and need to be addressed for training and development objectives.

Cultural Influences on Analysis   Culture is a two-edged sword. There is the culture of the organization that explains values and norms for behavior. Then there is the culture of each individual employee's background. People who come from America are going to see things differently from those who come from Brazil, India, or Russia. Cultural experiences may easily influence how employees behave on the job, and it is the task of the training organization to create the ability to merge the organization's culture with employee backgrounds to accomplish the organizational objectives.

Design

Training design is the response to the gap analysis performed in the first stage of the ADDIE model. The initial information from the assessment phase is decided upon for course content, delivery methods, and tactics for delivery. The result is an outline of what the training design will be and the order of presentation.

Goals and Objectives   Each training effort should begin with a statement of objectives. These objectives should answer the question, "What will participants be able to do when they have completed the training?" Identifying those specific goals will enable the subsequent creation of training content, including experiential exercises.

Cultural Influences on Design   Culture can play an important role in the design of training programs when it is known that a large portion of the training participant population will be from a specific cultural background. Customer service representative training may need to explain the reasons why customers in the United States want to have specific appointments made for repair technician visits. In other cultures, specific appointments are not an expectation.

Development

Development of training materials is the phase when pencil meets the paper and actual training materials and coursework are created. Courses and training materials may already be available off the shelf, or a customized or modified creation may occur. For training that is highly specific and customized to the organization, a course may be developed from scratch to fit the specific objectives to reach the desired outcome, such as in a new product launch for a product that has never existed. An example might be when the Apple Watch was introduced.

Learning Activities   Development can produce training that makes use of lectures, small-group exercises, large-group exercises, individual study and feedback, various audiovisual contributions, and other such techniques for getting participants involved with the learning experience.

Training Delivery   There is no one perfect teaching method for every situation. In fact, the method that should be used will depend on the training circumstances and the material being covered. There are teacher-centered instructional methods and learner-centered instructional methods. Instructional methods are the way learning materials are presented to students.

Self-Directed Study   Self-directed study, called *auto didacticism,* involves the learner making decisions about what to study and when to study it. Often, people who are self-studying will seek instruction from experts, teachers, parents, friends, or other community members.

Instructor-Led Training   Sometimes called *classroom training,* this model requires an instructor at the "head of the class" presenting learning material and leading learning exercises.

On-the-Job Training   Learning how to perform specific job functions or how to use equipment and tools required on the job is done on a day-to-day basis in this form of training. Often, on-the-job training involves a supervisor or co-worker showing and then supervising a new worker as tasks are learned and practiced.

Blended Learning   Blended learning involves the use of both classroom instruction and computer-based instruction programs. This has become a more popular form of learning since the dawn of the twenty-first century brought an expanded array of computer-based training programs. It may also refer to a combination of self-directed study and instructor-led training.

Learning Tools   Devices and systems used during the learning process are referred to as *learning tools.* They rely on computer technology.

E-learning   E-learning involves the use of electronic systems in the learning process. Computers and computer-based instructional programs are referred to collectively by the term *e-learning.*

Learning Portals   These are websites that act as repositories for training materials. They may be reference materials or entire training courses.

Learning Management Systems As defined by Wikipedia, learning management systems (LMSs) are "software applications for the administration, documentation, tracking, reporting and delivery of electronic educational technology education courses or training programs."

Webinars These are Internet-based seminars conducted using an instructor presentation, usually accompanied by visual aids such as slideshows using PowerPoint or another similar program.

Mobile Learning Mobile learning involves the use of tablet computers and smartphones to access training materials or course content along with reference materials important to the learning process. They can be used anywhere there is a phone or Internet connection.

Virtual-World Simulations As applied to the work environment, this type of learning is done by using replications of real-world conditions. Flight simulators are a good example. They offer what appears to be a real airplane cockpit with all the controls and gauges. Computers can be used to simulate actual flying conditions and interject scenarios that should best be practiced in training rather than when the plane is actually flying.

Social Media Internet sites such as Facebook, Instagram, YouTube, LinkedIn, and Twitter, among others, can be learning tools. These services allow the posting of documents, videos, and photos so students can share information and seek feedback about inquiries.

Cultural Influences on Development This is the extent to which culture plays a role in vocational training as it is related to values, expectations, and norms. It has been said that adult development (training) is influenced to a large degree by the cultural background of each individual participant. An example is an expectation for promptness. Training participants are expected to be prompt in their American classroom attendance, yet the same is not always true in other cultures.

Implementation

Once training is designed and constructed, the next phase involves putting it to use.

Pilot Testing This involves a presentation of the training program, with all materials collected to support the program. Someone is designated to observe and take notes about what portions of the program worked well and where there were problems with the materials or presentation. It is difficult for instructors to fill this role, so it is normally filled by the training developer/writer or someone else who is versed in training development and delivery.

Content Revisions Following the pilot test, there is a review of the problems that occurred in the program. Those instances where alterations are needed can be identified and changes made so the problems will not occur in future applications of the training.

Translation and Interpretation When training will be offered to multilingual audiences, it is necessary to translate the materials into the languages to be used. It is also important to review those translations to be sure the interpretations of the wording used will be acceptable and appropriate. Words and terms used in one culture are not always acceptable in a different culture.

Instructor Selection   Instructor selection is the identification of the person who will lead the training program. What level of instructor skills are required to present the training successfully? Are facilitation skills more important than skills in reading instructions? Candidate recruiting, screening, and selection are all part of this step in the process.

Logistical Considerations   What facilities are required? Will training need to be held in a classroom? Will Internet connections be required? Will the instructor be needing a computer? What about distribution of course materials? All these fall into the logistical category for consideration.

Announcing, Implementing, and Supporting   Once the program is prepared and ready for implementation, it must be announced to the target population so people who need the training can be selected for participation. There are issues of participant applications and registration to be handled. Also, there are support issues associated with tracking attendance during the program, logging grades, and staffing of any training exercise that is critical to the program.

Evaluation

Evaluation means grading. There may or may not be a pass-fail condition for the training program, but there will almost always be a requirement to track some form of evaluation for participants.

Evaluation Methods: Kirkpatrick's Four Levels   Donald Kirkpatrick was a professor emeritus at the University of Wisconsin. He first published his Four-Level Training Evaluation Model in 1959. The model was updated in 1975 and again in 1994 when he published his "Evaluating Training Programs."[83] The following are the four levels of evaluation he identified:

- **Reaction**   Measuring how participants react to the training
- **Learning**   Measuring how much a participant's knowledge has increased because of the training
- **Behavior**   Measuring how participant behavior has changed several weeks following the training
- **Results**   Measuring the outcomes, benefits, or results of the training (for example, increased retention, increased production, higher morale, reduced waste, increased sales, higher quality ratings, return on investment)

Computing the Return on Investment of Training   Return on investment (ROI) is determined as follows:

- Determine the total cost of training (for example, training development cost, resources cost, salaries of instructors, and participants).
- Determine the total value of the benefits achieved by the training (for example, increased production, lower waste).
- Determine the net benefit by subtracting the cost from the benefits.

- Determine the percentage of benefits over cost by dividing the cost into the net benefits.
- Multiply the result by 100 to restate the result as a percentage.

$$\text{Total Dollar Benefits} - \text{Cost of Training} = \text{Net Benefits}$$
$$(\text{Net Benefits} / \text{Costs}) \times 100 = \text{ROI of Training}$$

Career Development

Career development is the lifelong individual process that involves planning, managing, learning, and transitions at all ages and stages in work life. In organizations, it is an organized approach used to match employee goals with the business's current and future needs. An individual's work-related preferences and needs continuously evolve throughout life's phases. At the same time, organizations are also continuously adapting to economic, political, and societal changes.

Managing Career Development

There are two processes in career development: career planning and career management. With career planning, the focus is on the individual. Career management has its focus on the organization.

In career planning, assessing an individual's skills, talents, experiences, and potential abilities occurs to give direction to a person's career. HR professionals typically assist with these activities, but many self-assessment instruments are available online for individuals to use.

With career management, this involves implementing and monitoring employee career paths at an organizational level. The individual employee is actively involved; however, the organization is typically providing the development programs and opportunities associated with internal career progression opportunities and succession planning. The intention with career management from the organizational perspective is to assist with aligning existing workforce talent with new business objectives, to create an atmosphere of positive morale, and to retain needed talent.

Roles in Career Development

It is not just the individual employee and HR involved in career development. The direct line of management and the organization's leaders have a role to play, too.

Individuals bear the primary responsibility for their own career. Today, individuals are required to be proactive in planning their career progression and not rely on an organization to direct their career path. Being keenly aware of current assessed traits and skills, along with the needs for increased knowledge, skill, and experience associated with the individual's career ambitions, is largely the responsibility of an individual employee. Figure 4-16 shows the stages of an individual's career development.

That said, managers and supervisors perform four roles in assisting employees with their career development:

- **Coach**   Listening, clarifying
- **Appraiser**   Giving feedback, clarifying performance standards

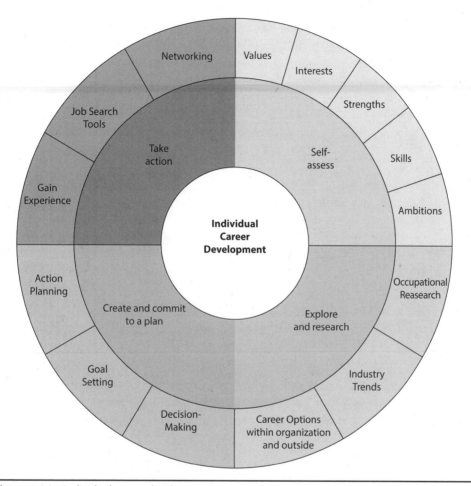

Figure 4-16 Individual career development

- **Advisor**   Suggesting options, making recommendations
- **Referral agent**   Consulting with employees on action plans and linking them to organizational resources

Forms of Career Development

Many large organizations create full-fledged career development programs. Some will be self-paced and require individual employees to opt in, and some are created with particular objectives in mind, such as management development programs, where high-potential employees are invited to participate. A typical model for a career development program will include the following stages:

- **Occupational preparation**   This stage is where occupations are assessed, an occupation is decided upon, and necessary education and skill levels are pursued.

- **Organizational entry**   This is the stage where a person obtains and decides on job offers from organizations they want to work for or internal changes within a current organization.

- **Early career establishment**   In this phase, an employee learns a new job, along with organizational norms and rules for fitting into the job, company, or industry. An employee gains work experience and career skills.

- **Midcareer**   In this phase, an employee evaluates their career objectives, with an understanding of their current life situation, and may choose to shift career direction.

- **Late-career**   In this last phase of career development, employees focus on retirement planning and thinking about their career legacy. Their choices in this phase are hugely different from the other career phases. They are more concerned with life considerations such as the hours they want to work and the extra effort they may want to provide, or what work assignments may cause additional mental stress. Climbing a career progression ladder is not normally in their career plans at this phase, yet mentoring employees in early career phases would be.

NOTE   By understanding the focus of each stage, HR professionals are better equipped to prepare and manage the transitions that employees will experience.

Employee Self-Assessment Tools   Coupled with the direct supervisory management evaluation, many employees are asked to self-assess their performance. This approach assists with creating a truly two-way dialogue in the evaluation interview and offers an opportunity for the employee to provide their own perception of their performance. Additionally, it engages employees in a proactive means of creating goals and objectives, along with triggering a discussion about career development. Figure 4-14 provides an example of a self-assessment—both a category rating along with open-ended questions to elicit a narrative commentary.

Apprenticeships   These are programs that allow untrained individuals to enter a trade or profession through formal on-the-job training, classroom training, and coaching programs. They are usually followed by journey-level status once conditions for ending the apprenticeship have been met. Journey-level status traditionally allows an individual to move from location to location or employer to employer within the trade, acknowledged as a skilled technician or professional. Trade unions often offer apprenticeship programs for electricians, plumbers, carpenters, and the like.

Job Rotation, Enlargement, and Enrichment   Job rotation involves an individual spending time in each of several job positions. The objective is to gain experience in each type of work but not to become an expert in any of them. Rotating jobs as an engineering technician, for example, might involve some time working on projects in civil engineering, electrical engineering, or mechanical engineering. Most fast-food businesses use job rotation with their staff. One shift an employee may take orders at the counter, the next shift they may only cook the French fries, and a third shift they might cook the meat patties.

Job enlargement involves taking on more work of the same type, perhaps additional client or customer assignments, while performing the same type of work for each one. Job enrichment involves taking on added responsibilities, often managerial in nature, expanding the job assignment's impact. As an example, a traffic enforcement police officer could take on the responsibility for investigating traffic accidents within a given geography.

Projects, Committees, and Team Participation Assignments to special projects, committees, and designated teams can provide excellent opportunities for growth in a career. These types of experiences can provide developmental opportunities helping an individual get ready for promotions or other assignments with greater responsibility. These are usually temporary assignments. Also, they offer exposure to parts of the organization or responsibilities that the individual will need to succeed in the next job assignment.

Internal Mobility There are often opportunities within an employer's organization that can be used for employee career development. They include the following:

- **Promotions** Promotions are usually defined in government regulations as a job move that involves an increase in job responsibility and an increase in compensation. Employers sometimes take issue with that definition and create their own.

- **Demotions** When an employee has difficulty performing well at a given level of responsibility, it is sometimes necessary to reduce that responsibility level by moving them to a lower-level job. Demotions are also frequently involved in the disciplinary process as an option that precedes termination of employment.

- **Transfers** Transfers are normally lateral movements from one job to another at the same level of responsibility and compensation.

- **Relocations and international assignments** Relocations are geographical movements from one job to another that can help career development by providing experiences that will be necessary when the incumbent is promoted to a new level of responsibility. Relocations may be required because the job assignments are not offered at the current work location. International assignments are also career enhancing because they offer exposure to new cultures and new employment challenges.

- **Dual career ladders** Companies offering dual career ladders allow mobility for employees without requiring that they be placed into the managerial enclave. Mostly associated with technical, medical, engineering, and scientific occupations, this type of program is a way to advance employees who are not interested in pursuing a management track. These individuals exhibit one or more of the following characteristics:

  - Have substantial technical or professional expertise beyond the basic levels

  - Have licensure or required credentials

  - Are known for innovation

  - May or may not be well-suited for management or leadership roles

An objective within a dual career ladder development program is to increase value to the organization, enabling the organization to increase employee compensation to improve employee retention and satisfaction. Lateral movement may occur within a dual career ladder program such as team membership, internal consultative roles, mentorships, or larger facility rotation. Figure 4-17 shows an example of a dual career ladder.

Individual Coaching/Counseling   When an individual is identified as someone who could advance to the executive level, it is sometimes helpful to provide individual coaching and/or counseling to them. This process can assist people in identifying their developmental needs and providing the skill development and practice necessary for achieving the desired level of performance.

Mentoring   Assignments that involve mentoring other individuals offer involvement with responsibility for the success of other people within the organization. Supporting those who seek to develop their job skills and helping them advance can be a growth experience for the mentor.

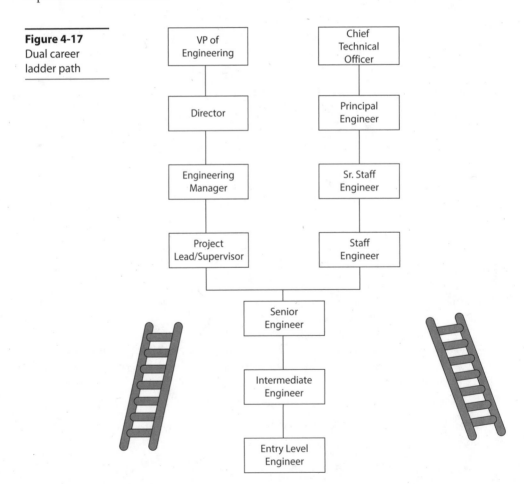

Figure 4-17
Dual career
ladder path

Universities, Colleges, Associations, Continuing Education Programs   There are countless programs at universities, colleges, and continuing education curricula that can support employee developmental efforts. It is possible for employers to encourage participation, with the employee underwriting the cost of such programs or the employer sponsoring employees in such programs. There are longer term degree programs, and there are certificate programs that generally tend to be shorter term. Executives will sometimes participate in advanced training for a few weeks or months to gain exposure to innovative theories and methods of management. Networking among executives can be advantageous in itself, offering valuable contacts at other employer organizations that can be accessed later.

Career Development Trends

The single biggest career trend in the last 10 years is that employees are taking responsibility for their own career development. What used to be left to managers and executive committees is now firmly placed in the lap of each individual employee. Employers are looking for problem-solvers. Volunteering to work with a difficult major customer to satisfy their needs can be a significant career development step. Things don't move in traditional paths anymore. Breaking ground with new jobs, task force membership, and difficult job assignments are all part of career development efforts for individuals who can solve problems for the employer.

Some contemporary trends in career development include the following:

- **Multiple jobs and careers**   Moving from one specialty to another to develop experience

- **Greater individual responsibility**   Moving from one job to another to accept greater responsibility (for example, going from managing a small hotel to managing a large hotel)

- **Nontraditional employment**   Working in jobs that have been traditionally done by the other sex (for example, airline pilot, nurse, secretary, truck driver)

- **Temporary contract and contingent work**   Developing experience through brief job assignments in various, untried subject areas or levels of responsibility

Developing Leaders

Leadership skills can be developed within existing employees. Many people can be taught to be leaders. This section discusses how that happens.

Leadership Development

Traditional leadership development programs have not been replaced. Instead, they have been polished and modified. The key to leadership success is that other people are willing to follow.

Organizational Perspective   From the employer perspective, leaders are essential to ensure the success of the organizational mission. Someone decides what the objective is for the current period. It might be a financial objective (returning 7 percent to stockholders through dividend distribution) or an organizational growth objective (opening a new branch in Chicago). With the objective in sight, leaders are needed to create the atmosphere for other people to provide support to the collective effort aimed at reaching the objective. The key to leadership is that others willingly volunteer their efforts each day.

Individual Perspective   From the individual perspective, leadership can be developed by identifying someone senior in the organization who can provide good counsel and advice as a mentor. Seek out and establish that mentor relationship. Solicit feedback and suggestions both before and after decisions are made and plans implemented.

Not all executives are successful, however. For a study on what can sometimes happen, refer to *Why Smart Executives Fail* by Sydney Finkelstein. It includes "Seven Habits of Spectacularly Unsuccessful People."[84]

HR's Role   HR professionals can facilitate leader development by coordinating mentoring programs, establishing and monitoring succession plans, and identifying and fulfilling training needs for employees identified for leadership development.

Obstacles to Leadership Development   The single biggest obstacle to leadership development is lack of senior management support for the effort. When senior executives fail to actively support the program, lower-level managers and supervisors will recognize that the program has a lower level of importance to the organization. In the end, what the boss wants to have happen will happen. Should leadership development not be on that list of what the boss wants, then leadership development will not happen.

Emotional Intelligence and Leadership Development   According to the American Society for Training and Development (ASTD), leaders "need to be self-aware of their own emotions and clearly understand their strengths and weaknesses. This understanding helps them stay in control of situations and avoid emotionally charged behaviors and decisions."[85]

Assessing Leadership Development Needs

The Center for Creative Leadership has offered some insight into competencies associated with organizational leadership (see Table 4-11).[86]

Leading the Organization	Leading Others	Leading Yourself
• Being a quick learner	• Building collaborative relationships	• Balancing personal life and work
• Change management	• Compassion and sensitivity	• Career management
• Decisiveness	• Confronting problem employees	• Composure
• Strategic perspective	• Employee development	• Culturally adaptable
• Strategic planning	• Inspiring commitment	• Self-awareness
	• Leading employees	• Taking initiative
	• Participative management	
	• Putting people at ease	
	• Respect for differences	

Table 4-11   Selected Leadership Competencies

Assessment Tools   A wide range of assessment tools are available for determining leadership skills.

Inventories   Inventories are testing devices that measure the quantity of leadership skills an individual displays. Questions pose hypothetical stories and ask the individual to rank responses or identify the most appropriate response in those circumstances. Inventories can be scored and scores compared to successful "norm groups." Multiple media presentations can be used in conducting inventory analysis. Written materials and video and audio recordings can present various scenarios for consideration. These tools are usually developed by psychologists who have studied the creation of these measurement devices.

Leadership Work Samples, Simulations, and Assessment Centers   The following are examples:

- **Assessment centers**   Actual work examples can be helpful in identifying leadership skills and skill development needs. They offer the individual easy-to-use references to understand what has yet to be done in terms of development.

  Simulations are quite like assessment center exercises. They construct artificial circumstances in which the individual must react to organizational situations. By practicing leadership approaches to these simulated conditions, the individual can gain feedback about successful behaviors and polish those behaviors that have positive outcomes.

  The most sophisticated assessment tool is the skill assessment center. Developed by American Telephone and Telegraph, Inc., in the 1960s, it is based on the Management Progress Study that began in the 1950s and continued for more than 30 years. In an assessment center, candidates are placed in situations where they must solve problems individually and within group settings. During group exercises, observing experts can identify leadership behaviors that are exhibited by each candidate and compare those behaviors with those seen in a control group of successful management people at the same level in the organization. On the other end of the spectrum of assessment tools is the questionnaire that attempts to assess skills through question-and-answer format. There are still other tools that fall within that range, including professional assessment by psychologist observation. There are advantages and disadvantages for each.

- **Situational judgment tests (SJTs)**   Situational judgment tests are like inventories in that they offer hypothetical scenarios to individuals and ask for choices of various possible reactions to those scenarios. The SHRM exams include SJTs to test behavioral competencies.

- **Assessment centers and simulations**   Assessment centers and simulations require a staff of professionals who have studied norm group reactions to the exercises candidates will be asked to participate in. After establishing a reference for the norm group behaviors, the staff of observers can identify behaviors used by the candidate group and compare them to the norm.

PART II

Emotional Intelligence Tools   There are three basic types of tools for determining emotional intelligence. Self-assessment is a skill list developed by introspection of the individual. This is usually accomplished by following a prepared list of considerations. Another individual assessment is a list of skills and needs developed by someone else who observes the individual interacting in different real-life circumstances. This can be a boss, supervisor, or mentor. A formal assessment center is usually accomplished in a formal setting with other candidates and requires a professional staff member trained in observation and feedback techniques.

Leadership Development Strategies

Successful leadership development strategies are aligned closely with business strategies. When organizations build a leadership development program that supports, trains, and then selects people who drive their business strategy, the organization thrives. There are no mixed messages. Everyone at all levels hears the same thing. Business strategies are paramount, and good leaders understand that and support them.

Leadership Development Methods   There are many methods for developing leadership skills. Here are some of the more common approaches.

More-Challenging Assignments   Stretching individual high-potential employees with extra responsibilities is a good way to expand skill levels. When the assignments require leadership skills, mentorship programs, coaching, and formal training can be just what is needed to smooth the way to success in the tasks.

Risk Management   Today, risks can be salient in financial regulation, markets, and products. There are also risks in employee management, industry evolution, and technological advances. Offering opportunities to lead an organizational effort to address one or more of these risks can result in skill enhancement.

Hardship Testing   The famous American management consultant, Peter Drucker, said that there are five types of hardship that can lead to enhanced leadership skills if the manager or executive experiencing them is successful in overcoming the hardship. Career setbacks can teach self-awareness, organizational politics, and identification of what one really wants to do. Personal trauma can teach sensitivity to others, coping with events beyond one's control, perseverance, and recognition of limits. Business mistakes and failures can teach how to handle relationships with humility and how to handle mistakes. Problem employees can teach how to stand firm and improve confrontational skills. Downsizing can teach coping skills, recognition of what's important, and organizational politics.

Real-Life Problem-Solving in a Controlled Environment   When problem-solving becomes a process that allows people to grow and get better, the organization has strong leadership. When problem-solving involves chaos, there is likely a large leadership deficiency. Exposing individuals to controlled situations and coaching them through the problem-solving process in the leadership role can give the real-world experience that cannot be totally replicated any other way.

Training Training programs can improve leadership skills, particularly for those people who are just beginning their formal learning experience on the subject. Training exercises, classroom experiences, and personal interactions with other learners are all helpful in the skill development process.

Action Learning Leadership Action learning involves defining the problem, taking action to solve the problem, and then analyzing the results of that action. It is a particularly good method of leadership development when the problem-solving is being done by a team.

Global Considerations in Leadership Development

If getting work done through the efforts of others is the definition of leadership, then that process is complicated considerably when international efforts cause multiple cultures to participate in that process. Working across cultural boundaries and in synchronization with other people who have different ways of getting things done can cause steep inclines in the effort to accomplish goals.

Global Competence and Leadership Development For organizations with a presence in multiple countries, cultural impacts are present every time someone from headquarters issues a new directive. Those instructions just may not be accepted well in remote locations where cultures understand the directive differently from the understanding at headquarters. It is critical that leaders consider all those cultural influences when attempting to solve problems and steer organizational movement. Without competence in global management and the leadership skills needed to gain cooperation and ultimately success with the problem's solution, steering the organization to success will be difficult or impossible.

Globalization and Leadership Development Programs Traditionally, international companies held key decision-making power at headquarters in the home country. It was home-country executives who ascended the executive ladder. Candidates from other countries and cultures, if there even were some, were not provided an opportunity to participate in the selection process. That worked well when foreign markets were just developing.

These days, there is a move to recognize that in developed markets, it is critical to accept cultural influence in the decision-making process. In the article, "A New Era for Global Leadership Development," Bill George says, "Developing global leaders with cultural sensitivities and collaborative skills requires greater focus on emotional intelligence, self-awareness, and empowerment than on traditional management skills."[87]

Culturally Related Challenges According to the Center for Creative Leadership,[88] there are six challenges faced by multicultural, international organizations:

- Developing managerial effectiveness
- Inspiring others
- Developing employees

PART II

- Leading a team
- Guiding change
- Managing internal stakeholders and politics

There are more similarities in leader challenges from one country to another than there are differences.

Functional Area 5: Total Rewards

Here is SHRM's BASK definition: "Total Rewards refers to the design and implementation of compensation systems and benefit packages, which are used to attract and retain employees."[89]

Key Concepts

- Approaches to gathering compensation and benefits-related market and competitive intelligence (for example, remuneration surveys, labor market trends)
- Remuneration and labor market data collection, interpretation, and analysis (for example, comparable worth, benchmarking, internal alignment, external competitiveness)
- Compensation philosophies (for example, lead, lag, match, lead-lag)
- Compensation plans for common (for example, salary, cost-of-living adjustment, merit increase, bonus structure) and special workforce groups (for example, domestic workers, expatriates, executives, sales, shift workers, part-time employees)
- Leave plans and approaches (for example, paid and unpaid leave, open leave, vacation, holiday, sick, parental, bereavement, jury duty, volunteer)
- Retirement planning and benefits (for example, pension plan, savings plan)
- Other benefits (for example, disability insurance, employee assistance programs [EAPs], flexible schedules, health and financial wellness programs, life coaches, share purchase plans, housing partnership, unemployment insurance, outplacement services)
- Other compensation (for example, deferred compensation, direct and indirect compensation, stock options, tuition assistance)
- Pay practices and issues (for example, pay increases, base pay, pay levels, banding, variable pay, pay compression, pay equity, pay transparency)
- Basic accounting and financial knowledge for managing payroll (for example, direct and indirect compensation, total compensation statements)
- Total rewards metrics and benchmarks (for example, insurance participation rates, compa-ratio)

The following are the proficiency indicators SHRM has identified as key concepts:

For All HR Professionals	All Advanced HR Professionals (SCP Exam)
Collects, compiles, and interprets compensation and benefits data from various sources	Designs and oversees organizational compensation and benefits philosophies, strategies, and plans that align with the organization's strategic direction and talent needs
Implements appropriate pay, benefits, incentive, separation, and severance systems and programs	Designs and oversees executive compensation approaches that directly connect individual performance and desired behaviors to organizational success
Complies with best practices for all laws and regulations governing compensation and benefits	Ensures the internal equity of compensation systems
Differentiates between government-mandated, government-provided, and voluntary benefits approaches	Re-evaluates the organization's total rewards package regularly and adjusts as needed
Performs accurate job evaluations to determine appropriate compensation and benefits	

Compensation and benefits plans play a key role in helping to attract and retain talent. HR professionals are responsible for the development and application of an organization's compensation and benefits philosophy, along with benchmarking to determine their competitiveness in the marketplace. A total rewards program will integrate and maximize monetary compensation, benefits, and other forms of compensation that are ideally designed to retain top talent. Total rewards encompass direct and indirect remuneration approaches that employers use to attract, recognize, and retain workers.

Total Rewards and Organizational Strategy

Compensation and benefits are the lifeblood of the employment relationship between the worker and the employer. But this relationship reaches beyond the scope of compensation and benefits alone, including recognition programs and assorted fringe benefits; thus, *total rewards* has become a popular term that best defines this aspect of the employment relationship.

Direct compensation, simply referred to as *compensation,* as a strategic objective, significantly impacts all the other HR functions, including staffing, performance evaluations, training and development, and employee relations. These HR functions in turn influence compensation. Compensation affects organizational processes, job satisfaction, productivity, and turnover. Compensation must be viewed not only based on what is legal and motivating but also on the ethical basis of what is fair and just.

Key terms used in this section include the following:

- **Total rewards**   Includes six elements (compensation, benefits, work-life effectiveness, recognition, performance management, and talent development) that collectively define an organization's strategy to attract, motivate, retain, and engage employees.[90]

- **Benefits** Benefits in kind (also called *fringe benefits* and *perks*) include various types of nonwage compensation paid to employees in addition to their normal wages and salaries. Examples of these benefits include housing (employer-provided or employer-paid), group insurance (health, dental, life, and so on), disability income protection, retirement benefits, daycare, tuition reimbursement, sick leave (paid and nonpaid), vacation (paid and nonpaid), Social Security, profit sharing, funding of education, and other specialized benefits.

- **Compensation** This includes all the rewards earned by employees in return for their labor. It includes direct financial compensation consisting of pay received in the form of wages, salaries, bonuses, and commissions provided at regular and consistent intervals.

- **Perquisites** Colloquially referred to as "perks," these are benefits of a more discretionary nature. Often, perks are given to employees who are doing notably well and/or have seniority. Common perks are company cars, company-paid mobile devices, free refreshments, leisure activities on work time (golf and so on), allowances for meals, and—when multiple choices exist—first choice of job assignments and vacation scheduling.

- **Incentives** These are systems of rewarding success and effort in the workplace by allowing employees to earn awards or recognition.

Developing a Total Rewards Strategy

Employers want to attract and retain good, qualified workers who are motivated to a degree of high productivity, but employers must make compensation decisions with competing pressures. Simply paying more or providing better company benefits may make some employees happy but will, in the long term, raise labor costs and make the company less competitive.

A total rewards strategy can be described as a four-step process that consists of assessment, design, implementation, and evaluation. Several factors affect the planning and design of a total rewards strategy. As an example, if the organization operates in a union environment, the planning and design elements will be affected by collective bargaining requirements. Important HR competencies needed to develop a successful total rewards strategy include excellent interpersonal and communication skills.

Assessment The assessment stage focuses on a competent evaluation of the organization's current compensation and benefits programs, if any. Attention is paid to the effectiveness of existing programs in fulfilling their purposes in an effective manner. Employee surveys are an important mechanism to develop good information regarding employee attitudes and opinions. Surveys typically address employee pay, benefits and growth, and development issues. During this stage, current policies and practices are also examined. An important result of the assessment phase is producing an assessment report that includes information on the current status of existing compensation and benefits coupled with recommendations for changes based on the assessment findings. Ultimately, the assessment report should address the following:

- Who should be eligible for coverage?
- What behaviors of value should be rewarded?
- What type of rewards will do the best job?
- How will changes, if any, be funded?

Design   The objective of this phase is to identify the best reward strategies for the organization based on the conclusions of the assessment report. To reach this objective, a team of HR leaders and senior management should be tasked with the job of identifying the best combination of pay and benefits needed to accomplish the goals stated in the assessment report. In addition to the direct pay and benefits possibilities, the project team responsible for the design effort should also explore additional benefits such as flexible work schedules, time off, and similar options as well as personal development opportunities that can be offered, such as training and development opportunities.

Implementation   Typically, HR is heavily involved in this phase. A new rewards program needs information planning and material describing the new program's features and benefits. In many cases, additional training will be required. The success of needed changes to an organization's rewards programs is largely dependent on the image communicated to the organization's workforce.

Evaluation   An organization's ultimate responsibility is to measure the success of its new rewards programs. Even the best of plans will often require additional attention. Slight modifications may be necessary, but, barring any new unforeseen elements, diligently following these four steps should ensure a successful result.

Objectives of a Total Rewards Strategy

All organizations need to have their compensation and benefits systems support the organization's mission and strategy. Although the degree of sophistication may vary, a good total rewards strategy should hold to some basic principles. That is, in the face of competitive market pressures, all pay decisions should have the following attributes:

- **Be legal**   They must be consistent with numerous federal, state, and local laws.
- **Be adequate**   They must be large enough to attract qualified employees to join the organization and stay.
- **Be motivating**   They should provide sufficient incentives to motivate employees to perform effectively.
- **Be equitable**   Employees should feel that their compensation is internally equitable relative to other employees in the organization and externally equitable relative to employees doing similar work in other organizations.
- **Provide security**   Employees want to feel that their monthly income is secure and predictable. They need to feel that their pay is somewhat insulated from changes in employment, profitability, individual performance, and personal health.
- **Be cost-benefit effective**   The organization must administer its compensation system efficiently and have the financial resources to support it on a continuing basis.

Organizational Mission and Strategy   Larger and more mature organizations generally have a written business plan that outlines the organization's mission and strategy. Normally, the compensation and benefits system are an outgrowth of the organization's business plan in these organizations.

A basic principle is that a business must generate sufficient revenue to cover its expenses. When the demand for workers exceeds the supply, there is an upward pressure on pay levels. The degree of competition, the level of market demand, and each industry's overall characteristics influence compensation and benefits programs. Other factors such as the organization's lifecycle stage also play a role. The bottom line is that the objective is to design and implement a total rewards plan that will attract the right people to the right jobs at the right time and the right place at the right cost.

Organizational Culture   Regardless of the other factors, a compensation system must fit the organization's culture. By "organizational culture," we mean a system of shared assumptions, values, and beliefs that governs how people behave in an organization. Every organization has a distinct value for each of these characteristics, which, when combined, define the organization's unique culture. Typically, organizations take one of two basic approaches toward their employees.

Entitlement-Oriented   These companies promote a caring, protective feeling and want employees to feel they are part of the family. Sometimes called a *fairness orientation,* or emphasis on people, these companies place a high value on how their decisions affect the people in their organizations. For these companies, it is important to treat their employees with respect and dignity. These organizations feel that employees are entitled to benefits such as health care, employee assistance, or disability insurance as a condition of employment. They place less emphasis on individual contributions and more emphasis on the success of the organization as a whole.

Contribution-Oriented   These companies are more performance driven. They put greater emphasis on job performance and the contributions of individual employees. They focus on results but not so much on how the results are achieved. A company that instructs its sales force to do whatever it takes to get sales orders has a culture that places a high value on outcomes. Their compensation systems emphasize performance-based pay, incentives, and shared responsibility for benefits.

Although few organizations have a compensation system based solely on a performance approach, the trend is moving further from an entitlement approach and closer to a performance approach. Most organizations have compensation systems with elements associated with both approaches.

Workforce   A rewards program must consider the type of workforce involved. An organization with many entry-level or unskilled workers will likely have a significantly different total rewards program than an organization with mostly high-level, skilled professionals. In either case, an important tool used to measure employee attitudes and opinions is a survey.

Equity   Equity is fairness and impartiality toward all concerned, based on the principles of even-handed dealing. Equity implies giving as much advantage, consideration, or latitude to one party as it is given to another. Along with economy, effectiveness, and efficiency, equity is essential for ensuring that the extent and costs of funds, goods, and services are fairly divided among their recipients.

Pay Equity   Pay equity is not equal access to jobs offered by an employer. This is called *employment equity,* which means that women, men, and minorities have equal opportunity when applying for jobs. Nor is pay equity the fact that a person working in company X is being paid $2000 less than the person of the same gender sitting nearby for exactly the same job. This is called *internal equity* and is unrelated to employment equity. So, what does *pay equity* mean? At first, it meant as equal pay for equal work. However, as organizations tried to achieve pay equity, they quickly realized that it was difficult to compare the same two jobs and their compensation since each one comprised a different set of tasks. The difficulties experienced by organizations with this approach prompted the government to adopt the following definition: "Equal pay for different but equivalent work."

This change ensures that there is no sexist bias in the comparison of compensation so that predominantly female jobs are paid equally to predominantly male jobs of equivalent value. The change also enabled comparisons between jobs of different types but equivalent in terms of tasks. An example of this would be to compare trade and service jobs with clerical jobs of equivalent value.

Internal Equity   Internal equity is a situation that results when people feel that performance fairly determines the pay for everyone with a certain job or that relative difficulty results in appropriate differences in pay rates between jobs. Worker dissatisfaction may arise when internal equity principles aren't met. Internal equity studies analyze the nature of a particular position, including skill, effort, responsibility, and working conditions. The internal equity study determines whether there is "pay equity" between like positions. This study ensures compliance with the Federal Equal Pay Act and state laws, thereby avoiding potential lawsuits. Additionally, an internal equity study makes good managerial sense in that employee morale, and consequently productivity, will increase.

External Equity   An effective employee compensation system must balance two factors: worker motivation and labor costs. In designing a company's pay plan, you must consider external equity as well as internal equity. External equity refers to comparisons with other competitive pay structures. An employer's goal should be to pay what is necessary to attract, retain, and motivate enough qualified employees. This requires a base pay program that pays competitively. Among others, internal data such as turnover rates and exit interviews can be helpful in determining the competitiveness of pay rates.

As is true for internal equity perceptions, global pay experts indicate that employee external pay fairness perceptions mostly focus on base pay, career development opportunities, and merit increases. Personal recognition perceptions were not as prevalent as base pay, career development, and merit pay. This is probably because it is not easy in the international marketplace for most employees to compare what is done in the employee's own organization to what is done in other organizations.[91]

Pay Strategies   Employers compete with other employers whose organizations have similar products and services and employ workers with the same experience and skills

Pay Strategy	Description
Lag market	This is the choice to pay less than other competitors. It is characteristic of organizations that experience moderate to high turnover in their market. Labor costs are controlled by setting initial pay rates lower than the surrounding market. Examples: janitorial, security, and fast-food employers.
Match market	This is the choice to meet and stay current with other competitors' pay levels. Wages and benefits are comparable to the surrounding market. The objective is to match the competition. Examples: insurance, recreation, and entertainment industries.
Lead market	This is the choice to pay more than other competitors. Higher wages and better benefits are provided with the objective of attracting the best qualified candidates. The objective is to increase workplace productivity, thus besting the competition. Examples: high-tech companies and select industry leaders.
Lead-lag market	This is the choice to treat employees differently, according to their value to the organization. Positions that are defined as key to the success of the organization are afforded a lead approach, while other positions that are more routine are treated with a more cost-saving lag approach. Example: a firm that has a lead approach for its marketing and research and development functions and a lag approach for the rest of the organization.

Table 4-12   Pay Strategies

and in the same geographical area. Typically, pay strategies are chosen that will provide the best competitive advantage to the employer. These strategies can be summarized in four ways, as shown in Table 4-12.

Ultimately, an effective pay strategy must accomplish the following objectives:

- *Attract talented employees.* Rewards should be used to entice talented qualified employees to the company or position. Companies should allocate a certain amount of funds to recruiting and hiring high-caliber employees.

- *Motivate employees to perform optimally.* Most programs focus on the motivational component of rewards. They use rewards to shape employee behavior in the most desired direction. This outcome should be carefully considered when designing a rewards program.

- *Foster personal growth and development.* Rewards should be used to encourage and promote personal growth and professional development. When rewards are used to encourage employees to engage in behavior that will increase their work performance, the company ultimately benefits from a more skilled workforce.

- *Increase employee satisfaction with their work.* Rewards can promote engagement with work, resulting in increased workplace satisfaction. They can motivate an employee to persist in the face of challenges, produce creative solutions to tackling tasks, and encourage them to derive more pleasure from their work.

- *Keep talented employees from leaving.* When employees love what they do and are rewarded for their performance, they are less likely to leave a company. Keeping talented employees on board should be a priority of any company. Therefore, companies should devote the resources necessary to ensure that their rewards programs meet the needs of their most talented employees.

Global Remuneration Issues and Challenges   HR and compensation professionals in organizations that operate on a global scale often find themselves faced with the task of managing compensation practices across multiple jurisdictions on a regular basis. Many factors increase the complexity of HR operations in a global context. Not only are additional proficiencies required daily, but there is the need for more collaboration with legal, finance, accounting, tax, and local and country management, which are all key elements in the global environment.

There are two key issues to keep in mind. The concept of "at-will" employment does not generally exist outside of the United States. In the United States, barring a contract to the contrary and in a nonunionized environment, employers are free to hire, fire, and change terms and conditions of employment without notice and without reason (if it is not an unlawful reason). Outside the United States, employment is typically a matter of contract, and employers cannot unilaterally change terms and conditions of employment. This limits the ability of an employer to make any changes for its non-U.S. workforce.

Different types of employees have different protections outside the United States. In the United States, the distinctions between type of employee are driven in large part by federal and state minimum wage and overtime laws (that is, exempt versus nonexempt status). Outside the United States, the distinctions for application of collective bargaining agreements (CBAs) and local labor laws on wage rates, vacation entitlements, and the like are not tied to whether an employee is equivalent to an exempt or nonexempt employee in the United States but rather vary by levels of workers. As an example, in Italy, an executive-level employee, as defined under the applicable CBA, will have different wage entitlements than a blue-collar worker. In France, levels of remuneration are dependent on the coefficient applicable to the position. In Japan, directors can be considered nonemployees, in which case they are generally not protected under the Labor Standards Law.

This presumes that the workforce is composed of employees, as opposed to independent contractors or other contingent workers. Where a company engages nonemployee workers, issues of misclassification of contractors as employees and joint employer liability for contingent workers can arise in almost all jurisdictions, and thus compensation levels for those workers should be carefully managed.[92]

Alignment with Global Staffing   Total rewards must support global talent acquisition and management strategies. Compensation practices must support the hiring and retention of an engaged and productive workforce, domestic and global.

Howard V. Perlmutter first formulated the differences among ethnocentric, polycentric, and regiocentric staffing, with the geocentric approach to international staffing added later.

The approaches shown in Table 4-13 directly affect the strategies, policies, and practices related to global compensation and benefits.

Global Orientation	Implications for Global Compensation and Benefits Strategy
Ethnocentric Tight control of international operations, little autonomy, and compensation and benefits developed at headquarters and rolled out globally	• This leads to transfer of headquarters total compensation policies, with inadequate consideration of local legal and cultural differences. • Directives to local country management may result in outward consistency but actual rejection of headquarters' practices.
Polycentric Subsidiary treated as its own entity; local compensation and benefits policies, programs, and practices	• Local cultural and legal compensation norms are more likely to be understood and implemented. • Remuneration policies are likely to be consistent and integrated within each subsidiary. • Incentives tend to maximize achievement of local rather than global objectives.
Regiocentric Operations managed regionally; communication and coordination high within the region but less between regions	• There is greater potential for consistency of remuneration approaches within a region. The proximity of countries may lead to the perception that remuneration practices are more similar than they really are. • Regional headquarters may suffer blind spots with respect to country differences, leading to ethnocentrism at the regional level.
Geocentric Organization seen as a single international enterprise with a strategic plan that's global in orientation	• Local compensation strategies are more likely to be consistent with global policies. • A desire for too much global consistency can lead to the imposition of inappropriate policies at the local country level. • The development of consistent and equitable remuneration policies among global managers will facilitate efficient and effective transfers.

Table 4-13   Purlmutter's Global Orientation on Global Compensation and Benefits Strategy

Influencing Factors in a Global Environment   Many forces influence global remuneration. They include labor market dynamics that exist in the business; regulatory, political, and cultural differences; taxation of compensation and benefits; operational legal and reporting structures in different geographies; and the role that mobility will play in future workforce strategy and deployment. Largely driven by these operational and country specifics, strategies for compensation and benefits delivery are then often capped by market practices.

Table 4-14 describes major issues and challenges, and it notes the general implications for global HR.

Special Considerations in a Total Rewards Strategy

Two factors must be addressed as part of developing a total rewards strategy. They are PESTLE factors and the employee lifecycle.

Factor	Description	Global HR Implications
Standardization versus localization	Strategies are standardized in keeping with the organization's overall compensation and benefits philosophy. Specific practices are localized to fit the context of the country, regional, or local conditions.	Organization has a long-term plan to support the organizational compensation and benefits philosophy, but local restrictions, tax regimes, and culture are considered.
Culture	Cultural differences require that the value of compensation and benefits programs be in "the eye of the beholder." Local benefits are more highly valued. Differences are often based on deep-seated beliefs, attitudes, and values that are local in nature.	Avoids headquarters biases or replication of headquarters country policies and procedures. Involves local contacts to understand the localized usual and customary compensation and benefits practices.
Competitive labor market	Compensation and benefits required to attract and maintain talent are determined by the competitive demand for that talent. However, the competition for talent may vary across countries and regions, depending on factors such as type of talent, geographic scope of talent market, industries in which the talent may be found, and the mix of remuneration components.	Rates of pay in the relative marketplace are based on the skills needed, the demand for talent, and the best way to compensate different types of workers. Appropriate combinations of pay and benefits are offered that appeal to current or perspective employees. People are employed with similar skills. When industry-specific expertise is in short supply or competition is high, the hires on the job are retrained or coached.
Collective bargaining, employee representation, and government mandates	Certain types and categories of employees in most parts of the world are protected from actions that impact their wages and employment conditions. Unions play a strong role in many countries and sometimes include provisions for management as well as employees. Work councils (not to be confused with unions) also offer worker protections.	Comply with requirements of third-party representation. Understand the implications for minimum wages, severance packages, and pensions. Adhere to related government regulations and mandates and industry-wide collective agreements.

Table 4-14   Issues and Challenges in Global Compensation and Benefits *(continued)*

Factor	Description	Global HR Implications
Economic factors	Many differences exist from one country to the next in terms of the influence of politics and power, the distribution of wealth across a country's citizenry, the unpredictability of events (that is, rapid changes in rates of inflation and currency levels), as well as the level of unemployment or scarcity of talent.	Unofficial sources of power in a community or region and official governmental personnel may have a large impact on what is considered acceptable. Educational facilities, internal training, childcare, or other local services contribute support to the local area. Local inflation/deflation or currency fluctuations are significant factors. Contingency plans may be required to mitigate the risks associated with potential changes in economic factors.
Taxation	Tax regulations differ widely from country to country. Some countries have no income tax, while others have income tax in excess of 50 percent. Some benefits that are taxable in one country are not taxable in geographically adjacent countries, and vice versa. There are complicated and ever-changing tax compliance requirements for nationals from one country working in another.	Experts in local compensation and benefits laws and practices, as well as country taxation, may be required, particularly for long-term assignees. This includes the taxation of cash and noncash compensation, benefits, and perquisites, including what is taxed, at what rates, and at what levels. A benefit may be unacceptable depending on how it is taxed.
Laws and statutory regulations	Laws and statutory regulations impact the remuneration of employees in many areas, such as work hours and compulsory time off (paid and unpaid). • Minimum wage • Overtime • Compulsory bonuses • Employment at will • Acquired rights There are significant country-to-country variances as well as some regional and local differences.	Requires an understanding of the differences and similarities in each market. Also, it includes the ability to recognize benefits that are government-provided, mandated by the government, or chosen by the employee. Usually this involves experts in local compensation and benefits laws and regulations as well as country taxation, particularly for expatriates.

Table 4-14 Issues and Challenges in Global Compensation and Benefits

PESTLE factors address political, economic, social, technological, legal, and environmental factors that may influence an organization's total rewards strategy. The following examples describe the conditions that may impact total rewards:

• **Political** The head of government or legislative body in control most likely has a particular agenda/position on employee pay as well as executive pay. Their approach and legislation impact an organization's total rewards.

- **Economic**   A city, state, or country economy as well as the global economy impact an organization's ability to provide total rewards. Pay may be frozen, and variable compensation may not be paid.

  Poor economies stunt organizational growth and, in turn, the hiring of new talent. The positive outcome of this may be that employee retention increases because of slow job growth/few external opportunities.

  Growing and prosperous economies benefit organizational bottom lines and encourage and promote hiring but accentuate the need for employee retention as more employees will probably be in the job market and look to leave for a better opportunity.

- **Social**   Citizens have views toward organizational pay, particularly that of the C-suite and the CEO. The information on the pay of these individuals is easily accessible if the organization is publicly traded. Even though compensation committees can control and impact executive total rewards, all too often compensation for the highest levels of an organization is viewed as exorbitant and leads to negative public opinion.

  Organizations come under significant scrutiny when their fired or ousted CEO receives a significant severance package on the way out the door. Many people fail to realize that this may have been contractually negotiated as part of the pre-employment negotiations. At a minimum, this translates to an unfavorable view and perception of the organization or the board of directors.

- **Technological**   An organization's ability to automate, streamline, and improve the efficiency of many transactions that accompany total rewards—from regular, periodic base pay to tax withholding to government-mandated reporting and filing—are directly impacted by technological advances. Organizations may outsource their technology requirements to third-party vendors that develop and manage applications. However, software may also be licensed so that organizations can perform the function in-house.

  A less common approach is for companies to develop the technology themselves. This usually is because they lack the money, the expertise, and/or the ability to maintain the technology.

- **Legal**   From a legal standpoint, HR needs to make sure the organization is in compliance with local, state, federal, and, when applicable, international laws related to pay (for example, minimum pay, tax withholding rates).

  HR needs to be proficient in compliance with total rewards–related acts and legislation where the organization does business (for example, cities, states, countries), as they are charged with providing (and expected to provide) expertise, particularly in the area of compliance.

- **Environmental**   An organization's response to the natural world or geography of where jobs will be located and what the corresponding total rewards package will be. Identical job duties performed in Manhattan and Little Rock will command vastly different total reward packages.

Any of these approaches can have a significant impact on employee total rewards, much of which is highly emotional to employees.

Employee lifecycle (ELC) refers to the various stages of the employment process. It starts with recruitment and ends with separation. The various stages of the ELC call for different HR management techniques for individual employees. As an example, compensation and benefit practices are increasingly planned and managed in response to the individual employee's lifecycle stage.

Some of the more commonly recognized lifecycle stages include the following:

- **Recruitment**   The employee lifecycle begins before the individual employee is even identified. HR considerations begin when the employer begins its planning (for example, identifying the job title, job description, and corresponding pay grade with its identified pay range) and engages in its initial search for potential applicants.

- **Selection**   This is where the qualified candidate is identified and hired.

- **Orientation and Onboarding**   During this stage, the initial sharing of information about the organization happens. Culture, history, policies and practices as well as benefits enrollment are all part of orientation. Most employers agree that complete integration into the workforce is most effective when it begins at orientation and continues during the onboarding stage. This is the start of the employee settling into the job, integrating with the organization's culture, getting familiar with co-workers and management, making sure they are aware of their responsibilities, and are comfortable in their new role.

- **Position Training**   While employees are hired or promoted in large part due to their knowledge and skill set, each unique job has its own duties. What are you doing to make sure your employees understand and know how to perform those duties and recognize how their contributions fit into the overall success of the organization?

- **Development, Engagement, and Retention**   This stage is the bulk of an employee's career. Effective organizations continue with ongoing training to keep skills current and workers more engaged, leading to longer retention.

- **Succession**   An employee who stays with the employer will likely want to advance within the workplace at an average to speedy rate. Managers, supervisors, and HR practitioners must be adept at recognizing changing interests and needs and be capable of matching the organization's interests with the individual's needs and more challenging assignments.

  Typically, as individuals move through their various lifecycle stages, the value of their contributions increases along with their total rewards.

- **Separation**   Whether an employee quits, retires, or is terminated by the employer, at some point the employment relationship will end. As planning begins the employee lifecycle, planning for succession and replacement needs also is an ongoing management activity supported by HR counsel and advice that ensures the orderly positioning of the organization toward new opportunities.

Studies show that organizations that can effectively adapt to employee lifecycle changes are organizations that succeed.

Communication of the Total Rewards Strategy

A typical total rewards package can include compensation, benefits, work-life balance, performance and recognition, personal development, and career opportunities. Recent strong global competition for talent and shortages of critical-skill workers, particularly in the fast-growing economies of Asia and Latin America, have driven a surge of interest in applying core total rewards principles to designing and delivering workforce programs. Critically, the total rewards framework is grounded in three core principles of sound design and delivery:

- *Align the total rewards strategy with the organization's business strategy and related workforce goals.* Effective workforce programs are an extension of an organization's business strategy, explicitly supporting key priorities and goals, and clearly communicating the level and nature of the contribution the organization expects from its people.

- *Optimize the money spent by allocating it among the programs that matter to employees and deliver the right return while being sensitive to cost and risk objectives.* Despite the magnitude of spending on reward programs, many organizations don't consistently measure returns or clearly understand the relationship between program costs and the value employees attach to them.

- *Design, communicate, implement, and deliver rewards that drive the specific employee behaviors you need to achieve your business strategy.* Identifying the right mix is not only a function of cost versus value but also of the culture and work environment your company is building and sustaining to meet strategic goals.

The Challenges of Transparency   How much to communicate about pay is a continual debate, one for which there is no clear answer. Sometimes the decision is made for the organization if it is a government entity and full public transparency is required. Those in favor of open communication feel that unless employees understand their organization's pay system and how their pay is determined, the organization will not achieve its primary objective of supporting the achievement of strategic business objectives. However, even proponents of reward program transparency recognize that a level of employee privacy must be preserved. The result of complete openness can foster jealousy and performance problems.

Effective total rewards communications have become even more important now when employees are faced with deciding between their economic needs (that is, their pay) and the level of health and retirement benefits they would like to receive.

Today, employers have an array of communication tools to choose from. Technology enables the creation of individualized reports informing employees about reward program eligibility and payouts. Computers make the dissemination of rewards information via e-mails, websites, webinars, DVDs, and other electronic media fast and cost-effective at work, at home, and, in fact, almost anywhere. Despite this, experts agree that rewards communications are, more times than not, done poorly; for the most part, employees do not understand how they are paid and what factors determine their eligibility for most reward programs.

Effective Communication of Total Rewards Considerations that affect the effective communications of total rewards include the following:

- **Type of information** Communications can be either required or voluntary:
  - **Required communications** Laws and regulations often mandate certain communications, such as disclosure and reporting requirements associated with pension benefits plans as well as payroll record and disclosure requirements. It is the organization's responsibility to ensure compliance with these legal requirements.
  - **Voluntary communications** Legal compliance is not sufficient to achieve a full objective of employee knowledge and understanding. Organizations must go beyond the legal minimum and fashion communication policies that clearly identify the message outlining policies and procedures as well as management expectations. To be effective, these communications should be of a two-way nature as a direct link between management, HR, and the organization's employees.
- **Communication plans** The larger the organization, the greater the need for a comprehensive communications plan. A good place to start is with a SWOT analysis (strengths, weaknesses, opportunities, and threats) considering both internal and external factors. Plans vary and should be written. They may include a description of the organization's compensation strategy; its policies, practices, and procedures; and any other pertinent important information.
- **Individualized compensation and benefits statements** Total compensation statements made their appearance in the workplace during the 1990s. Sometimes they were called *employee benefit statements, hidden paycheck statements, Benefacts,* or *total reward statements.* Regardless of the name, their purpose is to show true and total compensation value to employees. This is particularly important in a world where benefit premiums continue to increase while, at the same time, many employers plan to increase salaries minimally. The net result tends to create some negativity in the workplace and grumblings of job searches. The total compensation statement can provide a reassuring picture to employees and a tangible reminder of the organization's financial commitment to its employees. Total compensation statements contribute to improved employee morale. When employers take the time to present and explain these statements to their employees, they typically improve the employees' overall perceptions of the employer by increasing awareness of the company's total employee benefits (pay and benefits) offering. Total compensation statements also help to attract and retain quality employees by identifying a more rounded picture of both the direct and indirect compensation.
- **Self-service technologies** Employee self-service (ESS) software is an HR technology tool that gives employees the power to manage their own personal data. Employee self-service applications enable employees to view and

amend personal data (such as banking details), make requests for leave, easily access corporate policies, access the employee directory, view organizational structuring, access corporate communications, and much more. This gives employees a much higher level of control over the data that pertains to them. Enabling employees to provide input into decision-making is one of the top drivers of employee engagement according to the experts. From the tactical advantages that autonomy can bring to the strategic implications of giving greater responsibility to each employee for their career direction, employee self-service technology is an incredibly powerful tool for engagement when effectively utilized. Some ESS software is designed for employees to pull up their own total compensation statement on demand, as discussed earlier.

- **Consistent key messages**   An organization spread across multiple locations requires extra effort to present a clearly communicated consistent message. This is an even greater challenge when it is a global organization. Cultures become varied; the same message can be understood in different ways depending on the cultural perspectives. As a result, there is no one way to communicate the organization's compensation and benefits strategy. This results in a number of different approaches that have one objective in common—that is, to create open, effective communications designed to send and receive a clearly understood message.

Evaluation of the Total Rewards Strategy

The last phase of implementing a total rewards program, the evaluation, often is the most overlooked phase of total rewards. In this phase, the actual results of the executed total rewards strategies are compared against the desired results. The objective of this evaluation is to show top management that the company's investment in its total rewards system has paid off. To get the most from the evaluation phase, HR should be encouraged to measure the outcomes of the executed total rewards system and to interpret the findings correctly.

Measures, Metrics, and Analytics   Three terms often play a major role in the evaluation phase:

- **Measures**   The process of collecting and tabulating data. This is a standard unit used to express the size, amount, or degree of something.

- **Metrics**   Performance parameters based on the relationship between two or more measures. Metrics are a quantifiable measure that organizations use to track, monitor, and assess the success or failure of various business processes.

- **Analytics**   Convert a metric into a decision-supporting insight. This is information resulting from the systematic analysis of data or statistics.

The following key questions must be addressed to effectively conduct a total rewards strategy evaluation:

- Is the total rewards strategy in legal compliance?
- Is the total rewards strategy compatible with the organization's mission and strategy?

- Does the total rewards strategy fit the culture?
- Is the total rewards strategy internally equitable and externally competitive?
- Can the organization afford the compensation plan as designed?

The following evaluation guidelines are offered to ensure appropriate measures, metrics, and analytics are used in the evaluation phase of a total rewards strategy:

- Align HR measurements to the organizational strategic plan.
- Measure what can help improve employee performance or make better decisions.
- Avoid the problem of gathering data solely for its own sake.

Compensation Structure

People are willing to work in exchange for rewards they receive from the work they do. The objective is to provide a balance between what work is performed and the reward received for doing the work. *Total rewards* includes the financial inducements and rewards (direct pay, cash-based incentives, and benefits) as well as nonfinancial inducements and rewards such as the value of good job content as well as a good working environment. Employers strive to offer an attractive compensation package, including a fair base pay, incentives, and benefits, in addition to a good job match and working environment to attract employees and retain them.

Total rewards includes compensation that is both direct and indirect. Direct compensation (for example, cash) applies to a variety of pay programs that are, in one way or another, cash-based, whereas indirect compensation (for example, benefits) applies to programs primarily designed to provide recognition and benefits and, therefore, are indirectly cash-based. Examples of these two types of compensation are listed in Table 4-15.

Some of the direct compensation programs are discretionary (that is, cash awards, differential pay, and certain bonuses), while others are mandatory and governed by federal, state, and, in some cases, local law and regulation (base pay and incentives). Some of the indirect compensation programs are also discretionary—that is, they are employed

Table 4-15 Direct and Indirect Compensation	Direct Compensation ("Cash")	Indirect Compensation ("Benefits")
	Base pay (wages and salary)	Social Security
	Commissions	Unemployment insurance
	Bonuses	Disability insurance
	Merit pay	Pensions
	Piece rate pay	401(k) and other similar savings programs
	Differential pay	Health care
	Cash award	Vacations
	Profit sharing	Sick leave
	Gainsharing	Paid time off

at the option of the employer. They include paid vacation, paid sick leave (16 states and Washington D.C. now offer paid sick leave[93]), paid time off, 401(k) and similar retirement plans, and pensions. Finally, some benefits are mandatory and governed by federal law and regulation. Social Security, workers' compensation, and unemployment insurance are examples. Even discretionary programs are subject to regulation when they are implemented.

Compensation System Design

The compensation system design process, shown in Figure 4-18, includes four key activities: job analysis, job documentation, job evaluation, and pay structure.

Job Analysis

Before we address the process of a job analysis, we should first address what is a job. According to Dictionary.com, a job is either 1) a piece of work, especially a specific task done as part of the routine of one's occupation or for an agreed price or 2) a post of employment; full-time or part-time position.[94] Jobs comprise duties and responsibilities that are described in the job description. The information to create the job description comes from the job analysis.

Each job has a title based on typically accepted business and industry standards. Each job is different from other jobs such as receptionist, accountant, supervisor, and so on. A job such as an accountant may include many positions (that is, accounting specialist, forensic accountant, and so on). A position is a particular set of duties and responsibilities regularly assigned to an individual. Some job titles can be playful if that is consistent with the culture the organization is striving to create, such as "Help Desk Happiness Agent" and "Zookeeper" in a firm with no animals.

Job Analysis Defined   Job analysis is the process of collecting information about a job. It refers to the superstructure of the job. According to Herbert G. Heneman III "A job is a collection of tasks that can be performed by a single employee to contribute to the production of some product or service provided by the organization. Each job has certain ability requirements (as well as certain rewards) associated with it. Job analysis is the process used to identify these requirements."[95]

Job Analysis	Job Documentation	Job Evaluation	Pay Structure
Identify duties and qualifications of incumbents	Create job descriptions and specifications	Establish value of jobs in the organization	Establish pay grades and ranges for jobs

Figure 4-18   Compensation system design process

Job Analysis Considerations   The following considerations must be factors in conducting a job analysis:

- The facts identified must relate to the job and not the job incumbent.
- The duties and responsibilities must be for the job as it exists rather than what it is thought to be.
- Job facts must be verified to make sure they are accurate.
- Each duty must be analyzed to identify which duties are essential to the job function.
- When there is more than one job incumbent, only one job analysis should be required.

Job Analysis Methods   Multiple methods can be used to collect information as part of a job analysis:

- **Observation**   This involves the direct observation of employees performing the tasks of a job, recording observations, and translating them into the necessary knowledge, skills, and abilities. This method provides a realistic view of the daily tasks and activities performed in a job, but recognize that the presence of an observer can change the environment. Also be sensitive to when the observation is happening and whether it is capturing or missing critical activities. For example, the accounting function is busiest at the very beginning and very end of each month. Did you capture everything important if you observed on the fifteenth of the month?
- **Interview**   This involves a face-to-face interview, where the interviewer obtains the necessary information from the employee, peers, supervisor, or team/unit members about the knowledge, skills, and abilities needed to perform the job. The interviewer uses predetermined questions with new ones added as follow-up based on the response of the interviewee. This method is particularly good for professional jobs.
- **Highly structured questionnaire**   This involves questionnaires structured in a way that requires specific responses aimed at determining the frequency with which specific tasks are performed, their relative importance, and the skills required. This method defines a job with a relatively objective approach that also enables analysis that is easily adaptable to using computer models. It's good when many jobs must be analyzed and there are insufficient resources to do it.
- **Open-ended questionnaire**   This involves issuing questionnaires to job incumbents, and sometimes to their supervisors or managers, asking about the knowledge, skills, and abilities necessary to perform the job. After the answers are combined, a composite statement of job requirements is published from which a job description can be refined.

- **Work diary or log**   This method uses a diary or log maintained by the employee. Job information, including the frequency and timing of tasks, is recorded in the diary. Logs are usually kept over an extended period of time. They are analyzed, and patterns are identified and translated into duties and responsibilities. While data can be collected over a long period of time with this method, it can result in an enormous amount of information to be culled and summarized. Fatigue in maintaining the work diary or log may render the data gathered inaccurate.

- **Hybrid**   A combination of the preceding techniques may also be used. For example, an open-ended questionnaire can be shared with a supervisor ahead of time, to build trust and minimize any surprises. That questionnaire is then the basis for the in-person interview conducted at the work site. The interview is done at the work site so the working conditions may be observed, and based on what is seen, questions can be added.

Job Analysis Outcomes   Possible results from job analysis include the following:

- **Job description**   This is a functional description of what contents the job includes. It is a narration of the job contents, a description of the activities and duties to be performed in a job, the relationship of the job with other jobs, the equipment and tools involved, and the nature of supervision, working conditions, and job hazards, including physical and mental requirements.

- **Job specifications**   This focuses on the person doing the job (that is, the job holder). The job specification is a statement of the minimum acceptable qualifications that an incumbent must have to effectively perform a given job. It sets forth the experience, education, knowledge, skills, and physical and other abilities or attributes required to do the job successfully.

- **Job competencies**   Normally focused on "core" or "critical" competencies, these are the measurable or observable knowledge, skills, abilities, and behaviors (sometimes called KSABs) that are critical to successful job performance. Choosing the right competencies allows employers to do the following:
  - Plan how they will organize and develop their workforce.
  - Determine which job classes best fit their business needs.
  - Recruit and select the best employees.
  - Manage and train employees effectively.
  - Develop staff to fill future vacancies.

  Core competencies may be divided into three categories:
  - **Knowledge competencies**   The practical or theoretical understanding of subjects
  - **Skill and ability competencies**   The natural or learned capacities to perform acts
  - **Behavioral competencies**   Patterns of action or conduct

Job Analysis Uses   The following are the many uses of a job analysis:

- **Human resource planning**   It can be used to forecast HR requirements in terms of knowledge and skills.
- **Recruitment**   It can be used to find out how and when to hire people for future job openings.
- **Selection**   It is not possible to select the right person for the job without a proper understanding of what is to be done on a job.
- **Placement and orientation**   After selecting people, we must place them in jobs best suited to their interests, activities, and aptitude.
- **Training**   Effective training efforts cannot be initiated if there is any confusion about what the job is and what is supposed to be done.
- **Counseling**   Managers can properly counsel employees about their careers when they understand the different jobs in the organization. Likewise, employees can better appreciate their career options when they understand the specific needs of various other jobs.
- **Performance appraisal**   The worth of the person doing the job can be assessed by comparing what the person is supposed to be doing (based on job analysis) to what the individual has done.
- **Job design and redesign**   Once the jobs are properly understood, it becomes easier to locate weak spots and undertake remedial steps.

Job Documentation

Job documentation includes the creation of job descriptions, specifications, and competencies. In the context of a compensation system, job documentation does the following:

- Helps establish evaluation criteria for job performance
- Provides data used to compare pay with that of other organizations
- Helps the assignment of objective classifications or job titles to employees
- Communicates performance expectations to supervisors and employees
- Reduces an organization's liability exposure to discrimination charges or allegations
- Assists employers in recognizing and addressing reasonable accommodation and other legal compliance requirements

Job Evaluation

The systematic determination of the relative worth of jobs in an organization is known as *job evaluation*. The importance of job evaluation is that it is a critically important pay equity concept applied through a formalized process designed to prevent internal pay inequities as employers create structure within the organization's cost parameters while responding to its workforce expectations. Conducting a job evaluation is an essential first step in creating an appropriate wage structure that accommodates jobs of different worth, while it preserves the core objective of internal pay equity. Market surveys are a tool that enables organizations to understand and recognize market pressures with an objective of external equity.

Job-Content Based (Internal) Job Evaluation   Job evaluation options can be divided into job-content-based (internal) job evaluation and market-based (external) job evaluation. In job-content-based job evaluation, the relative worth and pay opportunities of different jobs are based on an assessment of their content (for example, responsibilities and requirements) and their relationship to other jobs within the organization. In a market-based evaluation approach, the relative worth and pay opportunities of different jobs are based on their market value or going rate in the marketplace.

Nonquantitative Job-Content Job Evaluation   Job evaluation methods can be nonquantitative or quantitative. The former method uses words, and the latter relies primarily on numbers. The primary objective of a nonquantitative method is to establish a relative hierarchy of jobs based on each job's relative worth. Nonquantitative methods often are referred to as *whole-job methods* because they rank jobs as a whole based on their perceived worth without placing a numerical value on each job. An example of a nonquantitative method would be to rank a clerical job below a supervisory job based on their relative, nonquantitative worth.

Quantitative job evaluation methods include *point-factor* and *factor comparison* methods. Quantitative methods evaluate factors on a defined measurable scale and provide a score as the result, which is a measurable comparison of one job to another (see Table 4-16).

- **Job ranking**   The job ranking method is often called a *whole-job* comparison because it is a comparison of the whole job compared to another whole job rather than a comparison based on each job's measurable factors. Job ranking using the whole-job method is quick and easy but not very precise. It is easy to explain, which is why it is popular, but it leaves unanswered why one job is worth more than another as well as how much of a "gap" exists between jobs.

  When there is a large number of jobs to evaluate, a *paired-comparison* method of ranking can be used. This method enables each job to be compared with every other job. Jobs are methodically compared to the next job and, depending on the perceived worth, moved up or below the next job. Ultimately, the job with the highest number of upward movements is the highest ranked. Other jobs are ranked accordingly.

Table 4-16 Job Evaluation Methods		**Nonquantitative Methods**	**Quantitative Methods**
	Job-to-job comparison	Job ranking	Factor comparison
	Job-to-predetermined-standard comparison	Job classification	Point-factor

- **Job classification**   Jobs can be compared to an outside scale. This also can be done on a whole-job basis called a *job classification* method. Job classification is the result of grouping jobs into a predetermined number of grades or classifications. Each classification has a class description. The federal government has a classification system known as the General Schedule (GS), which is the predominant pay scale for federal employees, especially employees in professional, technical, administrative, or clerical positions. The system consists of 15 grades, from the lowest level of GS-1 to the highest level of GS-15. There are also ten steps within each grade. The grade level assigned to a position determines the pay level for that job.

Classes can be further identified by using benchmark jobs that fall into each class. Benchmark jobs have the following characteristics:

- The essential functions and knowledge, skills, and abilities (KSAs) are established and stable.
- A significant number of workers are employed in these jobs.
- They are well-defined, and external market data is available for these jobs, so there's an acceptable basis for setting wages.

The job classification method is a nonquantitative job evaluation method. In the job classification method, a job may be compared to a similar job or to other jobs in the General Schedule to determine its relative ranking. This is considered a nonquantitative method called a *job-to-predetermined-standard comparison*. Job classification comparisons are a good method when evaluating many jobs and are understandable by employees. However, they may not be effective when jobs overlap, as they look only at whole jobs.

Quantitative Methods   The difference between nonquantitative job evaluation methods and quantitative job evaluation methods is that quantitative methods use mathematical data, whereas nonquantitative methods use qualitative data. The following are two quantitative methods:

- **Point-factor method**   A commonly used job evaluation method is the *point-factor method,* which uses specific compensable factors as its reference points to measure relative job worth. Compensable factors are significant job characteristics that contribute to the value of the work and organization as a whole. The following are two well-known systems used to identify compensable factors:
  - **The Hay plan**   Uses a standard criteria comprising three compensable factors: know-how, problem-solving, and accountability.
  - **The factor evaluation system (FES)**   Determines levels of duties and responsibilities using a point rating system to evaluate selected positions. Uses weighted factors to address the major position characteristics of responsibility, education/experience, job conditions, physical requirements, supervision, training, and so on.

The following five steps are involved in the point-factor method of job evaluation:

1. *Identify key jobs.* These are benchmark jobs—not necessarily the most important jobs in the organization, but jobs that are equitably paid, stable, and well-defined.

2. *Identify the compensable factors.* These factors are used to distinguish one job from another. Identifying six to eight factors is generally sufficient. Experience, responsibility, and education are most often used. Other factors that can be considered, depending on their general applicability, include physical demands, mental requirements, skill, working conditions, and supervisory responsibilities.

3. *Weigh the factors according to their overall worth.* Usually, the most heavily weighted factors are knowledge, responsibility, experience, education, degree of difficulty, and supervisory responsibilities.

4. *Divide each job factor into degrees that range from high to low.* Assign points to each degree. The number of points assigned to each degree should correspond with the weighting of the factors. As an example, if the factor for skill is weighted 40 percent, the factor of working conditions is weighted 10 percent, and both factors have five degrees, degree two for skill should have four times as many points as degree two for working conditions.

5. *Determine the total points.* This will usually determine the pay grade to which the job will be assigned. The final result will be determined using a table (see Table 4-17) that has a range of points from 50 (the least number, column 1) to 200 (the most, column 5). Based on the point values assigned, the job in this example is 126 on a scale of 50 to 200 points.

- **Factor comparison method**   The *factor comparison method* is more complex than the ranking, classification, or point-factor methods and is rarely used. It involves ranking each job by each compensable factor and then, as an additional step, identifying dollar values for each level of each factor to develop an actual pay rate for the evaluated job.

The factor comparison method is most often used in union negotiations as part of a labor contract and, in limited cases, where wages are steady over a period of time and the organization uses a flat rate for each job. A significant drawback of the factor comparison method is that no external market salary surveys report information by factor, which means the money assigned by factor is arbitrary and not confirmed with market data.

Market-Based (External) Job Evaluation
A market-rate system is not a true job evaluation system; however, in certain cases, market value can be used to price jobs—particularly when the organization is sensitive to competition. These prevailing rates are used to represent the relative worth of the jobs. In this approach, key jobs are measured and valued against the market, and the remaining jobs are inserted into a hierarchy based on their whole-job comparison to the benchmark jobs.

Point-Factor Job Evaluation Method						
Compensable Factor	**Weighted Percentage**	**Degrees/Points**				
		1	**2**	**3**	**4**	**5**
Skill	(40 percent)	20	32	48	72	100
Responsibility	(30 percent)	15	24	36	54	75
Effort	(20 percent)	10	16	24	36	50
Working Conditions	(10 percent)	5	8	12	18	25

Example:

Machine Operator	Compensable Factor	Degree	Points
	Skill	3	48
	Responsibility	2	24
	Effort	4	36
	Working Conditions	4	18
	Total points		*126*

Table 4-17   Point-Factor Job Evaluation Method

 NOTE   When matching a job with the competition, it is important to do the hard work to compare duties, scope, and reporting relationships and not simply rely on titles, because titles may be misleading.

Market-based evaluation can be particularly beneficial when an organization has similar jobs in various locations throughout the United States. The disadvantage of a market-based evaluation is that the data will be reliable only when gathered for a significant number of jobs in the organization. Market-based evaluation results are more vulnerable to legal challenge than job-content approaches. Another disadvantage is that market-based evaluations do not recognize internal job value and, as a result, are more likely to lead to discontent and frustration from within the organization.

Remuneration (Pay) Surveys   Many organizations rely on pay surveys as a systematic way to collect, evaluate, and classify their jobs; adjust pay structures; and provide market information to top management. Pay surveys collect data on prevailing market rates and provide information such as starting wage rates, base pay, pay ranges, overtime pay, shift differentials, and incentive pay plans.

Options to collecting pay survey data include whether the survey should be conducted internally or gathered externally. Organizations that want to maintain maximum control over their pay information may choose to sponsor a custom survey. The advantage of this approach is that the organization has the ability to design the survey, manage its administration, do its own data analysis, and customize its report specifically for its own use. Another advantage is that the organization is able to maximize its control over the transfer of data, thereby reducing the risk of an inappropriate disclosure of sensitive confidential information.

While choosing to conduct its own internal survey, an organization should contract with an outside consulting group or independent consultant to design the survey and process the data received in a confidential manner. Using an outside person or group relieves pressure on the organization and ensures compliance with Department of Justice antitrust guidelines. The downside of a custom internal survey is that it is a huge amount of work, plus you need to convince other organizations to participate.

External surveys have different options. National surveys are widely available through the U.S. Department of Labor and the Bureau of Labor Statistics. Many professional groups such as the Society of Human Resource Management (SHRM) and consulting firms conduct surveys of wage and job data for a wide range of professions and organizations. The expense of these surveys can be less if you plan ahead and are a participating organization, reporting your data for inclusion in the survey.

Data Analysis

Organizations have an interest in survey data based on their market exposure, completion, product or service, and employees.

Survey Data Analysis   To be accurate, survey data must be verified and may need aging, leveling, and/or factoring for location (geography):

- **Aging**   This is a technique used to make outdated data current, a phenomenon that regularly occurs with printed data as a result of the time lapse between when the data is collected, organized, and printed, and when you plan to use it. An example of aging occurs when pay movement or increases average 1.5 percent a year. If you use a pay survey that is 1 year old, to be reasonably accurate, you would increase the survey data by 1.5 percent.

- **Leveling**   Pay surveys provide summary descriptions of each job surveyed. In many cases, this description is close but not an exact match with the organization's job. To accommodate this separation between the two jobs, a leveling technique is used. Leveling consists of adjusting the survey number by an appropriate percentage needed to achieve a match. As an example, an organization's Engineering I job description indicates an approximate 10 percent less scope of responsibility than described in the same job in a pay survey. Reducing the pay survey job data by 10 percent would be an appropriate technique to provide an accurate match.

- **Geography**   While many surveys are developed with a specifically described geographical location identified, in cases where this is not done, it would be appropriate to determine the percent difference in job value for a given location and factor that into the comparison.

- **Documentation**   Any time you are engaging in aging, leveling, or adjusting for geography, you should document what you are doing and the reason for doing it.

Frequencies Distributions and Tables   Frequencies distributions and tables are used to sort salary data gathered from various remuneration surveys (sometimes called *pay* or *salary surveys*). A frequency distribution is a listing of grouped data, from lowest to highest. A frequency table lists the number of incumbents who receive a specific salary, as shown in Table 4-18.

Table 4-18	Frequency Distribution and Table		
Frequency Distribution and Table	Survey	Mean Salary	Number of Incumbents
	A	$60,000	2
	B	$65,000	1
	C	$70,000	3
	D	$75,000	4

The following are techniques used to organize data in a logical manner for ease and accuracy of interpretation.

Measures of Central Tendency   Measures of central tendency are another way to analyze salary survey data. Common measures of central tendency are mean (or *average*), median, mode, and quartiles and percentiles.

- **Mean (average)**   The arithmetic average or mean is the average value arrived at by giving equal weight to every participant's actual pay. This method is appropriate when the data to be determined is the average pay for a given job, as opposed to actual pay levels applicable to that job. This number is also known as the *unweighted average*.

- **Weighted average**   This number provides an average result taking into account the number of participants and each participant's pay. This result is known as the *weighted average*.

- **Median**   This number is sometimes referred to in pay surveys as the 50th percentile. This is the middle number in a range, with half the data points higher and the other half of the data points lower. The median is calculated by averaging the two middle numbers in a range when the range data is sorted from lowest to highest.

- **Mode**   This is the most frequently appearing number (or *wage* in a pay survey) in a range.

The following calculations are based on the data shown in Table 4-19:

- The unweighted average is $67,500 ($270,000 ÷ 4 organizations = $67,500).
- The weighted average is $69,500 ($695,000 ÷ 10 incumbents = $69,500).

Organizations	Number of Incumbents	Annual Salary	Total Salary
A	2	$60,000	$120,000
B	1	$65,000	$65,000
C	3	$70,000	$210,000
D	4	$75,000	$300,000
4 organizations	10	$270,000	$695,000

Table 4-19   Weighted and Unweighted Mean Calculation

Pay Structure

After an organization has determined its relative internal job values (that is, job evaluation) and collected appropriate market survey data through pay surveys, work begins on developing the organization's pay structure, including creating pay grades and establishing pay ranges.

Pay Grades   Pay grades, or job groups, are the way an organization organizes jobs of similar value. The valuation is a result of the job evaluation process. Jobs, even though dissimilar in function, of the same (or comparatively the same) value are paid within the same pay grade.

No fixed rules apply to creating pay grades; rather, the number of pay grades and their structure are more of a reflection of organizational structure and philosophy. Issues that should be considered include the following:

- The size and structure of the organization
- The "distance" between the lowest and the highest job in the organization
- The organization's pay increase and promotion policy
- The grouping of nonexempt and exempt jobs as well as job families (that is, clerical, technical, professional, supervisory, and management jobs)
- Creating sufficient grades to permit distinguishing difficulty levels but not so many that the difference between adjoining grades is insignificant

Well-structured pay grades enable management to develop a well-coordinated pay system rather than having to create a separate pay range for each job.

Pay Ranges   Pay ranges establish the upper and lower boundaries of each pay grade. Market data for a benchmark job (ideally, a "key" job that will link to market value) in each pay range helps to determine the range midpoint. The range spread reflects the equal dispersion of pay on either side of the midpoint to the lower and upper range boundary.

Quartiles and Percentiles   Quartiles and percentiles show dispersion of data throughout a range. These are commonly recognized reference points an organization uses to measure its position against the market as well as for internal compensation management purposes.

Range Spreads   The range spread is the dispersion of pay from the lowest boundary to the highest boundary of a pay range.

Range Spread Calculation

Range spread is calculated by subtracting the range minimum from the range maximum and dividing that figure by the range minimum. Range spread is expressed as a percentage.

$$\frac{\text{Maximum} - \text{Minimum}}{\text{Minimum}}$$

Example: The range spread for a pay range with a $30,000 minimum and a $45,000 maximum would be as follows:

$$\frac{\$45,000 - \$30,000}{\$30,000} = \frac{\$15,000}{\$30,000} = 50\%$$

Typical range spreads in organizations are as follows:

- Nonexempt jobs: 40 percent
- Exempt jobs: 50 percent
- Executive jobs: 60 percent

Generally, lower-level jobs have a narrow range between minimum and maximum pay ranges. Jobs at a lower level tend to be more skill-based, which provides for more movement opportunity than higher levels, where jobs are more knowledge-based and progression is slower.

Ranges should overlap so that progression is steady within a pay grade; as a worker's pay increases with movement to a higher range quartile, the opportunity for managed movement is possible in a measured way.

There also should be a large enough distance between range midpoints so that pay compression between a lower pay grade and a higher pay grade does not occur.

Compa-Ratios   Compa-ratios are indicators of how wages match, lead, or lag the midpoint—normally an indicator of market value. Compa-ratios are computed by dividing the worker's pay rate by the midpoint of the pay range. The compa-ratio formula is as follows:

$$\text{Compa-ratio} = \frac{\text{Pay rate}}{\text{Midpoint}}$$

Compa-ratios less than 100 percent (usually expressed as a compa-ratio less than 1.00) mean the worker is paid less than the midpoint of the range. Compa-ratios greater than 100 percent (1.00) mean that wages exceed the midpoint.

Broadbanding   Broadbanding is a recent concept that combines several pay grades or job classifications with narrow range spreads with a single band with a wider spread. Organizations usually adopt broadbanding to de-layer their organization, simplify their pay levels, or reduce management oversight requirements. As a result, broadbanding typically is more popular in large organizations than smaller ones.

While broadbanding has some advantages, it also has some disadvantages. In some cases, broadbanding does not work well with the organization's compensation philosophy. This is particularly true in organizations that focus on promotional opportunities. The reduction of pay grades as a result of broadbanding correspondingly reduces the number of opportunities for promotion.

Compensation Systems

A compensation system is the sum total of all monetary and nonmonetary benefits provided to employees in exchange for their willingness to work.

Base Pay Systems

After an organization has analyzed, evaluated, and priced its jobs, as well as designed its pay structure, the next step is to determine a type of base pay system that will help attract, motivate, and retain employees. In most cases, employees receive some type of base pay, either as an hourly wage (paid to hourly employees) or as a salary (a fixed wage that doesn't change regardless of the hours worked for exempt employees). Base pay system choices include single or flat-rate systems, time-based step rate systems, performance-based merit pay systems, productivity-based systems, and person-based systems. Each of these systems is designed to best achieve the objectives of attracting, motivating, and retaining employees, each under a different set of circumstances.

Single or Flat-Rate System   A flat-rate pay system compensates all workers at the same rate of pay, regardless of factors such as performance and seniority. Often, this is used for task-based jobs. It incentivizes workers to complete tasks as quickly as possible but can penalize those unable to meet the established standards and in some cases may encourage workers to sacrifice quality for speed. It is also common for some government jobs. All United States senators are paid the same amount, as an example, regardless of performance or seniority.

Time-Based Step Rate System   The time-based step rate system bases the employee's pay rate on the length of time in the job. Pay increases are published in advance on the basis of time. Increases occur on a predetermined schedule. This system has three variations, as described in the sections that follow.

Automatic Step Rate   In the automatic step rate system, the pay range is divided into several steps, each a predetermined range apart. At the prescribed time interval, each employee with the required seniority receives a one-step pay increase. This system is common in public-sector jobs and in a union environment. Being so automatic means you could have an employee on final warning for performance issues get a pay increase if the prescribed time interval was achieved.

Step Rate with Variability Considerations   The step rate with performance considerations system is similar to the automatic system, except that performance can influence the size or timing of the pay increase.

Combination Step Rate and Performance Structure   In the combination step rate and performance system, employees receive step rate increases up to the established job rate. Above this level, increases are granted only for superior job performance. To work, this system requires a supporting performance appraisal program as well as good communication and understanding by the workers paid under this system.

Performance-Based Merit Pay System   The performance-based merit pay system is based on an employee's individual job performance. It is the most popular pay method in the United States these days. A performance-based pay system is often referred to as *merit pay* or *pay for performance*. In this system, employees are typically hired at or near

Performance Rating	1st Quartile	2nd Quartile	3rd Quartile	4th Quartile
Exceeds Performance Objectives	0–7 percent	0–6 percent	0–5 percent	0–4 percent
Meets Performance Objectives	0–5 percent	0–4 percent	0–3 percent	0–2 percent
Needs Improvement	0–3 percent	0–2 percent	0–1 percent	0 percent

Table 4-20   Merit Guidelines Example

the minimum for their applicable pay range. Pay increases are normally awarded on an annual basis (or annualized if awarded on other than an annual basis) and influenced by the individual's overall job performance. A document identifying the percent pay increase linked to levels of performance and the individual's position in the applicable pay range is provided to employees as an incentive to increase their performance, thereby earning a higher percentage increase. This document is known as "Merit Guidelines," and Table 4-20 shows an example. In this table, each pay suggestion begins with zero to take into consideration the organization's ability to pay that particular year and acknowledging limited dollars and the achievements of other co-workers competing for the same limited merit dollars.

To be effective, the merit pay system must be understood by employees affected by the system. In addition to the merit pay system, a clear performance appraisal program is required to support the merit pay system, *so it truly is pay for performance.*

Productivity-Based System   In the productivity-based system, pay is determined by the employee's output. This system is mostly used on an assembly line in a manufacturing environment. It is not appropriate for other types of jobs. The following sections describe two types of productivity-based systems.

Straight Piece Rate System   With the straight piece rate system, the employee receives a base rate of pay and is awarded additional compensation for the amount of output produced.

Differential Piece Rate System   In the differential piece rate system, the employee receives one rate of pay up to the production standard and a higher rate of pay when the standard is exceeded. Both the straight piece system and the differential piece rate system focus on quantity rather than quality. As a result, other quality control measures must be defined to ensure the required quality standard is met.

Person-Based System   In the person-based system, employee capabilities, rather than how the job is performed, determine the employee's pay. For example, two employees do the same work, but one employee with a higher level of skill and experience receives more pay. Note that with this system, the pay is based on what the employee *can* do, not what they actually do. For example, a company might pay an employee more since they have the latest, hottest programming skill but not require them to actually use that skill. There are three types of person-based systems, as described here:

- **Knowledge-based system**   In the knowledge-based system, a person's pay is based on the level of knowledge the person has in a particular field. This system is often used for learned professions, such as lawyers and doctors.

- **Skill-based system**   Employees paid in the skill-based system are paid for the number and depth of skills they have that are applicable to their job. Heavy equipment operators are typically paid in this system.

- **Competency-based system**   In the competency-based system, pay is linked to the level at which an employee can perform in a recognized competency. In HR, a professional with specialty skills in organizational development or labor relations will typically be paid for their competency (for example, organizational development or labor relations) in the HR field.

Pay Variations

Pay ranges must be periodically evaluated and adjusted to reflect organizational and market changes. Market adjustments and cost-of-living adjustments are some of the techniques used to make these adjustments. When an individual's pay is outside the defined range, we call that a red circle or green circle rate.

Red Circle Rates   Individuals who are paid more than their assigned pay grade maximum are labeled red circled, which indicates to stop any increases to their base salary, as it is already too high for the work they are expected to perform. This can happen as a result of a merger or acquisition, a demotion, or inattention to pay grade maximums. Such individuals may be counseled and trained to move into a higher pay grade that's more in keeping with their current salary. Other organizations may leave them where they are and hope that over time market adjustments will eventually move up, so the red circled employee is once again within the range. A most unpopular third alternative is to take back base pay to drop the employee down to the range maximum.

Green Circle Rates   Green circle rates occur when a new employee is hired at a pay rate lower than the minimum rate for the applicable grade. It can also happen when a "fast-track" employee is promoted to a new job in a high pay grade under circumstances where the percentage pay increase needed to reach the new grade is excessive and might create an unwanted precedent. In this case, the pay increase may result in a pay level below the minimum level of the new pay grade, thus creating a "green circle rate." A third reason an employee might be green circled is that the company adjusted its pay grades upward in response to changes in the market. Those employees who were at the bottom of their pay grades prior to the adjustment may then fall below the newly defined minimum.

Situations such as this should be avoided whenever possible and should be allowed only as a last resort because they can create serious morale issues and, even worse, may create an arguable case of pay discrimination. Ideally, the first compensation dollars that become available should be applied to those employees who fell out of their range and should be brought back up to the minimum. In any case, such actions should be carefully considered and justified in writing after all the possible consequences are considered.

Pay Compression   Pay compression is the situation that occurs when there is only a small difference in pay between employees regardless of their skills or experience. Pay compression is the result of the market rate for a given job outpacing the increases historically given by the organization to high-tenure employees. As a result, employers can only hire newcomers by offering them as much, or sometimes even more, than much more senior professionals.

Pay inequities exist to some degree in all organizations. The most common causes are the result of talent acquisition, overtime, demotions, the demand for technical expertise, reorganizations, reassignments, and seniority. Some organizations conduct wage compression or parity studies to identify pay compression issues and their causes in an effort to achieve levels of internal equity so that people in relatively similar jobs receive equal pay.

Pay Adjustments

This term can be used to signify a pay increase for a number of reasons. In this section, we will examine cost of living adjustments, general pay increases, seniority increases, lump-sum increases, and market-based increases.

Cost-of-Living Increase   Technically, a cost-of-living adjustment (COLA) is an adjustment in pay, usually upward, linked to a predetermined scale, measure, or condition. Employment contracts, pension benefits, and government entitlements, such as Social Security, are linked to a cost-of-living index, typically to the consumer price index (CPI). A COLA adjusts salaries based on changes in a cost-of-living index. Salaries, which are typically adjusted annually, may also be tied to a cost-of-living index that varies by geographic location if the employee moves.

General Pay Increase   In some circumstances, nonunion employers may want to provide a general pay increase to their employees without the potentially precedent-setting basis of a COLA. A general pay increase is a pay increase given to all employees regardless of their job performance and not linked to market pressures. Usually, the only criteria is the desire to provide all employees with a pay increase subject only to the ability to fund the increase.

Seniority Pay Increase   Whenever a pay increase is given based solely on length of service, it is considered a seniority pay increase. As with a general pay increase, it is simply a basis on which to award a pay increase. Seniority pay increases are common in a unionized setting. In a nonunion setting, pay increases usually combine seniority with performance.

Lump-Sum Increase   A lump-sum increase (LSI) can be either a stand-alone performance bonus or a replacement for an annual base pay increase. Because a lump-sum increase is a single lump-sum payment, it creates no long-lasting commitment that ripples into other areas of the total rewards package, such as overtime, shift differentials, sick leave, vacation pay, or holiday pay.

A lump-sum increase is a single lump-sum payment subject to applicable tax and withholding that is not added to the employee's base rate of pay because of its character as a single lump-sum payment. This provides the full cash payment to the employee in a single lump sum. In a red circle rate situation, the lump-sum increase can be used for the amount that would otherwise exceed the range maximum without increasing the employee's base rate of pay beyond the range maximum. If there is concern an employee will accept the lump-sum payment and then leave for the competitor, divide the total by four and pay each fourth quarterly, requiring the individual be on the payroll to receive it.

Market-Based Increase   When employee retention is threatened because employee pay is not competitive with the market, employers can respond by creating a market-based increase to adjust a single employee's pay, or the pay for a group of employees, or to increase your entire compensation structure to better match market levels.

Differential Pay

Differential pay is additional compensation paid to an employee as an incentive to accept what would normally be considered adverse working conditions, usually based on time, location, or situational conditions. The same differential pay is given to all employees under the same circumstances or conditions. Differential pay benefits the employer by incentivizing employees to accept work they might not otherwise accept; it benefits the employee as additional compensation for accepting the work.

Time-Based Differential Pay   Also called a *shift differential,* time-based differential pay generally rewards the employee who works hours normally considered undesirable, such as a night shift. Time-based differential pay may be a specified flat dollar amount per hour or a percentage of the employee's regular rate of pay. Federal law does not legally require employers to pay a differential rate of pay, although state requirements may differ.

Geographic Differential Pay   Sometimes locations are undesirable because of their remoteness, a lack of amenities, climatic conditions, and other adverse conditions. To attract workers, in some cases employers will add a location-based differential to the employee's pay package. A geographic pay differential is additional compensation paid to an employee to account for variations in cost of labor and/or cost of living between locations. Some companies use the cost of goods and services as a factor to determine geographic pay differentials, but most companies use cost of labor as the primary factor to determine pay differences among locations.

Incentive Pay

SHRM-SCP

Incentive pay is a form of direct compensation where employers pay for performance beyond normal expectations to motivate employees to perform at higher levels. In structured incentives, sometimes called *production incentives,* workers understand ahead of time the precise relationship between performance and the incentive reward. In a casual approach, sometimes called *discretionary incentives,* workers do not know in advance when or how much of a reward will be given.

Types of Incentives   Typically, incentives are effective only if they are designed to a specific organization's operational conditions. To accomplish their objective, incentives need to add value to an organization's business objectives. Because of this, incentives generally are grouped into individual, group, and organization-wide applications, as discussed next.

Individual   The objective of an individual incentive program is to improve job performance. As such, the individual incentive program must be available to all employees in a particular group. An individual incentive program must be clearly designed and implemented as an incentive separate from an individual's base pay. Individual incentive programs can be either cash-based or non-cash-based.

- **Cash awards**   Cash award programs reward performance with extra pay based on job performance. The rewards are usually lump-sum rewards such as discretionary bonuses based on the judgment of a supervisor or manager, a performance-based bonus based on predetermined performance criteria, or formula-based bonuses based on a percentage of profits or other pre-established measurement.

- **Noncash awards**   Noncash awards include prizes, gifts, recognition awards, and other similar noncash items of value to the recipient. Sometimes these awards can be for length of service or contributions in addition to job performance. Although giving cash and noncash awards appears to be pretty straightforward, in fact, it can be more complicated than circumstances suggest. Some awards have tax implications, so advice might be required from accounting or your legal counsel as part of developing a cash or noncash incentive program.

Group   Used when teamwork is being rewarded, these programs are designed for groups of employees with the objective of rewarding group job performance considered necessary to accomplish a unit of work or when the desired result requires a team approach to the work. Group incentive programs can reward both short- and long-term work effort. Often, these programs include financial and nonfinancial measures as criteria for success. Group incentive programs include profit-sharing plans, gainsharing plans, and group performance incentives—for example, employee stock ownership plans (ESOPs).

- **Profit-sharing plans**   Profit sharing refers to various incentive plans that provide direct or indirect employee payments that depend on a company's profitability. These payments are in addition to the employees' regular salary and bonuses. In profit-sharing plans, the employer has the discretion to determine when and how much the company will pay into the plan. The contribution and any investment earnings accumulate in the plan on a tax-deferred basis. The IRS taxes these benefits only when employees receive distributions from the plan. A profit-sharing plan can be set up where all or some of the employee's profit-sharing amount can be contributed to a retirement plan. These are often used in conjunction with 401(k) plans.

- **Gainsharing plans**   Gainsharing plans are similar to profit-sharing plans except that gainsharing plans measure the increase in productivity achieved from one performance period to the next, whereas profit-sharing plans measure the profit to be shared from period to period. In a gainsharing plan, each member of the unit receives the same reward. Gainsharing measures usually apply to productivity terms, whereas profit-sharing measures typically apply to profitability. The following are three types of gainsharing plans:

  - **The Scanlon Plan**   The Scanlon Plan is the oldest and most widely used type of gainsharing plan. It is a combination of a classic gainsharing plan with an employee suggestion system. It's based on the historical ratio of labor cost to sales value of production. The distinctive characteristics of the Scanlon Plan are its philosophy of participative management, administration by a committee of employees and management, and its percentage method of payment. A distinguishing characteristic is that the organization does not have to be profitable for workers to receive an incentive.

- **The Rucker Plan** The Rucker Share-of-Production Plan is based on the premise that the ratio of labor costs to production value is historically stable in manufacturing. The Rucker Plan tracks the value added to a product as a measure of productivity. In the Scanlon Plan, a ratio is calculated that expresses the value of production required for each dollar of the total wage cost.

- **Improshare Plan** Improshare measures the change in the relationship between outputs and the time required to produce them. This plan uses past production records to establish base performance standards. A standard is developed that identifies the expected number of hours to produce something. Any savings between this standard and actual production are shared between the company and the workers. The organization and its employees usually share 50/50 in all productivity gains. It is minimally affected by changes in sales volume, technology and capital equipment, product mix, and price and wage increases. It's the easiest of the gainsharing plans to understand and install. It may be used in a wider variety of situations where a physical product is not produced.

- **Executive incentives** Executives are the people who run the business at the top of the pyramid. Executives form the highest level of management within their organization. In addition to their substantial management responsibilities within their organizations, they develop relationships with people outside their organization with the purpose of improving growth opportunities for their organizations. Their scope of activities and responsibilities impacts their compensation plans in two ways. First, their total compensation package includes their annual cash compensation plus the value of long-term incentives, which usually account for the larger share of their total package. Second, their incentives are generally linked to the performance of the entire organization's profitability and, in some cases, other nonfinancial measures, such as customer satisfaction and meeting certain other strategic objectives.

While there is no single compensation package designed for executives, their pay usually consists of a base salary that is "guaranteed," with other forms of variable (incentive) compensation dependent on performance factors.

- **Perquisites** Special privileges for executives are referred to as perks. These privileges include club memberships, company cars, reserved parking, and a host of other noncash benefits. The 1973 Tax Act greatly diminished these perks, but they remain a substantial element in an executive's compensation package.

- **Golden parachutes** These are provisions included in executive employment contracts that provide special payments or benefits to executives under certain adverse conditions, such the loss of their position or if they are otherwise adversely impacted by organizational changes. Most often, these impacts are the result of an organizational merger in which there is a change of control that displaces a senior executive. These "golden parachutes" may provide for accelerated payments or early vesting in nonqualified retirement plan options, among other possibilities.

- **Long-term incentives** Long-term incentive plans reward employees for attaining results over a long measurement period. For this purpose, long-term generally means more than 1 year and is typically between 2 and 5 years. Tax-deferred compensation plans, long-term cash plans, and certain stock-based plans are all considered long-term incentives.

  The form of payment from a long-term incentive plan is typically cash or equity. An employer might choose one or the other based on the goals of the plan, the recipients of the awards, and the availability of cash or equity for payment.

Organization-Wide Profit-sharing and stock ownership plans include the following:

- **ESOPs** An employee stock ownership plan (ESOP) is a retirement plan in which the company contributes to the plan either its stock or money to buy its stock for the benefit of the company's employees. The plan maintains an account for each employee participating in the plan. Shares of stock vest over time before an employee is entitled to them. With an ESOP, you never buy or hold the stock directly while still employed with the company. If an employee is terminated, retires, becomes disabled, or dies, the plan will distribute the shares of stock in the employee's account.

- **Incentive stock options** There are several varieties of stock options, all of which share some basic characteristics. A stock option is a right to purchase a share of stock in the future at a price determined at the grant (or based on a formula defined at the grant). Incentive stock options (ISOs) are a special subset of stock options, satisfying certain criteria promulgated by the Internal Revenue Service and discussed in Internal Revenue Code Section 422. As you design these plans, stay in contact with your accounting group for any changes in the code.

  One of the primary restrictions is that an ISO can be granted only to an employee; ISOs cannot be granted to outside directors, independent contractors, consultants, or any other nonemployees. Also, the recipient must exercise the ISO within three months of terminating employment.

- **Employee stock purchase plans (ESPPs)** An ESPP is a company-run program in which participating employees can purchase company shares at a discounted price. Employees contribute to the plan through payroll deductions, which build up between the offering date and the purchase date. At the purchase date, the company uses the accumulated funds to purchase shares in the company on behalf of the participating employees. The amount of the discount depends on the specific plan but can be as much as 15 percent lower than the market price.

  Depending on when you sell the shares, the disposition will be classified as either qualified or not qualified. If the position is sold 2 years after the offering date and at least 1 year after the purchase date, the shares will fall under a qualified disposition. If the shares are sold within 2 years of the offering date or 1 year after the purchase date, the disposition will not be qualified. These positions will have different tax implications.

- **Phantom stock plan**   A phantom stock plan is an employee benefit plan that gives selected employees (senior management) many of the benefits of stock ownership without actually giving them any company stock. This is sometimes referred to as shadow stock.

  Rather than getting physical stock, the employee receives "pretend" stock. Even though it's not real, the phantom stock follows the price movement of the company's actual stock, paying out any resulting profits[96]

- **Restricted stock unit**   A restricted stock unit (RSU) is compensation offered by an employer to an employee in the form of company stock. The employee does not receive the stock immediately but instead receives it according to a vesting plan and distribution schedule after achieving required performance milestones or upon remaining with the employer for a particular length of time. The RSUs are assigned a fair market value when they vest. Upon vesting, they are considered income, and a portion of the shares are withheld to pay income taxes. The employee receives the remaining shares and can sell them at any time.

- **Performance grants**   Public companies can also benefit from linking stock-based compensation to organizational performance. If done properly, such an arrangement can qualify as performance-based compensation, which avoids the deduction limits that can be imposed under Code Section 162(m). Such arrangements can also motivate recipients to achieve goals that are valuable to the organization and its shareholders. The accounting consequences of such arrangements can be tricky, and care should be taken to get the views of the organization's accountants.

In general, all incentive plans must meet the following criteria:

- *They must fit with other programs.* For example, individual sales reward programs must be compatible with larger team recognition and reward programs.

- *They must be in the employee's "line of sight."* Job performance measures should reflect the results the employee actually controls. For example, a laboratory technician's zero-defect completion of a prescribed number of test results within a specified period of time would be a "line of sight" accomplishment.

- *They must have a "sunset clause."* The incentive plan should be in effect for a specific time period with an identified end date for tracking and measurement purposes.

- *They must incorporate both short- and long-term perspectives.* The incentive plan should be structured to reward short-term goals (that is, increased production capacity) and long-term results (that is, achieving a strategic growth objective). The short-term perspective may be easier to visualize and achieve, but that may not encourage employees to think about long-term results.

Organizational requirements include the following:

- **A stable base pay plan**   A plan must be fair and equitable with long-term stability. Staff must be compensated competitively. An incentive plan will not support a base compensation system that is internally or externally inequitable.

- **An existing strategic plan** Long-term organizational goals, as expressed in the organization's strategic plan, must be clear, consistent, and measurable. There must be stability as measured through the organization's sales volume, expenses, profitability, and customer satisfaction.

- **Complete commitment** A great deal of effort goes into creating an incentive plan. The plan must be accepted at all levels of management. Continued coaching and training are necessary for long-term stability. Learning must be reinforced by strong support and commitment to achieve desired results using measured output to evaluate performance.

Challenges in Cross-Border Situations In addition to being organization specific, a successful incentive program has to be culturally sensitive. Cultural attitudes can vary widely from country to country. In addition, incentive programs are impacted by the laws and regulations that govern their application, which also vary significantly from one country to another.

Direct Sales Personnel There are several ways to compensate personnel who are responsible for sales, depending on the circumstances surrounding the sales activities. Compensation usually is both direct and indirect:

- **Direct** Compensation paid by cash and/or incentives (in turn, incentives can be cash-driven; for example, bonuses and commissions)

- **Indirect** Compensation paid through perks and entitlements (for example, cars and expense accounts, club membership, and allowances)

Factors that influence the design of a salesperson's compensation plan include the following:

- The time involved servicing the account as compared to the time spent in the sale of goods or services.

- The ability to objectively measure the sales activity.

- The nature of the sales activity. This is difficult to distinguish from the activity spent providing support services.

- The degree and type of motivation associated with the sales activity.

- The significance of the sales cost involved in the transaction.

- The comparative marketplace practice.

- The length of the production cycle.

Three types of compensation plans are most commonly used:

- **Straight salary** Of the three types of plans, the straight salary plan is the least used, but it more than likely will be found in situations where most of the time involved is spent servicing the account rather than selling the account.

It is also more likely when sales costs would otherwise be higher than acceptable to management as well as when, by comparison, the marketplace is more likely to compensate sales on a straight salary basis.

- **Straight commission**   This is the other extreme of the sales compensation spectrum. In this case, a person's entire salary is paid via commission. This most often occurs when the ultimate objective is increased sales volume with less emphasis or need for service as well as when the marketplace approach is also to compensate by way of a straight commission plan.

  In some cases, organizations that use a straight commission form of compensation will provide what is called a *draw* for novice or entry-level sales personnel. Typically, the draw consists of a nonrecoverable or guaranteed commission for a defined period of time, usually not more than 1 year. If, during this period, a salesperson does not earn a commission equal to or exceeding the draw, the salesperson does not owe the organization the difference. The period of time the draw is in place usually conforms with the organization's experience in developing the salesperson's selling capabilities to a point the individual is able to earn at least as much or more than the draw provides.

- **Salary plus commission and/or bonus**   In a salary-plus-commission arrangement, a portion of the total pay is a fixed salary; the remainder is variable commission. This is the most popular form of sales compensation in that it incorporates parts of both the fixed salary (which offers some stability with the individual's income flow) and the commission or the reward for sales success (thus, the incentive for greater future success).

Professionals   The characteristics unique to professional employees include a focus on their chosen fields of endeavor along with their interest in career progression within their chosen field. This requires a company's pay system to provide opportunity and to recognize employees' career progression. Two "tools" enhance management's capability to recognize professional growth:

- **The dual career ladder**   A typical career ladder describes the progression from entry-level positions to higher levels of pay for added managerial or supervisory skill, responsibility, or authority. The dual career ladder adds the option to promote employees on a technical track, not adding supervisory responsibilities. This program helps retain top talent by offering extended career opportunities with appropriate salary growth to employees in their chosen careers. Engineers, scientists, and actuaries are examples of jobs that could benefit from a dual career ladder.

- **Maturity curve**   This tool measures salaries based on years of related experience since the first educational degree or formal training requirement for job entry was earned. It is most often used to measure market pay for employees engaged in technical work such as engineering, and in particular in research and development, although it is also useful in many other areas, such as within a law firm. The process assumes that spending more years in the profession equates with more highly valued competencies.

Outside Directors   Any member of a company's board of directors who is not an employee or stakeholder in the company is an "outside director." Outside directors are paid an annual retainer fee in the form of cash, benefits, and/or stock options. Corporate governance standards require public companies to have a certain number or percentage of outside directors on their boards, as they are more likely to provide an "outside" perspective and offer unbiased opinions.

Metrics

Although many metrics can be applied to the subject of compensation, the following two are the most common metrics:

- **Compensation ratio**   Also known as *compa-ratio*, this is a measure of the relationship of current pay to the midpoints of the applicable pay ranges. Compa-ratios are computed by dividing a worker's pay rate by the midpoint of the range:

$$\frac{\textit{Employee's rate of pay}}{\textit{Pay range midpoint}}$$

  Example: Compensation ratio data enables managers to comparatively determine whether employees are equitably paid for their job performance.

- **Total company compensation expense**   This identifies all employment-related costs as a percentage of total operating costs:

$$\frac{\textit{Pay + Overtime + Benefits + Bonuses}}{\textit{Total Costs}}$$

  Example: Tracking total compensation as a percentage of total costs helps organizations manage the costs associated with human capital, including the use of fixed versus variable compensation.

Benefits and Perquisites

Benefit programs, also called *indirect compensation,* are designed to promote organizational loyalty, reward continued employment, enable employees to live healthy lives, help them care for their families, and help provide for retirement benefits. Examples of benefits include housing (employer-provided or employer-paid), group insurance (health, dental, life, and so on), disability income protection, retirement benefits, daycare, tuition reimbursement, sick leave (paid sick leave in a few states), vacation (paid and nonpaid), Social Security, profit sharing, funding of education, and other specialized benefits.

The term *perquisites,* more often referred to as *perks,* is used to refer to benefits that are more discretionary in nature. Perks often are given to employees who are doing notably well, hold senior positions, and/or have seniority. Common perks are take-home vehicles, hotel stays, free refreshments, leisure activities on work time (such as golf), and personal stationery.

Benefits Structure

Employee benefits represent a significant financial investment on the part of the employer. To effectively meet its purpose, the employer's total benefits programs must be cost-effective, meet their stated purpose, be affordable for both the employer and the employee, and comply with local, state, and federal law. To accomplish these objectives, data must be collected and analyzed to determine whether the employer's benefits programs actually meet their objectives. This process is known as a *benefits needs assessment* (that is, needs analysis).

Deciding Which Benefits to Offer   Employers must provide monetary compensation as well as certain legally mandated benefits to employees, but most benefits are optional. Providing benefits to your employees also allows you to offer benefits to yourself, and contributions that you make for benefit premiums are often tax-deductible for your business. In addition, if you need to attract employees with a special skill or talent, you're going to have to compete with other employers to get them, which may mean you'll need to offer some benefits to be successful.

So, how do you decide which benefits you should offer? Understanding which benefits you are required to offer is your first consideration because of the impact these requirements can have on your ability to offer optional benefits.

Some of the benefits employers are required to offer include time off to vote, serve on a jury, and perform military service. You must also comply with all of the requirements of workers' compensation, withhold for payroll taxes such as FICA and FUTA for Social Security and unemployment insurance, and contribute to state disability programs in states where such programs exist.

Employers don't have to provide paid holidays, vacation, or paid sick leave (except where required by state law), health benefits (except where required by state law), life insurance, or retirement plans.

The pros of offering benefits include the following:

- **Tax advantages**   You may be able to deduct plan contributions.

- **Recruiting advantages**   You can use benefits packages to attract good employees, and you can structure them in such a way to reward and thus retain your best employees.

- **Personal gain**   You may be able to get benefits for yourself for less money, if you also offer them to your employees, than you would procuring them privately for yourself.

- **Alternatives to pay**   Sometimes employees will accept benefits in lieu of higher salaries.

Cost is the biggest "con." Other challenges, particularly for smaller employers, include the following:

- You may have to pay higher rates than larger employers for group health care coverage because there are fewer employees among whom to spread risk.

- There may be difficulty providing life insurance coverage to certain employee groups.

- You may have fewer design choices when offering a retirement plan because of high administrative costs.
- You may be less likely to offer fringe benefits because of administrative complexity.

What benefits should be offered depends on the following:

- What you can afford
- What other businesses are offering
- How the benefit can help your business

Benefits Needs Assessment   A benefits needs analysis consists of several steps that include data collection and analysis, culminating in a report called a *gap analysis*.

Gap Analysis   The steps in this analysis are as follows:

- *Review the organization's overall culture and strategy.* The results of this effort will determine the potential coverage and scope of its benefits programs.
- *Collect and analyze the employer's workforce demographics.* This data is key to determining potential benefits needs.
- *Analyze the utilization and costs of existing benefits plans and programs.* The results of this data, coupled with the demographics data, will help determine the nature of coverage desired.
- *Determine the potential benefits coverage and costs.* This analysis will be an important factor for comparing the demographics and benefits utilization data.

The final step is to compare the organizational needs and budget with employee needs and any existing benefits coverage. The end result is a gap analysis—a document that will indicate what a benefits package should and should not include.

Types of Benefits
Employers have found that paid time off as a reward for service provides the employee with relief from the ongoing demands of work as well as benefits the employer with increased morale and commitment. Types of paid leave are described in the sections that follow.

Paid Time Off   Many employers combine vacation and sick leave into a single program called *paid time off* (PTO). PTO is a concept that allows employees to earn, typically by accrual over time, credits that the employee can then use whenever circumstances require that they be absent from work. PTO does not require justification for an absence; it simply requires an approval in the event of a planned absence or for the accrued balance to be used in an unplanned absence. In some states where PTO is offered, PTO accrual is treated in the same manner as vacation; that is, PTO is subject to the same rules that are applicable to vacation.

Vacation or Holiday Leave in the United States In the United States, there are paid holidays and vacations:

- **Paid holidays** While paid holidays are not legally required, employers find that both themselves and their employees benefit from them. The number of paid holidays vary from 6 to 12 a year, including New Year's Day, Memorial Day, Independence Day, Labor Day, Thanksgiving Day, and Christmas Day. Additional potential holidays include Martin Luther King, Jr.'s birthday, President's Day, Juneteenth, Columbus/Indigenous Peoples Day, Veteran's Day, and the day after Thanksgiving. Paid holidays are generally paid on the basis of the employer's schedule for a regular workday.

- **Paid vacation** The standard vacation is based on an accrual system measured on an employee's length of service. State laws vary on the management of vacation accrual. Some states do not allow a "use-it-or-lose-it" policy, while others are silent on the subject. In some cases, vacation can be carried over from year to year, with a provision for a reasonable cap. Many employers in states in which there is no rollover have a cash-out policy that allows an employee who hasn't taken their accrued vacation by the end of the year to receive cash back for their unused accrued vacation. Generally, employees must receive advance approval to use their vacation so as not to disrupt the employer's workflow.

Public or National or Bank Holidays Most countries provide vacation or holiday time to all employees regardless of job or status. Even in emerging countries, it is common for all employees to be provided a number of days for annual leave plus holidays. Generally, each country has paid public or national or bank holidays during which firms are required to close. Certain holidays may be observed on a local basis or only by certain industries. Public holidays may be required, or they may be only customary. In some Western European countries, most businesses shut down in August when most of their employees take their vacation.

Maternity and Paternity or Parental Leave At least some portion of parental leave is paid in most countries. In addition to maternity leave, some countries offer paternity and parental leave. A distinction is sometimes made between the two terms; they can, however, have the same meaning. Generally, parental leave is available to both mothers and fathers.

Leave Related to Illness There is also leave related to illness:

- **Leave in the United States** Organizations that otherwise have paid vacation policies usually also have paid sick leave policies to provide for time off because of illness or injury. These sick leave programs are primarily intended for the benefit of the employee, although in recent years sick leave programs have often been expanded to cover an employee's time off to care for a family member. Some states mandate that a portion of the employee's sick leave accrual must be allowed for family care.

- **Leave in other countries**   In most countries, it is common to take time off because of illness. Policies vary in terms of the number of days allowed away from work; the amount paid, if any; and in some cases, the applicable waiting period. Sick leave policies may be legally required, may be the result of collective bargaining, or may be determined by the employer.

Other Types of Leave   Some examples of other types of leave available in certain countries include the following:

- Paid leave to trade union officials for participating in trade union duties, union projects, or other activities.
- Paid leave to undergo training.
- In some cases, paid days off when workers get married. This extends to parents who are given paid time off when their children get married.
- In countries, predominantly Muslim, paid time off for prayer.
- Time off to carry out specified public duties such as campaigning as an official candidate in an election, voting, or jury duty.

Paid time off is mostly dictated by local laws. As such, it is important to know these laws and practices.

Family-Oriented Benefits   The composition of families in the United States has changed significantly in the past few decades. The number of traditional families, in which the man goes to work and the woman stays home to raise children, has declined significantly, while the percentage of two-worker families has more than doubled.

The growth in dual-career couples, single-parent households, and increasing work demands on many workers has accelerated the emphasis employers are placing on family-oriented benefits. Balancing family and work demands is a major challenge facing many workers at all levels of organizations. To provide assistance, employers have established a variety of family-oriented benefits.

Some of the family-oriented benefits offered in recent years include adoption benefits, childcare and elder care, flexible work hours, compressed workweeks, and telecommuting.

Flexible Work Hours   Flexible work schedules are those that vary from the standard work schedules of an organization. Since flexible schedules must meet the needs of both the employer and the employee, flexible work schedules are based on worker needs within set parameters approved by a supervisor. Table 4-21 lists some of the benefits and challenges of a flexible work schedule.

Compressed Workweeks   The compressed workweek is a special type of flexible schedule that involves working 40 hours per week but in fewer days than found in a typical 8-hours-per-day/5-day workweek. There are many different configurations to the compressed workweek. For instance, an employee can work 40 hours in 4 days (a 4/40 schedule) or 80 hours in 9 days (a 9/80 schedule). Table 4-22 describes some different configurations of a compressed workweek.

Flexible Work Schedule		
Benefits to Employee	**Benefits to Employer**	**Challenges**
• Schedule flexibility has been found to be highly associated with job satisfaction. • Employees who perceived having more flexibility on the job reported better sleep, more exercise, and a healthier lifestyle in general than those employees who did not perceive the availability of flexibility.	• Flexible work schedules positively affect work effort, job satisfaction, and improve worker productivity. • Flexible work schedules are positively related to employee engagement.	• Blending employees' schedule requests with business demands. • Using managers' time efficiently plus having enough supervisory coverage (the process of creating numerous schedules can be time-consuming, diverting managers' attention from other responsibilities). • Ensuring fair and equitable practices. • Maintaining customer loyalty (if, for example, the customers interact with different salespeople every time they come in).

Table 4-21   Flexible Schedule: Benefits and Challenges

Compressed Workweek		
Benefits to Employee	**Benefits to Employer**	**Challenges**
• Employees have positive view of the effects of a compressed workweek on home and work life. • Employees can schedule doctor appointments, deliveries, repair services, and such on the day that they are not in the office. • Employees save time and money by commuting less.	• Employers note reduced absenteeism among employees with compressed workweek schedules. • Some studies show improved productivity.	• Fatigue may increase with the initiation of a compressed workweek schedule, which may affect employee stress and, ultimately, productivity and performance. • The results of research have been mixed, with productivity either improving or staying the same after the implementation of a compressed workweek work schedule.

Table 4-22   Compressed Workweek: Benefits and Challenges

Health and Welfare   A group health plan is an employee welfare benefit plan established or maintained by an employer or by an employee organization (such as a union), or both, that provides medical care for participants or their dependents directly or through insurance, reimbursement, and the like.

Health plan coverage varies in other countries. Here are some examples:

- **Australia** In Australia, public coverage is guaranteed to all, but the state encourages wealthier individuals to use a private system by enforcing an additional 1 percent tax on those who fall above a certain income level but use the public system anyway. The Australian government's innovative techniques are evident in their death rate from conditions amenable to medical care, which was a startling 50 percent less than America's in 2003 and 25 percent less than the United Kingdom's.

- **Sweden** Sweden's low health care expenditures (US$5,331 per capita) in 2011 can in part be attributed to government initiatives that disincentivize sending patients to specialists when general practitioners can treat their illnesses. The Swedish government's success with cost efficiency explains why, even though public funding accounts for 85 percent of total Swedish health expenditure, this does not place an unreasonable constraint on taxpayers or the government.

- **United Kingdom** The United States and the United Kingdom are worlds apart in terms of health care. In the United Kingdom, the National Health Service (NHS) publicly covers various costs, including preventative services and mental health care. About 88 percent of prescriptions in the UK are exempt from charges. Despite American efforts to increase affordability and equity, the United Kingdom ranked first on indicators of efficiency in a recent Commonwealth Fund study. America could learn a lesson from the United Kingdom's successes at cutting administrative costs and closing loopholes that would otherwise cost the government millions.

- **Germany** With the oldest universal health care system in the world, 90 percent of Germans happily use the public system offered there, and just 10 percent of the population voluntarily uses the private system. Moving past the mythical trade-off between time and cost, Germany is one of the few countries to have quick access to specialty services with little out-of-pocket costs. Germany spends around half as much as America does on health care per capita, with few differences in quality of services between the two countries.

- **Netherlands** Interestingly, health insurance coverage is statutory in Holland but provided by private insurers competing for business. Insurers can decide by whom and how the care is delivered, which, to capitalists' great relief, allows the insured to choose between alternatives based on quality and costs. This system has proven to be highly effective. In 2010, 72 percent of Dutch adults saw their doctor the same or next day when they were sick, compared with only 57 percent of adults in America. Also, whereas one third of U.S. adults did not see a doctor when sick, went without recommended care, or failed to fill prescriptions because of costs, only 6 percent of adults in the Netherlands faced these issues.

- **Canada** In the realm of health care, America and its neighbor couldn't be more different. Canada's national health care system consists of a centralized body that sets standards that the 13 Canadian provinces must follow to receive funding. Hospitals are mainly private nonprofit organizations with their own governance structures, lending Canada an interesting balance between privatization and public ownership.[97]

Private Health Insurance   In other countries, health care is generally paid for through social insurance funded either by employers, by employees, through general taxation, or by some combination of these sources. By comparison, the United States is ahead of other countries in the use of high-end equipment and procedures. The United States also leads in the use of magnetic resonance imaging (MRI) machines, but the monetary cost of this technology is much higher in the United States than in other countries.

Other comparisons indicate that it is much harder for Americans to get same-day or next-day appointments and to get after-hour appointments. As a result, Americans use high-cost emergency rooms more frequently than those in other countries.

Most other countries have a single-payer system, but the United States has many different insurance companies with many different plans, plus overlapping programs such as Medicare, Medicaid, state plans, and programs for veterans.

Employee Assistance Programs   Employee assistance programs (EAPs) are benefit programs offered by many employers. EAPs are intended to help employees deal with personal problems that might adversely impact their job performance, health, and well-being. EAPs generally include short-term counseling and referral services for employees and their families. Supervisors may also refer employees (management referral) based on unacceptable performance or conduct issues.

EAP resources typically provide employees with confidential expert advice and support 24 hours a day, 7 days a week. Nearly all EAPs are outsourced, and most are priced on a per capita (that is, "per head") basis, whether services are used or not. EAPs address a broad and complex body of issues affecting mental and emotional well-being, such as alcohol and other substance abuse, stress, grief, family and financial problems, and psychological disorders. Many EAPs are active in helping organizations prevent and cope with workplace violence, trauma, and other emergency response situations.

Wellness Programs   These are programs intended to improve and promote health and fitness that are usually offered through the workplace, although insurance plans can offer them directly to their enrollees. Wellness programs allow employers to offer premium discounts, cash rewards, gym memberships, and other incentives to participate. Some examples of wellness programs include programs to help employees stop smoking, diabetes management programs, weight loss programs, and preventative health screenings.

Disability   The term *disability* represents a range of conditions differently measured, not only from country to country but also from program to program within a country. Yet, the general characteristics of the disabled are remarkably similar overall. They tend to be the older workers and those with relatively low educational levels and occupational status. When a country has a racial or national minority, members of the minority are more likely to be disabled than members of the majority population. Except in the aftermath of war, women have a higher incidence of disability than do men. The disabled are more likely to be unmarried and live alone than others in the working-age population.

Disability benefits have different meanings in different countries. Generally, disability benefits take the form of payments to individuals who are no longer able to work because of an illness or injury. Benefits may be short-term, long-term, or permanent—sometimes all of these choices.

Short-term benefits usually last up to 6 months; long-term benefits last longer. They usually start where short-term benefits end. Permanent disability may mean the same as a retirement income under health or medical circumstances.

Payments may come from employee contributions, employer contributions, government funding, or a combination of these sources. In some cases, funding may come from multiple agencies, depending on factors such as level of income, degree of disability, or even family status.

Life Insurance   In most countries, life insurance is provided by Social Security. Life insurance is mandated in some countries; in many cases, just a small amount is sufficient to cover burial but not sufficient to support a beneficiary. A majority of employers provide life insurance payable upon the death of the employee to a beneficiary as a voluntary company-provided benefit. Additional life insurance can often be purchased through an organization-sponsored group plan.

The situation in third-world countries is quite different from the norm in the United States and other richer countries. Poverty, disease, and living conditions directly affect the rate of mortality in many villages in third-world countries. Many people in those countries do not have sufficient food, live in war zones, and have to endure poor working conditions that are physically demanding. Money is used for basic needs such as food and clothing and maybe a roof over their head.

Employees in many Latin American countries receive life insurance that pays for up to 2 years' pay in the case of death. Employees in Peru with 4 or more years of service receive company-provided life insurance. Employees in the United Kingdom receive three to four times their annual salary as a life insurance benefit. Employees in the United States typically receive company-provided life insurance up to the equivalent of 1 year's salary with an option to personally purchase higher amounts of their choosing.

Workers' Compensation   Workers' compensation is a type of insurance paid for by the employer that provides wage replacement income and medical care benefits to employees who suffer work-related injuries or illnesses in return for giving up the employee's right to sue his or her employer for negligence. While the federal government mandates workers' compensation, the benefits are administered by the states. Individual states prescribe the rules governing coverage, eligibility, types of benefits, and the funding of benefits.

Workers' compensation defines a work-related disability as a physical condition that can result in an accident or illness and is caused, aggravated, precipitated, or accelerated by a work activity or environment. Workers' compensation only covers worker health problems that are identified as work-related disabilities, injuries, or illnesses.

Workers' compensation benefits include the following:

- Four types of workers' wage replacement benefits under certain circumstances:
  - **Income benefits**   These benefits replace income that might be lost because of a work-related injury or illness. Income benefits can include temporary income benefits, impairment income benefits, supplemental income benefits, and lifetime income benefits.

- **Medical benefits**   These benefits pay for necessary medical care to treat a work-related injury or illness.

- **Death benefits**   These benefits replace a portion of lost family income for eligible family members of employees who are killed on the job.

- **Burial benefits**   These benefits pay for some of the deceased employee's funeral expenses to the person who paid the expenses.

- Vocational rehabilitation or, in some cases, supplemental job displacement benefits

- Permanent and temporary partial or total disability benefits

- Survivor's benefits in cases of fatal work injuries or illnesses

Workers' compensation law in the United States is derived from European social insurance. It has evolved at the federal and state levels over the past century through a long series of reform (or redesign) initiatives.

Workers' compensation is a European concept, dating back to German Chancellor Otto von Bismarck. By the turn of the twentieth century, all European countries had workers' compensation laws. The German law required employees to pay part of the costs and called for highly centralized administration. Its coverage was broad, was compulsory, and provided for nonprofit mutual employers' insurance funds. Most industrialized nations now have national workers' compensation programs based on the German model.

In European Union (EU) countries, all workers are covered against the risk of wage loss because of temporary sickness through government agencies. Wage-replacement schemes consist of social insurance covering the loss of earnings because of old age, unemployment, temporary sickness, or permanent disability. Coverage typically lasts up to a year, with transition to longer-term disability insurance programs if needed.

Severance Packages   A severance package comprises the pay and benefits an employee may receive when leaving employment at a company. In addition to the employee's remaining regular pay owed, it may include some of the following:

- An additional payment based on length of service

- Payment for unused vacation time (unless mandated by state law) or sick leave

- Medical, dental, or life insurance

- Assistance in searching for new work, such as access to employment services or help in producing a résumé

- In some cases, a general release to be signed by the severed employee

Severance pay programs exist in most countries around the world. They typically provide lump-sum cash payments to workers who involuntarily or voluntarily separate from their employers. The size of the payment is usually related to the number of years worked with the last employer and is linked to the last salary in the job. Such payments were provided in many countries by employers before they were required by law. Organization-based severance pay schemes often also exist in parallel to legislated provisions.

Severance packages are required by law in many countries. Employers need to have a thorough understanding of the legal requirements associated with terminating an employee in countries where severance payments are a legal requirement. Some of the issues to address include the following:

- Requirements applicable to warnings for misbehavior or inadequate job performance
- Clearly stated reasons for the termination
- Specifically described severance payments with applicable conditions if any

Compensation for Termination Support is required for terminated employees in some countries, even when they have been terminated for cause. This can become expensive, as it often happens to at least some degree. If support requirements are ignored, it can be even more expensive because fines and penalties for noncompliance can be costly.

The amount of compensation paid to a terminated employee varies by country, but there may be some similarities within regions. Years of service is often a key factor when determining termination terms and end-of-service calculations. As an example, both Argentina and Bolivia require that a terminated employee receive 1 month's salary for each year worked, up to a defined maximum. Colombia also links the amount paid to the length of service. An employee who worked for a company 10 years is entitled to 45 days' pay, plus an additional 40 days' pay for each full year employed after that, up to a defined maximum. Other considerations include the employee's position, any employment agreements, and the employer's current policies and practices. Finally, organizations are responsible for ensuring that severance pay is compliant and fairly compensates terminated employees to avoid discrimination lawsuits and regulatory fines and penalties.

Retirement At some point, employees will reach an age where they no longer desire or are able to work. Retirement plans allow current employees to make financial provisions for the future. Retirement plans differ widely by country. Many retirement programs are mandated by the government and paid for through employee and employer contributions. Supplemental government support is sometimes provided.

The main goal is to provide retirement income to employees with some type of income payable periodically. Characteristics of the two most common types of plans, defined benefit plans and defined contribution plans, are summarized in Table 4-23.

Payments Most often, payments vary in terms of how they are made. They usually are made in the form of an annuity, paid monthly until death. In other countries, an amount may be paid in a single lump sum. The particular formulas for payment of retirement vary and are often complicated. They may be affected by the nature of the government funding strategies or variations that depend on such factors as age, level in the organization, and family characteristics.

Unemployment Insurance Unemployment insurance (UI) is a federally mandated program administered by the states that provides unemployment benefits to eligible workers who are unemployed through no fault of their own and who meet other eligibility requirements of applicable state law. UI benefits are designed to provide temporary financial assistance to unemployed workers. Each state administers its own unemployment

Type of Plan	Description
Defined benefit plan (DBP)	• The principal goal is to insure against loss of income in the event of retirement, death, or disability. • The benefit amount is determined based on a mathematical formula known well in advance. • The formula typically uses pay, age, and years of service as the primary variables in the event of a named contingencies, such as retirement, death, or disability. The employer is responsible for the funding.
Defined contribution plan (DCP)	• The principal goal is to accumulate savings through deferred compensation and investment earnings. • The employer promises to contribute periodically to each member's individual account. The amount contributed may vary based on pay, age, service, or member contributions. • The employee typically contributes to their own account. • The benefit is the account balance, payable in a lump sum, in installments, or as an annuity for life. • The benefit amount is determined based on what the employer contributed, what the employee contributed, and how well or poorly the investment grew over time.

Table 4-23   Types of Retirement Plans

insurance program within guidelines established by federal law. Eligibility for unemployment insurance, benefit amounts, and the length of time benefits are available are all determined by state law. In the majority of states, benefit funding is based solely on a tax imposed on employers. The amount a person receives is based on the person's salary up to a monthly maximum amount.

- **Eligibility**   To qualify for UI, individuals must meet requirements for wages earned or time worked during an established period of time referred to as the *base period*. In most cases, the individual must be unemployed through no fault of their own, must be available and actively seeking work, cannot be terminated for misconduct, and must not be unemployed because of a labor dispute.

  Individuals must file weekly or biweekly claims and respond to questions concerning their continuing unemployment. Any job offers or refusal of work must be reported for the period claimed.

- **Duration**   Most states grant UI benefits for up to 26 weeks, but this is often extended during periods of high unemployment by Congress with the approval of the president.

Social Security   First adopted in Germany in the 1880s to benefit the workers, Social Security was initially a compulsory sickness insurance for which the worker paid two-thirds of the cost and the employer one-third. In Great Britain, the National Insurance

Act was passed in 1911, and a compulsory unemployment insurance program as well as old-age insurance and sickness insurance programs were established. France adopted a program of voluntary unemployment insurance in 1905, and in 1928 made insurance plans for old age and sickness mandatory. Social Security was adopted in the United States in 1935 with the intent to move older workers out of the work force so younger workers could take their positions and lower the exorbitant unemployment rate of the Great Depression.

The following are the basic concepts behind Social Security:

- Social insurance in which people receive benefits or services in recognition of their contributions to an insurance program. These services typically include a provision for retirement pensions, disability insurance, survivor benefits, and unemployment insurance.

- Services that are provided by government or by a designated agency responsible for specific Social Security services. While this varies from country to country, it generally covers medical care; financial support during unemployment, sickness, or retirement; health and safety at work; aspects of social work; and even, in some cases, industrial relations.

- Basic security irrespective of participation in specific insurance programs where eligibility would otherwise be an issue. An example is assistance given to newly arriving refugees for basic necessities such as food, clothing, housing, education, money, and medical care.

Perquisites

There are several definitions of *perquisites,* or *perks.* Here is perhaps the most common from Wikipedia: "Any monetary or other incidental benefit beyond salary; a gratuity; a privilege or possession held or claimed exclusively by a certain person, group or class."[98]

The following are some of the more common perquisites identified by SHRM:

- **Free/discounted products or services**   Employees may be eligible for free products and services or discounts.

- **Mobile devices**   A cell phone, smartphone, personal digital assistant (PDA), or laptop may be provided for business needs.

- **Professional organizations/certifications**   Employee membership in professional associations and fees for professional certifications may be paid.

- **Training programs**   Employer payment for training programs may be available to many levels of employees.

- **Education fees**   Tuition assistance may be provided to employees. An employer may pay all or part of an employee's cost to attend college or university or technical school classes, allowing employees to continue to expand their knowledge and skills while working.

Some of the less common perquisites include the following:

- **Housing** Accommodations or related allowances are awarded to certain employees; these may be company-owned or company-leased. Allowances may be a fixed monetary amount or a percentage of basic salary. The specifics often depend on employee level. Furnishings may be provided.

- **Company car or cash car allowances** Cars are typically provided on status basis. Some countries offer a car allowance in lieu of a company car. In addition to the cost of the car, organizations often finance car maintenance, taxes, and insurance. Fuel costs are typically reimbursed for business purposes (except for senior executives, where all fuel costs are typically reimbursed). This is a common perk for outside sales staff.

- **Club memberships** Entrance fees as well as annual subscriptions for social or sports club memberships are paid by the employer.

- **Meal allowances** Lunch vouchers, meal tickets, meal subsidies, or subsidized/free lunches in the company restaurant/canteen may be granted to employees.

Some additional perquisites include financial and legal counseling and, to a lesser extent, medical check-ups, vaccinations, and immunizations; subsidized/low interest loans for the purchase of a house or car; and travel allowances. Perks may be negotiated with senior executives who, at times, can get quite creative in their employment contracts.

Metrics
As with other aspects of HR, knowing how to use metrics in regard to employee benefits is an important capability for every HR professional. Table 4-24 identifies three metrics applicable to determining the cost of benefits.

Legislation Affecting Compensation and Benefits

 A great many things influence the compensation of the employees of any organization. Some of these are external to the organization, such as the labor market and the law. Some are internal to the organization, such as organizational culture and policies. Some are part of the employee, such as skill and performance.

Complexities of Legal Compliance
The legal environment in which U.S. compensation administration is practiced consists of federal and state legislation and the regulations imposed by executive branches of these governments. In the case of some developing legal concepts, case law (court decisions) represents the public position. In these forms, government is stating public intentions or guides to decision-makers. Although private organizations tend to characterize these laws, regulations, and court decisions as constraints, they may also represent opportunities. In essence, the "rules" state that compensation must not be too low or (at times) too high but that within these limits compensation decisions should be left to the parties involved. Also, in the interest of fairness, certain groups have been protected, and all must be paid when wages are due.

Benefits Metric	Description	Formula
Benefits costs as a percentage of total payroll costs	Reflects the total cost of benefits compared to the total payroll costs for the organization.	$$\frac{\text{Total benefit costs}}{\text{Total payroll costs}}$$
Value: Pay and benefits combined make up total wage costs for an organization. This metric identifies the proportion of benefits costs to total payroll costs. It is most valuable when tracked over time to learn if the proportion is going up, down, or holding the same.		
Health care expense per employee	Percentage that measures the health care expense per employee for a given fiscal year. Total health care expenses include employee- and company-paid premiums, stop-loss insurance, and administrative fees.	$$\frac{\text{Total healthcare expenses}}{\text{No. of employees enrolled in a healthcare plan}}$$
Value: This measurement can show per-capita cost of employee benefits (for example, the average per person cost).		
Annual increase/decrease in benefits costs based on previous years and projected costs	Represents the expected increase/decrease in the organization's health care expense for a given fiscal year.	Compares the current health care expense per employee metric to previous years and project costs.
Value: This measurement alerts an organization to the increasing costs of benefits and helps the organization assess if actions should be taken to control benefit costs (for example, changing or reducing benefits, sharing more of the costs with employees, and so on).		

Table 4-24   Benefits Cost Metrics

As minimum and prevailing-wage laws place a floor under wage rates, Social Security, unemployment insurance, and workers' compensation can be described as placing a floor under benefits. Likewise, the Employee Retirement Income Security Act of 1974 (ERISA) and the 1980 amendments of it applying to multi-employer pensions can be considered assurance-of-benefit-payment laws.

Finally, in the United States, the network of state and federal laws is extensive. Some of the regulations apply only to firms with a specified minimum number of employees; others apply to all employee/employer relationships, regardless of enterprise size. Further, state laws may differ from federal laws. The general rule is to follow the regulation that most benefits or protects the employee when state laws differ from federal laws. (An organization can often do more than the law requires but cannot do less.)

Ultimately, HR practitioners must understand the employment laws, codes, and practices applicable in each of the countries and regions in which the organization operates. This necessitates due diligence on the part of HR practitioners that should include an understanding of the following:

- Standards and regulations set forth by international organizations, such as the International Labour Organization, the Organisation for Economic Cooperation and Development, the United Nations, and the European Union, as well as treaties and agreements, such as the United States, Mexico, and Canada

Agreement (USMCA) which replaced NAFTA when it was ratified in March 2020. Another treaty is Mercosur (a trade organization of Argentina, Brazil, Paraguay, Uruguay, and Venezuela).

- Country laws and regulations

- Regional and local laws and practices

- Extraterritorial application of national law

- Application of national laws to international-owned subsidiaries operating within a nation's borders.

Legal Areas for Compliance

The following legal areas for compliance represent key compensation and benefits topics applicable both in the United States and on a global scale. Keeping in mind the HR professional's responsibility to know, understand, and create compliance with the plethora of applicable laws, the following sections summarize these key topics.

Wage and Hour   To be compliant, employers need to understand the terms and conditions of wage and hour laws and how they apply to various classifications of workers wherever the operations are located. Basic wage and hour terms and conditions and key considerations include the following:

- **Minimum wage and increases**   How are minimum wages set (for example, hourly or monthly)? If any collective bargaining agreements are in force, do they impose different minimums or minimum wage increases?

- **Overtime pay and holiday pay**   What are the requirements for computing pay for legal overtime and locally worked holiday time (for example, time-and-a-half, less than time-and-a-half, double-time, or quadruple-time for overtime and holiday work; eligible if more than 40 hours in a week or after 8 hours on a single day)? If there are no statutory requirements for overtime and holiday pay, do collective bargaining agreements impose any? Who is entitled to overtime (for example, only hourly employees or managers as well)?

- **Equal pay**   What provisions are there to ensure that individuals doing the same work receive the same compensation?

- **Exemption**   What is the definition of "exempt" work under local law? Does the host country offer any special exemptions?

- **Cap on hours worked**   Is there a flat cap on hours worked (for example, weekly flat caps or hours of overtime per year)? Are there nominal caps that serve merely as reference points (for example, a 40-hour "standard" week but with "reasonable additional hours" allowed)?

- **Special issues under local law**   What miscellaneous local wage and hour rules are in place (for example, paid meal breaks, rules on break time, regulations on night work)?

PART II

Tax   Tax systems vary widely around the globe, from no-tax to high-tax regimes. Two commonly withheld taxes are national or federal tax and social tax. In some countries, income tax is dependent on whether an individual is considered a resident or a nonresident. Bonus payments may be treated differently from other taxable income. Many other variations exist.

Tax issues are quite complex for the employee on an international assignment as well as for the employee's organization. An employee may be subject to both host- and home-country taxes, depending on the countries involved and their tax treaties. Some countries permit residents to "break residency" while on an international assignment, thereby eliminating the need for them to pay into their home-country tax program. Generally, the structure of an employee's remuneration package should consider the various tax arrangements available.

Leave   This generally describes an employee benefit that provides paid or unpaid time off work. Country law may require employers to provide specific types of leave, such as time off for legal holidays, a certain amount of vacation each year, maternity and paternity or parental leave, and leave for an illness. Terms and conditions of minimum leave benefits are often stipulated by law. Many countries have generous leave laws. HR must be aware of the organization's legal obligations.

Social Security   Social Security (or social insurance) provides individuals with some level of income when faced with the contingencies of old age, survivorship, incapacity, disability, unemployment, or rearing children. Social Security may also offer access and coverage for curative or preventive health care. According to the International Social Security Association, Social Security can include social insurance programs, social assistance programs, universal programs, mutual benefit schemes, national provident funds, and other arrangements such as market-oriented approaches that, in accordance with national law or practice, form part of a country's Social Security system.

Health Care   Health care laws and regulations are complex. For example, some countries have a statutory universal access/universal coverage health care system. In other countries, employers offer employer-sponsored health insurance. Additionally, health care laws and regulations are often interlocking. Compliance typically cuts across government requirements and labor relations.

To varying degrees, health care affects all organizations, whether they conduct business in one location or multiple jurisdictions worldwide. Simply stated, employers must comply with health care regulations afforded their employees in a given country. Organizations must also comply with the medical privacy protections in force.

Disability   The concept of disability benefits varies across the globe. Generally, disability refers to payments made to employees who are physically unable to perform their jobs because of illness or injury. Sometimes it covers only incapacitation because of job-related injuries or illnesses; other times it also covers causes outside the workplace.

Short-term, long-term, and permanent disability are usually differentiated, and the source of funding and the length and amount of the benefit for each disability category may vary.

In addition, employers in some countries may be required to provide unpaid leave as a reasonable accommodation under disability antidiscrimination laws.

Severance To be compliant, a separation pay policy requires a detailed understanding of the complex laws governing severance and restructuring practices and protections for employees in different markets. Many countries have statutory protections regarding severance provisions. Where country laws dictate the terms of termination and end-of-service calculations, organizations have little room for discretion, even if the payments and benefits are significantly more generous than company policy would award in unregulated jurisdictions.

Pensions Upon retirement, workers in many countries continue to receive monetary compensation from their employer, the government, or a combination of both in the form of a pension. The provision of financial remuneration in retirement is critical for both individuals and societies. There is tremendous diversity in pension systems worldwide, as they are the unique product of each country's particular economic, social, cultural, political, and historical circumstances. Likewise, global pension funding issues are highly complicated.

Fiduciary Responsibility A fiduciary duty (or fiduciary obligation) implies a legal obligation of one party to act in the best interest of another. The obligated party is typically referred to as a *fiduciary* (for example, an individual or party entrusted with the care of money or property).

Countries worldwide regard fiduciary duties differently. Some regulations, for example, stipulate a broad view of fiduciary obligation, while other laws adopt more conservative approaches.

Chapter Review

This chapter covered five functional areas of professional HR knowledge and responsibilities. People are the heart of any organization. Until we get to the point where machines are able to run an organization autonomously, we will need to manage people resources. From overall HR strategy and talent acquisition to employee engagement and retention, HR professionals will have an important influence on their employer organizations. Employee learning and development and total rewards are two additional components of people requirements. Complexities abound. Satisfaction is just around the corner. Be ready to influence both the workforce and the employer organization. HR professionals have a unique position and huge responsibilities in this area.

Questions

1. Since 1978, the Uniform Guidelines on Employee Selection Procedures have required that many employers do what?

   A. Validate each step of their employment selection process.

   B. Submit their employment selection process to the EEOC.

   C. Review their employment selection process to be sure that there are sufficient veteran applicants.

   D. Publish their employment selection process each year.

2. What does PESTLE mean?

   A. Pests Eliminating Service Through Legitimate Extermination

   B. Payroll, employment, systems, training, liability, and employee

   C. Political, economic, social, technological, legal, and environmental

   D. Personnel, executives, systemic, training, legal, and ergonomics

3. The GS system used by the federal government is an example of which job evaluation method or system?

   A. A factor comparison method

   B. A classification system

   C. A point method ranking system

   D. A market comparison method

4. What is an employment brand?

   A. The market perception of what it is like to work for an organization

   B. A product name that appears on supermarket packages

   C. An industry-assigned label serial number

   D. A recruiting slogan

5. Soliciting applicant résumés to find minimally qualified applicants for a job opening is which of the following?

   A. The selection step of talent management

   B. The recruitment step of talent management

   C. Human resources planning

   D. A way to determine their salary requirements

6. Why is it important to measure turnover, retention rate, and reasons why people leave the payroll?

   A. They are all things the CEO wants to know.

   B. They can contribute to a monthly HR report to the executives.

   C. They are examples of reports HR professionals need clerical support to generate.

   D. They can all help control costs.

7. Why should a job offer always be in writing?

    A. It specifies details of compensation, benefits, and employment-at-will status.

    B. The federal Department of Labor requires it.

    C. State regulations specify that only with written offers can a job be filled.

    D. Actually, a job offer should not be made in writing because that constitutes a contract.

8. Employment interviews and written tests are considered to be what?

    A. Essential to the hiring manager's acceptance of candidates

    B. Selection devices that must be validated according to federal regulations

    C. HR purview only

    D. Always acceptable if the tests are bought "off the shelf" and not created in-house

9. Training for job selection interviewers is which of the following?

    A. Never needed

    B. Essential for all managers and supervisors who will participate in interviewing.

    C. Needed for supervisors who are new to employment selection interviewing

    D. A good idea for people who have been hired from a competitor organization

10. Why are written job descriptions a good strategic tool?

    A. They give incumbents a reference so they don't do something they aren't supposed to do.

    B. It is important to be able to follow responsibility trees in writing.

    C. Federal civil rights enforcement agencies insist on written descriptions.

    D. They provide reference for job seekers as well as incumbents, managers, and supervisors.

11. What is the key benefit to developing long-term goals?

    A. Showing the interaction of planning, people, and processes

    B. Separating the effects of culture against the intentions and goals

    C. Increasing the influence on internal factors

    D. Aligning the use of resources with intended strategic goals

12. What are the stages of the Strategy process?

    A. Formulation, buy-in, communication, evaluation

    B. Formulation, development, implementation, evaluation

    C. Development, communication, buy-in, implementation

    D. Senior management development, communication, implementation, evaluation

13. Herzberg's motivation-hygiene theory is based on which two categories of needs?

    A. Psychological and basic needs

    B. Motivational and security needs

    C. Extrinsic and intrinsic needs

    D. Safety and self-esteem needs

14. Which of the following is considered to be an HR strategic task in an organization?

    A. Developing an ergo training program to reduce repetitive injuries

    B. Ensuring backup and retention of records off-site

    C. Administering new hire orientation

    D. Providing analysis to management to forecast workforce needs

15. The Equal Pay Act prohibits wage discrimination on the basis of what?

    A. Race

    B. Sex

    C. Seniority

    D. Merit

16. You have been asked to develop a 5-year budget for the HR function. In what way would the existence of the organization's strategic plan be of help to you in the development of the multiyear budget?

    A. Because it's a budgeting activity, it will help in providing increase allotments for employees.

    B. The goals identified in the strategic plan will give you an idea of how to allocate monies for each year.

    C. The strategic plan will help you compete for training dollars versus marketing dollars.

    D. It will cause you to identify and prioritize the HR activities and the needed resources that align with the strategic plan's goals.

17. Which of the following laws does not directly relate to a company's compensation or benefits programs?

    A. Equal Pay Act

    B. Fair Labor Standards Act

    C. Port-to-Portal Act

    D. Uniform Guidelines on Employee Selection Procedures

18. Which of the following is not a pay differential?

    A. Hazard pay

    B. Shift pay

    C. Base pay

    D. Call-back pay

19. A home appliance manufacturer guarantees its installers a base wage plus an extra
$25 for each job completed to specifications. What system is the employer using?

    A. Merit pay system

    B. Productivity-based pay system

    C. Competency-based system

    D. Flat-rate system

20. An employee elects a $500 annual deferment in his Section 125 Flexible Benefits
Plan. His employer pays an FSA claim for $500 in March. In April, the employee
terminates his employment after deferring only $290 to his plan. What happens
in this situation?

    A. The employee must pay the company $290 for the amount in excess of his
    actual deferral.

    B. The employer may withhold $290 from the employee's final paycheck.

    C. The employee is entitled to the full reimbursement for $500.

    D. The employee becomes ineligible for the full FSA reimbursement.

21. According to COBRA, a company with 20 or more employees must offer which
of the following?

    A. Health insurance to its employees

    B. Continued medical insurance coverage to employees terminated for gross
    misconduct

    C. COBRA benefits to workers if the company terminates its health plan

    D. COBRA benefits to spouses of deceased workers

22. Which of the following is an action taken in the United States to lower budgets
that would most likely violate compensation laws in other countries?

    A. Reducing base salary levels

    B. Offering early retirement packages

    C. Delaying or not filling open positions

    D. Downgrading job titles

23. If a leave under FMLA can be reasonably anticipated, how much notice must the
employee give the employer?

    A. 7 days

    B. 14 days

    C. 30 days

    D. 90 days

24. An organization establishes an ESOP via which of the following?

   A. By deducting a small amount from the individual's pay for the purchase of stock

   B. By using stock as collateral to borrow capital from a financial institution

   C. By providing upper management with a bonus

   D. By having its profits distributed with favorable tax treatment

25. HR manager Sue makes sure that her HR staff has access to leading best practices and theories. What key element of Sue's leadership is she demonstrating according to Kouzes and Posner?

   A. Challenging processes

   B. Inspiring shared vision

   C. Enabling her staff to act

   D. Encouraging spirit

Answers

1. **A.** Each employment selection step must be validated if the employer has 15 or more workers on the payroll.

2. **C.** Political, Economic, Social, Technological, Legal, and Environmental are the components of PESTLE.

3. **B.** The GS system used by the federal government is probably the best known classification system.

4. **A.** An employment brand is a positive perception created in the job market for what it is like to work for that organization.

5. **B.** The employee lifecycle begins with recruitment, which is seeking qualified applicants.

6. **D.** Cost control is the reason for measuring turnover.

7. **A.** Explaining compensation, benefits, and employment-at-will status in writing will minimize any complications later.

8. **B.** Each employment interview and written test is considered a selection device. All must be validated according to the Uniform Guidelines on Employee Selection Procedures.

9. **B.** Essential for all managers and supervisors who will participate in interviewing. All interviewers must be properly trained so they will understand what questions they may and may not ask.

10. **D.** Having a written job description provides an anchor for all concerned parties when needing information about job duties and responsibilities.

11. **D.** Strategy is the identification of long-term goals, and having long-term goals allows management in an organization to align and appropriate resources to those goals in a consistent yet long-term manner.

12. B. The four stages of the Strategy process are formulation, development, implementation, and evaluation.

13. C. Hygiene factors are considered extrinsic and associated with job security, pay, working conditions, and relationships, whereas motivational factors are considered intrinsic, associated with recognition, achievement, and personal growth–related events in the job.

14. D. Answers A, B, and C are considered activities and functions of the HR department. Providing analysis for forecasting future workforce needs for, say, a new plant or office opening identified in the strategic plan would be considered an HR strategic task.

15. B. The Equal Pay Act requires that men and women be given equal pay for equal work in the same establishment. The jobs need not be identical, but they must require substantially equal skill, effort, responsibility, and similar working conditions. It is job content, not job title, that determines whether jobs are substantially equal.

16. D. Strategy assists all function leadership, including the HR function, to allocate and request resources that will be needed to implement initiatives that align with the organization's strategy.

17. D. In 1978, the Civil Service Commission, the Department of Labor, the Department of Justice, and the Equal Opportunity Commission jointly adopted the Uniform Guidelines on Employee Selection Procedures to establish uniform standards for employers for the use of selection procedures and to address adverse impact, validation, and recordkeeping requirements. The other choices are laws that directly relate to employers' compensation programs.

18. C. Hazard pay, shift pay, and call-back pay are all differentials. Base pay is the foundation of an employer's compensation program.

19. B. The employer is using an incentive program based on performance results, which is considered a productivity-based system. A merit-pay system does not address incentive pay. A competency-based system addresses capabilities, whereas a flat-rate system establishes a fixed rate of pay.

20. C. Flexible spending accounts are authorized under Section 125 (Cafeteria) plans. FSAs offer employees a pretax method to defer pay toward their group health plan costs as well as their out-of-pocket medical costs. FSA healthcare claims below the annual elected deferral must be paid by the employer when they are incurred, even though the employee's FSA payroll deductions have not created a sufficient balance to cover the expense.

21. D. COBRA provides up to 36 months' continuation of group health benefits in the event of a divorce or death of the employed spouse. None of the other choices is a valid COBRA provision.

22. A. Decreasing an employee's salary is illegal in most countries, particularly in Latin America and Europe. It is legal in the United States.

23. C. FMLA allows employers to require 30 days advance notice when the leave can be reasonably anticipated.

24. **B**. An employee stock ownership plan (ESOP) is an employee-owner method that provides a company's workforce with an ownership interest in the company. In an ESOP, companies provide their employees with stock ownership, often at no up-front cost to the employees. ESOP shares, however, are part of employees' remuneration for work performed. Shares are allocated to employees and may be held in an ESOP trust until the employee retires or leaves the company. The ESOP can borrow money to buy shares, with the company making tax-deductible contributions to the plan to enable it to repay the loan.

25. **C**. The HR manager is following Practice 3, enabling others to act, which is what Kouzes and Posner discuss in their research about exemplary leaders who encourage collaboration.

References

1. The SHRM Body of Applied Skills and Knowledge, pages 56–58.

2. Mintzberg, Henry. *The Rise and Fall of Strategic Planning,* Free Press, January 1994.

3. Porter, Michael E. *Competitive Strategy: Techniques for Analyzing Industries and Competitors,* Free Press, June 1998.

4. Porter, Michael E. *Competitive Advantage: Creating and Sustaining Superior Performance,* Free Press, June 1998.

5. Freemen, R. Edward. *Strategic Management: A Stakeholder Approach,* Cambridge University Press, March 1998.

6. https://www.professionalacademy.com/blogs-and-advice/marketing-theories-pestel-analysis

7. https://www.inc.com/encyclopedia/industry-analysis.html

8. Porter, Michael E. "How Competitive Forces Shape Strategy," *Harvard Business Review* (March–April 1979).

9. https://www.mckinsey.com/business-functions/strategy-and-corporate-finance/our-insights/enduring-ideas-the-ge-and-mckinsey-nine-box-matrix

10. Community Tool Box, "Developing Successful Strategies: Planning to Win," https://ctb.ku.edu/en/table-of-contents/structure/strategic-planning/develop-strategies/main

11. https://blog.marketresearch.com/6-ways-to-differentiate-your-business-from-the-competition

12. Porter, Michael E. *Competitive Advantage: Creating and Sustaining Superior Performance,* Free Press, June 1998, pages 11–15.

13. Mind Tools, "Porter's Competitive Strategies," https://www.mindtools.com/pages/article/newSTR_82.htm

14. Ibid.

15. https://www.thebalancecareers.com/business-strategy-tips-for-hr-manager-1916828

16. http://smallbusiness.chron.com/growth-strategies-business-4510.html

17. Timmons, J. *New Venture Creation: Entrepreneurship for the 21st Century,* Irwin, 1998, page 14.

18. Christensen, C.M., R. Alton, C. Rising, and A Waldeck. "The Big Idea: The New M&A Playbook," *Harvard Business Review*, March 2011.

19. https://www.shrm.org/resourcesandtools/tools-and-samples/toolkits/pages/mergersandacquisitions.aspx

20. Wheeler, Gary. "The Virtual HR Director LLC," https://vdocuments.net/aligning-hr-to-business-strategy.html?page=1

21. https://www.imaworldwide.com/resources-aim-methodology

22. Jones, Phil. *Communicating Strategy,* Taylor & Francis, March 2017.

23. https://hbr.org/2011/08/eight-ways-to-energize-your-te

24. https://onstrategyhq.com/resources/strategic-implementation/

25. Kubler-Ross, Elizabeth. *On Death and Dying: What the Dying Have to Teach Doctors, Nurses, Clergy and their Own Families,* Google Books, 1969.

26. Kirkpatrick, Donald L. *How to Manage Change Effectively: Approaches, Methods, and Case Examples,* Jossey-Bass Management Series, 1985.

27. https://peterstark.com/employee-responses-change/

28. https://www.fastcompany.com/3015083/6-steps-for-successfully-bringing-change-to-your-company

29. https://www.shrm.org/resourcesandtools/tools-and-samples/toolkits/pages/managingorganizationalchange.aspx

30. https://www.torbenrick.eu/blog/performance-management/how-to-ensure-successful-performance-measurement/

31. Rohm, Howard. "Balanced Scorecards," Balanced Scorecard Institute, 2018.

32. https://www.nap.edu/read/11344/chapter/5#22

33. https://www.business-case-analysis.com/financial-metrics.html

34. https://www.accountingtools.com/articles/what-is-variance-analysis.html

35. https://www.business.qld.gov.au/running-business/growing-business/trend-analysis

36. Kouzes, James M. and Barry Z. Posner. *The Leadership Challenge, Sixth Edition,* Jossey-Bass, April 2017.

37. Fox, Erica Ariel. *Winning from Within: A Breakthrough Method for Leading, Living and Lasting Change,* Harper Business, September 2013.

38. Goleman, Daniel. *Emotional Intelligence, Tenth Edition,* Bantam Books, September 2005.

39. Goldsmith, Marshall. *What Got You Here Won't Get You There,* Hachette Books, January 2007.

40. McGregor, Douglas. *The Human Side of Enterprise,* McGraw Hill, 2005.

41. Blake, Robert R. and Jane S. Mouton. *The New Managerial Grid,* Gulf Publishing Company, May 1978.

42. Hersey, Paul and Ken Blanchard. *Management of Organizational Behavior,* Prentice Hall, 2012.

43. Fiedler, Fred Edward. *A Theory of Leadership Effectiveness,* McGraw Hill, 1967.

44. Adair, John. *Action-Centered Leadership,* Gower Publishing Company, June 1979.

45. Katzenbach, Jon R. and Douglas K. Smith. *The Wisdom of Teams,* HarperBusiness, July 2006.

46. House, Robert J., Peter W. Dorfman, Mansour Javidan, Paul J. Hanges, and Mary F. Sully de Luque. *Strategic Leadership Across Cultures: GLOBE Study of CEO Leadership Behavior and Effectiveness in 24 Countries,* SAGE Publications, August 2013.

47. Hofstede, Geert. *Culture's Consequences: Comparing Values, Behaviors, Institutions, and Organizations Across Nations, Second Edition,* SAGE Publications, 2001.

48. The SHRM Body of Applied Skills and Knowledge, pages 59–60.

49. 2016 Survey Results, https://www.manpowergroup.com/talent-shortage-2016, accessed on March 5, 2018.

50. https://go.manpowergroup.com/talent-shortage

51. https://universumglobal.com/what-is-employer-branding/, accessed on March 6, 2018.

52. http://press.careerbuilder.com/2017-06-15-Number-of-Employers-Using-Social-Media-to-Screen-Candidates-at-All-Time-High-Finds-Latest-CareerBuilder-Study, accessed on March 6, 2018.

53. https://www.linkedin.com/pulse/20141016104025-615702-recruiting-vs-sourcing-a-day-in-the-life/, accessed on March 6, 2018.

54. https://www.mckinsey.com/business-functions/organization/our-insights/why-diversity-matters, accessed on March 6, 2018.

55. https://www.recruiter.com/i/6-key-metrics-to-measure-the-success-of-your-recruiting-process/, accessed on March 7, 2018.

56. Ford, Wayne D. *How to Spot a Phony Résumé,* The Management Advantage, Inc., 1998.

57. SHRM 2020 Learning System, People Book, page 100.

58. https://recruitee.com/articles/interview-red-flags

59. Willer, Dory, William H. Truesdell, and William D. Kelly. *aPHR Associate Professional in Human Resources Certification Exam Guide,* McGraw Hill, 2017.

60. Equal Employment Opportunity Commission, "Consideration of Arrest and Conviction Records in Employment Decisions under Title VII of the Civil Rights Act of 1964," www.eeoc.gov/laws/guidance/arrest_conviction.cfm, published on April 25, 2012.

61. U.S. Department of Justice, Bureau of Justice Statistics, "Prisoners in 2012—Advance Counts," www.bjs.gov/content/pub/pdf/p12ac.pdf, published July 2013.

62. Citing yearly compensation on a job offer letter has resulted in employers being obligated for the balance of the yearly amount when they terminated employees earlier than 1 year. Citing amounts in weekly or monthly terms can reduce that potential liability substantially.

63. https://www.eeoc.gov/laws/guidance/what-you-should-know-eeoc-and-arrest-and-conviction-records

64. The SHRM Body of Applied Skills and Knowledge, pages 61–62.

65. 2014 Modern Survey, Inc.

66. State of the Global Workplace, Employee Engagement Insights for Business Leaders Worldwide 2013, Gallup, Inc.

67. https://hbr.org/2014/11/a-primer-on-measuring-employee-engagement

68. https://www.qualtrics.com/support/wp-content/uploads/2017/10/Qualtrics-EBook-How-to-Design-an-Employee-Engagement-Survey.pdf

69. https://www.torbenrick.eu/blog/employee-engagement/infographic-what-is-the-business-case-for-employee-engagement/

70. Maslow, Abraham. "A Theory of Human Motivation," *Psychological Review* (1943), 50, 370–96.

71. Ouchi, William. *Theory Z: How American Management Can Meet the Japanese Challenge,* Basic Books, January 1981.

72. Pink, Daniel H. *Drive: The Surprising Truth About What Motivates Us,* Riverhead Books, April 2011.

73. Vance, Robert J. "Employee Engagement and Commitment," The SHRM Foundation, 2006, https://www.shrm.org/hr-today/trends-and-forecasting/special-reports-and-expert-views/Documents/Employee-Engagement-Commitment.pdf

74. 2016 SHRM/Globoforce Employee Recognition Survey, https://resources.globoforce.com/globoforce-blog/5-takeaways-from-the-new-shrm-globoforce-recognition-survey

75. https://www.workhuman.com/resources/reports-guides/unleashing-the-human-element-at-work-transforming-workplaces-through-recognition, May, 2022.

76. "How Employee Retention Impacts the Bottom Line," *Voice, The Engage for Success Magazine,* post by David Bator of TemboStatus (www.tembostatus.com/), November 12, 2014.

77. https://www.roberthalf.com/blog/management-tips/effective-employee-retention-strategies, accessed on March 8, 2018.

78. The SHRM Body of Applied Skills and Knowledge, page 63.

79. www.thechangeforum.com/Learning_Disciplines.htm

80. www.trainingmag.com/5-trends-future-learning-and-development

81. www.ntl.org

82. Cross, K. P. *Adults as Learners,* Jossey-Bass, 1981.

83. www.kirkpatrickpartners.com

84. https://www.researchgate.net/publication/ 357403465_Barriers_to_Participation_in_Adult_Learning

85. Finkelstein, Stanley. *Why Smart Executives Fail: And What You Can Learn from Their Mistakes,* Portfolio Trade, 2004.

86. https://www.td.org, search for "Leadership Development Through Emotional Intelligence and Meditation Premium Content," September 8, 2014, by Maynard Brusman.

87. www.bloomberg.com/bw/management/a-new-era-for-global-leadership-development-02172012.html

88. www.ccl.org/Leadership/pdf/research/ChallengesLeadersFace.pdf

89. The SHRM Body of Applied Skills and Knowledge, page 65.

90. *World at Work* website (www.worldatwork.org)

91. Scott, Dow, Tom McMullen, and Mark Royal. "Reward Fairness and Equity," World at Work, May 2011.

92. Eani, Susan. "The Essentials of Managing Global Compensation Practices," World at Work.

93. www.patriotsoftware.com

94. www.dictionary.com

95. Heneman III, Herbert and Timothy Judge. *Staffing Organizations, Sixth Edition,* McGraw Hill, 2008.

96. https://en.wiktionary.org

97. Jain, Sona. "7 Countries That Show Us How Health Care Should Be Done," June 11, 2013, http://mic.com/articles/46063/7-countries-that-show-us-how-health-care-should-be-done

98. https://en.wiktionary.org

Organization

The HR expertise domain of Organization Knowledge counts toward 18 percent for both exams. This domain covers the essential HR knowledge needed for relating to the organization. The following are the functional areas that fall within the Organization Knowledge domain:

- Functional Area 6: Structure of the HR Function
- Functional Area 7: Organizational Effectiveness & Development
- Functional Area 8: Workforce Management
- Functional Area 9: Employee & Labor Relations
- Functional Area 10: Technology Management

HR professionals are expected to know how to perform the following SHRM Body of Applied Skills and Knowledge (BASK) statements for the Organization Knowledge domain:

- **01** Create an effective HR function that is fully aligned to organizational strategy
- **02** Enhance the effectiveness of the organization at large
- **03** Ensure that the organization's talent pool has the skills and capabilities to achieve organizational goals
- **04** Promote positive relationships with employees
- **05** Leverage technology to improve HR functioning

Functional Area 6: Structure of the HR Function

Here is SHRM's BASK definition: "Structure of the HR Function encompasses the people, processes, theories, and activities involved in the delivery of HR-related services that create and drive organizational effectiveness."[1]

All career levels of HR are expected to know and support the different types of HR service models and understand how HR services are integrated. The HR organization must be structured to meet the needs of the organization and its stakeholders.

Gathering feedback, collecting data, and using the appropriate metrics to determine HR performance and satisfaction all enable HR professionals to evaluate HR's effectiveness and identify areas needing improvement and change.

Key Concepts

- Approaches to HR function/service models (for example, centralized, decentralized, global resources)
- Approaches to HR structural models (for example, center of excellence, shared services, business partners, matrix)
- Elements of the HR function (for example, recruiting, talent management, compensation, benefits)
- HR staff roles, responsibilities, and functions (for example, generalists, specialists, HR business partners)
- Outsourcing of HR functions (for example, recruiting, benefits administration, payroll, legal, contract management, investigations)
- HR-function metrics (for example, HR staff per full-time employee, customer satisfaction, key performance indicators [KPIs], balanced scorecard)

The following are the proficiency indicators that SHRM has identified as key concepts:

For All HR Professionals	Advanced HR Professionals (SCP Exam)
Adapts work style to fit the organization's HR service model to ensure timely and consistent delivery of services to stakeholders	Designs, implements, and adjusts the HR service model for the organization to ensure efficient and effective delivery of services to stakeholders
Seeks feedback from stakeholders to identify opportunities to improve HR function	Creates long-term goals and implements changes that address feedback from stakeholders to identifying opportunities for HR function improvements
Acts as HR point-of-service contact for key stakeholders within a division or group	Ensures that all elements of the HR function are aligned and integrated, and that they provide timely and consistent delivery of services to stakeholders
Consults with all levels of leadership and management on HR issues	Identifies opportunities to improve HR operations by outsourcing work or implementing technologies that automate HR functions
Coordinates with other HR functions to ensure timely and consistent delivery of services to stakeholders	Designs and oversees programs to collect, analyze, and interpret HR-function metrics to evaluate the effectiveness of HR activities in supporting organizational success

For All HR Professionals	Advanced HR Professionals (SCP Exam)
Ensures that outsourced and/or automated HR functions are integrated with other HR activities	
Analyzes and interprets key performance indicators (KPIs) to understand the effectiveness of the HR function	
Works collaboratively with departments outside of HR to deliver and support HR-related functions (such as working with IT to implement an HR information system)	

The Strategic Role of HR

The strategic role of HR professionals is to strengthen the relationship between the employees and the employer.

The Evolving Role of HR Professionals

The role of human resources has evolved over the years, probably more so than any other department function in an organization. In the old days, HR managers simply kept payroll records and benefit assignments straight. In the early twentieth century, HR as a specialized function began with a narrow focus of hiring and keeping records of employees—an operational and administrative function. Changes in HR have been stimulated by external changes, and a major change has been the need for HR professionals to participate in strategic planning and implementation of those strategic plans.

HR's staff typically provided the following three types of support:

- **Advice**   Advising line management on workforce matters, including policies and laws, providing solutions and procedural steps, offering assistance and guidance on employee issues, diagnosing problems or gathering facts, and providing resources

- **Service**   Maintaining records, hiring, training, answering, and clarifying information within a broad customer base, including management, employees, legal and regulatory agencies, applicants, retirees, families of employees, and vendors

- **Control**   An authoritative role involved in consistency of policy application, evaluation of employee performance, corrective action, and designing or implementation of employee programs

While the focus continues to have a foundational basis in the day-to-day operational role (acquisition, development, resolving issues, and communications), along with administrative transactional activities (maintaining a human resource information system [HRIS]), the significance of HR's contributions has become more apparent as a business strategist with a forward-thinking, long-term global focus that includes protecting the organization from potential risks. HR professionals have earned a seat at the executive round table, contributing to the organization's direction with strategic solutions for talent management, creating organizational culture, formulating and developing strategies, and balancing the external and internal environments to help the organization achieve its goals. The title of chief human resource officer (CHRO) is common in today's large organizations—a recognition that indicates HR has come a long way up the perceived value-added scale. In today's global competitive business climate, the HR role must contribute in quantifiable business terms, outlining a return on investment (ROI) that ensures the effective and efficient use of its human capital.

Table 5-1 provides a brief historical perspective of the evolution of the human resource function.

HR as a Profession A job is something you can go to every day, perform the assigned duties, and go home without any further attachment. Human resource management used to fall into this category. Now, however, HR professionals are placed into a role that demands strategic thinking and strategic planning, with an eye on overall organizational health and success. Early on, "personnel management" was a staff function.

Era	HR's Identity	Business Era	Issues for HR
Pre-1900	HR did not exist	Gilded Age—most small businesses and a few large corporations called "trusts"	Responsibilities mostly associated with payroll; hiring done by owners or accounting personnel
1900–19	Referred to as *Labor Relations*	Progressive Era	People could be replaced with machinery
1920–39	Referred to as *Employee and Industrial Relations*	World War I and civil service	Formalized processes brought in; workers' rights issues
1940–59	Referred to as *Personnel Administration*	World War II and scientific research	Efficiency productivity experts, benefits administration, more women in the workforce
1960–79	Referred to as *Personnel Management*	Civil Rights and government compliance	Legal compliance reporting and policing, policy application consistency
1980–99	Referred to as *Human Resources Management*	Knowledge and service economy; hostile takeovers; M&A; technology	HR theories for employee motivation, training and development, force reductions, immigration hiring
2000–09	Referred to as *People or Talent Management*	9/11 attack on U.S. and homeland security; global competitiveness	Cultural diversity, outsourcing, technology, cultural blending, talent acquisition, offshoring
2010–Present	Evolving: *HR Business Consultants within the Human Asset Department* is trending	Global economy; mobile technology age; climate change	Talent retention, organizational restructuring, employee engagement, cost containment, corporate social responsibility

Table 5-1 Evolution of Human Resources

Later "human resource management" became a management function. In recent years, HR management has become a strategic function helping the organization achieve its strategic goals.

HR in the Twentieth Century   Following the creation of a "personnel department" in the mid-twentieth century, people in that portion of the organization were expected to shift their focus toward a broader perspective of HR management. It became more than a personnel and payroll support function.

Administrative Services   HR workers were assigned duties including the following:

- Personnel records management
  - Benefits enrollment
  - Attendance tracking
  - Training recordkeeping
  - Employee data management, such as with an HRIS
- Employee award tracking
- Office party planning

Operational Services   Direct support of the operational units in the employer organization became necessary. The following were added to the HR responsibilities:

- Labor relations expertise
- Recruiting and staffing
- Training preparation and management such as operations and management skills
- Policy development
- Employee handbook management

HR in the Twenty-First Century   Now in the twenty-first century, HR professionals find themselves involved more with strategic planning and implementation.

Strategic Administrative Role   The functions handled in the twentieth century still exist, but they have morphed into a strategic support role. Personnel records management is now responsible for assessing employee benefit programs, as they contribute to the financial success of the organization. This includes impact analysis on employee recruiting and retention and its effect on the profit and loss performance of the company. Employee award tracking has evolved into a strategic assessment of programs that will improve employee retention and engagement. Office party planning has gone away in many organizations. In its place is the strategic assessment and selection of employee support programs, such as free or low-cost food services, and specific employee motivation programs.

Strategic Operational Role   Labor relations has grown over the years with the transitioning of union contract protections to laws that apply to most employers. Those protections, such as wage and hour restrictions, now are available to most employees in the country. The benefits offered by labor unions these days are less numerous than they used to be. Many of the old securities from labor contracts are now legal protections at both the state and federal levels.

Policy development involves a wide swath of topics—from employee benefit offerings to disciplinary processes. Those policies are being assessed based on their strategic impact on the organization and its mission. Once policies are developed, employee handbook content can be prepared that communicates those policies to the employee body. Even the designation *employee* is being altered by some organizations. Some of the terms now used include *cast member*, *crew member*, *associate*, and *staff member*.

Changes That Impact the HR Profession

The largest impact on the HR profession has come from state and federal legislative bodies creating new laws that contain employee protections that once were available only to union members within a bargaining unit.

David Ulrich presents his approach in terms of deliverables, or outcomes, for which HR should be responsible in new strategic roles: strategy execution, administrative efficiency, employee contribution, and capacity for change.[2] In the course of delivering in these four areas, he describes four corresponding roles for HR to play within a business: (a) as a strategic partner working to align HR and business strategy, (b) as an administrative expert working to improve organizational processes and deliver basic HR services, (c) as an employee champion, listening and responding to employees' needs, and (d) as a change agent managing change processes to increase the effectiveness of the organization. One of unique things about Ulrich's approach is that it includes all of the ways that HR can deliver value to an organization, rather than shifting focus from one area to another.

Workforce/Workplace Changes   According to an article in *Work Design Magazine*,

> "By 2027, global socioeconomic shifts will result in larger changes in worker type, available jobs, and ways of working. The rise of the middle class in emerging markets will have a large impact on the overall workforce. Currently, one-third of the global middle class is in Asia Pacific. By 2030, this proportion will double, due in large part to expansions of the middle class in countries like China and India. This growth will result in changes in buying habits, driving economic growth. According to a Morgan Stanley estimate, by 2030 middle-class spending will almost double that of 2010."

> "New patterns will emerge in occupations: jobs in service-oriented industries such as healthcare and hospitality sustain growth, but a significant portion of workers gravitate towards more flexible work arrangements and freelance jobs. There will be an influx of jobs enabled by emergent technologies."[3]

Globalization   Globalization is not a fad. It is a movement that will only solidify the ways of doing business as the days go by. The impacts it will have on employer organizations will be profound. Employee groups operating in remote locations with different laws and customs present challenges to professional HR managers. The role of diversity management will grow even bigger than it is today. Value added will be the operating expectation for every group, including HR. If something can't be measured and shown to add value, the HR organization will be hard-pressed to convince the C-suite that it should be done.

Ethics   In the past, HR professionals had to wrestle with different employment laws in the different states where they had employees working. Now more than ever before, it is necessary to wrestle with laws and customs in multiple countries. In some countries, there is an expectation that money will be offered to those approving work projects. That is unacceptable to an HR professional's ethics, so dilemmas will arise when the strategic repositioning of workforce groups becomes necessary. It is incumbent upon HR professionals to reconcile those differences so that the work can get done and the local expectations are satisfied without violating U.S. laws.

Organizational Growth or Retraction   Any time an organization increases or decreases its number of employees significantly, there are considerations for legal compliance and employee morale. When groups are small, there is a tendency for individuals to bond easily around the group's mission. As groups grow, that sense is diluted, and bonding can become more difficult. There can be issues related to who is promoted and who is not, or who is given a desirable work assignment and who is passed over. Leadership from HR professionals takes on critical importance. How they communicate and help employees through difficult periods of time will determine how well the organization can meet its strategic objectives.

When organizations reduce their employee headcount, other problems occur that require HR interventions and leadership. Layoffs, downsizing programs, relocations, and involuntary terminations can all result in employee dissatisfaction. How HR professionals handle these difficulties will determine how well the force reduction will reach its goals.

Movement of Decision-Making   As new workforce locations are opened in remote countries or even remote locations within the United States, there is a risk that they will experience the "out of sight, out of mind" syndrome. Managing people from a distance involves permitting and even encouraging decision-making by people at those locations. Working out what decisions should be local and what should be held for headquarters becomes an operational requirement with which HR can help.

Extended Organizations   When manufacturing, marketing, or administrative organizations find it necessary to create workforce placement in new, extended locations, HR can help facilitate those movements. Any expansion into an international environment will require some adjustments. It is not solely a need to hire people in the new location but also a need for cultural adaptation. That is a two-way process. New employees in the remote location must learn about the corporate culture and how to behave within it. The corporation must also learn about the local culture and design ways so that culture can be embraced by the organization.

New Organizational Structures   Expansion into international locations is not quite like expanding into additional U.S. locations. There are enough similarities from one U.S. location to another to make the transition easier than when international expansion is undertaken. New locations may mean a different organizational structure is required for the effective management of the remote location. The following are some organizational structures:

- **Functional structure** This type groups all workers within a function under the management of a chief executive for each function. Chief sales and marketing officer, chief operations officer, chief human resource officer, and chief financial officer are just examples. What one does determines where they are in the organization. For example, if you do marketing, you are in the marketing group. Those chief officers over these functions is the reason you may see some questions referring to the "C-suite."

- **Divisional structure** This aligns workers according to product, market, or region. An international expansion can sometimes result in an "Asian division" or a "Customer Product division." In this structure, employees have a direct solid-line relationship within the division they report to and a dotted-line relationship to the headquarters staff for their function.

- **Matrix structure** This requires two solid reporting lines—one to the divisional manager and one to the functional manager.

Changing organizational structures can be as difficult and challenging as merging cultures. Remember the merger of Continental Airlines and United Airlines? In May 2010, the two organizations agreed to a $3 billion merger.[4] Even 8 years later, the combined organization had yet to fully blend the two cultures. Union contract provisions for each group of employees were still separate and, in some cases, quite different from one another. Eight years in, and a new airline company had yet to emerge.

Increased Accountability The magazine *Inside HR* suggests the following: "Today, employees are collaborating in real time on projects across many time zones and geographies. People are working where they want and when they want—more than half of millennials say they want to work in a different country. Companies are moving towards organizational designs centered on project-based teams, matrixed structures and flat hierarchies."[5]

Possible future #1: expanded HR accountability

This potential future for HR includes increased accountability for workforce productivity, performance, collaboration, innovation, and culture. In this future, new core HR competencies would emerge requiring strong technical, analytical, and creative skills.

- HR would replace its one-size-fits-all policy focus with a focus on building flexible work environments that support myriad work styles, individual preferences, geographies, and time zones.

- HR would replace its focus on ensuring people work the requisite hours with a focus on building technologies that facilitate productivity, such as collaborative workspaces and virtual team rooms.

- HR would replace its focus on facilitating an annual performance review with a focus on deploying systems that increase performance and engagement, rather than just measuring them.

- HR would replace its focus on developing training curriculum with a focus on enabling real-time, "24/7" learning.

- HR would replace its focus on annual goal setting with a focus on providing managers with a real-time way to monitor and quantify work.

Possible future #2: decreased HR accountability

The second potential future for HR includes diminished accountability and a narrowing of mission. In this future, there are different possible paths:

- One possibility is HR will fail to step into the current accountability vacuum for productivity, performance, collaboration, and innovation and would cede enterprise leadership to other areas of the business. In this scenario, the business would drive the changes needed to support emerging work models, and HR would focus primarily on the administrative aspects of HR.

- Another possibility is HR will significantly increase its technical and analytical acumen and provide the business with the tools and data to be more self-sufficient and do for itself many of the things that HR once did for the business (recruiting of talent, measurement of performance, training of staff).

Understanding the Organization

Understanding one's organization is fundamental to an HR professional so that appropriate support may be provided. HR professionals need a thorough understanding of their organization's structure, the internal environment, and the external environment and industry in which it operates. This is why the business acumen competency is so critical to the HR professional. Understanding the operations of the business allows HR to become a trusted business partner when addressing operational needs for the business. Understanding the organization and its design allows you to do the following:

- Be fluent in the nomenclature of the business.
- Increase your credibility and the HR function's credibility.
- Connect the dots in the strategic planning process.
- Educate others in the organization about HR's contributions and value.
- Be proactive in affecting outcomes of the organization.

The Core Business Functions

Every organization, regardless of size, has basic key business functions: marketing and sales, operations, information technology, and finance and accounting. Larger organizations will have even more, including customer service and relations, research and development, and quality assurance. Each has a connection and collaboration associated with the human resource function. HR professionals need to form partnerships within their organization's key business functions to fully understand the key functional areas to support and become a strategic business partner. Understanding the core functions and business lines within the organization, including each area's perspectives, challenges, and goals, will be of great use to an HR professional.

Finance and Accounting   Like the sales and marketing functions, the finance and accounting functions go hand in hand yet are distinctively different. Finance has its focus on funding sources, such as bank loans and stock sales, along with budgeting for income generation and expenses. Accounting, on the other hand, is associated with the movement of the monies going in and out, such as payables and receivables processing, payroll, and taxes.

HR interfaces with finance and accounting by preparing and reviewing budgets.

Budgeting and Financial Analysis   Budgeting is the process of estimating the amount of income and expenses that will occur within a given period. It is usually done on an annual basis, although budgets can be created for multiple years and for shorter periods of time such as months and quarters. The accuracy of budgeting can be improved when there is some historical data on which to rely. Budgets in the short term can be easier to construct and are usually more accurate than long-range budgets. The reason, simply, is because many unforeseen influences can enter the picture over time. Fewer unpredictable influences tend to happen in shorter periods of time.

Whether an organization is a for-profit enterprise, a governmental agency, a nonprofit, or a volunteer service organization, there is a need for money management. Budgeting and financial analysis are critical to any organization large enough to have employees. Understanding how to plan for earnings and expenses, managing the process, and ultimately conducting analyses of what happened after the fact are key to any individual's success in a management role.

There are two key financial reports that any organization should be preparing and studying. One measures the income and expenses over a defined period such as a year, a calendar or fiscal quarter, or a month. This is usually called a *profit-and-loss statement,* or *P&L.* The second is a balance sheet that shows the assets (furniture, buildings, vehicles, cash, and accounts receivable) compared to the liabilities outstanding (accounts payable, taxes payable, credit card balances, and payroll payables). A balance sheet also shows the amount of equity owned by investors in the organization. Equity is the difference between income and liabilities in a for-profit organization. In a nonprofit organization it is called *net assets.*

 NOTE   This basic formula helps in understanding balance sheets: assets = liabilities + owner's equity.

There are four basic approaches to budgeting.

- *Zero-based* is a method of budgeting in which all expenses must be justified for each new period. The process of zero-based budgeting starts from a *zero base,* and every function within an organization is analyzed for its needs and costs.

- *Incremental* is a budget prepared using a previous period's budget or actual performance as a basis, with incremental amounts added or subtracted for the new budget period. It encourages "spending up to the budget" to ensure a reasonable allocation in the next period. It leads to a "spend it or lose it" mentality.

- *Formula* budgeting is based on some predetermined formula. For example, budgeting for one additional teacher for each additional 20 students that enroll.

- *Activity-based* is a method of budgeting based on an activity framework, using cost driver data in the budget setting and variance feedback processes.

HR professionals at management levels will participate in the creation of the HR department's budget to outline anticipated specific expenses, such as office supplies, equipment purchases, and software licenses, but also for other areas in the organization that have compensation and benefits associated with their budgets. Additionally, HR will provide projected budget expenses associated with plans that the organization's strategic plan may pursue that year. An example would be a strategic plan objective that creates a new incentive bonus plan for customer service representatives. HR will project how those additional earnings will impact 401(k) matching contributions.

Marketing and Sales   The marketing function has responsibilities for products, promoting, pricing, and locating/identifying the customer base. The sales function in an organization is normally the revenue generator. It is responsible for selling the organization's service or product.

Operations   Operations is considered the heartbeat of the organization. Operations will create the goods or services, acquire the resources, and make sure the customer receives those goods or services. This runs off five concepts: capacity, scheduling, inventory, standards, and control.

Information Technology   Information technology is the brain of today's organizations. The systems, tools, and information required for all other key functions to do what they do are the responsibilities of IT. IT's major focus is to support the integration of data from different systems and processes through an enterprise resource planning (ERP) system. This helps make an organization's data more visible for decisions and in real time. IT also is responsible for safeguarding the organization's data and electronic systems.

Research and Development   Research and development (R&D) varies by type of company. It exists not just in the private sector but also in the public sector. The private sector may focus on new product design and the development or expansion of the organization's mission to expand revenue. In the public sector, R&D would be in the form of research institutes and laboratories, mostly focusing on theoretical research that promotes science and new technologies of a public interest. Some organizations will have their R&D function in individual business units so that initiatives are focused specifically on that genre. R&D spending and investment vary by organization and industry. According to the 2013 Global Innovation 1000 Study by Booz & Company,[6] R&D spending ranges from 2 percent of revenue in telecommunications to 27 percent in computing and electronics. Globally, R&D spending has increased steadily since 1998.

Organizational Design

The design of an organization determines how it does business. The size and scope of the organization, its functions, its culture, and how it communicates and makes decisions are all part of its design. There are lifecycles for all organizations that take them through different phases of growth. Which phase an organization is in will define its structure and its goals. A startup will have a vastly different design than a more established mature organization, and the focus of HR will vary accordingly.

NOTE Chapter 4 covered the lifecycle of businesses.

Organizational Structures

Aligning the way the parts of an organization relate to each other is considered the organizational structure. HR professionals need to be familiar with organizational structures so they can act as a guide for management in selecting and determining which structure would be best to gain the highest performance consistent with the organization's strategy.

Structural Principles   The following six elements should be considered when designing your organizational structures:

- Departmental—functional, divisional, or matrix
- Chain of command
- Span of control
- Work specialization
- Formalization
- Centralized or decentralized decision-making authority

Choice of Department Structure   This is where tasks are divided into separate duties, grouping people and jobs together. The purpose is so that work can be optimally coordinated. There are three primary ways to divide work within an organization using departments.

Functional Structure   The first and most common is *functional*. A functional structure has individuals in groupings based upon the type of work they do. Departments are defined by the services they contribute to the organization in a functional structure.

Figure 5-1 Functional structure

A person who does marketing is in the marketing department. A person who does finance is in the finance department. The organizational chart in Figure 5-1 shows the solo functions of finance, marketing, and so on, reporting to the company president.

Divisional Structure The second option for structuring is *divisional*. This is sometimes also called a *product structure* or a *geographic structure* depending upon the criteria for dividing work. Groupings called divisions are created based upon the product or service they provide, or the geographical area they support. Within the division they are mostly self-contained with support services reporting into that division with a solid-line relationship. They will maintain a relationship with their functional counterparts at headquarters via a dotted-line relationship. An example of a company using a product structure is Gap Inc. They have different divisions for their various retail outlets, so three of their product divisions are Old Navy, Banana Republic, and Baby Gap. The organizational chart shown in Figure 5-2 depicts a geographic structure.

Matrix Structure The third option is a *matrix structure*, where there is at least a double solid line, so one worker has two direct supervisors. This structure requires outstanding communications. It is often chosen to facilitate the quick formation of new teams to meet client needs. One major accounting firm uses a matrix structure with three direct supervisors: one geographical, one functional, and one for an industry specialty. So, if I worked there, I would have my West coast, Human Resources, and Nonprofit sector supervisors. It can be a challenge for individuals getting direction and assignments from multiple bosses.

RACI Matrix RACI is an acronym standing for responsible (R), accountable (A), consulted (C), and informed (I). The RACI matrix is used by organizations to better

Figure 5-2 Geographic structure

define the roles and responsibilities of each member in the organization or on a team or supporting a team.

- There should be only one person *responsible* (R) for a work assignment. Having more than one person responsible for the same task increases the probability that there will be duplication of work or that some portions of the work will not be performed.

- *Accountable* (A) means an individual is designated to oversee the completion of the assigned tasks.

- *Consulted* (C) means there are appropriate subject-matter experts when necessary. They will suggest any deviations from the standard procedures that may be necessary.

- *Informed* (I) are those who have an interest in the task being performed. It could be a manager who oversees the given task or someone who cannot begin the next task until this one is completed.

Other Internal Environment Considerations

Beside understanding the functions within an organization, the HR professional needs to be keen to the important priorities and initiatives that are on the organization's agenda. This might include a shift in customer service performance, a new product or service being developed, or a new focus on vendor relationships. Understanding and knowing the hottest initiatives keeps HR "in the know" to relate its function and services to the initiatives underway.

The External Environment

Equally important to the internal environment is knowing the external environment. PESTLE is an acronym to follow in learning about the key factors that affect the external environment of an organization.

- **P = Political environment**   This political environment includes government regulations or any defined rules for that industry or business. It also involves studying tax policy, which includes exemptions (if any), employment laws, environment laws, and so on.

- **E = Economic factors**   This includes gauging the economic environment by studying factors in the macro economy such as interest rates, economic growth, exchange rate, and inflation rate. These factors also help in assessing the demand, cost of the product, expansion, and growth.

- **S = Social factors**   This forms the macro environment of the organization. It includes the study of demographics as well as the target customers. These factors help in gauging the potential size of the market. It includes studying population growth, age distribution, career attitude, and so on.

- **T = Technology**   Technology changes rapidly. It involves understanding factors that are related to technological advancements and the rate at which technology becomes obsolete.

- **L = Legal** We are required to know and apply the applicable laws that impact our organization.
- **E = Environmental** This involves examining our business practices and knowing how they impact the planet.

Chain of Command Chain of command defines what positions report to which other positions. As one goes higher up, authority increases and the decisions become more important. An excellent example of chain of command is to look at the military. A Private needs to follow orders while Generals make the most important decisions.

Span of Control Span of control refers to the number of individuals who report to a single supervisor. It's hierarchically in nature through a chain of command. For example, there is an executive at the top, then managers, then supervisors, and then direct reports, much like a pyramid. In organizations where many workers are skilled and require little supervision, they may report to one supervisor; this would be considered a *flat organization*. The ideal span of control varies depending on how simple or complex the work is, plus how experienced the staff is. An additional variable is how experienced the supervisor is.

Work Specialization Work specialization was first associated with the assembly line. It is where tasks are divided into specific jobs and workers are considered skilled labor. It may offer a more efficient manner of productivity; yet on the other hand, it can lead to worker boredom. Today's organizations using this organizational structure will typically rotate job functions on a regular basis, training the workers in skills that add variety to their tasks.

Formalization Formalization refers to how rigid or loose an organization's roles, rules, regulations, and policies are. Is it fluid and shoot from the hip, depending on the situation? Or are there umpteen written policies and procedures that are expected to be followed? Formalization is on a continuum and not an either-or dimension.

Centralized or Decentralized Decision-Making Authority To centralize or decentralize is the question. Centralizing the organization pulls decision-making into the core headquarters establishment. Decentralizing pushes the authority level to make decisions out to lower-level managers, usually closer to the customer. It is not an either-or but on a continuum of tight control by senior executive at headquarters at one end and much lower-level managers empowered to make decisions at the other. The latter is useful when it is important to have decisions made in close proximity to the local customers and your lower-level managers are skills. Holding power at headquarters is done when there is a concern for conformity and speed of decision making.

The centralizing and decentralizing continuum is also applicable to HR departments. With decentralized structures, corporate headquarters will create policy and develop programs; rollout and application are then carried out by the HR staff in the regional divisions. When the organization is centralized, HR headquarters would make the policy and coordinate the rollout activities or administration functions.

The HR Organization and Function

The function of HR is designed to serve the overall organization and its mission. The structure can take on different arrangements based on the size and needs of the organization. Let's explore the processes, the HR team, the department structure, and ways to demonstrate and measure HR's value.

HR Processes

Grouped in the following categories, these are the HR processes:

- Participating in the implementation and creation of the organization's strategy. Those processes might include the following:
    - Performance management
    - Job design
    - Organizational design
    - Communications
    - Knowledge management
    - HRIS selection, implementation, and integration
    - Strategic planning
    - Hiring

 NOTE You can find additional information on organizational strategy in Chapter 4.

- Creating and following strategy to source, recruit, hire, develop, manage, and retain talent, which might include the following processes:
    - Creating staffing plans
    - Attracting qualified talent
    - Selecting the best talent
    - Offering interviewing assistance to management
    - Onboarding and assimilating new hires into the organization
    - Developing and delivering programs such as training, total rewards, employee engagement, and communications
- Collecting data and analyzing it for specific organizational needs, which might include the following processes:
    - Capturing and tracking data to be analyzed
    - Identifying trends in the workforce and the external environment that affect the organization

- Identifying best practices and processes that would be helpful to the organization and its strategy
- Daily HR operations, such as the following:
  - The processing of data, information, recordkeeping, and requests, typically using an HRIS and applicant tracking system
  - Responding to employee and internal or outside requests

The HR Team

Here again, the HR team will vary depending on the organization's size and needs, yet the following are typical roles and responsibilities of an HR team:

- **HR leaders**   These are the most senior of the HR group, and many will be part of the executive team, such as the chief human resource officer (CHRO) or vice president of human resources reporting directly to the CEO or president. They have a seat at the "round table," where the role lends itself to correlating organizational challenges and strategies to the HR function.

- **Managers or directors**   This role is normally responsible for sections or units with the HR team such as the compensation director, the talent recruitment manager, and the training manager. They have a direct responsibility in coordinating and managing the activities of their specific function and the people who are within it.

- **Specialists**   This role on the HR team is usually singularly focused, with a specific knowledge and ability, such as the benefits specialist, the affirmative action specialist, or the HRIS specialist. They maintain and apply best practices in their specialty.

- **Generalists**   Also called *HR practitioners,* these are the jacks-of-all-trades. They may have roles and responsibilities that include expertise in more than one area. In today's large organizations, generalists are assigned a unit such as a department and may become known as the business partner for that unit, guiding the management of that unit with all aspects of HR and serving as a liaison to the HR specialists and management.

- **Business partner**   Also called *HR business partner, strategic business partner,* or *HR strategic business partner.* These are individuals with a lot of HR experience, adept at interacting with senior leadership to advance the strategy and success of the organization.

HR Structural Alternatives

Organizations will structure HR based on the areas of responsibility they are assigning to the HR function. An important factor is ensuring that the HR structure is aligned with the organization's strategic plan. This may sound redundant, yet it can't be emphasized enough that creating and sustaining HR's alignment with the organization's strategies is incredibly important. For example, if one of the organization's strategies is an initiative and goal to be the employer of choice for its technical engineers in its industry, then it is necessary to ensure that the structure of HR includes the formation of attraction, rewards, retention, and development functions to address those needs for the engineering department.

 NOTE When HR is aligned with the structure, the types of structure also include centralized versus decentralized, as discussed earlier in this chapter.

Shared Services

The shared services model is another structural alternative identified by Ulrich and Brockbank.[7] This model is used in organizations with multiple business units (or *divisions,* as most are called). Each division doesn't need to have its own expertise in every area, such as compensation and benefits. Each division selects what it needs from a menu of shared services, which are typically transactional, that the divisions agree will be shared (for example, affirmative action compliance and compensation administration).

The most common functions assigned for consolidation are health care, retirement, and compensation. Organizations that have implemented the shared services model have identified four favorable outcomes:

- Reduced administrative time by staff on tasks
- A reduction in administrative costs
- A consolidation of redundant functions
- Better tracking of employee data

 NOTE The greatest resistance from implementing a shared services concept generally comes from multinational organizations.

Centers of Excellence A center of excellence (COE) is a team, a shared facility, or an entity that provides leadership, best practices, research, support, or training for a focus area. This focus might be a technology (for example, Oracle), a skill (for example, negotiation), or a broad area of research (for example, cancer treatment). A COE, sometimes called a *center of expertise,* is an independent unit that provides services to internal customers within the organization. It is generally funded by fees that other functions using the COE have allotted from their budgeting. COEs may be located anywhere, wherever the internal customers can access the functions (for example, an in-house training university).

Third-Party Contractors   Outsourcing and co-sourcing are examples of structural alternatives used by the HR function. *Outsourcing* is where a third-party vendor provides selected activities, such as administration of benefits. *Co-sourcing* is when a third party provides dedicated services to HR, which may include having contractors within the HR's organization. An example would be a temporary employment agency on-site hiring and onboarding seasonal labor.

Measuring and Demonstrating HR Value

Organizations must measure and demonstrate the value they are delivering to their stakeholders—and so too does HR to its stakeholders within the organization. Measuring results serves to reinforce HR's role in showing its effectiveness to management. It can also strengthen HR's relationship within the organization by indicating the impact of its services. This affords it the position to seek investment when it comes to budget allocation. Measurement also indicates where things need to be improved. ROI is essential for HR to further the investment requests for its strategic plan serving the organization.

Performance Measures

Key performance indicators (KPIs) are used to measure value. A KPI gauges progress toward predetermined goals and standards of performance. An example is the number of new hires who have progressed through specific onboarding training, such as sexual harassment, ergonomics, and diversity practices.

Balanced Scorecards   A balanced scorecard is a performance metric used to identify and improve various internal functions and their resulting outcomes. It is used to measure and provide feedback. The balanced scorecard includes the four areas of customers, learning and growth, internal processes, and financial. You can use CLIF as an acronym to remember these four areas.

HR measurement using a balanced scorecard method would be focused on specific functions or initiatives (for example, recruiting), thus reducing the length of time to fill a position.

To be effective, a balanced scorecard must include the following:

- Accountability and measurable results
- Measures, metrics, and targets that are understandable and supported by data
- Measures that have actionable items associated with them that can be measured
- Meaningful measures that focus on results

A balanced scorecard must be carefully planned, focused on end results, and executed.

NOTE   You can find more information on balanced scorecards in Chapter 4.

HR Audits   An HR audit is a systematic and comprehensive evaluation of HR's policies, procedures, and practices that protect the organization, create best practices, and identify areas needing improvement. Audits also identify gaps in performance and outcomes and are usually identified in priority order to be corrected. There are different types of audits, such as those caused by legal embattlements with a lawsuit or regulatory compliance and those that are done to achieve a level of world-class acknowledgment such as being recognized for a best practice. Below is a table with the types of HR audits and their primary purpose.

Types of HR Audits	
Type	**Purpose**
Compliance	Determines the compliance with a law or regulation
Best practice	Compares its function with other organizations
Strategic	Reviews strengths and weaknesses of functions in terms of alignment with the organization's strategic plan and initiatives
Function-specific	Has a specific focus on a function or process (for example, records retention)

Metrics   There are many different metrics to select from, and the formulas can vary. It's important to use a formula consistent with other organizations when benchmarking HR practices. Here are the typical metrics used for measuring the HR value:

- Absence rate
- Applicant yield
- Cost per hire
- Human capital ROI
- Human capital value added
- Key talent retention
- Promotion pattern
- Success ratio
- Training ROI
- Transfer/relocation
- Turnover costs
- Turnover rate
- Vacancy costs

NOTE   You can find more information on metrics in Chapter 4.

HR's Role in Organizational Strategy

The role of HR as a function within the strategic plan of the organization has transformed from the traditional administrative and operations roles into becoming more strategic in nature, helping the organization plan how it will achieve its goals and objectives regarding talent management.

NOTE   You can find more information about strategy in Chapter 4.

HR and the Strategic Process

HR brings significant expertise, knowledge, and perspective to the organization's strategic planning process when it has a place in those planning meetings. What is discussed, decided, and shared in these types of planning meetings helps the senior management team have a full 360-degree view of the workforce and talent implications of plans. It also allows HR to ensure its goals and plans are aligned with the overall plans of where the organization is going.

HR's Role

HR plays an important role in the strategic planning process. It contributes perspective and ensures that all HR implications are considered, such as laws and regulations, community, union contracts, and so on. It plays a role in influencing and voicing an opinion for leadership and stakeholders at large, and it applies its strengths and technology to the direction set.

The administrative activities of HR are directly aligned with all aspects of the organization's strategy. Tasks that HR performs may be high in strategic value, such as orientation of new hires, or low in value, such as activities that third-party vendors can provide (for example, benefits administration). The core functions are what need consideration as to how they stack up to the value that HR lends to the organization's strategy and goals.

Leveraging HR's Strengths   The value of HR in an organization, specifically with the strategic planning process, is that HR knows the entire organization. This includes the functionality of the organization. This is because of the involvement it has in managing the talent, training, recruiting, risk management, policy administration, and so on. HR can be the ringmaster in helping coordinate and integrate the stakeholders listed here:

- **Employees**   HR needs to know the nuances of each geographical area in the organization and what laws or cultural issues are impacting each area.

- **Suppliers**   HR's knowledge of the suppliers and challenges they may pose, such as ethical behavior, is of great value within the strategic process.

- **Communities**   HR's role in corporate social responsibility and interacting with the communities of the organization in which it operates allows HR to identify potential conflicts or agreements with its communities associated with the new strategic plans on the table.

PART II

- **Government**   Yes, there is "big brother" to contend with, and it is HR's responsibility to ensure the organization stays in compliance with applicable employment laws and regulations.

- **Labor groups**   For those organizations with labor unions, HR has its finger on the pulse of the affected labor unions when a strategy is considered that may affect a workforce union group.

Contributing the HR Perspective   HR professionals can contribute an important perspective during the strategic planning process. Although the focus is to execute the organization's strategy, they have a ton of expertise and perspective they can add in the planning stages. For example, HR professionals can add value when the organization is formulating a strategy to expand into a new geographical area by pointing out their perspective and knowledge about the issues with local laws for employment in that area.

Negotiating and Influencing   Negotiation is when two or more parties work together to reach an agreement on a matter or with an issue. The HR professional needs to know and work the process, which has six phases:

- **Preparation**   Identify the needs and wants that would be concessions as well as the issues and positions that are considered "must gets."

- **Relationship building**   Personal character is involved here, and within the strategic planning process, this means having the trust of the others at the negotiating table.

- **Information exchange**   A thorough understanding of both sides of the issue is necessary.

- **Persuasion**   This means seeking what are the mutually beneficial options rather than going for the win-lose positioning. When HR professionals have a broader understanding of the other's interests, they can seek solutions that satisfy both sides of the issue.

- **Concessions**   Small concessions can count. The HR professional finds the "wants" that are not essential and decides whether giving them helps the negotiation process.

- **Agreement**   When both sides have agreed, confirm it in writing. With formal negotiations such as union contracts, legal investigations, and so on, these agreements must be in the form of a written document. Within the parameters of strategic planning, think of confirmation memos.

Influencing is an ability that goes hand in hand with credibility. Much more than just having knowledge and expertise, the HR professional needs to have credibility, which is part of building the personal relationship with trust mentioned earlier. HR professionals need to use their influence to provide the added value for the formulation of strategy to add what they know and their opinion of how the strategy can happen or what its challenges might be.

Due Diligence   Due diligence refers to digging in and looking at all factors surrounding a matter. It is being a detective, learning all the applicable data for a situation.

In strategic planning, this may involve researching the local employment laws for a new geographical area when you learn the organization is considering a geographical expansion. Due diligence also involves learning the landscape of the potential applicant pool for the new area and taking a 360-degree look at being an employer in that area. Chapter 4 discussed due diligence with mergers and acquisitions, which is the same process that would apply during the due diligence phase in strategic planning.

Aligning the HR Function and the Strategic Plan of the Organization

HR's administrative and operational activities are directly aligned with the organizational strategy and objectives. As we explained in Chapter 4 with the SWOT analysis tool, it is important for HR professionals to understand the business and industry they support and to know all the business function's own strategic plans.

HR Strategic Alignment   HR serves the entire organization and the needs of each business unit. Thus, having HR participate at each unit's planning session would be helpful, just as it is when HR sits as a participant to the senior team's strategic planning meeting. The same level of expertise, influence, and perspective is necessary at all levels of planning. When part of the organization's strategy involves entering a new market, HR's recruitment plans and sources will require a specific direction to be able to fulfill the workforce needs of the new markets. For example, the goals of HR's talent acquisition group may be focused on the nature of the talent required for the new market and how to manage the advertising that might go along with it. Forecasting the human resource needs is an important and essential role of HR in strategy.

Ensures That HR Fulfills Its Basic Mission   HR's basic mission is to help the organization achieve its vision with a highly engaged and talented workforce. That is the same with all other business units. Yet regarding HR's mission, it will cross into all business functions because there are employees in each of those functions. Bringing HR into the fold as a true business partner for each of those units in order to help them accomplish their goals and plans that support the organization is the bottom line of the mission of HR. HR must understand how all business units perform their work and their own priorities, values, and business plans in order to best help them design their processes.

Learn About Your Organization's History   Learning and talking "story" is an important function of HR, not just in attracting potential talent and onboarding them but in keeping the foundational values, desired culture, and history alive for the organization. HR professionals are the first impression in the talent arena and can be in the community too. Knowing the "story" of where the organization has been, how it began, and where it intends to go is necessary for keeping it alive and communicating it to all "who enter the double doors." Add to that the "story" of the industry and how the organization fits in, as well as the communities it exists in. Building this knowledge will help HR professionals make useful recommendations during the planning process.

Use Facts and Objective Data as Support   As a participant in the planning process, you'll need to have tangible evidence to back up your opinions and recommendations. An HR professional needs to be fluent in measuring strategic outcomes to be influential, have credibility, and build solid business cases for their recommendations.

Contribute to Measuring Strategic Success   Common measures used, besides the many discussed in Chapter 4, include the ones associated with human capital measurements. They are as follows:

- Productivity
- Employee attitudes
- Employee capability and capacity
- Human capital investment
- Leadership and management
- Total rewards
- Compliance and safety
- Employee relations
- Job recruitment
- Job creation
- Workforce retention
- Workforce profile

Developing the HR Strategy

HR needs to develop a strategy that is aligned with the capabilities needed to implement the organization's overall strategy. Becker, Huselid, and Beatty wrote in *The Differentiated Workforce*[8] that HR must shift its focus from employees to one of strategy, and it needs to commit to diverting a greater share of its resources from developing the entire workforce to developing strategic talent. It needs to "assess the big picture" and get out of the weeds.

The HR Strategic Process   Chapter 4 goes into detail on what creating strategy entails. For the HR strategic process, the steps are similar yet more specific.

1. Assess the big picture. Get an understanding of the organizational context and the previous strategic plans. Identify what goals will involve HR processes and support.
2. Do a SWOT analysis, which will review the matters affecting the people side of the business. A PESTLE analysis will also be used at this stage to assess the external environment in added depth. These analyses are explained in greater detail in Chapter 4.
3. HR's own mission and vision statements need to be either created at this phase or reviewed and updated if necessary. They need to reflect and fit into the organization's overall strategies.
4. Conduct a detailed HR analysis, which would include a thorough review of the current systems and processes in place. The goal in this phase is to identify gaps that may exist with current systems/processes and the future system needs.

Focus is generally on the total rewards, talent acquisition, performance management, and training/development functions. Here again a SWOT analysis and PESTLE analysis could be utilized. Addressing these gaps to align with the organizational direction is the crux of the HR strategy.

5. Determine what are the critical people issues. During this phase, the future talent needs and existing workforce will be compared, and again, the gaps are considered and addressed with a strategic plan of action. An example is when a plant is going to bring in new automated equipment. How does that affect the current workforce? Will there be a need for retraining to operate the new equipment? Will there be a need to reallocate workers to different jobs and/or downsize?

6. Develop HR's own goals, metrics, consequences, and solutions. At this phase, the specific actions HR will take and how they will be measured occur. Audits and balanced scorecards tools may be utilized (explained in Chapter 4).

7. Developing an implementation and evaluation plan is the last step. Here HR will provide clear direction on the resources, risks, timing, and support that each of their goals and initiatives will require. A project Gantt chart may be used as additional support for budget requests.

Functional Area 7: Organizational Effectiveness & Development

Here is SHRM's BASK definition: "Organizational Effectiveness & Development concerns the overall structure and functionality of the organization, and involves measurement of long- and short-term effectiveness and growth of people and processes and implementation of necessary organizational change initiatives."[9]

Organizational effectiveness and development (OED) is a complex effort whose objectives are to change the beliefs, attitudes, values, culture, and structure of organizations so that they can be in a better position to adapt to new technologies, markets, and challenges. These changes occur through planned interventions designed to accomplish better results. In simple terms, OD is a systematic approach that enables the company to implement improvements in a consistent way.

Key Concepts

- Group dynamics (for example, intergroup and intragroup, group formation, identity, cohesion, structure, influence on behavior, conflict, former, storming, norming and performing)

- Organizational design structures and approaches (for example, customer, functional, geographic, matrix, program)

- Organizational analysis (for example, performance analysis, McKinsey 7S model)

The following are the proficiency indicators that SHRM has identified as key concepts:

For All HR Professionals	Advanced HR Professionals (SCP Exam)
Ensures that key documents and systems (for example, job postings, job descriptions, performance management systems) accurately reflect workforce activities	Aligns HR's strategy and activities with the organization's mission, vision, values, and strategy
Supports change initiatives to increase the effectiveness of HR systems and processes	Regularly monitors results against performance standards and goals in support of the organization's strategy
Identifies areas in the organization's structures, processes, and procedures that need change	Establishes measurable goals and objectives to create a culture of accountability, continuous experimentation, and improvement
Recommends methods to eliminate barriers to organizational effectiveness and development	Consults on, plans, and designs organizational structures that align with the effective delivery of activities in support of the organization's strategy
Collects and analyzes data on organizational performance and the value of HR initiatives to the organization	Assesses organizational needs to identify critical competencies for operational effectiveness
	Designs and oversees change initiatives to increase the effectiveness of HR systems and processes
	Ensures that HR initiatives demonstrate measurable value to the organization

Overview of Organizational Effectiveness and Development (OED)

HR responsibilities have evolved into the area of establishing and monitoring meaningful organizational metrics. This is done to identify and analyze major operating, workforce, and cultural health information, which will help with organizational effectiveness and development efforts to add value to the organization. To do this, the HR professional must do the following:

- Recognize and support the alignment of key strategic and tactical business plans and program objectives. Each unit's tactical plans should be designed to support one or more strategic business objectives for the organization. Each unit's operational tactics need to be coordinated with other plans and objectives. In much the same manner, all HR and OED objectives must be aligned with the organization's overall strategy, with each other's activities, and with country-specific requirements.

- Focus on the organization's skills and capabilities; for example, all the organization's business units, including HR, need to identify, focus, and improve the organization's talent acquisition capabilities.

OED Process

The OED process is based on an action research model that begins with an identified problem or need for change and proceeds with assessing, planning an intervention, implementing the intervention, gathering data to evaluate the intervention, and determining whether satisfactory progress has been made or whether there is need for further intervention. The process is cyclical and ends when the desired developmental result is obtained.

The OED process begins when an organization recognizes that a problem exists that impacts the mission or culture of the organization and therefore change is desired. It can also begin when leadership has a vision of a "better way" and wants to improve the organization. An organization does not always have to be in trouble to implement organization development activities.

Once the decision is made to change the situation, the next step is to assess the situation to fully understand it. This assessment can be conducted in many ways, including documentation review, organizational sensing, focus groups, interviewing, and surveying. The assessment may be conducted by outside experts or by members of the organization.

After the situation is assessed, defined, and understood, the next step is to plan an intervention. The type of change desired determines the type of intervention needed. Interventions can include training and development, team interventions, structural interventions, and individual interventions. Examples are team building for management or employees and establishing change teams. Once the intervention is planned, it is implemented.

During and after the implementation of the intervention, relevant data is gathered. The data to be gathered is determined by the change goals. For example, if the intervention is training and development for individual employees, the data would measure changes in knowledge and competencies.

This data is used to determine the effectiveness of the intervention. It is reported to the organization's decision-makers, who then determine whether the intervention met its goals. If the intervention met its goals, the process may end, which is reflected by raising the development bar. If it did not, a decision is made on whether to continue the cycle by planning and carrying out another intervention or to end it.

OED Strategies

One approach depicts three basic strategies to achieving successful organizational change. The three strategies are not mutually exclusive, and all three could be used concurrently to bring about systemic change. One or the other, however, may be more conducive to the type of change needed in a particular organization. For this purpose, they are shown as being three different strategies.[10]

The Behavioral Strategy: Talent Development Talent development takes an employee training and development approach. It is based on the premise that employee learning would bring about the organizational change needed. Learning consists of gaining knowledge, skills, and new attitudes that lead to new behaviors. These new behaviors then lead to improved quality and performance.

The Technical Strategy: Performance Improvement Performance improvement takes a continuous improvement approach. Its premise is that processes in the areas of customer focus, product and service delivery, support, and supplier and partnering can be improved. This strategy also maintains that technology be continuously updated and aligned with the processes of production and service to make work more efficient and effective. Continuous process improvement with aligned technology leads to improved quality and performance. What follows is a table of various types of employee performance problems with possible solutions to the issues.[11]

Performance Problems		
Problem	**Description**	**Possible Solutions**
Behavioral	Often manifested as a communication problem, this involves a lack of collaborative effort between people or groups, inadequate team performance levels, or performance quality issues. This is frequently the result of inadequate leadership or unclear performance expectations, such as insufficient communication of performance standards or inconsistent use of metrics or accountability standards.	• Clarified expectations and work processes • Education • Consistent workplace practices • Strong leadership • Conflict-resolution practices
Cognitive	This problem results from deficiencies in knowledge or skills.	• On-the-job training, work expansion • Coaching/mentoring • Training
Technological	This is a problem with the equipment, materials, and information used to perform the work, including their accessibility, availability, and accuracy.	Address problems associated with inadequate, inaccessible, faulty, or inaccurate equipment, materials, or information that employees rely on to perform their jobs.
Process-related	This is a problem with how the work is done, which can stem from inefficient systems, outdated practices, a lack of process measurement data, impractical procedures, or cumbersome reporting structures.	• Review systems to obtain feedback and conduct regular audits. • Determine process measures and data collection techniques. • Identify problems before they become significant obstacles. • Design and implement process improvement strategies.
Cultural	This is a problem within the workplace atmosphere or environment that tends to be the most challenging to remedy. Matters concerning employee satisfaction, leader-employee relationships, leadership styles, corporate responsiveness to change, and policy flexibility are all examples of cultural changes.	• Typically, cultural shifts require multifaceted OED interventions. • Solutions derived from internal sources may be the most desirable, as credibility and familiarity levels are high. • Conversely, using an external tool or facilitator may provide a more holistic and objective perspective, thereby balancing the emotional components associated with internal relationships and performance history.

The Structural Strategy: Organizational Design The organizational design premise is that organization structure and design should be aligned (or realigned) consistent with the vision, direction, mission, or goals of the organization. Structural strategy will incorporate changes in the organizational chart. Employees, units, divisions, and departments can be realigned to optimize resources. For example, hierarchies can be flattened, and decision-making can be placed closer to the point of action. Significant work can be done in chartered, self-directed teams. Such realigned relationships lead to improved quality and performance.

OED Benefits OED is the practice of planned, systemic change in the beliefs, attitudes, and values of employees for individual and company growth. The purpose of OED is to enable an organization to better respond and adapt to industry/market changes and technological advances. The following are five benefits of OED, ranging from continuous improvement to increased profits:[12]

- **Continuous improvement** Companies that engage in organizational effectiveness and development commit to continually improving their business and offerings. The OED process creates a continuous cycle of improvement whereby strategies are planned, implemented, evaluated, improved, and monitored. Organizational effectiveness development is a proactive approach that embraces change (internal and external) and leverages it for renewal.

- **Increased communication** One of the key advantages to OED is increased communication, feedback, and interaction within the organization. The goal of improving communication is to align all employees to shared company goals and values. Candid communication also leads to increased understanding of the need for change within the organization. Communication is open across all levels of the organization, and relevant feedback is recurrently shared for improvement.

- **Employee development** The need for employee development stems from constant industry and market changes. To stay competitive, organizations are now required to regularly enhance employee skills to meet evolving market requirements. This is achieved through a program of learning, training, skills/competency enhancement, and work process improvements.

- **Product and service enhancement** A major benefit of OED is innovation, which leads to product and service enhancement. Innovation is achieved through employee development, which focuses on rewarding successes and boosting motivation and morale. In this scenario, employee engagement is high, leading to increased creativity and innovation. OED also increases product innovation by using competitive analysis, market research, and consumer expectations and preferences.

- **Increased profits** OED affects the bottom line in a variety of ways. Through raised innovation and productivity, efficiency and profits are increased. Costs are also reduced by minimizing employee turnover and absenteeism. As OED aligns objectives and focuses on development, product/service quality and employee satisfaction are increased. The culture shift to one of continuous improvement gives the company a distinct advantage in the competitive marketplace.

In its publication "Traits of Truly Agile Businesses," Accenture reported the results of a survey it conducted in 2013 that investigated business agility in strategy, organization, marketing, operations, and finance. Because of this research, five critical enablers of company agility emerged. Agile companies have leaders who do the following:

- **Actively build seasoned, diverse leaders and management teams**   Leaders ensure that managers up and down the organization are fully accountable and have the right competencies to handle a diverse set of circumstances.

- **Speed up decision-making**   They establish a culture of making critical decisions quickly, always ensuring that those decisions are tuned to market conditions.

- **Prioritize strategic decisions**   They distinguish between the decisions that affect everyday operations and the bigger decisions that concern the company's strategic direction.

- **Prepare their ecosystems to act quickly**   They arm their business ecosystems—suppliers, customers, and a range of third-party partners—with their sources, information, and tools to take decisive, well-orchestrated action and to quickly measure the results and correct their course when needed.

- **Invest in and make more use of data and analytics to run the business**   Leaders understand the competitive value of deeper insights and know how to mine many sources of data—not just their own—to obtain those insights.[13]

Opportunities for OED   In recent years, many companies became good at delivering their core products and services with limited resources by adopting a "do more with less" operating style. Many companies reaped some short-term benefits because of certain cost savings. However, some of these short-term benefits have the potential to inflict long-term problems on the organization's overall capabilities, organizational structure, business processes, and levels of workforce engagement. The unintended result of attempting to get along with less over the long term can, in many cases, become very problematic. These same problems can become opportunities for alert HR professionals. Examples include the following:

- **Diminished capacity, capability, and agility**   Not being properly staffed can directly influence a company's cost structure, cash flow, and ability to deliver goods or services. Diminished capacity and lagging response times will affect an organization's ability to remain competitive.

- **Misaligned organizational structure**   Many of these reorganizations produced structural gaps in roles, work processes, accountabilities, and critical information flows. Structural gaps can occur when companies eliminate jobs without eliminating the work, forcing employees to take on additional responsibilities, which can lead to job burnout. This can create problems because lower-level employees who step in may be ill-equipped to perform the required duties, and higher-level executives, who must take on more-tactical responsibilities, may feel that their leadership skills are being minimized. Businesses that do reductions in force need to get better at the concurrent reduction in tasks.

- **Broken business processes** Many organizations will admit that many core business processes are not documented, are not supported by technology, and relied too heavily on the "tribal knowledge" of long-term employees. This may create gaps in the firm's institutional knowledge management. Many businesses have not analyzed the impact from their cuts and the corresponding critical gaps that have developed. By failing to address these issues in a timely manner, companies risk losing core efficiencies, thus damaging the customer experience—a primary driver of revenue sustainability.

- **Declining workforce engagement** While doing more with less can improve productivity, it can also damage employee morale. More workers (managers and individual contributors alike) are juggling additional responsibilities, working longer hours, missing family time, and performing jobs that are one or two levels above or below their pay grade.

To ensure long-term viability, organizations need to realign their critical elements to fit the new economic realities without diminishing their core capabilities and competitive differentiation.

HR's Role in OED HR should be involved in major organizational changes from the beginning. HR's early involvement can facilitate the improvement of employee understanding of change and communication between management and nonmanagement employees. Positive outcomes of communication efforts can include the following:

- Identification and mitigation of potential risks

- Increased buy-in and satisfaction from employees

- Increased trust between management and non-managerial employees

- Identification of needed change-related training initiatives to improve employee skills and proficiency throughout the change process

- Increased leadership cohesiveness

In its 2014 publication "Future Insights," SHRM outlined the top OED trends according to an HR subject-matter expert panel, which identified several trends. HR professionals must do the following:

- Increase their focus on the development and engagement of highly professional talent and high-potential employees who possess deep expertise, drive innovation, and uniquely contribute to the organization's value proposition.

- Take responsibility to educate line management and help them acquire skills to become more proactive in managing and coaching talent.

- Become skilled in organizational design and change management required to effectively implement enhanced organizational structures.

- Develop superior communication and situational leadership skills, motivation, energy, and learning agility. Leaders must have the ability to recognize and respect cultural differences and to reconcile the issues cultural diversity creates.

- Integrate the workforce planning process with career planning and employee engagement to provide information and support for employees to help them identify and choose from available career paths and job opportunities.

- Interact with technology specialists to produce accurate models to use in planning and managing the workforce, including decision support tools and predictive analytics.

- Use creative development tools such as mobile technologies for just-in-time learning via "pulled" rather than "pushed" instruction.[14]

Organizational Gap Development

Organizational effectiveness and development involves more than just specialized interventions; its practice should be integrated into the organization's daily operations. When a "gap" begins to develop between what is going on in your organization compared to a standard or benchmark in your industry or other relevant comparator, you may be seeing a problem in the making.

Assessments and Targets

Identifying an organizational gap begins with isolating the area of interest. That may be customer service, employee skills, leadership skills, employee training, and countless other areas. Pick one. If your concern is employee skills, first identify the specific skill (running scientific machinery, answering employee benefit questions, or management communication skills, for example). Next, identify the benchmark or industry standard for the skill (number of hours managers spend working directly with employees each month, number of research grants obtained each quarter, or successful merger or acquisition for employee policies).

Change Readiness   Developing and implementing change programs should follow the articulation of specific needs. If efficiencies can be improved through implementing new technologies (for example, use of robots on the automobile assembly line to perform routine repetitive actions), plans can be made to implement that change.

Normally, implementation plans should involve these steps:

1. Documenting goals and specific actions required to achieve them
2. Meeting with employees to discuss the new vision and what changes it requires
3. Soliciting employee support and participating in the change process
4. Implementing your change
5. Measuring the results

Organizational changes should always be consistent with the employer's strategic plan. Changes should represent the means to achieve missions or goals. There should always be a link between the change and the organizational strategy.

Cultural Assessment   The greatest need for cultural assessment comes in the wake of mergers and acquisitions (M&As). When organizations try to combine their operations, there will inevitably be conflicts in policy, management style, and "the way we do things around here." One consulting firm, the Turknett Leadership Group, uses a written survey to gather input from employees on both sides of the corporate mix. Then, it conducts in-depth, one-on-one interviews with a sampling of employees from each group.[15] In those interviews, questions such as the following are asked:

- "Give me ten words you would use to describe the organization."
- "Who really gets ahead in this organization?"
- "What and who is really rewarded around here?"
- "What are some of the war stories or legendary events in the organization's history?"
- "What does the CEO or leader pay the most attention to? Where does the CEO's energy get expended, and what do they reward?"

With the answers to those and other similar questions, it will soon become apparent where work should be focused for cultural improvement.

Implementing OED Initiatives

According to SHRM, "Unfortunately, many OED interventions are incorrectly implemented in response to symptoms of the dysfunction rather than by following a thorough diagnostic analysis, or organizational assessment, to reveal core problems. To avoid this, employers must use caution and make certain a comprehensive data collection process is followed."[16] When correctly assessed, plans for intervention can be built and then implemented.

OED Initiatives

Organizational development involves more than just specialized interventions; its practice should be integrated into the organization's daily operations. One of the simplest tools OED practitioners use is the ADDIE model,[17] which is an instructional systems design framework that many instructional designers and training developers use to develop courses. It can be used when dealing with other problems and issues, too, and involves the following phases:

- Analysis
- Design
- Development
- Implementation
- Evaluation

OED initiatives often involve transformational change, including efficiency and effectiveness initiatives, organizational restructurings, organizational capabilities development, rebuilding trust initiative, and culture change. Nearly any aspect of the organization is fair game.

Workforce Support of OED Initiatives

To a large extent, whether employees support your OED initiatives will depend on the quality of leadership that shepherds the effort. However, it is a sure thing that unless employees do support your OED initiatives, there is little hope for success in that effort. Getting employee buy-in is critical.

OED Tools

Here are some tools and techniques that can help you in your OED initiatives.

Team Building   Achieving the state where individual team members trust one another to do their work and support others in the group is the objective of any team building program. Some groups work better together as teams than others. How the supervisor or manager treats each employee will influence how likely there will be a cohesiveness to the group. People want to work where they like the people they work with. They don't like to work with people who steal the credit for accomplishments of others, tattle to the supervisor about each small infraction of rules, or actively work to discredit others. Team building can overcome some of those behaviors, but not all. Progressive discipline is sometimes needed to eliminate really bad behavior before the group is willing to be a team. The question in the minds of employees who see the bad behavior all the time is, "Will the boss actually do something about it?"

Group Decision-Making   Group decision-making is a type of participatory process in which multiple individuals acting collectively analyze problems or situations, consider and evaluate alternative courses of action, and select from among the alternatives a solution or solutions.[18] In organizations, many decisions of consequence are made after some form of group decision-making process is undertaken. However, groups are not the only form of collective work arrangement. Group decision-making should be distinguished from the concepts of teams, teamwork, and self-managed teams. Although the words *teams* and *groups* are often used interchangeably, scholars increasingly differentiate between the two. The basis for the distinction seems to be that teams act more collectively and achieve greater synergy of effort. Here are some key points:

- The group has a definite leader, but the team has shared leadership roles.
- Members of a group have individual accountability; the team has both individual and collective accountability.
- The group measures effectiveness indirectly, but the team measures performance directly through its collective work product.
- The group discusses, decides, and delegates, but the team discusses, decides, and does real work.

There are several types of group decision-making methods:

- **Brainstorming**   This is freewheeling idea generation.
- **Dialectical inquiry**   Opposing groups debate the pros and cons of selected solutions or decisions.

- **Nominal group technique**   This is a structured decision-making process in which group members are required to compose a comprehensive list of their ideas or proposed alternatives in writing.

- **Delphi technique**   Group members are in different remote locations, and the group develops successive rounds of ideas, evaluation, refinement, and choices.

Diversity Programs   Changing workforce demographics are increasing the diversity of work teams in general and decision-making teams in particular. With these environmental changes, work teams that are diverse in terms of gender, race, ethnicity, national origin, area of expertise, organizational affiliation, and many other personal characteristics are increasingly common.[19]

Striving to increase workplace diversity is not an empty slogan; it is a good business decision. A 2015 McKinsey report on 366 public companies found that those in the top quartile for ethnic and racial diversity in management were 35 percent more likely to have financial returns above their industry mean, and those in the top quartile for gender diversity were 15 percent more likely to have returns above the industry mean.[20]

In a global analysis of 2400 companies conducted by Credit Suisse,[21] organizations with at least one female board member yielded higher return on equity and higher net income growth than those that did not have any women on the board.

In recent years, a body of research has revealed another, more nuanced benefit of workplace diversity: nonhomogeneous teams are simply smarter. Working with people who are different from you may challenge your brain to overcome its typical ways of thinking and sharpen its performance.

Quality Initiatives   Focusing on quality issues can happen in any workgroup within an organization. Of course, quality is important on the production line, but it is also important in the accounting department and in HR. What would be the consequence of HR publishing incorrect information about company benefit programs just before open enrollment? There are a few different ways to address quality.

Systems Theory   Systems theory is less of a management methodology as it is a way of analyzing and thinking about organizations. It puts forth the premise that organizations, like living organisms, are made up of numerous component subsystems that must work together in harmony for the larger system to succeed. Systems theory states that organizational success relies on synergy, interrelations, and interdependence between different subsystems. As arguably the most valuable component of a company, employees make up various vital subsystems within an organization. Departments, work groups, business units, facilities, and individual employees can all be considered component systems of the organizations.[22]

Systems theory is an alternative approach to understanding, managing, and planning organizations. Employee relations is a human resource discipline concerned with strengthening ties between employers and employees. Systems theory can provide a fresh perspective for approaching employee-relations initiatives, allowing managers to understand their employees' importance and position as a vital system in the organization, rather than viewing employees as an expense through the lens of accounting.

Quality Standards The International Organization for Standardization (ISO) has now published four standards for human resource management.[23] These are considered the benchmark against which all employers should measure themselves in these specific areas of HR:

- **ISO 30400, Human resource management – Terminology** This standard provides a common understanding of the fundamental terms used in human resource management standards.

- **ISO 30405, Human resource management – Guidelines on recruitment** This standard provides guidance on effective recruitment processes and procedures. It is designed for use by anyone involved in recruiting.

- **ISO 30408, Human resource management – Guidelines on human governance** This standard provides the guidelines to create an effective human governance system that can respond effectively to organizational and operational needs but also foster greater collaboration across all stakeholders, anticipate and manage risks in human resources, and develop a company culture that is aligned with its values.

- **ISO 30409, Human resource management – Workforce planning** This standard helps organizations respond more effectively to their current and projected requirements for staffing.

You can expect that more standards will be developed related to human resource management as time goes on.

Quality Control Tools The following are the seven tools of quality:

- **Cause-and-effect diagram** Also known as the *fishbone, the 5 whys,* or the Ishikawa diagram.

- **Check sheet** Chart of event/occurrence by date or time with stroke tally of times the event happened.

- **Control chart** Plot of quality conformance at times throughout the day.

- **Histogram** Column chart showing frequency/intervals on the y-axis and the event being measured along the x-axis.

- **Pareto chart** Column chart showing types of quality problems on the x-axis and frequency of occurrence on the y-axis, with the most frequency on the left.

- **Scatter diagram** Graph showing a plot of individual quality results using any two variables. Plot points can be used to determine the slope of a trend.

- **Stratification** Flow chart or run chart.

Theory of Constraints The Theory of Constraints (TOC) says that "a chain is no stronger than its weakest link." That means quality depends on the weakest point in the process, whether it is a machine, a person, a system, or a process. Quality failures can most often be traced back to that single point that constrains the quality results. It may also happen that there is more than one constraint interfering with the quality results.

Six Sigma   Six Sigma methodologies can be rolled out in a matter of months or over the course of years. From large international companies to midsize firms, many high-profile companies have implemented Six Sigma strategies as a way of saving corporate dollars, increasing quality, and leveraging the competitive edge.[24]

One of the guiding principles behind Six Sigma is that variation in a process creates waste and errors. Eliminating variation, then, will make that process more efficient, cost-effective, and error-free. This may sound like a straightforward concept, but its application in a complex and highly integrated business environment can be far from simple. The term *Sigma* refers to a scale of measurement of quality in processes such as manufacturing. When using this scale, Six Sigma equates to just under 3.4 defects per million opportunities (DPMO).

HR's Role in Implementation

HR can be called on to support OED changes in other portions of the enterprise, or it can take on an OED change program within its own department. HR can help by training managers and employees how the process will work, what the changes will be, and what expectations they should have for the results. They can provide tracking systems if necessary to document the program implementation.

Communicating OED Changes   Communication is relating the objectives of the organizational redesign to the organization's strategies and tactical plans. Employees need to understand how they will fit into the new organization, the new process, or the new work assignment. They will need to know that there is training, team building, or individual coaching on the horizon. Communication is more than an e-mail blast to everyone in the organization. It is conversation with groups and individuals. The OED development process will be more successful the more employees are included. This means greater and more mindful communications along the way. Make efforts to ensure that your communications are bidirectional—and that you are also listening.

Measuring Organizational Effectiveness and Development

First comes the goal or objective. Then comes the measurement. There are two types of measurements you can use to determine whether you have reached your goal:

- **Lagging indicators**   These confirm performance or lack of performance. They measure the results of past actions.

- **Leading indicators**   These predict performance. They measure actions that will affect future organizational effectiveness.

Demonstrating Value

If you think about it, it is easy to demonstrate value. Simply gather the results you have measured and show how your performance has met or exceeded the goals you set. Goals are established to create value for the organization. If you reach them, or better yet, exceed them, there is clearly value for the organization.

Cultural Assessment   Tools are available that companies can use to identify both their current and desired culture. One of the most well-known of these tools is the Organizational Culture Assessment Instrument (OCAI),[25] developed by Kim Cameron and Robert Quinn at the University of Michigan. Cameron and Quinn analyzed 39 organizational effectiveness indicators and identified two key dimensions:[26]

- Internal focus and integration versus external focus and differentiation
- Stability and control versus flexibility and discretion

Four organizational culture types emerged from these studies:[27]

- **Clan culture**   Similar to a large family, where people have a lot in common. The organization is held together by loyalty and tradition, and there is great involvement.
- **Adhocracy culture**   A creative working environment where employees take risks. Experiments and innovation are the bonding agents within the organization.
- **Market culture**   Results-oriented culture emphasizing finishing work and getting things done. The emphasis on winning keeps the organization together.
- **Hierarchy culture**   A formal, structured environment where procedures decide what people do. Formal rules and policies keep the organization together.

Functional Area 8: Workforce Management

Here is SHRM's BASK definition: "Workforce Management refers to HR practices and initiatives that allow the organization to meet its talent needs and close critical gaps in competencies."[28]

Workforce management is where HR will continually be evaluating the ability of the organization's workforce to meet the competency and talent needs of the organization. Development, productivity, staffing, and effectiveness initiatives will be the core functions of HR's responsibility within workforce management. Workforce management is setting up the organization for success with the right talent, with the right skills, in the right place, and at the right time. Workforce planning and employment are where you will find all the information about staffing, recruiting, interviewing, and employee performance management. Master these, and you will have a strong foundation for HR performance in your employment group.

Key Concepts

- Workforce planning approaches, techniques, and analyses (for example, forecasting, build, buy, borrow and bridge strategies, attrition, gap and solution, supply and demand, workforce profile, upskilling and reskilling employees, redesigning jobs, robotics, identifying high-potential employees)
- Best practices and techniques for knowledge management, retention, and transfer (for example, benchmarking, thought leadership)

- Techniques for organizational need-gap analysis (for example, examination of HR records, interviews, focus groups, surveys, exit interviews, digital skills assessments)

- Succession planning programs and techniques (for example, mentorship, cross-training, 9-box grid)

- Approaches to restructuring and downsizing (for example, mergers and acquisitions, reductions in force, layoffs, furloughs)

The following are the proficiency indicators that SHRM has identified as key concepts:

For All HR Professionals	Advanced HR Professionals (SCP Exam)
Assesses the competencies needed to support and grow the organization as well as identifies gaps and misalignment of staffing levels	Evaluates how the organization's strategy and goals align with future and current staffing levels and workforce competencies
Implements approaches to ensure that appropriate workforce staffing levels and competencies exist to meet the organization's goals and objectives	Develops strategies to maintain a robust workforce that has the talent to carry out the organization's current and future strategy and goals
Forecasts future workforce needs as well as plans strategies to develop workforce competencies that support the organization's goals and objectives	Coordinates with business leaders to create strategies that address the organization's leadership needs
Administers and supports approaches to ensure that the organization's long-term leadership needs are met	Develops strategies for restructuring the organization's workforce
Supports strategies for restructuring the organization's workforce	
Provides employees with continuous learning opportunities, including opportunities for upskilling and reskilling	

Organizational Workforce Requirements

Organizational staffing needs expand and contract with the level of organizational productivity requirements. It's not always a straight-line relationship that would indicate continuous steady growth. Living organizations inhale and exhale, and workloads grow and contract, often at irregular intervals. Workforce requirements expand and contract with those production requirements.

Workforce Requirements

Forecasting results can be converted into employee headcount and budget impact, and the consequences can demand other staffing needs. Adding production workers can cause an increase in payroll support work levels, for example.

Identifying job openings before they exist is the activity known as *forecasting*. It is best performed with the aid of staff and line managers who will be supervising the new positions. Given what is anticipated for growth (or force reduction), a manager can convert workloads into staff requirements. Determining the portion of jobs that will be part-time versus those that will be full-time is another contribution of the forecasting process.

Forecasting staffing needs is usually done in terms of the number of full-time equivalent (FTE) people. That unit value is also favored for budgeting activities. Here is the formula:

FTE people required = total functional workload / workload handled by one person

Organizational Structure

Aligning the way the parts of an organization relate to one another is considered the organizational structure. HR professionals need to be familiar with organizational structures so they can act as a guide for management in selecting and determining which structure would be best to gain the best performance.

Just a reminder there are six elements for consideration for your organizational structures (see the descriptions in the "Understanding the Organization" section, earlier in this chapter):

- Departmental—functional, divisional, or matrix
- Chain of command
- Span of control
- Work specialization
- Formalization
- Centralized or decentralized decision-making authority

Downsizing Downsizing is the act of reducing the size of a workforce. It may also be called a *reduction in force (RIF), layoff,* or unfortunately *rightsizing* or *smart-sizing*. It can be done for many different reasons, but usually due to decreased demand for the organization's products or services. The result is fewer people doing the work. In the past few decades, corporate downsizing has become a widely used tool.

The impact on individuals is immense. To help mitigate that impact, employers have sometimes offered incentive programs with cash buyouts based on the length of service and/or retirement qualification enhancements as well as outplacement services to help these people find their next employment. Offers have sometimes included support in a job search (providing an office, telephone, computer, e-mail, administrative support), formal outplacement service through a third-party vendor, and occupational training programs to provide new skills necessary for a career in a new field.

Regardless the absolute number or percentage of the workforce being let go, the entire organization will feel the impact. Firms need to be mindful to reduce what work they do when they engage in a RIF to become more efficient and not burnout the employees still on the payroll.

Restructuring

At times to stay competitive elements of the organizational structure may need to change. The act of restructuring to become more profitable, or better organized, is known as *corporate restructuring*. Additional changes can necessitate restructuring, such as a change of ownership, a bankruptcy filing, a divestiture, or a merger or an acquisition. *Divesting* is the action of selling off subsidiary business interests or investments to reduce debt or operations. A merger is when two companies are combined into one as a partnership while an acquisition is when one firm buys another.

Sometimes corporate restructuring occurs because of economic decline to reduce financial losses from the lack of revenue. The basic nature of restructuring is a zero-sum game. It can quickly reduce financial losses and simultaneously reduce the tensions between major stakeholders and the overriding condition prompting the distressed situation.

Divestiture   Organizations divest to refocus, rethink, and restructure their core business capabilities with a goal to be leaner and more cost-effective. They may also go through divestiture if ordered due to a court finding the company is a monopoly, such as AT&T in 1983 or Standard Oil much earlier in 1911. Going from big to smaller, or refocusing on the core product/service that the organization offers by selling off a separate line of business, can present a variety of challenges for HR. To minimize the disruption of operations and employees during divestiture, HR may need to redefine some of the organizational structure that is currently in place. Reviewing re-employment policies, severance packages, and employee classifications and job descriptions for either increased or decreased responsibilities are just a few considerations.

Merger and Acquisition   Mergers and acquisitions (M&As) are intended to enhance an organization by accessing market share or increasing assets. It is best to involve HR right from the get-go to plan for the effects that M&A has on an organization, such as due diligence, culture blending, job function redundancy, and comparison of benefits/compensation/job titles, along with effects on HR information systems, policies/procedures/ethics, and, if there is a union, collective bargaining.

The M&A process has four basic phases, as detailed in the following sections.

Preparation   You must first ascertain whether the HR staff has the necessary knowledge, strategic planning, and project management skills for managing the transition of a merger or acquisition.

Due Diligence Production   The due diligence stage is next, which includes scrutinizing not just the financials but many of the other risks associated with HR. Due diligence is the process of performing detective work to learn every detail possible about the other organization. The organization's workforce-related risks are just the tip of the iceberg. Factoring in people matters is more difficult to quantify and yet absolutely crucial.

Research and investigation are needed on the proposed M&A organization to determine the technology differences and needs, structural and talent risks, and cultural issues that will arise. The sheer recognition that two cultures must be brought together and blended to create a collaborative, high-performance new organization is daunting. Compliance, corporate governance, and legal claims/lawsuit information—those in process and those that appear on the horizon as a potential threat—would additionally be reviewed and understood at this phase. It is important to understand that oversimplifying these risks can lead to misguided integration planning, unexpected costs, and loss of critical talent.

Integration Planning   Here's where a good strategic planning process resulting in goals and objectives is necessary, along with project management implementation. A change management plan associated with a culture blending process, communication strategies, and consolidation activities occurs during this phase.

Implementation, Measurement, and Monitoring Results   The process is not complete when the organizations are finished with the M&A. HR plays a vital role in monitoring the pulse and mood, assisting with workforces that have blended successfully, and helping to troubleshoot new issues that may have occurred during integration. Employees, after all, will be the implementers of the changes to enable an organization to realize the goals of the merger. Creating metrics and milestones that measure the intended results the organization set out to achieve, with respect to the people-related value of the deal, is the last phase for HR.

Transition Tactics   During a major transition, management often expects leadership transitions to happen without major changes in the acquired business. When clarity and trust are most needed, it's possible that leadership may appear more focused on itself (individuals impacted personally by the transition) than on taking care of its anxious people. Employees can't help noticing the disconnection between leadership's actions and words, with potentially damaging effects of costly turnover of valued employees and serious morale and productivity problems. Poor people management and communication drain financial value from many changeovers.

Having a clear vision and consistent, frequent communication about organizational transition is vital. Creating a strategic blueprint should revolve around communication, not just to the workforce but also to other stakeholders such as the customers and communities served by the organization (plural in the case of an M&A). The best transition tactics revolve around trust and communication. Leadership groups must move forward together, fully aligned, and "owning" the strategic blueprint of the newly created vision in sharing its messages. If the messages and themes that are expressed to all parties are not consistent, then confusion, fear, and a lack of faith in the transition process will occur. Those signals could send tremors of uncertainty throughout the organization. The workforce can surely be counted on to fill a vacuum of information with worse-case scenario rumors, in terms of who will be retained, who will be let go, and how the everyday rules of the game will change.

Organizational Interventions

Aside from redesigning the organizational structure, the science of organizational development (OD) can be used to help solve problems with organizations through various interventions:

- Building teams
- Creating common values

- Creating a vision
- Creating a specific role for each organizational segment
- Facilitating problem-solving sessions focused on organizational structure

Workforce Planning

The exercise known as *workforce planning* is based on the notion that you want a balance between the work to be done and the workers available to do it. Over time, that balance will change, shifting toward one side of the equation or the other.

Workforce Planning Process

There are many approaches you can take to workforce planning. All of them ultimately boil down to one thing: analyzing the gap between what you estimate will be the staffing requirement and the staff you have available to meet that requirement. Once the gap is determined, then plans can be laid to identify action steps necessary to narrow that gap.

Supply Analysis This is a strategic evaluation to understand your current workforce and supply chain options, such as sourcing alternatives, plus plant and warehouse locations. Done well, a supply analysis is more detailed than knowing the total number of employees you currently have. It ought to include knowing where your workforce is and what KSAs and competencies they possess.

Trend and Ratio Analysis Projection Ratio analysis compares current results or historical results, but always at a point in time. Trend analysis compares historical results with current results and identifies what may happen in the future based on the trend of data in the past.

Turnover Analysis There are many reasons for employees leaving the payroll, including resignation, dismissal, death, long-term disability, and transfer to a subordinate company within the parent company. Identifying the reasons that employees are leaving provides the data needed to analyze trends and identify potential problems within the organization. If supervisors are causing high resignation rates, it may be appropriate to train the supervisors or take some other action to reduce the rate at which their subordinates are leaving.

Flow Analysis This can involve analysis of data, analysis of production line movement, or analysis of order processing, among other possibilities. How processes operate and how flows of products, data, or other items go through those processes are the objectives of this type of monitoring.

Demand Analysis

It is interesting to look forward to determine what customers, clients, or patrons will want in the future. Demand analysis is your best determination of your staffing needs for the future: What competencies and skill sets will be needed in which locations?

Judgmental Forecast This is a projection based on subjective inputs. This method is often used when there is a short time to draw a conclusion or when data is outdated or unavailable.

Statistical Forecast   This approach to analysis uses mathematical formulas to identify patterns and trends. Once identified, the trends are analyzed again for mathematical reasonableness.

Gap Analysis

Measuring the distance (or difference) between where you are and where you want to be is known as *gap analysis*. If you plan to train all employees in certain safety procedures, you can use gap analysis to determine what portion of the population has yet to receive the training, or any portion of the training.

Prioritizing the Gaps   Identifying the gaps is the first step. Then, it is a good idea to determine the relevant importance of each portion of the results that need attention. Safety training may be more important (and greater priority) than training on the new benefit forms. Product feature training may be higher priority than updates on vacation scheduling procedures. Setting priorities for all components of the gap is important.

Defining Tactical Objectives   In his article "Definition of Tactical Planning in Business," Neil Kokemuller states the following: "Tactical plans are sometimes called short-term action plans because they break down bigger-picture goals and strategies into narrower, actionable tasks. The key to a well-developed tactical plan is having specifically stated actions assigned to particular employees with specific deadlines."[29]

Therefore, identifying specific objectives to be worked on and determining who will do what by what date comprise the tactical planning component. The following action plan is an example of tactical objectives:

	Example of Tactical Objectives		
	Objective: Workforce Reduction of 500 People		
☒	**Action Step**	**Responsible Party**	**Estimated Completion Date**
	Prepare offer of voluntary separation with incentives	CHRO and CFO	1/15/26
	File WARN notice as required	CHRO	1/15/26
	Complete separation notices	CHRO	3/31/26

Solution Analysis

In problem-solving, once the problem has been identified, identifying potential solutions comes next. Every solution suggested should be written on a list, regardless of what you think of it. After identifying all the possible solutions via brainstorming, you can begin writing a list of criteria that are absolutely required of any solution you choose. These are the must-haves. Criteria tell us that no solution will work if it doesn't meet all these requirements. Next, compare each suggested solution with the list of criteria and scratch off the list any solution that does not fully meet all the criteria requirements. What is left will be a list of solutions that can each satisfy the criteria. You may then select from the surviving list of solutions.

When multiple solutions meet all the criteria, using regression analysis can help you decide which one is best for you. For example, it might be possible to solve the problem of turnover by creating a management skills training program. It also might be possible to solve the turnover problem by providing different employee benefits that are more appealing to the workers. It could also be that offering continuing education to employees would have an impact on turnover. Each of those solutions could work. You can determine how well each works by using regression analysis to calculate the contribution each could make to the problem of turnover control. This analysis considers that there is some value to be contributed by each different solution. If you can't choose all of them, where will you get the greatest impact for your investment of time and money?

The Staffing Plan

Once a list of organizational objectives is determined, it is possible to begin the process of determining the quantity of employees that will be needed in each function to accomplish those objectives.

Statement of Purpose

The purpose of your staffing plan should be simply stated. Universally, staffing involves the activities associated with filling job openings. Candidates can come from both internal and external sources. Therefore, the purpose can be stated like this: "Our staffing plan is designed to meet our employment needs with the right skills in the right jobs at the right time."

Stakeholders

Everyone who has something at risk if the job openings are not filled with qualified individuals at the proper time is considered a stakeholder. This includes the HR manager, the staffing manager, recruiters, operations managers and supervisors, production managers and supervisors, job candidates, interns, job advertising vendors, Internet sources, and more.

Everyone who has a "stake" in the success of your staffing efforts will fall into this grouping. Not all stakeholders will have the same level of interest or amount of risk involved, however. The supervisor trying to fill the job opening will have the most to gain or lose in the successful completion of the staffing efforts. The HR department's reputation will rise or fall depending on how well it develops the staffing plan and then implements its actions.

Activities and Tasks

What is involved in a staffing plan and its implementation? More or less it depends on the size of your organization. The larger the organization, the more complex the staffing plan will be. Larger organizations have more complex policies and procedures. Small organizations are more flexible and less encumbered by detailed policies.

Here are some of the activities you will find in staffing plans:

- Identify the organizational goals needing employee support.
- Identify the quantity of full-time equivalent (FTE) employees each goal will need.

- Specify the knowledge, skills, abilities (KSAs) and competencies each position will require.
- Identify candidate sources, considering diversity efforts and KSA requirements.
- Solicit qualified candidates to apply.
- Screen candidates for qualifications.
- Select candidates who will likely "fit best" into the job requirements.
- Forward candidate records to selecting manager for consideration.
- Schedule interviews with selecting manager and others, if warranted, in the department.
- Administer any other screening device or step such as written tests or skill demonstrations.
- Make employment selection decision.
- Follow up months later to assess the success of the employment selection.
- Make any procedural adjustments for the future based on that assessment.

Team Members

Staffing processes involve multiple individuals in organizations of any size. In large organizations, there will be individuals who specialize in given segments of the process. In smaller organizations, there will be greater emphasis on generalists who handle multiple functions.

For example, the HR department may have only one person, the HR manager, who is responsible for all phases of the staffing process. However, in the larger counterpart, there may be an entire staff of recruiters working for the HR department. There can even be psychologists involved in employment screening for some large, sophisticated organizations.

Resources

Staffing resources include all the people, assets, and funding needed to successfully place qualified people into the job openings. If there is a competitive marketplace where you must try to get your qualified candidates, your competitors may be trying to do the same thing. You will need to distinguish your organization from the competition so you can be successful in attracting the people you want on your staff.

There are internal resources from which you can make your staffing selections. Succession plans will help you identify who is "Ready Now" for promotion, who is capable of a lateral transfer, and who still needs some additional training or experience before being considered "Ready Now" for the job in question. While succession plans normally apply to the executive ranks, employee skills inventories can help you determine who is capable of filling job openings through a database of employee KSAs.

In organizations with labor union representation, it is common to have union-represented jobs filled based on employee seniority. Internal training centers can produce qualified job candidates with each graduating class.

Also, don't forget employee referrals. "I know someone..." can sometimes provide some very appropriate talent for the staffing needs.

External resources include state employment services, veterans' groups, state rehabilitation services for disabled job candidates, educational institutions, job fairs, Internet sources such as Indeed, Monster.com, LinkedIn, Craigslist, school alumni sites, and a host of other service vendors. Also, you shouldn't forget your own organization's website. Candidates coming directly to your website have a greater chance of wanting to work for your company, versus simply wanting a job. Your website can be an excellent avenue for job applicants to enter your selection process.

Communication Plan

A staffing plan won't be very effective unless people important to its success know what should be happening. Letting employees and people outside the organization know that you are hiring and the type of skill sets you want will boost the placement rate and reduce selection time.

Continuous Improvement

As with any other portion of the enterprise, staffing should be the focus of continuous improvement efforts. Small goals that are frequently reached can result in large progress over the course of longer time periods. The Japanese concept of *kaizen*—making frequent assessments of performance and then setting new improvement goals—will result in substantial performance improvement. Japan's automobile industry overtook the American market because Honda and Toyota presented better-quality products in the 1980s and 1990s.

Employee Development

Employee development programs are an important aspect of talent management, providing employees with opportunities to learn new knowledge and skills, preparing them for future responsibilities and job changes, and increasing their capacity to perform in their current jobs. Job rotation, job enlargement, and job enrichment represent some approaches to employee development. Another could be an apprenticeship program that relates to skills training.

NOTE The U.S. apprenticeship system is regulated by the Bureau of Apprenticeship and Training (BAT).

Higher education tuition reimbursement programs are also offered by many organizations as part of their employee development program. The pursuit of education is normally restricted to an employee's current occupation or an occupation that exists within the organization.

Other employee development programs that are increasingly on the rise within organizations are those associated with wellness training, stress management, and work-life balance.

Development of Employees

Next to strong retention efforts, employee development is a staffing effort that can lower overall costs and improve morale in the workforce. Giving people the opportunity to expand their skill set when they want, leads to their taking on more responsibility with higher levels of satisfaction. Blocking the wish for learning new skills can only lead to disappointment and discontent.

Talent Management

Talent management involves all the HR strategies and processes that are involved in attracting, developing, engaging, and retaining the KSAs of the workforce to meet the organization's needs. Talent management goals are simple: manage the HR initiatives that directly result in employee productivity and that address current and future business needs.

Skills Inventories   Skill inventories of your employees puts you ahead in your human resources planning. Knowing what skills your employees have allows you to compare that data with what you forecast you will need for the future. "Creating and maintaining current skills inventories allow employers to develop succession plans based on current employee skills sets and identify key employees for future openings critical to the company's leadership and business success. Skills inventories should be reviewed on an ongoing basis and employers should take steps to ensure employees keep their own skills inventory current and updated. By doing so, employers can help ensure the success of their strategic plans and achievement of their company's short- and long-term goals."[30] Utilizing skill inventories may also lend itself to creating talent pools to facilitate your succession planning.

Talent Management Strategies   It is less expensive to tap into the organization's internal talent pool than it is to conduct an external search for the skills needed in a particular job. Therefore, skill inventories are something that can pay off handsomely. Succession planning, if maintained well, can reduce the panic felt when key people are suddenly out of the picture due to death, resignation, long-term illness, or injury. Knowing in advance who has the skills and abilities to do the job, plus the interest and willingness, will accelerate placement efforts.

Addressing the Changing Needs of Employees   Nothing in the world is static for very long, and employee needs are no different. Life goes on, and work is just part of our lives. Therefore, when new babies arrive, someone gets seriously ill, or tragedy strikes and an employee has a death in the family, the employer will be faced with some attendance issues and some ongoing adjustment requests.

Flexible Staffing   Growing in popularity, telecommuting is an alternative to traditional staffing where everyone reported to a given work location every day. There are additional flexible staffing options:

- **Job sharing**   Job sharing is an employment technique that offers two or more workers the opportunity to collectively constitute one full-time equivalent (FTE) employee. One person works the job in the morning, and another works the same job in the afternoon—or each works half the days of the work week.

Considerations involve briefing the "job sharing partner" on the current issues to be dealt with during the next portion of work time. There are some financial considerations too. Each employee will require the employer's full contribution toward Social Security and Medicare. That may cost the employee more than if one person were to occupy the position. Job sharing also requires the organization to look at their policies for other benefits eligibilities: none, all, or prorated?

NOTE   Job sharing can increase morale and provide staffing in situations that otherwise might be difficult.

- **Shortened workweeks**   One option is four 10-hour days per week, aptly called 4/10s. Another option, called 9/80s, involves eight 9-hour days plus one 8-hour day every two weeks, which allows for an added day off work every other week.

- **Phased retirement**   As opposed to instant full-time retirement, phased retirement is another alternative to full-time employment, which allows an individual to take partial retirement while continuing to work a reduced schedule. It can take the form of job sharing, part-time, seasonal, temporary, or project work.

NOTE   A major advantage of phased retirement is that is allows employees to get used to working less and having more time to themselves. It prevents the sudden shock of not having a work routine that comes with traditional retirement. It also facilitates knowledge transfer from the employee about to retire to those who will be carrying on in the firm.

Alternative Staffing   When looking for alternatives to the FTE 40-hour workweek stereotype, you have some options:

- **Project employees**   Using project hires and contract labor is an alternative to full-time employment. Project hires are recruited and placed on the payroll with the understanding that their employment will be terminated once the project is completed. It is common in organizations that seek out projects from client organizations. A staff is hired for the project and then let go when the project ends.

  Contract labor refers to people who are hired for a specific period. An organization may believe that the workload will last until the same time next year. Therefore, it contracts with people to handle that workload for the year. At the end of the contract, those folks will come off the payroll, whether the project has concluded or not, unless the contract allows for a mutually agreed-upon extension until the project conclusion. The contract laborers could be "extended" (payroll status maintained) for a designated period if their labor is still needed.

- **Temporary employees**   One change to full-time employment is the use of temporary employees. It is not necessary to hire people by putting them on the payroll. Employers can expand their workforce quickly and easily by contracting with temporary talent agencies to satisfy their need for additional people. Temporary workers can be used on production lines, in accounting departments, or in any other portion of an organization experiencing a workload that cannot be handled by the permanent staff. Agencies pay their employees, take care of payroll withholding and tax reporting, add a profit margin, and then pass the final rate to the employer contracting for that help.

- **Payrolling**   When a job needs to be done and the organization does not want to hire someone onto its own payroll to do that job, an alternative is to contract with a vendor who will hire someone to do the job at the client organization. Contractor payrolling is used when you need to adjust to seasonal fluctuations, fill a vacancy while searching for a regular replacement, bridge the gap in personnel when there is unexpected growth, or use interns for a set period. It has many applications, and the greatest benefit is in protecting against charges that the person hired is not an independent contractor but an employee, a problem that cost the company Microsoft just under $100 million in payroll taxes, penalties, fines, and legal fees. This is usually a process used for less than an entire workforce. When single employees or small groups of employees are needed, payrolling services can solve the need.

- **Employee leasing through a professional employer organization (PEO)**   Similar to payrolling, employee leasing is a process of moving employees to another company's payroll as a service for a client organization. Typically, PEOs will take over the entire workforce in a client company. PEOs provide payroll services, tax tracking and depositing, retirement program management, health care benefit program management, and even employee counseling and support services. Employee leasing is the outsourcing of the human resource department and the payroll function together. Employees usually become employees of both organizations—the client where they perform their work as well as the vendor (PEO) that handles the payroll and HR functions for the client. In that case, it means both employers are liable for legal compliance. When working with a PEO, make sure you understand what your contractual obligations are and be clear if the workers are yours, the PEO's, or both.

- **Outsourcing and managed service providers (MSPs)**   Another alternative is outsourcing. Outsourcing is shifting a workload out of the organization through a contract with another employer organization, either in this country or somewhere else in the world. Managed service providers offer to manage functions as part of a strategic decision to move operations or support functions out of an employment organization to a vendor that can perform them less expensively. Such a decision is designed to allow the client company to focus on key activities within its core business while a vendor handles support activities for the client.

- **Temp-to-lease programs**   When a need exists for employees on a seasonal basis or for jobs that will last longer than a few days or weeks, it is possible for employers to lease their workers from a vendor organization. The vendor provides the underlying employment relationship with the worker. When temporary needs stretch into longer-term needs, it still may not be wise to increase payroll in the client organization. That's when contracting for temporary agency workers can be converted into long-term employee leases. These workers often have no benefits provided to them. The client organization pays an employment agency a fee in addition to the pay received by the worker assigned to the client. All payroll operations are maintained by the temporary service agency.

- **Rehires and transfers**   When workloads rise unexpectedly, it is sometimes difficult to bring in new hires quickly enough to respond to that increased demand. Rehiring recent retirees and laid-off workers and/or bringing in transfers from other portions of the organization can sometimes be good solutions. Rehired workers are already trained and can be productive immediately. Transfers from other portions of the organization have the advantage of already knowing the culture and, if coming from similar or identical types of work, can also be productive quickly.

- **Relocation**   Moving workers from one location to another outside the normal commute radius requires finding them new living quarters. This can be done on a temporary or an on-going basis. If relocation is used to respond to union strikes or increased workload, it will likely be a temporary condition. Employers sometimes rent blocks of rooms in long-term hotel facilities so workers can have cooking and laundry facilities along with living quarters.

Relocation not considered temporary can involve workers selling and buying homes, packing household belongings, and shipping them long distances, sometimes across the country or internationally. There are many variables in such action on the part of the employer. Enticing employees to accept relocation can be a high hurdle to overcome. Forcing the change for a spouse's employment, moving children from one school to another, and accepting a higher cost of living at the new location can require employers to provide financial incentives. Those incentives can include such things as the following:

- **Home purchase/lease escape fees**   One strategy is offering a guaranteed purchase of the employee's old home following an agreed upon appraisal of value. The employee can accept or reject the company's offer if it might be possible to achieve a higher selling price some other way. When there is a fee involved for canceling property leases, employers can pay that fee for employees.

- **Real estate processing fees**   Escrow fees for selling and buying real property can amount to many dollars. Paying these expenses for a relocating employee can lift that burden and remove another objection to relocating.

- **Mortgage subsidy**   In an inflationary economy, mortgage rates rise. It can sometimes be necessary for employers to pay a portion or all of the increased mortgage rate to get an employee to accept relocation.

- **Packing/shipping/unpacking** Paying the bill for a moving company to pack, ship, and unpack at the destination is another way to relieve employees of financial burden.

- **Funds for taxes on increased taxable income** When there are income tax consequences for employees because of a relocation, employers sometimes compute a "tax obligation roll-up" and pay that to the employee in a lump sum as withholdings.

Work-Life Balance According to the website www.worklifebalance.com, the proper definition of the term *work-life balance* is meaningful daily achievement and enjoyment in four life quadrants: namely, work, family, friends, and self. That doesn't mean an equal amount of time spent in each life area. It means whatever is necessary for personal satisfaction. Employers can help facilitate that achievement if they are sophisticated about employee management and contemporary issues.

Measuring Talent Management Effectiveness Talent management can be defined as putting the right people in the right positions at the right time…and keeping them there. This requires measuring that goes more than skin deep into the organization's policies and procedures.

An ADP whitepaper on the topic suggests that talent management should "connect investments in human capital with the immutable facts of financial performance." Here are some basic measurements it suggests organizations consider. All relate to the return on investment (ROI) employers can expect from their human capital.[31]

- Overall talent retention rate
- Cost to hire talent
- Revenue per full-time employee
- Time it takes to hire talent
- Time to full productivity per full-time employee
- Diversity statistics
- Impact of voluntary and involuntary employee loss rates on revenue
- Average tenure of new hires
- Number of senior positions and the depth of bench strength
- Number of promotions made from within the organization

Succession Planning

Succession planning systematically identifies, assesses, and develops talent as a key component for business success. It is an ongoing process that enables an organization to plan or recover when critical talent is lost. An effective succession plan includes a focus on identifying, developing, and preparing the placement of high-potential employees for future opportunities. It is foolish to assume that key players would provide adequate notice of resignation. Succession planning is not just for the planned events such as retirements; it serves for replacement planning, such as when a key player is relocating because of family or perished in an accident. Succession should be developed to anticipate managerial staffing needs or key employee positions that would interrupt the business process if an incumbent were to vacate.

 NOTE Be careful not to exclude employees from a succession plan solely based on their age.

A succession plan starts with the identification of which positions you want a contingency plan for backfilling. Some organizations look at only senior management. Others look at all management. SHRM urges a broad look, including critical nonmanagement positions as well. Next, add in any known or anticipated vacancy dates (as with retirements). Competencies for those positions are identified, and a gap analysis is conducted with the current workforce potential candidates. Individuals within are identified as high-potential employees, which might include their interest/aspiration in the position. Not every individual may be interested in moving into a more responsible position. Tentative plans are created for shortages, which may include seeking outside candidates.

HR is typically responsible for maintaining a candidate database of skills and career development plans, along with the monitoring of development activities. Additionally, HR is responsible for sourcing or creating training needs for candidates. Figure 5-3 provides a typical progression of steps in succession planning.

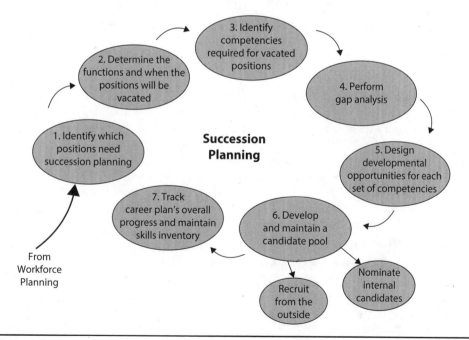

Figure 5-3 Succession planning

Knowledge Management

Knowledge management (KM) is a term that relates to the retention and distribution of organizational knowledge. It is the efficient process of capturing, developing, sharing, and handling of informational resources within a business. KM efforts will generally focus on competitive advantage, innovation, the sharing of lessons from the past, integration, policies, processes, and practices, plus the renewal cycle of continuous improvement in an organization. Its focus is on the management of internal knowledge held by incumbents as a strategic asset and the mentorship in sharing this knowledge.

Managing Organizational Knowledge

In managing organizational knowledge, organizations identify their collective knowledge to compete, including the creation, storage/retrieval, transfer, and application of knowledge that is pertinent to conducting business. Referred to as *knowledge assets,* these are some of an organization's most valuable assets. Knowledge assets include both explicit knowledge (for example, documented concepts, procedures, and processes) and tacit knowledge (for example, know-how) that are highly specific to an organization.

Knowledge Management Systems

Today, many organizations and industries are taking advantage of advanced technologies such as database tools and web-based applications to effectively manage their workforce's knowledge. Over the last two decades, organizations have leveraged these technologies in their KM initiatives. The goal of these technologies is to introduce a standardized process to promote a more efficient and effective flow of information and knowledge throughout the organization.

Knowledge Management Process   A knowledge management process is creating, sharing, using, and managing the information and knowledge within an organization. It is a multidisciplinary approach to achieving organizational objectives by making the best use of knowledge.

Uses of Knowledge Management Systems   There are various uses for knowledge management systems, yet they all focus on transferring knowledge seamlessly. "Document, document, document" has been the cry in IT for many years because IT has felt the pain of what it's like to have a programmer "keep the coding in their head" when that employee has abruptly and unexpectedly left their employment. An example of a KM system is a central database that stores customer data used for sales and marketing analytics. The resulting information that the sales/marketing folks place in the database is *knowledge,* which is then transferred and shared across the organization. A retrieval tool such as a query system could be used to have a new sales or marketing person learn who is the rep for a particular client and what the status is of that relationship in the sales cycle.

Strategies for Effective Knowledge Management Systems   Using information systems to manage the knowledge is often a difficult, time-consuming, and tedious task. The following internal and external strategies could help to ensure effective implementation and management of KM systems.

Internal Strategies

- *Identify business challenges.* This is related to knowledge management and then capturing essential pieces of knowledge. Focus on knowledge that is important to capture and feasible to maintain.

- *Obtain executive support.* Executives in the organization need to be on board with supporting knowledge management initiatives from both a strategic perspective and a financial perspective. The probability of success increases when the knowledge management effort is a top priority.

- *Get buy-in and input from the users.* Many KM initiatives have failed because the system designers neglect user feedback. Involve users at early stages in the design process and incorporate user input on system design requirements. Remember, the objective is to implement a system that users willfully use, not one that is technically sound but remains underutilized because of a lack of buy-in from potential users.

- *Celebrate small wins.* Use a "control tower" approach, where a specific function is mandated to develop a knowledge management action plans, such as accounts payable. This can result in a favorable approach to ensure small wins throughout the organization by showing how a function created their KM.

- *Manage employee behavior.* One of the signals of effective KM initiatives is evidence of employee participation. Project leaders should champion changes in KM practices and ensure that the technology provides added value. Moreover, employees should be actively involved in the knowledge management efforts because it is their knowledge that will be leveraged and retained for future.

- *Be patient.* Creating a knowledge management system is time-consuming. Managing knowledge is a difficult task with no fixed rules.

External Strategies

- *Attend KM-oriented training sessions and conferences.* KM is a new frontier for many organizations. Attending training sessions and discussing knowledge management problems and best practices with others will serve as an introduction to the challenges.

- *Establish a peer network.* Establish forums where colleagues can demonstrate the latest best practices.

- *Benchmark your knowledge management practices.* Benchmark your organization's knowledge management process against competitors to identify areas of strength and weakness.

- *Hire a knowledge management expert.* Knowledge management experts provide credibility to the organization's KM efforts, especially to stakeholders. Traditional management consultants may be insufficient because they lack the appropriate expertise needed to address KM issues.

Social Sharing of Knowledge   Knowledge sharing via enterprise social media (ESN) is increasingly being introduced into large organizations. ESN focuses on the use of online social networks among the employees who share the same roles and responsibilities, in large organizations, such as matrix positions (for example, HR business partners in each manufacturing plant who report to both the plant manager and the headquarters' HR director). Internally, an enterprise social software may be part of the organization's intranet. ESNs are also used externally and not just within a particular organization, such as software programmers seeking knowledge shared on blogs and networks to figure out how to code a particular challenge.

Functional Area 9: Employee & Labor Relations

Here is SHRM's BASK definition: "Employee & Labor Relations refers to any interactions between the organization and its employees regarding the terms and conditions of employment."[32]

Human resources management as a functional area within employer organizations didn't always exist in its current configuration. It began as a kinship department associated with accounting and was primarily responsible for taking care of payroll issues and for record-keeping. From that, it evolved into a labor relations department responsible for union interactions. In recent years, HR has had responsibility for legal compliance on employee matters, and today it's involved in strategic issues of employee resource management.

Key Concepts

- Employment rights, standards, and concepts according to the International Labour Organization (for example, labor rights, living wage and fair wage concepts, standard workday, unfair labor practices)
- Types and development of compliance and ethics programs (for example, design, implementation, required postings, performance measures)
- Types of alternative dispute resolution (ADR) and their advantages and disadvantages (for example, mediation, arbitration)
- Approaches to retaliation prevention (for example, open-door policy, open communication, nonretaliation policy, whistleblower protection, documentation)
- Techniques for workplace investigations (for example, consistency, interview plan, summary report)
- Progressive disciplinary procedures and approaches (for example, counseling, performance improvement plan, corrective action, verbal warning, demotion, termination)
- Techniques for grievance and complaint resolution (for example, grievance procedure, investigation, appeal)
- Causes of and methods for preventing and addressing strikes, lockouts, and boycotts (for example, unfair labor practices, economic grievances, strike response plan, hiring temporary workers, protection of nonstriking employees, supply chain contingency plans)

The following are the proficiency indicators that SHRM has identified for Employee & Labor Relations:

For All HR Professionals	Advanced HR Professionals (SCP Exam)
• Develops and implements workplace policies, handbooks, and codes of conduct	• Consults on and develops an effective organized labor strategy (for example, avoidance, acceptance, adaptation) to achieve the organization's desire impact on itself and its workforce
• Provides guidance to employees on the terms and implications of their employment agreement and the organization's policies and procedures (for example, employee handbook, code of conduct)	• Educates employees, managers, and leaders at all levels about the organization's labor strategy and its impact on the achievement of goals and objectives
• Advises managers on how to supervise difficult employees, handle disruptive behaviors, and respond with the appropriate level of corrective action	• Educates employees at all levels about changes in the organization's policies
• Conducts investigations into employee misconduct and suggests disciplinary action when necessary	• Coaches and counsels managers on how to operate within the parameters of organizational policy, labor agreements, and employment agreements
• Manages employee grievance and discipline processes	• Oversees employee investigations and progressive discipline actions
• Resolves workplace labor disputes internally	• Manages interactions and negotiations with employee representatives (for example, organized labor, governmental, legal)
• Supports interactions and negotiations with employee representatives (examples include organized labor, governmental, and legal)	• Serves as the primary representative of the organization's interests in activities related to organized labor management (for example, negotiations, dispute resolution)

The Employment Relationship

According to the government, people are either employees or not employees. That begs the question, "What is an employee?" A quick look in our glossary will reveal an employee is "a person in the service of another under any contract of hire, express or implied, oral or written, where the employer has the power or right to control and direct the employee in the material details of how the work is to be performed."

Toward "Employee Relations"

Organizational culture is often defined, at least in part, by the type of employee relations programs that exist. We are talking about structured programs designed to help employees feel part of the organization in positive ways. Creating a positive culture is not a simple matter and is an essential influential factor for recruiting and retaining talent.

HR devotes much effort and time to champion a positive culture with effective employee relations programs. The HR department also serves as an employee advocate. Culture is defined by the way an organization treats its employees, customers, and others. It is also influenced by the way power is distributed within the organization and the amount of power employees sense they have. What follows is an overview of different types of employee relationship programs.

Employer and Employee Rights

Under the laws of the United States, both employers and employees have rights related to their relationship.

Employer Rights Under the Law

Employers used to be able to treat employees in any way they wanted. That is what brought about the rise of labor unions. Unions protested ill treatment of workers and fought for employee benefits and wages. Over the decades, much of what the unions accomplished for their membership has been transported into laws that protect all employees, not just unionized workers. Equal Employment Opportunity (EEO) is a prime example. Employers may make their decisions about employees based on any factor that is job related. Things such as race, color, religion, sex, or national origin may no longer be considered in that decision-making process.

As things stand today, employers can do virtually anything they want if it doesn't violate law or public policy. That includes the covenant of good faith and fair dealing. Employers are expected to give workers more consideration the longer they have served the employer. Also, all workers are due fair treatment. That is a constant expectation.

Intellectual Property

While there are some exceptions, the general rule is that employers own the rights to work-related copyrights, patents, and trademarks developed by employees, even if the work was done on the employee's own time. In the absence of written agreements to the contrary, employers are ordinarily the owners of such work products by their employees.

Employee Rights Under the Law

There are dozens of labor laws on the books today. They have been created to provide protections to employees in the workplace. You can scan the list of federal laws in Chapter 3. Case law (refer to Appendix B) also brings influence on the subject. All U.S. employers are influenced in one way or another by these requirements.

Employees are usually given the "benefit of the doubt" when it comes to disciplinary treatment or complaint against an employer. Remember, they are always afforded consideration under the covenant of good faith and fair dealing. Employers must treat people fairly, even though they may be categorized as "employment at will" employees.

Employment at will is a form of employment relationship that has been amended over the years. Now, there are many restrictions to an employer's termination of a worker without cause, and fair treatment influences strongly employee attitudes and, in turn, production levels.

Relevant Employment Laws   Federal laws applying to employee relations include the following:

Railway Labor Act of 1926	Davis-Bacon Act of 1931
Norris-LaGuardia Act of 1932	Wagner-Peyser Act of 1933 (amended by Workforce Investment Act of 1998)
National Labor Relations Act of 1935	Federal Insurance Contributions Act of 1935 (Social Security Act)
Walsh-Healey Act of 1936 (Public Contracts Act)	Fair Labor Standards Act of 1938
Labor-Management Relations Act of 1947 (Taft-Hartley Act)	Portal-to-Portal Act of 1947
Immigration and Nationality Act of 1952	Labor-Management Reporting and Disclosure Act of 1959 (Landrum-Griffin Act)
Equal Pay Act of 1963	Civil Rights Act of 1964 (Title VII)
Service Contract Act of 1965	Age Discrimination in Employment Act of 1967
Fair Credit Reporting Act of 1970	Vietnam Era Veterans Readjustment Assistance Act of 1974
Uniform Guidelines on Employee Selection Procedures of 1976	Pregnancy Discrimination Act of 1978
Electronic Communications Privacy Act of 1986	Immigration Reform and Control Act of 1986
Worker Adjustment and Retraining Notification Act of 1988	Drug-Free Workplace Act of 1988
Employee Polygraph Protection Act of 1988	Civil Rights Act of 1991
Uniformed Services Employment and Reemployment Rights Act of 1994	Fair and Accurate Credit Transactions Act of 2003
Genetic Information Nondiscrimination Act of 2008	Lilly Ledbetter Fair Pay Act of 2009

- **Data privacy**   Privacy of employee-related data is a prime concern these days, especially with weekly revelations about computer hackers breaking into one database after another. The grand prize of all was reached when hackers accessed millions of records in the federal government's Office of Personnel Management database. Both current and former employee records were involved. The hack was attributed to Chinese government groups. It is among a growing list of invasions into personal information collections maintained by employers and governments around the country.

Some of the key requirements are shown here:

National Requirement for Employee Data Protection	
Jurisdiction	**Law or Agreement**
United States of America	Health Insurance Portability and Accountability Act (HIPAA).
	Genetic Information Nondiscrimination Act (GINA).

Jurisdiction	National Requirement for Employee Data Protection
	Law or Agreement
	Fair Credit Reporting Act (FCRA).
	Fair and Accurate Credit Transactions Act (FACT).
	Data breech notification requirements. All 50 states, the District of Columbia, Guam, Puerto Rico and the Virgin Islands have laws to notify individuals of security breaches regarding personally identifiable information.[33]
European Economic Area	European Union's data protection Directive 95/46/EC (the "EU Directive") recognizes personal data privacy as a fundamental right and establishes a comprehensive scheme to protect such information.[34]
Non-European Economic Area countries	Seventeen countries have comprehensive laws covering data protection and nondisclosure: Australia, Brazil, Canada, Chile, China, Egypt, India, Israel, Japan, New Zealand, Nigeria, South Africa, South Korea, Switzerland, Thailand, Turkey, and of course the United States.[35]

- **Separation of employment** Separation of employment includes every form of voluntary and involuntary employment termination category. Voluntary separations include resignation, retirement, and job abandonment. Involuntary separations include death, discharge, layoff/downsizing, or incapacitation.

Employment Contracts Employment relationships can exist under a contract or without a contract. Contracts may be either oral agreements or written documents. Either form of agreement will obligate each party to certain performance behaviors. Employers will be obligated for certain compensation, and employees will be obligated for certain work. Contracts spell out how they can be ended, meaning how the employment can conclude. Usually, there is a requirement for a "just cause" before an employer can dismiss a contractual employee.

Written employment contracts will typically contain several sections, such as the following:

- **Job description** Lists duties and responsibilities.
- **Statement of authority** Details expenditure limits, hiring authority, and what conditions require approval of the board of directors or other authority.
- **Agreement length** Identifies the beginning and ending dates of the contract.
- **Performance requirements** Documents performance requirements for compensation increases or bonuses. These can include revenue targets, sales targets, or other measurable performance standard.
- **Compensation and benefits** Details the base rate of pay, pay calculation (hourly, salaried, commissioned), how increases will be achieved, how bonuses will be achieved, how compensation will be paid (cash, stock, bonds, future payments), retirement program (company and employee contribution scheme), health care benefits programs (medical, dental, vision, individual or family),

perks (company car, airplane, driver, concierge, entertainment tickets for concerts and sporting events), and any other compensation condition upon which the relationship will be based.

- **Other important issues**   Can include agreements about who owns copyright and patent rights to things produced by the employee during the contract period, nondisclosure agreements for employer intellectual property protection, and noncompete provisions.

- **Termination provisions**   Can include personal behavior and ethics requirements and other reasons or "causes" for separating the employee from the organization. In many contracts, these reasons are specified in detail. If there is to be a "buyout" for time remaining on the agreement, that should be specified here. "Golden parachutes" are often large sums representing the buyout for early separation, such as in a merger.

Oral Employment Contracts   Oral employment contracts can be expressly made, or made by mistake, and still be valid and enforceable, much to the dismay of employers who fall into those traps.

Oral contracts can be created in some unusual circumstances. Supervisors and managers can inadvertently enter into oral contracts and should receive training to help them avoid such pitfalls.

The following are some examples of oral contracts:

- An in-house recruiter tells a job applicant that this is a great organization and anyone who keeps their record clean "can expect to have a lifelong career here." Within a year, the new employee's division was closed, and all employees were laid off.

- A manager tells a subordinate that "nothing short of stealing from the company" will be cause for termination. Within a year the employee was terminated for inadequate performance.

- A manager tells a new employee, "Sure, you can bet that you'll be here at least 5 years, so go ahead and sell your house in another state and move your family here." The employee was part of a downsizing 6 months later.

- A supervisor says to an employee, "Don't worry about your performance rating. Nobody pays any attention to them here anyway." Within a few months the employee was terminated because of poor performance.

At-Will Employment   Something unique to the employment relationship in the United States is what we call at-will employment. It developed out of common law. "During the late 19th and early 20th centuries a new set of legal rules emerged in the United States governing the relationship between employer and employee. These rules were called 'employment-at-will' and provided that, absent express agreement to the contrary, employment was for an indefinite time and could be terminated by either party, for any reason, or for no reason at all. This doctrine is a unique product of American common law, created by state and federal judges, and continues, substantially unchanged, until today."[36]

Currently, at-will employment exists in most states, and it is state law that usually governs these employee relationships. In other countries, using different legal systems, employment may be terminated only for cause. That means employers must justify their decisions to end the employment relationship with someone. The behavior of the individual is usually the justification.

At-will employment exists only in the absence of a contract that details the employment agreement between employer and employee. Those contracts can be related to a group, as union memorandums of understanding, or to individuals, such as chief executive officers. Since the 1930s, American courts have been instrumental in identifying conditions under which employers may not arbitrarily discharge people, even though they are at-will employees. Some of those restrictions include the following:

- Civil service rules
- Constitutional protections
- Protections against employment discrimination (based on race, color, national origin, religion, sex, age, genetic information, physical disability, mental disability, pregnancy, veteran status, use of family and medical leave)
- Whistleblowing protections

International Human Rights and Labor Standards   While the United States and other industrial countries lead the pack for employee rights, other countries also recognize the need to protect workers against inhumane treatment and bad employer conduct. The following are international organizations created to advance protections for workers.

- **International Labour Organization**   In 1919, the International Labour Organization (ILO) was created. The ILO was later adopted by the United Nations as a component of that international body; 187 of 193 UN member states also belong to the ILO.[37] There are four key principles of the ILO:
  - Freedom of association and the effective recognition of the right to collective bargaining
  - Elimination of all forms of forced or compulsory labor
  - Effective abolition of child labor
  - Elimination of discrimination in respect of employment and occupation
- **Organization for Economic Co-operation and Development (OECD)**   The OECD was formed in 1961 to stimulate economic progress and world trade. In 2022, there were 38 counties in the OECD. Current members are Australia, Austria, Belgium, Canada, Chile, Columbia, Costa Rica, the Czech Republic, Denmark, Estonia, Finland, France, Germany, Greece, Hungary, Iceland, Ireland, Israel, Italy, Japan, Latvia, Lithuania, Luxembourg, Mexico, the Netherlands, New Zealand, Norway, Poland, Portugal, Slovakia, Slovenia, South Korea, Spain, Sweden, Switzerland, Turkey, the United Kingdom, and the United States. Member countries produce two-thirds of the world's goods and services.[38]

By maintaining contact with many governmental and international agencies, such as the International Monetary Fund, the OECD has become a clearinghouse for a vast amount of economic data. It publishes hundreds of titles annually on a variety of subjects that include agriculture, scientific research, capital markets, tax structures, energy resources, lumber, air pollution, educational development, and development assistance.

- **World Trade Organization (WTO)**   The WTO has been headquartered in Geneva, Switzerland since its creation in January 1995. Its 159 member countries focus on global rules of trade between nations. Its main function is to ensure that trade flows as smoothly, predictably, and freely as possible.[39]

Treaties and Trade Agreements   Treaties are formal contracts between nations that, in the United States, must be approved by the U.S. Senate before they become binding on the government. Trade agreements are administrative arrangements made by the executive branch of the government that do not require approval of the U.S. Senate. Under international law, both types of agreement are considered binding, even though we only see treaties as enforceable under our laws.

Employee Relationship Strategy

Employee relations are methods for managing the employer-employee relationship. Strategically managing that relationship calls for consideration of four key elements:

- Union or nonunion status
- Communication
- Company culture
- Compensation and benefits

Union Acceptance/Avoidance Strategies   Employers that have not been unionized have a choice about how they will approach the idea of union organizing. It is possible that an employer would welcome or be neutral toward the idea. Where an employer believes the organization could be well served by having a single voice in representing the employee body, support for unionizing its workforce may be a positive approach. However, if the employer believes that a union would introduce a new lack of flexibility and stringent work rules, then avoidance could be the path of choice.

Accepting the notion of worker organization efforts is rather simple. It could even represent encouragement for the effort. Strategically, the employer would make it known that it supports the union-organizing effort.

Employers that believe unions would not add to their employee management programs will want to use strategies intended to show workers that unions are not necessary for their satisfaction on the job. Strategic programs such as honest open-door policies, sincere management attention to employee complaints, promotion from within, employee training programs, employee satisfaction surveys (with appropriate follow-up), competitive benefit programs and wage schedules, and similar policies can help deflect union-organizing efforts. Training supervisors to treat all direct reports with respect and dignity can also help reinforce the message a union is not needed here.

Global ER Strategies   Each national jurisdiction has its own legal requirements that act as a minimum threshold for employer-employee treatment. Once those minimums have been reached, it is appropriate for employers to ask whether their policies should go beyond to provide enhanced treatment benefits. Those are insurance programs such as medical, dental, and vision coverage. Sometimes the strategies include higher wage schedules or paid time off limits than absolutely required. Strategic use of employee benefits can be a strong argument against union-organizing success. Trying to find an appropriate treatment for employee values that can vary by culture in each different country is also a strategic application of union-prevention efforts.

Employee Recognition and Reward

The larger an organization grows, the greater the likelihood that its recognition programs will be structured. In small organizations, recognition can be given in many forms, often as events unfold and accomplishments are achieved.

Forms of Rewards   Employee recognition can include service anniversary awards (watches, clocks, plaques, certificates, pins), employee-of-the-month awards (designated parking space, plaque or bulletin board posting, special benefit like a dinner gift certificate), cost savings suggestions, sales achievement awards, team achievement awards, and individual achievement awards. Obviously, this is not an exhaustive list. You can add others and apply them as your organization finds a fit between the recognition and the accomplishment.

Recognition Systems   Employee recognition systems can be either formal or informal. Formal recognition systems involve programs designed to address systemic employee issues such as service awards, retirement awards, and employee-of-the-month recognitions. Informal recognition systems involve supervisor or manager spotlighting of employee accomplishments at an employee meeting or supervisor acknowledgment of an employee accomplishment by giving an extra paid day off.

Recognition and Rewards in Global Organizations   Cultural differences from one country to another mean that the esteem (or value) placed on specific rewards will also vary from one country to another. It may be that employees think a few extra days off are wonderful if they are in the United States. In China, they may place greater value on a free month of health benefits for their extended family. Before offering a recognition to employees in another country, it is a good idea to be sure the recognition will be perceived by the recipient as positively as it is by the manager offering it.

Feedback as Reward and Recognition   Culture doesn't usually get in the way of a supervisor telling an employee "Thank you" for a job well done. Almost everyone, regardless of their location, feels good when receiving positive reinforcement for their work performance. Managers and supervisors who make it a habit to give thanks to employees when it is truly deserved will find that it is quite the motivator. Everyone likes to feel appreciated.

Employee Communication

Here again, there are formal and informal communication systems. Formal systems include an employee bulletin or monthly newsletter and daily intranet blog updates for company work sites. Informal communication systems can involve manager distribution of periodic e-mails updating workers on specific happenings in the realm of employee relations. Employees are always interested in the subjects of benefits, customer feedback, and new customer contract activity. When the company is given an award for safety accomplishments or production goal achievements, the workers want to know about it. Being sure to communicate those things to employees is often the job of the HR manager.

Including Managers and Supervisors

As important as general employee communication, special communication to supervisors and managers cannot be overlooked. When new policies are issued, for example, managers and supervisors are interested because they will have to implement the policies and answer questions from employees about daily implications. It is common in larger organizations for managers and supervisors to participate in special meetings just for them. They are often venues for these organizational leaders to learn and provide feedback to senior management about what company policies and programs are working and what are not. Communication flows both directions in such a gathering.

Third-Party Influences on Employee Relations

When we think of employee relationships, we normally consider only the two primary parties: employers and employees. There are times, however, when third parties are involved in that process of conducting employee relationships.

Complex Labor Environments

Even in nonunion environments, there can be third parties in the employment relationship. Often those third parties are government agents responsible for enforcing legal compliance requirements having to do with things such as safety, child labor, equal employment opportunity, or workplace security. Things get complicated when labor unions are active representatives of employees in a portion of the organization and there are no unions in other parts of the company.

Labor or Trade Unions

Unions are groups of employees designated to represent interests of those employees through formal negotiation processes. They are responsible for conducting grievances as employee representatives and for protecting against an employer's failure to follow termination procedures.

Labor/Trade Union Strategies   Employers may find it an advantage to have a union represent their workers. Or, they may not want to have to deal with the regimental procedures necessary once a union gains a foothold in the organization. Either way, having a strategy for supporting or avoiding union representation is worthwhile.

Increasing Formal Internationalization of Unions   These days, unions are more often international entities such as the International Brotherhood of _____ (you can fill in the blank with just about any name). So many employer organizations are multi-national that unions are forced into the same mode of operation.

Pressing for National and International Compliance   Legal compliance requirements for unions vary from one country to another. It is incumbent upon employers who work with international unions to understand the requirements of each country in which they have represented employees.

Forming Networks and Alliances   The international labor-organizing effort is relatively new. It is building bridges between union organizations in individual countries to create international organizations with a wider influence. Also, the organizing effort continues to expand into new countries where there have not yet been union representation of workers. In Ireland, for example, the Irish Congress of Trade Unions is the single umbrella for trade unions in both Northern Ireland and Ireland.

Understanding Individual Labor or Trade Unions

Each trade union is organized to assist the members it attracts. Those members have a unifying interest in their employment relationship with one or more employers. In the case of trade workers (carpenters, electricians, plumbers), journey-level individuals can work for any union-represented employer. In the case of labor unions not in the trades (electrical workers, telephone workers, state government workers), employees usually work for a single employer doing similar types of work. For example, the Communication Workers of America (CWA) represents technicians in the telephone companies. The Service Employees International Union (SEIU) represents workers in health care (nurses, doctors, lab technicians, home health workers), property services (cleaning, security, building maintenance), and public service workers (bus drivers, state government workers, school workers).

Managing the Union Relationship

Traditionally, unions have been seen as adversaries of management. These days, more focus is being placed on cooperation between the two. That means employee representatives are often invited to participate in the decision-making process, along with managers and supervisors. When given an active participative role, unions can become allies of employers.

Work Councils

Work councils originally began in Germany in the 1920s and have been common in other European countries since the late 1990s. Either the employer or employees can request the formation of a work council. Member states are to provide for the right to establish European work councils in companies or groups of companies with at least five employees in the EU. Through work councils, workers are informed and consulted by management on the progress of the business and any significant decision at the European level that could affect their employment or working conditions. Members are usually elected from the employee body. Work councils focus their attention on issues dealing with employee status and rights.

Work Council Structures Work councils are composed of members from the employer's body of workers. In many organizations, those are also union representatives. Typically, a work council can be established once there are five employees in the employer's organization. The following table is an example of how representation of employees can be composed. Notice that there are always an odd number of members to facilitate achievement of a simple majority vote on issues. Members of senior management are not party to the work council.

Work Council Membership Size	
Number Employed	**Number of Works Council Members**
5–20	1
21–50	3
51–100	5
101–200	7
201–400	9
401–700	11
701–1000	13
1000–1500	15

Codetermination In organizations having systems of codetermination, employees are given seats on boards of directors and/or supervisory boards. Policy decisions related to employee treatment are addressed by the board of directors with this system in place.

HR and Work Councils Work councils are sometimes used in multinational corporations outside Europe. Oracle is one example. At Oracle, line managers and HR managers can make recommendations for hiring and firing, but the work council holds the approval stamp. In the United States, establishing work councils in the absence of labor unions is not recommended. The National Labor Relations Act prohibits "company unions," which is sometimes a label pinned on work councils.

Governments and Other Groups

Government laws and regulations weigh heavily on employee relations in today's workplace. In every country, laws govern minimum wage, paid time off allocations and use, safety and health issues, retirement programs, and union relations. It is incumbent upon HR managers to identify the specific legal requirements in each country where they have employees. Compliance, though complicated, can be critical to employee satisfaction.

Collective Bargaining

Collective bargaining is an issue governed by law. Regulations that implement the law specify how employers are to respond to employee union-organizing activities and ongoing negotiations for contract content. Collective bargaining is negotiation involving how employee relations will be conducted in the employer organization. It results in a formal contract document or resolution of formal workplace practice and procedures.

Contract Negotiation Process Negotiating a contract requires identifying the subjects to be addressed by the agreement. Then, each party prepares its preferred position on each subject. Next, the process of comparing those positions begins. Often, dollars are attached to contract subjects. For example, the length of work shift, the amount of overtime to be paid, and the cost of health care benefits all can be represented by dollar values. If the union wants greater benefits for its members, a dollar value can be assigned to that increase. Employers argue budget restraint and use dollar values to justify their reasoning.

EMyth Coach Remy Gervais identifies eight steps in the negotiation process. Here is a list of steps to follow in preparation for and during contract negotiations.[40]

1. **Determine your own motives and objectives.**
   What do you hope to gain from negotiating and why is it important? What do you have to offer in return?

2. **Decide on your starting position and your bottom line.**
   What's the ideal solution you want in the end? How much are you willing to deviate from that ideal outcome? What offer should you start with to give you space to negotiate to finish where you want? Determine your bare minimum for what you need to achieve on each bargaining issue.

3. **Identify the objectives and emotional motivations of the other person.**
   What do you think they want? Is there a hidden agenda? Are there areas on which you already agree?

4. **Plan your offers and possible counteroffers.**
   What are the probable scenarios that could happen? What are your non-negotiables and where can you compromise? Is there the option to have a point when you walk away?

5. **Start by stating and agreeing to the thing being negotiated.**
   Do you have the same goal? (e.g., the new bargaining unit contract, the settlement of an employee promotion or discipline review, etc.)

6. **Decide if you're going to make the first offer.**
   If you allow the other party to make the first offer, you'll be in a position to react. If you start, you'll be in a better leadership position. Even though you won't have the advantage of knowing their offer, you can set the parameters of the negotiation.

7. **Make your offers incrementally and strategically.**
   If you know your ideal outcome, monetary or otherwise, start *above that value* (if you want an increase) or *below it* (if you want a decrease). That's the only way you have any room to negotiate. Then as you go back and forth with offers and counteroffers, you may reach a desirable agreement before hitting your bottom line.

8. **Close the discussion at the right time.**
   If you've done your prep work, you've identified the lowest offer you'll accept. If you reach that point in the negotiation with no agreement, end the meeting. If you *do* reach an agreement that satisfies everyone, be ready to close the deal. Make it easy for them to do as little as possible by having everything ready to sign as quickly as possible.

HR's Role in Contract Negotiations   In large organizations, a segment of the HR department will be responsible for labor relations. That responsibility would include duties associated with contract negotiations. In smaller organizations, the HR manager may be the only person in the HR department. Then, that manager is responsible for contract negotiations. Often, there is direct support from the legal department or external legal counsel.

Each component of a contract agreement can be assigned a cost in dollars. Adding all those component costs can produce the total contract value. For example, health benefits will cost several hundreds of dollars each month to cover an employee and family members. The employer can agree to cover a percentage of that cost, with the balance being paid by the employee. A union will ask for more employer contribution to that formula, and if the employer agrees, the increased contribution can be assigned an incremental cost increase value. Adding that to other cost increases, such as increased pay schedules and overtime rates, will produce a total increase of contract costs. Each time a new proposal is made or received, a cost analysis should be made to determine the budgetary impact. Some costs will be perpetual, such as an increase in pay rates. Other costs can be limited to one time only, such as special bonus payments. Assembling this negotiation cost data is usually the responsibility of the HR manager.

Contract Administration and Enforcement

The thought that only large employers have union contracts is a myth. Many small employers work with union agreements. That is often the case in the construction industry, for example. Operating engineers, teamsters, and laborers, among other unions, will sometimes have agreements with governmental entities that only union-represented workers will be employed on projects funded by that entity. This is common practice for cities and counties, particularly in geographical areas where labor organizations are a strong political influence.

Memoranda of understanding (MOU) and collective bargaining agreements (CBAs) are the written contracts between employer and unions. MOU is a term usually found in the public sector, and CBA is a term normally used in the private sector.

Whether the employer is large or small, someone in the organization must be assigned the responsibility for coordinating work through unions and ensuring the employer abides by all the requirements of the union contract. Sometimes unions require that they process all job requisitions from their employer counterparts. Hiring through union "hiring halls," as it is sometimes called, is the practice of notifying the union of a job opening and receiving a qualified union member as the new hire designee. It is a simple process that can provide staffing quickly, often with only one telephone call or e-mail conveying the employment requisition.

Large employers will have labor relations staff groups that are assigned responsibility for day-to-day interactions with labor unions, as well as carrying responsibility for contract negotiations. Small employers will rely on a part-time job duty assignment for the labor relations function because it doesn't require full-time attention. Small employers sometimes rely on their labor attorneys to fill the role of contract negotiator and grievance handler, while job requisitions are processed on a part-time basis by another company employee.

Handling Grievances   Employee grievances can relate to any subject but always indicate a feeling of upset or discontent about something going on in the workplace, such as the way employees are being treated, organizational policies, and the big category of "fairness."

In union-represented organizations, the union contract or memorandum of understanding will usually explain the grievance procedure steps. They are designed to permit union members the opportunity to formally protest the application of any contract provision. Most will deal with working conditions such as hours of work, how shifts are assigned, or seniority practices. Note that *only* breaching contract provisions are grievable offenses, not everything management does in the workplace.

In nonunion organizations, employee handbooks will often detail the steps for submitting and processing an employee complaint.

Note that rarely will such complaints be called *grievances* in nonunion groups. That is usually a term reserved for union contracts. A more common term for nonunion groups would be *complaint procedure*.

Here are the typical grievance-handling steps you will find in most organizations:

1. **A written complaint**   The employee describes in writing what is causing the upset or discontent. It is a best practice to require inclusion of which contract provision has been perceived to have been violated.

2. **Supervisor-level discussion**   The employee's supervisor (or another group's supervisor) will discuss the complaint with the employee, reviewing facts and reasons for the decision that resulted in the complaint. If the explanation is sufficient, the grievance ends here. If the employee presents information that causes the decision to be changed, the grievance can also end here. It is typical from this step on to have a union steward present either with or for the employee.

3. **Management- or HR-level discussion**   If the supervisor and employee can't agree, the next discussion is with a management person or the HR department. If an agreement is reached, the matter is settled. If not, it can go to a final step with senior management.

4. **Senior management**   The final management step is usually with a senior management official. Sometimes that is the chief executive officer, but it can be with any other designated official who has authority to make any adjustments or decisions deemed appropriate in settling the grievance.

5. **Mediation or arbitration**   Contracts usually specify whether arbitration will be used to resolve union grievances. Ordinarily, employers and unions will split the cost of hiring an arbitrator. Contracts will also specify the procedures to be used in selecting an arbitrator.

When the Employee Relationship Falters

Things do not always move smoothly in an employment organization. There are times when management and employees do not see things in the same way. Sometimes, feelings get hurt, and people feel like they are being treated unfairly. Whether these conditions constitute a violation of union contract or company policy or are simply examples of miscommunication, they are very real for employees.

Preserving the Relationship at Difficult Times

When disagreements occur and upsets happen, HR managers should focus on preserving their relationships with union officials. The worst thing that can come from disagreements is failure of the communication channel. If parties cease to talk with one another, it is impossible to get back to a normal working relationship. Sometimes simply agreeing to disagree and move to the next step in the resolution process is the best that can be hoped for, but it carries with it an agreement to continue working toward cooperation in other areas.

Industrial Actions and Unfair Labor Practices

Either management or the union can initiate retaliatory action in the workplace as a response to the other party's failure to agree at the bargaining table. Industrial actions are designed to get the attention of the opposite party. Unfair labor practices are those activities that violate the National Labor Relations Act (NLRA). Note that you need to comply with the NLRA provisions even if you have no union.

Industrial Actions

Industrial actions can be initiated by either the employer or employees and almost always result from the breakdown in the negotiation process.

Employee-initiated industrial actions can include work slowdowns (where production rates are decreased from normal), work stoppage (where at least a portion if not all the facility stops its production), and "sickouts" (orchestrated absences by calling in "sick," such as the "blue flu" when police officers fail to report for duty).

Employer-initiated industrial action usually involves lockouts when employees are prevented from reporting to work because the employer has locked the facility or otherwise barred their access to the work area.

Unfair Labor Practices

The National Labor Relations Act (NLRA) explains that unfair labor practices can be blamed on either employers or labor unions. Common among issues evoking such claims are those revolving around the process of union elections. Unions commonly claim the employer is blocking their organizing efforts, and employers claim that the union is harassing employees and electioneering during workers' paid work time. Another issue that generates a great number of complaints is how management and union members behave during a work stoppage (strike).

Complaints of unfair labor practices are formally filed with the National Labor Relations Board (NLRB). The NLRB will investigate the complaints and issue a determination along with any order for corrective action or limitation on activities of the offending party.

In some instances, when an employer believes there has been a violation of civil law requirements, it will go directly to court requesting an *injunction* against the union to prevent the behavior that is causing the problem. That is common when striking union pickets block access to parking lots, loading docks, or employee building entrances. Municipal laws in many locations govern how public access to property must be maintained and how public sidewalks and roadways can be used appropriately.

In other instances, unions can seek court assistance when employers are being accused of inappropriate controls on picketers. Use of physical force by private security guards could be an example.

In either situation, the remedy sought through the court is an injunction preventing the offending behaviors. With an injunction in hand, it is possible to request help from law enforcement bodies such as the police department or sheriff's department to enforce the injunction.

HR's Role   Human resource professionals are usually the people responsible for monitoring activities in the workplace, seeing that the misbehavior of individuals gets documented, and communicating the messages from management and unions to one another.

Managing Conflicts with and Between Employees

Employee conflicts are not always limited to union grievances or discrimination complaints. Sometimes they happen because what happens "just isn't fair," and the American expectation is always that the workplace will operate fairly.

HR's Role in Managing Conflict   Howard M. Guttman of Guttman Development Strategies, Inc., has identified five roles the HR professional should play in managing conflicts within the employer organization:[41]

- *Be a custodian of team alignment.* HR professionals should hold a mirror to team members so they can see how well the team has done in reaching its goals. Part of that reflection should focus on individual accountability for participation and results.

- *Drive/monitor accountability.* Team members become accountable not only for their own performance but for that of their colleagues—even those who do not report to them.

- *Help assess the team's conflict-management behavior.* The HR professional can guide teams through an exploration of effectiveness in handling conflicts. Then jointly identify specific behavior changes for successful goal accomplishment.

- *Ensure the right capability set on teams.* A major role for HR is ensuring that, after the "should be as-is" analysis, teams receive the skills needed to fill any gaps.

- *Work to make sure that teams are high performers.* The internal HR consultant must wear many hats: consultant, coach, facilitator, trainer, and, perhaps most important, role model to support the team's continued success.

Conflict-Resolution Techniques   Some amount of conflict will always be present in the workplace. The fact that it exists is not necessarily an unhealthy thing. When it is resolved quickly and effectively, it can lead to personal and professional growth. In many cases, effective conflict resolution can make the difference between positive and negative outcomes. The "Leader's 5-Step Guide to Conflict Resolution"[42] recommends five steps in the conflict-resolution process:

1. *Affirm the relationship.* Make sure everyone at the bargaining table feels good about being there by treating all with respect and dignity.

2. *Seek to understand.* Stephen Covey's thoughts on listening are worth their weight in gold, teaching one to seek the others person's feelings, thoughts, and perspectives first.

3. *Seek to be understood.* After understanding, share one's feelings, thoughts, and perspectives, not in an attacking mode but in an effort for the other party to see one's views.

4. *Own responsibility by apologizing.* Seek to see where any, if not all, of the conflict is one's responsibility, learning to respond differently in the future. A genuine apology not only affirms the relationship but can do wonders in releasing hurt feelings.

5. *Seek agreement.* After both parties have apologized, accepting responsibility for their parts in the conflict, seeking agreement means reuniting on the common vision that drew both sides together in the first place, ideally agreeing that the cause is bigger than the conflict is for both parties.

One-on-One Resolution Rarely do two parties involved in conflict have the skills to dig themselves out of the pit they find themselves in. That requires help from a coach such as an HR professional. The coach will facilitate one-on-one discussions to help the two people identify what each wants and explore if it is possible to satisfy both parties. Identifying something that will be satisfactory to each party is what the coaching process is designed to accomplish.

Third-Party Resolution When something formal is required, mediation or arbitration might be the answer. Outside experts are trained and certified as mediators and arbitrators and are available for hire to bring two parties to a resolution of the conflict. It is important that each party to the process agree to accept the outcome as binding. The American Arbitration Association (www.adr.org) and the American Mediation Association (www.americanmediation.org) are two resources for HR professionals when these services are necessary.

Agency Complaints and Litigation Internal complaints give an employer the opportunity to resolve issues with employees before they fester further and generate formal external agency complaints. Wise HR professionals will make every effort to encourage employees to file complaints internally so they will have the opportunity to investigate and resolve them. Dealing with issues internally is always preferable to having employees reporting issues to third-party law enforcement agencies.

External complaints are those filed with state or federal fair employment practices agencies (for example, the federal Equal Employment Opportunity Commission), wage and hour enforcement agencies (for example, the U.S. Department of Labor or Wage and Hour Division), or safety enforcement agencies (for example, Organizational Safety and Health Administration or Mine Safety and Health Administration). When a formal complaint is filed with an external agency, it is often a signal that the employer may no longer speak with their own employee about that issue. All discussions with the employee after a complaint is filed must be handled through the enforcement agency. As a practical matter, that means the employer will face some limitations.

Before a response can be prepared explaining what happened and why, the employer will need to investigate to determine whether the complaint has merit. Based on that result and with the help from legal counsel, a formal response can be prepared explaining the employer's position.

Remember that these are law enforcement agencies with authority to require employers to take certain actions to remedy complaints if that is warranted. Your legal advisor is always your best ally when working with external agencies. There are usually complaint filing deadlines, designated response deadlines, and deadlines for implementing remedies. Those will vary depending on the agency involved and provisions of the relevant laws.

HR's Role in Complaints and Litigation HR managers are often the company's designated contact for employee complaints, and the HR professional will usually be the person responsible for conducting the investigation into the complaint's validity. Once the investigation has concluded, it is up to the HR professional to make recommendations to upper management regarding the outcome and any actions that should be taken. It may be necessary for the HR manager to recommend disciplinary action against the offending employee, or it may be that the HR manager must determine how to help an employee resolve a problem that is not a question of legal compliance but rather a problem of communication and misunderstanding.

Workplace Retaliation Every category of federal law that deals with employee relations provides prohibitions against employer retaliation for employees availing themselves of the legal protections against mistreatment. In 2021, the Equal Employment Opportunity Commission (EEOC) received 34,332 charges of retaliation from employees who had already filed complaints of discrimination based on a protected class. That was 56 percent of all charges filed with the commission that year.[43] People are feeling that filing a complaint with the EEOC has caused additional unfavorable treatment.

Conducting Investigations

Investigations are appropriate in several circumstances within an employer's organization. They can be helpful in a grievance-handling effort and are essential in determining the validity of discrimination complaints. Whenever there is a need to determine facts surrounding a complaint, an investigation should be conducted. Some form of this approach should be used when responding to complaints about safety or wages and work hours. Interviews may or may not be necessary, depending on the availability of records that can explain the facts.

Internal HR professionals are almost always given authority in state and federal law to investigate on behalf of the employer. If the organization wants to have an external investigator handle the fact finding, there are some limitations imposed by certain state laws. In California, for example, external investigators who are not licensed attorneys must be licensed private investigators. Other states have different requirements.

Legal advisors suggest that internal attorneys are not the best people to conduct investigations because they could be placed in the position of having to testify to their investigative activities while still providing legal advice to their employer.

Whoever is designated as the investigator should normally follow these steps:

1. *Obtain a written complaint.* The employee should write out a complaint that states they were treated differently from others in similar situations based on a legally protected category and that category should be identified. If this can be done, you will have been provided a prima facie case, which means it sounds good on its initial face.

2. *Conduct interviews.* Next, it is necessary to interview the complaining employee, the supervisor or management person who is named as the offending decision-maker, and any witnesses the employee says were there at the time. Sometimes it is a peer who has been the offending party. When that is the case, at least one interview of the offending party should be scheduled. The investigation should follow whatever leads are uncovered until the investigator is satisfied that all the facts have been uncovered that can be uncovered. Each step of the process should be documented in writing and maintained in a complaint investigation file.

3. *Make a determination.* Once the facts have been determined as best as possible, a determination needs to be made about the validity of the complaint. This is not a television moment of "beyond a reasonable doubt." You must decide upon the preponderance of the evidence. In a worst-case scenario that evidence may be 51 percent on one side and 49 percent on the other. If the complaint is valid, a remedy should be sought based on both legal and reasonable requirements. If the complaint is determined not to have valid grounds, that will be the determination. The decision should be documented in writing and included in the investigation folder.

4. *Give feedback.* The employee who filed the complaint should be given feedback about the investigation results and any decisions made as a result. It may or may not be advisable to provide specific information about disciplinary action taken against an employee. Your legal advisor can give you guidance about that in your specific circumstances.

Disciplining Employees

The progressive discipline model is a step-by-step process to give employees feedback so they will in turn modify unacceptable behavior. The progressive discipline model has been used in American workplaces for more than a century. It is written into many, if not most, union contracts as a requirement so management treats its members appropriately when problems arise.

Here are the typical steps in that process:

- **Oral warning** Observing the employee violating a policy, procedure, or instruction. In a personal discussion with the employee, the boss explains the problem and issues a verbal warning that the problem should not happen again. Even though labeled an oral warning, this conversation needs to be documented.

- **Written warning** Observing the employee doing the same behavior for which they received the oral warning. This is an "escalation" of discipline to the next step. A warning in writing should explain the infraction, why it is unacceptable, and what the consequences are. It should also explain the consequence of the same thing happening again.

- **Suspension** Although this step is not always included in the process, it is available for use to emphasize to the employee how serious the behavioral problem is. The rationale is to give the employee committing the breach of rules time away from the job to think about their behavior and their jeopardized future with the company. In many cases, a suspension will be unpaid time off (you should check with legal counsel and know your state laws). For example, California courts have ruled an unpaid suspension creates an undue hardship on the employee, so that is not a legal option in the Golden State. It can last from a day to several weeks. The length of time should be dependent on the seriousness of the behavioral problem and the employee's length of service.

- **Termination** The final stage of the disciplinary process is removing the employee from employment. Use of this step acknowledges that the employee cannot be salvaged.

NOTE You may skip steps depending on the severity of the infraction. Also, your disciplinary procedures should be applied consistently in similar situations. It is wrong to treat people differently when their situations are similar. That will surely land you in court or present you with a union grievance.

Employers can avoid locking themselves into strict disciplinary procedures if they provide a policy for discretionary disciplinary decisions based on the circumstances of a situation. Policies containing hard rules about steps to be used in the process can prevent flexibility and discretion.

Preventive Measures The best prevention is great communication. Be sure each employee is clear about the specific expectations you have for their performance. Help them understand how their personal contribution fits into the team and company efforts. Making sure people understand their personal importance to the employer's success is critical in preventing any behavior problems. It is only when expectations are not met that there are problems. Therefore, be sure everyone understands the expectations that relate to them.

Providing Due Process Due process is making sure employees receive all the protections to which they are entitled and not subject to arbitrary, capricious, or unfair treatment. It is part of what contributes to the Covenant of Good Faith and Fair Dealing. It means that every employee will be given an opportunity to hear that there is a problem with their behavior and be given a chance to improve. Progressive discipline provides employees with due process. It should be noted, even with progressive discipline as a policy, steps may be skipped if the employee behavior is particularly egregious, such as causing physical harm. It is a best practice to never fire on the spot. It is better to send an employee home and investigate to be sure of the facts, especially when a termination is being considered.

Constructive Discipline Constructive discipline is the positive outcome of the disciplinary process. It means that even though employees are being disciplined, they understand why, and the treatment is fair within the circumstances.

HR's Role in Discipline HR professionals are the coaches for line managers and supervisors. It is HR's responsibility to track disciplinary cases, counsel managers in how to handle disciplinary interviews, encourage employees when they discuss their problems, and nudge all parties toward a positive outcome. HR is the expert in how to perform discipline appropriately. As such, teaching supervisors is a key responsibility of the HR department. Encouraging employees with problems to do better is also part of the role HR plays.

Functional Area 10: Technology Management

Here is SHRM's BASK definition: "Technology Management involves the use of existing, new and emerging technologies to support the HR function, and the development and implementation of policies and procedures governing the use of technologies in the workplace."[44]

Enhancing the effectiveness of HR functions could not be done without the use of technology. HR information systems, applicant tracking systems, self-service portals to company-specific information such as employee handbooks, training programs, benefits—these form the backbone to having HR processes performed efficiently. HR professionals should fully understand the HR-related technology applications and the potential value of ever-increasing new technologies being developed. This functional area is about the use of technology to support the HR function, plus the development and implementation of policies and procedures governing the use of technologies in the workplace.

Key Concepts

- HR software and technology (for example, applicant tracking system [ATS], human resource information system [HRIS], learning management system, performance management system, big data analytics software, collaboration software, blockchain, artificial intelligence, machine learning)

- Data and information management (for example, data integrity, confidentiality, security, disclosure, backups, cloud-based software, cybersecurity, data)

- Approaches to electronic self-service for HR and people management functions (for example, scheduling, time keeping, contact information updates, benefit enrollment)

- Standards and policies for technology use (for example, bring-your-own-device policy, offsite network access policy, websites, computers for personal activity, Internet messaging, corporate and personal e-mail)

- Social media management (for example, internal social media platforms, social media policy, branding)

The following are the proficiency indicators that SHRM has identified for Technology Management:

For All HR Professionals	Advanced HR Professionals (SCP Exam)
• Implements and uses technology solutions that support or facilitate the delivery of effective HR services and storage of critical employee data	• Evaluates, advocates for, implements, and retires technology solutions to achieve HR's strategic direction, vision, and goals
• Implements technology that integrates with and complements other enterprise information systems, software, and technology	• Evaluates and selects vendors to provide HR technology solutions

For All HR Professionals	Advanced HR Professionals (SCP Exam)
• Develops and implements organizational standards and policies for maintaining confidentiality of candidate and employee data as well as limiting access as appropriate	• Designs and implements technology systems that optimize and integrate HR functional areas
• Uses technologies in a manner that protects workforce data	• Develops and implements technology-driven self-service approaches that enable managers and employees to perform self-service and people management functions
• Provides guidance to stakeholders on effective standards and policies for use of technologies in the workplace	• Assesses and implements automation technologies that augment human talent
• Coordinates and manages vendors implementing HR technology solutions	• Collaborates with business leaders to define the role of digitalization in the overall business, new products or services, new markets, and growth strategy
• Uses technologies to collect, access, and analyze data and information to understand business challenges and recommend evidence-based solutions	

HR and Technology

Technology is now foundational to any HR function in an organization. It captures more information and makes that information accessible to a variety of people with various data needs within the organization. It can make analyzing information far quicker and allows for detecting patterns, conditions, and issues. HR's technology provides communication support, which is particularly helpful with a workplace that is geographically broad. When technology doesn't work as planned or goes on the blink, it can cripple the functions of HR and the entire organization.

HR Technology Use

There is no one-size-fits-all technology blueprint for HR. Every organization is going to require HR technology that is specific to the organization's size, geographical and workforce particulars, plus industry. The technological platforms and applications will differ, yet the initial blueprint will have the same process flow guidelines for implementation. Think of the computer game *Minecraft*—the rules are the same, yet the various players' outcomes in building things are hugely different.

HR uses technology to allow more work to be accomplished with fewer people. By automating routine tasks, greater accuracy, speedier processing, data collection, and reports using that information for stakeholders are possible. This is the true value of HR's technology use. Examples of technology include the following:

- **E-signing** The use of electronic signatures to process authorization of documents
- **Electronic recordkeeping** A big advantage in the ever-growing field of legal record retention requirements

- **Mobile learning**   Offering instructional content delivered to wireless mobile devices to facilitate information sharing and learning
- **Intranet**   Access to information for the workforce for a broader style of communicating and understanding
- **Gamification**   Using technology to enhance learning by purposefully adding more fun
- **Blogs**   Used for communicating both internally and externally
- **Social media**   Used for customer service and for promoting information/communications for shared purposes
- **Self-service systems**   Portals that allow targeted groups of employees to access their information, such as benefits, payroll, and initiating selections and changes

Leveraging Advances in HR Technology

Technology is constantly changing the way HR functions and supports the organization in doing its business. HR professionals should be aware of the trends, the capabilities, and the issues associated with technology to be strategic partners and help their organization with its competitive advantage.

HR professionals can leverage technology to increase the efficiency of HR processes and functions by transforming data into sources of immense value to internal stakeholders. The world has embraced technology, and HR is no exception, adopting technology within organizations. The many advantages in doing so include streamlining processes and reducing administrative work; improving efficiencies; reducing costs, especially those related to compliance; providing real-time metrics to facilitate planning and decision-making; improving service to internal and external stakeholders; and enabling the sharing of information.

Information Management

HR's information, maintained within technology vehicles, is highly confidential to both the workforce and the organization. As such, there are challenges in how this information is managed and accessed. There is the complexity of having too much data—what to use and what not to use—and then there is real-time access, where users are interacting with information in real time. Transparency of data is another consideration—where is the information sourced and who will have access to it?

HR in the Era of Big Data

Technology has ushered in the era of "big data," which refers to huge amounts of dissimilar data, such as images and figures, tables, charts, and words. Users can access this data and do what is known as *data mining*—extracting data that serves their needs. In some large organizations, the HR function will have data specialists, such as compensation or affirmative action analysts, to gather and scrutinize data collected. In his article "The Promise of Big Data for HR,"[45] Alex Levenson discusses the likely paths for HR, which are as follows:

- **Collecting data**   New data collection about how employees do their jobs can provide process insights, thus reducing errors and increasing productivity and efficiencies.

- **Using data effectively** Data can be used to understand the motivation of employees, their engagement, and why they do what they do.
- **Strategic analysis** This involves mapping how information flows within organizations and how it impacts the way people rely on it to do their jobs.

Measures, Metrics, and Analytics

Analytics help HR professionals translate data into action and decisions. HR can use analytics to link HR outcomes to organizational results by starting with a foundation of accurate, consistent, integrated, accessible, and relevant data.

Sample Human Capital Metrics A sample of human capital metrics would involve using an employee database to track the knowledge, skills, and performance of employees; then using the analytics to identify the key performance indicators of high-potential employees to manage critical needs and projections for the workforce, perhaps because of anticipated retirements; and finally using the analytics to assess the marketplace for recruiting replacements and attracting the talent anticipated, along with the budget resources required for workforce planning.

Why Analytics Matters Analytics can improve organizational performance because it can improve and drive the planning and forecasting processes, shorten cycles, reduce costs, and direct resources for just-in-time needs.

HR Information Systems

A human resource information system (HRIS) is technology software that supports the functions of HR and is the workhorse of administration for HR data to be gathered, stored, maintained, retrieved, analyzed, and reported. Processing employee data, researching, answering questions—these were the activities that made up the major components of HR's time in the past. Enter HRIS technology and—poof—some time-consuming activities of typical HR professionals diminished. An HRIS offers increased efficiency and accuracy collecting, organizing, and disseminating critical personnel data.

HRIS records involve fields of data, including those shown in Figure 5-4. This is not an exhaustive list. Some employers maintain many other records.

Birthdate	Department	Home phone	Original job title
Building code	Educational degree	Home state	Original pay rate
Cell phone	Employee ID number	Home zip	Past job title
Certifications	Exempt/nonexempt	Job group/EEO code	Race/ethnicity
Current job title	Health care plan	Last employer	Sex
Current pay rate	Home address	Licenses	Social Security number
Dental plan	Home city	Name	Vision plan

Figure 5-4 Types of data included in employee records

HRIS Selection

Selecting and implementing an HRIS must be done right because errors in selection will have a profound impact. The HRIS software programs range from those serving employee groups up to 100 people to systems that can handle unlimited data fields and unlimited numbers of employees. Obviously, the prices of such software systems vary according to the capabilities they offer. The first thing to do in selecting an HRIS is to identify all the stakeholders and then perform a needs analysis to determine what features are needed for the stakeholders. A complete analysis will involve not only what the HR needs are but also what the user needs are when interacting with an HRIS.

Build, Customize, or Outsource Development   When deciding on an HRIS, you must consider whether the system is going to be developed internally by the organization's IT group or will be an off-the-shelf system such as PeopleSoft. Another choice is to outsource the HRIS to an external vendor because there are many available.

Integrated Solution or "Best-of-Breed" Option   A best-of-breed (BoB) option is the "best-fit" solution for each functional area in HR. Although a BoB option performs specialized functions better than an integrated system, this type of system is limited by its specialty area. To fulfill varying requirements, organizations sometimes use best-of-breed systems from separate vendors. An integrated solution features a common interface across applications.

The choice between an integrated or best-of-breed solution comes down to how to deliver the technology. Will it be on-premises, where the organization has software supported by internal IT staff, or will it be hosted, where the software is installed at the vendor's site and supported by external IT? There is also *software as a service (SaaS)*, which is where the organization does not purchase any software. Instead, it subscribes to a service that is accessed via the Internet and maintained by others.

Data Access   The data in an HRIS is not restricted to just the HR department. This is referred to as *democratization*, where HR data is provided with direct access by those who need it. Executives, finance, payroll, managers, hiring managers—there is a stakeholder for every source of data. This type of access brings with it both legal and ethical considerations, including the protection of employee private information and the dissemination of it. Creating restrictions on the access to different portions of an HRIS is imperative when considering its design and implementation.

Database Structure   An HRIS is a database with information stored in an organized manner. Access to the information in an HRIS typically happens through the following means:

- **HR portals**   A portal is a customized entry point via the intranet or Internet for employees and applicants that allows them to access information such as benefits enrollment.

- **Employee self-service (ESS) websites that often are accessed via the HR portal**   This is normally associated with transactional functions such as updating personal information, filing expense reports, and changing 401(k) selections.

- **Manager self-service (MSS)** These are tools that, like the ESS, allow supervisory management to conduct HR-related transactions via an HR portal, such as performance appraisals, job descriptions, and attaining reports or viewing information.

Data Protection Personally identifiable information (PII) is a crucial concern with HRIS and other systems in protecting employee data. PII has a high-priority status in today's world to be protected from hacking. Risk managers, IT managers, security managers, and audit managers all have a vested interest in HRIS data protection. Unauthorized use or loss of personnel data is a constant threat, and a breach of the HRIS could be catastrophic to an employer and those whose data has been compromised.

HRIS Implementation

Most implementations of HRIS systems use a project management approach. This involves a team of folks from both the internal IT department and the external IT consultants and HR professionals following a proven systematic framework over a period of time. Rushing the implementation of an HRIS is a disservice—take the time to be thorough when following the implementation steps. The steps follow this order:

- Assessing senior management support and determine the requirements
- Identifying the project parameters such as budget, technology limitations, and time
- Evaluating software packages against the requirements and parameters
- Gathering the project task committee, stakeholders, and implementation group
- Clarifying vendor requirements and putting out an RFP to vendors
- Screening the RFPs
- Selecting the best vendor/software

The Importance of Systems Integration Implementing an HRIS is complex and expensive, and headaches from unforeseen factors always come up. A systems integration approach that is thorough, looking at the entire process well before fingers are put on the keyboard, will be well worth it in the end. You need to look at all the software components involved and how the entire process will integrate into the HRIS. The two common approaches are the continuous integration, or *waterfall,* approach and the *big bang,* all-at-once approach.

Continuous Integration Approach With continuous integration, the various HRIS components are integrated as they are developed into the HRIS. The developers will build chunks or portions of the system and then integrate them into the whole. This results in an incremental building, which eventually creates the larger final HRIS. Throughout the development process, the HR functions can see the workings of what is created and massage the development process. This approach is less risky and allows for incremental learning by the users.

"Big Bang" Approach   Not until everything is ready will the individual components making up the HRIS be integrated—thus the label *big bang*. This approach allows for everything to be finished before testing begins. It can be time-consuming using this approach and cause system failures. Smaller organizations may adopt this approach, especially when using off-the-shelf or external HRIS implementations. With this approach, the learning curve for users is steeper, as everything about the new system needs to be learned at the same time.

Policies for Technology Use in the Workplace

Technology-use policies can raise some sticky issues for both the organization and the workforce. They can work well when organizations balance security, compliance, and privacy concerns. The key is being collaborative and thorough in the approach to creating policy and ensuring that policies are being updated to keep pace with the continuous growth of new and changing technologies.

Developing Workplace Policies

"A policy is a broad statement that reflects an organization's philosophy, objectives, or standards concerning a particular set of management or employee activities. Policies reflect the employer's employee relationship strategy. They are general in nature and are expressed through more specific procedures and work rules."[46]

The following nine steps are involved in developing workplace policies:[47]

1. Identify the need for a policy.

2. Identify who will take the lead responsibility for this policy development.

3. Gather information.

4. Draft the policy.

5. Consult with stakeholders.

6. Finalize and approve the policy.

7. Consider whether procedures will be required to implement the policy.

8. Implement the policy.

9. Monitor the policy's success, and then review and revise it if necessary.

Developing Employee Handbooks   An employee handbook is a document that communicates organizational history, mission, values, policies, procedures, and benefits. It should contain information about all the ways "we do things around here" and why we do them that way.

The steps for developing employee handbooks are similar to those involved in developing workplace policies:[48]

1. Review and make required revisions to the current company policies.

2. Create an outline of what to include in the employee handbook.

3. Create summarized versions of each policy and procedure.

4. Add each summary statement in the appropriate sections according to the outline.

5. Review the entire handbook.

6. Provide a finalized version to legal counsel for review.

7. Select a means of publication.

8. Distribute the handbook or provide a means to access it online.

9. Update the handbook as necessary.

Most organizations are finding it extremely helpful to have their employee handbooks available in electronic format. It allows for the updating (and announcement of updates) to be more frequent and an acknowledgment from employees that they are aware of the policy changes.

Bring-Your-Own-Device Policy   A *bring-your-own-device* (*BYOD*) policy applies to employee use of personal electronic devices for company purposes. Taking a clear position on employee-owned devices via a policy is critical. A policy should outline the terms for eligibility for BYOD, as well as protocols for using personal devices.

Allowing employees to work on their personal laptops, tablets, and smartphones instead of company-issued equipment has been a trend driven in part by society that now relies on the use of technology for both work and play. While allowing or asking employees to bring their own devices can lower costs and improve efficiency, effectiveness, and morale, it can also raise concerns of security and legal compliance. A well-crafted policy can minimize those concerns.

From an employee perspective, the largest concern is that BYOD could lead to a loss of employee privacy. Employees may worry that their company will have inappropriate access to their personal data, as well as to their photographs, contacts, and other information—and that they could lose all that information if the company attempts to remove or "wipe" business information from the worker's device, which typically happens after an employee's employment has ended.

On the organization's side, the primary concern is related to security. For example, devices may not have an automatic lock code or timeout function, and some people do not use passwords to protect their devices. Equally troubling are worries that employees may connect to their devices via unsecured Wi-Fi, share them with others, or simply lose them. All these possibilities raise the risk for the unauthorized disclosure or destruction of business data.

If nonexempt employees are asked to use their own devices for work, the organization opens itself up to exposure under the federal Fair Labor Standards Act and state overtime and wage payment laws. Nonexempt workers may respond to e-mails or text messages or to otherwise engage in work activities outside their scheduled work hours, which may require they be paid. Well-communicated policies on what work is allowed outside of scheduled hours (and if pre-authorization is needed) can help mitigate this financial exposure.

Collaboration

Because of the globally dispersed and diverse ways of working, technology vendors have created platforms that allow employees to collaborate more efficiently, such as programmers collaborating on coding. Organizations are recognizing this and adopting collaboration policies and tools to facilitate this new form of communication and productivity learning.

Groupware   Groupware is a specialized software application of a collaborative nature that facilitates interaction between people, helping them work together. Webinars, video-conferencing, and online collaboration tools such as Google Docs are just a few examples of groupware.

Effective Collaboration Policies and Approaches   Organizations have established practices that create greater effectiveness for these collaborations. Webinars may be arranged at times that are early in the morning for those on the West Coast and thus later in the day for those located in Europe, allowing participation and recognizing that it's outside the normal 8 A.M. to 5 P.M. routine. Also, the ability to record meetings using webinar technology allows those in Australia to view a meeting presentation made in Canada later instead of participating in the wee hours of the day, for example.

Of course, legal disclaimers and the rights and responsibilities should also be considered in policies that protect trade secrets and confidentiality.

Social Media

Social media policies and practices are land mines in today's world. With the ever-changing technology and new platforms popping up regularly, social media is an important technology trend that HR professionals need to stay on top of. Policies need to be aligned with the organization's ethical and cultural expectations and its core values. They must also reflect the organization's legal and reputational risks. What will the organization consider as an infraction of ethics with an employee's personal postings? Many situations have popped up challenging this issue within the last few years, causing newsworthy headlines.

Effective Social Media Policies and Approaches for Personal Posting   The types of personal posts that employers should be concerned with by their employees are the ones that disclose proprietary information, harass other employees or customers, reflect poorly on the organization, or are considered inappropriate comments (non-work-related included). There is a balance of restrictive and permissive aspects for personal posting, and a policy that establishes what constitutes both should be evaluated and updated on a frequent basis with legal review.

Networking

Social networks are the online clusters of individuals in groups with shared interests. These networking sites connect individuals with shared interests, regardless of their geographical location. An exchange of private and public messages can occur. They may be groups of professionals, such as alumni from a college, or informational, such as people with hobbies or those seeking information such as do-it-yourselfers.

Effective Networking Policies and Approaches Networking policies should protect the reputation of the organization and outline expectations of its employees, values, and ethics.

Communications

Policies and practices for communication in technology require a balance between protecting the organization's proprietary information, its security, and its legal interest and allowing the those in the workforce to do their job as well as exercise their First Amendment right to free speech. Here again, having expectations well thought out with examples will help the workforce know where the line is drawn concerning inappropriate communications.

Effective Communications Policies and Approaches Over the years, employers have discovered that the best approach to technology communication policies is constantly reminding employees of policies such as the monitoring of employee e-mails or browsing histories. Notifying employees, new hires, and even executives about the potential of monitoring can serve as a deterrent for inappropriate communications and resources. Further, when an organization regularly advises employees that their communications are not private, it makes it problematic for employees to contest confidentiality in lawsuits.

Chapter Review

In this chapter, you learned about the structure of the HR function within an organization. You also reviewed organizational effectiveness and development, workforce management, employee and labor relations, and, finally, technology management. These collectively compose the entity called an employment organization. Some new approaches are being used in these areas of HR management that the certified professional will need to be cognizant of and consider using in the operation of a contemporary HR department.

Questions

1. A large technology company has identified a group of key managers in various departments who were hired with employment contracts that included large equity options. The company went public 2 years ago and continues to see a steady increase in stock value. There is a realization that many of these managers may retire when they are eligible to exercise their stock options in 3 more years. What OD activity should HR be focused on related to this circumstance?

   A. Review the organization's retirement plan and begin counseling discussions.

   B. Expand the vacation policy for this group of managers.

   C. Design a succession plan and identify high-potential employees.

   D. Hire executive coaches to help this group of management with work-life balance.

2. The process of analyzing and identifying the need for human resources availability so that the organization can meet its objectives is known as what?

   A. Strategic planning

   B. PESTLE analysis

   C. Human resource planning

   D. Organization planning

3. The AB Trucking Company is expanding its routes and hiring more people. Those changes will mean that employees will have to take on different work assignments. How should the HR manager handle those changes with the workforce?

   A. Explain the coming changes to all employees and solicit their input for deciding how to assign the new routes. Prepare a project plan and make sure everyone has a chance to see it before the implementation date.

   B. Explain the coming changes and tell the truckers that assignments will be made based on seniority. The new people will be assigned last.

   C. Explain the coming changes and let the senior executives handle the questions about how new job assignments will be made.

   D. Explain the coming changes and let the employees discuss among themselves how they want to assign routes to the workforce.

4. Mergers and acquisitions (M&As) provide HR managers with special problems of cultural differences. To make sure the cultures don't clash after the merger, what should the HR manager do?

   A. Assign a subordinate to monitor the complaint levels and report on problems that are being addressed.

   B. Conduct meetings with key players from each organization to outline the cultural values of each organization and determine how best to protect them in the blended employer unit.

   C. Send memos to department heads that specify the new cultural characteristics and express the expectation that the department heads will "make it happen."

   D. Provide written complaint forms to all employees and express a willingness to listen to any comments the employees make about the merger.

5. Heather has just taken over for the HR manager in her group, and Heather's boss is asking for an update on the succession plan. Heather's boss wants to see the employee skill inventory as soon as possible. Heather didn't even know there was a succession plan. What should Heather be looking for in her files?

   A. A confidential record that lists each employee's skills and abilities

   B. A list of only the top-rated people in the group who have computer skills

   C. A list of everyone in the group identifying each person's skills and whether they are currently ready for promotion

   D. A list of people showing what individuals are capable of doing now, without regard for any future assignment

6. An employee in Cortez's organization came to him and suggested that she and her co-worker could consolidate their duties into one job and each work part-time, sharing the 40 hours each week so the work gets done as always. What would you say if you were Cortez?

   A. Unfortunately, the Fair Labor Standards Act and the Unified Job Consolidation Act say that sharing jobs is not permitted because it would violate union agreements.

   B. There is no reason that it couldn't work if Cortez believes the two people are capable and want to make it work.

   C. Having more than one person and one Social Security number on one job assignment won't work. It makes tax reporting impossible.

   D. It's not a good idea because it doubles the liability for workers' compensation and unemployment insurance.

7. The local county's workforce has been decimated in recent months because the pension plan is changing and folks wanted to get their higher-level calculation before the changes cut that formula. The result is a great deal of organizational intelligence has walked out the door. The senior staff are suggesting you hire back some of the key personnel as temporary workers until you can get replacements trained. Is that a good idea?

   A. Hardly ever. It gives the newly retired people a way to "double dip" and make more money than they would have if they had stayed on the job without retiring.

   B. Sometimes. If the temporary period is truly used to train a replacement, it could get the organization across the institutional knowledge gap, passing along that information to someone new.

   C. Always. There is no downside to bringing back retirees as temporary workers. So what if they make a bit more? The work gets done without interruption.

   D. Maybe, if there is a limit of 6 months on the temporary assignment in compliance with the Fair Labor Standards Act.

8. The Tasty Good Corporation downsized because of intense global competition and modified its strategic business plan for the year. What is the most important task the HR department's training and development function needs to do to support the change?

   A. Cost-justify training.

   B. Work with employees on accepting the change.

   C. Evaluate the effectiveness of all training programs.

   D. Link training and development to the new strategic plan.

9. You are coaching supervisors on how to handle difficult employees. What should you tell them about their documentation of performance and incidents?

   A. It should begin when they are ready to suspend the employee.

   B. It should begin with the first conversation about performance or an incident, no matter how informal.

   C. It should happen when they move from a verbal warning to a written warning.

   D. It should be done prior to terminating an employee.

10. Why has human resource management, as a function within employer organizations, developed into a critical business partnership?

    A. Strategic business success can be accomplished only if minor staff functions are given some consideration in planning conferences.

    B. Accomplishment of organizational objectives is dependent on strategic deployment of all resources, including human resources.

    C. With more technology supporting HR, it requires HR executives to contribute to strategic efforts and offer accountability for resource management.

    D. HR management is a function closely allied with accounting and finance, so strategic management of finance can't be complete without a contribution from HR.

11. As the HR professional in your organization, you've been asked to submit a recommendation for the best way to convert to the matrix form of organizational structure. What is the most important issue you might encounter?

    A. Matrix organizations don't have strict reporting relationships, so supervisors will be upset at their loss of control.

    B. Because the matrix organizations are "loose" in their management oversight, results may need to be monitored by executives more carefully.

    C. When matrix organizations are formed, it takes some time for people to get used to working in that type of configuration. Therefore, a "break-in" time is required.

    D. Unions object to matrix organizations because they impinge on union representation authority.

12. During a merger or acquisition, part of the process includes assembling data from the due diligence process. In many jurisdictions, much of the information about employer liabilities requires disclosure. This could include which of the following?

    A. The number of parking spaces that have disabled markings and the quantity of fire extinguishers in the building.

    B. The number and type of discrimination complaints as well as the number and type of lawsuits dealing with employee management issues.

    C. The number and type of safety classes held for employees each year.

    D. The amount of budget allocated to overtime versus straight time payroll.

13. You have been assigned to lead the team to choose and implement a new HRIS. You have done your homework and are prepared to make a recommendation to the rest of the team. What do you suggest?

   A. A big bang approach, so there is zero disruption until every component of the new HRIS is ready to roll.

   B. A bring your own device (BYOD) system to save money on computer hardware.

   C. A continuous integration approach so staff may start their learning, gain benefits of the new components sooner, and influence the yet-to-be-completed development.

   D. Handing over all the HRIS decisions to the IT department since that is their area of expertise.

14. Employees are sometimes caught up in downsizing efforts that are aimed at budget control. What are employers required to do when designing downsizing programs?

   A. Compare them to programs that were used by other employers with headquarters in their same city.

   B. Analyze their estimated results for age, race, and sex discrimination.

   C. Determine how many people will be affected from each department.

   D. Give the CEO and board of directors a written report on the downsizing impact on the organization's budget.

15. One of your employees has just been discovered stealing large amounts of money from the accounts receivable account. You have the evidence in hand. What should you do first?

   A. Reason with the employee and try to get them to give the money back.

   B. Suspend the employee for 2 weeks while the employee tries to stop taking drugs.

   C. File a police report of theft/embezzlement and criminal complaint against the employee and then terminate the employee.

   D. Call the insurance company to file a claim of loss.

16. One of the unions representing people in your organization has just called for a boycott of your products and services. What can you do about that?

   A. Negotiate with the union for them to cancel the boycott.

   B. Take the union to court and get a judgment against them.

   C. Begin an advertising campaign that explains how the union is wrong.

   D. Turn the entire problem over to the legal department.

17. A departmental manager has called you to report that a union steward has been behaving badly in grievance meetings. What can you do, if anything?

   A. Nothing can be done about that.

   B. Call the steward in for a chat. Explain that they will be disciplined if they don't change their behavior.

C. Advise the manager to suspend the steward for bad behavior.

D. Call the union president and discuss the problem. Ask the union president to control the steward's behavior.

18. HR in the twenty-first century embodies which of the following?

A. A tactical administrative role and a strategic operational role

B. A strategic administrative role and a strategic operational role

C. A strategic administrative role and a tactical operational role

D. A support role for corporate strategies only

19. What are three types of strategic differentiation?

A. Service differentiation, accounting differentiation, employee differentiation

B. Reputation differentiation, leadership differentiation, employee differentiation

C. Product differentiation, relationship differentiation, price differentiation

D. International differentiation, competitor differentiation, banking differentiation

20. BYOD policies must be carefully crafted to make sure which of the following is addressed?

A. That dogs brought in the workplace are well-behaved and always on a leash

B. Legal compliance with current technology

C. Security, legal compliance, and privacy of both employee and organization

D. That all levels of employees are offered to bring their dogs into the workplace

21. A detailed HR analysis during the HR strategic process serves what purpose?

A. Creating HR's goals and objectives

B. Reviewing the code of ethics

C. Identifying any HR gaps

D. Identifying key employees

22. What is the main reason HR is considered a valuable player in the strategic planning process?

A. Ability to provide programs

B. Total rewards administration

C. Access to employment laws

D. Knowledge of the entire organization

23. Besides activities, HR should also measure which of the following?

A. Progress against goals and objectives

B. Meetings

C. Results and outcomes

D. Projects and initiatives

24. What is the primary goal of an HR audit?

    A. Demonstrating value

    B. Controlling costs

    C. Identifying the existing gaps in HR processes

    D. Comparing human capital to organizational needs

25. Which form of measurement is an overall-yet-concise picture of the organization's performance?

    A. Balanced scorecard

    B. Internal audit

    C. ROI

    D. External audit

Answers

1. **C.** A succession plan is a key component for business success and should be part of every organization's human resource development program to be sure that there is no gap in knowledge that cripples an organization because of the departure of key human capital.

2. **C.** Human resource planning involves all facets of people management issues. Forecasting the need for more or fewer people, budget considerations, and recruiting sources all come into play. How HR can be used to support the organization's strategic plans is critical.

3. **A.** Whenever possible, involving employees in designing the plan for accommodating organizational changes will be the best for employee morale and acceptance of the change.

4. **B.** Involving key managers from each organization can provide a foundation for whatever cultural values the new organization wants to build.

5. **C.** The list should show what skills each person has now and whether they are ready for promotion now or need further experience or training before being ready for promotion.

6. **B.** Sometimes, using part-time workers to accomplish one job is a good solution. A great deal depends on the reliability of incumbents.

7. **B.** One reason these arrangements sometimes fail is that they go on and on and on. There is no real replacement training going on. The retired employee is doing the same work as before they retired, and nobody is being transferred, promoted, or hired into that job as a replacement.

8. **D.** Linking training and development activities to the new strategic plan is the first step to ensuring that activities and resources are aligned with the organization's new initiatives. We consistently want alignment between HR activities and the strategic plan.

9. **B**. A saying in our field is, "If it wasn't documented, it didn't happen." All performance discussions, even informal verbal-only ones, need to be documented immediately after the conversation.

10. **C**. Only if HR is willing to contribute to strategic planning and implementation and offer accountability for results will HR professionals be welcomed at the executive table.

11. **C**. Working on a team with representatives from many departments can take some time to get used to. There is a lag time between implementation and results simply because employees need time to get acquainted with the new working structure.

12. **B**. Liabilities such as lawsuits and discrimination complaints can pose future drains on budget and cash flow. The other party will want to understand what risks might exist because of these types of liabilities.

13. **C**. A continuous integration approach gives all the advantages listed. A big bang approach has you up the creek if you flip the switch and it doesn't work, and a BYOD policy does not replace the need for your HRIS. Finally, HR must never abdicate its involvement and responsibility for its own technology.

14. **B**. The Uniform Guidelines on Employee Selection Procedures and Age Discrimination in Employment Act (ADEA) requires analysis of the impact of selection decisions in downsizing.

15. **C**. Criminal behavior should be reported to the police. In the eyes of most employers, theft/embezzlement is cause for immediate dismissal.

16. **A**. Negotiation is the avenue to lifting the boycott.

17. **D**. Asking the union president to control the steward's behavior is likely to be the most effective approach. Since you can't discipline the employee for union activities, the president is the person who can help the steward understand the advantages of civil behavior.

18. **B**. As HR evolves in providing more value, HR professionals will find themselves involved more with strategic planning in an administrative role and operational role.

19. **C**. The three types of strategic differentiation are product, relationship, and price.

20. **C**. Security, legal compliance, and privacy need to be addressed in policies about employees using their personal electronic devices at work to protect both the organization and the employees' right to privacy.

21. **C**. HR analysis includes a thorough review of the current systems and processes in place to identify gaps that may exist with current systems, processes, and the future system needs. Addressing these gaps aligns with the basis of HR strategy.

22. **D**. The HR function has a finger on the pulse of the current workforce and outside influences on the workforce, which is why it adds value to the organization's strategic planning.

23. **C**. The deliverables, outcomes, and results that HR is responsible for producing are what David Ulrich suggests should be measured for HR's true effectiveness.

24. **C.** An HR audit is a comprehensive evaluation of HR's policies and procedures that identify gaps in performance and outcomes.

25. **A.** A balanced scorecard is a performance metric used to identify and improve internal functions and effectiveness in an organization.

References

1. The 2022 SHRM Body of Applied Skills and Knowledge, page 68

2. Ulrich, David. *Human Resource Champions: The Next agenda for Adding Value and Delivering Results*. Harvard Business Press, 1997

3. Williams, Jodi. "What changes in the workforce mean for the future of workplace design." *Work Design Magazine,* February 9, 2017

4. https://www.nytimes.com/2010/05/03/business/03merger.html

5. Hakikat, Emal. "How HR can fill the accountability vacuum," *Inside HR*, https://www.insidehr.com.au/how-hr-can-fill-the-accountability-vacuum/, April 7, 2014

6. 2013 Global Innovation 1000 Study, Booz & Company. https://cc.bingj.com/cache.aspx?q=Global+Innovation+1000+Study%2c+Booz+%26+Company+2013&d=4655263695797745&mkt=en-US&setlang=en-US&w=mt1ozgKV77NE-Ex1rBvVr9NNQrMsQodq

7. Ulrich, David and Wayne Brockbank. *The HR Value Proposition.* Harvard Business School Press, 2005

8. Becker, Brian, Mark Huselid, and Richard Beatty. *The Differentiated Workforce: Transforming Talent into Strategic Impact.* Harvard Business School Press, 2009

9. The 2022 SHRM Body of Applied Skills and Knowledge, page 70

10. The Office of State Personnel, North Carolina, March 5, 2008

11. 2015 SHRM Learning System for SHRM-CP/SHRM-SCP, Figure 4: Performance Problems, page 82

12. www.explorance.com blog. November 14, 2013

13. 2015 SHRM Learning System for SHRM-CP/SHRM-SCP, page 84

14. 2015 SHRM Learning System for SHRM-CP/SHRM-SCP, "HR's Role in OED," page 86

15. https://www.turknett.com/services-and-tools/organization-development/cultural-assessment-and-change/

16. https://www.shrm.org/resourcesandtools/tools-and-samples/toolkits/pages/introorganizationalandemployeedevelopment.aspx

17. Ibid.

18. www.referenceforbusiness.com/management/Gr-Int/Group-Decision-Making.html

19. https://smlr.rutgers.edu/sites/default/files/Documents/Faculty_Staff_Docs/UnderstandingTheDynamicsofDiversityInDecisionMakingTeams.pdf

20. https://hbr.org/2016/11/why-diverse-teams-are-smarter

21. https://www.credit-suisse.com/corporate/en/media/news/articles/media-releases/2012/07/en/42035.html

22. http://smallbusiness.chron.com/relationship-between-systems-theory-employee-relations-22465.html

23. https://enterpriseengagement.org/newswire/content/8483139/iso-releases-the-first-standards-on-human-resources-practices/

24. https://www.villanovau.com/resources/six-sigma/six-sigma-methodology-dmaic/#.Wxhc_e4vyUk

25. https://www.ocai-online.com/about-the-Organizational-Culture-Assessment-Instrument-OCAI

26. https://blog.hrcloud.com/is-it-time-for-your-company-to-do-a-cultural-assessment

27. https://www.ocai-online.com/about-the-Organizational-Culture-Assessment-Instrument-OCAI/Organizational-Culture-Types

28. The 2022 SHRM Body of Applied Skills and Knowledge, page 71

29. Lazzari, Zach . "Definition of Tactical Planning in Business," *Houston Chronicle,* http://smallbusiness.chron.com/definition-tactical-planning-business-14401.html

30. "Strategic Planning: How can a skills inventory be used for strategic HR planning?" SHRM Templates & Samples, www.shrm.org, September 6, 2012

31. ADP_NAS Effective Talent Management White Paper, www.adp.com

32. The 2022 SHRM Body of Applied Skills and Knowledge, page 73

33. www.ilo.org

34. https://www.wto.org/

35. www.ncsi.org

36. www.edpo.com

37. Simmons, Dan. "17 Countries with GDPR-like Data Privacy Laws," footnoteinsights.comforte.com, Jan 13, 2022

38. Moskowitz, Seymour. *Employment at Will & Code of Ethics: The Professional Dilemma,* 23 Val. U.L. Rev. 33 (1988). Available at http://scholar.valpo.edu/vulr/vol23/iss1/7 as of June 3, 2015

39. www.ilo.org

40. https://www.emyth.com/inside/8-steps-to-effective-business-negotiationhttps://www.coachyourselftowin.com/

41. Guttman, Howard M., https://www.guttmandev.com

42. https://www.thesocialleader.com

43. https://www.eeoc.gov/data/charge-statistics-charges-filed-eeoc-fy-1997-through-fy-2021

PART II

44. The 2022 SHRM Body of Applied Skills and Knowledge, page 75

45. "The Promise of Big Data for HR," People & Strategy, 2014

46. SHRM Learning System, 2017

47. DIY Committee Guide. "How to Develop a Risk Management Strategy," www.diycommitteeguide.org/resource/how-to-develop-policies-and-procedures, retrieved on August 29, 2017

48. SHRM. "How to Develop an Employee Handbook," May 22, 2015, https:// www.shrm.org/resourcesandtools/tools-and-samples/how-to-guides/pages/ developemployeehandbook.aspx, retrieved on August 29, 2017

6

Workplace

The HR expertise domain of Workplace Knowledge counts toward 14 percent for both exams. This domain covers the essential HR knowledge needed for relating to the workplace. The following are the functional areas that fall within the Workplace Knowledge domain:

- Functional Area 11: Managing a Global Workforce
- Functional Area 12: Risk Management
- Functional Area 13: Corporate Social Responsibility
- Functional Area 14: U.S. Employment Law & Regulations

HR professionals are expected to know how to perform the following Body of Applied Skills and Knowledge (BASK) statements for the Workplace Knowledge domain:

- **01** Manage a global workforce to achieve organizational objectives
- **02** Manage organizational risks and threats to the safety and security of employees
- **03** Contribute to the well-being and betterment of the community
- **04** Comply with applicable laws and regulations

Functional Area 11: Managing a Global Workforce

Here is SHRM's BASK definition: "Managing a Global Workforce focuses on the role of the HR professional in managing global and mobile workforces to achieve organizational objectives."[1]

Globalization is here. It has been coming for more than half a century. Today's technology has altered our lives so that the world and all it holds are always accessible on our personal smartphones. Employers, too, are now tapped into world suppliers, world customers, and world recruiting like never before in history. In fact, locating an employer that isn't tapped into these Internet resources is increasing harder to do.

Key Concepts

- HR structures that support global work (for example, immigration and mobility specialists, geographic centers of excellence, global job classifications, international business travel policies)

- Immigration and mobility (for example, laws, visa processes and requirements, sponsorship expenses)

- Best practices for international assignments (for example, performance expectations and evaluations, health and safety, compensation adjustments, socialization, assessing employee and family readiness, training on culture and resources, language training, education travel grants, rental subsidies, transition plans, repatriation)

- Methods for moving work (for example, offshoring, onshoring, near-shoring, remote teams)

The following are the proficiency indicators that SHRM has identified for managing a global workforce:

For All HR Professionals	For Advanced HR Professionals (SCP Exam)
• Maintains up-to-date knowledge of political, economic, social, technological, legal, and environmental (PESTLE) factors and their influence on the organization's universal workforce	• Recognizes and responds to global PESTLE issues that influence the organization's strategy and workforce
• Administers and supports HR activities associated with a global and mobile workforce	• Develops a comprehensive organizational strategy that addresses global workforce issues
• Balances the organization's desire for standardization of cross-border HR programs, practices, and policies with local needs	• Consults with business leaders to define global competencies and embed them throughout the organization
• Manages and supports the organization's immigration and mobility program in accordance with regulatory or compliance requirements	• Establishes and oversees the organization's immigration and mobility policy and program in accordance with regulatory or compliance requirements
• Manages the day-to-day activities with international (that is, expatriate) assignments	• Identifies opportunities to achieve efficiencies and cost savings by moving work across borders
	• Designs and oversees programs for international (that is, expatriate) assignments that support the organizational strategy and workforce

PART II

The Global Context

No longer are we *just* Americans, Mexicans, Canadians, or Swiss. Global interactions mean we must find ways to place our employer issues in a global context while still abiding by the cultural and legal requirements of each country in which we operate. It is taking on a larger viewpoint. Globalization changes how we see the world around us and we interact with all the dynamic forces. It includes increasing digital interconnections of people and things—at any time and any place.

Defining Globalization

Globalization is the trend of increasing interaction between people on a worldwide scale because of advances in transportation and communication technology.[2] Business and governmental requirements are also contributing factors in the new definition of globalization. Overall, it represents a compression of the world and intensification of the consciousness of the world as a whole.

Forces Shaping Globalization

A multitude of forces contribute to globalization. These include international economic influences (finance and development) and investment trading markets (Dow Jones, Nasdaq, commodities markets.) Environmental forces, political forces, global insecurity, and refugee crises all contribute to shaping the thing we call globalization.

Three Precepts of Global Force Interconnectedness   Three precepts of global force interconnectedness become apparent:

- PESTLE factors help us better understand global interconnections.
- Forces may be global, but impacts can be uniquely felt locally.
- We need to distinguish between large-scale forces and trends and more immediate events and "trendy" phenomena.

Globalization in the Twenty-First Century   Thomas L. Friedman reminds us that we used to build our towns and factories along rivers because they provided access to neighbors and their ideas, power, mobility, and nourishment. "But the rivers you want to build on now are Amazon Web Services or Microsoft's Azure—giant connectors that enable you, your business, or your nation to get access to all the computing power applications in the [worldwide Internet of Things], where you can tie into every flow in the world in which you want to participate."[3]

HR professionals no longer have the luxury of thinking only about their own local, state, or federal interactive requirements. International requirements are always nearby in terms of offshore manufacturing, importing rules and procedures, and exporting rules and procedures. Monetary impact comes from all parts of the earth. The international firms that are successful perform workforce recruiting and talent management, and they have policies influenced from multiple countries.

Some experts have pointed out that the workforce in emerging world economies is primarily young, while the workforce in developed countries is aging. The problems presented by each of those populations are quite different. HR professionals must be able to address both.

Shift from Developed to Emerging Economies

The long-term global economic power shift away from established developed economies is expected to continue into 2050, as emerging market countries continue to boost their share of the world's gross domestic product, or GDP, despite recent mixed performance in some of these economies.[4]

Diaspora   According to the *World Encyclopedia, diaspora* refers to any people or ethnic population forced or induced to leave its traditional homeland, as well as the dispersal of such people and the ensuing developments in their culture. It is especially used with reference to the Jewish population, who have lived most of their historical existence as a *diasporan* people.[5] In 2022, we saw this for the people of Ukraine in response to the invasion by Russia.

Demographic Dichotomy   The workforce in emerging economies is becoming disproportionately young, while the workforce in developed economies is rapidly aging (parallel demographic shift).[6]

Reverse Innovation   Innovations created for or by emerging-economy markets and then imported by developed-economy markets suggests that the "new" economies will have a greater influence over world economic events because they are selling their innovations to markets in developed countries also.

Global Recession and Global Warming

Episodes of severe weather in the United States, such as the abundance of rainfall and then drought across the West and especially in California, are brandished as tangible evidence of the future costs of current climate trends. A study by Hsiang et al. (published in the journal *Science*)[7] collected national data documenting the responses in six economic sectors to short-term weather fluctuations. This data was integrated with probabilistic distributions from a set of global climate models and used to estimate future costs during the remainder of this century across a range of scenarios. In terms of overall effects on the gross domestic product, the authors predict negative impacts in the southern United States and positive impacts in some parts of the Pacific Northwest and New England.

Hyperconnectivity

Hyperconnectivity is a state of unified communications (UC) in which the traffic-handling capacity and bandwidth of a network always exceed the demand. The number of communication pathways and nodes is much greater than the number of subscribers.[8] This is evidenced by the increasing digital interconnection of people and things around the clock from anywhere.

Measurability   If you can't measure it, why spend time working on it? Each of the issues we are discussing in this functional area can be measured if you take the time to think about them.

Moving Work

Globalization, more than anything else, has resulted in employers finding ways to do their work better, cheaper, and faster by looking outside traditional local recruiting sources. Here are some of the influences we see today:

- **Outsourcing**   The transfer of some work to organizations outside the employer's payroll. The vendor may be across the street or across the country.

- **Offshoring**   The transfer of some work to locations outside the home country borders. Those doing the work are still on your organization's payroll.

- **Onshoring (home-shoring)**   The relocation of business processes or production to a lower-cost location inside the same country as the business.

- **Near-shoring**   Contracting part of the business processes or production to an external company located in a country that is relatively close. For the United States, that would mean Mexico or Canada.

HR professionals play a critical role in supporting the decision-making effort involved in moving work from one location to another. In performing due diligence, HR professionals should conduct research on each of the following:

- **Talent pool**   Languages spoken, cultural differences, educational levels.

- **Sociopolitical environment**   Governmental regulations, plus the expense involved in following them. Quality of life and ethical environment can create certain expenses.

- **Risk levels**   IT security, political and labor conflicts, natural disasters, and security for individuals and property.

- **Cost and quality**   Wage structure, tax structure, communication facilities, Internet access.

Defining the Global Organization

 A global organization is a business that operates in two or more countries. It also goes by the name *multinational company*.

Defining the Role of Global HR

Global businesses should have a global HR function. At the same time, to compete successfully in diverse markets, most companies choose to recruit, train, and manage people locally, thus reflecting local culture, local labor markets, and the needs of diverse local business units.[9] Here are some key points regarding global business success to keep in mind:

- Business and talent strategies should be global in scale and local in implementation. Effective programs recruit, train, and develop people locally.

- Global HR and talent management is the second most urgent and important trend for companies around the world with 10,000 or more employees, according to Deloitte Insights' global survey.[10]

- Companies face the challenge of developing an integrated global HR and talent operating model that allows for customizable local implementation, enabling them to capitalize on rapid business growth in emerging economies, tap into local skills, and optimize local talent strategies.

Creating a Global Strategy

An increasing number of firms are deciding they need to create an overarching, global HR strategy as they expand around the world. This is because HR leaders must adhere to local laws but still meet the needs of regional staff, all while maintaining an across-the-board strategy.[11]

The Strategic Attraction of Globalization

Current attitudes toward globalization have resulted in new thinking called *guarded globalization*. Governments of developing nations have become wary of opening more industries to multinational companies and are zealously protecting local interests. They choose the countries or regions with which they want to do business, pick the sectors in which they will allow capital investment, and select the local, often state-owned, companies they want to promote. That's a different flavor of globalization: slow-moving, selective, and with a heavy dash of nationalism and regionalism.[12]

There are a multitude of reasons to expand a company internationally. Those reasons can broadly be characterized by moving away from something(s) domestically and being drawn to something attractive outside the domestic market. These are "push" and "pull" dimensions.

"Push" Factors   The following are examples of "push" factors influencing global organizations:[13]

- **Saturation of domestic demand and the need for new markets**   The market for a number of products tends to saturate or decline in developed countries. This often happens when the market potential has been almost fully tapped. For example, the fall in the birth rate implies contraction of a market for several baby products. Businesses undertake international operations to expand sales, acquire resources from foreign countries, or diversify their activities to discover lucrative opportunities in other countries.

- **Shortfalls in natural resources and talent supply**   When natural resources begin dwindling in developed countries, it seems reasonable for organizations to look to other countries for their raw materials. Creating a physical presence where the resources are located can help reduce the costs of acquisition. Moving to locations where talent can be found is a common solution for dwindling talent supplies in the home country.

- **Trade agreements**   Global expansion is driven by domestic competition from foreign competitors.

- **Technological revolution**   *Revolution* is the word that can best describe the pace at which technology has changed in the recent past and is continuing to change. Significant developments are being witnessed in communication, transportation, and information processing.

- **Globalized supply chain**   Moving production facilities closer to supplier locations can help reduce costs involved in moving raw materials before processing.

- **Domestic recession**   Domestic recession often provokes companies to explore foreign markets. One of the factors that prompted Hindustan Machine Ltd. (HMT) to seriously take up exports was the recession in the home market in the late 1960s.

- **Increased cost pressures and competition as a driving force**   Competition may become a driving force behind internationalization. There might be intense competition in the home market but little in certain foreign countries. A protected market does not normally motivate companies to seek business outside the home market.

- **Government policies and regulations**   Government policies and regulations may also motivate internationalization. There are both positive and negative factors that could cause internationalization. Many governments offer a number of incentives and other types of positive support to domestic companies to export and to invest in foreign locations. Tax subsidies or even tax forgiveness can be a strong magnet for international business moves.

- **Improving the image of the company**   International business has certain spin-offs too. It may help the company improve its domestic business; international business helps to improve the image of the company. There may be an advantage associated with exporting: when domestic consumers learn the company is selling a significant portion of the production abroad, they may be more inclined to buy from such a company.

- **Strategic vision**   The systematic and growing internationalization of many companies is essentially part of their business policy or strategic management. The stimulus for internationalization comes from the urge to grow, the need to become more competitive, the need to diversify, and the need to gain strategic advantages of internationalization.

"Pull" Factors   Here are some pull factors that make "foreign" markets attractive:[14]

- **Government policies**   When policies encourage foreign investment, domestic organizations may find it financially beneficial to locate to foreign markets. There may be tax advantages gained by expanding into foreign locations.

- **Strategic control**   Many multinational companies (MNCs) are locating their subsidiaries in low-wage and low-cost countries to take advantage of low-cost production. When it becomes easier to control things such as brand image by having a subsidiary in a foreign country, large organizations take that leap.

- **Taking advantage of growth opportunities**   MNCs are getting increasingly interested in several developing countries as the income and population rapidly rise in these countries. Foreign markets can flourish in both developed and developing countries.

- **Declining trade and investment barriers**   Declining trade and investment barriers have vastly contributed to globalization. Business across the globe has grown considerably in a free trade regime. Goods, services, capital, and technology all benefit significantly while moving across nations.

Regional trading blocs are adding to the pace of globalization. WTO, EU, USMCA, MERCOSUR, and FTAA are major alliances among countries. Trading blocs seek to promote international business by removing trade and investment barriers. Integration among countries results in efficient allocation of resources throughout the trading area, promoting the growth of some business and the decline of others as well as the development of new technologies and products and the elimination of old technologies.

Strategic Approaches to Globalization

When choosing a strategy for globalization, you need to consider the attractiveness of a number of factors:

- The organization's core capabilities and resources, both organizational and economic.

- The organization's strategic goals.

- The distance between current headquarters and the location under consideration. In this context, "distance" may include physical, legal, cultural, and sociopolitical similarities or differences.[15]

The following are some approaches to strategic globalization:

- Creating a new organization in a foreign country, which is called green field.

- Acquiring a subsidiary in a foreign country, perhaps through merger or acquisition, which is also called turnkey.

- Creating a new partnership.

- Outsourcing all or at least some of the production tasks to a supplier in a new work location.

- Repurposing a disused facility, which is called brown field.

- Adding capacity to existing domestic locations by offshoring.

Global Integration vs. Local Responsiveness   A key decision in becoming global is how to weigh global integration (GI) versus local responsiveness (LR). There is no single correct answer. GI emphasizes standardization of processes to achieve greater economies of scale. The sought-after efficiencies can lower the cost of operations, create greater price flexibility, and increase profits.

Local responsiveness emphasizes adapting to the needs, desires, and habits of a local market. It does so by allowing subsidiaries to develop unique products, structures, and systems.[16]

Adjustments for consumer preference is one strategy for the globalization of product marketing. H. J. Heinz adapts its products to match local preferences. Because some people of India will not eat garlic and onion, for example, Heinz offers them a version of its signature ketchup that does not include these two ingredients. On the other hand, such alterations are not needed in products hidden from consumer view. Intel's processing chips are an example. There is no need to modify the chips for various international cultures. The chips will work the same across all cultures. Such is a benefit of global integration.

Achieving Global Integration   Global integration means that decisions are made from a global perspective, and in some cases the firm operates as if the world were one market.

Achieving Local Responsiveness   Local responsiveness is achieved by delegating most of the decision-making responsibility to local units and by appointing a local manager to the top management teams of subsidiaries.

Global integration vs. Local Responsiveness Examples   BASF is a German-based corporation that is one of the largest chemical production companies in the world. It has more than 360 plants producing a host of chemicals in more than 90 countries for nearly all industries in the world that use chemicals. Its chemicals are standard, regardless of the country where they will be used. That is global integration.

Beverage companies produce various brands and flavors in local markets worldwide. For example, Coca-Cola offers Georgia Coffee in Japan, Café Zu in Thailand, Inca Cola in Peru, and the Burn energy drink in France. Making adjustments for local tastes is an example of local responsiveness.

Global-Local Models   A range of strategic choices is available within the global-local concept.

Upstream and Downstream Strategies   A simple metaphor like "upstream and downstream" can help identify the strategies you can apply:

- **Upstream**   Decisions are made at headquarters and apply to strategies for focusing on the standardization of processes and integration of resources. That can be a strategy for workforce alignment, organizational development, and sharing knowledge and experience across internal organization boundaries.

- **Downstream**   Decisions are made at the local level and target adapting strategic goals to local realities. That can be a strategy for agreements with local work groups, adjustments to standard policies related to working conditions that reflect local requirements, and adjustments to operations based on local requirements.

Identity Alignment and Process Alignment   As strategies, identify alignment and process alignment offer some possible benefits to multinational organizations:

- **Identify alignment**   This is based on the diversity of people, products/services, and branding, the differences among locations, and the adjustment of brand identity and products/services based on local culture. Some downside risks are that localized offerings can dilute the brand or product/service image, unless the corporate brand is well established, and local approaches can diffuse the core organizational identity. Think of McDonald's hamburgers. In most markets around the world, beef burgers are acceptable. In India, however, religion prevents a large portion of the population from eating beef. In that local market, products with chicken and fish are much more widely accepted.

- **Process alignment**   This is how well common internal functions can work across all locations. Are the same technologies used in all locations for accounting, HR, finance, and legal? Are the same performance measurements used in all locations? Is a unified HR system used in all locations? This can be a problem when one organization acquires another. There is great inertia within each organization for continuing to use its own systems. Blending them or replacing them can be and is often problematic.

The GI-LR Matrix: Strategic Options   For many years, scholars have been studying the relationships between global integration and local responsiveness.[17] The following table illustrates what they developed.

Global Corporate Strategies	
High	
Global Strategy	**Transnational Strategy**
• Treats world as a single global market	• Seeks to balance global efficiencies and local responsiveness
• Standardizes global products/advertising strategies	• Combines standardization and customization for product/advertising strategies
• Strong links between HQ and subsidiaries	• Strong links between HQ and subsidiaries and among subsidiaries
International Strategy	**Multidomestic Strategy**
• Domestically focused	• Handles markets independently for each country
• Exports a few domestically produced products to selected countries	• Adapts product/advertising to local tastes and needs
• Weak links between HQ and dependent subsidiaries	• Weak links between HQ and autonomous subsidiaries
Low	

(Left axis) **Need for Global Integration**

Need for Local Responsiveness

Low ◄─────────────► High

The following four terms are used in the table to describe the combinations of low or high need for Global Integration coupled with low or high need for Local Responsiveness:

- **International strategy**   All products/services, processes, and strategy at all levels are developed in the home country, even though the organization may export products or services to other countries.

- **Multidomestic strategy**   Headquarters has little influence over remote subsidiary units. They develop their own strategies and goals.

- **Global strategy**   Headquarters develops and disseminates strategies, products, and services. All offerings are the same worldwide. Local entities hardly influence the global image or products at all. Customizable elements are kept to a minimum.

- **Transnational strategy**   Remote locations are chosen for their access to supplies, vendors, and local markets. Subsidiaries are permitted to make adaptations to global products for appeal to local markets. Knowledge and practices are shared among all units in the organization. HQ assumes responsibility for certain factors such as advertising and strategies.

Perlmutter's Headquarters Orientations   Howard Perlmutter, an expert on globalization, identified a way of classifying alternative global management orientations, commonly referred to as Perlmutter's EPRG model. He states that businesses and their staff tend to operate in one of four ways:[18]

- **Ethnocentric**   These people or companies believe that their home country is superior. The way they have done business domestically has worked, so they export it exactly as is. It is a "we know best" attitude. When they look to new markets, they rely on what they know and seek similarities with their own country. Overseas subsidiaries or offices in international markets are seen as less able and less important than the head office. Typically, these companies make few adaptations to their products and undertake little research in the international markets.

- **Polycentric**   A polycentric orientation sees each country as unique and believes businesses are best run locally. Polycentric management means that the head office places little control on the activities in each market, and there is little attempt to make use of any good ideas or best practices from other markets. This is a country-by-country approach, and the various locations are essentially left alone by headquarters as long as they stay profitable.

- **Regiocentric**   This orientation sees similarities in large geographic regions and designs strategies around this. In a regiocentric approach, there is significant communication within the defined region, like Africa, and less communication with the rest of the organization outside of that region. For example, in South America, there are similar compensation practices among the countries in that region, where there is an expectation, sometimes even a statute, requiring a thirteenth, and in some places now even a fourteenth, monthly paycheck in December. There may also be major differences between countries within a region. For example, Norway and Spain are both in Europe but are very different in climate, culture, transport, and retail distribution, but they are still grouped together for management purposes.

- **Geocentric** As truly global players, geocentric companies view the world as a potential market and seek to serve it effectively. Geocentric management recognizes the similarities and differences between the home country and the international markets. It combines ethnocentric and polycentric views; in other words, it displays the "think global, act local" ideology. These companies are open to the best talent and practices, regardless of where they originate.

Sourcing and Shoring

As a product of globalization, work is moved to the most advantageous location. That can bring offshoring and outsourcing into play.

Offshoring This is the practice of placing production, customer service, IT development, or other elements of the organization in another country. Offshoring is sometimes chosen because it offers lower costs, production at a location closer to raw materials, or a better tax impact or other financial impact. There may also be direct financial incentives, such as government-sponsored loans or cash payments. Offshoring can also take advantage of time zone differences, and work can be done on a project without interruption should the appropriate workforce be scattered around the globe.

Disadvantages of offshoring can include a strong resistance from customers, who may even call the practice "unpatriotic." Other problems that sometimes arise are language difficulties, cultural differences, high turnover rates, quality control issues, and educational degrees that do not offer reliable skills or talents.

Onshoring When business processes, product manufacturing, or other functions are contracted out to another organization within the home country, it is called *onshoring*. Having home-country employees can often avoid the problems associated with offshoring.

Near-Shoring The practice of contracting part of the organization's business processes to a country that is close to the home country is known as *near-shoring*. A company in the United States selecting manufacturing subcontractors in Mexico for making its automobiles or washing machines is a good example. These arrangements are influenced to a great degree by trade agreements and social or economic stability.

Outsourcing Almost always, outsourcing is evidenced by contracts with vendors in the home country or in other countries that can provide products or services more cheaply than can be offered at headquarters. A prime example is the use of call centers to support customer service and order processing.

HR's Role in Globalization

Any time a strategic decision is contemplated that involves placing a workforce in a distant location, HR has some responsibility in that process. What is the workforce talent pool? What are the local laws and customs that will influence operations? What will be the approach to product quality in the new location?

HR Global Abilities   Experts say that some of the core competencies international HR careers demand are the same as those for domestic HR professionals—the skills are just on a heightened scale. For example, global HR managers need effective communication skills, including the ability to listen well.[19] It is common for international HR professionals to be multilingual. This is often a job requirement. Here are some questions you should include in performing due diligence for HR management in a new distant work location:

- What is the wage structure?
- What is the tax structure for payroll in addition to operational taxes?
- What is the real estate situation?
- How will telecommunications, Internet, and transportation be provided?
- How much government regulation will be involved in managing a workforce?
- How ethical are the government, political influences, and business environments?
- What is the quality of life in the new location?
- Is there a history of labor unrest or political upset?
- Have there been any natural disasters? What is that likelihood for more?
- How can IT security be addressed?
- What are the challenges for intellectual property rights and personal and property security?
- Is the economy stable? How widely does the currency exchange value fluctuate?
- What cultural differences are there?
- Is there a qualified labor force available?

HR Global Tasks   On a global level, HR professionals must work toward helping the organization achieve its maximum value. Strategically, HR must help balance the priorities of headquarters and subsidiaries. How can human resources be distributed and balanced within budget restrictions and still maximize goal achievement? On a tactical level, HR professionals must facilitate management groups so that different disciplines and professions can achieve joint goals within differing cultural and socio-political environments.

HR Global Skills   HR professionals must be capable of doing a lot of things that require professional HR skills. Here are some of the skills HR professionals must possess in the global workplace:

- **Develop a strategic view of the organization**   How does value get created? What can HR contribute to the strategic plan development of the organization?

- **Develop a global organizational culture**   Training plays a key role, and HR needs to be the training provider. How can communication issues be overcome?

- **Secure and grow a safe and robust talent supply chain**   Work for a ready supply of leaders at each global location. Monitor the availability of qualified workforce candidates at all levels. Support efforts to develop a strong employer brand.

- **Use and adapt HR technology**   Ensure HR technology can be applied at all locations globally. Work with IT professionals to ensure technology supports both domestic and global operations.

- **Develop meaningful metrics**   Develop and implement consistent measurement devices and their application at all global locations. Be sure it is obvious that employee investment supports strategic goals.

- **Develop policies and practices to manage risks**   Ensure the health, safety, and security of employees. Protect physical assets and the intellectual property of the organization. Ensure all legal requirements are being met at all global locations, including safety requirements, nondiscrimination requirements, payroll requirements, benefit requirements, and ethical requirements.

Auditing Global HR Practices   It is important to know how your global HR practices are actually serving your organization and its people. To determine that, you will need to assemble a global compliance audit project team. Consider these types of representatives in your team selection process:

- Headquarters (that is, home country) HR representative
- Foreign location (that is, host country) HR representative
- Legal counsel, determine if in-house or outside best meets your needs
- Compliance officer
- Outside international HR expert
- Corporate audit department representative

An audit of global HR practices would be advisable if you have received a lawsuit challenging your HR practices, you are going through a merger or acquisition, you are undergoing corporate restructuring, you want to be sure you are complying with antibribery and insider trading laws, or you simply want to be sure your practices are being followed.

An audit should begin by identifying the countries involved. Next, define the focus of the audit. Will it look at legal compliance, union contracts, corporate policies, or simply best practices? It is possible to take in all of these focal areas, but that becomes more complex.

Will your audit look only at local host country employees, or will you include expatriates, consultants, independent contractors, international transfers, temporary workers, or some other group? Will the audit engage in examining international payroll tax laws or data security issues?

Build a checklist of areas to be examined. Then, expand that into a matrix that includes individual team member assignments, expected completion date for each component, and the ultimate audit report completion. Be sure you include time for a review process by identifying who will be involved in the review and approval sequence and how long each contributor will have to submit approval or additional report requirements. Finally, determine who will receive the final report when it is issued. What role will the report have in legal filings with organizations such as the Securities and Exchange Commission (SEC) and other similar oversight groups?

Becoming a Multicultural Organization

 Organizations cannot become multicultural by proclamation. It takes a concerted effort.

Developing a Global Mindset

Personal development precedes organizational development. First, leaders must develop their own global mindset. Then they will be able to help guide their organization into the same way of thinking. Here are five steps toward that goal:[20]

- **Recognize your own cultural values and biases**   Developing a strong self-awareness has shown to foster a nonjudgmental perspective on differences, which is critical to developing a global mindset.

- **Get to know your personality traits, especially curiosity**   Five specific traits affect your ability to interact effectively with different cultures:

  - Openness

  - Flexibility

  - Social dexterity

  - Emotional awareness

  - Curiosity

  Ask yourself how open you are to different ways of managing a team. Are you flexible enough to attempt a different feedback style? How easy is it for you to strike up a conversation with people from different countries?

- **Learn about the workplace and business expectations of relevant countries and markets**   Learn about the typical workplace habits, expectations, and best practices in other countries and cultures.

- **Build strong intercultural relationships**   Just like when learning to speak a second language, it's helpful to immerse yourself with people from other parts of the world to develop a global mindset. These relationships facilitate valuable learning about what works and what doesn't. The ability to form relationships across cultures is not a given, but the more positive intercultural relationships you develop, the more comfort you'll have with diverse work styles and the less you'll resort to stereotyping.

- **Develop strategies to adjust and flex your style**   What has made you successful in a domestic or local context likely won't help you reach the same level of success on a global scale, which is why learning to adapt your style is often the hardest part of mastering a global mindset. This step involves expanding your repertoire of business behaviors by learning to behave in ways that may be unusual to you but highly effective when interacting with others.

Defining a Global Mindset   We would define global mindset as one that combines an openness to and awareness of diversity across cultures and markets with a propensity and ability to see common patterns across countries and markets.

Benefits of a Global Mindset   The main benefit of a global mindset is the organization's ability to combine speed with accurate response. The organizational global mindset can bring about benefits that can manifest themselves in one or more competitive advantages.

Acquiring a Global Mindset   Acquiring a global mindset requires you to recognize situations in which demands from both global and local elements are compelling; you need to be open and aware of diversity across cultures and markets with a willingness and ability to synthesize across this diversity.

Definition of Culture   *Culture* is the beliefs, customs, arts, and so on of a particular society, group, place, or time. It's a particular society that has its own beliefs, ways of life, art, and so on, and it's a way of thinking, behaving, or working that exists in a place or organization (such as a business).

How Types of Culture Affect an Organization   Here are five types of corporate culture.[21] Can you find one that best describes your organization?

- **Team-first corporate culture**   Team-oriented companies hire for culture fit first, skills and experience second. A company with a team-first corporate culture makes employee happiness its top priority. Frequent team outings, opportunities to provide meaningful feedback, and flexibility to accommodate employee family lives are common markers of a team-first culture. Netflix is a great example; its decision to offer unlimited family leave gives employees the autonomy to decide what's right for them.

- **Elite corporate culture**   Companies with elite cultures are often out to change the world by untested means. An elite corporate culture hires only the best because it's always pushing the envelope and needs employees to not merely keep up but lead the way (think Google). Innovative and sometimes daring companies with an elite culture hire confident, capable, competitive candidates. The result? Fast growth and making big splashes in the market.

- **Horizontal corporate culture**   Titles don't mean much in horizontal cultures. Horizontal corporate culture is common among startups because it makes for a collaborative, everyone-pitch-in mindset. These typically younger companies have a product or service they're striving to provide yet are more flexible and able to change based on market research or customer feedback. Though a smaller team size might limit their customer service capabilities, they do whatever they can to keep the customer happy—their success depends on it.

- **Conventional corporate culture**   Traditional companies have clearly defined hierarchies and are still grappling with the learning curve for communicating through new mediums. Companies where a tie and/or slacks are expected are, most likely, of the conventional sort. In fact, any dress code at all is indicative of a more traditional culture, as are a numbers-focused approach and risk-averse decision-making. Your local bank or car dealership likely embodies these traits. The customer, while crucial, is not necessarily always right—the bottom line takes precedence.

- **Progressive corporate culture**   Mergers, acquisitions, or sudden changes in the market can all contribute to a progressive culture. Uncertainty is the definitive trait of a progressive culture because employees often don't know what to expect next (see almost every newspaper or magazine). "Customers" are often separate from the company's audience because these companies usually have investors or advertisers to whom they answer.

Cultural Layers

There are differing interpretations of culture because it's like an onion, consisting of many layers.[22]

Schein's Model   In 1980, the American management professor Edgar Schein developed an organizational culture model to make culture more visible within an organization.[23] Schein divided organizational culture into three different levels:

- **Artifacts and symbols**   Artifacts mark the surface of the organization. They are the visible elements in the organization such as logos, architecture, structure, processes, and corporate clothing. These are not only visible to employees but also visible and recognizable for external parties. If you see the Eiffel Tower in a movie, you immediately know the scene is set in Paris.

- **Espoused values**   This concerns standards, values, and rules of conduct. How does the organization express strategies, objectives, and philosophies, and how are these made public? Problems can arise when the ideas of managers are not in line with the basic assumptions of the organization.

- **Basic underlying assumptions**   The basic underlying assumptions are deeply embedded in the organizational culture and are experienced as self-evident and unconscious behavior. Assumptions are hard to recognize from within.

Cultural Dimensions

Social scientist Geert Hofstede suggests that the following six unique cultural dimensions can be seen anywhere. Cultures are ranked on a scale of 1 to 100 for each dimension.[24]

- **Power distance**   This dimension displays how a culture accepts or rejects inequality, particularly in relation to money and power. In some cultures, inequality and hierarchal statuses are a way of life. High power distance means these inequities are accepted. Low power distance has an expectation for social mobility and treating one another as equals, regardless of where one is within the corporate hierarchy.

- **Individualism versus collectivism**   This dimension focuses on the unification of culture. In individualistic cultures, the population is less tightly knit, and there is an "every man for himself" mentality. Cultures that value collectivism more put the group needs over the individual's needs.

- **Masculinity versus femininity**   In this dimension, a culture is measured on a scale of masculine to feminine, which represents a culture's preferences for achievement, competition, and materialism versus preferences for teamwork, harmony, and empathy. This dimension looks at people filling roles via traditional expectations at one end of the spectrum and at the other filling roles based on each individual's skills and passions.

- **Uncertainty avoidance**   Have you ever been in a situation where a new idea or element is introduced? How did you react to that? For this dimension, cultures are gauged on their response to ambiguity and new ideas and situations. Change in the future can be a terrifying notion for some, while others will see it as an exciting possibility.

- **Long-term orientation versus short-term orientation**   When dealing with the present and future, a culture either will look to innovate when facing new challenges or will look to the past for answers.

- **Indulgence versus restraint**   In the final dimension, all cultures acknowledge that the natural human response in life is the urgent need to gratify desires. However, each culture will answer this need by either enjoying (indulgence) or controlling (restraint) those impulses.

Hall's Theory of High- and Low-Context Cultures   Anthropologist Edward T. Hall defines intercultural communication as a form of communication that shares information across different cultures and social groups. One framework for approaching intercultural communication is with high-context and low-context cultures, which refer to the value cultures place on indirect and direct communication.[25] High-context cultures need direct explicit communication due to the participants not knowing one another in depth. Low-context cultures may use more indirect communication since the participants know one another well and have an abundance of shared experiences that may be referenced.

Hofstede's Dimensions of Culture As mentioned earlier, Geert Hofstede developed a cultural dimensions theory as a framework to understand cross-cultural differences better.[26] It describes the effects of a society's culture on the values of its members and how these values relate to behavior.

Hofstede developed his original model using factor analysis to examine the results of a worldwide survey of IBM employees concerning their reported values between 1967 and 1973.

Trompenaars and Hampden-Turner's Dilemmas Anglo-Dutch gurus Fons Trompenaars and Charles Hampden-Turner have become the go-to guys on multinational mergers. Their recipe: making opposites attract.[27]

If you followed dilemma theory to its logical conclusion, you would attribute every pernicious culture clash, and most other management problems, to the human habit (especially common in Western cultures) of casting life in terms of all-or-nothing choices: winning-versus-losing strategies, right-versus-wrong answers, good-versus-bad values, and so on. As a manager, when you unconsciously approach a business issue (or any issue) as a contest between good and evil, you lose sight of the potential benefits the "evil" side has to offer. It's far better to interpret, say, the battle between English and French management styles or American dominance and European resistance as a dilemma that can be reconciled when both sides see they have something to learn from the other.

Cross-Cultural Challenges for HR

With the rapid increase in the globalization of business, workforces are becoming increasingly diverse and multicultural. Managing global workforces has increased pressure on HR managers to recognize and adapt to cultural differences, which when ignored can result in cross-cultural misunderstandings. With the growing significance of developing economies in the global business environment, human resource management is facing increased challenges in managing cross-border cultural relationships.[28]

Challenges of Culture As workplaces become more complex and the mingling of cultures becomes more demanding, HR professionals must keep an eye open for these specific challenges:[29]

- Colleagues from some cultures may be less likely to let their voices be heard.
- Integration across multicultural teams can be difficult in the face of prejudice or negative cultural stereotypes.
- Professional communication can be misinterpreted or difficult to understand across languages and cultures.

- Navigating visa requirements, employment laws, and the cost of accommodating workplace requirements can be difficult.
- There may be different understandings of professional etiquette.
- There may be conflicting working styles across teams.
- Decision-making may slow down as teams work through cultural differences.

Dilemma Reconciliation   The essence of the reconciliation of a dilemma lies in the recognition that a dilemma is a nonlinear problem and therefore needs a nonlinear problem-solving approach. It replaces "either-or" thinking with "and-and and through-and-through" thinking.[30]

Creating Cultural Synergy   *Cultural synergy* is a term coined by Nancy Adler[31] of McGill University. It describes an attempt to bring two or more cultures together to form an organization or environment that is based on combined strengths, concepts, and skills. High-synergy organizations have employees who cooperate for mutual advantage and usually tackle their problems by following a simple structure that focuses on identifying the problem, culturally interpreting it, and, finally, increasing the cultural activity. Contrary to this, there are low-synergy organizations that work with employees who are ruggedly individualistic and insist on solving any problem alone.

Managing Global Assignments

Only 51 percent of companies track the actual total cost of international assignments, yet 69 percent say there is pressure to reduce mobility program costs, according to a report on global mobility trends and practices.[32] In addition, 76 percent of companies do not compare the actual versus estimated cost at the end of an assignment, and a whopping 94 percent do not measure the program's return on investment.

Strategic Role of Global Assignments

Global assignments can contribute to the organization's strategic plan. They offer cross-training for senior managers and executives. This can enhance cultural exposure and even cultural emersion. Global assignments also provide an opportunity to assess global presence and expansion plans.

Types of Assignments

Specialists in international human resource management identify different types of global assignments. Technical assignments occur when employees with technical skills are sent from one country to another to address a particular skill shortage. Developmental assignments, in contrast, are typically used within a management development program to equip managers with new skills and competencies. Strategic assignments arise when key executives are sent from one country to another to launch a product, develop a market, or initiate another key change in business strategy.[33]

Managing Allegiances

Sometimes people are torn between their parent company and their local company. According to authors Kate Hutchings and Helen De Cieri, those allegiances can be understood by using the following chart:[34]

Forms of Expatriate Allegiance			
Allegiance to the Parent Firm	High	Expatriates who leave their hearts at home	Expatriates who see themselves as dual citizens
	Low	Expatriates who see themselves as free agents	Expatriates who "go native"
		Low	High

Allegiance to the Local Firm

Global Assignment Guidelines

The companies that manage their expats effectively come in many sizes and from a wide range of industries. Yet they all follow three general practices:[35]

- When making international assignments, they focus on knowledge creation and global leadership development. Many companies send people abroad to reward them, to get them out of the way, or to fill an immediate business need. At companies that manage the international assignment process well, however, people are given foreign posts to generate and transfer knowledge, to develop their global leadership skills, or to do both.

- They assign overseas posts to people whose technical skills are matched or exceeded by their cross-cultural abilities. Companies that manage expats wisely do not assume that people who have succeeded at home will repeat that success abroad. They assign international posts to individuals who not only have the necessary technical skills but also have indicated that they would be likely to live comfortably in different cultures.

- The companies who utilize expatriates best end their assignments with a deliberate repatriation process. Returning to the home country can have its own culture shock moments. Most executives who oversee expat employees view their return home as a nonissue. The truth is, repatriation is a time of major upheaval, professionally and personally, for two-thirds of expats. Companies that recognize this fact help their returning people by providing them with career guidance and enabling them to put their international experience to work.

What Managers Should Know   Global human resource managers can use the high failure rates of international job assignments to support investing in up-front and ongoing programs that will make international assignments successful. Selecting the right person, preparing the expat and their family, measuring the employee's performance from afar, and repatriating the individual at the end of an assignment all require a well-planned, well-managed program. Knowing what to expect from start to finish as well as having some tools to work with can help minimize the risk.[36]

The Global Assignment Process

The following five stages are involved in the global assignment process:

- **Stage 1: Assessment and selection**   Determining who will be appointed to the international job opening depends on who meets the job requirements in the best way. There may be a formal assessment, or there may be only a single selecting manager who makes the decision.

- **Stage 2: Management and assignee decision**   The selecting manager determines how long the assignee will have to accept or reject the appointment.

- **Stage 3: Predeparture preparation**   Before anyone leaves the home country, there are important considerations to be processed and questions answered. What are the immigrant requirements in the destination country? What visa requirements must be processed? What provisions will be made for the employee's family members (school or spouse work appointment)? What about selling a home before departure? Will a home be purchased in the destination country?

- **Stage 4: On assignment**   When the employee arrives at the new job location, there is a "settling-in" process. Are the living arrangements going to be satisfactory? Where is the local grocery store? What about dentists, optometrists, and physicians? What about transportation? Potentially, you need to ensure the employee has the ability to drive on the other side of the road when using an automobile, after you make sure they have a license that is recognized in that country.

- **Stage 5: Completing the assignment**   When the expat comes home, there should be a debriefing process that could last several days. Inquiries should be made about the employee's opinion of the job environment, the work itself, the support received from the employer, and what things could be done differently.

Navigating the Global Legal Environment

There are always labor-management laws to be considered regardless of where one works in the world. They vary greatly in their control over the workplace, but both the employee and the employer should understand them for the destination country so no one violates one of these laws, even by accident.

World Legal Systems

Around the globe there are several different types of legal systems, and they don't always agree with one another. Civil law, common law, and religious law are the three primary kinds of legal systems in the world today.

Civil Law   Civil law systems have drawn their inspiration largely from the Roman law heritage that, by giving precedence to written law, have resolutely opted for a systematic codification of their general law. This is the most widespread system of law in the world.

Common Law   Common law systems are legal systems founded not on laws made by legislatures but on judge-made laws, which in turn are based on custom, culture, habit, and previous judicial decisions throughout the world.

Religious Law   The Muslim law system is an autonomous legal system that is of a religious nature and predominantly based on the Koran.

Key Concepts of Law

While laws bring us some level of consistency in the treatment of the same or similar events, there are some key elements you should recognize in all of them.

Rule of Law   The rule of law is the principle that law should govern a nation, as opposed to being governed by decisions of individual government officials.

Due Process   Due process acts as a safeguard from arbitrary denial of life, liberty, or property by the government outside the sanction of law.

Jurisdiction   Legal jurisdiction applies to government agencies as well as courts. State courts have jurisdiction only in their state. Federal courts have jurisdiction over federal matters. Federal case law is determined by appellate courts, and those decisions apply only within the jurisdiction of the appellate court. The U.S. Supreme Court has jurisdiction over all matters of the U.S. Constitution.

Levels of Law

Each governmental strata can offer its own laws.

Within a Nation   At the national level, there can be laws created that apply to the entire country and others that apply only to a subset of the nation.

National Laws   Federal laws apply to all governmental subsets, such as states in the United States. Nondiscrimination rules apply to all states equally. Of course, there are qualifying thresholds, such as the number of employees that can cause certain employers to be exempt from the provisions of the law, but all those who qualify by employee head count will be expected to comply with the national law.

Subnational   Called a state, canton, or province, each smaller entity within the federal umbrella can create its own laws. These laws apply only within its own jurisdiction.

Between and Among Nations   When nations agree that the same laws should apply to each of them, one of the following types of rule would come into existence.

Extraterritorial   Extraterritorial jurisdiction (ETJ) is the legal ability of a government to exercise authority beyond its normal boundaries. Any authority can claim ETJ over any external territory they want. As an example, most embassies or consulates claim ETJ within their space. This is the stuff that wars are fought over. The European Union and the World Trade Organization are examples.[37]

Regional/Supranational   A supranational organization is an international group or union in which the power and influence of member states transcend national boundaries or interests to share in decision-making and vote on issues concerning the collective body.

International This is a body of rules established by custom or treaty and recognized by nations as binding in their relations with one another. For example, EU law is divided into primary and secondary legislation. The treaties (primary legislation) are the basis or ground rules for all EU action. Secondary legislation—which includes regulations, directives, and decisions—is derived from the principles and objectives set out in the treaties.

Functional Area 12: Risk Management

This is SHRM's BASK definition: "Risk Management is the identification, assessment and prioritization of risks, and the application of resources to minimize, monitor and control the probability and impact of those risks accordingly."[38]

Risk Management is a broad functional category. There are so many types of risk management that it is hard to list all of them. Some areas of risk management are liquidity, banking, crisis, supply chain, insurance, software, and strategic reputation risk management. In human resource terms, risk management involves right hiring, health insurance, avoiding discrimination, appropriate employee behavior, workplace safety, asset security, and more.

There are two vastly different philosophies about risk management. The first, where we will focus, is identifying and protecting things of value against loss, most often with insurance. Do be aware of a second philosophy about risk, which is captured in the old saying, "Nothing ventured, nothing gained." You have to put some chips on the table if you want any chance of winning more. This second philosophy sees all managers as risk managers by each daily decision made.

Key Concepts

- Enterprise risk management processes, best practices, and risk treatments (for example, understanding context, identifying risks, analyzing risks, prioritize risks, avoidance, reduction, sharing, retention)

- Approaches to qualitative and quantitative risk assessment (for example, single loss expectancy, annualized loss expectancy)

- Risk sources (for example, project failures, insufficient resources) and types (for example, hazard, financial, operational, strategic)

- Legal and regulatory compliance auditing and investigation techniques (for example, audit or investigation plan, corrective actions)

- Quality assurance techniques and methods (for example, after-action analysis, industry-specific standards)

- Business recovery and continuity-of-operations planning (for example, business continuity and disaster recovery plan, evacuation procedures and simulations)

- Emergency and disaster preparation and response planning (for example, communicable disease, natural disaster, severe weather, terrorism, manufactured disaster, communication mechanisms, evacuation plans)

- Safety and security concerns and prevention (for example, workplace violence, active shooter, theft, fraud, corporate espionage, sabotage, kidnapping and ransom, insider threat, data breach)

- Workplace/occupational injury and illness prevention as well as investigations and workplace solutions (for example, identification of hazards, safety training)

- Approaches to a drug-free workplace (for example, drug testing, treatment of substance abuse)

The following are the proficiency indicators that SHRM has identified for Risk Management:

For All HR Professionals	For Advanced HR Professionals (SCP Exam)
Monitors PESTLE factors and their influence on the organization	Develops, implements, and oversees formal and routinized processes for monitoring the organization's internal and external environments to identify potential risks
Administers and supports HR programs, practices, and policies that identify and/or mitigate workplace risk	Monitors and evaluates labor market, industry, and global trends for their impact on the organization
Implements crisis management as well as contingency and business continuity plans for the HR function and the organization	Examines potential threats to the organization and guides senior leadership accordingly
Communicates critical information about risks and risk mitigation to employees at all levels	Develops, implements, and oversees a comprehensive enterprise risk management strategy
Conducts due diligence investigations to evaluate risks and ensure legal and regulatory compliance	Develops crisis management as well as contingency and business continuity plans for the HR function and the organization
Conducts workplace safety and health-related investigations	Communicates critical information about risks and risk mitigation to senior-level employees and external stakeholders
Audits risk management activities and plans	Ensures that risk management activities and plans are audited and that the results are used to improve risk mitigation strategies
Maintains and ensures accurate reporting of internationally accepted workplace health and safety standards	Oversees workplace safety- and health-related investigations and reporting
Incorporates anticipated level of risk into business cases	Establishes strategies to address workplace retaliation and violence
	Leads after-action debriefs following significant workplace incidents
	Evaluates the anticipated level of risk associated with strategic opportunities

Establishing the Context of Risk

Risk management may impact nearly every aspect of HR management in one way or another. We make an implicit risk management decision in every hiring interview and every performance appraisal discussion. Employee satisfaction can be captured through monitoring of complaints. Safety can be expressed in terms of workers' compensation experience. The cost of employee health benefits is impacted by employer programs that support smoking cessation, exercise, and good diet. Computer security programs can block unauthorized access to confidential employee and business records. All of these issues potentially impact the profit or loss of an employer's organization. Even nonprofits and governmental agencies have budgets they are expected to manage within. Huge, unexpected expenses related to risks can cause instant budget failure. HR professionals can have a great impact on the organizational finances by preventing large losses through proper risk management programs.

Focusing Risk Management

Risk management covers many functional areas in the employment world. Some of them are as follows: complying with federal and state employment laws, identifying workplace hazards, developing safety plans to protect employees and the public, and preparing job descriptions to be used both as a communication tool and as a means to address the physical and mental requirements of each job. Risk management explores how technology can help manage the liability that comes with operating an employment organization. Finally, risk management addresses the rapidly evolving field of social media, Internet, technology, and e-mail use.

There are business risks, and there are employment risks. Risk management addresses issues related to employees, customers, clients, the public, and vendors/suppliers. Risk management is the process of managing liabilities related to these populations in ways that will protect the employer organization and not be so heavy-handed that the organization can't function well in performing its mission. HR professionals are the key to striking a balance in that delicate effort—developing, implementing/administering, and evaluating programs, procedures, and policies to provide a safe, secure working environment and to protect the organization from potential liability. There are lots of exciting things to think about.

Defining Risk

The International Organization for Standardization (ISO) defines risk simply as "the effect of uncertainty on objectives." Risk is the potential for what could happen—either losing or gaining something of value, although most discussions focus on the downside. To be most effective, risk management needs the broadest focus, encompassing risks to strategic goals and to daily operations. Ideally, risk management becomes part of the mindset of all within the organization. "We are all risk managers now," says Tom Mumford, a leader of the engineering firm KBR.[39] As individuals, we value our health, our financial well-being, the people we care for, and our happiness. As organizations, we value investment in our workers' training, worker skills, physical plant, assets such as supplies and product material inventories, customer/employee data, financial records, and community goodwill.

Categories of Risk   Risk comes in many forms and can be related to many different issues. There are risks of decision-making, but there are also risks of standing outside as a target for lightning strikes.

What Is Unknown and What Is Not Known About the Unknowns
Planning for risk management is based on the ability to identify anticipated risks. If you are unable to identify the risks in the future, you are not reasonably able to determine how to mitigate them. The Jahari window is a model of disclosing relationships by identifying what you know and what you do not know. Borrowing from its headers, consider these examples:

Risk Determinations	
Things You Know The union agreement ends on September 30	**Things You Don't Know** Whether or not the union will agree to our proposals
Things You Know You Don't Know The extent of the union demands for benefits	**Things You Don't Know You Don't Know** The surprises that will happen at the bargaining table

Kaplan and Mike's Categories
Robert S. Kaplan and Annette Mikes are two Harvard Business School professors who suggested in a June 2012 *Harvard Business Review*[40] article that risks can be managed using a model containing three categories of risks:

- **Preventable risks**   These are internal risks that are controllable and should be eliminated or avoided. They include illegal, unethical, or inappropriate actions and breakdowns in operational processes. These are manageable through rule-based compliance approaches. The best controls involve active prevention such as monitoring operational processes and guiding people's behaviors and decisions toward desirable norms via policies and training.

- **Strategic risks**   Such risks are identified and accepted in the process of strategic planning. These cannot be managed through a rule-based control model. Instead, it is necessary to reduce the probability that the assumed risks actually materialize and to improve the employer's ability to manage or contain the risk events should they occur.

- **External risks**   These risks generally cannot be prevented from happening. Therefore, organizations should forecast what those risks might be and develop ways in which their impact can be minimized. Using key-player discussions to identify how best to handle such risks will take the form of war gaming (simulations) for the near-term issues or scenario analyses for long-term issues. Both offer value from stepping out of individual and group comfort zones, looking around at the bigger picture, and taking the time to plan for the unexpected.

Enterprise Perspective Risk management can best be performed with an enterprise perspective. Looking at risks solely within a department or division won't reveal the importance of those risks to the entire organization without taking the wider view. When risks are identified, the potential impact on each department can be assessed as well as the impact on the enterprise as a whole. If the risk involves illegal activity, even though only one department is involved, the entire enterprise will be tainted by the bad publicity generated by the bad behavior.

HR and Risk The HR department plays a key role in risk management and mitigation. From benefit program management to employee complaint investigations, HR professionals help protect the employer from serious harm and the employees from abuse.

ISO Principles, Framework, and Process

The International Organization for Standardization (ISO) is based in Geneva, Switzerland and is the world's largest developer and publisher of international standards, with a membership in 2022 of 167 national standards bodies. In the United States, the oversight organization is called the American National Standards Institute. It publishes standards applying to everything from the size of nuts and bolts (ISO 225:2010) to how to measure the cost per hire (ANSI/SHRM 06001.2012).

Establishing the Context of Risk Management

In 2011, the U.S. Department of Homeland Security (DHS) published a paper on its risk management process.[41] It states the following: "It is critical to define the context for the decision that the risk management effort will support. When establishing the context, analysts must understand and document the associated requirements and constraints that will influence the decision making process, as well as key assumptions." Here are the key variables DHS says should be considered:

- **Goals and objectives** Clearly defined goals and objectives are essential to identifying, assessing, and managing those areas that may threaten success.

- **Policies and standards** Ensure that risk management efforts complement and consider any risk management policies, standards, or requirements the organization has in place.

- **Scope and criticality of the decision** The risk analysis and management effort should be commensurate with the criticality of the decision.

- **Decision-makers and stakeholders** These interests should be engaged and represented throughout the risk management process.

- **Decision time frame** The time frame in which a decision must be made and executed will dictate a number of the attributes of the risk management effort, including how much time is available for conducting formal analysis and decision review.

- **Risk management capabilities and resources** At the beginning of the process, it is useful to identify the staff, money, skill sets, knowledge levels, and other resources available for risk analysis and management efforts.

- **Risk tolerance**   Risk management efforts often involve trade-offs between positive and negative outcomes. How much risk taking is acceptable in your culture?
- **Availability and quality of information**   Consider the anticipated data limitations, including expected levels of uncertainty, so decision-makers can adjust their expectations accordingly.

Risk Criteria   According to ISO 31000, risk criteria are terms of reference and are used to evaluate the significance or importance of an organization's risks. They are used to determine whether a specified level of risk is acceptable or tolerable. Risk criteria should reflect your organization's values, policies, and objectives; should be based on its external and internal context; should consider the views of stakeholders; and should be derived from standards, laws, policies, and other requirements.

Moral Hazard   Moral hazard is a situation in which one party gets involved in a risky event knowing that it is protected against the risk (most often by insurance) and the other party will incur the cost. For example, shareholders may want to have managers distribute all profits to them. Managers may be more interested in using profits to increase manager compensation.

Principal-Agent Problem   The problem of motivating one party (the agent) to act on behalf of another (the principal) is known as the *principal-agent problem*. For example, shareholders expect managers to oversee profit generation so distributions can be made to the shareholders. Managers may want to hold back some profits to hedge against future problems involving dropping revenues.

Conflict of Interest   A conflict of interest is a conflict between the private interests and the official responsibilities of a person in a position of trust. For example, a manager is responsible for the impartial selection of vendors to maximize value to the employer, but the manager has a close relative bidding on the contract. Selecting the vendor who is the relative may represent a conflict of interest for the manager.

Identifying and Analyzing Risk

Risk identification is the process of recognizing and defining risks. Risk analysis is the systematic process to comprehend the nature of the risk and to determine the level of risk.

Risk Assessment Phase

Risk assessment involves evaluating and comparing the level of risk against predetermined standards, target risk levels, or other criteria. For example, the risk identified is associated with managers and supervisors sexually harassing someone in the workforce. Compared to a standard of zero tolerance for such behavior, the risk may be deemed to be strong, even if there is only one occurrence.

Identifying Risks

Risk identification is the process of determining risks that could potentially prevent the program, enterprise, or investment from achieving its objectives. For example, an employee complains one manager is sexually harassing employees. The risk has been identified.

Risk Identification Approaches   There are many tools and techniques for risk identification. Here are some of them:

- **Brainstorming**   This is a freewheeling generation of ideas without criticism or evaluation of any ideas until later.

- **Delphi technique**   Here a facilitator distributes a questionnaire to experts, and responses are summarized (anonymously) and circulated among the experts for comments. This technique is used to achieve a consensus of experts and helps to receive unbiased data, ensuring that no one person will have undue influence on the outcome. The experts are not physically together. This process helps to avoid "group think."

- **Interviewing**   This is a discussion with individuals using questions to stimulate responses.

- **Root-cause analysis**   This is for identifying a problem, discovering the causes that led to it, and developing preventive action.

- **Checklist analysis**   This involves comparing each item on the checklist with a set of pre-established criteria.

- **Assumption analysis**   This technique may reveal an inconsistency of assumptions or may uncover problematic assumptions.

- **Diagramming techniques**   This includes cause-and-effect diagrams, system or process flow charts, or influence diagrams (graphical representations of situations, showing the casual influences or relationships among variables and outcomes).

- **SWOT analysis**   This is a structured planning method used to evaluate the strengths, weaknesses, opportunities, and threats (SWOT) involved in a project or in a business venture.

- **Expert judgment**   Individuals who have experience with similar projects may use their judgment through interviews or risk facilitation workshops.

Analyzing Risks

Risk analysis involves evaluating vulnerable assets, describing potential impacts, and estimating losses for each hazard. When you buy common stocks, you do so in the hopes their value increases while understanding the potential exists for them to lose some or all of their value.

Risk Analysis Tools   It is helpful to have some tools with which to assess risks to your organization. The following are some of the more popular tools available.

Risk Scorecard   The U.S. Army Materiel Systems Analysis Activity (AMSAA) is an analysis organization of the United States Army. AMSAA developed a "reliability scorecard" that uses eight critical areas to evaluate a given program's reliability progress.

Each element within a category can be given a risk rating of high, medium, or low (red, yellow, or green) or not evaluated (gray). The scorecard weights the elements, normalizes the scores to a 100-point scale, and calculates an overall program risk score and eight risk scores:

- Reliability requirements and planning
- Training and development
- Reliability analysis
- Reliability testing
- Supply chain management
- Failure tracking and reporting
- Verification and validation
- Reliability improvements

Risk Matrix   A simplified example, using a single element from the previous list, is shown here:

Overall Risk Assessment		
Reliability Risk	0–25%	25–75%	75–100%
	Low Risk	Medium Risk	High Risk

In general terms, risks can be classified as low, moderate, high, or extreme, as shown next:

		Impact			
		Negligible	**Marginal**	**Critical**	**Catastrophic**
	Certain	High	High	Extreme	Extreme
	Likely	Moderate	High	High	Extreme
	Possible	Low	Moderate	High	Extreme
Likelihood	**Unlikely**	Low	Low	Moderate	Extreme
	Rare	Low	Low	Moderate	High

Evaluating Risks

A risk evaluation system is a combination of practices, tools, and methodologies within a risk management system used to measure the potential impacts of risk events on the performance metrics of an organization. Therefore, evaluating risks is the act of measuring potential impacts that various risks will have on the organization's ability to accomplish its objectives. For example, you can identify a risk as the possibility of a work stoppage when the union contract expires. Evaluation of that risk can tell you how well you may expect to keep your business operating using only management personnel during the strike.

Key Risk Indicators

A *key risk indicator (KRI)* is a measure that indicates how risky an activity is. It is different from a key performance indicator (KPI). The KRI indicates the possibility of a future adverse impact. A KPI measures how well something is being done. KRIs are metrics used to monitor identified risk exposures over time. Therefore, any piece of data that can perform this function may be considered a risk indicator. The indicator becomes "key" when it tracks an especially important risk exposure (a key risk) or it does so especially well (a key indicator), or ideally both. An example is the forecasting of the financial impact of expanding the workforce into international offices in multiple countries. Will that be repaid with profits over time, or will it interfere with profitability? Then, how can HR management impact those potential results?

Risk Register

A risk register acts as a central repository for all risks identified by the organization and, for each risk, includes information such as source, nature, treatment option, existing countermeasures, recommended countermeasures, and so on. ISO 73:2009, "Risk management – Vocabulary," defines a risk register to be "a record of information about identified risks. It can sometimes be referred to as a risk log." Check with your legal counsel on the advisability of created such a log prior to doing so.

Managing Risks

Once risks have been identified and logged, the next logical step is planning for handling those risks believed to bring negative impacts on the enterprise that cannot be accepted.

Responses to Upside and Downside Risks

Upside and downside risks are two sides of the same coin. Possible adverse outcomes represent downside risk. When there is uncertainty about a desirable outcome, there is upside risk.

Eliminate Uncertainty   Risk can be managed if the uncertainty is eliminated. If you know there will be an undesirable outcome, there is no risk. It is a certainty. You simply avoid entering into the activity that will produce that outcome because you know it will take place. If someone sets fire to a building, that person knows for a fact the fire will happen. There is no risk; there's simply an undesirable outcome. If you can eliminate the uncertainty of an event, you can control the risk. Usually eliminating all uncertainty is not an option.

Redefine Ownership   Only the person or organization that owns the circumstances will own the risk. If you can redefine ownership of the problem, you can reduce your risk exposure. Here are two possibilities for doing so:

- **Share**   Sharing the risk of being an employer can be done, for example, by entering into a joint-employer relationship with an employment leasing agency, sometimes called a *professional employer organization (PEO)*. That won't eliminate risk for either party, but it will double the resources available to combat whatever risk may exist because of having an employee workforce.

- **Transfer** Transferring risk is done by purchasing insurance policies. Employers are able to reduce their exposure to employee liability through the purchase of employment liability insurance. It can lower the potential for financial loss when employees are found to have engaged in inappropriate behaviors, such as harassment, for example. It is much the same as purchasing fire insurance to protect against financial loss if there is a fire in the workplace.

Increase or Decrease Effect A way to decrease the effect of fire in the workplace is to install a water sprinkler system. This way, if a fire does happen, the sprinkler system can limit the damage from or the effect of the fire. Employee training programs can act in the same way. Teaching employees about the dangers of harassing behavior can help reduce their personal exposure to liability while at the same time lowering the employer's liability exposure.

Take No Action In most circumstances, when faced with various possible courses of action, one of those options is to take no action. When a risk is identified and defined, it may be judged to be in the best interest of the organization to do nothing. Usually this is considered if the impact expected would be minimal or the level of certainty for the outcome is low. In the case, the options are as follows:

- **Accept** "We will take the risk" is sometimes heard, meaning the decision is to take no action to eliminate the hazard and just wait to see how things develop. If a safety hazard is identified that would not cause serious harm and can be repaired within the near future, it may be best to simply identify the risk by putting out orange cones, for example, rather than prohibiting all access to the area. Remediation of the hazard will take place in time. The risk of injury is minimal, and the level of certainty can be lowered by putting out the cones.
- **Ignore** When a safety hazard is identified, considered, and ignored, there is no credence given to the level of risk or the certainty of loss. Think about the air bag failures that Takata Industries ignored for several years. That was a decision that didn't work out so well for the company.

Implementing the Risk Management Plan

A risk management plan results from analysis of the circumstances that foresees risks, estimates impacts, and defines responses to issues.

Defining Risk Management Performance Objectives All business enterprise exists in the world of balancing risks and rewards to produce value. Risk management performance objectives should be part of the overall list of performance objectives generated at each level of the organization. Just like equal employment opportunity (EEO) compliance or time reporting, risk management for each component of the organization should be identified by those responsible for the component/department/division.

Integration Is our risk management process aligned with our strategic decision-making process and existing performance measures? Is our risk management process coordinated and consistent across the entire enterprise?

Communication   Does everyone use the same definition of risk? Are all employees involved in some way with the risk management process, sensing a degree of owner-ship that will result in organizational success? Proper risk management plans will involve employees in training programs and daily discussions, if only brief, about the "risks facing us today." These are sometimes called *tailgate meetings,* where safety topics are common. Tailgate meetings typically only last 5 or 10 minutes, and then everyone is off to do their work for the day. At higher levels of the enterprise, the topic of risk management should be present on each staff meeting agenda. That way, it becomes a common topic of conversa-tion, and everyone begins to take some level of ownership in the results.

Emergency Preparedness and Business Continuity

A primary safety axiom is that proper planning can save lives and property. It is a good idea to have a written plan specifying what actions will be taken in any of many various scenarios. There are some basic alternatives for dealing with a disaster, large or small.

We are talking about the entire universe of emergency planning.

Crisis Management Planning and Readiness Process   The first step toward having an emergency response plan is to conduct a risk assessment for your work location. Look at the physical facilities, emergency exits, fire suppression systems, electrical and gas shut-off access, hazardous materials used in the workplace, protective equip-ment needed for operations, employee training for special equipment, use of proper lock-out/tag-out procedures when working on electrical equipment, ease of access and departure from the site, and proper handling of carcinogenic substances such as copy machine toner. Answer hypothetical questions such as, "What would we do if someone with a gun walked through our front door?"

Engage key personnel in the development process. Ask people on the production line and in the office what they would do in some circumstances. Get input from experts and nonexperts alike. Then list the responses that should happen for each emergency you listed.

Finally, once the plan is developed, be sure everyone in the workplace knows about it and what to do if an emergency happens.

Manage Risk   Initially, it is important to identify the risks. Then you can move on to identifying how to deal with them effectively. So, what types of risks are we concerned with in the world of human resource management, and what type of involvement does HR have with those risks?

Types of Organizational Risks	
Type of Risk	**HR Involvement**
Safety Risks	Develop safety plans, routine workplace inspections, corrective action oversight, employee training, and insurance company interface.
• Injury hazards	
• Illness hazards	
• Workplace violence hazards	
• Transportation disaster (loss of multiple employee/executive personnel)	

Types of Organizational Risks

Type of Risk	HR Involvement
Equipment Risks • Production failures • Protection failures	Inclusion in safety plans, production line procedures when failure occurs, and inclusion of protection failure issues in safety plans.
Facility Risks • Systems failure (heating/cooling/sprinklers) • Security access failure	Provision for action plans in the event of system failures, anticipation of security issues, and preventative measures.
Employment Risks • Background check/wrongful hiring • Wrongful retention • Employee behavior problems (harassment/discrimination/embezzlement/ethics failure) • Loss of key personnel	Establish criteria for screening new hires' background/behavior issues, prepare procedures for handling behavior problems and termination procedures and discuss with executives about scenario involving loss of key personnel.
Employee-as-Agent Risks • Management interaction with public • Community involvement	Discuss with or train all managers in the legal agent-relationship definition and how they can represent the organization in community groups.
Business Risks • Business continuation • Data security (employee records/customer records/financial records) • Government intervention	Ensure essential records backup, including employee, payroll, medical, investigation, and complaint records. Work with finance and sales/marketing to cover preservation of financial and customer records (orders). Create a plan to preserve HR records when government agencies audit the organization.
Natural Disaster Risks • Fire, volcanic eruptions • Flood (rising or falling water), tsunamis, hurricanes and tropical storms • Earthquake, tornado • Temperature (heat or cold) • Drought	Develop procedures for reacting to natural disasters with differences based on the type of disaster.
International Risks • Differences in laws • Differences in customs	Identify the differences in legal response requirements by country. Identify the expectations of each country's customs during disaster responses.

Develop Contingency Plans If there is a flood or fire and your workplace is destroyed, the computers, hard drives, onsite backup systems, and filing cabinets may no longer be available. How will you open your business tomorrow morning?

Employers must have a plan for how they will continue operating their organization. What about customer records, accounting records, client data, and payroll information?

This is an area of responsibility where HR professionals should work with others in the organization, such as professionals in information technology (IT) and accounting. It should be common practice for backups to be made of all technology systems, especially a human resource information system (HRIS). Also, those backups, or at least duplicates of them, should be stored offsite at some secure location. It is necessary for the survival of your organization that it be able to continue operations as quickly as possible with all the records it requires for that to happen.

How will you communicate to employees where they should report to work after such a disaster? Do you plan to use e-mail, text messages, or telephone calls to contact everyone and pass along instructions? How will you keep supervisors and managers informed? Who will handle media inquiries about the disaster and your plans for the future?

Test and Implement Plans   A key element of disaster recovery is practicing the contingent plan to see whether it will actually work. That's what fire drills are all about. People in the military constantly gripe about having to drill all the time. Those drills are nothing more than rehearsals for the time that the actual event will happen and the practiced behavior responses will become essential. The same holds true for civilian organizations. Employees need to practice evacuating their work location so they know for sure which exit they should use and what their assigned rallying point is once outside the building. If there is a disaster involving the loss of key personnel, an emergency response plan should be activated. Ideally, it will have been rehearsed so everyone involved understands their roles and how to play them. Who will be the spokesperson for the company when media representatives come asking for answers to their questions? Who will be responsible for interacting with government officials if that becomes necessary? Who will be guiding the instruction of managers and distributing information to the general employee group?

Debrief and Learn   Make plans and then test them by rehearsing. Evaluate the results of the rehearsal and adjust the plans based on those experiences. Identify where improvements can be made and then make them. Debriefing is the process of meeting to discuss what happened during the practice exercise. Debriefing should gather input from individuals as well as the collective input of managers and employees.

Debriefing is the opportunity to be sure all of the communication channels are open and working accurately. Are all telephone number lists up to date? Are other contact points noted and verified? What are the emergency contact points for government resources (fire/ambulance/police/sheriff)? If the plan involves coordination with other organizations, they should be represented in the debriefing session so their input can be gathered and evaluated.

Evaluating Risk Management

At least once per year, all formal risk management plans should be reviewed and adjusted if it is thought necessary. Those reviews are usually chaired by either the chief HR officer or the chief legal officer in the organization.

Providing Oversight

The role of risk management oversight is commonly assumed by the board of directors. It applies to all forms of risk for the entire enterprise. Since the board is the organizational element responsible for the overall success of the company, identifying how risk management is being handled becomes a key element of the board's responsibilities.

Evaluating Effectiveness of Risk Management Policies and Processes

Obviously, the most effective feedback or evaluation comes from having actually experienced the danger (risk) that plans had been developed to address. When disaster strikes, debriefing sessions or critique meetings should be held to establish what worked well and what needs improvement.

Healthy organizations will conduct periodic tests of their risk management plans through exercises designed to probe every element of reaction to the problem anticipated. There should be critique sessions held following each test to determine what updates should be made to the plans. Then, after a reasonable interval, the plans should be tested again. Some plans (evacuation/earthquake/shelter-in-place) should be tested quarterly. Other plans can be tested once a year, or even less frequently. Some tests can be as simple as the CEO walking into an executive staff meeting and announcing that a test scenario will be run in which the top five executives of the enterprise have all been killed in a plane crash. What will the remaining employees do as a result of hearing "The exercise begins now"? Tests of risk management plans must be customized to the plan.

After-Action Debriefs and Incidents Investigations   How to determine the effectiveness of risk management plan test exercises depends on what the plan involves. Fire reactions and building evacuation can be evaluated by using a stopwatch and exercise referees who keep track of when each group of employees has assembled at their emergency contact point outside the building. When testing plans for handling embezzlement or product failure/recalls, the exercise will not be as dramatic. However, it should be evaluated after it has completed to determine whether people followed the plan and what issues they discovered need improvement.

If the employee arriving first one morning finds an alligator sitting on the building's front porch blocking the normal route employees use to enter the building, a risk management response is needed. Clearly you cannot and ought not spend your time pre-thinking an infinite number of issues that could happen. The reaction may be as simple as directing workers (from a safe distance) to a different entrance and calling animal control. However, the point is the incident demands a response to prevent serious harm to humans. After-incident investigations can shed light on how well a plan worked and people reacted. If the plan was good but people didn't implement it properly, there may be a training need. More frequent practice could be called for. The investigation should provide direction for resolving any remaining issues.

Whistleblowing   When a whistleblower reports inappropriate behavior going on within the organization, it can result in a public relations nightmare. One of the conditions for which emergency plans are prepared should be disclosure of bad behavior, such as a cover-up of illegal activity or simply behavior that is ethically wrong and embarrassing to the employer. What can be made of the story by media representatives will be potentially damaging to the company. Someone will need to be positioned to speak for the company on such issues. There needs to be a predesignated group of key employees who will decide quickly how to address the problem and explain the company's reaction to it when addressing the media.

Evaluating Compliance

Compliance with government regulatory requirements is a complex realm. There are compliance requirements for many different topics, as shown in the following table.

Examples of Government Compliance Issues	
Government contracts for providing service	Government contracts for construction (buildings/roads/dams)
Government contracts for selling goods (pencils/jet engines/Brussels sprouts)	Government requirements for safety reporting
Requirements for logging driving hours for over-the-road truckers	Requirements for logging batch identifications for drug manufacturers
Requirements for handling of meat in slaughterhouses	Labeling requirements for food processors
"Organic" produce category requirements	Bus driver licensing
Health ordinance requirements for restaurants	Banking requirements for cash-handling limits
IRS requirements for tax records and reporting	Affirmative action requirements for government contractors
Employee demographic reporting requirements on EEO-1/EEO-4	Wage and hour requirements/prohibitions for child labor
Minimum wage requirements	ERISA compliance for retirement and welfare plans

Promoting Continuous Improvement

In 1985, Tom Peters authored a book titled *Thriving on Chaos*.[42] In it, he highlighted the Japanese management concept of *Kaizen*, the never-ending quest for perfection. American managers have retitled the concept as *continuous improvement*. Whatever it is called, the idea is to strive each day for a little better quality, quantity, and effort. Peters became famous for, among other things, his suggestion that management by walking around (MBWA) was the most effective approach and produced the greatest positive organizational results. Managers can't be expected to think of everything, and those who work directly with the process are best able to identify how improvements can be made. Employees are truly the best resource for identifying better ways of doing things.

Functional Area 13: Corporate Social Responsibility

Here is SHRM's BASK definition: "Corporate Social Responsibility (CSR) represents the organization's commitment to operate ethically and contribute to economic development while improving the quality of life of the workforce and their families as well as of the local and global community."[43]

As an HR professional your role is to help the organization and its employees to integrate corporate social responsibility (CSR) into the everyday business activities of the organization. CSR reflects how the organization integrates and aligns with its communities as a helping hand for sustaining economic prosperity, social equity, and environmental protection.

Key Concepts

- HR-related activities that support sustainability (for example, human rights, safety practices, labor standards, performance development, diversity, equity and inclusion, compensation, supply chain management)
- Organizational philosophies and policies (for example, development, integration, shared value)
- Steps to implement CSR strategy (for example, developing a business case, obtaining executive approval, selecting recipients, identifying and analyzing performance indicators, recruiting and organizing participants)
- Approaches to community inclusion and engagement (for example, representation on community boards, joint community projects, employee volunteerism)

The following are the proficiency indicators that SHRM has identified as key concepts:

For All HR Professionals	For Advanced HR Professionals (SCP Exam)
Acts as a professional role model and representative of the organization when interacting with the community	Develops a CSR strategy that reflects the organization's mission and values
Identifies and promotes opportunities for HR and the organization to engage in CSR activities that align with the organization's CSR strategy	Coordinates with business leaders to integrate CSR objectives throughout the organization
Identifies opportunities to incorporate environmentally and socially responsible business practices and shares them with leadership	Coordinates with business leaders to develop and implement appropriate levels of corporate self-governance and transparency
Helps staff at all levels understand the societal impact of business decisions and the role of the organization's CSR strategy in improving the community	Partners with business leaders to develop strategies that encourage and support environmentally and socially responsible business decisions
Maintains transparency of HR programs, practices, and policies, where appropriate	Aligns CSR activities with the organization's CSR strategy and engages the organization's workforce and the community at large
Coaches managers to achieve an appropriate level of transparency in organizational practices and decisions	Uses metrics to measure and report how the organization's CSR programs enhance the employee value proposition, positively impact HR programs, or contribute to the organization's competitive advantage

The Ever-Changing and Growing CSR

HR can no longer see CSR as an isolated defensive or tactical action. CSR is now seen as a comprehensive strategic initiative for the organization, aligned with business strategy. CSR now has a global reach and impact, enriching and broadening its communities and beyond. As cultural and political landscapes and opinion shift, so does the need for CSR in an organization.

Is Sustainability the New CSR?

Sustainability practice is in every aspect of doing business today and needs to be ingrained in an organization's culture, becoming an ongoing process and way of doing business. Sustainability is a key focus for many organizations as government and regulatory pressures, societal demands, and even climate change have increased its demands on companies. For organizations, this means a conscious way of doing business and how it impacts their communities, employees, and environments. In addition, businesses must assess social and environmental risks and opportunities with their business decisions.

This approach is referred to as the *triple bottom line,* which focuses on the "three Ps" of positive results for people, the planet, and profit. These three Ps represent the environment (planet), economic success (profits), and social health, safety, and well-being (people). Sustainability, such as environmental stewardship, workplace responsibility, human rights protection, and good corporate citizenship are increasingly part of an organization's social legitimacy. The HR function is critical to achieving success in a sustainability-driven organization.

Redefining Sustainability

Sustainability and the associated accountability efforts within sustainability (behavior that is cognizant of depleting resources that the organization is intertwined with) have also become front and center for CSR. Time, labor, and finances are where HR is involved with the design or implementation of programs. An example of a program would be re-entry into the workforce by former stay-at-home parents. "Green initiatives" along with "environmental footprints" are now prime attention grabbers within CSR. HR departments reducing their paper printing needs by converting to online paperless activities such as employment and benefit forms, employee handbooks, and newsletters are green initiatives. Creation of a paid-time-off volunteerism policy for employees is another popular CSR initiative.

Today's CSR

Corporate social responsibility involves keeping a watchful eye within the organization's communities, including local, national, and even international. CSR strives to enhance the organization's reputation. Strategic relationship and behaviors are elements involved in CSR activities, such as being a member of the Chamber of Commerce or sponsoring a local nonprofit fundraiser, thus creating a *corporate citizenship.* Multiple departments may have responsibility, yet HR is typically the department primarily at the core, absent an organization's official CSR or public relations department.

Forces Shaping Today's CSR

The external forces that typically drive goals and objectives in CSR can be better understood by looking at Figure 6-1.

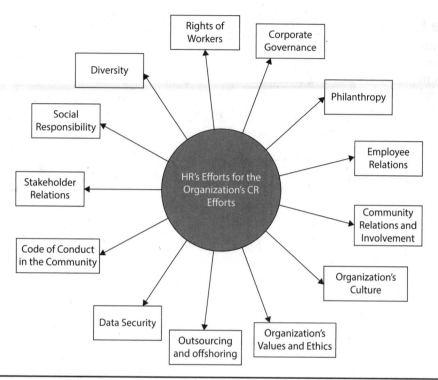

Figure 6-1 Corporate Social Responsibility

According to McKinsey & Company, when identifying the goals and objectives for CSR, it is ideal to use the same analysis tools as used with strategic planning to identify the long-term investment and involvement for the organization.

Creating a CSR Strategy

As mentioned, the CSR of an organization needs to be carefully aligned with the organization's business goals and strategies. As with all strategy initiatives, careful planning must be undertaken. Research into frameworks and existing benchmarks should be involved, and so should the reports of CSR initiatives.

Frameworks, Guidelines, and Examples

Gaining a clear perspective of the work is the best starting point for developing a CSR strategy. Several international organizations have provided frameworks and templates, along with guidance for organizations:

- The Global Reporting Initiatives' G4 Guidelines
- The United Nations Global Compact, which developed a broad statement of principles on which a CSR strategy can be based

- The International Organization for Standardization and Social Accountability International (SAI), which created standards addressing specific sustainability issues and social responsibilities

The most widely accepted frameworks and guidelines are briefly described next. Although this are a good starting point to develop your organization's CSR strategy, be sure to tailor it to your organization's industry and unique environments. Review your CSR annually and benchmark it against those of similar organizations.

OECD Guidelines for Multinational Enterprises   The Guidelines for Multinational Enterprises established in 1976 by the Organisation for Economic Co-operation and Development (OECD) is one of the first to address corporate governance. Since 1976, the guidelines have had many revisions and are updated regularly. The OECD guidelines cover the following:

- Transparency governance and disclosure
- Environment
- Consumer interests
- Workforce relations
- Bribery
- Science and technology application and access

United Nations Global Compact   Introduced in 2000, the United Nations Global Compact has ten principles addressing human rights, labour, environmental, and anticorruption issues. When an organization commits to uphold these principles, it also agrees to annually report on the progress, including specific actions taken.[44]

The UN Global Compact's Ten Principles

Human Rights
> Principle 1: Businesses should support and respect the protection of internationally proclaimed human rights.
> Principle 2: Make sure they are not complicit in human rights abuses.

Labour
> Principle 3: Businesses should uphold the freedom of association and the effective recognition of the right to collective bargaining.
> Principle 4: Eliminate all forms of forced and compulsory labour.
> Principle 5: Abolish child labour.
> Principle 6: Eliminate discrimination in respect to employment and occupation.

Environment
> Principle 7: Businesses are asked to support a precautionary approach to environmental challenges.

Principle 8: Undertake initiatives to promote greater environmental responsibility.

Principle 9: Encourage the development and diffusion of environmentally friendly technologies.

Anti-Corruption

Principle 10: Businesses should work against corruption in all its forms, including extortion and bribery.

Caux Principles   The Caux Round Table (CRT) principles believe that the world business community should play an important role in improving economic and social conditions. In 1986, a network of business leaders from Japan, Europe, and the United States (aka the Caux Round Table members) began meeting because of mounting trade tensions. In 1994, they developed and formalized a set of international business standards based on the values of human dignity and working together for the common good. These became known as the *Caux principles,* which was one of the earliest employer-led efforts for an international code of ethics. The key Caux principles[45] are as follows:

- **Principle 1: Respect stakeholders beyond shareholders.** Contribute value to society and act with honesty and fairness toward customers, suppliers, competitors, employees, and the community.

- **Principle 2: Contribute to economic, social, and environmental development.** Maintain investments in the community and its economy that support the environment and social well-being as well as organizational income.

- **Principle 3: Build trust by going beyond the letter of the law.** Know the spirit and intent of the law and abide by them rather than just the letter of the law.

- **Principle 4: Respect rules and conventions.** Respect local cultures and traditions everywhere the organization operates.

- **Principle 5: Support responsible globalization.** Perhaps the most controversial of the Caux principles, this calls for reforming domestic rules and regulations where they impinge upon global commerce. It supports open and fair multilateral trade.

- **Principle 6: Respect the environment.** Protect environmental needs while conducting business so the next generations will have the advantage of a secure planet.

- **Principle 7: Avoid illicit activities.** Corruption of all kinds, bribery, money laundering, drug trafficking, human trafficking, and other illegal and illicit activities are not condoned.

ISO 26000   The ISO is the world's largest developer of voluntary international standards. ISO 26000 is the international standard developed to help organizations effectively assess and address those social responsibilities that are relevant and significant to their mission and vision; operations and processes; customers, employees, communities, and other stakeholders; and the environment. ISO 26000 provides guidance on key themes of social responsibility across a wide spectrum of topics; it's a quality standard, though not a certification. The principles have social and environmental responsibility and guidance for action/implementation. ISO 26000 addresses seven core subjects of social responsibility (Organizational Governance, Human Rights, Labor Practices, Environment, Fair Operating Practices, Consumer Issues, and Community Involvement and Development), as shown in Figure 6-2.[46]

SA8000   Social Accountability International (SAI) is the international nongovernmental organization that created SA8000, which is an auditable certification standard that encourages organizations to develop, maintain, and apply socially acceptable practices in the workplace. It is one of the first certification standards (1997), focusing on human rights and labor relationship, which provides process and performance criteria. It is based on both United Nations and International Labour Organization (ILO) standards.

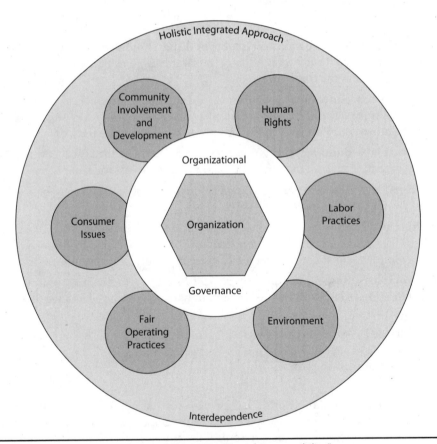

Figure 6-2   The seven core subjects of ISO 26000, "Social Responsibility"

Over 4750 facilities with approximately 2.1 million employees around the globe have adopted SA8000, and as of the third quarter of 2021,[47] 55 countries and 57 industries are represented. It is frequently used as a tool for ensuring human rights in extended supply chains (aka slave labor). It not only focuses on standards of performance but also on systems that need to be in place for management. Nine elements comprise the SA8000 standard:

- Child labor
- Forced or compulsory labor
- Health and safety
- Freedom of association and right to collective bargaining
- Discrimination
- Disciplinary practices
- Working hours
- Remuneration
- Management systems

GRI G4 Sustainability Reporting Guidelines The Global Reporting Initiative (GRI) G4 Sustainability Guidelines are the universally accepted standard for global reporting on a company's sustainability effort and progress. The main goal is for organizations to identify and report on a business's economic, environmental, and social impacts that influence the decisions of its stakeholders. The guidelines are divided into two parts:

- Reporting Principles and Standard Disclosures (criteria for preparing the sustainability reporting)
- Implementation Manual (explanations for applying the principles for the reporting)

The GRI has other supplementary guidelines, listed here:

- Assistance with G4 efforts.
- Guidelines for specific business sectors. Examples include oil and gas, financial services, food processing, and media.
- Interactive guides that are online for assisting with specific concerns and issues such as risk management and supply chain.
- A sustainability disclosure database providing URL links to corporate CSR reports and scorecards.

The G4 list is organized into the categories[48] listed here:

The G4 Sustainability Reporting Guidelines: Categories	
Category: Economic	**Category: Environmental**
1. Economic Performance 2. Market Presence 3. Indirect Economic Impacts 4. Procurement Practices 5. Anticorruption 6. Anticompetitive Behavior	1. Materials 2. Energy 3. Water and Effluents 4. Biodiversity 5. Emissions 6. Effluents and Waste 7. Environmental Compliance 8. Supplier Environmental Assessment

Subcategory: Human Rights	Subcategory: Labor Practices and Decent Work	Subcategory: Product Responsibility	Subcategory: Society
1. Assessment 2. Child Labor 3. Forced or Compulsory Labor 4. Freedom of Association & Collective Bargaining 5. Human Rights Grievance Mechanisms 6. Indigenous Rights 7. Investment 8. Non-discrimination 9. Security Practices 10. Supplier Human Rights Assessment	1. Diversity and Equal Opportunity 2. Employment 3. Equal Remuneration for Women & Men 4. Labor Grievance Mechanisms 5. Labor/ Management Relations 6. Occupational Health & Safety 7. Supplier Assessment for Labor Practices 8. Training & Education	1. Compliance 2. Customer Health & Safety 3. Customer Privacy 4. Marketing Communications 5. Product & Service Labeling	1. Anticompetitive Behavior 2. Anticorruption 3. Compliance 4. Grievance Mechanisms for Impacts on Society 5. Local Communities 6. Public Policy 7. Supplier Assessment for Impacts on Society

KPMG Survey of Corporate Responsibility Reporting KPMG has been tracking the trends in corporate responsibility reporting since 1993. KPMG provides a detailed examination of what is being reported and the quality of the reporting. KPMG reporting is helpful with the following:

- Identifying areas that organizations need to address and how to report on and measure the results and outcomes.

- Providing support in making the business case for a sustainability strategy for an organization. This section of the reporting has interviews with industry leaders who discuss how to best maximize the value of sustainability.

You can find more information on KPMG reporting surveys at www.kpmg.com.

Philanthropy and Volunteerism

Corporate philanthropy has been around for decades and was typically the influence of senior management within a corporation. Although corporate philanthropic activities such as monetary donations, percentage of sale, and cooperative programs are still widely in existence, the tide has shifted to a more strategic focus on donations, one that affiliates with the organization's relevant business or branding. A good example of this is the cosmetic company Avon, which is widely known as a corporate sponsor for breast cancer research. The company's customer base is relevant to the majority of affected individuals with breast cancer, women.

Employee Volunteerism

One aspect of CSR is employee volunteerism. It has been growing in popularity in organizations, and for good reason. Volunteerism can positively impact employee engagement. Surveys have indicated that when employees frequently participate in company-sponsored volunteer programs, they are more likely to feel a strong connection and sense of belonging at work, which is good for engagement and retention. While volunteering sounds like a win-win for everyone, in practice there can be some pitfalls that HR professionals should avoid. Be clear and communicate ahead of time if the volunteer time will be paid or not and ensure that the activities are truly voluntary.

A risk for employers centers around Fair Labor Standards Act (FLSA) compliance. An employer cannot require an employee to "volunteer." As an example, let's say a company organizes a disaster relief effort for a community recently hit by a hurricane and asks for employees to volunteer to help hand out water and blankets or provide meals. If getting involved is truly voluntary, then that is perfectly fine. But once it's required of any employee, the employee is no longer a volunteer, and it's considered time on the payroll clock. Companies sometimes get so caught up in pushing employees to get involved that they cross this line, even though their intentions are good. A firm choosing to pay employees for their service time solves this compliance issue.

Another related risk for for-profit companies is that there is no such thing as "volunteering" for a for-profit company. If the company "suffers or permits" an employee to work, the employee has to be paid at least minimum wage under FLSA. This issue has shown up recently related to the use of unpaid interns.

Organizations need a program and policy around volunteerism so employees and management completely tow the FLSA line and understand what can and should not be expected of the workforce. Without a policy, there can be misunderstandings and ill will on the part of employees. Having a policy or process helps to clarify expectations.

Functional Area 14: U.S. Employment Laws & Regulations

Here is SHRM's BASK definition: "U.S. Employment Law and Regulations refers to the knowledge and application of all relevant laws and regulations in the United States related to employment—provisions that set the parameters and limitations for each HR functional area and for organizations overall."[49]

As an HR professional, you are responsible for the compliance and alignment with employment laws and regulations for your HR programs and policies. You may be educating the workforce and leadership, coaching executives on various matters and options, and tracking compliance with required reporting. It's one of the most important focuses of the HR professional in an organization. For doing business in the United States, this knowledge is vital. If you do not want to be tested on this information, schedule your exam at a test center outside of the United States. This Functional Area 14 content is not included outside of the USA.

Key Concepts

The key concepts within this functional area are grouped into seven broad categories of U.S. laws, regulations, and Supreme Court cases relating to employment, as listed next. The examples listed here from the SHRM BASK[50] do not comprise an exhaustive list, nor do the categories. Please refer to Appendix B in this book for case law by chapter. Also know that state, municipal, and other local-level laws, regulations, and state court cases are not included because they will not be tested on the SHRM-CP exam nor on the SHRM-SCP exam.

- **Employment and authorization to work** For example, Immigration Reform and Control Act of 1986, Form I-9 and E-Verify, green cards and visa types (examples include H-1B, F-1), employment at will, background checks, Fair Credit Reporting Act of 1970 (FCRA), Deferred Action for Childhood Arrivals policy

- **Compensation** For example, Davis-Bacon Act of 1931, Walsh-Healey Public Contracts Act of 1936, Fair Labor Standards Act of 1938 (FLSA, Wage-Hour Bill, Wagner-Connery Wages and Hours Act) and amendments, including the 2020 overtime rule, Equal Pay Act of 1963 (amending FLSA), McNamara-O'Hara Service Contract Act of 1965, Employee Retirement Income Security Act of 1974 (ERISA), Affordable Care Act's Break Time for Nursing Mothers (2010), Lilly Ledbetter Fair Pay Act of 2009, Ledbetter v. Goodyear Tire & Rubber Co. (2007)

- **Employee relations** For example, National Labor Relations Act of 1935 (NLRA, Wagner Act, Wagner-Connery Labor Relations Act), Labor Management Relations Act of 1947 (LMRA, Taft-Hartley Act), Labor-Management Reporting and Disclosure Act of 1959 (LMRDA) and amendments, Electronic Communications Privacy Act of 1986, Worker Adjustment and Retraining Notification Act of 1988 (WARN), Employee Polygraph Protection Act of 1988, NLRB v. Weingarten (1975), Lechmere, Inc. v. NLRB (1992)

- **Job safety and health** For example, Occupational Safety and Health Act of 1970 (OSHA), Drug-Free Workplace Act of 1988, Health Insurance Portability and Accountability Act of 1996 (HIPAA), guidelines on sexual harassment, Workers' Compensation

- **Equal employment opportunity**   For example, Civil Rights Acts of 1964, including Title VII, Executive Order 11246 of 1965, Age Discrimination in Employment Act of 1967 (ADEA) and amendments, Equal Employment Opportunity Act of 1972, Rehabilitation Act of 1973, including sections 501 and 503, Vietnam Era Veterans' Readjustment Assistance Act of 1974, Uniform Guidelines on Employee Selection Procedures (29 CFR Part 1607) (1978), Pregnancy Discrimination Act of 1978 (PDA), Americans with Disabilities Act of 1990 (ADA) and amendments, Genetic Information Nondiscrimination Act of 2008 (GINA), Executive Order 13672 (2014), Griggs v. Duke Power Co. (1971), Phillips v. Martin Marietta Corp. (1971), McDonnell Douglas Corp. v. Green (1973)

- **Leave and benefits**   For example, Consolidated Omnibus Budget Reconciliation Act of 1985 (COBRA), Family and Medical Leave Act of 1993 (FMLA, expanded 2008, 2010). Uniformed Services Employment and Reemployment Rights Act of 1994 (USERRA), Patient Protection and Affordable Care Act (PPACA), including rules for breaks and lactation rooms for nursing mothers, Americans with Disabilities Act of 1990 (ADA) and amendments, including leave as a reasonable accommodation, EEOC v. Verizon (2011), National Federation of Independent Business v. Sebelius (2012)

- **Miscellaneous**   For example, drug screening, medical marijuana

The following are the proficiency indicators that SHRM has identified for U.S. Employment Laws and Regulations:

For All HR Professionals	For Advanced HR Professionals (SCP Exam)
Maintains a current working knowledge of relevant domestic and global employment laws	Maintains current, expert knowledge of relevant domestic and global employment laws
Ensures that HR programs, practices, and policies align and comply with laws and regulations	Establishes and monitors criteria for organizational compliance with laws and regulations
Coaches employees at all levels in understanding and avoiding illegal and noncompliant HR-related behaviors (for example, illegal terminations or discipline, unfair labor practices)	Educates and advises leadership on HR-related legal and regulatory compliance issues
Brokers internal or external legal services for interpretation of employment laws	Oversees fulfillment of compliance requirements of HR programs, practices, and policies
	Ensures that HR technologies facilitate compliance and reporting requirements (for example, tracking employee accidents, safety reports)

SHRM-
SCP

PART II

Organizational Compliance

Compliance is a necessary expense for employers, both in and out of the federal contracting world. In the first few years of this century, the federal government has enacted the following rules regarding employee management. You can find all of these explained in Chapter 3.

- 2000: The Needlestick Safety and Prevention Act
- 2001: The Economic Growth and Tax Relief Reconciliation Act
- 2001: The USA Patriot Act
- 2002: The IRS Intermediate Sanctions
- 2002: The Sarbanes-Oxley Act
- 2002: The Homeland Security Act
- 2003: The Fair and Accurate Credit Transactions Act
- 2006: The Pension Protection Act
- 2008: Jobs for Veterans Act
- 2008: Americans with Disabilities Act Amendments Act
- 2008: The Genetic Information Nondiscrimination Act
- 2008: The Mental Health Parity and Addiction Equity Act
- 2008: The National Defense Authorization Act
- 2009: The Lilly Ledbetter Fair Pay Act
- 2009: The American Recovery and Reinvestment Act
- 2009: The Health Information Technology for Economic and Clinical Health Act
- 2010: The Dodd-Frank Wall Street Reform and Consumer Protection Act
- 2010: The Patient Protection and Affordable Care Act
- 2012: The FAA Modernization and Reform Act

In addition to these federal laws, states have been busy working on their own versions of employee protections. Those protections vary widely, and HR professionals find themselves faced with having to track and adapt to changing requirements from one state to another. International enterprises have even more challenges with compliance requirements. Other countries have quite different views of employee management requirements. HR professionals must constantly be monitoring the legal updates to be sure they are allocating proper budget amounts for compliance work and covering all of the requirements placed on them by these different jurisdictions.

U.S. Laws and Regulations

Chapter 3 details the federal laws most commonly impacting HR professionals who are responsible for compliance in interstate commerce organizations. You should be familiar with all of these requirements, regardless of your specific corporate obligations.

If your organization contracts, or subcontracts, with the federal government, there are additional compliance reporting requirements overseen by the Office of Federal Contract Compliance Programs (OFCCP).

Employee Records Management

There are increasing obligations for records management in today's climate. It used to be that "good management practices" were the guiding element in determining how an employer established records creation and retention. That's not so any longer.

There are three reasons why proper recordkeeping is a requirement for employers. First, it simply makes good business sense to have accurate information handy and organized when you want to use it. Second, most business owners and managers will eventually encounter the need to produce documentation about employee performance and work history. Having the proper records to retrieve is vital when the need presents itself. Third, some employee records are required by federal or state governments and must be kept somewhere. Organizing them by employee name makes access easy.

There are some important cautions to be given about the subject of identifiable employee information. Generally, state laws permit employees the right to examine their personal employment records. This simply allows individuals the opportunity to confirm information in the file and identify any specific information that is believed to be incorrect. Employees are not universally guaranteed the right to copies of all file contents, however. As the employer, you usually have the right to control the time and location of these examinations as long as you are reasonable in doing so. The objective, of course, is to ensure accuracy of information about each person. In most states, ownership of the personnel file and its contents rests with the employer who maintains it.

Access to information about employees should be strictly limited to those people in your business with a need to use the information in their jobs. Many states are aggressive protectors of employee privacy, and random or unauthorized access to personnel files can bring on severe penalties. Make sure that you store personnel files in a secure location and that they are not left unattended, even during the business day. When asked by people outside the company to provide "verification" of certain employment information about your employees, make it a practice to confirm only the information your employees have authorized you to release. Employment verifications are usually required to support such things as mortgage applications, credit applications, and the like. Employee authorization should be in writing and specify the information they want you to reveal. Tell your employees the policy is designed for their protection.

Job applicants may not have decisions about their applications made based on protected categories such as race, color, sex, religion, national origin, and so on. Therefore, having any information on the application that identifies these categories is inappropriate and may be considered illegal. It is permissible, and for some employers required, to request demographic data from job applicants. This information is directed to a location separate from the hiring manager, however, to avoid even the suspicion of discrimination.

For employees it is necessary to have information in the personnel file that would be considered illegal to gather prior to the job offer being made. For example, you need a birth date to enroll your employee in health insurance and life insurance programs. As long as such information is used for legitimate purposes, employers will have no problem (see Chapter 3).

Personnel File

A *personnel file* is often a collection of record files maintained by various people in various locations. The central file is usually maintained by the HR department. However, additional employee records could be located in the training department, in the labor relations department, and in the desk of the immediate supervisor. Each of these files contains different information, yet they all comprise personnel records. Taken together, they represent the personnel file. While the discussion here is of various documents, we fully realize, depending on the sophistication of your technology, that many of these records may indeed be electronically stored.

The following should be in a personnel file when circumstances require them:

Employment Request for Application

- Employee's original employment application
- Prescreening application notes
- College recruiting interview report form
- Employment interview report form
- Education verification
- Employment verification
- Other background verification
- Employment offer letter
- Employment agency agreement if hired through an agency
- Employee handbook acknowledgment form showing receipt of handbook
- Checklist from new employee orientation showing subjects covered
- Veterans/disabled self-identification form
- Transfer requests
- Relocation offer records
- Relocation report
- Security clearance status
- Payroll
- W-4 form
- Weekly time sheets
- Individual attendance record
- Pay advance request record
- Garnishment orders and records
- Authorization for release of private information
- Authorization for all other payroll actions

Performance Appraisals

- New employee progress reports
- Performance appraisal forms
- Performance improvement program records

Training and Development

- Training history records
- Training program applications/requests
- Skills inventory questionnaire
- Training evaluation forms
- In-house training notification letters
- Training expense reimbursement records

Employee Separations

- Exit interview form
- Final employee performance appraisal
- Exit interviewer's comment form
- Record of documents given with final paycheck

Benefits

- Emergency contact form
- Medical/dental/vision coverage or waiver/drop form
- Vacation accrual/taken form
- Request for nonmedical leave of absence
- Retirement application
- Payroll deduction authorizations
- COBRA notification/election
- Hazardous substance notification and or reports
- Tuition reimbursement application and or payment records
- Employer concession and or discount authorization
- Annual benefits statement acknowledgment
- Safety training/meeting attendance/summary forms

Wage/Salary Administration

- Job description form
- Job analysis questionnaire
- Payroll authorization form

- Fair Labor Standards Act exemption test
- Compensation history record
- Compensation recommendations
- Notification of wage and or salary increase/decrease

Employee Relations

- Report of coaching/counseling session
- Employee Assistance Program consent form
- Commendations
- Employee written warning notice
- Completed employee suggestion forms
- Suggestion status reports

The following should *not* be in a personnel file:

Medical Records

- Physician records of examination
- Diagnostic records
- Laboratory test records
- Drug screening records
- Any of the records listed previously in the discussion on HIPAA
- Any other medical records with personally identifiable information about individual employees

Investigation Records

- Discrimination complaint investigation information
- Legal case data
- Accusations of policy/legal violations

Security Clearance Investigation Records

- Background investigation information
- Personal credit history
- Personal criminal conviction history
- Arrest record

Insupportable Opinions

- Marginal notes on any document indicating management bias or discrimination (for example, comments about an applicant's race, sex, age, disability, national origin, or other protected class membership)

PART II

Medical File

The federal Health Insurance Portability and Accountability Act of 1996 (HIPAA) requires employers and health care providers to protect medical records as confidential, separate, and apart from other business records. That means you may no longer retain medical information in a personnel file. Here are some examples of information you should extract from your personnel files and place in separately protected files as medical information:

- Health insurance application form
- Life insurance application form
- Request for medical leave of absence, regardless of reason
- Personal accident reports
- Workers' compensation report of injury or illness
- OSHA injury and illness reports
- Any other form or document that contains private medical information for a specific employee

Questions about employee access to review their personnel file come up frequently. Each employer should have a policy addressing such questions that complies with state requirements. Federal law does not address the question. Government employees and private sector employers are usually controlled by state laws. Therefore, multistate employers must comply with requirements in all of the states in which they operate.

Investigation File

Any time a complaint is lodged or law enforcement agencies get involved with individual employees, it may be necessary to investigate what are the facts. Each time that happens, a written record should be created that documents what investigative steps were taken and what actions resulted from them. Complaints of illegal employment discrimination are a good example.

These files will have specific employee-identifiable information that may be of a sensitive personal nature. Facts may involve criminal activity or behavior that could result in civil action. For the sake of privacy, each investigation file should be held under the same security provisions as medical records. Only those people having a need to access the content of the files should be allowed access. Records should be secured at all times so passersby cannot pull open a file drawer and remove documents.

Recordkeeping Legal Compliance

As with many HR issues, retention requirements do change from time to time. Be sure you confirm the requirements for your situation before destroying any records. Because these requirements are fluid in nature, we suggest you confirm your specific needs through discussion with your employment attorney.

The following table lists some of the most common federal requirements for record retention:

Federal Records Retention Requirements		
Record Required	**Retention Period**	**Requirement Citation**
Wages, Hours, Working Conditions		
Payroll records • Name • Address • Social Security number • Occupation • Hours worked each day (nonexempt employees) • Wages paid • Payday records • Straight time and overtime • Payroll deductions • Union collective bargaining agreements • Qualified benefit plans • Trust records • Employee notices • Sales and purchasing records	Four years from date of last entry (according to the IRS)	Fair Labor Standards Act of 1938 (29 U.S.C. Sec 201-219)
Payroll records • Basic time and earnings cards • Wage rate tables • Work time schedules • Order, shipping, billing records • Records of additions to or deductions from wages • Unemployment compensation contributions	Two years from the date of last entry	Fair Labor Standards Act of 1938 (29 U.S.C. Sec 201-219)
Payroll records • Any report required by the Secretary of Labor • All backup data required to prepare required reports (including vouchers, worksheets, receipts, dispute resolutions)	Five years after filing report based on records	Labor Management Reporting & Disclosure Act of 1959 (29 U.S.C. Sec 433-436)

Federal Records Retention Requirements

Record Required	Retention Period	Requirement Citation
Occupational Safety and Health Records		
• Log of occupational injuries or illnesses resulting in medical treatment (other than first aid), loss of consciousness or restriction of work or motion, transfer or termination of employment	Five years minimum following injury or illness	Occupational Safety and Health Act of 1970 (29 U.S.C. Sec 51, *et sec.*, 29 C.F.R. Sec 1904-2, 1904.4, 12904.6)
• OSHA 300 report posted each year from February 1 through April 30 • Hazardous condition exposures • Medical tests and screening • Employee medical records • Allegations of employee exposure • Heavy equipment operation records	Five years after the year reported; up to 30 years after employment ends	29 C.F.R. 1904.2, 1904.4, 1904.6 Occupational Safety and Health Act of 1970 (29 U.S.C. Sec 51 *et sec.*, 29 C.F.R. Sec 1904.32(a)(1), 1904.32(b)(6))
Nondiscrimination, EEO, and Affirmative Action Records		
• Employment records (hiring, promotion, demotion, transfer, layoff, termination, compensation changes, training selection) • Payroll records (name, address, birth date, occupation, rate of pay, days worked each week, compensation earned each week) • Job descriptions • Union agreements and contracts • Retirement, pension, and insurance plans • Seniority and merit system descriptions and records	One year from the date of personnel action, or until any discrimination charge is resolved. Three years for affirmative action employers unless employer has fewer than 150 employees or does not have a government contract at least $150,000; then, the retention requirement is 2 years from the date of making the record or the personnel action taken.	Civil Rights Act of 1964, Title VII (42 U.S.C. Sec 2000e-5, 2000e-17) Age Discrimination in Employment Act of 1967 (29 U.S.C. Sec 621-634)
• Employment requisitions • Job advertisements • Job applications and testing documents • Affirmative action plans and all supporting evidence of good faith efforts to implement the plans • Standard Form 100 (EEO-1, EEO-4, EEO-3, EEO-5)	One year (same as Title VII) Three years for affirmative action employers with the same exceptions shown for Title VII	Civil Rights Act of 1964, Executive Order 11246 (41 C.F.R. 60-1.12; 60-2.32; 60-250.80; 60-741.80)

(continued)

PART II

Federal Records Retention Requirements

Record Required	Retention Period	Requirement Citation
• Interviewer records and notes • Selection decisions • Physical exam reports	Three years for affirmative action employers with the same exceptions shown for Title VII	Vietnam Era Veterans Readjustment Assistance Act (41 C.F.R. 60-250; 60-1.12)

Family and Medical Leaves

• Basic payroll data showing additions/deductions from wages and total compensation paid • Dates for FMLA leave • Hours for FMLA leave • Notices given to employees regarding FMLA • Employee requests for FMLA leave • All benefit documents and information about paid/unpaid leave status • Benefit premium information • Any dispute or complaint from employee about FMLA leave	Three years from the making of the record	Family and Medical Leave Act of 1993

Income Tax Records

• All payroll-related records (including general ledgers, cash, books, journals, voucher registers, and so on) may be retained in magnetic tapes, discs, and other machine-readable data media used in accounting processing; microfilm systems must be complete, used consistently in the business, and properly indexed; retrieved data must be legible, and taxpayer must provide IRS with written procedures governing the system and its operation.	Fifteen years (assessment period of 3 years plus collection period of 10 years plus 2 years for payment of refund)	Treasury Regulations Sec 1.446-1(a)(4); 1.6001-1(a); 1.6001-1(b); 1.6001-1(e); 301.6501(a)-1; 3016501(e)-1; 301.6511(d)-1; 301.6501(c)-1; 31.6001-5
• Name, address, account number, total amount, and date of each payment • Period of services covered by each payment • Amount of wages subject to withholding • Amount of tax collected • Explanation for any discrepancy between total income and taxable income • Fair market value and date of each noncash payment • Form W-4 for each employee • All other supporting documents relating to each employee's individual tax status	W-4 kept for as long as in effect, plus 4 years	IRS Sec 6502(a); 3402

Federal Records Retention Requirements

Record Required	Retention Period	Requirement Citation
Unemployment Tax		
• Total pay, including amounts withheld for any reason • Wages subject to tax • Contributions to state unemployment funds	Four years after tax is due or paid	Federal Unemployment Tax Act (Internal Revenue Code Sec 3301-3311)
Social Security and Medicare Tax		
• Name, address, and Social Security number of all employees • Total amount and date of each payment and period covered by payment • Amount of total wages subject to tax • Amount of employee tax collected for each pay period • Explanation of any difference between total pay and taxable pay • Details of adjustment or settlement of taxes • Records of tips received by employees, including statements of tips provided by employees • All employer filing records	Four years after tax is due or paid, whichever is later	Treasury Regulations Sec 6001-2
Work Authorization Records		
• Form I-9 for each employee hired after November 6, 1986 • Forms I-9 kept in a file separate from other personnel records • Student work permits	Three years from date of hire, or one year after termination of employment, whichever is later	Immigration Reform and Control Act of 1986 (8 U.S.C. Sec 1324a, *et seq.*)
Polygraph Exams		
• Statement of reasons for conducting the examination • Copy of statement given to examinee about time and place of examination • Copies of opinions, reports, and so on given to employer from examiner	Three years after exam	Employee Polygraph Protection Act (29 U.S.C. Sec 2001-2009; 29 C.F.R. Sec 801.1-801.75)
Public Works Contracts: Prevailing Wages		
• Contract number and period each employee was engaged on the contract • Detailed pay records for each employee for each day worked • Record showing all employees paid prevailing benefits or their equivalent value	Two years	Davis-Bacon Act (40 U.S.C. Sec 276a-276a-5)

PART II

(continued)

Federal Records Retention Requirements		
Record Required	**Retention Period**	**Requirement Citation**
• Wage and hour records for all "laborers and mechanics" employed in construction and repair of public works facilities • Records showing all employees paid at least the prevailing minimum wage • Age certificate for each employee younger than 18	Three years	Walsh-Healey Act (41 U.S.C. Sec 34-45) Service Contract Act
Pension Plans		
• Records sufficient to determine benefits due to employees • Welfare and pension records • Supporting documents for ERISA filings	Permanent Five years Six years after filing	Employee Retirement Income Security Act of 1974 (29 U.S.C. Chapter 18, Sec 1001-1381) Welfare and Pension Plans Disclosure Act (29 C.F.R. 308)
Union-Related Records		
• Collective bargaining agreements • Organizing records • Correspondence with union	Seven years from conclusion of contract	National Labor Relations Act
Other Personnel Records		
Some personnel records should be retained for even longer than required by individual laws; here are our recommendations: • Attendance records • Employee training • All verification of job applicant references • Verification of previous employment requests • HIPAA employee advisory record	Three years after termination	Best practices
• Employee awards • Employee commendations • Disciplinary action records • Requests for transfer	Five years after termination	Best practices
• Job descriptions • Performance evaluations • Wage attachments or garnishment notices	Six years after termination or update	Best practices

Federal Records Retention Requirements		
Record Required	**Retention Period**	**Requirement Citation**
• Employer property records showing employee issue of property	Duration of employment	Best practices
• Employment applications • Job offer letters • Records of pay changes since date of hire • Benefits beneficiary designation or changes • Benefits request form • Performance evaluations • Policy receipts with employee signatures • All employee training logs • Leaves of absence taken • Notices of union membership/dues deduction • Education records • Termination records • Exit interviews	Permanent	Best practices

Records Destruction   Once a record has reached its expiration date (been retained for the period required by law), it should be destroyed. Destruction of paper records is something that should be done by shredding so that records cannot be reconstructed by someone rifling through the trash bin.

Commercial records storage and destruction companies can be found almost everywhere in the United States. For a fee, they will come to your work site, collect the paper records you want to have destroyed, and either shred them in their truck while at your location or take them back to a central location where the documents will be shredded. Some specialize in certain industries such as medical records.

Electronic employee records may be destroyed by crushing or incinerating the storage media, by overwriting and rendering the data unrecoverable, or by demagnetizing. The destruction companies mentioned above are happy to help.

Chapter Review

In this chapter, you studied workplace issues such as the managing a global workforce, risk management, and corporate social responsibility. All of these are based on the foundation of employment law and regulations that are highlighted here and thoroughly reviewed in Chapter 3. You saw how contemporary HR organizations are influenced by global issues, even if they are not themselves multinational. HR professionals will be expected to increasingly know and manage according to these influences as years pass and societies change.

Questions

1. What is a diaspora?

    A. Any medical condition that presents as an upset stomach

    B. Any people or ethnic population forced or induced to leave their traditional homeland

    C. Any common grouping of workers who commute across international borders

    D. Any group of people who are collectively working to upgrade their personal skills

2. What does guarded globalization mean?

    A. Developing nations are wary of opening more industries to multinational companies and are zealously protecting local interests.

    B. Countries are slow to invest in globalization.

    C. Developing nations believe it is unwise to export too much of their national resources.

    D. Developed countries choose not to participate with certain developing countries in trade exchanges.

3. What did Perlmutter identify?

    A. Certain countries don't behave fairly in international trade agreements.

    B. Developing countries are the best type of trade partners.

    C. Unknowns must be revealed before international trade can begin.

    D. International alternative management orientations can be classified into four categories.

4. HR's role in setting up a global business presence involves which of the following?

    A. Updating the employee handbook for the new location languages

    B. Providing accounting with the payroll tax withholding rates for the new location(s)

    C. Providing due diligence in issues related to the workforce

    D. Issuing newsletter updates about the progress being made in opening distant locations

5. When placing an employee on an international assignment, it is important to do what?

    A. Provide ongoing support for the individual and their family in the new location

    B. Provide anything needed before the family lands in the new location

C. Provide help with language issues before the move takes place

D. Provide publicity in the corporate newsletter showcasing the newly appointed employee and the assignment

6. What does ISO-26000 provide guidelines on?

   A. Risk management and mitigation

   B. Globalization for emerging markets

   C. Diversity

   D. Social and environmental responsibilities

7. Title VII of the 1964 Civil Rights Act defines all the following as protected classes except what?

   A. National origin

   B. Religion

   C. Age

   D. Sex

8. Which of the following does the GRI provide?

   A. Standards for sustainability reporting guidelines

   B. Standards for the employee value proposition (EVP)

   C. Standards for protected class hiring quotas

   D. Standards for minimum safety protocols

9. When determining how long to retain an employee record, which of the following is the best practice?

   A. Follow the retention for the most applicable law, like FLSA.

   B. Hold onto the document for the longest required retention period from any of the applicable laws.

   C. Research the various applicable laws, add up the various years of required retention, then divide by the number of laws to retain for the average.

   D. Just retain forever and not worry about it.

10. Employee medical documentation should be what?

   A. Shared with the supervisor so they may be fully informed

   B. Filed under "H" in the personnel file for health information

   C. Filed under "M" in the personnel file for medical information

   D. Kept separate and secure, away from the primary personnel file

11. Which statement best describes federal contractors and the legislative and regulatory environment?

    A. Federal contractors have additional compliance requirements monitored by the OFCCP.

    B. Federal contractors have additional compliance requirements monitored by the NLRB.

    C. Federal contractors have identical compliance requirements with non-contractors, both monitored by the OFCCP.

    D. Federal contractors have identical compliance requirements with non-contractors, both monitored by the NLRB.

12. Employment risks are the potential for losing things of value. They can include which of the following?

    A. Confidential employee data and complaint investigation records

    B. Job requisition information and published news articles on the organization

    C. Executive biographical summaries and SEC required reports

    D. Visitor comment cards and building maintenance records

13. What are key risk indicators (KRIs)?

    A. Indicators of how well something is being done

    B. Indicators of how much insurance covers the employer

    C. Indicators of potential future adverse impact

    D. Indicators of company risks compared to competitor risks

14. What is a risk register?

    A. A financial account of insurance costs

    B. A record of information about identified risks

    C. A computer device to monitor IT performance

    D. A record of automotive repairs due to accidents

15. What is the first step toward having an emergency response plan?

    A. Be sure all emergency exits are properly marked.

    B. Write a policy for evacuation in an emergency.

    C. Conduct a risk assessment for your work location.

    D. Assign development for the emergency plan to an HR person.

16. Contingency plans explain what?

    A. How to handle whistleblower exposure

    B. How to bring the organization into governmental compliance

    C. How to respond to discrimination complaints

    D. How the organization will continue running in the event of a catastrophe

17. Which CSR guideline framework was one of the first initiatives relating to corporate governance?

   A. United Nations Global Compact

   B. OECD

   C. The Caux principles

   D. ISO 26000

18. Which social responsibility subject does *not* belong to the ISO 26000?

   A. Animal rights

   B. Labor practices

   C. Consumer issues

   D. The environment

19. What set of sustainability guidelines was created by a network of business leaders from Japan, Europe, and the United States?

   A. ISO 26000

   B. OECD Guidelines for Multinational Enterprises

   C. SA8000

   D. The Caux principles

20. What should *not* be in an employee's personnel file?

   A. Job description

   B. Benefit enrollment forms

   C. Performance improvement program records

   D. Insupportable opinions

Answers

   1. **B.** The relocating of any specific population by inducement or force is a diaspora.

   2. **A.** Protecting local interests is part of guarded globalization.

   3. **D.** Perlmutter classified management orientations into four categories.

   4. **C.** Global business expansion involves more than translating the employee handbook. Due diligence embraces everything from legal requirements to policy differences.

   5. **A.** Expatriate employees need support, as do their family members.

   6. **D.** ISO-26000 provides guidelines on social and environmental responsibilities.

   7. **C.** The five protected classes from Title VII are sex, national origin, race, religion, and color.

   8. **A.** The GRI provides standards for sustainability reporting guidelines.

   9. **B.** It is a best practice to retain employee documents according to the guidelines of the longest applicable legislation.

10. **D**. Employee medical information needs to be safeguarded by being kept separate and secure, away from the primary personnel file.

11. **A**. Federal contractors and subcontractors have additional compliance reporting requirements overseen by the Office of Federal Contract Compliance Programs (OFCCP).

12. **A**. Confidential employee data and complaint investigation records are both considered confidential and private. Losing them would be losing something of value.

13. **C**. KRIs are forecasts of future bad things that could happen.

14. **B**. A risk register is a log of identified risks.

15. **C**. Emergency response plans depend on a risk assessment that the response plan is built to address.

16. **D**. Contingency plans outline how the organization will continue operating in the event of a catastrophe.

17. **B**. Corporate social responsibility (CSR) is an overall umbrella guideline. The Guidelines for Multinational Enterprises established in 1976 by the Organisation for Economic Co-operation and Development (OECD) is one of the first to address corporate governance in this area.

18. **A**. Animal rights are not part of the ISO 26000 standard on corporate social responsibility.

19. **D**. The Caux principles were created by a joint effort of business leaders from several countries.

20. **D**. Insupportable opinions, regardless of the source, should never be part of an employee's personnel file.

References

1. 2022 SHRM Body of Applied Skills and Knowledge, page 78

2. https://en.wikipedia.org/wiki/Globalization, retrieved on March 10, 2018

3. Friedman, Thomas L. *Thank You for Being Late: An Optimist's Guide to Thriving in the Age of Accelerations,* Farrar, Straus and Giroux, 2016, pages 120–121

4. https://www.pwc.com/jp/en/press-room/world-in-2050-170213.html, retrieved on March 10, 2018

5. http://www.newworldencyclopedia.org/entry/Diaspora, retrieved on March 10, 2018

6. https://quizlet.com/114411913/shrm-cp-hr-in-the-global-context-flash-cards/, retrieved on March 10, 2018

7. http://science.sciencemag.org/content/356/6345/1362, retrieved on March 10, 2018

8. Google search, retrieved on March 10, 2018

9. Stephan, Michael et al. "The Global and Local HR Function," Deloitte Insights, https://www2.deloitte.com/insights/us/en/focus/human-capital-trends/2014/hc-trends-2014-global-and-local-hr.html, retrieved on March 12, 2018

10. Ibid.

11. https://www.adp.com/spark/articles/2016/12/create-a-global-human-resources-strategy.aspx, retrieved on March 12, 2018

12. Bremmer, Ian. "The New Rules of Globalization," *Harvard Business Review,* Jan–Feb 2014, https://hbr.org/2014/01/the-new-rules-of-globalization, retrieved on March 12, 2018

13. "Push and Pull Factors in Business," www.ukessays.com/essays/business-strategy/push-and-pull-factors-in-business.php, retrieved on March 12, 2018

14. Ibid.

15. *Mastering Strategic Management,* https://opentextbc.ca/strategicmanagement/chapter/types-of-international-strategies/, retrieved on March 12, 2018

16. SHRM Learning System 2020 Workplace, page 27

17. SHRM Learning System 2020 Workplace, page 28

18. https://www.managementstudyhq.com/eprg-framework.html, retrieved on March 13, 2018

19. Koch, Jennifer. "Must-have Global HR Competencies," Workforce, 10/1/1996, https://workforce.com/news/must-have-global-hr-competencies, retrieved on March 13, 2018

20. https://trainingindustry.com/articles/strategy-alignment-and-planning/5-ways-to-develop-a-global-mindset/, retrieved on March 13, 2018

21. https://blog.enplug.com/corporate-culture, retrieved on March 14, 2018

22. Lee, Kiefer and Steve Carter. *Global Marketing Management, Third Edition,* OUP Oxford, 2012

23. https://www.toolshero.com/leadership/organizational-culture-model-schein/, retrieved on March 14, 2018

24. http://daily.unitedlanguagegroup.com/stories/editorials/six-cultural-dimensions, retrieved on March 14, 2018

25. https://online.seu.edu/high-and-low-context-cultures/, retrieved on March 14, 2018

26. https://en.wikipedia.org/wiki/Hofstede%27s_cultural_dimensions_theory, retrieved on March 14, 2018

27. https://www.strategy-business.com/article/17251?gko=444c1, retrieved on March 14, 2018

PART II

28. http://summit.sfu.ca/item/774, retrieved on March 14, 2018

29. http://www.hult.edu/blog/benefits-challenges-cultural-diversity-workplace/, retrieved on March 14, 2018

30. http://cognitive-edge.com/blog/a-non-linear-approach-to-reconciling-business-dilemmas/, retrieved on March 14, 2018

31. https://www.mcgill.ca/desautels/category/tags/nancy-adler

32. https://www.shrm.org/resourcesandtools/hr-topics/talent-acquisition/pages/half-of-employers-report-not-tracking-global-mobility-costs.aspx, retrieved on March 14, 2018

33. http://www.oxfordreference.com/view/10.1093/oi/authority.20110803095855152, retrieved on March 14, 2018

34. Hutchings, Kate and Helen De Cieri. *International Human Resource Management: From Cross-Cultural Management to Managing a Diverse Workforce*, Routledge, 2007

35. https://hbr.org/1999/03/the-right-way-to-manage-expats?referral=03758&cm_vc=rr_item_page.top_right, retrieved on March 14, 2018

36. https://www.shrm.org/resourcesandtools/tools-and-samples/toolkits/pages/cms_010358.aspx, retrieved on March 14, 2018

37. https://www.investopedia.com/terms/s/supranational.asp, retrieved on March 15, 2018

38. 2022 The SHRM Body of Applied Skills and Knowledge, page 80

39. 2020 SHRM Learning System, Workplace, Book 1, page 106

40. Kaplan, Robert S. and Anette Mikes. "Managing Risks: A New Framework," *Harvard Business Review* 90, No. 6, June 2012

41. "Risk Management Fundamentals, Homeland Security Risk Management Doctrine," U.S. Department of Homeland Security, April 2011, https://www.dhs.gov/xlibrary/assets/rma-risk-management-fundamentals.pdf

42. Peters, Thomas J. *Thriving on Chaos*, Harper & Row Publishers, 1987

43. 2022 SHRM Body of Applied Skills and Knowledge, page 85

44. Ten Principles of UN Global Compact, www.unglobalcompact.org

45. CRT Principles for Responsible Business, www.cauxroundtable.org

46. ISO 26000, "Social Responsibility: 7 Core Subjects," https://www.iso.org/iso-26000-social-responsibility.html

47. https://sa-intl.org/sa8000-search/#stats

48. 2020 SHRM Learning System, Workplace, Book 2, page 204

49. 2022 SHRM Body of Applied Skills and Knowledge, page 89

50. 2022 SHRM Body of Applied Skills and Knowledge, pages 98–802

Behavioral Competencies

The SHRM Certified Professional (SHRM-CP) and the SHRM Senior Certified Professional (SHRM-SCP) identify and detail nine behavioral competencies that will be tested on both exams. They make up 50 percent of the scored questions. The nine behavior competencies are segregated by SHRM into three clusters: Leadership, Interpersonal, and Business.

A *competency* is a cluster of interrelated attributes, including knowledge, skills, abilities, and other characteristics (KSAOs), that lead to behaviors identified as being needed to perform a specific job effectively. Competencies can be either technical (the knowledge required to perform a specific job) or behavioral in nature. A behavioral competency is the application of knowledge to job-related behavior. Thus, technical competencies for HR professionals reflect *what* knowledge they are expected to apply to their jobs, and a behavioral competency is about *how* they apply the knowledge. You can find more in-depth information about some of the behaviors within the knowledge topics in Chapters 4 through 6.

In each of the nine behavioral competencies, we have included the outline of SHRM's Body of Applied Skills and Knowledge (BASK) key concepts[1] (foundational knowledge), which are descriptions of what HR professionals are expected to know to perform their job. It is important to understand SHRM's definitions as they may differ from definitions used in your workplace.

Leadership Cluster

The Leadership cluster represents 17 percent of both exams' scores. Three competencies fall within the Leadership cluster:

- Behavioral competency 1: Leadership and Navigation
- Behavioral competency 2: Ethical Practice
- Behavioral competency 3: Diversity, Equity, and Inclusion (DE&I)

Regardless of experience level or job title, all HR professionals need to demonstrate and display strong leadership skills and ability, keeping in mind the focus of a strategic mindset.

Behavioral Competency 1: Leadership and Navigation

The first competency in the SHRM-identified behavioral competency model is Leadership and Navigation. This competency focuses on understanding leadership plus the knowledge and skills needed to be an effective HR leader, along with being an HR business partner in your organization and contributing to initiatives and processes for the organization. Additionally, an effective HR professional builds trust, influences, motivates, and has the required level of emotional intelligence to demonstrate those behaviors.

Four subcompetencies comprise the Leadership and Navigation competency. They are defined by SHRM[2] as follows:

- **Navigating the organization**   Working within the parameters of the organization's hierarchy, processes, systems, and policies
- **Vision**   Defining and supporting a coherent vision and long-term goals for HR that support the strategic direction of the organization
- **Managing HR initiatives**   Implementing and supporting HR projects that align with HR and organizational objectives
- **Influence**   Inspiring colleagues to understand and pursue the strategic vision and goals of HR and the organization

Key Concepts

- Leadership theories (for example, situational leadership, transformational leadership, participative leadership, inclusive leadership, leader-member exchange theory, servant leadership, transactional leadership, trait theory, contingency theory)
- People management techniques (for example, directing, coaching, supporting, delegating, mentoring)
- Motivation theories (for example, goal-setting theory, expectancy theory, attribution theory, self-determination theory, Herzberg's two-factor theory)
- Influence and persuasion techniques (for example, personal appeal, forming coalitions, leading by example, rational persuasion)
- Personal leadership qualities (for example, vision, self-motivation, self-discipline, risk-taking, commitment to continuous learning, growth mindset)

Definition

According to SHRM, "*Leadership and Navigation* is defined as the knowledge, skills, abilities, and other characteristics (KSAOs) needed to create a compelling vision and mission for HR that align with the strategic direction and culture of the organization, accomplish HR and organizational goals, lead and promote organizational change, navigate the organization, and manage the implementation and execution of HR initiatives."[3]

Proficiency Indicators for All HR Professionals

The Leadership and Navigation competency for all HR professionals focuses on understanding leadership and the skills and knowledge needed to be a leader: influencing, building trust, emotional intelligence, and motivation. Yet, first there needs to be an understanding as to the difference between managing and leading. Both are needed to get work done through people. Knowing when and how to lead, setting the vision and strategy for the future, understanding when to manage, and tending to the day-to-day operational details are the keys to effective leadership and navigation. All HR professionals are expected to conduct themselves according to these expectations.

Conforming to Organizational Culture

Organizations develop their own models of leadership, creating a set of expected behaviors, attitudes, and beliefs that become the leadership norm for the organization to complement the organization's mission and strategies. The result is a leadership culture. Managers and leaders are then expected to conform to that identified model, a *norm,* to guide their interactions in managing people.

Organizations desire to identify the type of leadership that is most effective in their workplaces. This self-awareness can then be used to identify individuals with leadership potential and to create leadership development programs. The identified norms ought to be used when sourcing new hires to stay consistent with the desired leadership culture.

Collaborating with Stakeholders

There are five steps to collaborating with stakeholders:

1. *Know the stakeholders.* The first step toward any collaboration process is identifying stakeholders and their roles. Understanding who you are working with is critical to collaborating effectively.

2. *Identify what is at stake.* Every stakeholder is involved for a specific reason. Use their role and motivation to your advantage. For example, if you are working on an office reconfiguration for HR, consider including the IT and facilities managers in every conversation that relates to the new room design, not just those explicitly regarding the movement of PCs. Why? Because they may be affected by the decisions made in those conversations pertaining to the location of cables, connectivity, and other associated matters such as overtime for IT or facilities personnel.

3. *Understand each stakeholder's issues and language.* Communicating effectively with stakeholders is linked to their motivation. For example, for decision-makers, every project is an investment because they are normally responsible for their share of the resources. To collaborate effectively, you should discuss plans in relation to the planned outcomes or return on investment (ROI).

4. *Set the specific expectations.* Once you know who stakeholders are, what their challenges and issues are, and how to talk to them, you can better express your expectations for their involvement, such as when they are expected to provide input for the project and how to provide feedback.

5. *Value their input.* One reason stakeholders can become frustrated is they do not feel "heard." Helping stakeholders to see how their input was incorporated or even why it was not used is essential. It makes them an active part of decision-making without abdicating the decision to them.

Accomplishing Tasks

Leaders get things done through people, which means managing people and their tasks to produce desired outcomes. Chapter 4 discusses in detail the techniques, skills, and theories to manage and motivate people to accomplish tasks.

Managers do the following with groups:

- Plan activities
- Organize and identify resources required, including people
- Direct work in a way that ensures the best use of resources
- Coordinate to achieve efficiency
- Control resources and activities through monitoring, measuring, and correcting as needed

Leaders perform the following roles with groups:

- They model desired values in all their actions.
- They challenge the status quo and harness the talent in the organization to solve problems, accept change, and move in new directions when needed.
- They inspire and influence people toward achieving a common vision and goals.
- They maintain employees' motivation and focus.
- They foster growth and develop people to their full potential.

If an organization has ineffective management, it will fail to meet its goals. On the other hand, if organizations lack leadership, they often lack innovation and the ability to adapt to change.

Demonstrating Agility and Expertise

Although the concept of learning agility is not new, it is gaining momentum. There is a clear message from the mounting research around demonstrating agility: you should either be hiring for it, developing it, or perhaps doing both. The traits to look for are simple: self-driven motivation to learn, seeking out and using feedback, and an openness to try something new and different (to welcome discomfort). It is not easy, yet having developmental experiences is what leads to a new level of expertise and innovation. Success as a leader depends on a willingness and ability to learn because it enables leaders to acquire new behaviors quickly and effectively, which enables adaptability and resilience. While this overarching concept of learning agility may have always been important, it seems even more so now given the constant turmoil of today's business environment. This can explain why some of the world-renowned management experts are saying now is the time to put your bets on learners.

Setting the Vision

Leaders create energy. They inspire, empower, and support others. Most importantly, they set the vision. Setting a vision of what can be serves as a powerful inspiration—a North Star for a leader—to move everyone in an organization in the same direction toward that vision's achievement. That vision needs to be clear and achievable—something that inspires others to want to be a part of it. Leaders must continually point to this North Star and remind everyone that this is where we are all headed. The behavior that is most essential with this leadership ability is going to involve inspiring and motivating others.

Leading the Organization Through Adversity

"The best developer of a leader is failure," said Richard Branson, chair of Virgin Airlines. Business history is full of examples of leaders whose organizations ran into adversity and bounced back to become more successful than before. A fitting example is Steve Jobs, who was fired from Apple Computer and then rehired when it was on the brink of despair. When Steve Jobs returned to Apple, he had a new view of the market that caused him to lead Apple into introducing products like the iPod, which ended up redefining the industry. This was all through his vision and ability as a leader to paint a picture of what could be, design the strategy, and send in the resources. The rest is history.

Promoting Consensus

Getting people to move together as a unified team toward a common goal has always been challenging. However, with consensus building, management can ensure they have the support of the entire team as they steer the organization in the chosen direction.

This concept is known as *consensus management*. It is not a new concept (Native Americans have been utilizing it for hundreds of years), and now organizations like Starbucks have successfully incorporated it into their management processes. Consensus management is the process where team members work as a group to develop a solution and agree to support whatever decision is made in the best interests of the whole. It requires asking for input from each person on the team, carefully considering that feedback, and making an earnest effort to address any concerns that are raised. This is most commonly accomplished by holding a consensus meeting, where staff members are empowered to voice their support and concerns. The key to success here is that everyone agrees to support the consensus decision once it is made, regardless of their personal feelings.

Serving as a Transformational Leader

Leadership today is associated with a group role, placing value on behaviors characterized as authentic leadership or transformational leadership.

The following are key elements of this type of approach to leadership:

- **Power**   Leaders can be recognized as formal or informal in their style. They often empower other team members giving greater autonomy, act as their champion, and support their efforts.

- **Orientation**   Transformational leaders think in terms of long-range vision, strategy, and values rather than short-term objectives. They believe in challenging, developing, and investing for the long term.

- **Emotional intelligence**   Their knowledge and skills allow transformational leaders to be self-aware, to control their actions and emotions, and to understand others' perspectives and the drivers of other people's behavior.
- **Ethical grounding**   Transformational leaders walk the talk of the organization's values, encourage others, and will sacrifice for those values.

Proficiency Indicators for Senior HR Professionals

 Senior HR professionals are expected to possess the following skills over and above the basic behaviors already reviewed.

Leading HR Staff

Leading the HR staff to become a true business partner is one of the most important leadership roles for HR professionals. Demonstrating the behaviors to be a strong HR leader is one of the best training tools for the HR leader. In their book *The Extraordinary Leader: Turning Good Managers into Great Leaders,*[4] Jack Zenger and Joseph Folkman studied the strengths and weaknesses of HR leaders and concluded the following:

Strong HR leaders demonstrate the following behaviors:

- Develop and coach others
- Build positive relationships
- Model their values and fulfill their promises and commitments
- Have functional expertise

Weak HR leaders display these behaviors:

- Focus internally rather than externally, failing to look outside the HR function to the organization's internal and external stakeholders
- Lack strategic perspective, focusing on short-term objectives and daily tasks
- Do not anticipate or react well to change
- Resist "stretch" goals and act as a drag on the organization's attempts to innovate

As an HR professional, consider what your own leadership style is and where you may need to shore up your leadership skills to lead the HR department more effectively so you and HR can have a more significant role in your organization.

Facilitating Strategic Change

Facilitating strategic change as an HR leader involves employing the three *C*s of change leadership: communicate, collaborate, and commit.

- **Communicate**   Unsuccessful leaders tend to focus on the "what" behind the change. Successful leaders communicate the "what" *and* the "why." Leaders who explain the purpose of the change and connect it to the organization's values or explain the benefits create stronger buy-in and urgency for the change.

- **Collaborate**   Bringing people together to plan and execute change is critical. Successful leaders work across boundaries, encourage employees to break out of their silos, and refuse to tolerate unhealthy competition. They also include employees in decision-making early on, strengthening their commitment to change. Unsuccessful change leaders fail to engage employees early and often in the change process.

- **Commit**   Successful leaders make sure their own beliefs and behaviors support change, too. Change is difficult, but leaders who negotiate it successfully are resilient, persistent, and willing to step outside their comfort zone. They also devote more of their own time to the change effort and focus on the big picture. Unsuccessful leaders fail to adapt to challenges, express negativity, and are impatient with a lack of results.

Serving as the Voice for HR

There is a new agenda for HR in today's business environment, and it is a radical departure from the prior status quo. It used to be that HR was charged with playing policy police and regulatory watchdog, handling the volumes of paperwork involved in hiring and firing, managing the bureaucratic aspects of benefits, and administering compensation decisions made by others. HR's activities were often disconnected from the real work of the organization. Today, HR is defined not by what it does but by what it delivers—results that enrich the organization's value to customers, stakeholders, and employees.

More organizations have dispersed their HR staff as business partners within the business units to be closely aligned with the needs of those business units so that HR can help deliver organizational excellence. This closeness to the internal customer helps HR to serve in the following four ways:

- Become a true business partner within the unit with line management in strategy execution

- Become an expert in the way work is organized and executed, delivering administrative efficiency

- Become a champion for employees, representing their concerns to line management and at the same time working to increase employee contribution and engagement

- Become an agent of continuous transformation, shaping processes and a culture that together improve the organization

Ensuring Accountability

As an HR leader, modeling desired behavior and outcomes with the HR staff is vitally important to other employees and management in the organization. When *leaders* are visibly holding their own direct reports *accountable,* this sends a powerful leading-by-example message. People struggle to be *accountable* when roles and processes are ambiguous. Having clear roles, responsibilities, and expectations is a vital step in holding others accountable. As an HR professional, how well are you measuring up to doing what you say you are going to do and when? Holding yourself accountable to delivering the outcomes and the outlined leadership behavior norms is just as important.

Changing Organizational Culture

When you're embarking on changing organizational culture, the first step is defining the values and behaviors you are seeking to change. *Culture* is defined as the beliefs and behaviors that govern how people act in an organization, and it is now believed to be a major determinant of a company's success or failure. Culture is considered a potential competitive advantage if it is a strong, positive one.

According to the Deloitte Global Human Capital Trends 2016 report,[5] here are ten tips for driving a culture change:

1. Define desired values and behaviors.
2. Align culture with strategy and processes.
3. Connect culture and accountability.
4. Have visible proponents.
5. Define the non-negotiables.
6. Align your culture with your brand.
7. Measure your efforts.
8. Do not rush it.
9. Invest now.
10. Be bold and lead.

Championing the HR Function

To champion the HR function, HR professionals must build trust, credibility, and relationships.

To champion high performance from the workforce, HR's functions must be deliberately designed to support and be linked to the organization's mission, vision, strategy, and goals. When HR is seen as the lever that drives performance upward, then HR lives up to its purpose in providing value.

Creating Buy-in for Organizational Change

When you are enacting an organizational change, the executives most likely already gave a green light for the change you are tasked to implement. You need to create more buy-in for other levels in the organization to help proceed with the change. The following are the steps to take to create buy-in.

Work from the Top Down   In addition to obtaining buy-in from the C-suite, consider bringing mid-level management into the change plans early. Gaining support from leaders at different levels of the organization will make your pitch stronger and ensure managers are knowledgeable and equipped earlier for questions from their own employees.

Be Transparent   Communication is key to prevent unfounded concerns and gossip about how the change is going to affect people. Be open and transparent early and often. This includes being clear about what is going well and what is not working. Be upfront and specific about what failed throughout the process and what was learned.

Ask for Input   It is vital for employees to know their opinions and ideas are acknowledged when voiced. It can prove a challenge to collect and address feedback and questions from everyone. Be creative in forming a solution to both gather and disseminate communications in both directions. Perhaps have a key contact within each unit to help you communicate details and gather feedback at certain phases of the change process.

Change is key to helping organizations innovate and grow, and your organization's workforce is the needed component for helping changes take place. Ensuring that they are informed and can provide input throughout the transition is essential in earning their support.

Summary

In this portion of the chapter, we explored the expertise in leadership and navigation that enables HR professionals to keep their organizations focused on strategies and goals that lead the workforce talent by creating collaboration and fostering a vision with influence, emotional intelligence, and motivation.

Behavioral Competency 2: Ethical Practice

It is important for HR professionals to understand the demand for ethical practice. Everyone expects a level playing field, and that requires employers to be doing what is expected for employees, customers, and shareholders.

The following three subcompetencies comprise the Ethical Practice competency, as defined by SHRM:[6]

- **Personal integrity**   Demonstrating high levels of integrity in personal relationships and behaviors

- **Professional integrity**   Demonstrating high levels of integrity in professional relationships and behaviors

- **Ethical agent**   Cultivating the organization's ethical environment and ensuring that policies and practices reflect ethical values

Key Concepts

- Ethical business principles and practices (for example, transparency, authenticity, conflicts of interest)

- Privacy principles and policies (for example, anonymity, confidentiality, opt-in/opt-out policies)

- Internal ethics controls (for example, protection of employee confidentiality, standards for employee investigations)

Definition

According to SHRM, "*Ethical Practice* is defined as the KSAOs needed to maintain high levels of personal and professional integrity, and to act as an ethical agent who promotes core values, integrity and accountability throughout the organization."[7]

Personal integrity is a personal choice to uphold certain moral and ethical standards. *Professional integrity* defines the professional who consistently and willingly practices within the guidelines of a chosen profession under the obligation of a code of ethics. *Ethical agent* means someone who, with strong internal guidance, practices ethical behavior and encourages others to do the same.

What Are Ethics?

Ethics are the rules or standards that govern conduct of individuals within a profession. They are based on a moral philosophy. That philosophy holds that there are differences between right and wrong or good and bad. Ethics are the standards people use to guide their decision-making with the intent that outcomes are fair to those involved.

Unethical behavior is that which is inconsistent with the stated values, norms, and beliefs of the organization's stakeholders.

Proficiency Indicators for All HR Professionals

Ethical practice for all HR professionals relies on these key behaviors. All HR professionals are expected to conduct themselves according to these requirements. SHRM has published a professional "Code of Ethics" for HR professionals (https://www.shrm.org/about-shrm/Pages/code-of-ethics.aspx). It is something you should read, understand, and follow in your daily job.

Maintaining Confidentiality

Confidentiality refers to data, whereas *privacy* refers to people. Therefore, because HR professionals work frequently with confidential information, maintaining that confidential status is critical. Handling such information requires respect for the intimate and classified nature of the information. Keeping those secrets is an expectation of all HR professionals.

Acting with Personal, Professional, and Behavioral Integrity

Personal conduct of HR professionals must meet a standard as high or higher than others are expected to meet. Integrity is the inner expectation people have for themselves that causes them to act in accordance with a code. That code expects honesty and forthrightness in all activities. Frequently, organizations publish written ethics codes, specifying exactly the expectations that exist for personal behavior.

Responding Immediately to All Reports of Unethical Behavior or Conflicts of Interest

When other people are suspected of acting unethically, it is up to the HR professional to react appropriately. This may involve a formal investigation, or a simple coaching of the individual involved. Doing nothing is not an ethical option.

Empowering All Employees to Report Unethical Behavior or Conflicts of Interest Without Fear of Reprisal

Employees at all levels must feel welcome to report observations of unethical behavior exhibited by others, even their bosses or others higher in the organization. If employees do not feel safe speaking up when they see wrong-doing, it becomes a cancer that can grow and consume the organization over a short period of time.

Showing Consistency Between Espoused and Enacted Values

Everyone in the organization must be able to witness the leaders doing what they demand of others. Organizational values are valid only if they are supported by daily decisions from the executive suite. People notice those things and will be slow to support values that are not supported by executives. "Do as I say, not as I do," does not work. Starting with senior management and then cascading throughout the organization, you want to foster a culture where "walking the talk" is the norm.

Acknowledging Mistakes

Denial is a reaction that may work in court, but it rarely proves helpful in the context of employment. If an HR professional has made an error, it is always preferable for them to admit the mistake and extend an offer to correct it. Most of us appreciate people who admit that they have goofed. We do not appreciate someone stonewalling us. Building confidence and trust in the HR department depends on people admitting and correcting mistakes when they happen.

Driving the Corporate Ethical Environment

Charles D. Kerns writes in Pepperdine University's *Graziadio Business Review*,[8] "Values drive behavior and therefore need to be consciously stated, but they also need to be affirmed by actions. Driving ethical behavior with values and attitudes requires that there be alignment among values, attitudes, and behavior." Table 7-1 shows examples of this alignment between each of the virtuous values, associated attitudes, and behavior.

Applying Power or Authority Appropriately

Abusing power is the shortest route to violating a trust. If employees are to trust and support an employer organization, the leaders must wield power and authority appropriately and with discretion. Decisions must be made in ways that support the employment relationship rather than undermine it. Power can be corrupting; successful HR professionals are people who understand the concepts of fairness and equality.

Mitigating the Influence of Bias

The most difficult image to see is the self-image. We tend to see ourselves as we think we are rather than as others see us. That is simply human nature. It is important for HR professionals to make special efforts to seek feedback from those they interact with so they can adjust their behavior as appropriate. Identifying personal bias is not always easy. Once it's identified, assuring that personal bias does not influence business decisions is even more difficult. It is not uncommon for individuals to create justifications for their decisions that deny impact of personal bias when in actuality bias is driving the decision.

Value	Attitude	Ethical Behavior
Wisdom and knowledge	Experience promotes wisdom, which helps convert information to knowledge.	Using knowledge to solve problems ethically and to do what is right.
Self-control	Self-control means effectively managing reactions to challenging situations and temptations.	Putting personal motivations aside and acting with objectivity by doing what is right.
Justice	Acting justly and fairly is a long-term driver of ethical behavior; remember the "Golden Rule."	Establishing just and mutually agreed-upon criteria that's administered fairly to all people.
Transcendence	The belief in a power and source outside oneself reduces self-serving actions and increases humility.	Putting institutional and/or stakeholder interests above self-interests. Identifying a personal purpose that is aligned with the organizational mission.
Love and kindness	Treating people with kindness helps increase the reservoir of positive affection and love.	Recognizing and encouraging others for their contributions.
Courage and integrity	Ethics requires the courage to do the right things consistently without regard to personal consequences.	Making unpopular decisions based on fair consideration of the facts.

Table 7-1   Values, Attitude, and Ethics and How They Relate

Bias is ingrained and can come from individual experiences reaching back into childhood. Once a person is treated unfairly by someone in a protected group (for example, race, gender, age, disability), the sense of ill treatment unfortunately may carry over into future relationships and decision-making.

Maintaining Appropriate Levels of Transparency in Organizational Practices

Transparency means the opposite of secrecy. Related to HR professionals, transparency means making information available to employees, stakeholders, and even sometimes the public, to explain policies and even benefit issues. The latest legislative push has been directed at compensation transparency. That means employers are required to permit employees to discuss their compensation openly and that of others in the group. Expectations have changed, and openness is now the order of the day. In truth, such openness makes it more difficult to cover up differences in pay between men and women in the same job or how job schedules are assigned to a racially mixed group of workers.

Ensuring That All Stakeholder Voices Are Heard

An obvious prerequisite is the identification of all stakeholders for the organization. *Stakeholder* is defined broadly as anyone or any organization or group we impact or are impacted by. Then, as issues arise, we can reach out to each stakeholder for input to the discussion. The downside of not doing this is that people will feel left out and ignored. None of us wants to be ignored. Therefore, you should invite participation and input.

Managing Political and Social Pressures when Making Decisions

HR professionals are in the unique position of brokering compromise between opposite views on issues such as benefits versus budget restrictions, cultural celebration versus production requirements, and confidentiality of records versus transparency of investigation outcomes. There are always going to be pressures from those of higher rank in the organization and sometimes from outside social standings. Many employers are being pressured to permit employee recreational use of marijuana while federal law continues to hold the substance illegal. Reconciling these differences is often the job of the HR professional. Sometimes, it takes the wisdom of Solomon.

There comes a time in most people's lives when there is pressure from a supervisor, manager, executive, or other influential player who would have you do something unethical. While the action may not be illegal, you recognize it as crossing the ethical line. The question is, "What will you choose to do?" Going against the wishes of the powerholder may negatively impact your career. Agreeing to the unethical action may cause harm to someone else. How you choose to handle that conundrum will determine your personal and professional ethics. Professional HR managers must put their jobs on the line from time to time to stand up for ethics. Remember the military comparison. Just because your boss tells you to shoot someone else, you remain responsible for your own actions. "Because my boss gave me an order" is no excuse for doing something you know is wrong.

Proficiency Indicators for Senior HR Professionals

At the senior level in the profession, ethical practice takes on greater importance because of the impact of the decisions being made. These added elements are additions to the basic ethics requirements for all HR professionals.

Empowering Senior Leaders to Maintain Internal Controls and Create an Ethical Environment to Prevent Conflicts of Interest

Executives must be leaders, but they must also follow policies and values established by the CEO and board of directors. From time to time, pressures arise to do something expedient that would violate a policy or a corporate value. An example is making an exception to the corporate commitment for equal pay when an executive chooses to hire a highly qualified female candidate at a rate below market value simply because she appears willing to accept the lower offer. Such exceptions can undermine the organization's declaration that it values equal pay treatment for all its workforce. Senior leaders need to understand they have a responsibility to oppose such violations of values.

Maintaining Contemporary Knowledge

With changes in local, state, and federal laws added to the changes in research about employee management issues, professionals in human resource delivery positions are challenged every day to keep their knowledge current. It is a never-ending process. If you happen to fall behind, your organization's reputation can suffer, it can lose its ability to recruit top talent, and it can miss important compliance requirements. Maintaining current knowledge is crucial.

Establishing Credibility

Acceptance at the executive table requires HR professionals to be accepted as credible contributors among organization executives. Credible reputation is based on the ability to inspire belief. Belief is created when experience shows there is more honesty and accuracy than missed expectations. Credibility goes beyond talk and promise. It is based on demonstrated accomplishments.

Challenging Conflicts of Interest

Conflicts of interest occur with more frequency than one might imagine. When the purchasing manager has stock in the vendor organization, there is a potential conflict of interest. When the HR professional has a personal interest in the recasting of a compensation policy because it can result in a substantial pay increase, there is a potential conflict of interest. When the CEO wants to hire her neighbor's daughter on a summer internship even while the company is laying off workers, there is a potential conflict of interest. These situations should be identified and challenged by the HR professional. Conflicts of interest undermine the organization's values and can occur at every level in the organization.

Withstanding Pressure when Developing Strategy

One conflict of interest that arises frequently for management personnel is interest in protecting or growing their slice of the organization. Getting more budget dollars, more headcount, or more time on the executive committee agenda can be a strong motivating force leading to bias in decision-making about organizational policy. HR professionals must constantly be aware of motivations that cause managers and executives to take policy positions. Counteracting such bias takes skill and commitment to the organization's well-being.

Setting the Standard

HR professionals contribute to performance standards by demonstrating behavior that is both legal and ethical. It is hard for employees, let alone managers and supervisors, to follow behavior standards when they see people in HR doing things that violate those standards. If people in HR have poor attendance or tardiness records and suffer no penalty, other departments begin to wonder why they should not also ease up on disciplinary action for the same type of issues with standards in their own area.

Balancing Organizational Success with Employee Advocacy

HR professionals juggle more than one client. The organization relies on HR to help establish and enforce standards and rules. The organization's employees also rely on HR to be their advocate. Complaints of sexual harassment often put HR into that dual role. When a claim is made, it is HR who must conduct an appropriate investigation by gathering all the relevant evidence available then rendering a decision based upon the preponderance of that evidence. This assures employees have been treated fairly and helps control legal liability. When management is at fault, employees depend on HR to be honest and reach an investigation finding that supports their valid complaint.

Developing HR Policies

One of the most critical parts of the HR management function is the development of employment policies. In organizations such as government agencies, there are extensive rule books that describe procedures and policies for almost any conceivable requirement. In entrepreneurial organizations, initially there are no policies. They must be written without the benefit of historical references within the organization. HR professionals get to work with executives to identify policy needs and then draft new policies. They have responsibility for gathering data that compares with alternative policies. Data supporting whatever policy is recommended should stand out above other alternatives. Data includes input from executives and managers, analysis of industry standards and expectations, and even competitor policies. Cost analysis or forecasting for each option is often helpful.

Creating HR Strategy

Louise Allen offers this: "Deeper knowledge and understanding of your business goals and business model can identify potential threats and opportunities in the quantity and quality of human resource required by your organization. This in turn identifies the key components of your HR strategy and the virtuous circle of providing whatever your organization needs for success."[9] So, once you have your business goals and business model well in hand, the question becomes, "How can we get HR functions to support those business requirements?"

Like any other creative effort, there will be multiple drafts and reviews before a final strategy is approved. Remember always that HR has a value-added mission to support the organizational reasons for being if it is to survive. If that is not done, executives may decide to outsource the HR functions to an outside third party who will provide the necessary support.

Making Decisions Aligned with Organizational Strategies and Values

Consistency of policy interpretation is critical to employees feeling they are being treated fairly. Americans have an innate belief that employers should treat their workers fairly. "Fair" is not a legal requirement, except for the common law requirement that employers offer "good faith and fair dealing." Every individual will be carrying around their own measuring tool to assess decisions based on how fair they are. When a decision does not pass their fairness test, discomfort, disgruntlement, and discord soon follow. When one department terminates someone for poor attendance and another department only gives a warning to an employee with a similar attendance record, there will be cries of unfairness. It is up to HR professionals to ensure that these disparate treatments do not happen.

You should be able to write down your organization's strategies and values. Based on those lists, you may assess the quality of decisions made in any department on any issue.

Communicating the Vision

Once executives have developed and described the organization's vision, it is up to HR to support and communicate that vision to the workforce. That communication often happens through training sessions. They can be classroom events, online seminars, webinars, or some other form of training. Every employee needs to understand and support the vision their leaders put forth. If the vision includes treating employees with dignity, then an open-door policy with access to managers and executives on a timely basis may be appropriate. Treating customers with respect may also be part of the vision. Training employees to be courteous in their approach to customers is part of the vision implementation requirement.

Maintaining a Culture of Ethics

"Do as I say and not as I do" does not work as an ethical model. People will comply with almost any requirement if they see their superiors also complying with that requirement. If the company does not allow ordinary employees to telecommute and it becomes known that managers are telecommuting, a schism develops in the workforce. How serious it is will depend on how many employees find the behavior contrast distasteful and whether discipline has resulted in some cases. Remember, a perception of fair treatment is a strong requirement in the employment relationship. Lose that, and expect to see turnover rates increase.

Aligning All HR Practices

Ethical behavior requires all interests under the control or influence of HR professionals be joined in the effort to support those ethical decisions. Think about what HR professionals must cover:

- Legal and regulatory compliance
- Labor union relationships
- Employee motivation
- Employee performance management and discipline oversight
- Global mindset
- Organizational leadership
- Support for creation and implementation of organizational vision, mission, policies, and other behavioral expectations
- Recruiting and hiring
- Employee training
- Diversity programs
- Workforce leadership and coaching managers on leadership issues
- Oversight of ethical expectations
- Employee communication
- Consultation on business decisions representing the employee viewpoint
- Periodical review of employee programs to ensure effectiveness

Usually, on the job, several of these areas of HR influence will be in play at the same time. Balancing them with one another is an expectation of a certified HR professional.

Summary

In this portion of the chapter, we explored ethical requirements for HR professionals. Ethics permeates each segment of HR duties and responsibilities. If HR managers do not demonstrate personal and organizational integrity, employees are likely to also demonstrate an absence of integrity. Transparency, honesty, and confidentiality are key components of an effective ethics program. For some people, ethics is simply doing the right thing in each circumstance. For others, ethics represents compliance with professional standards of conduct. Every day, an HR professional is likely to encounter one or more ethical dilemmas. How you react to those problems will determine what your organizational culture really is, not what you claim it to be. Decision-making is integral to ethics requirements. It starts with the most senior executive and then applies to each subordinate manager, supervisor, and employee.

HR professional behavioral standards are expected to conform to the HR Professional Code of Ethics, published by SHRM.[10] Key components of the code include the following:

- Professional responsibility
- Professional development
- Ethical leadership
- Fairness and justice
- Conflicts of interest
- Use of information

Behavioral Competency 3: Diversity, Equity & Inclusion (DE&I)

This topic has become so important, it was elevated to a competency from a Functional Area in 2022 and had equity added to what had been Diversity and Inclusion. This change is to increase our awareness and challenge us to take more proactive action. DE&I leverages the unique backgrounds and characteristics of all employees to contribute to organizational success. DE&I encompasses the qualities, life experiences, personalities, education, skills, competencies, and collaboration of a variety of people.

The following three subcompetencies comprise the Ethical Practice competency:[11]

- **Creating a diverse and inclusive culture**   Cultivates a work environment in which every person in the organization feels welcomed, respected, supported, and a sense of belonging
- **Ensuring equity effectiveness**   Ensures fair treatment in access, opportunity, and advancement for all individuals in the workplace
- **Connecting DE&I to organizational performance key concepts**   Demonstrates the importance of DE&I efforts to achieving organizational goals and key objectives

Key Concepts

- Characteristics of a dynamic workforce (for example, multigenerational, multicultural, multilingual, multitalented, multigendered)
- Approaches to developing an inclusive workplace (for example, executive sponsorship, leadership buy-in, allyship, unconscious-bias training, employee resource groups, mentorship, diversity metrics, psychological safety, using preferred gender pronouns)
- Workspace solutions (for example, lactation room, prayer room, Braille and screen reader, closed captioning, wheelchair ramp, gender-neutral restrooms)
- Barriers to success involving conscious and unconscious bias (for example, gender-based discrimination, racism, including systemic racism, stereotypes, ageism, ableism, ingroup/outgroup bias, affinity bias, gender identity bias, sexual orientation bias, social comparison bias, extroversion/introversion bias, neurodiversity bias, microaggressions, personal barriers such as imposter syndrome and identity covering, cultural taxation)
- Techniques to measure and increase equity (for example, SHRM Empathy Index, diversity of employees at all organizational levels, pay audits, pay equity reports, pay transparency, employee surveys)
- Benefits and programs that support DE&I (for example, caregiver options, workplace flexibility policies, paid leave options, tuition reimbursement programs, global festivities and events calendar)
- DE&I metrics (for example, gender diversity, race diversity, retention rates for diverse employees, diversity of external stakeholders)

Definition

According to SHRM, "*Diversity, Equity & Inclusion (DE&I) is defined as the KSAOs needed to create a work environment in which all individuals are treated fairly and respectfully, have equal access to opportunities and resources, feel a sense of belonging, and use their unique backgrounds and characteristics to contribute fully to the organization's success.*"[12]

Proficiency Indicators for All HR Professionals

The following are the basic behaviors required of all HR professionals in the area of DE&I:

- Recognizes, supports, and advocates on behalf of a diverse workforce with representation across race, gender, sexual orientation, ethnicity, religious beliefs, country of origin, education, abilities, and the intersectionality of the elements of diversity
- Identifies and implements workspace solutions

- Identifies, confronts, and addresses evidence of bias, stereotyping, microaggressions, and subtle acts of exclusion in the workplace
- Provides professional development, mentoring, coaching, and guidance on cultural and diversity differences and practices to employees at all levels of the organization
- Identifies and communicates the benefits of DE&I to employees and leaders
- Develops and maintains knowledge of current trends and HR management best practices relating to DE&I
- Implements HR programs, practices, and policies that encourage employees to embrace opportunities to work with those who possess diverse experiences and backgrounds
- Supports a workplace culture and team that invite interpersonal risk-taking, support mutual respect and trust, and do not embarrass or punish team members for speaking up

Overview: Key Terms

The three important key terms to fully understand within this behavior competency are *diversity, equity,* and *inclusion.* It is helpful to define them to understand how to incorporate them into the organization's culture and management.

Diversity

With DE&I, we are valuing individuals' unique perspectives and their diversity of thought. This is far beyond Equal Employment Opportunity Commission compliance. Our perspectives are highly influenced by our cultural backgrounds and experiences. Food, housing, recreation, and life activities are tied to the culture in which one grows up and matures. Thought processes and references are determined by the experiences people have had and the interactions with others that were part of those experiences. If we were rewarded early on for our imagination and innovation, it is easier for us to generate ideas later in life. If we were encouraged to contain our behavior within strict boundaries of social decorum and not deviate much from those expectations, it will be more difficult for us to be inventive or creative later in life.

Organizational leaders will be most effective when they understand each individual's background to understand how to encourage them to fully participate in the organization.

Equity

In this context, we are not talking about the value attributable to the owners of a business. "Equity" is one of those terms that everyone seems to understand at some visceral level, but few people share the same definition. Merriam-Webster's "simple definition" of equity is "fairness or justice in the way people are treated." But then, what exactly is fairness? How do we define justice? If these concepts are not absolutes, but shaped by everyone's worldviews and experiences, then the definition may stay a moving target. Equity is about each of us getting what we need to survive or succeed—access to opportunity, networks, resources, and supports—based on where we are and where we want to go.[13]

Inclusion

Inclusion is the characteristic of a workplace referring to behaviors within the organization that determine how individuals are valued, engaged, and respected. Inclusion is also linked to "fairness," equal access to resources and opportunities, plus being included within a group or structure. You can see the link between inclusion and equal employment opportunity (EEO). While EEO is a legal obligation, inclusion goes further by valuing the importance of being part of the group in every way. Inclusion is being welcomed not in spite of who I am but because of who I am.

While it's not incorporated into the competency name yet, many organizations are adding "belonging" to DE&I. That expands the concept for an affinity for a group, situation, or place. Belonging is a sense of fitting in and feeling like a key member of the team.

Visible and Invisible Traits

Some traits will be visible, while many may be invisible. Visible traits are external physical characteristics that are easily recognizable.[14] Examples include ethnicity/race, nationality, gender, age, skin color, culture, body size/type, and language.

Invisible traits are those attributes not readily seen. These include diversity of thought or perspective, life experience, values and beliefs, working-style preferences, and socioeconomic status.

Then, to keep things from being simple, some traits may be visible or invisible. Examples include religion, veteran status, sexual orientation, and disabilities. It is estimated 70–75 percent of disabilities are not readily visible.

Diversity Without Inclusion

Through a strong outreach program, it is possible that an organization can recruit a diverse group of employees. It is possible that some of those employees may not be made to feel like a part of the company because they are not invited to fully contribute their ideas or suggestions. They may not be invited to participate in after-hours activities or assigned the key jobs or projects. Sadly, some folks may not be comfortable with co-workers because they look different or come from a different culture.

Any exclusion, whether subtle or overt, can lead to a feeling of being an outsider. Therefore, diversity does not innately result in inclusion. Inclusion comes from conscious effort. Inclusion depends on more than a lack of bias. It depends on commitment to ensuring each person is welcomed as a participant in every facet of work life. With diversity, I may simply get invited to the party. With inclusion, when I arrive at the party, I will be sincerely welcomed in, offered a beverage, and asked to dance.

Diversity and Globalization

Not every culture in the world has the same view of diversity, equity, and inclusion as found in the United States. Some countries are theocracies, monocracies, or other monogenic countries. Whatever the circumstance, lack of variety in cultural experience makes it more difficult to accept, let alone encourage, recruiting a diverse group of job candidates. When it comes to selecting new hires, this cultural bias may play a part in the hiring decision. That bias usually is not intentional, yet it exists, and its results are seen in a high percentage of people in the organization that look and think alike. It may be based on religion, race, or even gender. The differences in cultural experience are measured along a broad spectrum. From one country to another, the pointer along that spectrum line can shift dramatically.

Global Legal Distinctions

Legal requirements for equal employment opportunity, equity, and diversity vary widely from one country to another. In some cases, imposition of quotas for some groups exists. Here are a few random examples. Equal employment opportunity requires some serious study of local and federal requirements in each political area where you may have employees located.

- **Australia**   The Aussies require employers with 100 or more workers to report their gender equity plans and submit reports on the participation of women in their workforce and their board of directors.

- **Canada**   Seven provinces and the federal government have pay equity legislation that requires employers to provide equal pay for work of equal or comparable value.

- **Germany**   There are absolute quotas for the employment of severely disabled people based on the size of the employer workforce. Employers with 60 or more employees must have 5 percent of their workforce composed of severely disabled employees. Smaller quotas apply to smaller organizations.

- **Great Britain**   The practice of a fixed retirement requirement at age 65 has been rescinded by law.

- **South Africa**   There is a legal prescription for annual turnover thresholds. Exceed those limits, and affirmative action requirements will apply for recruiting and hiring. Protected groups include Black people, women, and people with disabilities.

The Benefits and Costs of Diversity

The European Commission, Directorate-General for Employment, Industrial Relations, and Social Affairs conducted a study using input from 200 companies in four European countries.[15] The study identified some specific benefits and costs associated with employment diversity policies and programs.

The benefits of active diversity policies were determined to include the following:

- Strengthened cultural values within the organization
- Enhanced corporate reputation
- Helped attract and retain exceptionally talented people
- Improved motivation and efficiency of existing staff
- Improved innovation and creativity among employees
- Enhanced service levels and customer satisfaction
- Helped overcome labor shortages
- Reduced labor turnover
- Resulted in lower absenteeism rates

The costs of diversity programs were determined to include the following:

- **Costs of legal compliance**   Recordkeeping systems, staff training, policy communication.
- **Cash costs of diversity**   Staff education and training, facilities and diversity support staff, monitoring and reporting processes.
- **Opportunity costs of diversity**   Loss of benefits because a scarce resource cannot be used in other productive activities (diversion of top management time, productivity shortfalls).
- **Business risks of diversity**   Slower decision-making and plans taking longer than planned to implement or failing completely. This is known as the *execution risk*. Sustainable diversity policies are an outcome of a successful change in corporate culture.

The Four Layers of Diversity

According to *Color Magazine,*[16] the four layers of diversity can be compiled into the four layers model, developed by Lee Gardenswartz and Anita Rowe, which has radiating rings from a center where personality constitutes the core:

- **Personality**   This includes an individual's preferences, perceptions, learning styles, behavioral predispositions, and beliefs. Personality is shaped early in life and is both influenced by, and influences, the other three layers throughout one's lifetime and career choices.
- **Internal dimensions**   These include aspects of diversity over which we have no control (though "physical ability" can change over time because of choices we make to be active or in cases of illness or accidents). This dimension is the layer in which many divisions between and among people exist and which forms the core of many diversity efforts. These dimensions include the first things we see in other people, such as race, gender, and age, and on which we make many assumptions and base judgments.
- **External dimensions**   These include aspects of our lives that we have some control over, which might change over time, and which usually form the basis for decisions on careers and work styles. This layer often determines, in part, with whom we develop friendships and what we do for work. This layer also tells us much about whom we like to be with and decisions we make in hiring and promotions at work.
- **Organizational dimensions**   This layer concerns the aspects of culture found in a work setting. While much attention of diversity efforts is focused on the internal dimensions, issues of preferential treatment and opportunities for development or promotion are impacted by the aspects of this layer.

The *Color Magazine* article tells us, "The usefulness of this model is that it includes the dimensions that shape and impact both the individual and the organization itself.

While the 'Internal Dimensions' receive primary attention in successful diversity initiatives, the elements of the 'External' and 'Organizational' dimensions often determine the way people are treated, who 'fits' or not in a department, who gets the opportunity for development or promotions, and who gets recognized."

Proficiency Indicators for Senior HR Professionals

Senior HR professionals are expected to possess the following skills over and above the basic behaviors already reviewed.

- Advocates to leadership to increase workforce diversity with representation across race, gender, sexual orientation, ethnicity, religious beliefs, country of origin, education, abilities, and the intersectionality of the elements of diversity

- Partners with business leaders to develop, implement, and oversee enterprise-wide programs, practices, and policies that lead to an inclusive and diverse workforce

- Ensures HR staff members have up-to-date knowledge of current trends and HR management best practices relating to DE&I

- Assesses an organization's inclusiveness, diversity, and retention of diverse talent using DE&I metrics

- Creates and manages HR programs, practices, and policies that encourage employees to embrace opportunities to work with those who possess diverse experiences and backgrounds

- Develops policies and programs to create a workplace culture and team that support and reinforce the principles of psychological safety

- Provides a culture that encourages employees to be their authentic selves, promotes courageous and honest DE&I-related conversations, and supports allyship among employees

Developing a Diversity, Equity, and Inclusion Strategy

Three reasons mark the need for a strategy to be used in creating and implementing a diversity, equity, and inclusion program for any organization:

- **Reason 1: Priority**   Without a strategy, the DE&I efforts will always take a backseat to other more immediately urgent matters.

- **Reason 2: Complexity**   DE&I programs are not simple. The complexity requires organization-wide strategies if a successful implementation is to be achieved.

- **Reason 3: Resistance**   DE&I programs require organizational change, regardless of the organization. There will be more change in some organizations than in others. Change is hard. Therefore, making the changes needed for successful DE&I programs will take some significant effort to overcome the initial resistance.

Once the decision has been made to develop and implement a diversity, equity, and inclusion program in your organization, you will need to identify the strategic steps you must take to achieve success.

Executive Commitment

Changing organizational behaviors and individual attitudes are results that do not come easily. If they are to be achieved at all, you need the support and backing of senior management. Otherwise, you might as well not even start. Without the constant challenge and reinforcement from senior management for your program, objective, and rationale, there can be no hope for reaching your established goals. "What the boss says is what gets done." If leadership is not fully behind the program, it will just waste organizational resources and not accomplish what is hoped.

Making the Business Case for DE&I   The Conference Board published some thoughts in 2008 that still hold true today:[17]

- **Business acumen and external market knowledge**   This becomes the foundation of understanding how a DE&I program can support business needs. It includes the following characteristics:
    - Executives understand and are current on global and local trends/changes and how they inform and influence DE&I.
    - Executives gather and use competitive intelligence.
    - Executives understand diverse customer/client needs.
    - Executives understand and are current with global sociopolitical environments.
    - Executives understand context and lessons learned.
- **Holistic business knowledge**   This requires understanding of the impact of the financial, economic, and market drivers on the bottom-line results. Additional requirements include the following:
    - Executives understand core business strategies.
    - Executives possess solid financial acumen.
    - Executives use information from multiple disciplines and sources to offer integrated ideas and solutions on issues important to the organization.
- **Diversity, equity, and inclusion return on investment (ROI)**   This is where the fiscal impact of the DE&I program becomes evident. Requirements include the following:
    - Determine and communicate how DE&I contributes to core business strategy and results.
    - Create insights on how DE&I contributes to both people and HR strategies as well as business results.
    - Design and develop DE&I metrics that exhibit the ROI impact.

Preliminary Assessment

A quick way to determine how you are doing with your DE&I program is to conduct an employee survey. It may take some professional help to identify the specific information you want to gather and the form of the inquiries you craft for each. Some questions and data you want to collect may best be first discussed with your legal counsel, such as questions on religion, sexual orientation, and gender identity. But surveying the workforce will help you understand the "state of the enterprise" about diversity, equity, and inclusion.

Infrastructure Creation

If you are just beginning to address the issues of diversity, equity, and inclusion, it is important to recognize that there is going to be a need for some changes in the way you do things within the organization. Sometimes those changes can be uncomfortable for people, and that demands you be ready to give them the support they need to get past their discomfort to participate in the successful implementation of your program.

Diversity Councils Diversity councils are groups of employees who discuss issues of diversity, equity, and inclusion. The duties of these councils can vary widely—from being an advisory-only group to a group having some or total responsibility for implementing or overseeing program elements such as complaint handling and community involvement.

Employee Resource Groups Employee resource groups (ERGs) can have many names. One common name is *employee affinity groups*. Whatever the name, these are groups of similar employees coming together voluntarily to express opinions and requests for consideration that apply to their group. Some examples of employees benefiting from ERGs are Black employees, Hispanic employees, Asian employees, employees who are veterans, LGBTQIA+ employees, Women engineers, and employees using English as a second language. There are countless possibilities.

Strategic Alliances DE&I programs can make use of linkages to community groups that support expanding or reinforcing outreach efforts for particular groups of people. It may be that you need more women in professional jobs. Identifying and then building relationships with these community groups can take some time but will contribute authenticity to your DE&I program. They can also be sources for your open job placement opportunities when those occur. Community organizations range from groups of persons with disabilities to veteran groups and various racial and gender support groups. Some are social, but many are also focused on increasing employment opportunities for their qualified membership.

System Changes

DE&I programs by their very nature require changes to the way employers operate. Systemic changes will be needed. That is why there is often discomfort associated with DE&I programs. They take us out of our usual and customary routines and demand that we expand our experiences and embrace things that are different.

DE&I programs are most effective when they evolve from standalone programs to instead fully integrated practices in the way you conduct your HR functions and responsibilities. This means making changes to recruitment, selection, orientation, onboarding, training, development, promotions, engagement, retention, total rewards, and employee relations.

Supply Chain Management and Relations   Vendor and supplier relations are important to DE&I programs because we want to spend our dollars with other businesses that share our values and commitment to DE&I. Outreach programs to encourage participation of minority- and female-owned businesses are part of the DE&I process. Include businesses owned by veterans or people with disabilities to participate in the contracting or bidding process. There are some governmental jurisdictions that require contractors to meet participation goals for vendors and suppliers to be sure that these various groups have a "piece of the pie." Employers who demonstrate active solicitation from all portions of the vendor community will also have successful relationships with the vendors, ensuring that they will be able to meet future requirements as well as current demands for contract participation.

According to the Society for Human Resources Management, "Beyond that, nurturing a diverse supplier base—including coaching minority-, veteran-, and women-led enterprises on ways to improve their offers—enhances the buying company's image. It can also foster economic strength, as many of these companies tend to hire from within their communities."[18]

Marketing, Branding, and Customer Relations   Broad appeal and brand awareness are the goals of most marketing programs. Establishing a brand that is recognized and valued by multiple cultures is also desirable. Doing that with an eye on healthy customer relations may require addressing each group in special ways. For example, if a portion of the customer base is Hispanic, having customer service representatives who speak Spanish can help reinforce those customer relationships. The same is true of any other ethnic or cultural group.

In some portions of the country, there are large populations of Vietnamese, Chinese, and Korean people. Serving these groups in their own language can build positive relations and increase brand loyalty. Some large companies choose to locate their customer support function in Salt Lake City, Utah. Why? Salt Lake City has a population of bilingual members of The Church of Jesus Christ of Latter-day Saints who have learned a second language to facilitate their faith missions. Providing literature in the primary language of the customers is another way to address their needs and increase diversity, equity, and inclusion of the various nationality groups. Also, providing employment posters in the primary languages of the employees is a requirement in many instances. That is why in some places, such as San Francisco, employment posters can be found in English, Spanish, Chinese, and Tagalog (a language spoken in the Philippines).

Training

Training programs for both managers and nonmanagement employees can be a key component of the DE&I program. It is more than sensitivity training. It involves the communication of key organizational values. Also, training can help raise the skill levels of supervisors to more effectively deal with DE&I issues.

Initial employee training during the onboarding process can help new workers understand "how we do things around here." Communicating and instilling values of diversity, equity, and inclusion early on can help those lessons last for the duration of the employee's tenure.

Measurement and Evaluation

Diversity programs can be measured by looking at demographics of employee composition. How diverse is the incumbent group? How diverse is the recruiting effort? Count the number of recruiting resources that represent various racial or ethnic groups. Are there groups representing women, veterans, and people with disabilities? Recruiting and hiring are just exercises unless they result in employee retention. Another measurement is turnover rate. What percentage of new hires are still on the payroll after a year?

Equity can be measured by comparing salaries using compa-ratios. Promotions can be tracked as well as access to developmental opportunities.

Inclusion is a bit more difficult to measure. It can be effectively done, however, with employee surveys. To what extent do employees feel their direct supervisor includes them in decisions about their job activities? Do employees feel they are part of the decision-making process when policy changes are being considered? Again, check with your legal counsel concerning which questions on inclusion you can use on your survey.

Why Diversity Initiatives Falter

If you are going to emphasize diversity, equity, and inclusion in your organization, it is not enough to develop a statement to post on the wall next to your company values. How you define diversity, equity, and inclusion needs to be in terms clear enough that your workforce can both understand and reiterate the definition as well as "walk the talk" in all functions of work, demonstrated by leadership, policies, systems, and programs. Without defining your terms, you cannot expect everyone will have the same understanding.

Conducting annual diversity, equity, and inclusion training is helpful, but it is not enough. Too often, these initiatives fail because they are delivered as a strong-arm tactic. Many firms see adverse effects from mandatory training because of the use of negative messages in their training, like headlining a legal case for diversity and highlighting stories of huge settlements, which gives an implied threat: "Discriminate, and the company will pay the price." Threats, or "negative incentives," rarely win converts. What's more, these tactics may create covert resentment. Organizational development (OD) specialists have told us for years that people often respond to compulsory training with anger and resistance. Do people who undergo training usually shed their biases? Researchers have been examining that question since before World War II. While people are easily taught to respond correctly to a questionnaire about bias, they soon forget the right answers. The positive effects of diversity training rarely last beyond a day or two, and several studies suggest that it can activate bias or spark a backlash. Frank Dobbin and Alexandrea Kalev studied 829 midsize and large U.S. firms, and their report, "Why Diversity Programs Fail,"[19] concluded that "companies do a better job of increasing diversity when they forgo the control tactics and frame their efforts more positively." In their statistical research, looking at the percent of change over 5 years among managers in their study, they found the largest positive change occurred when mentoring was used.

Summary

In this portion of the chapter, you learned about SHRM's newest behavioral competency of Diversity, Equity, and Inclusion. We explored the expertise in DE&I that enables HR professionals to keep their organizations focused on valuing the unique perspectives a wide variety of individuals bring to an organization.

Interpersonal Cluster

The Interpersonal cluster represents 16.5 percent of both exams' weighted scores. There are three competencies that fall within the Interpersonal cluster:

- Behavioral Competency 4: Relationship Management
- Behavioral Competency 5: Communication
- Behavioral Competency 6: Global Mindset

This cluster covers the behaviors, attributes, and knowledge required for HR professionals to perform collaboratively and with interpersonal aspects of their roles.

Behavioral Competency 4: Relationship Management

HR's most notable role has been, and continues to be, the "people" job; therefore, managing relationships is a core function for an HR professional. Those who are good at using their relationship skills will foster greater collaboration, understanding, and communication with stakeholders.

Five subcompetencies comprise the Relationship Management competency. SHRM defines them[20] as follows:

- **Networking**   Effectively building a network of professional contacts both within and outside of the organization
- **Relationship building**   Effectively building and maintaining relationships both within and outside of the organization
- **Teamwork**   Participating as an effective team member that builds, promotes, and leads effective teams
- **Negotiation**   Reaching mutually acceptable agreements with negotiating parties within and outside of the organization
- **Conflict management**   Managing and resolving conflicts by identifying areas of common interest among the parties in conflict

Key Concepts

- Types of conflict (for example, relationship, task, inter- and intra-organizational)
- Conflict-resolution strategies (for example, accommodation, collaboration, compromise, competition, avoidance)
- Negotiation, tactics, strategies, and styles (for example, perspective taking, principled bargaining, auction, interest-based bargaining, position-based bargaining)
- Trust-building techniques (for example, emotional intelligence, relatability, vulnerability, transparency, recognizing individual strengths)

Definition

According to SHRM, "*Relationship Management* is defined as the knowledge, skills, abilities, and other characteristics (KSAOs) needed to create and maintain a network of professional contacts within and outside of the organization, to build and maintain relationships, to work as an effective member of a team, and to manage conflict while supporting the organization."[21]

Basic Proficiency Indicators

All HR professionals must be able to establish and maintain positive relationships with people both inside and outside the organization. HR touches all parts of the organization and reaches into a myriad of external groups, including vendors and professional colleagues in the larger HR community. We want to establish a positive relationship with all the people with whom we have contact.

Establishing Credibility

Without credibility, the HR professional has little to offer. When seen as someone who cannot be relied on to offer accurate information and advice, the HR professional will find managers avoiding them. You must be the "go-to" expert on all matters involving human resources. That means when you do not know an answer, say so and promise to do the necessary research and get back to your contact with accurate information. Do it in a timely way because help that is delayed often is not any help at all. Managers need information quickly so they can deal with the issues they have facing them. Remember, it takes only one incident where you give bad advice for your reputation to be damaged. It will take a long time to get it back on the positive side, and there is no guarantee of success in recapturing trust.

Treating Stakeholders with Respect and Dignity

As an HR professional, you have many stakeholders. We reviewed them in Chapter 5. Remember, all organizational employees are stakeholders, too. The same goes for all your managers and executives. Do not forget your boss. Your boss is also a stakeholder. Working with some of these folks will be delightful. Others not so much. Each deserves your respect for the role they play and the person they are. Your job as an HR professional is to treat each individual with dignity and respect. Even if there is someone who has committed a terminable offense and you are helping the supervisor terminate them, being kind can go a long way toward decent treatment. Ask yourself each time, "How would I like to be treated?" Then do that. No one deserves to be belittled or shamed for any reason. Even if you must call the police to deal with a serious behavioral issue, you can still be an adult in your approach to that person who is causing the problem.

Building Engaging Relationships

Building relationships is a skill HR professionals must develop. Some people do it naturally, and others must work at it. Here are some suggestions from an expert in communication.

How to Build Engaging Relationships

Proactive communication with your team can serve your business significantly. Done consistently, you will have access to one of the best, most authentic focus groups for your brand. You will be given qualified, firsthand perspective into your services and processes. You will also gain better knowledge of your staff and their strengths. Another bonus is that your team will become more inspired and loyal knowing you care about their feedback.

The key is listening. Meet with your HR professionals one at a time. Go into this kind of communication without preconceived thoughts. Listen mindfully and do not dominate the conversation. This is your time to collect insights and information. Remember that you are the final decision-maker, but now is your opportunity to gather data to help in creating strategies to improve your business. Do not be defensive. Remember this person is on your team. When your meeting concludes, let your employee know how appreciative you are and *then* correct or add anything you think will benefit their knowledge of the business.

Here are some tips to get started:

- Meetings with each employee should be held on a regular basis, such as monthly.

- Dedicate a specific time for these discussions and *make them a priority, not to be changed* on your schedule. This helps convey their importance. If you have a dedicated hour and are done in 45 minutes periodically, that is fine. The goal is to schedule meetings that you can attend and not have to reschedule.

- Be prepared. Your employee has probably thought a lot about this meeting. They will be more engaged in this and future conversations if you are taking this meeting seriously.

- Ask purposeful questions so at the end of your meeting you have learned something. (In other words, what is the one thing that we do that customers appreciate? What new technology do you think our clients would respond to?)

- Keep to your allotted time so you establish structure and consistency. Meetings consistently running long may lead to irritation and burnout.

- Reconfirm the next scheduled meeting as your last agenda item so your team knows these conversations are now part of the business culture.

- Ask staff to save any follow-up comments or notes for the next meeting, unless urgent. This will keep you both organized and avoid pop-in meetings that can also lead to burnout.

- Realize you are building a new process, and it will take time. Do not push yourself to meet with everyone or act on suggestions right away. It is better to be consistent with meetings and actions to effect change that truly improves your business.

This same process can work with your customers/clients and even vendors.[22]

Demonstrating Approachability

How do you feel when you walk up to someone and they do not recognize you? They continue their current conversation or, worse, turn away from you. It hurts when people do not acknowledge you. Others feel the same when we treat them in that way. While it is not always easy, particularly with people who are known to be difficult to work with, it is important for HR professionals to treat others with professionalism. Being discourteous is a sure way to become known as someone who cannot be approached easily.

Ensuring Alignment with HR Strategy

Without doubt, HR strategy will embrace employees, managers, suppliers, customers, and even stockholders. Each of these groups is important to the successful achievement of the company goals. Strategy is the way those goals will be accomplished. And people are always going to be the force that implements the strategy. There is a direct link to strategic completion of goals with the relationships that can cause that to happen. HR professionals touch each of the stakeholder groups along the way. It is therefore critical that HR professionals be conscious of how they impact their relationships and thus the impact they have on strategic implementation of action plans.

Providing Customer Service

Customers in the corporate sense are those people external to the organization who buy our products or services. They are the clients of governments and nonprofits who receive services. Customers and how we provide for them are the reasons that our organizations exist. No customers equals no need for HR.

For HR, our primary customers are our organizational employees and managers. We provide the products (for example, insurance programs, career pathing) and services (for example, complaint investigations, onboarding) on which our customers rely. How we service these people will determine their view of the HR group, plus the individuals within that group. If HR is always telling people, "You can't do that," it will not be long before the phones in the HR department stop ringing. People do not like hearing that they can't do something. They much prefer hearing, "Let's see what we can do."

Explore with them what is possible and what is not. Your employees will leave with a more positive feeling having received an explanation of the reasons behind each option or prohibition. You will have provided good customer service, even if they did not get exactly what was requested.

Promoting Successful Relationships

These are some basic methods for promoting successful relationships:

- Help employees understand organizational goals and strategies for achieving them.
- Give each employee an understanding about how they personally can contribute to achieving those goals.
- Acknowledge positive accomplishments when they are extraordinary.
- Highlight employee achievements within the organization.
- Say "thank you" when people do the right thing.
- Compliment the boss for the achievements of people in the group.

Managing Internal and External Relationships

Internal relationships take the form of employee and management encounters. Often, HR is serving these people in some way. Managing those relationships can be best accomplished by offering a positive experience, even if the message HR is required to deliver is not one people want to hear. How it is delivered, its tone, and its level of kindness will go a long way to preserving the relationships.

External relationships exist with shareholders, regulators, enforcement agencies, media contacts, and even membership in community service clubs like Rotary, Kiwanis, Masons, and Lions. Do not forget your local chamber of commerce. Knowing what information can be shared and responding when appropriate will establish positive relationships with each of these groups. There is an expectation that HR professionals are "the face of the corporation" whenever someone is dealing with you in an official capacity. Even if you are on a community baseball team, you carry the flag of your employer organization. People see you as the official representative of that employer. You are an agent in that regard. You carry a large burden when that happens. You must be ready to carry it with pride and professionalism.

Championing Organizational Effectiveness

Being a cheerleader for effectiveness in your organization is another role you must play as an HR professional. When you see things that are not working because of organizational structure or "red tape," it is incumbent upon you to intervene and suggest change. That can be a bit tricky when people have a sense of "owning" the portion of the organization that is not working well. Working with your HR boss to identify means for influencing improvements is often an effective way to approach the situation. This is another area where spotlighting success is a terrific way to get other people to agree to do something similar in the future when similar problems exist.

Serving as an Advocate

Employees sometimes need an advocate. When there are policy issues that need attention and large groups of employees are providing feedback that the current policy is inadequate or no longer applicable to the times, HR is responsible for consolidating those employee views and presenting them to senior management. When a discrimination complaint is filed and the investigation suggests the manager is at fault, HR will be responsible for providing the feedback and advocating for a remedy on behalf of the employee. Sure, there is always a need to act as an advocate for what is right, but there are also circumstances that call for an advocate when people just need to be heard. Potentially unsafe working conditions that have yet to be recognized by management can be a reason for HR's involvement. One employee working alone may not be as effective as when HR becomes an advocate for employees in general to deal with the problem.

Fostering Team Building

HR sometimes provides team building training and facilitation programs. Sometimes HR researches and recommends outside vendors for such programs. Every day HR can support team building by recognizing team accomplishments. Offering rewards for team accomplishments can be effective, and providing acknowledgment and thanks for those accomplishments can be equally if not more effective. An important HR role in fostering team building is in guiding supervisors on effective behaviors for high-performing teams, helping them create internal team cultures that include high trust, common vision, team unity, and accountability.

Building a Network of Contacts

Effective HR professionals compile a host of contacts who can help with the wide range of HR problems that may come up from day to day. Who do you call when you need a contact for employee assistance programs, workers' compensation reimbursement problems, or addiction rehabilitation programs? Who can help you set up an employee relocation program or provide in-home medical care following a difficult surgery? Each day another issue will come up, and you will be faced with having to do some research to determine what contact will help you solve your problem with or for the employee. Over time, all those vetted contacts will combine to represent a large database of references when you need them.

Proficiency Indicators for Senior HR Professionals

SHRM-SCP Beyond the basic proficiency indicators, senior HR professionals are challenged to master additional behaviors.

Designing Metrics

Senior HR managers are usually involved in establishing the measurements that will appraise how well they and their department are serving employees. Whether you are calculating turnover rates or revenue to expense ratios, there are some critical aspects of HR management that should be measured. Those measurements provide feedback to the

HR department but also offer reassurance to the senior executive team that HR is keeping its commitment to accomplish its key goals. Designing those metrics is a way for HR to demonstrate its willingness to be accountable for its own performance. All other portions of the organization are measured in some ways, so the HR department should be as well.

Networking

Developing a professional network outside the organization is as important as maintaining healthy relationships with managers and employees inside the company. Other senior HR professionals at other industry organizations can help suggest solutions to problems you are having that they have already solved. As cultural norms evolve, other HR professionals can provide sounding boards for policy questions and benefit program adjustments. Maintaining a professional network of HR friends is increasingly important as time goes on. Not everyone can solve all the problems. Relying on help from other professionals is an effective way to leverage your time and resources.

Championing Customer Service

While it is a basic HR behavior to champion organizational effectiveness, it is an advanced behavior to champion customer service. Sometimes it is necessary to fight for employee treatment when budget dollars must be allocated. Adding a new paid day off to the offering will expand budget expense by a certain amount. What will be the offsetting benefit to the corporation for making that extra offering? Identifying the business needs is first. Then comes the presentation and response to executive questions about your recommendations. Serving your customers is a key role as an HR professional.

Negotiating with Stakeholders

It is not only employees with whom we deal. You will interact frequently with insurance providers, union representatives, state and federal enforcement agencies, and the board of directors if you are at an executive level. All are stakeholders in how an organization is run. From time to time, you will need to negotiate with each one. For example, changing working condition provisions in a union contract can be calculated to have a dollar impact on the budget. Settling discrimination complaints and workers' compensation cases with outside agencies will also have budget impact. Establishing a new policy sometimes requires approval of the board of directors. Persuading them to adopt the new policy is often also an exercise in convincing them to accept the budget impact it will cause.

If you are in an organization that bills its HR costs back to internal client departments, there will be negotiations to support and justify those billings. You will be called upon to discuss your department's performance on a regular basis.

Designing a Customer Service Culture

It is the expectation, and typically the norm, that HR professionals provide great customer service each day. It is necessary to create a sense that providing outstanding customer service is "just the way we do things around here." When your HR department believes that, and behaves collectively to deliver it, your internal clients and boss will be happy.

Forbes published a list of key customer service action plan items for those who have yet to develop their own program:[23]

- *Articulate your central philosophy in a few meaningful words.* "The needs of our patients come first."

- *Distill a list of your core values.* Identify how customers, employees, and vendors should be always treated.

- *Reinforce your commitment to these values constantly.* Do this daily or weekly, not annually.

- *Make it visual.* Put your values on e-mails, water bottles, coffee mugs, on the breakroom wall, and in-customer packages.

- *Make your philosophy the focus of orientation.* Make sure your employee-orientation messages are reinforced by actual work experiences.

- *Train, hire, support, and, if necessary, discipline to enforce what is important.* Be sure the messages are consistent.

Creating Conflict-Resolution Strategies

Put two people together in a working environment, and eventually there will be some level of conflict. Put many people together, and those conflicts will happen frequently. According to SHRM, "The human resource team has a leadership responsibility to develop and implement workplace conflict policies and procedures and to create and manage conflict-resolution programs. HR also initiates employee communication on conflict and tracks the metrics and costs of conflict-resolution efforts. Many HR professionals receive conflict-resolution training, often as part of their professional development, and many are accustomed to conducting such training or enlisting outside training resources for supervisors and managers.

"HR professionals often become involved in settling workplace conflicts, particularly if the employees and their supervisors cannot achieve a resolution. If HR cannot resolve a conflict, an outside specialist may be needed to work out a settlement."[24]

Overseeing HR Decision-Making Processes

The entire HR department must be capable of making decisions that are consistent with legal requirements and company policy. Documentation of those decisions is essential for the employer to be able to defend its actions at some later time. Then, it is necessary to train managers and supervisors to make good decisions and properly document them. Managers and supervisors hate documentation. It takes time that they do not believe they have—and some just hate writing anything. HR is accountable for overcoming those impediments and ensuring that the proper standards are met.

Developing Strategic Relationships

Remember, relationships both inside and outside the organization can be strategic. That means they can help you meet your corporate goals. The senior HR professional is responsible for developing relationships that can contribute to those strategies. Think in terms of the insurance program representatives for health care, life insurance, and long-term disability care. How about employee assistance contractors, relocation moving companies, and human resource information system (HRIS) software vendors? Each of these is an important relationship that senior HR managers should develop and maintain.

Fostering an Intra-organizational Culture

Encouraging understanding of other cultures is something HR can facilitate within the organization. International interests are obviously going to require such action and support, but within the employee group, there are more cultural backgrounds added to our populations. Embracing and supporting the integration of those cultures into your employee body is a significant role for senior HR managers. Collaborating with employee affinity or employee resource groups can help achieve that goal. Those might include women engineers, Hispanic managers, or Black technical professionals, just as examples. Hosting meetings of employees who come from outside the headquarters' country can help make people feel more comfortable in their new surroundings. Helping them understand how to contribute their cultural features to problem-solving at the company will go a long way to expanding the warm welcome you want them to feel, plus make it easier for their contributions to be accepted.

Designing Strategic Opportunities

HR should have a prominent attachment to each corporate strategic action item. Even if HR is not specifically mentioned, the link to HR must be identified by the senior HR executive. HR must then develop its own strategic plan for supporting those links. Just how that will happen is the process of designing strategic opportunities. You must be creative and invent ways that you can support your customers in other departments. You must identify ways to actively support their strategic goals by connecting them back to the HR functions. Those actions on your part will prove to your colleagues in other departments that you stand ready to support them as a business partner and that you will help them succeed in their goals.

Proactively Developing Relationships

It does no good to sit on the sidelines and wait for someone to come to your office with a help request. You must actively extend yourself to your customers. Offer to attend their departmental staff meetings so you can help people understand the new policies or benefits programs. Help them understand how the new health care laws or income taxes will impact them. Providing information to employees will help your client managers maintain a calm work environment for their employees. Upset only grows through lack of factual input. You can help alleviate such upset by extending your offer to participate personally.

Proactively developing external relationships is also important. Getting to know your vendors and learning about the way they do business can help you analyze how you use them now and in the future. The objective in all relationships is to be well enough acquainted so that, when necessary, you can pick up the phone and discuss whatever business problem you face.

Summary

You now know about the behavioral competency of Relationship Management. You learned that establishing and maintaining relationships is critical to the HR mission and purpose in an organization. Supporting stakeholders in reaching the strategic goals of the organization can make those achievements less difficult and more rewarding.

Behavioral Competency 5: Communication

Being an effective communicator is one of the most important building blocks to a successful HR career. First, career-level HR professionals will need to hone their oral and written communication skills to manage employee and candidate communications, grievances, training, and presentations, along with investigations. More senior-level HR professionals will require a higher level of communication skills that will be used in developing presentations, programs, policies, and various analyses or other outcomes, along with interactions with a variety of internal and external stakeholders.

Three subcompetencies comprise the Communication competency and are defined by SHRM as follows:[25]

- **Delivering messages**   Developing and delivering to a variety of audiences communications that are clear, persuasive, and appropriate to the topic and situation
- **Exchanging organizational information**   Effectively translating and communicating messages among organizational levels or units
- **Listening**   Understanding information provided by others and seeking feedback

Key Concepts

- Elements of communication (for example, source, sender, receiver, message, feedback)
- General communication techniques (for example, planning communications, listening actively, checking for understanding, asking questions)
- Communication techniques for specialized situations (for example, giving feedback, facilitating focus groups, facilitating staff meetings, using skits or storytelling, creating communication plans, translating technical jargon, facilitating communication from an anonymous source, informal communication)
- Communications media (for example, phone, e-mail, face-to-face, report, presentation, social media, town hall meetings, videoconference)
- Elements of nonverbal communication (for example, eye contact, body language, proximity, gestures)

Definition

According to SHRM, "*Communication* is defined as the knowledge, skills, abilities, and other characteristics (KSAOs) needed to effectively craft and deliver concise and informative communications, to listen to and address the concerns of others, and to transfer and translate information from one level or unit of the organization to another."[26]

Proficiency Indicators for All HR Professionals

All HR professionals are expected to conduct themselves according to the following behaviors associated with the competency of Communication.

Communicating Clearly

Communication is a vital tool for critical change management. To be effective with change management from any leadership position within an organization, and especially in the HR function, requires what may feel like over-communication. This is done to ensure everyone hears and understands the message and then acts accordingly, hopefully embracing it. Here are the basics of a communication model:

> *Who* (the communicator) ➜ *says what* (the message) ➜ *in what way*
> (the medium used) ➜ *to whom* (the intended receiver) ➜ *with what effect*
> (the feedback).

Whether the communication is spontaneous (someone dropping into your office) or carefully planned out (an all-hands meeting), the same model is applied to ensure the intended impact. At each step of the model, something can go wrong, derailing the intent or purpose of the communication. Clarity of intent is incredibly important in HR communications, regardless of whether they are planned or informal/spontaneous. A communicator's ability to be clear builds credibility and helps avoid rumor mills or "noise" within an organization.

Kouzes and Posner, in their book *The Leadership Challenge*,[27] describe the following behaviors that contribute to the "credibility factor" with communicators:

- Accuracy, derived from their expertise and preparation
- Consistency
- Reliability, doing what a person says they will do
- Courage to disagree when appropriate and necessary
- Integrity
- Creativity
- Maintaining confidentiality
- Creating an atmosphere that is comfortable

Listening

The most effective communicators are excellent listeners. They can interpret and confirm what is being said and use this content to drive the conversation further. For example, accurate understanding may be confirmed using follow-up questions such as, "If I heard you right, you think the records are incorrect. Help me understand what makes you think they are incorrect."

Communicators must also be good observers of nonverbal messages. They can promote a more open and better discussion by using a nonthreatening manner to draw in a person who may be indicating resistance to speak (for example, sitting with legs crossed, arms crossed high, and a scowl on the face). Use an open-ended question that may sound to the receiver as agreement, to help elicit their openness—for example, "Chris, you are one of the best people to ask this question due to your length of time in your job. What do you think I should review first?" Listening has another big benefit in communications: focused, authentic attention builds trust and goodwill with others, allowing you to get to the heart of what really matters.

Delivering Critical Information

The delivery of a message, especially a critical message, involves choosing the communication channel that best fits the message and the intended receiver's needs, along with a delivery style that supports the receiver's understanding of the message. Timing plus anticipation of the intended receiver's reactions are important considerations. Not getting to the core point of the message within the first couple of sentences is highly ineffective. When delivering critical information, get to the factual point quickly. An example would be the following: "Lee, the ABC project deadline for a week from Friday is not going to be met unless we change something. I believe if we switch Jan from the implementation group over to analytics, plus have everyone work overtime 2 hours each night next week, we have a better chance of making the deadline."

Providing Constructive Feedback

In delivering constructive feedback, you need to consider ways to be precise but also help the person to hear and apply the feedback. This can be done by framing the message in terms of the goal of the activity, what is lacking, and what specifically needs improving and what improvement would look like.

The following might be made in a coaching session aimed at helping a manager improve their ability to conduct discipline meetings:

> "You want Jim to know the reason for the meeting and the desired outcome. I have observed that when Jim rambles at length and repeats various excuses, you lose focus on the point that he is not meeting quota. Jim must correct his quota deficiency. Yes, allow Jim to respond and explain, but keep it short and draw him back to what he can do and what he is accountable to produce."

The employee's understanding of the feedback can be confirmed by asking the employee to state what their understanding is and to demonstrate the performance or by observing the employee at work.

PART II

Ensuring Effective Communication

Impactful communicators are prepared to shorten their message to key points if the audience is rushed or bored, tailor their message if the audience has more trouble understanding or accepting a certain point, or expand their message if the audience shows great interest. They engage their audience with not just their words and supporting documentation but also with their voices and nonverbal body language. Their gestures are appropriate to the message, such as shaking their head up and down for positive agreement/understanding or side to side to signal disapproval. They establish eye contact and have vocal qualities that amount to speaking clearly, at a pace and volume that can be heard.

Knowing Your Audience

Understanding an audience's needs and perspective relies on building awareness of common interest. This requires seeing situations through the eyes of the audience or intended receiver—an essential skill set utilizing emotional intelligence. As discussed earlier, knowing how your message will be framed and delivered for understanding and acceptance will increase its impact. Consider the audience and their needs and perspective when shaping your communication. This is easier with a cognitive and emotional connection.

Leading Meetings

Communication in meetings often focuses on conveying information, receiving updates, soliciting opinions, improving engagement and morale, and coordinating activities. While these are essential communication activities, meetings can become time wasters that are resented if they are a one-way street and/or are felt to be a waste of time. All meeting facilitators would benefit from starting each meeting with the purpose and goal of the meeting and why the people present are attending. Here are additional tips for leading effective meetings:

- Set a clear agenda with defined items. Circulate the agenda before the meeting and specify what individuals may need to do to prepare for the meeting.
- Allot time according to the agenda and stay within the time limit as a show of respect for others' time.
- Start on time. Come early to allow social exchanges that strengthen relationships, but start covering the agenda at the published time.
- Take time to resolve conflicts but postpone discussion of conflicts that may be difficult to resolve until after the meeting.
- Review any decisions and assignments at the meeting's end.
- Send an e-mail summary if needed for more complex agendas.

Proficiency Indicators for Senior HR Professionals

 Beyond the basic proficiency indicators are the following additional behaviors that senior HR professionals are challenged to master.

Negotiating with Stakeholders

When negotiating with stakeholders, it is imperative that you begin the dialogue by asking open-ended questions about the issue at hand, their position and perspective, and the desired outcomes they have. The more information you gather, the better you will understand what is motivating their position, and the more targeted and effective your negotiations will be. By building an authentic dialogue using open-ended questions, you will be creating a level of trust that helps you work out an agreement, facilitated by the feeling of genuine connection. Stakeholders need to feel that you hear and understand their point of view.

Soliciting Feedback

Significant communication events need to be evaluated as soon as possible to determine whether the communication has met its objective or failed. Within the change management process, feedback is the phase of communicating that makes sure the desired outcome or action targeted is going to happen. Allowing the audience a question-and-answer period is most helpful after a presentation. Even within a one-to-one communication, when you're delivering critical information, asking for feedback is a wise thing to do (for example, "Leslie, will you please give me a recap of our discussion and your next actions?")

A review of what occurred for all major communication initiatives and meetings ought to include these evaluating questions:

- Did the intended audience react as anticipated?

- Was there confusion and, if so, about what?

- Where did the audience seem most engaged and why?

- Where did the audience seem least interested?

- Were the medium and materials used supportive and understood by the audience?

- What questions were asked? Were there interruptions and when?

Developing Communication Strategies

While not all communications require extensive planning, the costs of not planning are high. Impactful communicators create strategies for critical or complex communications. These strategies can include the following considerations:

- *How will the communication take place?* Face to face? By phone? Zoom or equivalent? In writing, using e-mail, text, or another method? It is going to be difficult to assess the intended receiver's (or receivers') reactions when they are not personally in front of you. In these cases, communications should be reviewed by multiple people who can point out areas where there may be ambiguity or potential confusion. Complex topics addressed in presentations usually provide visual support materials that allow the audience to see and digest information, especially those involving numerical data. Discussions about sensitive issues may be conducted best in person, or at least by phone or videoconference call, rather than by e-mail.

- *When will the communication take place?* Some messages require the planning and releasing phases or portions of the message to different groups in a specific sequence. As an HR professional, you also need to consider organizational timing. What other communications might be occurring at this time that can distract from your message? What is the importance of your message compared to the other required communications at this time?

- *Where will the communication take place?* For sensitive discussions, the setting should safeguard confidentiality. For group communication events, the setting should be comfortably accommodating for the group size. Be sure to minimize the risk of distractions and interruptions with sensitive discussions.

- *Who will communicate?* Some communications will be better delivered by a presenter with authority in the organization, such as the chief human resources officer (CHRO). Others require expertise and the ability to respond to technical questions, such as the HRIS manager. Still others require communicators who are adept at listening, understanding an audience's changing needs, and responding in a positive, unthreatened way, such as the workers' compensation specialist. Get the right presenter for the situation.

- *What form of media will be used?* HR communications should consider the appropriateness of the media used to deliver the messages and intended receivers' ease with different media types, such as reading level, ability to use and access to technology, and the effects of time zones.

Communicating using various media presents certain challenges and different types of planning. The following table provides the advantages and challenges of various means of communication.

Media	Advantages	Challenges
Face to face (or small group)	• Provides immediate verbal and nonverbal feedback • Useful for complex, sensitive issues (e.g., conflicts, negotiations, problem-solving)	• Takes time. • Requires good listening skills. • Requires care to avoid conveying wrong message. • May take multiple meetings if intended audience not all in the same location. Different questions at different sessions may lead to inconsistency.
Phone call	• Provides more opportunity for feedback, questions • Can reach intended audience, regardless of location	• Requires good listening skills since there are no visual cues. • Faces more competition for attention.
Voicemail	• Saves time (when used to relay content, not make direct contact)	• Does not provide feedback or confirmation of understanding.

Media	Advantages	Challenges
E-mail	• Saves sender time • Allows detail • Includes multiple parties easily • Documents communication	• Requires more care to create accurate message and convey correct tone. • Does not necessarily provide desired feedback. • Can be missed or perceived as nuisance.
Short messaging (e.g., texting, chat)	• Saves time for both parties • Can be broadcast to announce information (e.g., promotional, emergency)	• Limits content that can be communicated. • Can be missed or perceived as intrusive.
Social media	• Can be broadcast to large audiences • Reaches certain audiences efficiently and can elicit immediate feedback (e.g., quick surveys)	• May not reach all audiences. • Requires review since the message will be widely viewed.
Written report	• Allows full presentation of topic • Can reach a large audience and encourage thoughtful responses • Provides documentation of communication	• Takes time and care to create. • May need to conform to organizational expectations (templates). • Takes time to get a response. • No guarantee it will be read.
Oral presentation	• Can allow immediate questions and feedback and adjustment of message • Can incorporate visuals, video, handouts	• Requires skill and time to practice. • Requires time and expense to create support materials.

Mastery of Delivery

Framing is often used in discussions of communication. The term reflects the process of getting an audience to see communicated topics and facts in a particular way. *Reframing* is changing the way an audience sees or feels about the content of the intended message. When an HR professional manages an employee's discouragement over a change in the workplace by pointing out benefits and opportunities for them created by the change, the HR professional is reframing the facts. Effectively framing the message requires clarity and explanation. This in turn requires the following:

- Articulating the objective and desired outcome of the communication
- Identifying the benefit to the intended audience
- Identifying the key points of the message and placing them in a logical order
- Providing an explanation for each point that helps the intended audience see these facts within the desired framing

Summary

In this portion of the chapter, we discussed the importance of and ability to effectively exchange and communicate information, both oral and written, with stakeholders. When HR information is communicated with clarity and effectiveness, the intended receivers better understand the value and purpose of what is being communicated, be it policies, practices, decisions, or changes. This in turn can have a positive effect with the audiences HR serves, both internal (such as employee satisfaction) and external (such as candidate attraction).

Behavioral Competency 6: Global Mindset

Even organizations that do not actively participate in direct international exchanges have a stake in how those relationships influence their own organization. What suppliers do can influence the pricing of products used both in manufacturing and by consumers. Follow along as we explore the nuances of a global mindset in this section. According to SHRM, "In the context of today's increasingly global workforce, HR professionals must be able to effectively and respectfully interact with colleagues, customers, and clients of varying backgrounds and cultures."[28]

Three subcompetencies comprise the Global Mindset competency. They are defined by SHRM as follows:[29]

- **Operating in a diverse workplace** Demonstrating openness and respect when collaborating with people from different cultural traditions
- **Operating in a global environment** Effectively managing globally influenced workplace requirements to achieve organizational goals
- **Advocating for a diverse and inclusive workplace** Designing, implementing, and promoting organizational policies and practices that encourage cultural diversity and inclusion in the workplace.

Key Concepts

- Cultural norms, values, and dimensions (for example, the Hall, Hofstede, Schein, and Trompenaars models)
- Techniques for bridging and leveraging individual differences and perceptions (for example, employee resource groups, reverse mentorship, sensitivity training, focus groups)
- Best practices for creating and managing globally diverse workforces (for example, translating policies and procedures into local languages, accounting for multiple time zones when scheduling meetings)

Definition

According to SHRM, *Global Mindset* is defined "as the knowledge, skills, abilities, and other characteristics (KSAOs) needed to value and consider the perspectives and backgrounds of all parties, to interact with others in a global context, and to promote a culturally diverse and inclusive workplace."[30]

Proficiency Indicators for All HR Professionals

Behaviors all HR professionals should be able to demonstrate include the following.

Having a Strong Set of Core Values
While Adapting to Conditions, Situations, and People

While appreciating and accepting input from other cultures is a beneficial management technique, having a solid foundation in the cultural expectations where we conduct business is paramount. U.S. culture is different from the culture in Israel or Chile. Each has its strong points; each can contribute to the success of our enterprise. Yet, if you are based in the United States, it is critical for that success to be based on compliance with U.S. requirements and culture.

Maintaining Openness to the Ideas of Others

It only makes sense to take advantage of all the knowledge and abilities people can offer. Therefore, does it really matter whether they are U.S. citizens or from other countries? If they can offer positive input to the discussions you have about employee issues, shouldn't you be listening? The answer, of course, is "yes." There is no expectation that you will accept 100 percent of their input 100 percent of the time. That is no more realistic than taking 100 percent of the input of U.S. employees. Overlooking valuable resources can cause you to fall short of your effectiveness goals.

Demonstrating Nonjudgmental Respect for the Perspectives of Others

By listening more and talking less, you can learn more from other people about their mindset. Listening shows respect for what people have to say. It does not obligate anyone to agree with what is being said. It does require strong resistance to preparing rebuttal arguments while pretending to listen. When we listen to others, we gain the nuggets of value they have to offer.

Working Effectively with Diverse Cultures and Populations

One of the drivers of our need to communicate across cultures is the ability we now have to work remotely. It is therefore easier to have people participate from distant locations than it used to be. How we keep the technology-enabled communication effective is now the problem.

Although it is not a cultural issue, the difference in time zones is a large issue when collaborating with people in other parts of the world. Why? There are often delays in responses when we reach out, waiting for the workday to begin for others.

Even within the same language there are sometimes issues because of spelling differences. *Labor* in U.S. English is spelled *labour* in Great Britain and Australia. Sometimes that can confuse things. Part of the communication challenge is to be aware of these differences and encourage people to collaborate with one another. Thinking that someone in a different culture is stupid because they cannot spell correctly will block acceptance of any value they have to offer. And believing that someone in a different country is not very smart because they have trouble with vocabulary when speaking English ignores the fact that they are multilingual. Only about 15 to 20 percent of Americans consider themselves bilingual, compared to 56 percent of Europeans surveyed in 2006 by the European Commission.

Conducting Business with Understanding and Respect for Differences

Our global interactions bring us into contact with customs we may find strange, even unacceptable in our own culture. For example, "Many foreigners new to Saudi Arabia must adapt to significant limits to public interaction and contact between men and women, even in business environments. Saudi Arabia is one of the most gender-segregated countries in the world. Public places such as shopping malls, restaurants, and the workplace have entire areas that are female-only. Female businesswomen meeting male counterparts in public locations are expected to be accompanied by another male."[31]

Appreciating the Commonalities, Values, and Individual Uniqueness of All Humans

We each market ourselves based on our uniqueness. Our language skills, our business background, and our specific skill demonstration all become our self-expression of who we are. If we do that, wouldn't other people as well? Of course they do. The trick for HR professionals is to train themselves to recognize, and even encourage, self-expression from others. Getting to know who you deal with is the first stage of developing a healthy relationship. Any sales expert will tell you that it is critical to determine what the customer wants and then speak to that. In HR terms, determining a person's background, experiences, and cultural influences is important to creating a healthy relationship with them. Find out what is important to people and then speak to that topic, and you will build a long-term relationship.

Possessing the Self-Awareness and Humility to Learn from Others

"JetBlue airlines founder and former CEO, David Neeleman, spent one day each week flying on JetBlue planes, collaborating with his crew serving passengers drinks and snacks and cleaning planes between flights. By doing this, Neeleman showed his humility and that work he was expecting others to do well was not beneath him. Result: The word spread about Neeleman's leadership and helped JetBlue become an employer of choice. Two years after JetBlue was founded, it was growing so fast it needed to hire 2,000 new employees. The company received an astounding 130,000 employment applications!"[32] Humility is letting your experiences speak for themselves and not believing that you are more important than you are.

Embracing Inclusion

Embracing inclusion begins with recognizing our biases and working to prevent them from blocking other people's contributions. Racial and religious biases are two of the biggest biases in our population today. To embrace inclusion, we must be able to reach out to people of different races and religions. Even though our laws say that we may not use these group memberships in our employment decisions, the biases we carry can often result in unseen discrimination. As HR professionals, we are responsible for leading the way with our organization's staff members and getting them to recognize their own biases. Decision-makers must keep these thoughts in the front of their thinking when selecting people for job openings, assigning training opportunities, and making other employment decisions.

Adapting One's Perspectives and Behaviors to Meet the Cultural Context

In recent times a new term has crept into our lexicon regarding cultural acceptance and inclusion. That term is *cultural quotient (CQ)*. It joins intelligence quotient (IQ) and emotional quotient (EQ) in how we think about people. "CQ is a system consisting of three interactive components: cultural knowledge, cross-cultural skills, and cultural metacognition."[33] Sometimes cultural metacognition is described as cultural mindfulness. This is the ability to recognize cultural context, analyze the cultural issues, and develop strategies to work within them.

Navigating the Differences Between Commonly Accepted Practices and Laws

Here are just a few examples of differences around the world. When meeting someone for the first time in Japan, it is customary to present a small gift. Giving gifts in Germany is usually not done and may even be considered offensive. Gifts are seldom presented in the United Kingdom or Belgium. When conducting business meetings in the Middle East, it is expected that small talk will be exchanged before beginning a business discussion.

There are scores of legal differences between countries of the world. Here are just three areas of labor law that have different expectations:

- **Laws on paid time off** Germany and Spain mandate 34 days of paid vacation and holidays for every worker each year, Italy and France require 31 days of paid time off, Belgium and New Zealand require 30 days, Australia mandates 28 days, and Canada's federal law requires 19 paid days off. Even Japan, which has a reputation for working employees to their limits, requires 10 paid holidays for every worker.[34] In the United States, by contrast, paid time off is mandated only under a few circumstances. For example, states such as California require paid time off for parental leave when the employee has a new child.

- **Laws on paid vacations** The United States is the only country with an advanced economy that does not guarantee any paid vacation to its workers. In the United States, no company is required to provide paid vacations to employees or pay its employees for federal or state holidays. This is considered an optional employee benefit that employers can choose to provide. The law does not mandate additional pay for employees who work on holidays unless such work is overtime as defined in state or federal law.[35] Paid holiday entitlement in the European Union is set at a minimum of 4 weeks (20 days) per year, exclusive of bank holidays; however, many countries are more generous. Sweden, France, and Denmark offer the most, at 5 weeks (25 days) for a standard Monday to Friday job.

- **Laws limiting hours worked**   In the United States, the Fair Labor Standards Act defines when overtime must be paid and how much that amount will be. There are few upper limits to employees working overtime. In Mexico, the constitution establishes a maximum of 8 work hours for shift workers, a maximum of 7 work hours for the night shift, and a maximum of 9 hours of overtime per week. For every 6 days of work, Mexico's workers must have 1 day off.

In the European Union, the maximum average working week (including overtime) is capped at 48 hours. The minimum daily rest period is 11 consecutive hours in every 24, and breaks are required when the working day exceeds 6 hours. The European Union requires a minimum weekly rest period of 24 hours plus an 11-hour daily rest period every 7 days.[36]

If you have employees working in other countries, it is critical that you understand the labor laws in those countries. Payroll requirements are also an obligatory focus for HR professionals.

Operating with a Global Mindset

Glen Fisher describes mindsets as "differing ways that the subject at hand is perceived, understood, and reasoned about."[37] Stephen Rhinesmith says, "A mindset is a filter through which we look at the world."[38] Being open to all cultural contributions doesn't mean accepting everything that comes along. Like any problem-solving effort, it is important to establish criteria that represents the filter you will use in identifying the way forward or the solution to your problem.

National norms are one thing; local needs may be slightly different. A classic example can be found in holiday observance. The United States generally observes the following federal holidays: New Year's Day, Martin Luther King, Jr. Day, Presidents Day, Memorial Day, Independence Day, Labor Day, Thanksgiving Day, and Christmas Day. On the local level, Columbus Day in the Eastern portion of the country is an important holiday. October 10 is now celebrated as Indigenous People's Day by some. Some locations have holidays like Founder's Day and Armistice (or Veterans) Day. In other countries, the same types of examples can be identified. Walpurgis Night, the Friday after Ascension Day, Mother's Day, and Father's Day are celebrated. In Brazil, holiday celebrations include Our Lady of Apparition, All Souls Day, and Public Proclamation Day. In Rio de Janeiro, people celebrate holidays such as Umbanda, the Festival of the Goddess of the Sea, and June Bonfire Festivals (Festas Juninas).

Operating with a Fundamental Trust in Other Humans

Ralph Waldo Emerson said, "Our distrust is very expensive."[39] Without trust, influence wanes, intimacy erodes, relationships crumble, careers derail, organizations fail to prosper (and, also crumble), and, in short, nothing much works. Wherever trust is missing, opportunity is lost—opportunity to collaborate, exert influence, deepen intimacy, build understanding, resolve conflict, expand peace, and succeed at the very things that matter most, individually and collectively. This is why building trust is the foundation of every peace negotiation, every business collaboration, and every truly meaningful endeavor.[40]

According to Roderick M. Kramer, human beings are predisposed to trust others. And touch is one way we indicate acceptance of trusting another person. The American handshake is one example. It not only says "hello" and "goodbye," it also says many other things, including "I trust we will have a good relationship."[41] Sometimes we are too eager to trust. It is important, Kramer says, to temper our trust with some conscious examination of the circumstances. HR professionals are key players in building trust with stakeholders by demonstrating that HR will do what it says it will do. Making and keeping commitments is part of a trusting relationship.

Taking the Responsibility to Ensure Inclusion

Respecting individual differences will benefit the workplace by creating a competitive edge and increasing work productivity. Diversity management benefits associates by creating a fair and safe environment where everyone has access to opportunities and challenges. Management tools in a diverse workforce should be used to educate everyone about diversity and its issues, including laws and regulations. Most workplaces are made up of diverse cultures, so organizations need to learn how to adapt to be successful.[42]

Incorporating Global Business and Economic Trends into Business Decisions

Incorporating sustainable development principles into a business's mission can improve its reputation and regain public trust, increase profit margins, open new business opportunities, and reduce risks associated with less sustainable processes. Businesses are influenced to incorporate sustainable development into supply chains by consumer demand and, in some cases, by investor pressure.[43]

HR professionals must be sensitive to economics when analyzing strategies for employee benefits, payroll issues, policy development, and business impact. It is no longer acceptable for HR professionals to work in a vacuum and just make recommendations without support from a business case analysis.

Proficiency Indicators for Senior HR Professionals

In addition to the "basic" behaviors all HR professionals are expected to master, these behaviors are essential for the success of senior HR professionals.

Setting a Strategy to Leverage Global Competencies for Competitive HR Advantages

Increasingly today, business leaders are concluding that competency in human resources is a core requirement for success. Are your human resources ready and able to answer key questions like the following?

- Do you need radical change, or will you move forward with incremental adjustments?
- Will you "rock the boat" today and add more uncertainty to your strategy, or should you wait until things are more settled?

- Is it less risky to mitigate the uncertainty of large and complex organizational changes or the potential downside of the status quo?
- Does your future business need new skills and competences, or are you comfortable with the talent you have today?

Businesses need to answer these questions, and, increasingly, HR plays a key role in doing this. Suddenly, HR performance is positioned to influence the overall business performance of a company. HR leaders find themselves under heavy pressure, which calls for new skills, competencies, and profiles across the HR profession. There is also a special focus on HR senior management in charge of driving organizational medium- and long-term changes.[44]

Using a Global Economic Outlook to Determine Impacts on the Organization's Human Capital Strategy

Many converging issues are driving the need to rewrite "the rules." Technology is advancing at an unprecedented rate. Individuals are quick to adapt to ongoing innovations, but organizations move at a slower pace. Many still retain an industrial age structure and practices that are long outdated. Even slower moving are public policy issues such as income inequality, unemployment, immigration, and trade.

It is these gaps among technology, individuals, businesses, and public policy that are creating a unique opportunity for HR to help leaders and organizations adapt to technology, help people adapt to new models of work and careers, and help the company adapt to and encourage positive changes in society, regulation, and public policy.[45]

Maintaining Expert Global and Cultural Knowledge/Experience

Learning is a continuous process. It is not enough to attend an hour-long webinar about the culture in the country where your company wants to conduct business. It is necessary to keep up with changes in that culture and in the expectations for legal compliance and customer service. HR staffs should maintain that intercultural knowledge and experience. When someone with those talents moves on to another job, it is necessary to identify a qualified replacement so that the needed components of HR strategic contributions can be maintained.

Maintaining Expert Knowledge of Global Economic Trends

How will the global economy impact the countries in which you do business? What are the economic trends in those countries? Who has the knowledge necessary to deal with these issues? What backups do we have for that key contact person? What role does HR play in educating employees about these trends? Answer these questions, and you will be on your way to being in control of your strategic contributions.

Understanding Global Labor Markets and Associated Legal Environments

International trade and workers' rights are two of the most complex issues in which HR can get involved. Laws vary widely around the world when focused on employee rights and treatment. Due diligence is necessary if you plan to expand into a new country.

Your international labor attorney can become your best friend when that happens. You need to understand the nuances of labor laws in a new country so you can properly adjust the focus of your company's policies. This is an example of how important HR's contribution can be to the strategic decision-making process. Identifying workforce-related costs in the new country can contribute to a business decision-making exercise that will determine whether the move will be profitable.

Fostering the Organization's Cultural Norms

According to SHRM, "[It] is important to have a culture based on a strongly held and widely shared set of beliefs that are appropriately supported by strategy and structure." That is a mouthful. It means that culture evolves from shared beliefs. And if those beliefs are not supported by strategy and organizational structure (for example, reporting relationships), the beliefs will ring hollow with employees and others outside the organization.

If a company says, "We believe in customer service at the highest level," and then does not behave as though customer service is important, the culture will wind up being based on poor customer service. Managers who say, "People are our most important asset," and then cut into policies affecting working schedules and job assignments will have a decidedly negative impact on the organization's culture. It is not what we say that impacts culture as much as what we do.

Proving the ROI of a Diverse Workforce

The consulting firm McKinsey & Company conducted some studies related to the question of return on investment from corporate diversity efforts and determined the following:[46]

- Companies in the top quartile for racial and ethnic diversity are 35 percent more likely to have financial returns above their respective national industry medians.

- Companies in the top quartile for gender diversity are 15 percent more likely to have financial returns above their respective national industry medians.

Managing Contradictory Practices to Ensure Cross-Cultural Harmony and Organizational Success

If you accept the definition of culture as the patterns of behavior and beliefs shared by a group, then you can examine the impacts of those behaviors within the group. When cultures clash (for example, religious dress codes, beards, or holiday observances), HR professionals are usually called upon to intercede and find some common-ground resolution that will fit for the entire organization. Doing so respects individual cultural expectations while preserving the employer's need to get work done.

How these conflicts are resolved usually involves gathering data from individuals and examining what common ground exists between conflicting viewpoints. Involving those same individuals in discussions about the issues, with HR playing the facilitation role, can often result in acceptance of the common ground as a way forward.

Integrating Perspectives on Cultural Differences and Their Impact on the Success of the Organization

Some of the elements found to have the strongest impact on cross-cultural or multicultural business include the following:[47]

- **Communicating**   Explicit versus implicit
- **Evaluating**   Direct negative feedback versus indirect negative feedback
- **Leading**   Egalitarian versus hierarchical
- **Deciding**   Consensus versus top-down
- **Disagreeing**   Confrontation versus avoidance
- **Persuading**   Holistic versus specific
- **Scheduling**   Organized time versus flexible time
- **Trusting**   Task versus relationship

Setting the Vision That Defines the Strategic Connection Between Diversity and Organizational Success

Organizational leaders are the ones on whose shoulders rest the need to set and communicate the vision for the company. They must set forth the clear desire to embrace diversity and acknowledge that diversity brings its own set of problems. With an eye on the need to resolve those conflicts, leaders can create a culture of diversity acceptance, knowing they will get a *fair chance* to express their needs and have those needs respected. Leaders, including HR professionals, must communicate that people should not expect to have all their needs met as they are expressed but, through discussion and negotiation, can meet them in ways acceptable to others in the workforce as well.

Building Cross-Cultural Relationships and Partnerships

Regardless of their background, when cultural representatives interact, they can build strong cross-cultural partnerships if they observe the following seven tips recommended by Juliette C. Mayers:[48]

1. *Seek to understand.* Do not make assumptions. Ideally you want to learn about different cultures through a variety of credible sources, such as your own personal relationships, books, travel, research, and ongoing education.

2. *Keep an open mind.* Avoid stereotypes. Expand your base by building a broad cross-section of relationships such as gender, race, sexual orientation, country of origin, and people who think differently from you.

3. *Start with "who you know."* The best place to start is with others who you know inside and outside of your organization, business, and social organizations.

4. *Attend multicultural networking events.* Professional organizations, cultural events, conferences, diversity forums, minority business expos, and community events are all great places to network. Talk to others while there instead of focusing on your phone.

5. *Get involved.* Volunteer and partner with groups and organizations where you can add value, while interacting and getting to know others from different backgrounds. It will take time to build trust and to establish authentic relationships, so think long term.

6. *Keep your word.* Establishing trust is the key to sustained successful relationships. If you say you are going to do something, do it!

7. *Assume positive intent.* Be positive. At some point miscommunication is likely to occur. When this happens, do not give up. Assume positive intent and continue your journey. Persistence is the key. Stay the course, and establish yourself as someone with genuine interest in maintaining relationships across cultures.

Summary

In this segment, we examined global and cultural needs and their impacts when organizations are operating in other countries. Differences in the speed of work and the way in which respect is shown and expected all play a part in how we help our groups develop the common culture we want to have moving into the future. Each culture has positive contributions to make, and through discussions, those contributions can be discovered and highlighted.

Business Cluster

The Business cluster represents 16.5 percent of both exams' weighted scores. The following three competencies fall within the Business cluster:

- Behavioral Competency 7: Business Acumen
- Behavioral Competency 8: Consultation
- Behavioral Competency 9: Analytical Aptitude

This cluster covers the behavioral competencies for HR professionals to ensure HR contributes to the strategic direction of the organization, understands the business and the environment in which it operates, designs and implements business solutions to meet human capital needs, contributes to and leads change management initiatives, and gathers and analyzes data to inform business decisions.

Behavioral Competency 7: Business Acumen

Understanding how the business (organization) runs, what makes it financially viable, and how it can be guided to greater effectiveness is a role for HR managers that gains importance each day.

Three subcompetencies comprise the Business Acumen competency and are defined by SHRM as follows:[49]

- **Business and competitive awareness**   Understanding the organization's operations, functions, products and services, and the competitive, economic, social, and political environments in which the organization operates
- **Business analysis**   Applying business metrics, principles, and technologies to inform and address business needs
- **Strategic alignment**   Aligning HR strategy, communications, initiatives, and operations with the organization's strategic direction

Key Concepts

- Business terms and concepts (for example, competitive advantage, profit and loss, revenue, financial projections, quality, service level agreements, strategic plans, fixed and variable costs, supply and demand, net income, key performance indicators [KPIs])
- Analyzing and interpreting business documents (for example, strategic plans, contracts, grants, standard operating procedures, business plans, organizational charts, business continuity plans)
- Elements of a business case (for example, executive summary, benefits, alignment with the organization's strategic goals)
- Business intelligence techniques and tools (for example, analytical processing, business intelligence portals, predictive analytics, advanced analytics, trend analysis, scenario planning, balanced scorecard)
- Financial analysis and methods for assessing business health (for example, balance sheets, budgets, cash flow statements, profit and loss statements, overhead, cash flow, cash reserves, return on investment [ROI], SWOT [strengths, weaknesses, opportunities, threats] analysis, sales pipeline, market position)

Definition

According to SHRM, *Business Acumen* is defined "as the knowledge, skills, abilities, and other characteristics (KSAOs) needed to understand the organization's operations, functions, and external environment, and to apply business tools and analyses that inform HR initiatives and operations consistent with the overall strategic direction of the organization."[50]

Proficiency Indicators for All HR Professionals

The following are the basic behaviors required of all HR professionals for Business Acumen.

Building Strategic Relationships

Strategic relationships are symbiotic. They provide each person or entity with something that they need. Strategic relations can exist with vendors, customers, regulators, and other oversight groups. HR can contribute to those relationships through its policies, planning, and management of the HR functions. Everything HR does should support the organization's strategic planning objectives.

Understanding the Business Operations

Business operations are ongoing activities involved in the production of value for the organization's stakeholders. HR contributes to an organization's business operations by supporting its people assets in ways that enhance the organization's strategic goals and objectives.

Learning the Business and Operational Functions

"Operations management (OM) is the business function responsible for managing the process of creation of goods and services. It involves planning, organizing, coordinating, and controlling all the resources needed to produce a company's goods and services. Because operations management is a management function, it involves managing people, equipment, technology, information, and all the other resources needed in the production of goods and services. Operations management is the central core function for every company. This is true regardless of the size of the company, the industry it is in, whether it is manufacturing or service, or is for-profit or not-for-profit."[51] HR professionals should create "people" policies and practices that contribute to the organization's operational success.

Understanding the Industry

Industries are collections of enterprises doing similar things or serving similar segments of the economy. Examples include energy, retail, restaurant, communications, consumer products, and business services. Organizations within an industry either compete with one another for a portion of the market or serve those who are competing. HR policies and procedures should be constructed to enable rapid response to industry demands and competitive adjustments.

Making the Business Case for HR Management

HR should contribute key elements to organizational success. This requires the development of a business case. There are specific content requirements for a business case. The following are the ten elements of an HR business case:[52]

1. **Problem statement**   In one paragraph or less, clearly state the specific business problem.

2. **Background**   Be sure to include significant information regarding skills, budgeting, and performance that contribute to the business problem and how long you have had the problem. Indicate, in general terms, what is required to resolve or reduce the problem.

3. **Project objectives**   Use a maximum of seven bullet points to state what the proposed solution is trying to accomplish. Some examples may include purchasing hardware and software and selecting a new vendor.

4. **Current process**   Identify the organizational processes and units impacted by the proposed solution, such as the training department when training is required, as well as other impacted units and relationships with clients, external partners, and the competition.

5. **Requirements**   List resources needed to complete the project, such as staff, hardware, software, print materials, time, and budget.

6. **Alternatives**   Outline at least four options to implementing the proposed solution. Be sure to include basic requirements for each and estimate project risks, ramp-up time, training costs, and project delays.

7. **Compare alternatives**   Compare and contrast each of the alternatives with the proposed solution and the other alternatives. State similarities and differences, benefits, detriments, and costs associated with each option.

8. **Additional considerations**   List critical success factors other than return on investment (ROI) metrics; for example, list the effects on partnership agreements with specific vendors or the potential need for help desk or customer support.

9. **Action plan**   Propose specific action steps. State your short-term (first 3 months) and long-term (3 months to conclusion) action plans, including major milestones. This section should also include proposed metrics to measure success.

10. **Executive summary**   Write a clear, one-page summary of the proposed solution. Tailor it to your audience and offer a high-level overview of research that leads you to make the proposal. Many put the executive summary at the beginning, either first thing or right after the problem statement.

Marketing HR

HR challenges have increased in recent times. Identifying, attracting, and holding onto qualified talent are the top priorities in many industries. The trades (carpentry, plumbing, electrical) are in crisis because they do not have a supply of qualified talent from which to draw. That leads to the need to be innovative in how to "grow your own" or support training programs that will graduate qualified people who can be hired. HR plays a key role in those strategies. Letting people inside the organization know that HR is working on their behalf to accomplish these types of critical functions is important to creating HR credibility within the organization.

Applying Organizational Metrics

Metrics are measurements. Organizational metrics are measurements of individual functions or specific business processes within the organization. Applying metrics involves identifying the items to be measured that are critical indicators of success for the organization. Then, once the measurements have been identified, it is necessary to prepare a plan for implementing or applying them. What gets measured gets attention, so choose your metrics with care and do not try to measure everything. If everything is measured, then nothing becomes a priority.

Using Organizational Metrics

HR can employ organizational metrics easily enough. Here are two basic measurements that impact HR:

- **Revenue per employee**   Divide the revenue by average employee head count.
- **Expense per employee**   Divide the expense element (or total expense) by average employee head count.

These can be applied to the total organization or to individual elements (divisions, departments) within the organization.

Metrics can be tactical or strategic. Tactical metrics include reasons why people accept job offers, levels of satisfaction with their boss, and number of new hires made within the target date on each requisition. Strategic metrics include goals or targets met within a defined period (month, quarter, year), value received for HR programs compared to forecast value, and achievement rates for revenue or expense targets and goals.

Leveraging Technology

Technology plays an indispensable role in today's employment world. Yet technology without proper consideration of its impact on the workforce is not helpful. Technology can have a positive effect on human resources. It can play a key role in communicating, interacting, collaborating, and training. Making sure technology is working for you and not against you is the process of leveraging technology to its greatest advantage.

Training used to be done in a classroom environment. People would have to travel to the training location, and if the training was longer than a single day, they would stay in a hotel or long-term housing, eat meals out, do laundry, and perform other activities that allowed them to remain in the training for the time required. Technology today allows most training to be done electronically, so traveling to a central training site is no longer necessary. People can stay at home and participate in training while on the job or away from the workplace. That saves time and money. Measuring the savings is one way to support HR's contribution to organizational economic performance.

Proficiency Indicators for Senior HR Professionals

Senior HR professionals are expected to possess the following skills over and above the basic behaviors we have already reviewed. If you are studying for the SHRM-SCP exam, pay close attention to these requirements.

Developing ROI for All HR Initiatives

Return on investment (ROI) is a way of expressing the financial benefit gained from any given business activity. You can talk about ROI of a new "paid time off" policy when looking at the impact on absence rates and expenses. You can examine ROI for offering employees access to their employment record on the organization's computer network. You can also allow employees to enter their own data changes (name change due to marriage, birth of a new child for health care enrollment, and updating educational achievements when receiving a new degree). Such programs can reduce the payroll expense in the

HR department and thereby offer an opportunity to compare the payroll savings with the expense associated with the technology program permitting employee record access.

Assessing Risks/SWOT

There are two sources of risk for any organization: internal and external. Internal risks come from strengths and weaknesses. External risks come from opportunities and threats. Together, they form the acronym SWOT:

- **Strengths** These are positives inside your organization. They are advantages you and your team have that will help you reach project goals. It is important to know your special skills that give you an advantage. Lack of strengths in a specific area can define a risk.

- **Weaknesses** These are negatives inside your organization—anything internal to your organization or team that could prevent you from meeting objectives, or something that gives you a disadvantage relative to others. Not having enough staff with the skill sets you need is an example.

- **Opportunities** These are positive potentials outside your organization—external facts that could lead to a positive outcome in meeting objectives. Overlooking opportunities can be described as representing specific risks.

- **Threats** These are negative potentials outside your organization—external elements that could jeopardize your company, project, department, or industry.

Aligning HR Strategy, Goals, and Objectives

According to SHRM, "Identifying and implementing workforce strategies in a challenging global economy is a high-priority issue for top executives. To be successful, HR professionals and business leaders together must grapple with the many variables that affect the organization's ability to attain its strategic objectives. They must develop quantitative and qualitative approaches to attract, engage, and retain human capital efficiently and effectively."[53]

Once HR strategy, goals, and objectives are all in alignment, the outcomes are more likely to be positive. Creating action plans to implement strategies and then achieving specific goals and objectives become easier once they are identified and written down. Even more important, other managers in the organization will see how HR can support them in their efforts toward achieving their goals and objectives.

Demonstrating Business Language Fluency

It has become clear that for HR professionals to be accepted as strategic business partners with other executives in the organization, they need to be able to talk about what they do using business terminology. Therefore, expressing the budget impact for a new employee benefit program and then showing the offset that can be accomplished by reducing turnover costs will speed acceptance and credibility for HR. Business language includes profits, losses, cost impact ratios, industry position impact for given programs, and revenue impact ratios for HR programs that can be sold outside the organization.

Examining Organizational Problems

Problem identification is a critical step in the process of finding solutions. Too often, people rush to express their thoughts about solutions without first identifying the specific problem they face. Problem identification is a process of questioning what is getting in the way of achieving specific goals and objectives. For example, what is preventing us from getting more employee enrollment in the company retirement savings program? Why is the turnover rate in the accounting department above normal? How can we reduce the cost of training managers in the new safety requirements? Once the problem is identified, you can begin working on solutions, but not before.

Sometimes, people rush to recommend solutions without a problem having surfaced. That situation presents a solution in search of a problem. If you are to be part of the executive team in your organization, you should get into the habit of clearly laying out the problem before rushing to identify solutions.

Developing Solutions

Problem-solving techniques are many and varied. They all basically have these steps in common:

1. *Define the problem.* What is it that gets in the way of us reaching our goals?

2. *Identify options.* What might we do to eliminate the problem? These are the solutions we think might work.

3. *Evaluate the options.* Develop a list of criteria any solution must meet to be acceptable and then compare each of the options identified against that list of criteria. Any option that does not pass this test must be discarded. What remains is a list of those options that can work.

4. *Choose an option and implement it.* Make a judgment about what might be best of all the options that pass the criteria screening. Identify what is necessary for the successful implementation in the form of an action plan.

5. *Evaluate the solution.* Ask if the chosen solution solved the problem. Did it create other problems? What other follow-up action might be required?

Evaluating Proposed Business Cases

Business case analysis (BCA) looks at the programs, solutions to problems, or other action plans with the eye on how they will impact the business. In every analysis, consideration must be given to the impact the activity or plan will have on the overall business operation. What is the impact on profit or loss? What is the impact on corporate image in the marketplace? What is the impact on product liability? What is the impact on employee retention? Not all of these will be the focus of any one evaluation, but all are eventually going to be part of some business case analysis at some time.

Business case analysis is a means of projecting accountability for taking any action. Business case analysis demands accountability. Any senior HR professional these days must be accountable for the success or failure of their programs. Putting their job on the line is something HR professionals are expected to do every day. It is no longer acceptable to duck accountability by excusing results as unmeasurable "people" issues. If it cannot be measured, it should not be done.

Benchmarking the Competition

According to Ross Beard, "Competitive benchmarking can be defined as the continuous process of comparing a firm's practices and performance measures with that of its most successful competitors."[54] For HR professionals, that may mean identifying compensation levels through periodic compensation surveys. It could involve comparative analysis of insurance benefits being offered in other organizations within the industry compared to those offered in your organization. What "leading-edge" programs are being offered by competing companies? Might they work here? What would be the business impact of adapting such programs?

Communicating Global Labor Market Direction

Communicating global labor market direction first requires identifying what that direction might be. Is there a trend for exporting manufacturing jobs to Asian countries? Is there a trend to return manufacturing jobs to the United States? What trends are politically motivated, and what are economically motivated?

Once identified, the trends can be articulated and communicated to executives within the organization. There is an impact on technology workers because it is suddenly no longer economically viable to produce computer components offshore. Maintaining a competitive edge in the marketplace requires following those economic benefits and moving production units to locations where the work can be done for less money. The executive team needs input from HR professionals that will allow them to make these types of decisions.

Maintaining Expert Knowledge

HR is responsible for identifying sources of expert knowledge that can be used when job openings occur in any department of the organization. It is also critical that HR protect its own expert knowledge. That is often done through specifying a certification requirement when searching for HR professionals. When expert knowledge leaves through normal turnover, the organization's goals and objectives can be negatively impacted if there is no backup available. Finding a replacement fast is often needed. That means HR must have done its homework and already identified sources for candidates with that knowledge.

Developing HR Business Strategies

In the beginning, there are corporate strategies. These are normally developed by executives representing each of the major organizational work units, such as legal, operations, research, sales, information technology, engineering, accounting, and, of course, HR. Once organizational strategies are clearly defined and documented, each individual work unit can begin developing its specific strategic plans to support the larger organization.

Administrative support entities are unique in that they serve all operational units in the organization. What they do impacts the internal client groups. Therefore, strategic planning for support groups must be focused on the services they offer to internal clients. That means fancy HR initiatives and the latest fashionable HR programs should take a back seat to delivering the HR support needed by the client groups. Once clients are satisfied, HR professionals can spend time thinking about upgrading to the latest versions of HR management programs.

For each strategy there should be at least one action item in the action plan. Implementing a strategy is necessary to reflect its reason for existing. If you do not plan to act on the strategy, scratch that strategy off your list because it is going to use energy for monitoring and maintenance without delivering any practical value to your group.

Maintaining Knowledge of Economic Factors

Human resource management is a function that embraces pieces of each organizational unit, carrying some influence over the success or failure of those portions of the internal client functions. If staffing is not done in a timely way by HR management, the production and accounting organizations cannot perform their tasks successfully.

HR's influence is dependent upon knowledge of economic factors. The annual company budget is dependent upon knowing the cost of compensation in all departments. HR holds the key to those numbers and any appropriate adjustments that will be required in the coming year. The cost of employee benefit plans is also something that HR oversees but shares with client organizations inside the company. If HR professionals do not understand the economic impact of these expenses, the support they provide to other groups cannot be sound or effective. It would be like the legal staff providing bad legal advice to other departments.

HR is often responsible for a large portion of the employer's compliance efforts—from safety to equal employment opportunity. Done improperly, the economic impact to the business can be quite severe, including fines and legal judgments.

Evaluating Critical Activities

Each effort we make in our jobs should be subject to review and evaluation. Review involves checking to be sure we have included the topic in our action planning. Evaluation is the effort to determine the value achieved by the action taken.

Balanced Scorecard

Developed by Robert Kaplan and David P. Norton, a *balanced scorecard*[55] helps evaluate effectiveness. The balanced scorecard contains four dimensions: financial performance of an organization, its customer service, its internal business processes, and its capacity to learn and achieve growth. Within these four areas, managers need to identify the key performance indicators the organization should track. The financial dimension reflects a concern that the organization's activities contribute to improving short-term and long-term financial performance.

(continued)

The customer service perspective measures such things as how customers view the organization, as well as customer retention and satisfaction. Business process indicators focus on production and operating statistics, such as order fulfillment and cost per order. The final component relates to the human resource and its potential to learn and grow. This perspective seeks to focus on how well resources and human capital are being managed for the company's benefits.

The balanced scorecard provides a balanced picture of current performance as well as the triggers for future performance. The scorecard helps managers align their business units, as well as their financial, physical, and human resources, to the firm's overall strategy.

What needs emphasis is that the HR evaluation should not be confined only to the people dimension of the scorecard. The HR professional should be judged on all the dimensions of the scorecard. HR executives tend to believe that their success should be judged only by the extent to which they meet employee needs. As the scorecard indicates, employee commitment is only one criterion for effective HR performance, and HR professionals will be held accountable for all the dimensions just like other managers.

Knowing the Business

It is up to HR to understand the business it supports. Are there seasonal workflow fluctuations? Are there peaks and valleys for employment activity? How important are specific educational backgrounds for future employees? What colleges will provide the skills that new hires will require? How much do employee benefit programs contribute to employee retention programs?

How do labor relations efforts work in this employer organization? What type of employee benefits are needed to attract and retain the type of qualified people needed?

Brainstorm the specific questions you must ask so that you understand the business you are supporting. Revisit these questions and others at least annually. Invite critical updates from internal client executives at any time during the year.

Setting Technology Strategy

The information technology (IT) department is responsible for corporate technology initiatives. But HR professionals are responsible for IT developments within their own realm of influence. What programs will permit employees to access and update their own employee records in the HRIS? What types of programs will give employees the opportunity to do online comparisons of various benefit programs they may want to consider? How can new policies be introduced online so training costs can be controlled?

Overall, HR professionals are given the responsibility of identifying the strategy they will apply for IT within the HR department. Knowing how that will impact and contribute to company strategies is something the HR professional must undertake.

Serving as a Strategic Contributor

For years HR professionals have been clamoring for "a seat at the table," meaning they want to "meet with the big boys and girls" in the corporate suite. Being part of the planning up front reduces clean-up of problems later that could have been avoided if HR had earlier involvement. That seat is not something that is just given to HR. It is something HR must earn. Proving that HR belongs at the executive table can be done only through demonstration of strategic contributions to the corporation. HR professionals have been welcomed into the "C-suite" (corporate executive suite) discussions when they have been able to show they add value to the discussions and programs.

Influencing Government Policy

Compliance with government regulations is often delegated to the HR department. Occupational Safety and Health Administration (OSHA) rules about safety require compliance efforts for all employers, regardless of size. Department of Labor (DOL) regulations about wages and hours of work, federal contracting, and the Equal Employment Opportunity Commission (EEOC) all require compliance efforts.

Employers can influence government policy by monitoring the *Federal Register* postings of proposals for regulatory changes. Identifying how those proposals will impact their employer is a service HR professionals can provide. Submitting those studies with editorial comments to the agency proposing the changes will help by giving "real-world impact" input to the government. Testifying at government hearings at the local, state, and federal levels is another way to offer input to government changes governing employee management issues.

Developing Business Strategy with Top Leaders

HR professionals have a great deal to offer their organization's strategic planning process. Participating with the top leaders of the organization in that effort will cement HR's relationship with the executive team. Offering to take on responsibility for key strategic plans will ensure the executive team invites HR back to participate in the future.

Defining Strategy for Managing Talent

We know now that any HR strategy must complement overall employer strategy. Managing talent is a strategic contribution to the organization's interest in maintaining a workforce needed to produce products or services for financial success.

Talent management requires recruiting, selecting, onboarding, training, evaluating, and matching talent to needs. HR can develop a strategy for each of these components of workforce oversight.

Summary

In this section, we identified the need for HR professionals to gain and exercise the knowledge and skills associated with business acumen. Assessing financial impacts of business proposals related to employee management is an important HR contribution to executive discussions and proposal considerations. All HR programs should be assessed periodically using business management tools, including profit and loss sheets and balance sheets.

HR professionals cannot have credibility with other executives unless they have this ability to analyze programs using business considerations and business and competitive awareness, and they must be able to align strategies in HR with corporate strategies.

Behavioral Competency 8: Consultation

Providing advice and counsel to clients is one of the biggest, most important roles for HR professionals. There are some important components of that effort you should be developing.

Five subcompetencies comprise the Consultation competency, as defined by SHRM:[56]

- **Evaluating business challenges** Working with business partners and leaders to identify business challenges and opportunities for HR solutions
- **Designing HR solutions** Working with business partners and leaders to design HR solutions and initiatives that meet the business needs
- **Advising on HR solutions** Working with business partners and leaders as they implement and support HR solutions and initiatives
- **Change managing** Leading and supporting maintenance of or changes in strategy, organization, and/or operations
- **Service excellence** Providing high-quality service to all stakeholders and contributing to a strong customer service culture

Key Concepts

- Organizational change management theories and models (for example, Lewin's change management model, McKinsey 7S model, Kotter's 8-step change model, the Kubler-Ross change curve)
- Organizational change management processes (for example, obtaining leadership buy-in, building a case for change, engaging employees, communicating change, removing barriers)
- Consulting processes and models, including the contributions of consulting to organizational systems and processes (for example, discovery, analysis and solution, recommendation, implementation)
- Effective consulting techniques (for example, understanding organizational culture, understanding areas and limits of one's own expertise, setting reasonable expectations, avoiding overpromising)
- Key components of successful client interactions (for example, listening, empathy, communication, follow-up)
- Methods for design and delivery of HR service functions and processes (for example, issue tracking, client service)

Definition

According to SHRM, *Consultation* is defined "as the knowledge, skills, abilities, and other characteristics (KSAOs) needed to work with organizational stakeholders in evaluating business challenges and identifying opportunities for the design, implementation, and evaluation of change initiatives and to build ongoing support for HR solutions that meet the changing needs of customers and the business."[57]

Proficiency Indicators for All HR Professionals

Every HR professional should have the ability to behave in ways that will offer their organization these competencies.

Applying Creative Problem-Solving

Of course, there are "old" problems that keep cycling back, demanding our attention, such as insurance benefit open enrollment each year. Yet there are even more "new" problems that arise requiring more than compliance. Those problems demand unique approaches that can keep our organizations running smoothly with attention to new requirements. The conversion of HR's role to include oversight of electronic employee records is the best example. Each organization has its own needs, and cultural expectations demand that the HRIS respond to those needs.

Creative problem-solving for such a companywide effort should involve representatives from all aspects of company life. Together, identifying the problem ("How do we convert paper record systems into an HRIS?") and exploring possible solutions can result in a superior approach that would not have been possible absent some creativity.

Remember the basics of creative problem-solving and assume the role of facilitator so you can guide your colleagues to a proper conclusion.

Steps to Creative Problem-Solving

The following is a set of sequenced steps to creative problem-solving:

1. *Identify the problem.* Rushing into generating a list of solutions without everyone being clear about what problem you are trying to solve will result in a lot of wasted time. It is likely that your committee will generate solutions for many different problems, without any idea how they all fit together.

2. *Generate a list of possible solutions.* This can be done by brainstorming or some other technique you personally prefer. Teach people in your group how to apply the technique you choose and then go to town. Get as many solutions on your list as you can. You can evaluate them in the next step. For now, just make the list as long as possible.

(continued)

3. *Create a list of criteria for acceptable solutions.* It is necessary to have an idea about how to evaluate the solutions you generate so you can compare each against the criteria and determine which will meet all the requirements and which must be scratched from the list.

4. *Re-evaluate your list of remaining solutions.* Select the one you want to use as your problem solution. Assign responsibilities for communication of the new solution to managers and employees.

5. *Coordinate implementation of the solution across the company.* A pilot program could determine whether the solution will really work as expected. If so, you can expand the pilot into a full-blown introduction companywide.

6. *Evaluate the results.* It is important to measure the results to determine whether they meet your expectations.

Serving as an In-House Expert

No one in the organization knows as much about employee programs as the professionals in the HR department. Being an in-house expert is just part of what HR professionals do. Remember that being accurate is one of the job demands. Loss of credibility can happen in a heartbeat, so be sure you are correct before answering questions. Do your homework. Study each of the subject areas you are assigned. They can include wage and hour rules, union contract provisions, discrimination prevention requirements, management skills training, employee relocation services, HRIS administration, and so many more. Become the expert people will look to for answers when they have questions. Again, you should know all applicable U.S. employment laws (found in Chapter 3) and any local laws that apply.

Analyzing Specific Business Challenges

Have you ever had one of your external customers tell the sales and marketing organization that you must attest that your organization is compliant with equal employment opportunity and affirmative action requirements? It is not unusual for customer organizations, particularly local governmental entities, to say they require adherence to stricter requirements than those imposed by the federal government. There are many reasons for such a difference, many of which are not founded in law. They may require release of sensitive employee data to "prove" your organization is doing what the customer's requirements demand. In these situations, along with your sales and marketing people, you could determine whether you are willing to release the data required or push back with objections and negotiate. When the customer is adamant about its submission demands, you are faced with a question about whether you will comply, forego business with that customer, or find an alternative solution that satisfies all parties. All along the way, you must identify issues, provide assessment of those issues to others in the decision-making group, and offer recommendations with your rationale. Can you develop a solution that satisfies the customer while still protecting the privacy of your workforce? The final decision is not going to be made by HR for many of these types of issues. Yet the final decision depends on high-quality staff work by HR professionals.

Generating Organizational Interventions

What happens when the production department and the maintenance department have a conflict over access to machinery? Production wants to use the machinery for production. Maintenance wants to use the machinery for updates and repairs. Both cannot prevail without some compromise. HR can help identify how union and wage and hour rules can be used to support a solution to the problem. Scheduling maintenance work during a shift that is not used for production is one approach. HR can facilitate the resolution by knowing legal requirements and offering support to both groups and their own missions. In the end, the only thing that matters is having the company reach its objectives.

Developing Consultative and Coaching Skills

Everyone needs personal help from time to time, even managers and executives. One of the most satisfying and productive HR roles is that of counselor and coach.

Ten Tips for Building Relationships with Your Clients During Meetings[58]

1. *Do your homework.* Be sure you know each organizational unit's mission and goals.

2. *Listen before you talk.* Ask questions to be sure you understand the client's needs. Tell them you will be taking notes as the meeting progresses. That is to capture key points and any follow-up items during your conversation.

3. *Learn about your client's vision of the future.* Where will their portion of the organization be in another few years? Will their role be changing within the company?

4. *Provide anecdotes and examples.* Help your clients understand the nuances of HR requirements and options. Always try to relate your message specifically to your clients through conversation and with a storytelling approach. Describe similar situations and offer examples of how others handled situations successfully.

5. *Offer to work with other advisors.* The legal staff or accounting department should be involved in the discussion. Be willing to work with others so your advice can satisfy the client's needs.

6. *Save your client's time and effort.* Your client is busy like you are. If you can help them save their time and budget dollars, you will be doing them a favor.

7. *Use technology.* Suggest web portals or apps that can help the client with their problem(s).

8. *Build a team approach.* Whenever possible, make use of your HR colleagues as a backup to your personal participation in the discussions.

9. *Find out how clients prefer to be contacted.* Not everyone prefers e-mail contact. Some would rather have text messages or even a voice phone call. If the client does not have a preference and you do, ask if you can contact them the way you find best for you.

10. *Follow up.* After the meeting, follow up with your client to thank them for their time and suggest you are available for additional discussions if they would like to have more sessions.

There are also steps you can take to practice your coaching skills in addition to those you use for consultation.

Coaching Skills[59]

- *Listen with curiosity.* Convey a genuine interest in what others have to say.

- *Take in what you hear.* Concentrate on what the other person is saying. Do not be thinking about what your next comment will be.

- *Reflect with accuracy.* Active listening is a skill that HR professionals must develop. Comments like "So, what you're saying is…" and "What I'm hearing is…" are good ways to recap what you think you heard. If it is incorrect, the other person can make the necessary correction by saying, "No. What I really meant was…."

- *Ask open-ended questions to explore more fully.* Who, what, when, where, and how are the way to begin questions that cannot be answered with a simple "yes" or "no." They require an explanation and allow the coach to get additional information that will be helpful in providing the advice necessary.

- *Provide feedback for development.* Understand the individual's strengths and weaknesses and know that feedback is what we all need to be sure we are on track with the journey to our goals. Feedback is not an accusation or complaint. Feedback consists of suggestion and rationale, reinforcement, and praise.

Guiding Employees

Every day, employees will walk into the HR department with questions. Today it will be about life insurance. Tomorrow it will be about a discrimination complaint. Later in the week it will be someone asking how to correct some of the information in their employee records. Guiding employees to a solution they can implement themselves is going to free you to help others more quickly than if you took on the problem resolution yourself.

Employees are sometimes confused. They do not usually know the law and its application. Sometimes they do not know company policy. Guiding them through understanding where to find the answers they need is a good approach. You may have an employee who wants to file a discrimination complaint because their boss has just told them either their work performance must improved or there will be further steps toward a performance improvement program. Not everything that's labeled discrimination actually is discrimination, but employees might not know the difference. You can help them understand the legal requirements for something to be illegal discrimination.

Sexual harassment problems are usually just the opposite. People will say, "I need to tell you something, but I don't want you to do anything about it." You must guide them to understand that once you are aware of the problem, you have a fiduciary obligation to do something about it. You cannot keep this information to yourself.

Proficiency Indicators for Senior HR Professionals

SHRM-SCP Senior HR professionals have much more impact on the business because they participate in developing strategies that will contribute to the company achieving its goals.

Creating Talent Management Strategies

Managing talent depends on knowing what talent needs exist in the incumbent workforce now and into the future?

A strategy is a plan for how you will reach your goal. If the goal is to determine what talent needs exist that cannot be met by your incumbent workforce, then the strategy can reflect how you will obtain that talent from external sources. Finding new recruiting sources for minorities, women, disabled, and veterans can be helpful. Utilizing the resources of specific groups such as the Institute for Electrical and Electronic Engineers (IEEE), technical school graduates, or the United States Chef Association can tap into specific talent and skills that you may require. Identify the needs you have and then explore how those needs might be met with a campaign aimed at specific groups.

Listening

Listening is an often-underrated skill. Most people do not do it very well. Senior HR professionals must develop this skill so it can be used to help internal clients and even the multitude of outside contacts.

You will recall our discussion earlier about the communication cycle. It requires a message to be sent from the speaker to the listener. Then, it requires feedback from the listener to the speaker to be sure the message was received and understood in its entirety. The communication cycle embodies the concept of active listening. It requires listening for the meaning of the message, not just the words being used. Feedback to the speaker will allow the speaker to confirm the listener's understanding or give the speaker an opportunity to correct the misunderstanding.

Feedback amounts to comments like "What I hear you saying is…" or "You're telling me…." It is often helpful as the speaker to request feedback from the listener. This is helpful for supervisors and managers who are giving instructions to workers. After the instruction, say something like, "Now, tell me what you are going to do" or "so I know I have clearly conveyed what I intended, please tell me what you understood and what action you will be taking."

Developing a Human Capital Vision

A vision is a statement of what you want for the future. Steve Jobs had a vision that Apple's desktop computer would be the best on the market. He also had a vision that Pixar could become a leader in animated entertainment. He articulated those visions and developed strategic plans to support them. And guess what? They happened.

It is always amazing to hear people talk about "overnight successes." The fact is, not very many successes develop overnight. They take years and suddenly appear to have just happened because they broke through the background clutter and are now visible as a force in the world.

Human capital changes faster in some industries than in others. Yet it changes. When USS-POSCO, the joint venture of U.S. Steel and POSCO steel in South Korea, decided to work together, there were some basic requirements they had to meet for the success they wanted. They completely refurbished the factory that U.S. Steel had in Pittsburg, California. It was changed from a steel smelting operation to a plant that would "cold-roll" steel for customer use. Cold-rolled steel is used to make refrigerators, computer housings, automobile parts, and "tin" cans for the food industry. The smelting and hot rolling was to be done in South Korea; then the rolls of steel would be shipped to Pittsburg, California, where they would be rolled again but without heating. Some of the stock would be zinc coated to produce galvanized steel. The thing is, none of this could be done by people manually operating the machinery that squeezes the steel into smaller and smaller in thicknesses. It is all controlled by computer. That meant employees had to undergo six months of training in statistical process control, machinery, and hydraulic operations. The talent requirements for the new factory shifted from laborer and crafts-people to technicians. They had to find employees with new skills from sources different from where they had recruited before.

Your vision for human capital in the future of your organization will demand a new strategic plan for attaining the goals associated with that vision.

Maximizing ROI for the Organization

HR Professionals Magazine identifies several elements in the effort to maximize return on investment for an organization:[60]

- **Perceptual elements** How we learn and retain new knowledge (auditory, visual, kinesthetic, and verbal)
- **Psychological elements** How we process new information and make decisions/solve problems (analytic/global, reflective/impulsive)
- **Environmental elements** How the work environment contributes to or detracts from productivity (loud or quiet, bright or low light, warm or cool temperature, informal or formal seating)
- **Physiological elements** How we remain energized and stay alert at work (time of day, intake, mobility)
- **Emotional elements** How quickly we complete challenging and complex tasks (internal or external motivation, single- or multiple-task persistence, conformity, structure)
- **Sociological elements** How we prefer to work and interact effectively with others (alone/in pairs/in small or large groups, authority, variety)

Making sure the organization receives the greatest financial return on its investment in HR is the duty of every senior HR professional.

Using Appropriate Analytical Tools

Data analysis is a growing responsibility of the HR professional. Particularly at the senior HR level, determining and interpreting the data are critical functions. The question is, how do we perform those analyses?

A sample of the software available for use in data analyses includes Orange Data Mining, R Software Environment, Weka Data Mining, Tableau Public, Arcadia Data, Microsoft R, ITALASSI, Shogun, Trifacta, ELKI, Scikit-learn, Data Applied, Lavastorm Analytics Engine, Gephi, DataMelt, TANAGRA, Julia, RapidMiner Starter Edition, SciPy, KNIME Analytics Platform, and Dataiku DSS. Most of these are languages that will require programming assistance.

This readily available data has led to a boom in companies dedicated to building data visualization and analysis tools that can be used by almost anyone within the business. Gone are the days of waiting for an analyst to generate a report that is out of date the minute you get it or spending weeks mired in Excel. The global business intelligence (BI) and analytics software market has grown to 23.22 billion in 2022, according to Marketwatch.com.[61]

Identifying Creative Solutions

Senior HR professionals are the key players in their organizations who can explore alternative solutions for difficult, often new problems. Sure, the old problems about helping employees understand the benefit plan choices will still be around, but now there are issues such as protecting the HRIS data from external hackers. Dealing with industrial espionage, key employees walking away for jobs at competitor companies, and key vendors closing shop are just three of the types of problems you can face in today's world.

How you deal with these problems will determine whether you are going to survive as an HR department without turnover in key HR personnel. Creative approaches are the ones that explore options. Executives want to know what is possible, not what is impossible. It is up to senior HR executives to help them find those alternatives.

Supervising HR Investigations

One element of HR management that should be consistent is the investigation of employee complaints. There are some legal experts who believe that the employer's legal staff should conduct all the investigations. Other people within the legal community counsel that HR should be the investigating group so there is a separation of investigator and legal counsel.

However you approach the issue in your organization, you will want to be sure that every complaint investigation is managed in the same systematic and rigorous way. Methodology is important. Touchstones during the investigation are important. Discrimination complaints must meet certain requirements. If an employee says she has been discriminated against because of her sex, it is necessary to determine what happened that has resulted in her paying a penalty of some kind. And what was that penalty? If those basic elements are present, the *prima facie* case has been established. Then the investigation must gather evidence to show that the complaint can be substantiated.

Should our organization treat each complaint on its emotional value rather than its evidentiary value, our liability will be increased. Ultimately, the complaint will migrate to state or federal enforcement agencies and sometimes to the courts. Senior HR managers must supervise those conducting the investigations to remedy problems when that is appropriate and to explain that the employee does not have the evidence to support her claim if that is the appropriate outcome.

Recognizing HR Liabilities

According to SHRM,[62] the following are the top ten employment liabilities in the modern workplace. Some of these may be covered by insurance, and others will not be subject to insurance protections. Some coverage will depend on specific policies designed to cover risks of discriminatory treatment, among other issues.

1. **Wage and hour claims**   Violations of FLSA and state counterparts can cause employer exposure to financial remedies.

2. **Class action lawsuits**   More frequently these days employees are banding together to consolidate their complaints into a class action lawsuit. This means the exposure for employers is higher as a result.

3. **FMLA violations**   Not following the Family and Medical Leave Act can bring financial remedies that could be quite costly.

4. **Whistleblowers**   These are employees who file complaints that something illegal is happening at the employer's organization.

5. **Data breaches**   This is loss of employee data that could lead to identity theft.

6. **Social media**   Beware of negative reviews of company policies or employment practices.

7. **Alternative work arrangements**   Telecommuting, job sharing, and other alternative work schedules can lead to FMLA complaints and more.

8. **Discrimination complaints**   Violations of civil rights laws bring exposure for financial remedies.

9. **Sexual harassment**   Also a violation of civil rights law, workplace behavior that is sexual in nature can bring employer liability.

10. **Gender and sexual orientation claims**   Most recently defined of the civil rights protections, this type of complaint and financial remedy is just gaining traction.

Coaching Executives

More than any other, this skill will allow HR managers to leverage influence in the employer organization. Teaching line executives how to evaluate problems that have HR implications is a way to help them deal with issues within their own organizational unit. There is also the personal element of coaching. Executives sometimes need help to adjust their personal approach to managing employees. Sometimes they do not see what their behavior is doing adversely to the workforce. Helping them understand that impact and exploring alternative approaches can give the executive a path to greater effectiveness.

Designing Strategic HR and Business Solutions

Strategy is the plan you will implement to achieve your goals. HR strategy should always support business solutions. HR must help the organization meet its goals. Proving that link is the duty of a senior HR professional. When problems arise that were not anticipated, HR professionals should be key players in developing the appropriate solutions so company goals will be achieved.

Summary

The Consultation behavior competency has explored the things HR professionals say and do that will provide quality support to other departments. Collaborative interactions can be rewarding and satisfying when the impact is measured and found to contribute to company goals.

Behavioral Competency 9: Analytical Aptitude

The days of "winging it" are in the past. HR professionals are now able to access vast amounts of data to help them in their decision-making. This area of behavioral competency looks at the gathering, assessing, and using of information in the decision-making process.

Four subcompetencies comprise the analytical aptitude competency, as defined by SHRM:[63]

- **Data advocate**   Understanding and promoting the importance and utility of data
- **Data gathering**   Understanding how to determine data utility and identifying and gathering data to assist and inform organizational decisions
- **Data analysis**   Analyzing data to evaluate HR initiatives and business challenges
- **Evidence-based decision-making**   Using the results of data analysis to inform and decide the best course of action

Key Concepts

- Survey and assessment processes (for example, development, administration, validation)
- Sources of data (for example, interviews, focus groups, employee surveys, customer surveys, marketing data, analytical reports)
- Data analysis techniques and methods (for example, data cleansing, data mining, visualization, big data analysis, statistical analysis, predictive analysis)
- Basic concepts in statistics (for example, descriptive statistics, correlation) and measurement (for example, reliability, validity)
- Interpretation of data and charts (for example, bar charts, line graphs, scatterplots, histograms)
- Using data to support a business case (for example, interpretation, visualization, graphical representation, storytelling)

Definition

According to SHRM, Analytical Aptitude is defined "as the knowledge, skills, abilities, and other characteristics (KSAOs) needed to collect and analyze qualitative and quantitative data and to interpret and promote findings that evaluate HR initiatives and inform business decisions and recommendations."[64]

Proficiency Indicators for All HR Professionals

Anyone working at the professional level in human resource management is expected to access and interpret information the organization's leaders need to make accurate decisions about the workforce. What follows are the basics in this area of competency.

Making Sound Decisions

It is a rare circumstance for all information needed to be available for decision-making. In most situations, only partial data is available. Yet, despite that, HR professionals are expected to be able to make good, workable decisions in a timely way. For example, from a long list of possible health insurance vendor programs, HR must select only a handful to present as options for employee enrollment. That requires using whatever might be known about the vendor programs, costs of each program, availability in the geography required, and employee likelihood that each program would be deemed attractive. Only some of that information is available, but the selection of a "short list" must happen anyway. If the decisions are not good, employees will reject the options, and morale and even production levels could be impacted. Turnover may be impacted whether the decisions made by HR are good or bad, and that is just one example of the importance of sound decisions in the presence of uncertainty.

Assessing the Impact of Laws

Federal and state laws may change every year. When those laws impact HR issues, it is important to determine what specific impact they will have on your organization. When minimum wages increase, there is direct financial impact that can be computed and presented for consideration in the budget planning process. When new benefits are mandated, such as paid sick leave, the costs can be estimated and provided for budget consideration. If new requirements are placed on nondiscrimination, it may be necessary to train all managers and supervisors in those new legal provisions. If the company decides to move into federal contracting or subcontracting, the financial and recruiting impacts must be estimated.

Chapter 3 lists the federal laws involved based on the payroll head count of any employer organization that engages in interstate commerce. When a company hires its first employee, it becomes subject to dozens of federal laws governing employment. Hire more than 14 people, and the exposure to legal requirements continues to grow.

HR professionals are expected to monitor these legal developments and forecast how the organization will comply with those requirements.

Transferring Knowledge

What do benefit enrollment, payroll, and discrimination complaints have in common? The answer is they all can involve historical data for proper handling. Using knowledge gained in handling one issue within the HR arena to apply to another issue (or even several other issues) is both efficient and smart. Equally important is the need to pass along to others the information gained in handling problems with one issue so that it might help in other areas.

Applying Critical Thinking to Information Received from Organizational Stakeholders

Determining what information can be used to support organizational success is dependent on being able to identify what is important from what is not. Many pieces of information flow into our realm every day. Most of that data does not have value in the HR decision-making process. Therefore, you must sort the valuable from the less valuable.

Of the numerous phone calls you receive on a given day...

- One is an alert that the union will be challenging an employee suspension.
- One is an invitation to speak at the local service club luncheon.
- One is a subordinate in the HR department complaining about the lack of hand towels in the restroom.
- One is the boss explaining that the budget estimates are due a week earlier than planned.
- One is an update on the progress made in planning the office holiday party.
- One is from the union president wanting to discuss disciplinary policy.

As each call comes in, your priorities may have to shift, and the information you get from one issue may be helpful in some way when addressing other issues. You must store, sort, and retrieve each of these pieces of data, applying critical thinking to each in determining what will be helpful and what will not be helpful.

Gathering Critical Information

When a problem has been identified, such as "The board of directors has just approved a policy that will give paid sick leave to all employees," it falls to HR to figure out how to implement that policy. Implementation begins with gathering data. How many employees are going to be impacted? What has been the average absence rate in the past year? What portion of that absence has been due to illness of the employee? What portion has been due to illness of an employee's family member? Will the new policy apply to family members as well as the employee?

Identify the information you want to have and then get it. If it is not available for some reason, you may need to make some educated guesses about what it might have been if it were available.

Analyzing Data

Once you have the data you think you need, begin the sorting process to determine what will be helpful and what will not. Then assess the data for accuracy. Do the best you can to determine whether any data collection errors have been introduced to the process. Were there typos or transpositions? When the data is clean, begin analyzing what it tells you.

Analyzing Best Practices

Having in hand an analysis of the data, you now need to define what the best practices are for your issue. What are other similar employers doing about the same issue?

Who can you contact to get information about other employers' handling of this issue? Once you have determined what other employers are doing, you will know what each considers to be the best practice in the situation.

Delineating Best Practices

Compare the best practices you identified from contacting other employers and researching industry data or using some other source. Once you know how others handle a situation, you can decide if their solution could work for you too, either as is or modified to your particular circumstances. Information sources can include the following:

- Your organizational history
- Industry data
- Specific data from another company
- Peer-reviewed research
- Internet information available to the general public
- Response to survey requests sent to other employers

Combine all the input you can gather and construct a description of the best practices being followed by employers like your own.

Identifying Leading Indicators

Leading indicators provide evidence as to whether HR is achieving its goal expectations. Human resource management has common measurement areas. Productivity, employee engagement, recruiting, retention, and budget are some examples:

- **Productivity** Translated into dollars, employee productivity offers opportunity for significant savings in company expense. When one employee can produce more this year than last year, the budget will benefit.
- **Engagement** Results from employee surveys can indicate the state of morale and positive feelings about the employer. In turn, these factors can reduce turnover, improve attendance, and improve employee loyalty.
- **Recruiting** Perception of an employer's reputation can impact people's willingness to respond to recruiting efforts.
- **Retention** Employee turnover can represent a sizable amount of expense. Reducing that turnover, or increasing retention, can directly reduce costs.
- **Budget** Some executives see HR as an overhead expense. HR can achieve success in this area via expense management and hitting budget targets.

Analyzing Large Quantities of Information

Vast amounts of data flow to the HR department each year, including financial data, recruiting data, internal employee data, and training needs data, just to name a few. It is necessary for HR professionals to sort the important information from the less important information. Data can grind the HR organization to a halt. Without prioritization and sorting, the total amount of data can be so overwhelming that it is not possible to deal with all of it. HR professionals must be able to determine which information should be acknowledged and which can be ignored.

One technique for dealing with large quantities of information is to only dip into that data in search of specific answers to specific questions. Systems can be developed to house data, permit retrieval by authorized individuals, and allow access to answers as questions arise. Protecting the data with security procedures can meet obligations for privacy. When done well, systems can permit data management that will prevent sinking the HR organization.

Once the data is sorted and stored, HR has the responsibility to analyze what the data says. What portions of the organization are experiencing the highest turnover rates? What departments have the lowest absence rates? What is the cost of each benefits program? What should be offered in the next round of union negotiations and why? Who has yet to be trained in sexual harassment prevention? Identifying the problem, defining it properly, gathering the right data, then analyzing that data for potential insights and solutions are the key steps in applying analytical aptitude.

Proficiency Indicators for Senior HR Professionals

Evaluation done at the senior level of HR tends to focus more on the impact of policy and strategy. That evaluation can contribute to discussions held by executives about the organization's market position, employee issues, and financial performance.

Maintaining Expert Knowledge

HR knowledge is constantly changing. New scientific studies are being conducted each year, and new laws are being enacted by federal, state, and local entities. It falls to the senior HR professional to know all these things and to keep that knowledge current. It is often helpful to seek regular input from the legal staff and the accounting staff. Knowing requirements and how they relate to organizational goals can help in identifying areas that need adjustments.

Senior HR professionals must not only keep current in their knowledge but also must be able to understand what that knowledge means to the organization's objectives and how it will impact performance.

Interpreting Data and Make Recommendations

It is easy to identify the cost of benefit plans and suggest changes if costs warrant them. It may be a bit more difficult to interpret data about employee satisfaction and formulate recommendations for changes in policies or practices that might be appropriate.

The key question to ask is, "What impact will this data have on our organization?" Answering that question will then suggest what should be done to influence different outcomes. For example, monitoring recruiting efforts for veterans might tell you your identified sources for qualified people is not producing the results you need. The impact on your organization is that you will fall short of the target you set for hiring veterans if you do not change something. Your monitoring has told you that you need to make adjustments and find new sources for qualified veterans.

Making Decisions with Confidence

Decision-making has two components. One is the willingness to make decisions. The other is the quality of the decisions (that is, whether the decisions actually work). Senior HR professionals are expected to be able to make decisions, often in the face of uncertainty. Not all the data will be available to guide you when you would like to have it. Sometimes, the quality of data you do have will be questionable. In the face of all the uncertainty, you are still expected to draw conclusions and make choices that will guide the senior executives in your organization.

When policy changes are not an absolute requirement but an option, how will you formulate recommendations? Consider, for example, adding protections in your EEO and affirmative action policy that apply to your LGBTQIA+ staff. Aside from federal contractors, most other employers have the choice about including LGBTQIA+ in their policy statement. The question is, should you? What will be the outcome if you do include that group among protected categories of people? What recommendation will you make to the senior executives? Likely you will not have all the data you would like to have about the impact of such a policy change. Yet you are still expected to make a professional determination about the question.

Setting the Direction of HR

Where is your HR organization going? What are its objectives? How should those objectives be redefined from year to year? To determine the answers, it is necessary to evaluate risks and economic and environmental factors.

Keeping a list of issues that will have an impact on your organization can help determine any adjustments in goals needed during the year. Economic impacts can come from change in benefit plan costs, increases in payroll expense, and increases or decreases in turnover rates. Environmental factors can include legislation, competition, compensation, and employee relations. Legislation impacts HR by imposing requirements such as records retention and compliance requirements, such as the Americans with Disabilities Act. Competition impacts can come from the effort to recruit the same type of talent found in competing organizations. Employee relations brings policy issues, early retirement programs, and different international expectations among the employee workforce. Compensation factors include the effort to maintain competitive positioning in the job market compared to other similar employer organizations while concurrently keeping pay affordable.

How HR responds to each of these factors will determine how well it can meet its stated objectives. Altering the direction HR will take can result in the need to change its objectives.

Seeking Information

Obtaining information can be done strategically and systematically. Senior HR professionals are interested in gathering data that can help them run their HR organization, as well as data that can be shared with other executives.

Strategic data might include the results of employee attitude surveys. One strategy is to incorporate employee views into decisions about specific employment-related policies and programs. Knowing how employees feel about specific issues can provide the guidance needed for decision-making about those policies and programs. Vacation policies, leave of absence practices, educational support programs, and telecommuting policies are all examples of issues that can benefit from employee input during the decision-making process.

Systematic data gathering can be done using routine systems such as direct employee accessing and updating of the HRIS records. Regular sampling of employee attitudes can be done automatically once the system has been set in place to generate questionnaires to a sampling of the workforce. Questionnaires can be modified as needed to assess opinions about evolving issues.

Data is essential to decision-making. When routine visitations are made to topics such as employee benefits, compensation, and performance appraisal systems, having data-gathering processes in place to accumulate the information needed makes those discussions easier. Informed decisions are better than those made in the dark.

Analyzing Information for Evaluation

Raw data might be interesting, but it is usually easier to use if it is summarized and transformed into statistics and charts. The number of hours employees are absent because of illness may be interesting, but it is more useful to look at it when it has been summarized into statistics such as absence rates. Displaying the relationship between two or more different data items means more when viewed over time.

Other examples of data that can be useful when evaluated over time can include anything that would permit trend plotting. Median compensation paid to a given job category, average employee training hours per year, and percentage of employees still on the job 1 year after hiring are all examples of data relationships that can be plotted on a graph to represent trends over time. Figure 7-1 shows an example displaying EEO complaints per year.

Figure 7-1
Sample data summary display with trend line

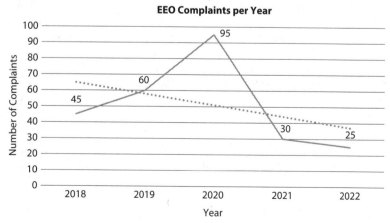

Sponsoring Process Improvement Initiatives

There is usually more than one way to accomplish a goal. The same can be said of most processes used in the workplace. You tend to use processes because they exist, not because they are the best. What exists and works well takes no effort to change. If you want to make changes, you must invest effort.

Improving processes is not always encouraged precisely because it takes time and effort. It may also take other resources such as budget dollars. For example, the recruiting links we have on our company website are used by people interested in our job openings. If we wish to modify the process to include an invitation to self-identify disabled and veteran status during the application process (which is now required of all federal contractors), we must involve the people who write the code for these additional steps in the process.

HR can offer support or withhold support for such changes in processes having to do with employee data. Designing a new employee survey can take considerable time. Hiring an outside consulting firm to do that can cost considerable money. HR can decide to either support or oppose the creation of a new employee survey based on all the factors known at the time.

Sponsoring initiatives to improve processes is an HR opportunity to influence and improve the overall workings of company systems. These initiatives can be responding to a spontaneous employee suggestion ("The handling of new employee orientation would be better if...") or a structured response (from a study group assigned to assess and improve the performance evaluation process).

Communicating Impact for Data Analysis

Data has no value until it is communicated to those who can use it. HR professionals play a critical role in employer organizations because they have ownership of many data elements regarding employment activities. How HR professionals decide to pass along that data will determine the effectiveness of HR and the impact of the data.

For example, when it is determined that certain recruiting sources are more productive than others, helping the hiring managers understand where candidate riches are is a role HR can play. When HR explains to senior managers the cost of discrimination complaints, even though they are investigated internally and do not result in external agency complaints, it falls to the executive team to take any policy actions that HR recommends.

Building Effective and Creative Policies

When local, state, or federal legislation specifies how employees are to be treated, HR should craft policies that will ensure the organization is in compliance. When there is no legislation, but regulatory rules specify the handling of employee issues, again HR professionals should guide their organizations to implement policies that will ensure compliance.

When managers are making decisions that treat similarly situated employees quite differently, it is time for HR to step in and create policies that can be recommended for standardizing that treatment when those conditions arise.

When no one knows how things should be done and the circumstances will recur, it should be no wonder that HR is expected to step in and create policies that will address those situations.

Using Environmental Factors in Decision-Making

Looking at external political, economic, sociological, technological, legal, and environmental factors can influence decision-making within organizations. Responsible business leaders look for ways to minimize the impact of their decisions on the environment. That means, for example, that energy consumption and energy sources come into play. Should the company invest in solar or wind power generation to offset carbon-based generation sources? Should systems be developed that will permit the recycling of water in the production of company products? If so, perhaps the overall use of "new" water can be reduced.

Customers are voting with their wallets these days. Organizations that consider the impact on environmental factors will win the race for consumer dollars when compared with sources or products and services that ignore such things.

Challenging Assumptions

Analytical Aptitude is not complete until you review your work and identify assumptions that have been made. What happens if you do not check for assumptions? Well, here are some examples:[65]

- IBM focused on mainframe sales in the 1980s while servers and PCs had greater sales.
- Blockbuster held onto retail stores when streaming and DVD sales exploded.
- Nokia did not recognize smartphones as important but held onto standard cell phones.

The impacts of these oversights were serious financial penalties. In HR terms, it behooves you to keep track of the leading-edge trends; otherwise, your competitors will be able to attract the talent you would like to have. What are you doing for paid parental leave, employee lounge areas for rest breaks, or paid health care benefits that include dental and vision coverage? Are you considering adding optional pet insurance? You can bet your competitors are considering all these things as tools for recruiting and retaining tomorrow's workforce.

Providing a Strategic View

According to Ross Beard, "Critical analysis of the strategic management process focuses on the way managers develop strategies to achieve company goals. Since carrying out the strategy requires the support of the whole company, you must evaluate how well you achieve such an acceptance of your strategy. You can build consensus by demonstrating to employees that the strategy looks after their interests, while motivating employees to look beyond their own interests to the well-being of the group. An example is profit-sharing, which rewards each team member but only to the extent that the team as a whole performs well."[66]

HR professionals provide critical input to strategic development and implementation of the strategic plan. Your problem analysis and decision-making are not complete until you evaluate how the decision will fit into the strategic plan.

Summary

In this section of the chapter, we examined the behaviors associated with Analytical Aptitude. All HR professionals will find it necessary to use these behaviors when performing their jobs. Looking past the obvious to what is driving people to do what they do is essential. Gathering data, assessing that data, and using the information to make quality decisions are tasks all HR professionals should be able to perform. There is no more "shooting from the hip." Conscious exploration of alternatives and impact now drive the modern HR function.

Chapter Review

This chapter has been about behavioral competencies that apply to HR professionals. These are things that HR professionals are expected to be able to say and do given any set of circumstances they may face. Proper responses depend on experience, careful thought, and knowledge. It is not enough to memorize facts. What is important is how those facts can be blended with the situation to respond properly. That is called situational awareness. HR professionals must be capable of working with problems within their context. It is not enough to say, "You can't use that written employment test." There needs to be an analysis of why the test was wanted by the hiring manager in the first place. Situationally, there may be some valid alternative approaches to the real problem of identifying the talent needed. Behavioral competencies are a critical part of an HR professional's life.

 NOTE The exam will have 10 percent knowledge-related questions pertaining to the nine behavioral competencies, and 40 percent will be situational judgment–type questions stemming from scenarios. The following questions are intended to help you review your understanding of this chapter's content and to simulate actual situational judgment practice exam questions. You will find more situational judgment scenario-based exam-like questions in the two practice exams available with this book.

Questions

1. Cathy is the HR manager in her organization. She has just been told she must find a supplier for employee service awards. As it turns out, she is well acquainted with all the local companies offering such products. Cathy's husband Connor owns one of them. Given that circumstance, what should Cathy do about placing an order?

   A. Since Cathy knows she can get a good deal from her husband Connor's company, she should select it as the vendor.

   B. The professional HR code that deals with conflicts of interest would prevent Cathy from selecting her husband's company because it could appear as favoritism for personal gain, whether this is the case or not.

   C. If Cathy treats her husband's company as an equal in consideration of vendors, there should be no problem.

   D. Cathy should seek vendors outside the local area just to avoid any contamination of her ultimate selection.

2. Darlene has been recently promoted to senior HR representative. In the first week in her new position, one of her internal clients comes to her with a request to approve an expense voucher. When she reads the voucher, she sees it will be a payment to a foreign government agency to help facilitate her company's sale of a product to their country. What ethical issues, if any, should Darlene recognize?

   A. There are no ethical issues. It is a legitimate government payment like any permit application process in this country.

   B. There is an ethical issue. HR should support every sales effort regardless of where it is taking place around the globe. Yet Darlene is right to be concerned. She has approval authority only up to a certain amount. In this case, she will "fudge" the limit and sign off anyway to start the process of building trust with this new client.

   C. There are no ethical issues. There is nothing in this transaction that would raise any questions about ethics.

   D. There is an ethical issue. It looks like Darlene will be giving a bribe to someone in the foreign government. That is both illegal and unethical.

3. Just as you reach your desk, the phone rings. On the other end of the line is an employee saying one of the company's executives sexually assaulted her. After a 3-month-long investigation, you have gathered volumes of testimony from the employee's co-workers. Try as you might, there were no witnesses to be found who saw the alleged assault. Of course, the executive has denied all charges. He did not even contend a consensual encounter was behind the current complaint. He just says, "Nothing happened."

   During the complaint investigation you discover this accused executive is the key contact for your company with a major international customer. What will you do at the conclusion of the investigation, if the employee's version of events has more credibility than the executive's in this complaint? There are no witnesses to the assault, but co-worker statements support the employee's credibility. The company sees itself as an ethical organization, and it rewards managers for ethical behavior on occasion.

A. The key contact status is a major mitigation of the sexual harassment charges. The company cannot afford to lose the customer's business. It would be appropriate to support retention of the executive in the current job until some other person is able to take over as key contact with that customer.

B. Immediate suspension is appropriate in this circumstance. There is no ethical barrier to taking that action.

C. Ethics are not an issue in this type of situation. The best business decision is to keep the executive in his job and reassign the complaining employee to some other work group.

D. Postponing any discipline or corrective action with the executive because of his key contact status with a key customer is wrong. It amounts to treating the executive differently from the way other management people have been treated in similar circumstances. Inconsistency in treatment is unethical. You decide to recommend appropriate discipline based on the evidence you have and comparable other cases. It does not matter how much pressure you are getting to do otherwise.

4. Jose has always been a good employee. He arrives at work promptly and works hard throughout his shift, as is his custom. His manager gives him top marks for his attitude and performance. The manager says, "If I had more like Jose, we would never have to worry about production."

Then one day, Jose gets a call and must rush home for a family emergency. Later, about quitting time, he remembers he did not clock out. He calls his friend Guillermo and asked him to punch out for him. Guillermo says, "Sure, no problem."

A few days later, Jose's manager is reviewing the timecards and finds Jose's timecard overstates his actual work hours for that week. Jose did not work the afternoon, but his timecard says he did. Is this a termination offense? Are there any ethical issues for you as the HR director?

A. There are ethical issues if what has happened involves a cover-up at any level. Jose's lack of intention to deceive by having a friend clock him out at the end of the day may be a mitigating factor to the company policy. Endorsing the cover-up by giving Jose a "pass" on his behavior would be unethical. Falsifying timecards is still a serious issue.

B. Falsifying timecards is a disciplinary issue, not an ethical issue.

C. HR should not be involved in this situation. It is up to Jose's manager to dole out whatever discipline is appropriate.

D. What is the big deal? Jose is a good performer. Cut him some slack. Keep him happy since we want to keep him. Everyone has a family emergency at some point.

5. When Achmed became an HR professional, there were only four people in the HR department. The other three staff members were women. Achmed has trouble working with women and giving them the respect they deserve. Nonetheless, he attempts to be careful to make sure that does not interfere with his personal job interactions.

   Achmed should do which of the following to be sure his bias does not impact his job-related decision-making?

   A. Often bias will not surface except in rare circumstances. Achmed should not be worried. He knows his colleagues will tell him if he has become too obnoxious.

   B. What does it matter if he is a bit heavy-handed with the women he interacts with on the job? In the end, it is really his decision that counts. If it does not reflect a bias, there should be no issue.

   C. Ask for feedback from women with whom he interacts. Request that they tell him how he can improve his interpersonal skills. Ask for input about his fairness in approaching the problem being discussed. He can work to identify when his bias is trying to break through and influence his decision-making.

   D. The best approach is for him to wait for women to get upset with him so he can get good input about his bias.

6. Juanita is the HR representative for her assigned department. She oversees all the HR issues that come up. Recently, Juanita saw an article in the news about a new requirement that will likely impact her company's workers. She decides that the company lawyers will probably take responsibility for digesting that information and distributing it to the HR professionals. What would you tell Juanita about her decision?

   A. Her decision is a good one. She obviously does not have time to spend scouring through the news for new HR requirements. Also, it is the lawyers' responsibility to follow legal changes, right?

   B. Her decision is a good one. She does not have responsibility for tracking new legal requirements that apply to HR management issues.

   C. Her decision is not a good one. She should accept responsibility for detecting and studying new legal requirements as they apply to the HR profession. Certification requirements point out that it is the HR professional, as well as the legal staff, who should be monitoring these changes.

   D. Her decision is not a good one. It is not the inside attorney who should be monitoring these new requirements; it is the outside attorney. What else does that consulting attorney do if not tracking legal requirement changes related to the HR staff?

7. Diversity, equity, and inclusion (DE&I) programs should also reach out to which of the following?

   A. Employees of competitor firms

   B. Government auditors for validation of the employer's program

   C. News organizations that can provide justification for a diversity program

   D. Veterans and disabled people for their viewpoints and experiences

8. DE&I programs do which of the following?

   A. Explain that minorities and women must be hired at a certain minimum rate.

   B. Provide managers with legal mandates for recruiting only minorities for certain key positions.

   C. Make it possible for all employees to contribute more fully to the workforce.

   D. Supersede EEOC and affirmative action programs.

9. You have been serving as an HR professional for more than 20 years now. In your current assignment, you have been working to identify the organization's values and strategies. You have also been working to assess HR policies to be sure they support those organizational values and strategies. Is this an appropriate use of your time?

   A. Yes. If HR policies do not support values and strategies, it will be difficult to get the employee body to work toward the organizational values. If strategies for the organization are different from HR policies, employees are likely to be left out of the journey to the organization's vision.

   B. Yes. If HR policies do not support values and strategies, it will mean employees will find it hard to link their jobs to the organizational values.

   C. Yes. If HR policies do not support values and strategies, the executive team will begin asking questions about the importance of the HR department to the organization. Somewhere along the line the HR department may become irrelevant.

   D. No. If HR policies do not support values and strategies, there is no problem. HR policies are in place so they can be interpreted in each case as events develop. Nothing is written in stone. It is all good.

10. It is May and the start of your "season of the interns." Your company is a federal contractor and always hires student interns to expose them to actual workday requirements of the job and, if they are good, make them job offers for after they graduate. Yesterday, your CEO came to you and said his next-door neighbor's daughter needs a job, and he said she could work here. He wants you to put her on the payroll. What should you do?

    A. There is no ethical conflict. The executives of the company get to decide how the company will be staffed. Hiring by directive is an acceptable and ethical strategy.

    B. You should explain the ethics of not getting a job requisition number to start with. Once that is done, you can hire the neighbor's daughter and close the job requisition without a problem.

C. You should explain the ethics of following the company's hiring process. Federal contractors would find it particularly problematic when complying with recruiting and hiring regulations come into play. You need to assess how ethical it would be to open a job requisition and then close it with only one candidate without any announcement of opportunity to others. Share how the neighbor's daughter may apply.

D. You can ignore the normal process and just do what the CEO has asked you to do. The boss is in charge. Anything he wants can be done.

11. Stacie is a new HR analyst, and this is her first professional HR job. Her first assignment is to determine how other companies in the area are handling the problematic high cost of housing. It is negatively impacting employee recruiting. What should Stacie keep in mind more than anything else?

   A. Never disclose any information to other companies.

   B. Do not discuss the issue with any of the organization's own employees.

   C. Her credibility will be based on the quality of the work she produces.

   D. She should call her boss each time a question comes up about the project.

12. Renaldo has just been appointed director of HR. At the same time, the company has announced a merger that will result in a new line of business. How can Renaldo make the transition easier for the merging of company employees?

   A. Negotiate with the new company executives how the employment policies of the two companies can be merged and on what timeline.

   B. Negotiate with the new company executives what service awards will be presented to people in the new organization.

   C. Negotiate with the current company executives what office space they will be giving up to the new people.

   D. Negotiate with the current company executives how parking spaces will be allocated.

13. HR professionals must be open to the ideas of others based on which of the following?

   A. The financial backing they can offer

   B. The similarities they have to U.S. expectations

   C. Decisions made at headquarters that demand conformity to policies

   D. Experience, data, facts, and reasoned judgment

14. What is the best way managers and HR professionals can learn from others?

   A. Encourage employees to send in anonymous suggestions for improvement.

   B. Invite employees to correct the manager's decision-making methods.

   C. Express self-awareness, openness, and humility.

   D. Tell them you understand their culture pretty well.

15. Why should industry characteristics be part of an HR professional's study list?

   A. Industry requirements can vary considerably based on the type of products and services they demand. The better you understand your industry, the better HR support you may give.

   B. Industry associations demand that HR professionals submit information about employee compensation and benefit programs.

   C. Industry competitors are going to get greater revenues if you do not adjust your programs based on how competitors are doing their work.

   D. Industry representatives dictate the HR programs that must be adopted by each corporate employer.

16. Shirley is new to her job as director of human resources. The CEO has asked her to prepare a business case supporting HR's representation in executive strategic planning sessions. What should Shirley do to create that business case?

   A. She should give the job to her lieutenant as a developmental assignment.

   B. She should follow the ten-element process, from problem identification to action planning.

   C. She should identify at least five reasons why HR needs to be included in the planning process.

   D. She should call a friend at a competitor's company and ask what they did.

17. Anton has been VP of HR for 3 years now. He has been gradually adding metrics to the HR department since he took over as leader. Are there practical limits to the number of metrics that should exist in an organization?

   A. Yes. If there are too many critical metrics, nobody will get anything done other than generating data for the measurements. Those things that get measured become priorities. If almost everything is made a priority, then nothing is a priority.

   B. No. Any quantity of measurements is acceptable if each one can be linked to another department. Metrics are here to stay.

   C. Yes. More than ten metrics will choke an HR department and bring its production to a standstill.

   D. No. Any amount of metrics is acceptable if none of them cost more than 1 percent of the HR budget to monitor.

18. Greg has just been invited to present an analysis of employee benefit programs that the executive team wants to consider using, starting at the beginning next year. How should he do that?

   A. Conducting an ROI analysis is the best approach.

   B. Getting anecdotal evidence from competitors who are using the programs is the best approach.

   C. Getting vendor input is critical to arriving at the best approach.

   D. Preparing a narrative analysis is the best approach.

19. Latisha is a new HR analyst. She has been tasked with training her contacts in client departments on the changes in medical insurance benefits programs for this year. How should she handle that assignment?

    A. Provide managers the option to sit in on the training or skip the program, knowing how busy her client departments are.

    B. Study the benefits programs so she is an expert in the provisions of each plan and all the changes that will be made this year; then prepare and share a summary in a meeting where her audience may ask questions.

    C. Take the literature from the insurance companies and distribute it to the client managers in the training session.

    D. Ask the registration clerk to come along to the training sessions to answer questions about the plans.

20. Craig has been the manager of HR at his company for 2 years. He is now facing the task of making use of all the employee data that is available to him. What should he do?

    A. Delegate the project. Get a clerk to gather all the data and find a way to handle it.

    B. Bring in a consultant to write a computer program that will digest the employee data and spit out comparisons that will help in decision-making.

    C. Review the data personally and determine which analytical tool he should use to "crunch the numbers" and get some comparative results.

    D. Send the data to a consultant offsite for review and analysis.

21. Sue has just been appointed to the HR staff as an entry-level professional. What should she recognize about the need for analytical aptitude in her decision-making?

    A. She must be able to interpret information and make business recommendations to those who will decide on the organization's direction.

    B. She must rely on HR analysts to provide her with evaluation of the issues she faces. Then she should make any policy decisions needed.

    C. She must recognize that any situation with less than total descriptive information cannot be addressed by analytical aptitude.

    D. She must depend on her external contacts to provide the evaluation of HR policies in other organizations.

22. Reed is a senior HR analyst in his organization. What impact do you think new state and federal laws will have on his work?

    A. It depends on whether the new laws have local impact. HR cannot make that determination. It is important for HR professionals to get outside legal input.

    B. It is the legal staff that should be paying attention to the new laws. HR really has no significant role to play in that regard.

    C. Each new piece of legislation that impacts HR issues is important and must be a consideration for Reed's analysis work.

    D. These days, having an attorney on the HR staff is a good idea. Reed should always rely on that HR staff lawyer.

23. When inputs to HR on any given workday become so varied and intense, the HR professionals must do what?

   A. Handle issues in the order they were received. "First in, first served" should be the customer service motto.

   B. Perform triage and determine the priority for each new issue. Then deal with issues in priority order.

   C. Priorities, once set, should not be changed. Commitments must be honored and receive attention as originally determined.

   D. Handle payroll issues first, followed by benefits issues and union issues.

24. Tila has just been asked to draft a new policy for employee engagement efforts and programs. What key components should her analysis include?

   A. HR, accounting, production, and budget

   B. Office staff, production staff, recruiting staff, and legal staff

   C. Productivity, engagement, recruiting, retention, and budget

   D. Competitors, industrial associations, congressional actions, and budget

25. There is so much data involved in HR problems. How is a new HR professional supposed to handle it all?

   A. Every HR professional must be a certified professional statistician so all the data analysis can be certified as accurate.

   B. There is no need for HR professionals to be certified professional statisticians; they just need to be able to do a defensible regression analysis with three or more variables.

   C. When the data elements get to be overwhelming, HR professionals should just pick the most important for their analysis and ignore the rest.

   D. Refining problem statements so they are more specific is one important way to reduce the data overload problem.

Situational Judgment Scenario-Based Questions

Scenario 1 (Questions 26–29): You answer your phone, and it is Nancy, the CEO's executive assistant. She wants to know whether you could come talk with Marian, the CEO, in 15 minutes. When you reply you will be right up, Nancy hesitates and then adds that she wants you to keep who you are meeting with to yourself. You are intrigued but assure Nancy you will comply with her request.

When you get to the CEO's office, Marian is not there, but Nancy asks you to take a seat in her office, saying Marian will be right back. Sure enough, Marian soon arrives and asks whether she may speak freely and in confidence. You respond, "Absolutely." Marian goes on to say she wants your advice, as she thinks she needs to fire one of her C-suite members, so of course she needs to do it right. You are surprised that you have been asked for this help and not the vice president of human resources, Bob, but you keep listening.

The CEO has received e-mails from three different employees claiming different degrees of sexual harassment, all naming the same member of the C-suite. These allegations of behavior are different from what Marian has experienced with this executive.

26. What is one of your first questions for the CEO?

    A. Is the C-suite member's performance otherwise okay?

    B. Is this C-suite member a key financial contributor?

    C. What investigatory steps have been taken?

    D. What succession plan do you have in place for this C-suite member?

27. Marian gives you printouts of the three e-mails she referenced and asks you to talk to "who you think you need to talk to, please." Who will that include?

    A. The three employees

    B. The three employees and the accused

    C. The three employees, their supervisors, and the accused

    D. The three employees, their supervisors, the accused, and anyone else who becomes relevant based upon your interviews

28. Marian tells you that if you have any resistance setting up your meetings, you should share that you are doing this at her request. She asks that you meet with her again to give a verbal update as soon as you have news to report. In that second meeting, you share more details from e-mail writers, that every supervisor reported their employee was credible, and that the accused was shocked, outraged, and refused to cooperate once he understood the purpose of the meeting. Based upon this data gathering, what do you report to the CEO?

    A. You will make a recommendation based on the preponderance of the evidence.

    B. You cannot make a recommendation without more information from the accused.

    C. You need your vice president, Bob, to make such an important recommendation.

    D. You want to turn your notes over to the firm's legal counsel to make the recommendation.

29. Marian says you have provided her with enough information and looks forward to quickly receiving your written report. She asks whether you have any additional related comments. How do you respond?

    A. "No, but thank you for the learning assignment."

    B. "Yes, we should do sexual harassment prevention training for all supervisors within the company."

    C. "Yes, why didn't this assignment go to Bob?"

    D. "No," but you wonder the reason this assignment did not go to Bob.

Scenario 2 (Questions 30–33): You have been tasked to prepare a report that Pat, the VP of human resources, has requested for the senior leadership team. You will need to figure out what data is available, how to display it, and how to interpret what it means.

30. Which of the following would be the least helpful to include?

    A. Current organizational turnover rates

    B. Historical organizational turnover rates

    C. Your industry turnover rates

    D. National turnover rates

31. Looking at the data you have gathered on your organizational turnover rates, you determine it would be best to share the data by what feature?

    A. Department

    B. Title

    C. Length of service

    D. Whichever way shares greater insight

32. Looking at the data you have gathered on your organizational turnover rates, you determine it would be best to share the data using which of the following?

    A. A bar chart

    B. A matrix

    C. A Pareto chart

    D. A Six Sigma

33. Looking at the data you have gathered on your organizational turnover rates, you want to be sure to include which of the following when you share the data?

    A. All the detailed data you collected, so senior management may draw their own conclusions

    B. All the detailed data you collected, so senior management will appreciate all the hard work you have done

    C. Your insights about the various turnover rates and whether they are good or bad

    D. Your insights about the various turnover rates, whether they are good or bad, plus recommendations on how to improve the rates

Scenario 3 (Questions 34–37): You have been a director of human resources in California for 7 years now. Your firm has just completed an acquisition of a new operations group in Texas that has more employees working at it than your California operations, so overnight the firm has more than doubled in size. You just got your hands on the current Texas employee handbook and are comparing it to the one you recently updated in California. While the California handbook has a policy that bans firearms from all work locations, the Texas handbook is silent on the issue. Another difference is that California's handbook states a zero-tolerance policy for any violence, and again the Texas handbook is silent on the issue.

As you FaceTime with the local human resources manager, Catherine, prior to your planned trip to Texas next week, she tells you about an operations technician, Gene, who was terminated last week for making threats toward a co-worker, as they were both interested in the same woman, who is the company's receptionist.

34. You have so many questions about this. What follow-up question do you want to ask Catherine first?

    A. What is the name of the receptionist?

    B. What security measures are in place at the Texas plant and are they adequate?

    C. What is the name of the co-worker who had threats made against him?

    D. Do you have good operations technician applicants available?

35. What is one of the first steps you are going to take regarding the differences in policies?

    A. Make all the handbooks the same, following the Texas lead, since it has more employees who are familiar with those policies.

    B. Make all the handbooks the same, following the lead of California, since that is the company that did the acquiring.

    C. Make all the handbooks the same, following the lead of California, since California is famous for having more complicated employment laws for compliance.

    D. Engage Catherine in conversation about the areas of silence for better understanding.

36. You realize your options for the policies are to keep your policies separate, adopt one of the two for all, integrate the two, or start fresh. What will influence you most in your choice of approach?

    A. The approach you can implement the fastest to get through the change quickly

    B. The values of the combined company going forward

    C. The mission, vision, and values of the combined company going forward

    D. The mission and vision of the combined company going forward

37. What is your best approach to convince the new leadership team of your proposed newly integrated policies related to firearms and workplace violence?

    A. Talk in individual sessions with each leader to explain the risks to the corporation and employees, away from the peer pressure of the group.

    B. Discuss the topic at a meeting of the leadership team, outlining the general risk and what some mitigating measures are.

    C. Share examples and facts from the news and about growing workplace violence and its financial risk with the leadership team and then offer your prepared solutions for your firm.

    D. Share examples and facts from the news and about growing workplace violence and its financial risk with all the stakeholders of the firm.

Scenario 4 (Questions 38–42): Nadine, the director of marketing, is having a serious performance problem with a key marketing analyst, Andrew. Andrew has been with the firm for 3 years and is a 41-year-old minority. Andrew's initial 6-month review was satisfactory. After that, the appraisals have continued to be satisfactory, but marginally so.

You talked Nadine out of firing Andrew for employment at will and got her to agree to put Andrew on a performance improvement plan (PIP). You convinced Nadine that for the PIP to work, she would need to make expectations for work quantity and quality clear to Andrew and to meet with him weekly to provide regular feedback.

38. It is now 30 days later, and Nadine wants to meet with you concerning Andrew. What will you want to know from Nadine?

    A. How is Andrew's performance in terms of quality?

    B. How often did Nadine meet and give feedback?

    C. How is Andrew's performance in terms of quantity?

    D. How often did they meet, and how is Andrew's overall performance?

39. Thirty-two days after Andrew's PIP began, you meet with Nadine. She reports that Andrew's quality is about the same as before and his quantity of analytical reports has gone up slightly. She met with him initially to put him on the PIP and then just met with him a second time 3 days ago. Nadine wants to fire Andrew. What is your counsel to Nadine?

    A. Agree completely and offer to prepare the final check, plus remind Nadine it is best practice to have another manager present when she terminates Andrew.

    B. Agree completely and offer to prepare the final check and be in the room with Nadine when she terminates Andrew.

    C. Disagree, saying termination now is premature since there has been some improvement and there has been imperfect feedback.

    D. Disagree, saying termination now is premature since there is not time to get a special termination check this week.

40. In that meeting 32 days after the start of Andrew's PIP, you gently ask Nadine to help you understand the reason she did not engage in more feedback meetings with Andrew. She tells you work has been overwhelming, especially with marginal performers on her staff, and that she had to go out of state for 2 weeks to arrange for hospice for her father. What is your response?

    A. Condolences for her father's condition and a gentle reminder of her managerial duties.

    B. Condolences for her father's condition and your advice on how best to proceed with Andrew.

    C. Condolences for her father's condition, your advice on how best to proceed with Andrew, and a reminder of your employee assistance program.

    D. Knowing you are to stay professional and do not want an awkward moment, you give her a gentle reminder of her managerial duties.

41. If Nadine wants to go forward with the termination, what advice do you want to give to her?

    A. Advise Nadine that since all the performance appraisals are satisfactory and improvement was made during the 30-day PIP, you think the paper trail is insufficient to warrant going forward with the termination at this time.

    B. Advise Nadine that since all the performance appraisals are satisfactory and improvement was made during the 30-day PIP, suggest finding an alternate job in another department for Andrew.

    C. Advise Nadine that since all the performance appraisals are satisfactory and improvement was made during the 30-day PIP, she should set up a meeting with your legal counsel for suggested actions.

    D. Advise Nadine that since all the performance appraisals are satisfactory and improvement was made during the 30-day PIP, and because she is going through a lot right now, you will handle the termination for her to provide excellent internal customer service to her.

42. What further advice do you want to give to Nadine, knowing Andrew is in at least two protected groups?

    A. Do not terminate too hastily since Andrew has the right to file a complaint with EEOC, alleging his termination was biased based on his protected-class status.

    B. Do not get too stressed over Andrew's termination since you have personal issues going on and Andrew is an at-will employee.

    C. Do not terminate too hastily since the director could instead ask Andrew if he would like to resign.

    D. Do not get too stressed over Andrew's termination since your human resource group has prescreened a number of qualified marketing analyst applicants.

Scenario 5 (Questions 43–46): You are an HR manager in a state that will have decriminalized marijuana starting in 3 months. You are getting comments from supervisors concerned that they will lose productivity and will have a break room that smells of "wacky tobacky." They dread the change coming.

43. What is one of the first steps you are going to take in response to this situation?

    A. Gather data from SHRM chapters in states where marijuana has already been decriminalized to learn what they did.

    B. Research the exact wording of the law in your state.

    C. Confirm the law has not changed at the federal level.

    D. Conduct an employee survey to ask how many employees plan to partake.

44. You are revising your internal policies to include your corporate response to marijuana. Part of that process will include which of the following?

   A. Presenting all the options for a response to your leadership team so they may decide.

   B. Presenting all the options for a response to your vice president of HR so she may decide.

   C. Running the draft of your new policies past some respected colleagues in other departments for additional viewpoints outside of HR, making it clear what they are reading is still a draft.

   D. Post the draft of your new policies in the break room and set up a suggestion box next to it for comments.

45. What is a key message you want everyone to understand in your new policies?

   A. All employees should be reminded that in 3 months the company parties are going to get a lot more fun.

   B. All employees should be reminded they must be mentally and physically able to execute their responsibilities safely.

   C. All employees should be reminded of the sick time policy.

   D. All employees must be reminded of the attendance policy.

46. The manager with the greatest concerns approaches you with an article in hand stating that marijuana is still a controlled substance under federal law. In response, you do what?

   A. Say thanks for the article, but you already knew that.

   B. Give thanks for the article and realize since marijuana is illegal at the federal level, there is no need to change your policies.

   C. Assure the manager that the federal law is changing any day now.

   D. Say thanks for the article and assure the manager you know the federal and state laws and because of that your new policies will state there will be no ADA or ADAAA accommodation for medical use of marijuana.

Answers

1. **B**. Cathy should exclude her husband Connor's company from participating in the vendor selection process simply because of the appearance of a conflict of interest.

2. **D**. Bribery is possible, and it is one of the specific problems a code of ethics will address and caution against. At the very least, before approving the transaction, Darlene should investigate the true nature of the payment demand from the foreign government or its representative.

3. **D**. Withstanding political pressure from above and fighting for consistent treatment of management employees who have been accused of similar misbehavior is the ethical approach to the solution. The company will just have to take its lumps until another key contact can be appointed and learns the job. The loss of new revenue in the process may not be considered.

4. **A**. A review of company policy related to falsifying timecards or any other records should be undertaken. Then a review of similar cases of friends clocking out for another employee should be made. Once all the background information has been gathered, you can proceed with any appropriate discipline. Ensuring that treatment is the same for Jose as it has been for others in similar circumstances will help avoid ethical conflicts or favoritism claims. Communications reminding the work group of your timecard policies, specifically never handling another's timecard, is also in order.

5. **C**. Requesting feedback from others is a good way to see things through the eyes of other people. Sometimes it is difficult to determine the impact we are having on those we interact with on the job. Asking for feedback is the solution. Achmed can be specific about the type of feedback he wants or can just ask for general observations. Achmed can also increase his personal awareness of his bias trying to break through when he interacts with women.

6. **C**. Part of a senior HR professional's duties is to keep current on all new HR requirements that may come to influence the workplace. Juanita should accept the responsibility and do her homework. It is a requirement of certification. If Juanita abandons her role in maintaining current knowledge about HR requirements, she can have no assurance that her organization will be in compliance should that become necessary. It is not just the legal staff that is responsible for tracking such things but also the professional HR staff.

7. **D**. Veterans and disabled workers have been overlooked populations for many years. Including them in recruiting and employment programs is a way to strengthen diversity, equity, and inclusion programs.

8. **C**. Diversity, equity, and inclusion programs attempt to gain value from the contributions of all employees.

9. **A**. If there is a disconnect between policies versus values and strategies, the organization will find it difficult, if not impossible, to demonstrate its values and implement the stated strategies. Having consistent HR policies should be one of the strategies itemized by the organization.

10. **C**. Federal contractors must meet certain outreach and recruiting requirements. The CEO's request would present an ethical problem for you. Do you abide by the company's policies and meet federal requirements, or do you abandon all that and do what the boss wants? Explaining the situation to the CEO is the best option. Then he can make an informed decision.

11. **C**. Credibility, both personal and departmental, will rest on the quality of work Stacie produces in this and all future assignments.

12. **A**. Negotiating the merger of employment policies is critical to the successful merger of different workforce groups.

13. **D**. The entire spectrum of possibilities must be considered. Input from experience, data, and facts, combined with reasoned judgment, will best support cultural strength.

14. **C**. "Walk a mile in another's shoes" is a motto for better leadership. Finding out how it feels to perform jobs done by subordinates will bring more understanding than a stack of memos.

15. **A**. Retail is different from restaurants. Consumer products are different from business services. Knowing the specifics for your industry is important because it has needs unique to the work being done. Knowing your own industry will make you a stronger partner.

16. **B**. There are ten elements in the process of preparing a business case. She needs to follow those steps to generate the best analysis for her CEO.

17. **A**. Be mindful that measurements create a focus and raise that which is being measured to a priority. If everything becomes a priority, then nothing is a priority distinguishing it from everything else.

18. **A**. A return on investment analysis will provide the financial information necessary to clarify the best benefit program out of the options available.

19. **B**. Latisha must be able to answer all the basic questions that might arise in the training sessions. She also must be willing to take unanswered questions and research them so she can provide answers to the people interested in the answers.

20. **C**. Craig must prepare a list of data elements that will be important for comparisons and reporting. He then should select the analytical tool that can best perform those comparisons.

21. **A**. As a new HR professional, Sue must interpret the information she has about the problem situation and design recommendations to those in upper management.

22. **C**. Even if there is a legal expert available for advice to the HR staff, Reed must be able to understand the new laws and how they will impact HR programs and policies.

23. **B**. Priorities must constantly be reassessed and issues handled in the order that new priorities dictate.

24. **C**. While not the only areas to be considered, the significant areas every problem analysis should include are productivity, engagement, recruiting, retention, and budget.

25. **D**. Reducing data overload can be done quickly by narrowing the scope of the problem statement. It is going to be easier to handle data analysis for the cost of a new "paid time off" policy rather than trying to deal with the cost of all benefits.

26. **C**. It is never a good idea to terminate an employee based on allegations. It certainly is not a best practice. An investigation to get to the truth is required.

27. D. You want to be inclusive to gather as many facts as possible. That includes the employees. It also includes their supervisors to get a sense of motivation to make a false allegation, plus the accused. If anyone in their statements mentions a witness, then your investigation should expand to include any witnesses as well.

28. A. Once an investigation is undertaken, you are required to make a decision based on the preponderance of the evidence, meaning which viewpoint has more than 50 percent of the credible evidence on its side.

29. B. This is the right response to increase the odds of all supervisors understanding what harassment is and the steps to prevent it going forward.

30. D. It is the least useful measurement of the four.

31. D. You may need to experiment with all three variables to detect patterns and gain the insight as to what is going on in your organization.

32. A. A bar chart showing differences by department, title, or length of service will best tell your story.

33. D. Part of the value you are bringing to senior management from human resources is your interpretation of the data. That is a strong contribution, and it's even stronger when coupled with suggestions on what steps to take next.

34. B. Your first concern under duty of care is to make sure your new employees at the Texas facility are secure.

35. D. While both states are within the United States, there could be some significant cultural differences regarding firearms. It is best to understand a situation before making changes. There may be local gun use laws that you do not know about to take into consideration as well.

36. C. This answer is the most complete.

37. A. Sharing facts is good, but on a topic that could be sensitive, creating a safe space and being available to hear various viewpoints individually is key. Individual meetings prior to a group meeting facilitate greater sharing.

38. D. Yes, you want to know how Andrew is performing across all his defined measurements *and* you want to know that he was getting the regular feedback that was part of the commitment to help him improve.

39. C. The PIP commitment was for weekly feedback, and that did not happen. Despite a lack of weekly feedback, Andrew's performance is slightly better. We do not know how much better it could have been if management had kept its commitment during the PIP.

40. C. The director of marketing has just shared something very personal, so your best response is to acknowledge it with your condolences, remind Nadine of a resource available (EAP), and share your expertise on the matter at hand.

41. A. It is completely acceptable to extend the PIP 30 or even 60 days to give Andrew a fair shot at getting better with the regular feedback he was told he would get.

42. **A.** Since your current documentation does not justify a termination now, Andrew might indeed file a complaint with this outside federal agency.

43. **A.** It is a best practice to have a policy making it clear you will not tolerate someone being under the influence in your work environment. Learning how other HR professionals have already dealt with this issue is a smart step to take.

44. **C.** You need to take the lead, but getting additional input from a variety of perspectives can only make your final policy better.

45. **B.** Whether it is over-the-counter cough syrup, prescription drugs, alcohol, or marijuana, as the HR Manager you represent the employer and have a fiduciary responsibility to ensure that employees on your property are safe to execute their responsibilities.

46. **D.** This is a manager who needs assurance and additional facts. You will put this manager more at ease giving additional information, such as information on the ADA.

References

1. 2022 SHRM Body of Applied Skills and Knowledge (BASK), page 9

2. 2022 SHRM Body of Applied Skills and Knowledge (BASK), pages 12–16

3. Ibid.

4. Zenger, Jack and Joseph Folkman. *The Extraordinary Leader: Turning Good Managers into Great Leaders*, McGraw-Hill Education, May 2009

5. https://www2.deloitte.com/insights/us/en/focus/human-capital-trends.html

6. 2022 SHRM Body of Applied Skills and Knowledge (BASK), pages 17–20

7. Ibid.

8. Kerns, Charles D., Ph.D. *Graziadio Business Review*, Pepperdine University, Volume 6, Issue 3, 2003

9. Allen, Louise. "Developing HR Strategy," *Personnel Today*, November 19, 2002, retrieved on September 15, 2017

10. Code of Ethics, Society for Human Resource Management, https://www.shrm.org/about-shrm/Pages/code-of-ethics.aspx, retrieved on November 10, 2022

11. 2022 SHRM Body of Applied Skills and Knowledge (BASK), pages 21–23

12. 2022 SHRM Body of Applied Skills and Knowledge (BASK), page 22

13. Stanford SOCIAL INNOVATION Review, "What the Heck Does 'Equity' Mean?", https://ssir.org/articles/entry/what_the_heck_does_equity_mean

14. SHRM Learning System 2020, Workplace, page 68

15. "The Costs and Benefits of Diversity: A Study on Methods and Indicators to Measure the Cost-Effectiveness of Diversity Policies in Enterprises," European Commission, Directorate-General for Employment, Industrial Relations and Social Affairs Unit D/3, October 2003

16. www.colormagazineusa.com

17. https://www.conference-board.org/pdf_free/councils/TCBCP005.pdf

18. "Global Diversity and Inclusion: Perceptions, Practices and Attitudes," Society for Human Resources Management, 2009, http://graphics.eiu.com/upload/eb/ DiversityandInclusion.pdf

19. Dobbin, Frank and Alexandrea Kalev. "Why Diversity Programs Fail," *Harvard Business Review,* July/August 2016

20. 2022 SHRM Body of Applied Skills Knowledge (BASK), pages, 26–31

21. Ibid.

22. Nelson, Sheri. The Local Shop, https://welcometotheshop.com

23. Solomon, Micah. "7 Secrets of Building a Customer-Centric Company Culture," *Forbes,* https://www.forbes.com/sites/micahsolomon/2014/07/20/customer-centric-culture/#2ccd76db7582

24. SHRM Managing Workplace Conflict Toolkit, https://www.shrm.org/ resourcesandtools/tools-and-samples/toolkits/pages/managingworkplaceconflict.aspx

25. 2022 SHRM Body of Applied Skills and Knowledge (BASK), pages 32–35

26. Ibid.

27. Kouzes, Jim and Barry Posner. *The Leadership Challenge, Fifth Edition,* Wiley Publishing, 2012

28. 2022 SHRM Body of Applied Skills and Knowledge (BASK), pages 36

29. Ibid.

30. Ibid.

31. "(Hello) and Welcome to our Guide to Saudi Arabian Culture, Customs, Business Practices & Etiquette," https://www.commisceo-global.com/resources/country-guides/saudi-arabia-guide

32. Stallard, Mike. "Leading with Character: Humility," Connection Culture Group, http://connectionculture.com/post/leading-with-character-humility

33. Why You Need Cultural Intelligence (And How to Develop It)," *Forbes,* https:// www.forbes.com/sites/iese/2015/03/24/why-you-need-cultural-intelligence-and-how-to-develop-it/?sh=4da15f1f17d6

34. McDonnell, Steve. "Foreign vs. U.S. Labor Laws," *Chron,* http://smallbusiness .chron.com/foreign-vs-us-labor-laws-77421.html

35. Ibid.

36. Ibid.

37. Fisher, Glen. *Mindsets: The Role of Culture and Perception in International Relations,* John Wiley, 1988

38. Rhinesmith, Stephen H. "Global Mindsets for Global Managers," https://go.gale
    .com/ps/i.do?id=GALE%7CA13528770&v=2.1&it=r&linkaccess=abs&issn=105
    59760&p=AONE&sw =w&userGroupName=anon~cf8d96ca

39. Emerson, Ralph Waldo. "Essays: Man the Reformer, A Lecture Read before the
    Mechanics Apprentices' Library Association, Boston, January 25, 1841," https://
    www.bartleby.com/5/103.html

40. Warrell, Margie. "How to Build High Trust Relationships," *Forbes,* https://
    www.forbes.com/sites/margiewarrell/2015/08/31/how-to-build-high-trust-
    relationships/#54ac927415cf

41. Kramer, Roderick M. "Rethinking Trust," *Harvard Business Review,* June 2009

42. Farnsworth, Derek et al. "Diversity in the Workplace: Benefits, Challenges, and
    the Required Managerial Tools," University of Florida, 2015

43. Willis, Jennifer. "Sustainable Development is Good for Business," June 6, 2017,
    https://cligs.vt.edu/blog/sustainable-development-is-good-for-business.html

44. Fogh-Andersen, Karen. "7 Pivotal HR Competencies for Global Business in
    2017," Stanton Chase, March 2017, https://www.stantonchase.com/wp-content/
    uploads/2017/03/SC_WP_7_HR_Competencies_A4-1.pdf

45. "2023 Deloitte Global Human Capital Trends: Rewriting the rules for the
    digital age," https://www2.deloitte.com/us/en/pages/human-capital/articles/
    introduction-human-capital-trends.html

46. Hunt, Vivian, Dennis Layton, and Sara Prince. "Why Diversity Matters,"
    McKinsey & Company, January 2015, https://www.mckinsey.com/business-
    functions/organization/our-insights/why-diversity-matters

47. "Understanding Intercultural Competence," SHRM, October 13, 2022, https://
    www.shrm.org/resourcesandtools/tools-and-samples/toolkits/Pages/default.aspx

48. Mayers, Juliette. "Seven Tips for Building Cross-Cultural Relationships,"
    April 22, 2012, https://inspirationzonellc.com/seven-tips-for-building-cross-
    cultural-relationships/

49. 2022 SHRM Body of Applied Skills and Knowledge (BASK), page 40

50. 2022 SHRM Body of Applied Skills and Knowledge (BASK), pages 41

51. Sanders, Nada. *The Definitive Guide to Manufacturing and Service Operations:
    Master the Strategies and Planning, Organizing, and Managing How Products and
    Services Are Produced,* Pearson Education, 2014

52. Mayberry, Ed. "How to Build an HR Business Case," SHRM, October 28, 2008

53. "Aligning Workforce Strategies with Business Objectives," SHRM, September 14,
    2015, https://www.shrmpr.org/aligning-workforce-strategies-with-business-
    objectives/

54. Beard, Ross. "Competitive Benchmarking 101," https://www.youtube.com/
    watch?v=UoN5jA7nJ74

55. Kaplan, Robert S. and David P. Norton, The Balanced Scorecard: Translating Strategy into Action, Harvard Business Review Press, 1996.

56. 2022 SHRM Body of Applied Skills and Knowledge (BASK), page 41.

57. Ibid.

58. Alter, Michael. Accounting Web, https://www.accountingweb.com/practice/clients/top-ten-ways-to-take-a-consultative-approach-to-client-meetings.

59. Bacharach, Yael. Five Essential Skills for Successful Coaching, Inc., https://www.inc.com/yael-bacharach/five-essential-skills-for-successful-coaching.html.

60. Atkinds, Richard. How to Maximize Human Capital ROI, HR. Magazine, http://hrprofessionalsmagazine.com/how to maximize human capital roi/.

61. https://www.marketwatch.com

62. Andrew, Walter J., and Michael S. Levine. SHRM, Top 10 Employment Liability Concerns, https://www.shrm.org/hr-today/news/hr-magazine/pages/07815-employment-liability.aspx

63. 2022 SHRM Body of Applied Skills and Knowledge (BASK), page 51.

64. Ibid.

65. Herbold, Bob. "Challenge Assumptions. Don't Be Afraid of Taking a Different Tack," Entrepreneur, April 6, 2014, https//www.entrepreneur.com/article/232767,downloaded on November 6, 2017.

66. Markgraf, Bert. "Critical Analysis of Strategic Management, "http://smallbusiness.chron.com/critical-analysis-strategic-management-65195.html, accessed on November 6, 2017.

PART III

Appendixes

List of Common HR Acronyms

AA	1) Affirmative Action; 2) Adverse Action
AACU	American Association of Colleges and Universities
AAO	Affirmative Action Officer
AAP	Affirmative Action Plan
AAR	Average Annual Return
ABF	Asset-Based Financing
ABM	Activity-Based Management
ABMS	Activity-Based Management System
ACA	Affordable Care Act
ACH	Automated Clearing House
AD&D	Accidental Death and Dismemberment
ADA	Americans with Disabilities Act
ADAAA	Americans with Disabilities Act Amendments Act
ADEA	Age Discrimination in Employment Act
ADL	Activities of Daily Living
ADP	Automatic Data Processing
ADR	Alternative Dispute Resolution
AFL-CIO	American Federation of Labor and Congress of Industrial Organizations
AFSCME	American Federation of State, County, and Municipal Employers
AI	Appreciative Inquiry
AIDS	Acquired Immunodeficiency Syndrome
AJB	America's Job Bank
ALC	Alien Labor Certification
ALEX	Automated Labor Exchange
ALN	Asynchronous Learning Network
ALJ	Administrative Law Judge
ALM	Asset Liability Management

AMPS	Auction Market Preferred Stock
ANSI	American National Standards Institute
AP	Accounts Payable
APA	American Psychological Association
APB	Accounting Principles Board
aPHR	Associate Professional in Human Resources
APR	Annual Percentage Rate
APV	Adjusted Present Value
APY	Annual Percentage Yield
AR	Accounts Receivable
ARRA	American Recovery and Reinvestment Act
ASB	Accounting Standards Board
ASHHRA	American Society for Healthcare Human Resources Administration
ASO	Administrative Services Only Plan
ASTD	American Society for Training and Development
ATB	Across the Board
ATO	1) Administrative Time Off; 2) Asset Turnover
ATOI	After Tax Operating Income
ATS	Applicant Tracking System
ATU	Annual Tax Unit
AWL	Actual Wage Loss
AWOL	Absent Without Leave
AWW	Average Weekly Wage
BARS	Behaviorally Anchored Rating Scale
BAT	Bureau of Apprenticeship and Training
BB	Base Benefits
BCP	Business Continuity Plan
BCR	Benefit/Cost Ratio
BIA	Business Impact Analysis
BFOQ	Bona Fide Occupational Qualification
BLBA	Black Lung Benefits Act
BLS	Bureau of Labor Statistics
BNA	Bureau of National Affairs
BOD	Board of Directors
BOT	Board of Trustees
BPA	Blanket Purchase Agreement
BRB	Benefit Review Board
BU	Bargaining Unit
C&B	Compensation and Benefits
C&P	Compensation and Pension
CAA	Congressional Accountability Act

CAFTA	Central American Free Trade Agreement
CAI	Computer Assisted Instruction
CAO	Chief Administrative Officer
CAPEX	Capital Expenditures
CASB	Cost Accounting Standards Board
CBA	Controlled Business Arrangement
CBO	Congressional Budget Office
CBP	Cafeteria Benefit Plan
CBT	Computer-Based Testing
CC	Civil Code
CCH	Commerce Clearing House
CCHR	Canadian Council on Human Resources
CCI	Consumer Confidence Index
CCL	Center for Creative Leadership
CCP	Certified Compensation Professional
CCPA	Consumer Credit Protection Act
CDC	Center for Disease Control
CDL	Commercial Driver's License
CEA	1) Commodity Exchange Authority; 2) Certificate of Educational Achievement
CEBS	Certified Employee Benefits Specialist
CEO	Chief Executive Officer
CEPS	Cash Earnings Per Share
CEU	Continuing Education Unit
CFAT	Cash Flow After Taxes
CFO	Chief Financial/Fiscal Officer
CFR	Code of Federal Regulations
CGQ	Corporate Governance Quotient
CGT	Capital Gains Tax
CHRC	1) Canadian Human Rights Commission; 2) Criminal History Records Check
CHRO	Chief Human Resources Officer
CIO	1) Chief Investment Officer; 2) Chief Information Officer
CISO	Chief Information Security Officer
CMO	Chief Marketing Officer
CO	Compliance Officer
COB	Close of Business
COBRA	Consolidated Omnibus Budget Reconciliation Act
COL	Cost of Living
COLA	Cost of Living Adjustment

COO	Chief Operating/Operations Officer
CPA	Certified Public Accountant
CPE	Continuing Professional Education
CPG	Consumer Packaged Goods
CPHR	Chartered Professional in Human Resources
CPI	Consumer Price Index
CPI-U	Consumer Price Index for All Urban Consumers
CPI-W	Consumer Price Index for Urban Wage Earners and Clerical Workers
CPM	Critical Path Method
CR	Corporate Responsibility
CRM	1) Client Relationship Management; 2) Customer Relationship Management; 3) Credit Risk Management
CROGI	Cash Return on Gross Investment
CSHO	Compliance Safety and Health Officer
CSO	Chief Security Officer
CTO	Compensatory Time Off
CTS	Carpal Tunnel Syndrome
CUPA	College and University Personnel Association
CUSFTA	Canada-U.S. Free Trade Agreement
CV	Curriculum Vitae
CWHSSA	Contract Work Hours and Safety Standards Act
CWSP	College Work-Study Program
D&I	Diversity and Inclusion
D&O	Directors and Officers
DB	Defined Benefit
DBA	1) Davis-Bacon Act; 2) Doing Business As
DBPP	Defined Benefit Pension Plan
DC	Defined Contribution
DCA	Dollar Cost Averaging
DCAA	Defense Contract Audit Agency
DCF	Discounted Cash Flow
DCPP	Defined Contribution Pension Plan
DCAP	Dependent Care Assistance Program
DEFRA	Deficit Reduction Act
DFA	Department of Finance and Administration
DFEH	Department of Fair Employment and Housing
DINKS	Dual Income No Kids
DJIA	Dow Jones Industrial Average
DMADV	Define, Measure, Analyze, Design, Verify
DMAIC	Define, Measure, Analyze, Improve, Control

DRIP	Dividend Reinvestment Plan
DRP	Disaster Recovery Plan
DSI	Discretionary Salary Increase
DSPP	Direct Stock Purchase Plan
DOB	Date of Birth
DOC	United States Department of Commerce
DOD	United States Department of Defense
DOH	Date of Hire
DOI	Date of Injury
DOJ	United States Department of Justice
DOL	United States Department of Labor
DOLETA	Department of Labor Employment and Training Administration
DOT	1) Dictionary of Occupational Titles; 2) United States Department of Transportation
DTI	Department of Trade and Industry
DVOP	Disabled Veterans Outreach Program
DW	Dislocated Worker
DWC	Division of Workers' Compensation
E-VERIFY	United States Department of Labor New Hire Screening System
EAC	Employee Advisory Committee/Council
EAP	Employee Assistance Program
EAPA	Employee Assistance Professionals Association
EB	Extended Benefits
EBITDA	Earnings Before Interest, Taxes, Depreciation, and Amortization
EBO	Employee Buyout
EBRI	Employee Benefits Research Institute
EBS	Employee Benefits Security
EBSA	Employee Benefit Security Administration
EBT	Earnings Before Tax
ECI	Employment Cost Index
ECOA	Equal Credit Opportunity Act
ECPA	Electronic Communications Privacy Act
EDA	Economically Depressed Area
EDI	Electronic Data Interchange
EDP	1) Electronic Data Processing; 2) Employee Development Plan
EE	Employee
EEO	Equal Employment Opportunity
EEO-1/EEO-4	EEO-1 or EEO-4 Report/Standard Form 100 Report
EEOC	Equal Employment Opportunity Commission
EEOICPA	Energy Employee Occupational Illness Compensation Program Act

PART III

EFT	Electronic Funds Transfer
EFTA	European Free Trade Area
EGTRRA	Economic Growth and Tax Relief Reconciliation Act
EI or EQ	Emotional Intelligence
EIC	Earned Income Tax Credit
EIN	Employer Identification Number
EMT	Executive Management Team
EO	Executive Order
EOB	Explanation of Benefits
EOD	End of Day
EOI	Evidence of Insurability
EOY	End of Year
EPA	1) Equal Pay Act; 2) Environmental Protection Agency
EPLI	Employment Practices Liability Insurance
EPPA	Employee Polygraph Protection Act
EPS	Earnings per Share
ER	Employer
ERISA	Employee Retirement Income Security Act
ERTA	Economic Recovery Tax Act
ESA	Employment Standards Administration
ESL	English as a Second Language
ESO	Employee Stock Option
ESOP	Employee Stock Option Plan
ESOT	Employee Stock Ownership and Trust
ESP	Exchange Stock Portfolio
ESS	Employee Self-Service
ETA	1) Employment and Training Administration; 2) Estimated Time of Arrival
EU	European Union
EV	Enterprise Value
EVA	Economic Value Added
EVM	Earned Value Management
EX	Exempt
FAAS	Financial Assurance and Accountability Standards
FACT	Fair and Accurate Credit Transactions Act
FAQ	Frequently Asked Questions
FAS	Financial Accounting Standards
FASAB	Financial Accounting Standards Advisory Board
FASAC	Financial Accounting Standards Advisory Committee
FASB	Financial Accounting Standards Board

FCC	Federal Communications Commission
FCCPA	Federal Consumer Credit Protection Act
FCPA	Foreign Corrupt Practices Act
FCRA	Fair Credit Reporting Act
FDA	Food and Drug Administration
FDCPA	Fair Debt Collection Practices Act
FDIC	Federal Deposit Insurance Corporation
FEA	Fair Employment Act
FECA	Federal Employees' Compensation Act
FEIN	Federal Employment Identification Number
FELA	Federal Employment Liability Act
FEMA	Federal Emergency Management Agency
FEP	Fair Employment Practice
FERS	Federal Employees Retirement System
FES	Factor Evaluation System
FFY	Federal Fiscal Year
FHA	Federal Housing Administration
FICA	Federal Insurance Contributions Act
FICO	Fair Isaac Credit Organization
FIE	Foreign Invested Enterprise
FIFO	First In, First Out
FKI	Foundational Knowledge Items
FLRA	Federal Labor Relations Authority
FLSA	Fair Labor Standards Act
FMLA	Family and Medical Leave Act
FMSHA	Federal Mine and Safety Health Act
FMV	Fair Market Value
FOIA	Freedom of Information Act
FOM	Field Operations Manual
FOREX	Foreign Exchange
FR	Federal Register
FRA	Federal Reserve Act
FRB	Federal Reserve Board
FROI	First Report of Injury
FRS	Financial Reporting Standards
FSA	Flexible Spending Account
FSB	Fortune Small Business
FSET	Federal State Employment Tax
FSLMRA	Federal Service Labor-Management Relations Act
FT	Full-Time
FTA	Free Trade Agreement

PART III

FTC	Federal Trade Commission
FTD	Federal Tax Deposit
FTE	Full-Time Equivalent
FTP	File Transfer Protocol
FUA	Federal Unemployment Account
FUTA	Federal Unemployment Tax ACT
FY	Fiscal Year
GAAC	Government Accounting and Auditing Committee
GAAFR	Governmental Accounting, Auditing, and Financial Reporting
GAAP	Generally Accepted Accounting Principles
GAAS	Generally Accepted Auditing Standards
GAGAS	Generally Accepted Government Accounting Standards
GAO	General Accounting Office
GAS	Governmental Accounting Standards
GASB	Governmental Accounting Standards Board
GATB	General Aptitude Test Battery
GATT	General Agreement on Tariffs and Trade
GDP	Gross Domestic Product
GED	General Equivalency Diploma
GIC	Guaranteed Investment Contract
GICS	Global Industry Classification Standards
GIF	Guaranteed Investment Fund
GINA	Genetic Information Nondiscrimination Act
GIPS	Global Investment Policy Standard
GIS	Geographic Information System
GL	1) General Ledger; 2) General Liability
GLB	Gramm-Leach-Bliley Act
GLSO	Group Legal Services Organization
GM	Gross Margin
GNP	Gross National Product
GPHR	Global Professional in Human Resources Certification
GPROI	Gross Profit Return on Investment
GPS	Global Positioning System
GR	General Revenue
GS	General Schedule
GSI	General Salary Increase
GTL	Group Term Life Insurance
HAS	Highest Average Salary
HAZMAT	Hazardous Material
HB	House Bill
HC	Human Capital

HCE	Highly Compensated Employee
HCFA	Health Care Financing Administration
HCM	Human Capital Management
HCN	Home-Country Nationals
HCO	Health Care Organization
HCSA	Health Care Spending Account
HCTC	Health Coverage Tax Credit
HHS	Department of Health and Human Services
HICP	Harmonized Index of Consumer Pricing
HIPAA	Health Insurance Portability and Accountability Act
HIPC	Health Insurance Purchasing Cooperatives
HITECH	Health Information Technology for Economic and Clinical Health Act
HIV	Human Immunodeficiency Virus
HMO	Health Maintenance Organization
HR	Human Resources
HRA	Health Reimbursement Account
HRCI	Human Resource Certification Institute
HRCS	Human Resource Competency Study
HRD	1) Human Resources Development; 2) Human Resources Department
HRIS	Human Resources Information System
HRLY	Hourly
HRM	Human Resources Management
HRMS	Human Resource Management System
HROD	Human Resources and Organizational Development
HSA	Health Savings Account
HTML	Hypertext Markup Language
HUD	United States Department of Housing and Urban Development
I-9	United States Immigration Form I-9
IAG	International Auditing Guidelines
IAS	International Accounting Standards
IASC	International Accounting Standards Committee
ICC	International Chamber of Commerce
ICE	United States Immigration and Customs Enforcement
IFEBP	International Foundation of Employee Benefit Plans
IHRIM	International Association of Human Resource Information Management
IIPP	Injury and Illness Prevention Plans/Programs
ILAB	International Labor Affairs Bureau
ILO	International Labor/Labour Organization
IME	Independent Medical Examination

PART III

INA	Immigration and Naturalization Act
INS	Immigration and Naturalization Service
IOS	International Organization for Standards
IPA	Inflation Protected Annuity
IPI	Industrial Protection Index
IPMA	International Personnel Management Association
IPO	Initial Public Offering
IPS	1) Inflation Protected Security; 2) Investment Policy Statement
IRA	Individual Retirement Account
IRB	Internal Revenue Bulletin
IRC	Internal Revenue Code
IRCA	Immigration Reform and Control Act
IRR	Internal Rate of Return
IRS	Internal Revenue Service
ISO	1) International Organization for Standardization; 2) Incentive Stock Option
ISP	Internet Service Provider
ISSA	International Securities Services Association
IT	Information Technology
ITA	United States International Trade Administration
ITIN	Individual Taxpayer Identification Number
IUR	Insured Unemployment Rates
IVR	Interactive Voice Response
J&S	Joint and Survivorship
JAN	Job Accommodation Network
JD	1) Job Description; 2) Juris Doctorate; 3) Job Date
JGTRRA	Jobs and Growth Tax Relief Reconciliation Act
JEEP	Joint Ethics Enforcement Plan
JIT	1) Just in Time; 2) Job Instruction Training
JOA	Joint Operating Agreement
JPAC	Joint Public Advisory Committee
JPEG	Joint Photographic Experts Group
JSSA	Jury Selection and Service Act
JTPA	Job Training Partnership Act (replaced by WIA)
JV	Joint Venture
JVA	Jobs for Veterans Act
KI	Knowledge Items
KM	Knowledge Management
KPI	Key Performance Indicator
KSA	Knowledge, Skills, and Abilities
KSOP	401(k) Employee Stock Option Plan
LA	Labor Area

LAN	Local Area Network
LAR	Legislative Appropriations Request
LAUS	Local Area Unemployment Statistics
LBB	Legislative Budget Board
LBO	Leveraged Buyout
LCA	Labor Condition Application
LCD	Labor Cost Distribution
LDI	Liability-Driven Investment
LDP	Last Day Paid
LDW	Last Day Worked
LEI	Leading Economic Indicators
LEO	Long-Term Equity Options
LEPO	Low Exercise Price Option
LF	Labor Force
LFPR	Labor Force Participation Rate
LFY	Last Fiscal Year
LGBTQIA+	Lesbian, Gay, Bisexual, Transgender, Queer or Questioning, Intersex, Asexual, and more
LHWCA	Longshore and Harbor Workers' Compensation Act
LIFO	Last In, First Out
LLC	Limited Liability Company
LLP	Limited Liability Partnership
LMA	Labor Market Area
LMI	Labor Market Information
LMRA	Labor Management Relations Act
LMRDA	Labor Management Reporting and Disclosure Act
LMS	Learning Management System
LO	Learning Objectives
LOA	Leave of Absence
LOC	Letter of Commitment
LOI	Letter of Intent
LOR	Letter of Response
LOS	Length of Stay
LOW	Lack of Work
LP	Limited Partnership
LR	Labor Relations
LRO	Labor Relations Officer
LT	Lost Time
LTC	Long-Term Care
LTCM	Long-Term Capital Management
LTD	Long-Term Disability

PART III

LTFP	Long-Term Financial Plan
LTIP	Long-Term Incentive Plan
LTO	Long-Term Option
LTV	Loan-to-Value Ratio
LWDI	Lost Work Day Incident
LWO	Leave Without Pay
LWP	Leave With Pay
M&A	Mergers and Acquisitions
MBO	Management by Objectives
MBTI	Myers-Briggs Type Indicator
MER	Management Expense Ratio
MEWA	Multiple Employer Welfare Arrangement
MHPA	Mental Health Parity Act
MHPAEA	Mental Health Parity and Addiction Equity Act
MIRR	Modified Internal Rate of Return
MIS	Management Information System
MLA	Minimum Liquid Assets
MLM	Multilevel Marketing
MLP	Master Limited Partnership
MLR	Monthly Labor Review
MLS	Mass Layoff Statistics
MNC	Multinational Corporation
MOC	Market on Close
MOF	Ministry of Finance
MOOCs	Massive Open Online Courses
MOU	Memorandum of Understanding
MPPAA	Multiemployer Pension Plan Amendments Act
MRD	Minimum Required Distribution
MSA	1) Medical Savings Account; 2) Metropolitan Statistical Area; 3) Merit Salary Adjustment
MSDS	Material Safety Data Sheet. Changed to SDS in 2012.
MSFW	Migrant and Seasonal Farm Worker
MSHA	Mine Safety and Health Act
MSP	Managed Service Provider
MSPA	Migrant and Seasonal Agriculture Worker Protection Act
MSPB	Merit Systems Protection Board
MSPR	Medicare Secondary Payer Rules
MST	Marketable Securities Tax
MTD	Month to Date
MTHLY	Monthly

NAAEC	North American Agreement on Environmental Cooperation
NAALC	North American Agreement on Labor Cooperation
NAB	Nonaccrual Basis
NAFTA	North American Free Trade Agreement. Replaced by the USMCA in 2020.
NAFTA-TAA	NAFTA Transitional Adjustment Assistance
NAICS	North American Industry Classification System
NASDAQ	National Association of Securities Dealers Automated Quotations
NASDR	National Association of Securities Dealers Regulation
NATO	North Atlantic Treaty Organization
NAV	Net Asset Value
NAVPS	Net Asset Value Per Share
NAWW	National Average Weekly Wage
NCCI	National Council on Compensation Insurance
NDNH	National Directory of New Hires
NEO	New and Emerging Occupations
NEX	Nonexempt
NFA	Net Financial Assets
NFE	Net Financial Expense
NFI	Net Financial Income
NFO	Net Financial Obligations
NHCE	Non-Highly Compensated Employee
NI	Net Income
NIH	National Institute of Health
NIOSH	National Institute of Occupational Safety and Health
NL	No Load
NLRA	National Labor Relations Act
NLRB	National Labor Relations Board
NMB	National Mediation Board
NMHPA	Newborns' and Mothers' Health Protection Act
NMS	Normal Market Size
NOA	Net Operating Assets
NOI	Net Operating Income
NOL	Net Operating Loss
NOPAT	Net Operating Profit After Taxes
NPV	Net Present Value
NRA	Nonresident Alien
NRET	Nonresident Withholding Tax
NSC	National Security Council
NSTA	National Securities Trade Association
NSX	National Stock Exchange

NT	Near Term
NVI	Negative Volume Index
NYSE	New York Stock Exchange
O*NET	Occupational Information Network
OA	Operating Assets
OAS	Option-Adjusted Spread
OASDHI	Old Age, Survivors, Disability, and Health Insurance
OASDI	Old Age and Survivors Disability Insurance
OASI	Old Age Survivors Insurance
OBRA	Omnibus Budget Reconciliation Act
OCF	Operating Cash Flow
OD	Organizational Development
ODDS	Online Data Delivery System
OE	Operating Expense
OEBS	Office of Employee Benefits Security (replaced by PWBP)
OER	Operation Expense Ratio
OES	Occupational Employment Statistic
OFCCP	Office of Federal Contract Compliance Programs
OHCA	Organized Health Care Arrangement
OI	Operating Income
OIS	Occupations Information System
OJT	On-the-Job Training
OL	Operating Liabilities
OM	Options Market
OMB	Office of Management and Budget
OOB	Out of Business
OOH	Occupational Outlook Handbook
OPM	Office of Personnel Management
OR	Operating Revenue
OSHA	1) Occupational Safety and Health Administration; 2) Occupational Safety and Health Act
OT	Overtime
OTC	Over the Counter
OTI	OSHA Training Institute
OTS	Office of Thrift Supervision
OWBPA	Older Workers Benefit Protection Act
P&L	Profit and Loss
PAR	Public Accounting Report
PBGC	Pension Benefit Guaranty Corporation
PBO	Projected Benefit Obligation
PBSI	Performance-Based Salary Increase

PBT	Profit Before Tax
PC	1) Personal Computer; 2) Politically Correct
PCAOB	Public Company Accounting Oversight Board
PCE	1) Preexisting Condition Exclusion; 2) Private Commercial Enterprise
PCI	Per Capita Income
PCN	Parent-Country Nationals
PD	Position Description
PDA	1) Pregnancy Discrimination Act; 2) Personal Data Assistant; 3) Public Displays of Affection; 4) Payday Advance Loan
PDF	Portable Document Format
PDQ	Position Description Questionnaire
PE	Price to Earnings Ratio
PEG	Price to Earnings Growth
PEO	Professional Employer Organization
PEPPRA	Public Employee Pension Plan Reporting and Accountability Act
PERT	Project Evaluation and Review Techniques
PESTLE	Political, Economic, Social, Technological, Legal, and Environmental
PFK	Pay for Knowledge
PHI	Protected Health Information
PHR	Professional in Human Resources Certification
PHRca	Professional in Human Resources California Certification
PIK	Payment in Kind
PIP	Performance Improvement Plan
PL	Public Law
PM	1) Profit Margin; 2) Performance Management
PMSA	Primary Metropolitan Statistical Area
PMV	Private Market Value
PNG	Portable Network Graphics
POA	Power of Attorney
POB	Public Oversights Board
POD	1) Payable on Death; 2) Professional and Organizational Development
POP	1) Premium-Only Plan; 2) Public Offering Price
POS	Point of Service Plan
PPA	Pension Protection Act of 1987
PPACA	Patient Protection and Affordable Care Act
PPE	Personal Protective Equipment
PPI	Producer Price Index
PPO	Preferred Provider Organization
PR	Public Relations
PRC	Peer Review Committee
PSI	Performance Salary Increase

PART III

PT	Part-Time
PTO	Paid Time Off
PTSD	Post-Traumatic Stress Disorder
PV	Present Value
PW	Present Worth
PWBA	Pension and Welfare Benefits Administration
PWBP	Pension and Welfare Benefit Program
PWC	Public Works Commission
PWD	Prevailing Wage Determination
PY	Program Year
QA	Quality Assurance
QAIP	Quality Assurance and Improvement Plan
QBU	Qualified Business Unit
QC	Quality Control
QCEW	Quarterly Census of Employment and Wages
QCR	Quarterly Contributions Report
QDRO	Qualified Domestic Relations Order
QMAC	Qualified Matching Contributions
QMCSO	Qualified Medical Child Support Order
QME	Qualified Medical Examiner
QNEC	Qualified Nonelective Contributions
QPAM	Qualified Professional Asset Manager
QR	1) Quarterly Report; 2) Quality Review
QREC	Quality Review Executive Committee
QTD	1) Qualified Total Distribution; 2) Quarter to Date
QWI	Quarterly Workforce Indicators
R&C	Reasonable and Customary
R&D	Research and Development
RA	Resident Alien
RAP	Regulatory Accounting Principles
RCR	Recruiting Cost Ratio
RE	Residual Earnings
REA	Retirement Equity Act
RFB	Request for Bid
RFI	Request for Information
RFID	Radio Frequency Identification
RFP	Request for Proposal
RFQ	Request for Quote
RIC	Regulated Investment Company
RICO	Racketeer Influenced and Corrupt Organizations Act
RIF	Reduction in Force

RIPA	Retirement Income Policy Act
RMP	Risk Management Plan
RNFA	Return on Net Financial Assets
ROA	Return on Assets
ROC	Return on Capital
ROI	Return on Investment
ROIC	Return on Invested Capital
ROM	Range of Motion
RONA	Return on Net Assets
ROOA	Return on Operating Assets
ROR	Return on Revenue
ROS	Return on Sales
ROTA	Return on Total Assets
ROTC	Reserve Officer Training Corps
RPI	Retail Price Index
RR	Retention Rate
RRSP	Registered Retirement Savings Plan
RSU	Restricted Stock Unit
RTO	Reverse Takeover
RTW	1) Return to Work; 2) Right to Work
RWA	Risk-Weighted Asset
RYR	Recruitment Yield Ratio
S&P	Standard and Poor's
SAAR	Seasonally Adjusted Annual Rate
SAR	1) Summary Annual Report; 2) Stock Appreciation Right; 3) Student Aid Report; 4) Search and Rescue; 5) Suspicious Activity Report; 6) Sales to Active Ratio
SARSEP	Salary Reduction Simplified Employee Pension
SAS	Statement of Accounting Standards
SAT	Scholastic Aptitude Test
SB	Senate Bill
SBA	Small Business Administration
SBAP	Small Business Assistance Program
SBBA	Sales and Buy-Back Agreement
SBD	Small Disadvantaged Business
SBJPA	Small Business Job Protection Act
SBLC	Standby Letter of Credit
SBO	Small Business Ombudsman
SC	Securities Commission
SCA	McNamara-O'Hara Service Contract Act
SCM	Supply Chain Management

SDI	State Disability Insurance
SDS	Safety Data Sheet
SE	1) Salaried Exempt; 2) Self-Employed
SEA	Securities Exchange Act
SEC	Securities and Exchange Commission
SEP	Simplified Employee Pension
SEPPAA	Single Employer Pension Plan Amendments Act
SERP	Supplemental Executive Retirement Plan
SESA	State Employment Security Agency
SFAS	Statements of Financial Accounting Standards
SHRM	Society for Human Resource Management
SHRM-CP	SHRM Certified Professional
SHRM-SCP	SHRM Senior Certified Professional
SIA	Securities Industry Act
SIB	Securities and Investment Board
SIC	Standard Industrial Classification
SIPA	Securities Investment Protection Act
SITC	Standard International Trade Classification
SJI	Situational Judgment Items
SLA	Service Level Agreement
SLOB	Separate Lines of Business
SMARTER	Specific, Measurable, Achievable or Attainable, Relevant or Realistic, Time-based, Evaluated, Revised
SME	Subject Matter Expert
SMI	Supplemental Medical Insurance
SMM	Summary of Material Modifications
SMS	Standard Metropolitan Statistical Area
SMT	Senior Management Team
SNAP	Supplemental Nutrition Assistance Program
SNE	Salaried Nonexempt
SOC	Standard Occupational Classification
SOL	Statute of Limitations
SOP	Statement of Position
SOX	Sarbanes-Oxley Act
SPD	Summary Plan Description
SPHR	Senior Professional in Human Resources Certification
SPX	Standard and Poor's Index
SRA	Supplemental Retirement Annuity
SRO	Self-Regulatory Organization
SROI	Subsequent Report of Injury
SS	Social Security

SSA	Social Security Administration
SSB	Securities Supervisory Board
SSD	Social Security Disability
SSDI	Social Security Disability Indemnity
SSI	Supplemental Security Income
SSN	Social Security Number
STD	Short-Term Insurance with Disability
STEEPLED	Social, Technological, Environmental, Economic, Political, Legal, Ethics, and Demographics
STF	Summary Tape File
STIP	Short-Term Industry Projections
STW	School-to-Work
SUB	Supplemental Unemployment Benefit
SUTA	State Unemployment Tax Act
SWOT	Strengths, Weaknesses, Opportunities, and Threats
T&D	Training and Development
TAMRA	Technical and Miscellaneous Revenue Act of 1988
TANF	Temporary Assistance to Needy Families
TBD	To Be Determined
TCA	Test Center Administrators
TCN	Third Country National
TDA	Tax-Deferred Annuity
TDB	Temporary Disability Benefits
TEA	Transportation Efficiency Act
TEFRA	Tax Equity and Fiscal Responsibility Act
TER	Total Expense Ratio
TESSA	Tax-Exempt Special Savings Account
TEUC	Temporary Extended Unemployment Compensation
TEV	Total Enterprise Value
TIL	Truth in Lending
TIP	Transportation Improvement Program
TL	Time and Labor
TN	Temporary Visitor Visa
TOC	Theory of Constraints
TOM	Traded Options Market
TPA	Third-Party Administrator
TPD	Temporary Partial Disability
TPL	Third-Party Liability
TQM	Total Quality Management
TRA	Tax Reform Act
TRASOP	Tax Reduction Act ESOP

PART III

TSA	1) Tax-Sheltered Annuity; 2) Transportation Security Administration
TSB	Targeted Small Business
TSP	Thrift Savings Plan
TTD	Temporary Total Disability
TUR	Total Unemployment Rates
TVI	Trade Value Index
TWA	Time-Weighted Average
UAW	United Auto Workers
UBTI	Unrelated Business Taxable Income
U&C	Usual and Customary
UCA	Unemployment Compensation Amendments Act
UCC	Uniform Commercial Code
UCI	Unemployment Compensation Insurance
UCR	Usual, Customary, and Reasonable
UFW	United Farm Workers
UGESP	Uniform Guidelines on Employee Selection Procedures
UGMA	Uniform Gifts to Minors Act
UI	Unemployment Insurance
UIC	Unemployment Insurance Commission
ULP	Unfair Labor Practice
UN	United Nations
UNCITRAL	United Nations Commission on International Trade Law
UR	1) Utilization Review; 2) Unemployment Rate
URL	Uniform Resource Locator (website address)
URO	Utilization Review Organization
USCIS	United States Citizenship and Immigration Services
USDA	United States Department of Agriculture
US DOL	United States Department of Labor
US DOJ	United States Department of Justice
USC	United States Code
USMCA	United States Mexico Canada Agreement, 2020
USERRA	Uniform Services Employment and Reemployment Rights Act
USITC	United States International Trade Commission
USM	Unlisted Securities Market
USTC	United States Tax Court
UTMA	Uniform Transfers to Minors Act
VA	Veterans Administration/Affairs
VBIA	Veterans Benefits Improvement Act
VEBA	Voluntary Employees' Beneficiary Association
VETS	Veterans Employment and Training Service
VETS-4212	VETS-4212 Report (replaced VETS-100)

VEVRA	Vietnam-Era Veterans Readjustment Act
VOC-ED	Vocational Education
VOC-REHAB	Vocational Rehabilitation
VPN	Virtual Private Network
VPT	Volume Price Trend
VWAP	Value-Weighted Average Price
VWPT	Value-Weighted Price Trading
VWPX	Volume-Weighted Price Uncrossing
WACC	Weighted Average Cost of Capital
WAI	Wealth-Added Index
WARN	Worker Adjustment and Retraining Notification Act
WC	Workers' Compensation
WCB	Workers' Compensation Board
WDC	Workforce Development Center
WHCRA	Women's Health and Cancer Rights Act
WIA	Workforce Investment Act
WIP	Work in Progress
WKLY	Weekly
WOTC	Workforce Opportunity Tax Credit
WPE	Workforce Planning and Employment
WPI	Wholesale Price Index
WPOA	Wagner-Peyser Act
WPPDA	Welfare and Pension Plan Disclosure Act (repealed by ERISA)
WRA	Weighted Risk Assets
WRAEA	Workforce Reinvestment and Adult Education Act
WTO	World Trade Organization
WTW	Welfare to Work
XML	Extended Markup Language
XRA	Expected Retirement Age
YTD	Year to Date
YTM	Yield to Maturity
ZBB	Zero-Based Budgeting

PART III

Case Law by Chapter

There are three types of federal laws. First are the acts taken by Congress to legislate mandates. Congressional actions, when completed, become the "law of the land." Second are the implementing regulations promulgated by the federal agencies and departments that specify in detail how the congressional laws will be administered. Third are the court interpretations of those congressional actions and regulatory rules. When the U.S. Supreme Court, or an agency such as the National Labor Relations Board (NLRB), issues a ruling about how the laws should be applied and interpreted, the ruling becomes "case law." It establishes precedent that must be followed by everyone within the court's jurisdiction. This appendix lists cases that interpret important issues that have influence on human resource management and summarizes key case law decisions. We recommend that you review each case in its entirety by going to the link listed and searching by the citation title. HR professionals should have a working knowledge of these cases and their impact on the workplace. This information may appear on the certification exam in one way or another.

Chapter 4: People

Year	Citation	Decision
1987	*Leggett v. First National Bank of Oregon* (739 P.2d. 1083) https://law.justia.com	The employer invaded the privacy of the employee when a company representative contacted the employee's psychologist (to whom the employee had been referred by an employee assistance program [EAP]), inquiring about the employee's condition.
2000	*Erie County Retirees Association v. County of Erie, Pennyslvania* (2000) https://caselaw.findlaw.com/us-3rd-circuit/ 1210474	If an employer provides retiree health benefits, the health insurance benefits received by Medicare-eligible retirees cost the same as the health insurance benefits received by younger retirees.
2005	*IBP, Inc. v. Alvarez* (546 U.S. 21) https://www.law.cornell.edu	Time spent donning or doffing unique safety gear is compensable, and the FLSA requires payment of affected employees for all the time spent walking between changing and production areas.

Year	Citation	Decision
2008	*LaRue v. DeWolff* (No. 06-856, 450 F. 3d 570) https://www.law.cornell.edu	When retirement plan administrators breach their fiduciary duty to act as a prudent person in administering the investments of retirement funds, the employee whose retirement account lost money can sue the plan administrators.
2009	*Kennedy v. Plan Administrators for DuPont Savings and Investment Plan* (No. 07-636) https://law.justia.com	This decision awarded retirement benefits to an ex-spouse even though she had agreed to disclaim such benefits, because the retiree had never changed the beneficiary designation on the retirement plan. This points out the need for retirement plan administrators to pay attention to divorce decrees and qualified domestic relations orders.

Chapter 5: Organization

Year	Citation	Decision
1971	*Griggs v. Duke Power Co.* (401 U.S. 424) https://www.law.cornell.edu	When an employer uses a neutral test or other selection device and then discovers it has a disproportionate impact on minorities or women, the test must be discarded unless it can be shown that it was required as a business necessity.
1973	*McDonnell Douglas Corp. v. Green* (411 U.S. 792) https://law.justia.com	In a hiring case, the charging party has to show only that 1) the charging party is a member of a Title VII protected group, 2) he or she applied and was qualified for the position sought, 3) the job was not offered to him or her, and 4) the employer continued to seek applicants with similar qualifications. Then the employer must show a legitimate business reason why the complaining party was not hired. The employee has a final chance to prove the employer's business reason was really pretext for discrimination.
1974	*Espinoza v. Farah Manufacturing Co.* (414 U.S. 86) https://law.justia.com	Noncitizens are entitled to Title VII protection. Employers who require citizenship may violate Title VII if it results in discrimination based on national origin.
1974	*Corning Glass Works v. Brennan* (417 U.S. 188) https://law.justia.com	Pay discrimination cases under the Equal Pay Act require the employee to prove that there is unequal pay based on sex for substantially equal work.

Year	Citation	Decision
1975	*Albermarle Paper v. Moody* (422 U.S. 405) https://law.justia.com	This decision requires the employer to establish evidence that an employment test is related to the job content. Job analysis could be used to show that relationship, but performance evaluations of incumbents are specifically excluded.
1976	*Washington v. Davis* (426 U.S. 229) https://www.law.cornell.edu	When an employment test is challenged under constitutional law, intent to discriminate must be established. Under Title VII, there is no need to show intent, just the impact of test results.
1976	*McDonald v. Santa Fe Transportation Co.* (427 U.S. 273) https://law.justia.com	Title VII prohibits racial discrimination against whites as well as blacks.
1987	*Johnson v. Transportation Agency, Santa Clara County, California, et al.* (480 U.S. 616) https://law.justia.com	The employer was justified in hiring a woman who scored two points less than a man because it had an affirmative action plan that was temporary, flexible, and designed to correct an imbalance of white males in the workforce.
1987	*School Board of Nassau County v. Arline* (480 U.S. 273) https://law.justia.com	A person with a contagious disease is covered by the Rehabilitation Act if the person otherwise meets the definitions of "handicapped individual."
1988	*Watson v. Fort Worth Bank & Trust* (487 U.S. 977) https://law.justia.com	In a unanimous opinion, the Supreme Court declared that disparate impact analysis can be applied to subjective or discretionary selection practices.
1989	*City of Richmond v. J. A. Croson Co.* (488 U.S. 469) https://law.justia.com	Affirmative action programs can be maintained only by a showing that the programs aim to eliminate the effects of past discrimination.
1989	*Price Waterhouse v. Hopkins* (490 U.S. 288) https://law.justia.com	This decision established how to analyze an employer's actions when the employer had mixed motives for an employment decision. If an employee shows that discrimination played a motivating part in an employment decision, the employer can attempt to prove as a defense that it would have made the same employment decision even if discrimination were not a factor.
1989	*Wards Cove Packing Co. v. Atonio* (490 U.S. 642) https://law.justia.com	An employee is required to show the disparate impact violation of Title VII in specific employment practices, not the cumulative effect of the employer's selection practices. When a showing of disparate impact is made, the employer only needs to produce evidence of a business justification for the practice, and the burden of proof always remains with the employee.

(continued)

Year	Citation	Decision
1993	*Harris v. Forklift Systems, Inc.* (510 U.S. 17) https://law.justia.com	In a sexual harassment complaint, the employee does not have to prove concrete psychological harm to establish a Title VII violation.
1993	*St. Mary's Honor Center v. Hicks* (509 U.S. 502) https://law.justia.com	Title VII complaints require the employee to show that discrimination was the reason for a negative employment action.
1993	*Taxman v. Board of Education of the Township of Piscataway* (91 F.3d 1547, 3rd Circuit) https://law.justia.com	Race in an affirmative action plan cannot be used to trammel the rights of people of other races.
1995	*McKennon v. Nashville Banner Publishing Co.* (513 U.S. 352) https://law.justia.com	"After-acquired" evidence collected following a negative employment action cannot protect an employer from liability under Title VII or the Age Discrimination in Employment Act (ADEA), even if the conduct would have justified terminating the employee.
1996	*O'Connor v. Consolidated Coin Caterers Corp.* (517 U.S. 308) https://law.justia.com	To show unlawful discrimination under the Age Discrimination in Employment Act (ADEA), a discharged employee does not have to show that he or she was replaced by someone outside the protected age group (that is, younger than 40).
1997	*Robinson v. Shell Oil* (519 U.S. 337) https://law.justia.com	Title VII prohibition against retaliation protects former as well as current employees.
1998	*Faragher v. City of Boca Raton* (524 U.S. 775) https://law.justia.com	This ruling distinguished between supervisor harassment that results in tangible employment action and that which does not. When harassment results in tangible employment action, the employer is liable. Employers may avoid liability if they have a legitimate written complaint policy, it is clearly communicated to employees, and it offers alternatives to the immediate supervisor as the point of contact for making a complaint.
1998	*Oncale v. Sundowner Offshore Service, Inc.* (523 U.S. 75) https://law.justia.com	Same-gender harassment is actionable under Title VII.
1998	*Bragdon v. Abbott* (524 U.S. 624) https://law.justia.com	An individual with asymptomatic HIV is an individual with a disability and therefore is protected by the Americans with Disabilities Act (ADA). Reproduction is a major life activity under the statute.
1998	*Wright v. Universal Maritime Service Corp.* (525 U.S. 70) https://law.justia.com	Collective bargaining agreements must contain a clear and unmistakable waiver if they are to bar an individual's right to sue after an arbitration requirement.

Year	Citation	Decision
1999	*Kolstad v. American Dental Association* (527 U.S. 526) https://law.justia.com	Title VII punitive damages are limited to cases in which the employer has engaged in intentional discrimination and has done so "with malice or with reckless indifference."
1999	*West v. Gibson* (527 U.S. 212) https://supreme.justia.com	This decision endorsed the position of the Equal Employment Opportunity Commission (EEOC) that it has the legal authority to require federal agencies to pay compensatory damages when the EEOC has ruled during the administrative process that the federal agency has unlawfully discriminated in violation of Title VII.
2001	*Circuit City Stores, Inc. v. Adams* (532 U.S. 105) https://law.justia.com	The court ruled that a pre-hire employment application requiring that all employment disputes be settled by arbitration was enforceable under the Federal Arbitration Act.
2002	*Ronald Lesch v. Crown Cork & Seal Co.* (334 NLRB 699) https://law.justia.com	This NLRB decision lifted some restrictions on the employer's use of employee participation committees.
2002	*EEOC v. Waffle House* (534 U.S. 279) https://law.justia.com	The Supreme Court ruled that even if there is a mandatory arbitration agreement in place, a relevant civil rights agency can still sue on behalf of the employee.
2002	*Phoenix Transit System v. NLRB* (337 NLRB 510) http://www.nlrb.gov/cases/ 28-CA-016043	This NLRB ruling struck down an employer rule prohibiting employees from discussing among themselves an employment complaint—in this instance, a complaint of sexual harassment—on the grounds that the prohibition was not limited in time and scope and interfered with a protected concerted activity.
2004	*NLRB v. Weingarten, Inc.* (420 U.S. 251, 254 1975) overturned by *IBM Corp. v. NLRB* (341 NLRB No 148, June 9, 2004) https://law.justia.com	NLRB ruled by a 3-2 vote that employees who work in a nonunionized workplace are not entitled to have a co-worker accompany them to an interview with their employer, even if the affected employee reasonably believes that the interview might result in discipline. This decision effectively reversed the July 2000 decision of the Clinton board, which had extended Weingarten rights to nonunion employees.
2007	*Toering Electric Company v. NLRB* (351 NLRB 225) https://casetext.com/admin-law/ toering-electric-co	NLRB ruled that an applicant for employment must be genuinely interested in seeking to establish an employment relationship with the employer to be protected against hiring discrimination based on union affiliation or activity. This creates greater obstacles for unions attempting salting campaigns.

(continued)

PART III

Year	Citation	Decision
2007	*Oil Capitol Sheet Metal, Inc., v. NLRB* (349 NLRB 1348) https://www.nlrb.gov/case/17-CA-019714	This NLRB decision provided employers relief in salting cases by announcing a new evidentiary standard for determining the period of back pay; it required the union to provide evidence that supports the period of time it claims the salt would have been employed.
2011	*Staub v. Proctor Hospital* (131 U.S. 1186) https://law.justia.com	The Supreme Court applied the "cat's paw" principle to a wrongful discharge case, finding that an employer was culpable because the HR manager did not adequately investigate supervisors' charges against the fired employee.
2011	*AT&T Mobility, LLC v. Concepcion* (563 U.S. 333) https://law.justia.com	The Supreme Court ruled that some state statutes restricting the enforceability of arbitration agreements in a commercial context may be preempted by the Federal Arbitration Act.
2011	*Kepas v. eBay* (131 S. Ct. 2160) https://law.justia.com	The Supreme Court refused to review a lower court decision that held in an employment case that a cost provision was severable from the balance of an arbitration agreement. The cost provision was unenforceable, but the agreement to arbitrate was enforceable.
2011	*Specialty Healthcare and Rehabilitation Center of Mobile v. NLRB* (15-RC-008773) https://www.nlrb.gov/case/15-RC-008773	NLRB indicated that, in nonacute health care facilities, it will certify smaller units for bargaining unless the employer provides overwhelming proof of a community of interest.
2011	*UGL-UNICCO Service Company v. NLRB* (01-RC-022447) https://www.nlrb.gov/case/01-RC-022447	NLRB reestablished the successor bar doctrine, allowing unions a window of 6 months to 1 year of presumed majority support after the transfer of ownership of a business.
2012	*D.R. Horton, Inc., v. NLRB* (12-CA-25764) https://www.nlrb.gov/case/12-CA-25764	NLRB ruled that requiring employees to agree to a class action waiver as a term and condition of employment violates Section 7 of the National Labor Relations Act (NLRA).

Chapter 6: Workplace

Year	Citation	Decision
1971	*Phillips v. Martin Marietta Corp.* (400 U.S. 542) https://law.justia.com	Sex discrimination means employers may not have different policies for men and women with small children of similar age.
1977	*Hazlewood School District v. United States* (433 U.S. 299) https://law.justia.com	An employee can establish a *prima facie* case of class hiring discrimination through the presentation of statistical evidence by comparing the racial composition of an employer's workforce with the racial composition of the relevant labor market.

Year	Citation	Decision
1977	*Trans World Airlines, Inc., v. Hardison* (432 U.S. 63) https://law.justia.com	Under Title VII, employers must reasonably accommodate an employee's religious needs unless doing so would create an undue hardship for the employer. The court defines hardship as anything more than *de minimis* cost.
1978	*Regents of University of California v. Bakke* (438 U.S. 265) https://law.justia.com	Medical school admission set asides (16 of 100 seats) are illegal if they discriminate against whites and there is no previous discrimination against minorities established.
1979	*Steelworkers v. Weber* (443 U.S. 193) https://law.justia.com	Affirmative action plans are permissible if they are temporary and intended to "eliminate a manifest racial imbalance."
1982	*Connecticut v. Teal* (457 U.S. 440) https://law.justia.com	An employer is liable for racial discrimination when any part of its selection process, such as an unvalidated examination or test, has a disparate impact, even if the final result of the hiring process is racially balanced. In effect, the court rejected the "bottom-line defense" and made clear that the fair employment laws protect the individual. Fair treatment for a group is not a defense to an individual claim of discrimination.
1984	*EEOC v. Shell Oil Co.* (466 U.S. 54) https://law.justia.com	The Supreme Court affirmed authority of EEOC commissioners to initiate charges of discrimination through "Commissioner Charges."
1986	*Meritor Savings Bank v. Vinson* (477 U.S. 57) https://law.justia.com	This defined "Hostile Environment Sexual Harassment" as a form of sex discrimination under Title VII. It also further defined it as "unwelcome" advances of a sexual nature. The victim's failure to use the employer's complaint process does not insulate the employer from liability.
1988	*DeBartolo Corp. v. Gulf Coast Trades Council* (known as DeBartolo II) (485 U.S. 568) https://law.justia.com	The Supreme Court ruled that bannering, hand billing, or attention-getting actions outside an employer's property were permissible.
1991	*United Automobile Workers v. Johnson Controls, Inc.* (499 U.S. 187) https://law.justia.com	The Supreme Court held that decisions about the welfare of future children must be left to the parents who conceive, bear, support, and raise them, rather than to the employers who hire their parents.
1992	*Electromation Inc., v. NLRB* (Nos. 92-4129, 93-1169, 7th Circuit) https://law.justia.com	NLRB held that action committees at Electromation were illegal "labor organizations" because management created and controlled the groups and used them to deal with employees on working conditions in violation of the NLRA.

(continued)

PART III

Year	Citation	Decision
1993	*E. I. DuPont & Company v. NLRB* (311 NLRB 893) https://law.justia.com	NLRB concluded that DuPont's one fitness committee and six safety committees were employer-dominated labor organizations and that DuPont dominated the formation and administration of one of them in violation of the NLRA.
1995	*PepsiCo, Inc. v. Redmond* (No. 94-3942 7th Circuit) https://law.justia.com	This was the case in which a district court applied an inevitable disclosure doctrine, even though there was no noncompete agreement in place. An employee who had left his position in marketing PepsiCo's All Sport sports drink to work for Quaker Oats Company and market Gatorade and Snapple drinks was enjoined from working for Quaker because he had detailed knowledge of PepsiCo's trade secrets pertaining to pricing, market strategy, and selling/delivery systems.
2003	*Grutter v. Bollinger* (539 U.S. 306) https://law.justia.com	The diversity of a student body is a compelling state interest that can justify the use of race in university admissions as long as the admissions policy is "narrowly tailored" to achieve this goal. University of Michigan did not do so for its undergraduate program, but the law school admissions program satisfied the standard.
2004	*General Dynamics Land Systems Inc., v. Cline* (540 U.S. 581) https://law.justia.com	The ADEA does not protect younger workers, even those older than 40, from workplace decisions that favor older workers.
2004	*Pennsylvania State Police v. Suders* (542 U.S. 129) https://law.justia.com	In the absence of a tangible employment action, employers may use the Faragher-Ellerth defense in a constructive discharge claim when supervisors are charged with harassment.
2005	*Smith v. Jackson, Mississippi* (544 U.S. 228) https://law.justia.com	The ADEA, like Title VII, offers recovery on a disparate impact theory.
2005	*Leonel v. American Airlines, Inc.* (400 F.3d 702, 9th Circuit) https://law.justia.com	To make a legitimate job offer under the ADA, an employer must have completed all nonmedical components of the application process or be able to demonstrate that it could not reasonably have done so before issuing the offer.
2007	*Ledbetter v. Goodyear Tire & Rubber Co.* (550 U.S. 618) https://law.justia.com	A claim of discrimination must be filed within 180 days of the first discriminatory employment act, and the clock does not restart after each subsequent act (for example, issuance of a paycheck with lower pay than co-workers if based on sex). Congress overruled this decision with the passage of the Lilly Ledbetter Fair Pay Act of 2009, which says the clock will restart with each paycheck and may reach back as far as when the incident of discrimination began. The 180 days expands to 300 days in deferral states.

Year	Citation	Decision
2009	*Ricci v. DeStefano* (No. 07-1428) https://law.justia.com	The key take away from the *Ricci v. DeStefano* ruling is that "Under Title VII, before an employer can engage in intentional discrimination for the asserted purpose of avoiding or remedying an unintentional disparate impact, the employer must have a strong basis in evidence to believe it will be subject to disparate-impact liability if it fails to take the race-conscious, discriminatory action."
2013	*Vance v. Ball State University* (No. 11-556) https://law.justia.com	This case determined that an employee is a "supervisor" of another employee for the purposes of liability under Title VII of the Civil Rights Act of 1964 only if he or she is empowered by the employer to take tangible employment actions against the other employee.
2013	*University of Texas Southwestern Medical Center v. Nassar* (No. 12-484) https://law.justia.com	Retaliation claims brought under Title VII of the Civil Rights Act of 1964 must be proved according to principles of "but-for-causation," not the lesser causation test applicable to bias claims.
2020	*Bostock v. Clayton County* https://law.justia.com	Supreme Court ruled Title VII of the Civil Rights Act of 1964 forbids job discrimination on the basis of sexual orientation or transgender status.

PART III

Chapter 7: Behavioral Competencies

There is no case law related to these competencies.

For Additional Study

This appendix lists additional resources that can be helpful in your studies for the SHRM-CP and SHRM-SCP exams and for future reference as an HR professional. The resources listed may apply to several domains. In addition to these resources, a useful list to consult is the "100 Best Business Books of All Time." Putting that phrase into your favorite search engine will produce multiple websites to explore, such as forbes.com, goodreads.com, and amazon.com, with useful reading for your development.

Ashbaugh, Sam and Rowan Miranda. "Technology for Human Resources Management: Seven Questions and Answers." Public Personnel Management, 31(1), pp. 7–17, 2002.

Badgi, Satish. *Practical Guide to Human Resource Information Systems.* Delhi: Phi Learning Pvt. Ltd., 2012.

Becker, Brian E., Mark A. Huselid, and David Ulrich. *The HR Scorecard: Linking People, Strategy, and Performance.* Boston: Harvard Business School Press, 2001.

Benjamin, Steve. "A Closer Look at Needs Analysis and Needs Assessment: Whatever Happened to the Systems Approach?" *Performance Improvement* vol. 28, no. 9, pp. 12–16, Wiley Periodicals, Inc., 1989.

Bennett-Alexander, Dawn D. and Laura B. Hartman. *Employment Law for Business, Tenth Edition.* New York: McGraw Hill, 2022.

Bingham, B., S. Ilg, and N. Davidson. "Great Candidates Fast: On-Line Job Application and Electronic Processing: Washington State's New Internet Application System." Public Personnel Management, 31(1), pp. 53–62, 2002.

Bliss, Wendy (Series Advisor). *The Essentials of Finance and Budgeting.* Boston: Harvard Business School Press and Alexandria, Virginia: Society for Human Resource Management, 2005.

Blosser, Fred. *Primer on Occupational Safety and Health.* Washington, D.C.: The Bureau of National Affairs, 1992.

Carrell, Michael R. and Christina Heavrin. *Collective Bargaining and Labor Relations, Third Edition.* New York: Merrill, 1995.

Cherrington, David J. *The Management of Human Resources, Fourth Edition*. Englewood Cliffs, New Jersey: Prentice-Hall, 1995.

Coffey, Robert E., Curtis W. Cook, and Phillip L. Hunsaker. *Management and Organizational Behavior, Second Edition*, Boston: Austen Press, 2007.

Dawes, S. "Human Resource Implications of Information Technology in State Government." Public Personnel Management, 23(1), pp. 31–46, 1994.

DeLuca, Matthew J. *Handbook of Compensation Management*. Englewood Cliffs, New Jersey: Prentice-Hall, 1997.

DeMers, A. "Solutions and Strategies for IT Recruitment and Retention: A Manager's Guide." Public Personnel Management, 5/(1), pp. 27–37, 2002.

DeNisi, Angelo and Ricky Griffin. *HR*. Boston: Cengage Learning, 2011.

Doherty, Neil. *Integrated Risk Management: Techniques and Strategies*. New York: McGraw Hill Education, 2000.

Feldacker, Bruce. *Labor Guide to Labor Law, Fifth Edition*. Englewood Cliffs, New Jersey: Prentice-Hall, 2014.

Fitz-Enz, Jac. *How to Measure Human Resource Management, Second Edition*. New York: McGraw Hill Education, 1995.

Glaser, Judith E. *Conversational Intelligence*. Brookline, MA: Bibliomotion, Inc., 2014.

Grant, Phillip. *Multiple Use Job Descriptions: A Guide to Analysis, Preparation, and Applications for Human Resources Managers*. Westport, Connecticut: Praeger, 1989.

Hayes, John. *The Theory and Practice of Change Management*. London: Palgrave Macmillan, Sixth Edition, 2022.

Herzberg, Frederick. *The Motivation to Work*. Piscataway, NJ: Transaction, *Tenth Reprint*, 2010.

Kahan, Seth. *Getting Change Right: How Leaders Transform Organizations from the Inside Out*. San Francisco: Jossey-Bass, 2010.

Kaplan, Robert S. and David P. Norton. *The Balanced Scorecard: Translating Strategy into Action*. Harvard Business Review Press, 1996.

Kavanaugh, Michael, Mohan Thite, and Richard D. Johnson (Eds.). *Human Resource Information Systems: Basics, Applications, and Future Directions*. Thousand Oaks, California: Sage Publications, 2011.

Kirkpatrick, Donald L. and James D. Kirkpatrick, *Evaluating Training Programs, Third Edition*, San Francisco: Berrett-Koehler Publishers, 2006.

Knowles, Malcolm. *The Adult Learner: The Definitive Classic in Adult Education and Human Resource Development, Ninth Edition*, Oxford: Butterworth-Heinemann, 2020.

Kotter, John P. *Leading Change*. Harvard Business Review Press, 2012.

Kushner, Gary. *Health Care Reform: The Patient Protection and Affordable Care Act of 2010*. SHRM/Kushner and Company, 2010.

Kutcher, David. "What Is a RFP, Where to Find RFPs, and Are RFPs Relevant?" *Confluent Forms*. May 13, 2013. Retrieved February 7, 2014, from www.confluentforms.com/2013/05/requests-for-proposals-rfp.html.

Lanier, Sarah A. *Foreign to Familiar, Second Edition*, McDougal Publishing, 2022.

Lawler, Edward E., III. *Strategic Pay: Aligning Organizational Strategies and Pay Systems*. San Francisco: Jossey-Bass, 1990.

Lewis, Jackson. *Employer's Guide to Union Organizing Campaigns*. New York: Aspen Publishers, 2007.

Mantel Jr., S., J. Meredith, S. Shafer, and M. Sutton. *Project Management in Practice, Seventh Edition*, Hoboken, New Jersey: John Wiley & Sons, 2020.

Mathis, R., J. Jackson, John H. Jackson and Sean Valentine. *Human Resource Management, Fourteenth Edition* Boston: Cengage Learning, 2019.

Maslow, Abraham H. *A Theory of Human Motivation*. Eastford, Connecticut: Martino Fine Books, 2013.

McGregor, Douglas. *The Human Side of Enterprise* (annotated edition). New York: McGraw Hill Education, 2005.

Michaud, Patrick A. *Accident Prevention and OSHA Compliance*. Boca Raton, Florida: Lewis Publishers, 2017.

Milkovich, George T., Jerry M. Newman, and Dr. Barry Gerhart. *Compensation, Tenth Edition*. Boston: McGraw-Hill Education, 2016.

"Models and Techniques of Manpower Demand and Supply Forecasting: A Strategic Human Resource Planning Model." Retrieved February 7, 2014, from http://corehr.wordpress.com/hr-planning/53-2/.

Pink, Daniel H. *Drive: The Surprising Truth About What Motivates Us*. Riverhead Books, 2011.

Porter, Michael E. *Competitive Strategy: Techniques for Analyzing Industries and Competitors, Sixth Edition*, New York: Free Press, 2008.

Richardson, Blake. *Records Management for Dummies*. Hoboken, New Jersey: For Dummies, 2012.

Rogers, Everett. *Diffusion of Innovations*. New York: Free Press, 2003.

Scott, Mark, JD, CFE. "Managing Risks in Vendor Relationships." *The Fraud Examiner*. March 2012. Retrieved February 7, 2014, from www.acfe.com/fraud-examiner.aspx?id=4294972428.

PART III

Senge, Peter M. *The Fifth Discipline: The Art & Practice of The Learning Organization.* Crown Business, 2006.

"SHRM Code of Ethical and Professional Standards in Human Resource Management." www.shrm.org.

Tolbert, Pamela and Richard Hall. *Organizations: Structures, Processes, and Outcomes, Tenth Edition* New York: Pearson, 2016.

Truesdell, William H. *Secrets of Affirmative Action Compliance.* Walnut Creek, California: Management Advantage, Inc., 2017.

Ulrich, David. *Delivering Results: A New Mandate for Human Resource Professionals.* Boston: Harvard Business Review, 1998.

Waddill, Deborah and Michael Marquardt. *The e-HR Advantage: The Complete Handbook for Technology enabled Human Resources.* Boston: Nicholas Brealey America, 2011.

Watkins, Michael D. *The First 90 Days, Proven Strategies for Getting Up to Speed Faster and Smarter.* Harvard Business Review Press, 2013.

The following material is available on www.youtube.com:

Goleman, Daniel. "Daniel Goleman Introduces Emotional Intelligence."

Goleman, Daniel. "Focus: The Secret to High Performance and Fulfilment."

Welch, Jack. "Jack Welch on People Management."

About the Online Content

This book comes complete with TotalTester Online practice exam software with 268 practice exam questions.

System Requirements

The current and previous major versions of the following desktop browsers are recommended and supported: Chrome, Microsoft Edge, Firefox, and Safari. These browsers update frequently, and sometimes an update may cause compatibility issues with the TotalTester Online or other content hosted on the Training Hub. If you run into a problem using one of these browsers, please try using another until the problem is resolved.

Your Total Seminars Training Hub Account

To get access to the online content, you will need to create an account on the Total Seminars Training Hub. Registration is free, and you will be able to track all your online content using your account. You may also opt in if you wish to receive marketing information from McGraw Hill or Total Seminars, but this is not required for you to gain access to the online content.

Privacy Notice

McGraw Hill values your privacy. Please be sure to read the Privacy Notice available during registration to see how the information you have provided will be used. You may view our Corporate Customer Privacy Policy by visiting the McGraw Hill Privacy Center. Visit the **mheducation.com** site and click **Privacy** at the bottom of the page.

Single User License Terms and Conditions

Online access to the digital content included with this book is governed by the McGraw Hill License Agreement outlined next. By using this digital content you agree to the terms of that license.

Access   To register and activate your Total Seminars Training Hub account, simply follow these easy steps.

1. Go to this URL: **hub.totalsem.com/mheclaim**

2. To register and create a new Training Hub account, enter your e-mail address, name, and password on the **Register** tab. No further personal information (such as credit card number) is required to create an account.

   If you already have a Total Seminars Training Hub account, enter your e-mail address and password on the **Log in** tab.

3. Enter your Product Key: **ghw4-j9cc-kppw**

4. Click to accept the user license terms.

5. For new users, click the **Register and Claim** button to create your account. For existing users, click the **Log in and Claim** button.

   You will be taken to the Training Hub and have access to the content for this book.

Duration of License   Access to your online content through the Total Seminars Training Hub will expire one year from the date the publisher declares the book out of print.

Your purchase of this McGraw Hill product, including its access code, through a retail store is subject to the refund policy of that store.

The Content is a copyrighted work of McGraw Hill, and McGraw Hill reserves all rights in and to the Content. The Work is © 2023 by McGraw Hill.

Restrictions on Transfer   The user is receiving only a limited right to use the Content for the user's own internal and personal use, dependent on purchase and continued ownership of this book. The user may not reproduce, forward, modify, create derivative works based upon, transmit, distribute, disseminate, sell, publish, or sublicense the Content or in any way commingle the Content with other third-party content without McGraw Hill's consent.

Limited Warranty   The McGraw Hill Content is provided on an "as is" basis. Neither McGraw Hill nor its licensors make any guarantees or warranties of any kind, either express or implied, including, but not limited to, implied warranties of merchantability or fitness for a particular purpose or use as to any McGraw Hill Content or the information therein or any warranties as to the accuracy, completeness, correctness, or results to be obtained from, accessing or using the McGraw Hill Content, or any material referenced in such Content or any information entered into licensee's product by users or other persons and/or any material available on or that can be accessed through the licensee's product (including via any hyperlink or otherwise) or as to non-infringement of third-party rights. Any warranties of any kind, whether express or implied, are disclaimed. Any material or data obtained through use of the McGraw Hill Content is at your own discretion and risk and user understands that it will be solely responsible for any resulting damage to its computer system or loss of data.

Neither McGraw Hill nor its licensors shall be liable to any subscriber or to any user or anyone else for any inaccuracy, delay, interruption in service, error or omission, regardless of cause, or for any damage resulting therefrom.

In no event will McGraw Hill or its licensors be liable for any indirect, special or consequential damages, including but not limited to, lost time, lost money, lost profits or good will, whether in contract, tort, strict liability or otherwise, and whether or not such damages are foreseen or unforeseen with respect to any use of the McGraw Hill Content.

TotalTester Online

TotalTester Online provides you with a full-length simulation of the SHRM-CP and SHRM-SCP exam, with 134 questions each. Exams can be taken in Practice Mode or Exam Mode. Practice Mode provides an assistance window with references to the book, explanations of the correct and incorrect answers, and the option to check your answer as you take the test. Exam Mode provides a simulation of the actual exam. The number of questions, the types of questions, and the time allowed are intended to be an accurate representation of the exam environment.

To take a test, follow the instructions provided in the previous section to register and activate your Total Seminars Training Hub account. When you register, you will be taken to the Total Seminars Training Hub. From the Training Hub Home page, select your certification from the Study drop-down menu at the top of the page to drill down to the TotalTester for your book. You can also scroll to it from the list on the Your Topics tab of the Home page, and then click on the TotalTester link to launch the TotalTester. Once you've launched your TotalTester, you can begin testing yourself in Practice Mode or Exam Mode. All exams provide an overall grade and a grade broken down by behavioral competency or functional area.

The TotalTester Online practice exam software includes several practice exam options. Select the SHRM-CP Practice Exam or the SHRM-SCP Practice Exam TotalTester icons to launch a full-length, 134-question, timed practice exam. These exams are intended to simulate the actual SHRM-CP and SHRM-SCP certification exams. Only one full-length exam is available for each, and these exams cannot be customized.

Separate TotalTesters are also provided for the Knowledge Domain Questions and the Situational Judgment Questions, although all question types will be delivered together in the real certification exams. The Knowledge exams and the Situational Judgment exams can be customized as described next.

Knowledge Exams

The Knowledge exams can be taken in Practice Mode or Exam Mode. Practice Mode provides an assistance window with references to the book, explanations of the correct and incorrect answers, and the option to check your answer as you take the test. Each time you take a test, a different set of questions will be generated from the total pool of questions. The number, distribution, and types of questions are intended to be an accurate representation of the Knowledge questions you will encounter on the real exam.

Note that the 3 hour and 40 minute time allotment is the total time you will receive to complete all questions on the full exam, including the Situational Judgment questions. Be sure you are able to complete the Knowledge exams in Exam Mode with enough time left over to complete a Situational Judgment exam.

The option to customize your quiz allows you to create custom exams from selected functional areas or chapters, and you can further customize the number of questions and time allowed.

Situational Judgment Exams

The Situational Judgment exams can also be taken in Practice Mode or Exam Mode. Practice Mode provides an assistance window with references to the book, explanations of the correct and incorrect answers, and the option to check your answer as you take the test.

Whether taken in Practice Mode or Exam Mode, each Situational Judgment exam will always present the same questions in the same order. The number of questions and types of questions in the Situational Judgment exams are intended to be an accurate representation of the Situational Judgment questions you will encounter on the real exam. As with the Knowledge exams, the 3 hour and 40 minute time allotment is the total time you will receive to complete all questions on the full certification exam. Whether you begin with the Situational Judgment exam or the Knowledge exam, be sure you are able to complete both exams within the total time allotment.

The option to customize your quiz allows you to create custom exams from selected behavioral competencies, and you can further customize the number of questions and time allowed.

Technical Support

For questions regarding the TotalTester or operation of the Training Hub, visit **www.totalsem.com** or e-mail **support@totalsem.com**.

For questions regarding book content, visit **www.mheducation.com/customerservice**.

401(k) plan A salary reduction, individual retirement plan for employees. Contributions reduce one's taxable income, and investment income accumulates tax-free until the money is withdrawn.

ADDIE model A five-step instructional design process consisting of analysis, design, development, implementation, and evaluation.

administrative exemption Exemption from overtime pay and other FLSA provisions based on several qualifying factors, including minimum pay requirement, plus the exercise of discretion and independent judgment performing work directly related to the management of general business operations.

administrative services–only plan Health insurance programs in which the employer assumes all of the risk.

adverse impact Illegal employment discrimination that results when a neutral-appearing policy has a discriminatory effect on a protected class. Also known as *disparate impact*.

adverse selection Pertaining to health care benefits when employees enroll in coverage they expect to need and other employees do not enroll because they do not expect to need the coverage. Orthodontia coverage is an example.

adverse treatment A legal category of illegal employment discrimination involving individual treatment or "pattern and practice" treatment of groups of workers.

affinity group A group of employees who share a diversity dimension. Also called an *employee resource group*.

affirmative action Use of special outreach and recruiting programs to ensure participation of qualified job candidates when the incumbent workforce is significantly less than the computed availability.

aggregate stop-loss coverage Insurance to help protect a health plan against the risk of large total claims from all participants during the plan year.

aging A technique used to make outdated data current.

alternative dispute resolution (ADR) A variety of processes that help parties resolve disputes without a trial. Processes include mediation, arbitration, neutral evaluation, and rent-a-judge services.

amendment Modification of a U.S. law or the U.S. Constitution.

analytics   The discovery and communication of meaningful patterns in data.

andragogy   The study of how adults learn.

applicant tracking system (ATS)   A software application that automates the management of the recruiting process through various steps.

apprenticeship   A system of training a person in a trade or profession, with on-the-job training for technical skills, by pairing them with a skilled worker.

arbitration   The process of submitting a labor dispute to a third party for resolution. The third party is called an *arbitrator*. Both parties agree beforehand to accept the arbitrator's decision, making that decision binding.

assessment center   A method for assessing leadership aptitude using various diagnostic processes evaluated by observers.

assets   The properties an organization owns, both tangible and intangible.

at-will employment   A legal doctrine that describes an employment relationship where either party can end the relationship at any time for any reason, except if there is a law to the contrary Also known as *employment at will* or *employment at will doctrine*.

auditory learner   This is a person who learns best through listening.

automatic step rate plan   A pay plan where an employee automatically has base pay adjusted upward based on their time in the title.

average   Arithmetic average, or mean, showing the typical value in a set of data. Calculated by dividing the sum of values in the set by the number of values.

back pay   Payment of salary or wages that should have been paid initially, usually as a form of remedy for a complaint of discrimination.

background check   Investigation of an individual's personal history, including employment, education, criminal record, and financial records.

balance sheet   A statement of a business's financial position at a specific point in time in terms of assets, liabilities, and owner's equity.

balanced scorecard   A big-picture view of an organization's performance as measured against goals in the four areas of customer and stakeholder, learning and growth, internal processes, and financial.

BARS   Stands for *behaviorally anchored rating scale* and is a form of performance management best applied when a large number of workers are in the same job title.

base-pay systems   Methods for establishing regular wages. The various base-pay systems include single or flat-rate systems, time-based step rate systems, performance-based merit pay systems, productivity-based systems, and person-based systems.

behavioral expectation scale (BES)   Performance evaluation using behavioral anchors describing expected employee behavior.

behavioral interview   A technique that queries job applicants to describe their specific behaviors or actions they've taken in particular past situations as a basis for determining each individual's demonstrated skill sets.

behavioral observation scale (BOS)   Performance evaluation using frequency of behavioral observation.

bell curve   Used to describe the mathematical concept called "normal distribution."

benchmarking   Process by which an organization identifies performance gaps and sets goals for improvement via comparing data and processes against those of other organizations.

benefits   Payments or services provided to employees, typically covering health care, retirement, life insurance, sick pay, disability, and paid time off.

benefits-needs assessment or analysis   Collection and analysis of data to determine whether the employer's benefits programs actually meet their objectives.

bereavement leave   Paid or unpaid time off to attend a funeral.

bias   Prejudice in favor of or against one thing, person, or group compared with another, usually in a way considered unfair.

big data   Extremely large data sets that may be analyzed computationally to reveal patterns, trends, and associations.

bill   A proposal presented to a legislative body in the U.S. government to enact a law.

blended learning   A formal education program in which a student learns via a combination of instructor-led training and self-directed study.

blue ocean strategy   The pursuit of creating a new market space where there are no competitors.

bona fide occupational qualification (BFOQ)   A factor that is reasonably necessary to carry out a particular job function. Two examples are religion and gender. Race is never a BFOQ.

bonus   A one-time financial payment above and beyond base pay.

boycott   A protest action that encourages the public to withhold business from an employer that is targeted by a union.

brain drain   The departure of educated or professional people from one country, economic sector, or field for another, usually for better pay or living conditions.

branding   1. The process of conveying key organizational values. 2. Marketing.

broadbanding   The combining of several pay grades or job classifications into a single pay band with a much wider spread.

budgeting   Forecasting income and expenses by category over a specific period of time.

Bureau of Labor Statistics (BLS)   A Department of Labor agency that collects and publishes labor market information.

business acumen   Knowledge and understanding of the financial, accounting, marketing, and operational functions of an organization.

business case   A documented argument intended to convince a decision-maker to approve some kind of action, usually identifying a specific problem coupled with a specific solution.

business concept   An idea for producing goods or services that identifies the benefits that can be achieved for prospective customers or clients.

business continuity   The ability to continue conducting business following an unplanned interruption.

business ethics   Generally accepted norms and expectations for business management behavior.

business intelligence (BI)   An umbrella term that refers to a variety of software applications used to analyze an organization's raw data to make better decisions. BI is a discipline made up of several related activities, including data mining, online analytical processing, querying, and reporting.

business unit   A segment of a company (such as accounting, production, marketing, or sales) representing a specific business function. This can also be called a department, division, or functional area.

cafeteria benefit plan   Benefits approach where employees may choose the benefits they desire, subject to certain limitations and total cost constraints.

career development   A concept that individuals expand their knowledge, skills, and abilities as they progress through their careers.

career management   Planning, preparing, and implementing employee career paths.

career mapping   Process by which organizations use visual tools or guides for career possibilities and paths, sequential positions, roles, and phases in a career.

career pathing   Process in which employees are given a clear outline for moving from a current position to a desired position.

career planning   Activities and actions that individuals follow for a specific career path.

case study   Simulation of real-world problems that calls for an application of skill or knowledge to resolve.

cash award   Reward for exceeding performance goals; a formula-based bonus using a percentage of profits or other preestablished measurement.

cash flow statement   A mandatory part of a company's financial reports since 1987; records the amounts of cash and cash equivalents entering and leaving a company.

cause-and-effect diagram   Total quality tool that identifies possible root causes for an effect or problem. Also called a *fishbone diagram, Ishikawa diagram,* or *the five whys.*

center of excellence (COE)   Refers to a team, a shared facility, or an entity that provides leadership, best practices, research, support, or training for a focus area.

central tendency error   When managers and interviewers rate all or most of the employees or interviewees as average.

certification of a union   Formal recognition of a union as the exclusive bargaining representative of a group of employees.

chain of command   The order in which authority and power in an organization is wielded and delegated from top management to other employees.

change agent   The internal role of HR managers when they are guiding an organizational change intervention.

change management   Transitioning individuals, groups, teams, and institutions to a desired future state.

change program   Strategic approach to organizing and implementing specific changes (for example, policies or procedures) within an organization.

childcare services   Programs designed to help working parents deal with the ongoing needs of preschool or school-aged children.

civil law   A legal system based on written laws, rules, and regulations.

clawback   A provision of the Dodd-Frank Act that requires executives to return ill-gotten bonuses.

cloud computing   Application software on offsite central servers that is accessed using Internet-enabled devices.

coaching   Focused guidance, usually one-to-one, intended to develop and enhance on-the-job performance or behavior.

code of conduct   1. Principles that guide behavior and decision-making in an organization. 2. An employment policy listing personal behaviors that are acceptable in the workplace, plus behaviors identified as unacceptable.

cobot   A robot intended to physically interact with employees in the workplace.

code of ethics   Principles of conduct that guide expectations for behavior and decisions.

cognitive learning   The refining of knowledge by adding new information through engaging the senses and thereby expanding prior knowledge.

collective bargaining   A formal process of negotiating working conditions between an employer and a union.

collective bargaining agreement (CBA)   Union contract outlining working conditions agreed to between a union and an employer.

combination step rate and performance   Pay practice where employees receive step rate increases up to the established job rate. Above this level, increases are granted only for superior job performance.

common law   Law developed over time from the rulings of judges as opposed to law embodied in statutes passed by legislatures (statutory law) or law embodied in a written constitution (constitutional law.)

communication skills   Verbal and written abilities that enable an individual to transmit and receive messages.

commuter assistance   Financial assistance programs designed to help defray employee public transportation costs associated with going to and from work.

comparable worth   The principle that men and women should receive equal pay for jobs that require comparable skills and responsibilities, even if the titles differ.

compa-ratio   An indicator of how wages match, lead, or lag the midpoint of a given pay range computed by dividing the worker's pay rate by the midpoint of the pay range.

compensation   Financial payments in the form of base pay, commissions, bonuses, merit pay, piece rate, differential pay, overtime, tips, profit sharing, or gainsharing in exchange for work.

compensation philosophy   Written statement documenting an organization's guiding principles and values about employee compensation.

compensatory damages   A monetary equivalent awarded for pain, suffering, and emotional distress as a result of a legal proceeding.

competency   Measurable or observable knowledge, skills, abilities, and behaviors critical to successful job performance.

competency-based interview   An interview where the style of question forces candidates to give situational examples of times in the past when they have performed particular tasks or achieved particular outcomes using certain skills.

competency-based pay system   System where pay is linked to the level at which an employee can perform in a recognized competency.

compliance   Being in accordance with all applicable federal, state, and local laws.

compliance evaluation   Formal audit of a federal contractor subject to oversight by the Office of Federal Contract Compliance Programs (OFCCP.)

compliance program   Systematic procedures instituted by an organization to ensure that the provisions of the regulations imposed by a government agency are being met.

compressed workweek   An alternative work schedule where employees work fewer days but more hours per day.

computer employee exemption   Exemption from overtime pay and other FLSA provisions based on several qualifying factors, including minimum pay requirement, job duties involving computer programming, software analysis, and software engineering.

computer-based testing (CBT)   Testing delivery method via a computer.

conciliation   A nonbinding dispute resolution using a neutral third party to help disputing parties reach a mutually agreeable decision.

concurrent validity   Gathering predictor and criteria data to validate a selection procedure at the same time.

conflict of interest   A situation in which a person or organization has two or more competing interest.

construct validity   The degree to which a test measures what it claims to measure for psychological traits.

constructive discharge   An employee resignation as a result of the employer making working conditions intolerable.

constructive discipline   Discipline that imposes increasingly severe consequences and penalties if unwanted behaviors reoccur. This is also called *progressive discipline*.

consumer price index (CPI)   The average of prices paid by consumers for goods and services.

content validity   Validity inferred from the similarity between the predictor and the requirements of the job. Also called *face validity*.

contingency plan   A coordinated set of steps to be taken in an emergency or disaster.

contingent workers   Workers who do not have an ongoing expectation of full-time employment, such as part-time workers, independent contractors, temporary workers, consultants, leased employees, and subcontractors.

continuous improvement   A total quality management (TQM) principle looking for ways to always to make processes and outcomes better.

contract labor   Work performed under the terms of a legally enforceable contract.

contract negotiation   The process of give and take related generally to content details and provisions of an employment contract, such as a union agreement or memorandum of understanding (MOU).

contrast effect   An error made in interviewing when strong candidates are interviewed after weak candidates, causing them to appear more qualified because of the contrast.

contrast error   In an interview or performance appraisal process, this is an error caused by the effect of previously interviewed or appraised applicants on the interviewer.

control chart   A chart that illustrates variation from normal in a situation over time.

controlling   A management function involving monitoring the workplace and making adjustments to activities as required.

cooperative learning   A strategy in which a small group of people work on solving a problem or completing a task in a way that each person's success is dependent on the group's success.

copyright   A legal form of protection for authors of original works.

core competency   A unique capability that is essential or fundamental to a particular job.

corporate citizenship   A self-regulatory mechanism where an organization monitors and ensures its active compliance with the spirit of the law, ethical standards, and international norms.

corporate governance   The mechanisms, processes, and relations by which corporations are controlled and directed.

corporate social responsibility (CSR)   Strategic goals achieved through local community relationships around social needs and issues.

cost-benefit analysis (CBA)   A business practice in which the costs and benefits of a particular situation are analyzed as part of the decision process.

cost containment   Efforts or activities designed to reduce or slow down the cost of expenses and increases.

cost-of-living adjustment (COLA)   Pay increase given to all employees regardless of performance or organizational profitability. It is usually measured against the consumer price index (CPI).

cost per hire   The total cost to hire each new employee.

covering   Defensive behavior of diverse employees when the culture expects assimilation rather than promoting inclusion.

credit reports   Reports obtained from one of the major credit reporting agencies that explains the individual's personal rating based on financial history.

criteria data   Information collected for validity testing in the selection process (usually early job performance).

criterion-related validity   A validation study in which the predictor data is statistically correlated with the criteria of performance.

cross-functional work team   A group of people from different functions working together to generate production or problem resolution.

cultural artifact   A visible symbol or object that conveys information and the shared beliefs of members.

cultural noise   The hinderance of successful communication between people due to different cultures.

cultural relativism   The principle that an individual human's beliefs and activities should be understood by others in terms of that individual's own culture.

culture   Societal forces affecting the values, beliefs, attitudes, customs, and actions of a group of people, giving rise to the group's sense of identity.

DART   Incident rate for occupational illnesses or injuries, standing for *days away* from work, *restricted* work activity, and job *transfers*.

dashboards   A data visualization tool that displays the current status of metrics and key performance indicators (KPIs).

database   A systematically organized or structured repository of indexed information (usually as a group of linked data files) that allows for easy retrieval, updating, analysis, and output of data.

database management system (DBMS)   A computer program that catalogs, indexes, locates, retrieves, and stores data, maintains the data's integrity, and outputs it in the form desired by a user.

deauthorization of a union   Removal of "union security" from the contract. The union remains as the exclusive bargaining representative, and the collective bargaining agreement remains in effect, but employees are not forced to be members or pay dues to the union.

decertification of a union   Removal of a union as the exclusive bargaining representative of the employees.

defamation   Making slanderous or libelous statements about a person's reputation or credibility.

defined benefit plan (DBP)   A pension plan that provides retirement income to retirees based on a formula that is based on age, years of service, and an average annual income for a set number of years.

defined contribution plan (DCP)   An individual retirement fund created for each employee into which the company and the employee make contributions.

Delphi technique   A systematic forecasting method that involves structured interaction among a group of experts on a subject. The Delphi technique typically includes at least two rounds of experts answering questions and giving justification for their input. It is a useful tool to avoid group think.

demand analysis   Estimation of what customers, clients, or patrons will want in the future.

demonstration   Showing how something is done.

dental plan   Insurance program that covers some or all of the cost of dental services for subscribers.

departmentalization   The way organizations group jobs to coordinate work.

developmental activities   The part of human resource management that specifically deals with the training and development of employees.

differential pay   An addition to base pay that results from special job circumstances such as shift assignment, on-call requirements, temporary responsibility assignments, hazardous conditions, and similar "extras." Can be a percentage of base pay or a flat dollar amount.

differential piece rate system   Employees receive one rate of pay up to the production standard and a higher rate of pay when the standard is exceeded.

dilemma reconciliation   Process of seeking solutions to issues involving cultural differences.

direct threat   A medical condition that poses a significant risk or substantial harm to the health or safety of the individual or others.

directing   Managing or controlling people to do what is wanted or needed.

disability   A medically determinable impairment of body or mind that restricts, or causes loss of, a person's functional ability to carry on major life activities.

disaster recovery plans   A set of procedures used to protect and recover a business from a natural or other disaster that has impacted the organization or employer.

discipline   Forms of punishment to ensure obedience with policies.

disparate impact   Adverse effect of a practice or standard that is neutral and nondiscriminatory in its intention but nonetheless disproportionately affects individuals with a disability or belonging to a particular group based on their age, ethnicity, race, sex, or other protected class. Also known as *adverse impact.*

disparate treatment   Type of discrimination that occurs when an individual is treated differently from others based on protected group membership.

distance learning   Using technology to deliver educational or instructional programs away from a physical classroom.

diversity   Differences in people's characteristics, including but not limited to race, religion, color, national origin, sex, ethnicity, age, education, socioeconomic status, beliefs, personality, thought processes, job function, and work style.

diversity council   Task force created to work on diversity, inclusion, and equity initiatives in an organization.

diversity dimensions   Framework for diversity, including personality, internal dimensions, external dimensions, and organizational dimensions.

diversity, inclusion, and equity   The practice of embracing differences of race, culture, and background, ensuring that everyone is a valued participant in the workplace.

diversity of thought   Different types of cognitive processes.

divestiture   The sale of an asset.

domestic partners   Two adults who have chosen to share one another's lives in an intimate and committed relationship of mutual caring.

downsizing   Reducing the number of workers, usually due to economic necessity or restructuring. Also called *reduction in force (RIF).*

dual career ladders   A system that enables a person to advance up either a management or a technical career development path in an organization.

due diligence   The first step in mergers and acquisitions involving a broad scope of research and investigation of the other company.

due process   Conduct of legal proceedings, strictly according to established principles and procedures, to ensure fair treatment that is neither arbitrary nor capricious.

dues check off   A collective bargaining agreement provision that allows direct payment of union dues to the union by the company's payroll function. Requires an annual signed statement by the employee authorizing this to happen.

duty of care   1. Principle that employers should take all steps reasonably possible to ensure the health, safety, and well-being of employees (and families on international assignments) from foreseeable injury. 2. The responsibility or the legal obligation to avoid reasonably foreseeable acts or omission likely to cause harm to others.

effectiveness   Measurement of the entire cycle of acquiring inputs, transforming inputs into useful products, selling them, and then obtaining more inputs.

efficiency   A ratio of inputs to outputs. A measure of how well an organization creates products from materials and energy.

elder care   Programs to help employees deal with responsibilities for care of family elders.

election bar   Condition where the NLRB will say no to a request to hold an election to install a union.

e-learning   Internet-based training programs that can be instructor-led or self-paced.

emotional intelligence (EI or EQ)   The capacity to be aware of, control, and express one's emotions and to handle interpersonal relationships judiciously and empathetically.

employee   1. A person in the service of another under any contract of hire, express or implied, oral or written, where the employer has the power or right to control and direct material details of how the work is to be performed. 2. In the United States, workers who have earnings reported on a Form W-2.

employee assistance program (EAP)   A benefit program that provides counseling and related services to help employees and their families with personal problems.

employee complaints   Written or verbal statements of dissatisfaction from an employee that can involve charges of discrimination, lack of fairness, or other upset.

employee engagement   1. The degree employees are fully absorbed by and enthusiastic about their work so they take positive action to further the organization's reputation and interests. 2. Employees' emotional commitment to the organization demonstrated by their willingness to put in additional discretionary effort.

employee leasing   Contracting with a vendor who provides qualified workers for a specific period of time at a specific pay rate.

employee lifecycle   A human resources model that identifies stages in employees' careers to help guide their management and optimize associated processes.

employee relations program   A method for managing the employer-employee relationship.

employee resource group (ERG)   A group of employees who share a diversity dimension. Also called an *affinity group*.

employee stock ownership plan (ESOP)   A retirement plan in which the company contributes its stock, or money to buy its stock, to the plan for the benefit of the company's employees.

employee stock purchase plan (ESPP)   A program allowing employees to purchase company stock at a discounted price.

employee survey   A questionnaire used to gather opinions of employees about their employment experiences.

employee-management committee   A problem-solving group of management and nonmanagement employees focused on specific issues within the workplace.

employee value proposition (EVP)   An employer's attempt to influence candidates and employees' perceived value of the total rewards (tangible and intangible benefits) they receive from the organization as part of their employment.

employment at will or employment at will doctrine   A legal doctrine that describes an employment relationship where either party can end the relationship at any time for any reason, except if there is a law to the contrary. Also known as *at-will employment.*

employment branding   A targeted strategy to manage the awareness and perceptions of employees, potential employees, and related stakeholders to be seen as an "employer of choice."

employment policies   Rules by which the workplace is managed.

Employment Practices Liability Insurance (EPLI)   Liability insurance to protect employers against claims alleging legal rights of the employment relationship (even for job candidates) have been violated.

employment reference checks   Verification of references, both personal and professional, provided by a job candidate on an application form or résumé.

employment testing   Any tool or step used in the employment selection process. Commonly includes written tests, interviews, résumé reviews, or skill demonstration.

encryption   Scrambling sensitive information so that it becomes unreadable to everyone except the intended recipient.

enterprise resource planning (ERP)   Business management integrated software system of an enterprise that supports multiple activities.

environmental footprint   The effect that an entity has on the environment.

environmental scanning   A process of studying the environment to pinpoint potential threats and opportunities.

e-procurement   An electronic web application for transacting and purchasing supplies and services.

Equal Employment Opportunity (EEO)   Laws that provide equal access to employment opportunities based on qualifications regardless of federal or state protected-class membership.

Equal Employment Opportunity Commission (EEOC)   The government agency responsible for enforcing federal laws related to employment discrimination.

equal pay   Providing equal compensation for jobs that have the same requirements, responsibilities, and working conditions regardless of the incumbent's gender. Also known as *pay equity*.

equity   1. The difference between income and liabilities reported on a balance sheet. 2. Equal treatment.

essential functions   The fundamental, crucial job duties performed in a position and the reason the job exists. They are the primary job duties a qualified individual must be able to perform with or without reasonable accommodation.

ethical universalism   The concept that there are fundamental ethical principles that apply across cultures.

ethics   Principles and values that set expectations for behaviors in an organization.

ethnocentric   An international business approach where how things are done in the home country is the consistently preferred approach. This includes key management positions worldwide to be filled by home country employees.

eustress   Pleasant or curative stress that contributes to enthusiasm and a zest for living.

evacuation plan   A written procedure for moving employees out of the work location to a safer location in case of an emergency.

evaluation   1. The ability to judge. 2. Also a synonym for performance appraisal.

E-Verify   A government database that employers access to confirm a match between a new employee's name and their Social Security number.

executive coaching   The coaching of senior-level management by a third party.

executive exemption   Exemption from overtime pay and other FLSA provisions based on several qualifying factors, including supervision and minimum pay requirements.

executive incentives   Variable compensation additives for executive employees that may include company stock and use of company facilities such as vacation timeshares. These are usually variable based on the profitability of the company.

exempt employees   Employees exempt from overtime compensation and other FLSA or state law protections.

exempt job   A job with content that is exempt from FLSA provisions, including pay for overtime. Exemption can be based on several designated factors.

exit interview   A discussion with a departing employee to explore how they feel about their experience as an employee and what recommendations they might have for the employer.

expatriate   Employee working in a foreign country. Also known as an *international assignee (IA)*.

external coaching   Coaching that is provided by a third party.

external equity   The conditions and rewards of employment, compared with those of the employees of other firms.

extraterritoriality   The extension of a country's laws over its citizens outside that country's national boundaries.

extrinsic rewards   Rewards such as pay, benefits, incentive bonuses, promotions, time off, and so on.

face validity   Validity inferred from the similarity between the predictor and the requirements of the job. Also called *content validity*.

factor comparison   A process that involves identifying the compensable factors for each job, plus identifying dollar values for each factor to develop an actual pay rate for the evaluated job.

fast-track program   A career development program that identifies high-potential leaders for rapid career growth.

featherbedding   The practice of a union requesting more employees than the actual work requires.

fee-for-service plan   Allows health plan members to go to any qualified physician or other health care provider, hospital, or medical clinic and submit claims to the insurance company.

fiduciary responsibilities   Th duties of the person who manages a pension fund or savings program. Must follow the prudent person rules.

field test items   Questions on the SHRM certification exams that are not scored. These items are included on exam for the first time to statistically determine their validity and reliability.

final warning   The last step in the disciplinary process progression prior to removing the employee from the payroll.

first impression error   Occurs when a manager or interviewer bases their entire assessment of an employee or applicant on the first impression the employee or applicant made.

flat-rate or single pay system   A system in which each worker in the same job has the same rate of pay, regardless of seniority or job performance.

flexible spending account (FSA)   Allows employees to set aside a preestablished amount of money on a pre-tax basis per plan year for use in paying authorized medical or child care expenses.

floating holiday (FH)   Designated paid time off that can be used at any time during the year with the employer's approval.

flow analysis   How processes operate and how flows of products, data, or other items go through these processes.

focus group   A group of people brought together with a moderator to share their opinions on a specific topic. Focus groups aim at a discussion instead of individual responses to formal questions and produce qualitative data (preferences and beliefs.)

force-field analysis   A technique for identifying and analyzing the positive factors of a situation that help ("driving forces") and negative factors that hinder ("restraining forces") an entity in attaining its objectives.

forced choice   An evaluation method in which the evaluator selects from pairs of statements that represent "most like" and "least like."

formalization   The extent to which work roles are structured in an organization and the activities of the employees are governed by rules and procedures.

four-fifths rule (4/5ths rule)   A calculation to determine whether adverse impact is present. The protected group must be hired at a rate of at least 80 percent of the non-protected group.

framing   Composing a communication message so the intended audience sees the presented facts in a certain way and is persuaded to take a certain action.

frequency distribution   Listing of grouped pay data from lowest to highest.

frequency table   Number of workers in a particular job classification and their pay data.

full-time   Employees who work a designated number of hours per week, usually 30 to 40 hours.

fully funded plan   A health insurance program paid for entirely by the employer.

functional HR   A structure where HR generalists are located within business units such as HR business partners and implement the policies and interact with management and employees in the unit and where headquarters HR staff create policies and strategy.

functional structure   A common type of organizational structure in which the organization is divided into groups based on the type of work they perform, such as IT, finance, HR, and marketing.

functional work team   A group of people from the same function working together to generate production or resolve problems.

gainsharing plan   Extra pay provided to individual employees or groups of employees based on increases in productivity.

gamification   Extending elements of game play (point scoring, competition with others, rules of play, and so on) to other activities that encourage fun and employee engagement.

Gantt chart   A project planning tool that scopes and monitors the activities of a project, the timeline, and accountability.

gap analysis   Measurement of the difference between where you are and where you want to be.

gender   Culturally and socially constructed difference between men and women.

gender identity   Internal personal sense of being male or female, which may or may not be the same as one's sexual assignment at birth.

general duty clause   A provision in OSHA regulations that imposes an employer responsibility to ensure a safe and healthy working environment for its employees free from recognized hazards that cause or are likely to cause death or serious harm.

general pay increase   A pay increase given to all employees regardless of their job performance.

geocentric   A staffing policy to place the best person in the job regardless of their country of origin.

geographic structure   An organizational structure in which work is organized by different geographic regions.

geographic-based differential pay   Adjustment to base pay programs based on cost-of-living requirements in various geographic locations where employees work.

gig worker   Independent contractors who move from job to job (gig to gig) and are employed for a particular need or a defined time.

giganomics   The creation of employment through the piecing together of several separate work projects, or "gigs."

glass ceiling   A discriminatory practice that has inhibited women and other protected class members from advancing to executive-level jobs.

global integration (GI) strategy   An international business strategy that emphasizes consistency, standardization of processes, and a common culture across worldwide operations.

global mindset   An openness to and awareness of diversity across cultures and markets.

Global Professional in Human Resources (GPHR)   A global competency-based credential that validates the skills and knowledge of an HR professional who operates in a global marketplace.

global remittance   A transfer of money from migrant workers to their home country.

globalization   1. Growing interconnectedness and interdependency among people, markets, and organizations worldwide. 2. The worldwide movement toward economic, financial, trade, and communications integration.

glocalization   An international organization with equally strong global integration and local identity.

golden parachute   A provision in an executive employment contract that provide special payments or benefits to the executive under certain adverse conditions, such as the loss of their position.

good-faith bargaining   The requirement for both parties to meet, make offers, and counter proposals in an effort to reach an agreement.

governance   1. Establishment of policies and continuous monitoring of their proper implementation by the members of the governing body of an organization. 2. Process to ensure compliance with all applicable laws.

graphic rating scale   Performance management using numbers assigned to behavioral dimensions to evaluate employees.

green circle rate   Pay at a rate lower than the minimum rate for the assigned pay range.

grievance   A formal employee complaint handled by a structured resolution process in a company with a union-represented work group.

grievance procedure   Step-by-step process an employee must follow to get their complaint addressed when represented by a union. The process is defined in the collective bargaining agreement.

gross domestic product (GDP)   The total value of goods and services produced in a country.

gross profit margin   Ratio of gross profit to net sales.

group incentive program   Pay to all individuals in a workgroup for achievement by the entire workgroup.

group term life insurance   A benefit providing a lump-sum payment to beneficiaries upon the death of an employee.

group think   Decision-making that allows one individual to dominate, leading to unquestioned consensus and poorer decisions.

halo effect   This occurs when an evaluator scores an employee high on all job categories because of performance in a single area. May also apply in an interview.

harassment   Persecution, intimidation, pressure, or force applied to employees by supervisors, co-workers, or external individuals that interferes with the employee's ability to perform the job assignment.

Hawthorne Effect   Named for the Hawthorne studies, this is the phenomenon of employees changing their behavior when they are observed.

Hay method   A widely used job evaluation method that addresses three compensable factors (know-how, problem solving, and accountability) to determine how many points should be assigned to different jobs.

hazard   Situation that has the potential for harm and may lead to a danger, emergency, or disaster.

hazard pay   Additional pay for working under adverse conditions caused by environment or because of specific circumstances.

headcount   Number of individuals carried on a firm's payroll.

health insurance purchasing cooperative   Purchasing agent for a large group of employers.

health maintenance organization (HMO)   Health care program where the insurer is paid on a per-person (capitated) basis and offers health care services and staff at its facilities.

health reimbursement account (HRA)   Employer-funded medical reimbursement plan.

health savings account (HSA)   A tax-advantaged medical savings account available to taxpayers in the United States who are enrolled in a high-deductible health plan.

high-context culture   A culture of people that emphasizes complex interpersonal relationships and close connections over a long period of time, with a rich history. Therefore, the context of their interactions is not always clear to those outside the culture.

high-deductible health plan   A program that helps employers lower their costs and allows employees with set aside money to pay for out-of-pocket medical and medical-related expenses.

histogram   A graphic representation of the distribution of a single type of measurement using rectangles.

horn effect   This effect occurs when an employee receives a low rating in all areas because of one weakness influencing the evaluator. May also apply in an interview.

host-country national (HCN)   A worker hired by a multinational firm to work in their own country. Also called a *local national*.

hostile environment harassment   Occurs when an employee is subject to unwelcome advances, sexual innuendos, or offensive gender-related language or visuals that is sufficiently severe or pervasive from the perspective of a reasonable person.

HR audit   An objective look at the company's HR policies, practices, procedures, and strategies to ensure compliance, protect the company, establish best practices, and identify opportunities for improvement.

HR business partner   HR staff that acts as an internal consultant to senior management.

HR Certification Institute (HRCI)   A nonprofit professional certifying organization for the human resources profession.

HR professional certification   Status awarded to HR professionals by a recognized certifying agency after satisfying qualifying requirements.

HR service model   An approach for delivering HR services to support an organization.

HRCI Body of Knowledge (BOK)   The description of a set of concepts, tasks, responsibilities, and knowledge associated with HRCI credentialing.

HRIS   Stands for *human resources information system,* a computer-based collection of personal data.

human capital   The value of the capabilities, knowledge, skills, experiences, and motivation of a workforce in an organization.

Human Resource Business Partner (HRBP)   A global, competency-based credential designed to validate generally accepted professional-level core HR knowledge and skills.

human resource development (HRD)   Systematically planned activities that help the organization's workforce meet current and future job and skills needs.

human resource management (HRM)   Organizational systems to ensure that human talent is used effectively and efficiently to accomplish organizational goals.

identity alignment   The extent to which diversity is accepted and embraced in an organization.

IIPP   Injury and illness prevention program.

imminent danger   Under OSHA, any condition with a high probability that an accident may occur that results in death or serious physical harm.

incentive   An inducement or supplemental reward that serves as a motivational device for a desired action or behavior.

incentive pay   Pay designed to promote a higher level of job performance than otherwise included in the basic design of the job.

incentive stock option   An award of rights to purchase company stock in the future at a price determined at the time of the grant.

inclusion   1. The state of including or of being included within a group or structure. 2. Each person in an organization feeling welcomed, respected, supported, and valued as a team member. 3. Culture where employees are treated fairly, differences are valued and respected, and opportunities and resources are equally available to all employees.

income statement   A summary of financial performance with reported revenues, expenses, and profits of the organization over a certain period.

independent contractor   One who independently contracts to do work according to their own methods and is subject to their principal's control only as to the end product or final result of their work.

indirect compensation   Social Security, unemployment insurance, disability insurance, pension, 401(k), and other similar programs as well as health care, vacation time, sick leave, and paid time off (for holidays, for example).

individual development plan (IDP)   A written document that outlines goals and professional growth for an employee.

individual incentive program   An offer to individual employees in a workgroup to receive extra pay based on achievement of clearly defined objectives.

information management (IM)   Application of management techniques to collect information, communicate it within and outside the organization, and process it to enable managers to make quicker and better decisions.

injunction   A court order prohibiting a given action, such as a strike or boycott, that could cause irreparable damage.

inpatriate   An employee working at corporate headquarters who originated in a different country.

insourcing   Delegating a job to someone within a company, as opposed to someone outside of the company (outsourcing).

instructional method   An approach to training that is either teacher-centered or learner-centered.

intellectual property (IP)   Knowledge, creative idea, or expression of the human mind that has commercial value and is protectable under copyright, patent, service mark, trademark, or trade secret laws from imitation, infringement, and dilution.

intercultural wisdom   Knowing what you do not know about the values, behavior, and communication styles of people from other cultures.

internal coaching   A training or developmental process whereby organizational leaders support the achievement of a personal or professional goal.

internal equity   Employees' perception of their responsibilities, rewards, and work conditions as compared with those of other employees in similar positions in the same organization.

internal investigation   Gathering information dealing with an issue that needs to be clarified.

international assignee (IA)   Employee working in a foreign country. Also known as an *expatriate*.

inter-rater reliability   Degree of agreement between two evaluators.

intrinsic motivation   Stimulation that drives an individual to adopt or change a behavior for their own internal satisfaction or fulfillment.

intrinsic reward   A reward such as meaningful and fulfilling work, autonomy, or positive feedback that may lead to high levels of job satisfaction.

investigation   A detailed search for facts involving records, witnesses, and other inputs.

investigation file   A collection of documents related to complaints or charges of discrimination, policy violation, or criminal behavior assembled by an employer about an employee or event.

involuntary separation   An individual leaving the payroll for an involuntary reason, such as performance deficiencies, policy violations, or unauthorized absence.

ISO 9000 standards   Standards and guidelines on quality management and quality assurance developed by the International Organization for Standardization (ISO).

item response theory (IRT)   Method used to pre-equate the difficulty level of questions on an exam.

J curve   Introducing change typically decreases productivity. The hope is a gradual return and then a surpassing of prior levels of productivity. When productivity is plotted over time, the shape of the data resembles an angled letter *j*.

Jahari window   A framework designed to help people better understand their relationship with themselves and others, using anchors of known or not known, to self or to others in a two-by-two matrix.

job analysis   A systematic process to identify and determine the particular job duties, requirements, working conditions, and responsibilities for a given job that produces a job description, job specification, and perhaps competencies.

job application   A form used to gather information significant to the employer about an individual candidate for employment.

job bidding   An internal process that allows employees to express interest in a position before there is a vacancy.

job classification   A system for objectively and accurately defining the duties, responsibilities, tasks, and authority level of a job.

job-content-based job evaluation   A job evaluation method in which the relative worth and pay of different jobs are based on their content and relationship to other jobs within the same organization.

job description   A document that describes a job and its essential duties, responsibilities, and working conditions.

job enlargement   Broadening the scope of a job by expanding the number of similarly valued tasks.

job enrichment   Increasing the depth of a job by adding responsibilities, most often managerial tasks.

job evaluation   A systematic determination of the relative worth of jobs in an organization.

job evaluation method   A quantitative or nonquantitative method allowing for sorting or categorizing jobs based on their relative worth to the organization.

job ranking   Establishing a hierarchy of job values, based on each job's measurable factors.

job rotation   The process of shifting a person from job to job.

job sharing   When two or more employees work part time in the same job to create one full-time equivalent position.

job specification   A statement of employee characteristics and qualifications required for satisfactory performance for a specific job.

judgment-based forecasting   The use of simple estimates, the Delphi technique, focus group or panel estimates, or historically based estimates in human resource management.

judgmental forecast   Projection based on subjective inputs.

jurisdiction   Power or right of a legal or political agency to exercise its authority over a person, subject matter, institution, or territory.

key performance indicator (KPI)   A key business statistic such as number of new orders, cash collection efficiency, or return on investment (ROI) that measures a firm's performance in a critical area.

key risk indicator (KRI)   A measure used in management to indicate how risky an activity is.

kinesthetic learner   This is a "hands-on learner" or "doer" who concentrates better and learns more easily when tactile senses and movement are involved.

knowledge   Facts and information gathered by an individual.

knowledge items   Key concept topics associated with the 14 HR functional areas. Knowledge items comprise one of the two types of exam questions on the SHRM-CP and SHRM-SCP. (The other question type is situational judgment items.)

knowledge management   The way an organization identifies, stores, and shares institutional knowledge in order to be competitive.

knowledge-based system   A system in which pay is based on the level of knowledge an employee has in a particular field.

KSAs   The *knowledge, skills,* and *abilities* needed to perform a job.

KSAOs   The *knowledge, skills, abilities,* and *other characteristics* needed to perform a job.

K-W-L table   A display of what students know (K), what they want to know (W), and what they actually learned (L).

labor cost differential   An adjustment to pay structures based on local competitive comparisons.

labor union   An organized association of workers formed to collectively protect and further their rights and interests, such as working conditions and pay. Also called a *trade union.*

lagging indicator   A measure describing an activity that has already happened.

layoff   Suspension or termination of employment (with or without notice) by the employer.

leadership   1. The action of leading a group of people or an organization. 2. The individuals who are the leaders in an organization, regarded collectively. 3. The activity of leading a group of people or an organization to achieve its goals, or the ability to do this.

leadership concepts   The study of leadership styles and techniques.

leadership development   The teaching of leadership qualities to management or executive-level employees, including communication, ability to motivate others, and management techniques.

leading indicator   A measure that precedes, anticipates, or predicts future performance.

learning curve   Graphic illustration of the rate of learning.

learning management system (LMS)   A comprehensive system that tracks training content, employee skill sets, training histories, and other career development activities.

learning object (LO)   A defined learning element that may be used in other contexts in the organization (for example, animated graphics and training aids).

learning organization   An organization that quickly responds and adapts to changes in the environment.

leniency error   This occurs when ratings of all employees fall at the high end of the range.

leveling   1. Adjustments to survey numbers by an appropriate percentage needed to achieve a match with specific jobs. 2. Determining value of a job not in market surveys.

liabilities   An organization's debts and other financial obligations.

local national   A worker hired by a multinational firm to work in their own country. Also called a *host-country national (HCN).*

local responsiveness (LR) strategy   An international strategy that adapts to the needs of local markets, allowing an organization's units to meet the needs of their unique markets via products, structures, and systems.

location-based differentials   Adjustment to base pay programs based on work location remoteness, lack of amenities, climatic conditions, and other adverse conditions.

lockout   Employer action that prevents workers from entering the workplace to do their normal jobs.

long-term care insurance   Insurance to help cover the cost of long-term care at home, in an assisted living facility, in a nursing home, or as an inpatient in a hospice.

long-term disability (LTD)   Begins where short-term disability ends if employee is still disabled. Continues some of an employee's income.

long-term incentive   A reward for attaining results over a long measurement period.

low-context culture   A communication style that relies heavily on explicit and direct language. Typical when people have limited history with one another.

lump-sum bonus   A one-time performance bonus. Also called a *performance bonus.*

managed care plan   Insurance that provides plan subscribers with managed health care, with the purpose of reducing costs and improving the quality of care.

management by objectives (MBO)   A method of performance appraisal that specifies the performance goals that the employee and manager identify in advance.

management skills   The abilities required to succeed at a management job, such as leadership, communication, decision-making, behavior flexibility, organization, and planning.

mandatory bargaining issue   An issue that must be discussed by the employer and union when negotiating a contract of representation.

market-based job evaluation   Benchmark jobs are measured and valued against other companies, and the remaining jobs are inserted into a hierarchy based on their whole-job comparison to the benchmark jobs.

marketing   The process of encouraging people to purchase the organization's products or services.

mathematically based forecasting   Staffing ratios, sales ratios, or regression analysis used in human resource management analysis of data elements.

matrix structure   Organizational structure in which employees have at least two direct supervisors.

maturity curve   Measures salaries based on years of directly related experience in the profession, such as research or teaching.

mean (average)   Average of arithmetic values. Calculated by adding together all values and then dividing by the number of values.

measuring   Collecting and tabulating data.

median   The number in the middle of a range.

mediation   The nonbinding use of an independent and impartial third party in the settlement of a dispute, instead of opting for arbitration or litigation.

memorandum of understanding (MOU)   An addendum to a union contract for a represented group of employees and designated employer(s).

mentoring   An experienced individual helping another who has less experience.

mergers and acquisitions (M&A)   The joining together of two separate organizations (merger) or the acquiring of another organization (acquisition).

merit pay   An adjustment to an employee's salary based on their performance. Also called *performance pay, performance-based pay,* or *pay for performance.*

metric   A standard of measurement by which the efficiency, performance, progress, or quality of a plan, process, or product can be assessed.

minimum premium plan   A health insurance program paid for in part by the employer and in part by the employee.

mission statement   A statement describing what an organization does, who its customer/client base is, and how it will do its work. It is the reason for being in business.

mobile learning   Learning across multiple contexts, through social and content interactions, using personal electronic devices.

mode   The number that appears most frequently in a range or data set.

modified duty   Temporary alteration of job duties that can be performed by an employee who is medically restricted for a designated period of time.

moral hazard   Lack of incentive to guard against risk where one is protected from its consequences due to another party incurring any resulting loss.

motivation   Factors that initiate, direct, and sustain behavior over time.

motivation concepts   Notions about what motivates individuals, which have come about as a result of scientific studies. Examples of researchers involved with such studies include Herzberg, Maslow, and McGregor.

multicriteria decision analysis (MCDA)   1. A group decision-making tool where the group defines characteristics of a successful decision and then scores alternatives against that defined criteria. 2. A subdiscipline of operations research that explicitly considers multiple criteria in decision-making environments.

multinational enterprise (MNE)   An enterprise operating in several countries.

multiple linear regression   A statistical technique based on an assumed linear relationship between a dependent variable and a variety of explanatory or independent variables.

national origin   The country of one's birth or one's ancestors' birth, regardless of whether that country still exists. A protected category of Title VII of the Civil Rights Act of 1964.

near-shoring   Conducting business in a foreign country with close proximity to the home country.

needs analysis   See *needs assessment*.

needs assessment   Determining through analysis what gaps exist between a standard or an objective and existing capabilities.

negative emphasis   The rejection of a candidate based on a small amount of negative information.

negligent hiring   A legal tort claim against an employer for injury to someone inside or outside the organization in a way that should have been predicted by the employer if a proper background check had been completed.

negligent retention   A legal tort claim against an employer for keeping someone on the payroll who is known to be a danger to others inside or outside the organization.

negotiation   When two or more parties work together to reach agreement.

net assets   The difference between income and liabilities.

net profit margin   Ratio of net income (gross sales minus expenses and taxes) to net sales.

networking   Developing mutually beneficial contacts for the purpose of exchanging information.

nominal group technique   Development of forecasts based on input from a group of people.

noncash award   A prize, gift, or award presented in recognition of service, production, or other designated criteria.

nonexempt employee   Employees covered by the protections of the U.S. Fair Labor Standards Act (FLSA).

nonexempt job   A position under the provisions of the FLSA.

objective   An end-result intention.

objective measurement   Impartial assessment of a result.

occupational category   A grouping of job titles with similar levels of responsibility or skill requirements.

occupational illness   A physical or mental malady caused by job-related conditions.

occupational injury   A physical or mental injury caused by a single incident in the work environment.

offboarding   Moving employees out of the organization, off the payroll.

offshoring   The relocation of functions or work to another country.

onboarding   1. The process of deliberately assimilating new employees into the company faster by purposely sharing information about the company's culture, unique vocabulary, and additional details of how work is successfully accomplished. 2. Moving employees onto the payroll, into the organization.

onshoring   Bringing work back to the home country from overseas.

on-the-job training (OJT)   Training that takes place while the employee is performing the job. This usually involves a co-worker or supervisor demonstrating and providing coaching or training while job content is being learned.

open-door policy   An alternative dispute resolution technique allowing employees to bypass the chain of command and approach any member of management with a perceived complaint.

oral employment contract   Verbal agreement involving promises of working conditions in the employment relationship.

oral warning   Verbal notice that a rule or policy has been violated and further discipline will result if the behavior is repeated.

organization exit   Final formal meeting between management and an employee leaving the firm; usually called an *exit interview.*

organizational culture   Shared beliefs on how an organization should treats its employees, customers, and others.

organizational development   The process of enhancing effectiveness and efficiency via planned interventions.

organizational learning   Organization-wide continuous process that enhances its collective ability to accept, make sense of, and respond to internal and external change.

organizational restructuring   Change to an organization's internal and external relationships or departmentalization.

organizational values   The operating philosophies or principles that guide an organization's internal conduct as well as its relationship with its customers, partners, and shareholders. These are core values.

organizing   1. Union efforts to convince employees to support and vote to recognize a union as the designated bargaining agent for a workgroup. 2. The process of bringing order out of chaos.

orientation   An introductory process or program for new employees to their jobs, organization, co-workers, and facility.

outplacement   A program that assists employees in finding new jobs when their job is eliminated.

outside sales exemption   Exemption from overtime pay and other FLSA provisions based on several qualifying factors, including the primary duty being making sales or obtaining orders for products or services. Work must be customarily and regularly engaged away from the employer's place of business.

outsourcing   Contracting for services with a third party rather than having them performed in the organization.

overtime pay   An additional amount of money paid in accordance with federal law to hourly employees who work more than 40 hours in a workweek. Paid at 1.5 times regular hourly pay. State laws may vary on how overtime pay is calculated.

paid holidays   Designated days each year that are awarded to employees as paid time off.

paid leave   Paid time off for a specific designated reason.

paid sick leave   Accrued paid time off for medical reasons and usually based on length of service.

paid time off (PTO)   An account of hours in which an employer pools sick days, vacation days, and personal days that an employee can use as the need arises.

paid vacation   Accrued paid time off, usually based on length of service.

paired comparison   Method of evaluation in which each employee or job is compared with each other employee or job.

Pareto chart   A quality control tool that displays variances by the number of their occurrences in a bar graph with the highest values on the left.

partially self-funded plan   A health insurance program where the employer funds the claims payments and contracts with another organization to administer the health plan.

part time   Employees who work fewer than the number of hours required to be considered full time.

pass rate   The number of people, shown as a percentage, who were successful in passing an exam.

pay compression   When new employee wages are very similar to or even higher than those being paid to current employees. Also known as *salary* or *wage compression*.

pay differential   Additional compensation paid to an employee as an incentive to accept what would normally be considered adverse working conditions, usually based on time, location, or working conditions.

pay equity   The providing of equal compensation for jobs that have the same requirements, responsibilities, and working conditions regardless of the incumbent's gender. Also known as *equal pay*.

pay for performance (P4P, PfP)   The notion that employees are compensated based on the results they achieve on their job. Also called *merit pay* or *performance-based pay*.

pay grade   The way an organization organizes jobs of a similar value into a job group as a result of the job evaluation process.

pay range   Pay amounts constrained by the upper and lower boundaries of each pay grade.

pay survey   A survey that collects information on compensation and benefit practices in the prevailing market. Also called a *salary survey* or a *remuneration survey*.

payroll   The function of recordkeeping and computation of compensation for each employee that results in issuance of a check or electronic deposit and the collection and deposit of payroll taxes and other withholdings.

payroll system   Usually, a computerized software program designed to accept work time data and generate paychecks or electronic deposits.

Pension Benefit Guaranty Corporation (PBGC)   A federal corporation established under ERISA that insures the vested benefits of pension plan participants.

percentile   A distribution of data into a percentage range, such as top 10 percent.

performance appraisal   A process of evaluating and providing feedback on how employees perform their jobs.

performance bonus   Compensation in excess of base pay that is paid in recognition for exceeding performance objectives. May also be called a *lump sum bonus*.

performance grant   Stock-based compensation that is linked to organizational performance.

performance improvement plan (PIP)   A written plan detailing over a defined period how an underperforming employee's performance results must improve.

performance management   The process used to identify, measure, communicate, develop, and reward employee performance.

performance measure   A method for identifying quantities and qualities for job performance.

performance standard   An indicator of what a job is to accomplish and how it is to be performed.

performance-based merit pay system   A system where pay increases are determined based on individual job performance.

perk   See *perquisite.*

permissible bargaining issues   Issues that may be discussed by the employer and union during contract negotiations. They are neither required nor prohibited. Strikes may not happen over permissible bargaining issues. Also called *voluntary bargaining issues.*

perquisite   Better known as a *perk.* A special privilege for executives, including club membership, company car, reserved parking, use of the company airplane, enhanced medical coverage, or a similar benefit. Some perks, like the use of a company car, may also extend to the sales force.

person-based pay   Pay system in which an employee's characteristics, rather than performance, determine pay. Also called *person-based pay system.*

person-based pay system   Employee capabilities rather than how the job is performed determine the employee's pay. Also called *person-based pay.*

personal protective equipment (PPE)   Equipment worn by employees as protection against injury or illness hazards on the job.

personnel file   One or more sets of documents held by an employer that contain information about the employee, including but not limited to employment status, performance evaluations, and disability accommodations.

PESTLE analysis   A framework used to analyze and monitor external environment factors through the lens of political, economic, social, technological, legal, and environmental forces.

phantom stock plan   Employee benefit program giving selected senior management employees pretend stock rather than actual stock, with the same financial benefits over time.

phased retirement   Partial retirement while continuing to work a reduced schedule.

PHR   Stands for *Professional in Human Resources,* HRCI's credential for experts in employment regulations and legal mandates.

PHRca   Specific HRCI credential that demonstrates HR knowledge for the state of California.

picketing   Public protest used by unions to inform the public about a problem with an employer.

pilot program   A small-scale, short-term experiment that helps an organization learn how a large-scale project might work in practice. This is also called a *feasibility study* or *experimental trial*. Often used to test training to improve a course prior to implementation for its target audience.

plateau curve   A horizontal part of a learning curve in which learning is seemingly stalled.

point-factor system or point-factor job evaluation   A job evaluation method identifying specific compensable factors with various weightings to measure relative job worth.

point-of-service plan   A type of managed care plan that is similar to PPO plan but with a gatekeeper.

policy   A statement describing how an organization is to be managed.

polycentric   Literally meaning having more than one center. It is an international business approach where the business in each country operates relatively independently.

portal to portal   From "door to door." This is usually applied to employees traveling from home to work or from home to a remote job site.

predictor   Data collected in the selection process to determine validation. Examples include job applications, tests, and interviews.

preferred provider organization (PPO)   Health care program, including an in-network and out-of-network options, for fee-for-service health care.

premium   1. A payment for health coverage. 2. A payment for achievement of specific objectives. 3. Excess over apparent worth.

premium-only plan (POP)   Authorized under the IRS Code, Section 125, a POP allows employer-sponsored premium payments to be paid by the employee on a pre-tax basis instead of after-tax. Also called a *Section 125 plan*.

premium pay   Payment at a rate greater than straight pay for working overtime or another agreed-upon condition.

prepaid legal insurance   Employer financial support for the cost of routine legal services, such as developing a will, real estate matters, divorces, and other services.

prescription drug plan   A medical insurance program that covers some or all of the cost of prescription drugs for subscribers.

primacy error   The tendency of an employee performance evaluator or an interviewer to rely on early cues for first impressions or data collected early in the evaluation period.

principal agent problem   A conflict arising when people entrusted to look after the interests of others use the authority or power for their own benefit instead.

procedure   A method to be used in fulfilling organizational responsibilities and policies.

process alignment   The linking or integration of an organization's structure and resources with its strategy and business environment.

process-flow analysis   A diagram of the steps involved in a process.

product structure   A way to organize work based on the products or services generated.

productivity-based pay system   A system in which pay is determined by the employee's production output.

professional employer organization (PEO)   A vendor who, as a co-employer, provides qualified workers to a client organization.

professional exemption   Exemption from overtime pay and other FLSA provisions based on several qualifying factors, including minimum pay requirement, advanced knowledge or education, and use of professional discretion and judgment.

Professional in Human Resources (PHR)   Credential that demonstrates mastery of the technical and operational aspects of HR practices and U.S. laws and regulations.

profit-and-loss statement (P&L)   A financial statement that summarizes the revenues, costs, and expenses incurred during a specific period of time.

profit-sharing plan   A plan in which direct or indirect payments are made to employees, depending on the employer's profitability.

program evaluation and review technique (PERT)   A project management tool used to organize, coordinate, and schedule tasks and people.

progressive discipline   Discipline that imposes increasingly severe consequences and penalties if unwanted behaviors reoccur. This is also called *constructive discipline*.

prohibited bargaining issue   An issue that may not be discussed by the employer and union during contract negotiations. This is an illegal issue under the NLRA.

project hire   An employee who is hired for the duration of a project. Once the project is completed, the employee is dismissed or laid off. Also called a *term employee*.

project management   Guiding the implementation of a program from beginning to end.

project team   A group of people with specific talent or experience, brought together to resolve a problem or accomplish some other organizational goal.

promotion   An increase in responsibility, usually with an increase in compensation too. Typically involves a change of work title.

proof of identity   A document such as a passport or driver's license that contains a photo of the individual that proves that person is who they claim to be.

proof of work authorization   A document such as a Social Security card or an alien registration number that proves the individual is authorized to work in the United States.

protected class   People who are covered by federal or state antidiscrimination laws.

prudent person rule   Basic principle for investment decisions by institutional investors and professional money managers. Managers must not take more risk than a reasonably knowledgeable, prudent investor would under similar circumstances.

punitive damages   Damages intended to deter a defendant from engaging in conduct similar to that which was the basis of a lawsuit.

qualified domestic relations order (QDRO)   A court-issued order that instructs a plan administrator to pay all or a portion of a pension plan benefit to a divorced spouse or child.

qualified privilege doctrine   Allows past employers to share job-related information on past employees during a background check without fear of defamation.

qualifying event   A circumstance that triggers the beginning of COBRA eligibility.

quartiles   Distribution of data into four equal quadrants: bottom quarter, lower-middle quarter, upper-middle quarter, and top quarter.

quid pro quo harassment   Insisting on sexual favors in exchange for some work-related benefit or to avoid some work-related punishment. Most often perpetrated by a person with power abusing that power over someone with less power in the organization. Literally means "this for that."

Rabbi trust   A financial vehicle for holding assets to fund an employer's deferred compensation obligations.

range spreads   Dispersion of pay from the lowest boundary to the highest boundary of a pay range.

ratio analysis   Comparison of current results or historic results at a specific point in time.

realistic job preview (RJP)   A recruiting approach used by an organization to communicate the favorable and less favorable aspects of a job and its work environment so a candidate may make a better informed decision when offered a position.

reasonable accommodation   Adjustment or modification to a job condition or workplace that will allow a qualified individual to perform the essential job duties without imposing an undue burden on the employer.

reasonable cause   One possible determination from a state or federal enforcement agency concerning an investigation of a charge of illegal discrimination.

recency error   An error that occurs when an evaluator gives greater weight to recent events of performance.

recognition   Acknowledgment of the accomplishments of individual employees.

recordkeeping   Documentation involving any aspect of employee management, from discussions to personal employee information.

recruitment   Process of seeking out qualified job candidates to encourage them to apply for open positions.

red circle rate   Pay at a rate higher than the maximum for the assigned pay range.

redeployment   Assignment to a different job, often at a remote work location.

reduction in force (RIF)   Reducing the number of workers, usually due to economic necessity or restructuring. Also called *downsizing*.

regiocentric   An international business approach where operations are similar and communications active within a large contiguous geographical region such as Asia, South America, or Europe.

regression analysis   A statistical process of estimating the relationships among variables, measuring whether the relationship exists and its strength. Used as a tool to help make predictions.

regulation   Rule or order issued by an administrative agency of government that usually has the force of law behind it.

rehire   A former employee who is hired back onto the payroll.

reliability   The repeatability or consistency of a measurement.

remediation   A process by which an unacceptable action or behavior is corrected.

remuneration survey   A survey that collects information on compensation and benefit practices in the prevailing market. Also called *salary survey* or *pay survey*.

repatriation   Returning employees to their home country following a work assignment in a different country.

replacement planning   Succession planning using a snapshot assessment of existing qualified talent for key positions.

request for proposal (RFP)   A written document asking for vendor input along with cost estimates for the scope of defined work.

residual risk   Exposure to loss or uncertainty remaining after other known risks have been countered, factored in, or eliminated.

responsibility   A required part of a job or organizational obligation.

restructuring   Redesigning the organizational structure, altering reporting relationships, or changing the legal ownership of a firm.

results measurement   A method for monitoring the amount of progress that has been accomplished toward a stated goal or objective.

retention 1. A measurement of the quantity of employees remaining with the employer over a given period of time. 2. The ability of an organization to keep its employees.

retiree An ex-employee who met the qualification requirements for retirement under the organization's definition or plan.

return on investment (ROI) The calculation showing the value received versus the investment cost.

return to work Clearance to return to active employment activities following an illness, injury, or other absence.

reverse innovation Innovation first seen or used in emerging-economy markets before spreading to developed-economy markets. Also known as *trickle-up innovation.*

right to work (RTW) Allows states to forbid union shops, thus making union membership and union dues optional. Considered bad for unions. More than half the states are RTW states.

risk 1. A probability or threat of damage, injury, liability, loss, or any other negative occurrence that is caused by external or internal vulnerabilities. 2. Uncertainty where outcomes may include opportunities, losses, or threats.

risk appetite The level of risk or uncertainty a person or corporation is willing to accept in order to execute a strategy.

risk control 1. The probability of loss arising from the tendency of internal control systems to lose their effectiveness over time and thus expose (or fail to prevent the exposure of) the assets they were instituted to protect. 2. An action taken to manage a risk.

risk management System to identify and manage potential risks or liabilities to the organization.

risk position Extent of exposure to a particular risk. Usually expressed in monetary terms.

risk scorecard A tool used to gather various characteristics of risk.

risk tolerance The capacity to accept or absorb uncertainty or risk.

role-play A technique for simulating individual participation in real-life roles involving performance or action for the purpose of solving a problem.

root cause analysis Analysis that begins with the results and then works backward to identify the fundamental cause or causes.

rote learning Learning primarily through memorization.

Rucker plan or Rucker Share of Production plan A companywide incentive plan in which compensation is based on a ratio of income to value added by employees engaged in the production process.

rule of law   The concept that no individual is above the law, no matter how powerful. The concept includes laws that are written and publicly disclosed.

safety audit   The process of evaluating the workplace for safety hazards and determining any needed corrective action.

salary compression   When new employee wages are very similar to or even higher than those being paid to current employees. Also known as *pay* or *wage compression.*

salary survey   A survey that collects information on compensation and benefit practices in the prevailing market. Also called a *pay survey* or a *remuneration survey.*

sales personnel incentive program   A program that provides bonuses or commissions based on predetermined formulas involving the successful selling of products or services.

salting   When a union gets union-sympathetic people hired at a non-union company for the purpose of encouraging union organizing.

scaffolding   A method used by teachers to model skills and thinking for students, allowing the students to take over those expressions based on the initial structure provided by the teacher.

Scanlon plan   Cost-saving productivity-incentive plan in which any saving (computed per unit of output) compared with an agreed-upon standard labor cost is shared equally between the workers and the firm. A component of the plan includes an employee suggestion plan.

scatter diagram   A graphical tool that depicts the relationship among variables.

SDS (safety data sheet)   Hazardous chemical information form describing how onsite chemicals are used, processed, and stored. Formerly called a *material safety data sheet.*

seasonal employee   A worker hired for a specific seasonal surge in work levels, common in the retail industry and also agriculture and other food processing businesses.

Section 125 cafeteria plan   Authorized under the IRS Code, Section 125, this plan allows employer-sponsored premium payments to be paid by the employee on a pre-tax basis instead of after-tax. Also called a *premium-only plan (POP).*

selection   The ultimate choice in a field of multiple choices. This is usually applied to the choice of the most suitable job candidate for a position.

selection screening   The process of eliminating job candidates based on specified criteria of job requirements. This is accomplished through the use of job applications, interviews, tests, and demonstrations.

self-directed team   A group of people with a specific assignment permitted to select their own leadership, methods, and direction to take toward the problem or task.

self-funded plan   A health insurance program where the employer assumes all of the risk as a self-insured entity.

Senior Professional in Human Resources (SPHR)   Credential for those who have mastered the strategic and policy-making aspects of HR management.

seniority   Length of service in a job, employer organization, industry, or union.

seniority pay increase   A pay increase given based solely on length of service.

service level agreement (SLA)   Contract between a service provider and a customer; it details the nature, quality, and scope of the service to be provided. This is also called a *service level contract*.

severance package   Voluntary payment by some employers to laid-off employees. It may include pay, job retraining, outplacement services, and paid benefits premium assistance.

shared services HR model   An HR organizational structure where specific functions of HR expertise develop HR policies, and units of HR can determine what they need from a menu of services.

short-term disability (STD)   Coverage that begins where sick leave ends. This covers some or all of an employee's income for up to a specified period (usually 6 months).

sick leave   Paid leave for a specified number of hours or days absent from work because of a medical condition.

simple linear regression   A technique in which a straight line is fitted to a set of data points to measure the effect of a single independent variable. The slope of the line is the measured impact of that variable.

simulation   An imitation of a real-world system or process. A learning exercise designed to be as realistic as possible without the risk of a real-life circumstance.

single or flat-rate pay system   A system in which each worker in the same job has the same rate of pay, regardless of seniority or job performance.

situational judgment items   Questions covering the KSAOs (knowledge, skills, abilities, and other characteristics) associated with the SHRM BASK's behavioral competencies on the SHRM-CP and SHRM-SCP exams.

situational judgment test (SJT)   A type of psychological test that presents the test-taker with realistic, hypothetical scenarios and asks the individual to identify the most appropriate response or to rank the responses in the order they feel is most effective.

Six Sigma   A data-driven quality approach and method for eliminating defects.

skill-based system or skill-based pay system   A system in which pay is based on the number and depth of skills an employee has applicable to their job.

skills inventory A database of employee knowledge, skills, and abilities useful for succession planning.

SMART goal model or SMART model A model for creating goals that are specific, measurable, attainable/achievable/action-oriented, relevant/realistic, and timed (SMART).

social media Contemporary methods of communicating with other individuals or groups. A term applied to Internet services such as Facebook, Pinterest, LinkedIn, and Twitter, as just a few examples.

socialization Acquiring socially acceptable attitudes and behaviors that conform to the standards of the organization.

Society of Human Resource Professionals (SHRM) The world's largest HR membership organization devoted to human resource management, representing more than 300,000 members in over 165 countries.

Software as a Service (SaaS) Software that is delivered over the Internet to contracted customers on a pay-for-use or subscription basis.

Solomon four-group design Experimental research design where participants are randomly assigned to four groups. Two groups are pretested. One pretest group and one non-pretest group participate in the experimental treatment, then all four groups are measured.

solution analysis Statistical comparison of various potential solutions.

sourcing The process of finding qualified applicants or suppliers of goods or services.

span of control The number of subordinates reporting to a single direct supervisor.

specific stop-loss coverage A health plan protected against the risk of a major illness for one participant, or one family unit, covered by the plan.

SPHR See *Senior Professional in Human Resources*.

staffing Filling job openings with qualified applicants.

stakeholder An individual with an interest in an organization's success or outcomes.

stakeholder concept 1. All people, organizations, or entities that affect an organization or are affected by an organization. 2. A conceptual framework of business ethics and organizational management that addresses moral and ethical values in the management of a business or other organization.

standard The yardstick by which amount and quality of output are measured.

standard deviation The average amount of variability in a data set.

state employment service The agency responsible for assisting citizens with job placement and unemployment benefits in each state.

statistical forecast The use of mathematical formulas to identify patterns and trends.

stay interview   A structured interview with existing employees for the purpose of determining what aspects of their job causes retention or can be improved to increase probability of future retention.

stereotyping   Broadly classifying people into groups based on characteristics that may not be accurate. For example, "Everyone loves bacon" doesn't take into account food restrictions of Judaism and Islam.

stock option   The right, but not obligation, to buy company shares at a specific strike price on or before a specified date, usually 10 years into the future.

straight piece rate system   A pay plan where an employee receives a base rate of pay and is awarded additional defined compensation based on the amount of output produced.

strategic fit   A situation that occurs when a specific project, target company, or product is seen as appropriate with respect to an organization's overall objectives.

strategic planning   Identifying organizational objectives and determining what actions are required to reach those objectives.

strategy   1. A method or plan chosen to bring about a desired future, such as achievement of a goal or solution to a problem. 2. The art and science of planning and marshalling resources for their most efficient and effective use. 3. Specific direction that outlines objectives to achieve a long-term plan.

stress interview   Emotionally charged interview setting where the interviewee is put under purposeful psychological stress to evaluate how they perform under pressure.

strictness   An error in which a manager is too strict in evaluating employee performance, leading to decreases in motivation and performance.

strike   When a group of employees refuse to work. Also called a *work stoppage*.

structured interview   A fixed-format interview in which all questions are prepared beforehand and are put in the same order to each interviewee.

subject matter expert (SME)   A person who is well versed in the content of a specific knowledge area.

substance abuse   Personal use of alcohol or drugs in excess of the amount prescribed by a medical professional, or any use of illegal substances. Abuse generally results in an impairment of the individual's physical or mental capacities.

succession planning   A plan for the replacement of key employees.

Summary Plan Description (SPD)   A legally required communication document under ERISA defining a benefit, including a summary, eligibility, and how to make a claim or appeal.

supplemental unemployment benefits (SUB)   Unemployment benefits in addition to government benefits offered by some employers.

supply analysis   1. Strategic evaluation of job candidate sources, plant locations, and other factors. 2. Workforce planning step of evaluating what staff you have in which locations with what skills.

supply chain   Entire network of entities directly or indirectly interlinked and interdependent in serving the same consumer or customer.

suspension   Management-imposed temporary hiatus of active employment, usually as a disciplinary step, that can be paid or unpaid.

sustainability   1. The ability to maintain or support an activity or process over the long term. 2. Using resources wisely for current and future generations.

SWOT analysis   A process in strategic planning that looks at an organization's internal strengths and weaknesses, plus external opportunities and threats.

systems thinking   Understanding how independent units within a larger organization interact with and influence each other.

talent management   The management and integration of all HR activities and processes to meet current and future organizational needs.

talent retention   The retention of key talent, those employees who are the strongest performers, have high potential, or are in critical jobs.

taskforce   A group of workers assembled to address a major organizational issue.

teacher exemption   Exemption from overtime pay and other FLSA provisions based on several qualifying factors, including the primary duty of teaching in an educational establishment.

team   A group of workers focused on specific organizational issues.

temp-to-lease   Conversion of a temporary agency–provided employee to regular employee status in the client organization.

term employee   An employee who is hired for the duration of a project. Once the project is completed, the employee is dismissed or laid off. Also called a *project hire*.

termination   End of the employment relationship.

test center administrators (TCAs)   Trained proctors who supervise the Prometric testing centers.

theory of constraints (TOC)   Concepts and methodology aimed mainly at achieving the most efficient flow of material in a plant through continuous process improvement.

third-country national (TCN)   An employee working for an international firm who is a citizen of neither the home nor host country.

third-party administrator plan　Health insurance program in which the employer assumes all of the risk but hires an independent claims department.

time-based differential pay　Shift pay for employees who work undesirable shifts such as night shifts.

time-based step rate pay or system　A system that determines pay rate based on the length of time in the job based on a predetermined schedule.

total quality management (TQM)　A management system for achieving customer satisfaction using quantitative methods to improve processes and reduce errors.

total rewards　1. Financial inducements and rewards as well as nonfinancial inducements and rewards, such as the value of good job content and a good working environment. 2. Direct and indirect renumeration to attract and retain workers.

total rewards strategy　An integrated reward system encompassing three key elements employees value from their employment: compensation, benefits, and work experience, including development. This system is used to attract and retain talent.

totalization agreement　An agreement between several nations that avoids double taxation of income for workers who divide their working career between two or more countries.

trade union　An organization whose membership consists of workers and union leaders, united to protect and promote their common interests. Also called a *labor union*.

trainability　The readiness and motivation to learn.

training　The process whereby people acquire skills, knowledge, or capabilities to perform their jobs.

training effectiveness　A measurement of what students are expected to be able to do at the end of the training course or module.

training techniques　Training approaches or methods, including virtual, classroom, on-the-job, and one-on-one tutoring.

transactional leadership　A leadership style that focuses on either rewards or threat of discipline in an effort to motivate employees.

transfer　Movement of a current employee to a different job in a different part of the organization.

transfer of learning　The ability of a trainee to apply the behavior, knowledge, and skills acquired in one learning situation to another.

transformational leadership　A leadership style that motivates employees by inspiring them and giving them greater autonomy.

transparency   When an organization's dealings, information, practices, transactions, and agreements are open to disclosure and review by others.

travel pay   Extra pay provided for travel time, either under legal requirement or by other agreement.

trend analysis   Comparison of historical results with current results to determine if something is developing or changing in a general direction.

trickle-up innovation   Innovation first seen or used in emerging-economy markets before spreading to developed-economy markets. Also known as *reverse innovation*.

triple bottom line   Financial, social, and environmental effects of a firm's policies and actions that determine its viability as a sustainable organization.

tuition reimbursement   Employer financial support for employee continuing education efforts.

turnover analysis   The gathering and studying of data to understand the turnover rate.

turnover rate   The percentage of employees exiting the organization during the time period under measurement.

unfair labor practice (ULP)   Legally prohibited action by an employer or union, such as refusal to bargain in good faith.

Uniform Guidelines on Employee Selection Procedures   Federal antidiscrimination regulations that specify how job selection tools must be validated.

unweighted mean or average   Raw mean or average of data that gives equal weight to all factors, with no regard to individual factors.

utilization analysis   Comparison of the percentage of minorities and women available in the surrounding labor force compared to the percentage hired.

validity   The extent to which a test, process, or procedure measures what it says it measures.

value   The resulting benefit created when an organization meets its strategic goals.

value chain   Interlinked value-adding activities that convert inputs into outputs, which, in turn, add to the bottom line and help create a competitive advantage.

value drivers   1. Entities that increase the value of a product or service by improving the perception of the item and essentially providing a competitive advantage. 2. Actions, processes, or results that are needed to deliver a desired value.

values   1. Social beliefs shared among organizational members that regulate behavior and guide decision making. 2. Beliefs, principles, or standards of behavior to direct and govern employees' behavior.

variable pay   Performance-based pay that includes individual performance bonuses, executive bonuses, profit sharing, gainsharing, group incentives, and other incentives tied to productivity as opposed to base pay.

variance analysis   Process aimed at computing the difference between actual and budgeted or targeted levels of budget, performance, or outcomes and identification of their causes.

vestibule training   A training technique replicating the real workplace in an off-the-job simulation.

vesting   When company contributions made to a retirement benefit for an employee become nonforfeitable.

veteran   A former member of the U.S. military service from any branch.

veto   The action of rejecting a bill or statute in the U.S. legislature.

vicarious liability   Legal doctrine of obligation that arises from the relationship of one party with another. A company may be held liable for the actions of its employees.

vision care plan (VCP)   Medical insurance program that cover some or all of the cost of vision care (exams and corrective lenses) for subscribers.

vision statement   A statement that describes the desired future of an organization.

visual learner   This is a person who best absorbs ideas, concepts, data, and other information using the sense of sight.

voluntary bargaining issues   See *permissible bargaining issues*.

voluntary separation   An individual leaving the payroll for voluntary reasons, including retirement, obtaining a different job, returning to full-time education, or personal reasons.

vulnerability analysis   An analysis of factors that could threaten company assets, coupled with the probability of occurrence and the resulting impact.

wage compression   When new employee wages are very similar to or even higher than those being paid to current employees. Also known as *pay or salary compression*.

weighted mean or average   A mean or average result taking into account the number of different values.

Weingarten rights   The right of a union employee to have a union representative present during an investigatory interview.

well-being   A good or satisfactory condition of existence; a state characterized by health, happiness, and prosperity.

whistleblowing   Employee reporting and making public organizational actions that are illegal or immoral.

wildcat strike   An illegal work stoppage by union workers.

work council   An organization outside the United States that represents employees on a local level. A work council may be a useful collective bargaining tool for employees who require an organization that is more familiar with their particular situation than a national labor union.

work-life balance (WLB)   A comfortable state of equilibrium achieved between an employee's primary priorities of their employment position and their personal lifestyle.

work stoppage   When a group of employees refuse to work. Also called a *strike*.

workers' compensation   A program that provides medical care and compensates an employee for part of lost earnings as a result of a work-related injury, regardless of who was responsible for the accident.

workforce analysis   Assessment of the workforce looking at supply and demand and how to close any gap between the two.

workforce management   Managing employees' work activities and responsibilities, work hours, planning, scheduling, and tracking results of the work effort.

workforce planning and employment   The process of recruiting, interviewing, staffing, ensuring equal employment opportunity, affirmative action, new employee orientation, retention, termination, and employee records management performed by an employer.

workplace accommodation   The reasonable modification of a job or way of doing a job so that a person with a disability may have equal access to opportunity in all aspects of their work and perform the essential functions of the job.

workplace violence   Personal behavior that ranges from shouting to hitting, or worse, taking place on an employer's premises.

work-to-rule   When union employees perform only the tasks described in their job descriptions and nothing more.

workweek   A defined period of 168 consecutive hours (7 days times 24 hours) that always begins at the same hour of the same day each week.

written employment contract   A written agreement involving promises of duration, pay, and conditions in the employment relationship.

written warning   A written notice that a rule or policy has been violated and further discipline will result if the behavior is repeated within the defined period.

yellow dog contract   Now illegal, a requirement for employment where employees agreed not to support or join a union.

yield ratio   A recruiting metric for evaluating the different steps in the selection process. Expresses in ratio format the number of applicants at one stage of the hiring process required to produce enough applicants at the next stage.

zero-based budgeting   A model of budgeting that is based on expenditures being justified for each budget year built from the ground up, not based on a prior budget.

zero-sum   When whatever is gained by one side is lost by the other.

INDEX

A

ability competencies, 227
ability tests, 157
ACA (Affordable Care Act), 64–65
Accelerating Implementation
Methodology (AIM), 107
accountability
conflict management, 348
HR increases/decreases for,
284–285
senior HR professionals, 447
accounting function, 286–287
acquisition strategies, 105
action learning leadership, 207
action plans in HR business
case, 496
active-centered leadership, 128
activities
critical, 501
staffing plans, 321–322
unplanned, in job
descriptions, 141
activity log, 112
activity-based budgeting, 287
actual damages in Civil Rights Act
(Title VII), 56
ADA. *See* Americans with
Disabilities Act (ADA)
ADA Amendments Act
(ADAAA), 53
ADAAA (ADA Amendments
Act), 53
ADDIE model, 194, 309
address of residence, in interview
questions, 153
ADEA (Age Discrimination in
Employment Act), 60–61, 61
adhocracy culture, 314
administrative services, 281
adult learning
obstacles, 192
retention, 191
styles, 190–191, 192–193
adverse impact in talent selection
process, 157
adversity, 445

advisor role
career development, 199
change management, 115
HR staff, 279
advocates, 473
Affordable Care Act (ACA), 64–65
after-action debriefs, 409
Age Discrimination in
Employment Act (ADEA),
60–61, 61
age in interview questions, 153
agency complaints, 349–350
agility, 306, 444
aging technique in compensation
analysis, 233
agreement in negotiations, 298
agreement length section in
employment contract, 336
AIM (Accelerating Implementation
Methodology), 107
alien of extraordinary ability visas,
70–71
aliens, 35
alignment
business acumen, 494
conflict management, 348
employee engagement, 169
global staffing, 215
globalization, 382
HR function and strategic
plans, 299
with HR strategy, 471
identity, 382
organizational structure, 316
process, 382
strategic, 494
allegiances in global
assignments, 393
alliances
diversity, equity and
inclusion, 465
labor/trade union strategies, 342
alternative staffing, 325–328
alternative work arrangements, 512
alternatives in HR business
case, 496

AMA (American Management
Association), 130
Amazon Web Services, 375
American Bell, 108
American Health Benefit
Exchanges, 65
American Management
Association (AMA), 130
American National Standards
Institute, 400
American Telephone and
Telegraph, 205
Americans with Disabilities Act
(ADA), 52–56
ADA Amendments Act
(ADAAA), 53
enforcement, 55–56
essential job function, 54
job accommodation, 54
major life activities, 53
provisions and protections, 52
recordkeeping requirements,
54–55
substantially limits, 53
U.S. Supreme Court
interpretation of, 52
AMSAA (U.S. Army Materiel
Systems Analysis Activity), 402
analysis
business case analysis
(BCA), 499
data analysis methods,
118–119
gap, 250, 320
job, 140, 225–228
PESTLE, 94–96, 135, 218–219,
290–291
risk, 402–403
SWOT, 96, 402, 498
trend, 119, 319
Analytical Aptitude competency,
513–522
definition, 12, 513
key concepts, 513
proficiency indicators, 514–522
subcompetencies, 12, 513

P